Chronicle of Sipsòng Panna

History and Society of a Tai Lü Kingdom
Twelfth to Twentieth Century

Foon Ming Liew-Herres

Volker Grabowsky

Renoo Wichasin

Mekong Press

Chiang Mai

Mekong Press was initiated in 2005 by Silkworm Books with the financial support of the Rockefeller Foundation. In 2007, the Mekong Press Foundation was registered as a nonprofit organization to encourage and support the work of local scholars, writers, and publishing professionals in Cambodia, Laos, Vietnam, and the other countries in the Greater Mekong Subregion. Books published by Mekong Press (www.mekongpress.com) are marketed and distributed internationally. Mekong Press also holds seminars and training workshops on different aspects of book publishing, and helps find ways to overcome some of the huge challenges faced by small book publishers in the region.

ISBN 978-616-90053-3-9

The publication of this book was funded by the Rockefeller Foundation.

Published in 2012 by

Mekong Press

6 Sukkasem Road, T. Suthep

Chiang Mai 50200 Thailand

info@mekongpress.com
http://www.mekongpress.com

Typeset by in Gentium 10 pt. by Silk Type

Printed and bound in China

5 4 3 2 1

Contents

Maps and Tables

Maps

Tables

Abbreviations and Signs

AD	Anno domini
BE	Buddhist Era
Ch.	Chinese
ch.	chapter
CKC	Chiang Khaeng Chronicle
CKC-WTP	Chiang Khaeng Chronicle, Wat Ta Pao version Preservation of Lao Manuscripts Programme, Vientiane
CMC	Chiang Mai Chronicle
CMC-HP	Chiang Mai Chronicle, Hans Penth version. Wyatt, David K. and Aroonrut Wichienkeeo 1995 Aroonrut Wichienkeeo and David K. Wyatt 2005 (1999)
CMC-N	Chiang Mai Chronicle, Notton version. Notton, Camille 1932
CMC-TPCM	Chiang Mai Chronicle, *Tamnan phün müang chiang mai*. Udom et al. 1995
CS	cūlasakarāja (*cunlasakkalaca*)
CTC	Chiang Tung Chronicle
CTC-JSC	Chiang Tung Chronicle – Jengtung State Chronicle. Sāimöng Mangrai, Sao 1981
CTS-PMCT	Chiang Tung Chronicle – *Phongsawadan müang chiang tung* Thawi Sawangpanyangkun 1990
DKH	Department of Culture and History, Government of Sipsòng Panna Tai Autonomous Prefecture (Xishuang Banna Dai Autonomous Prefecture)
DMB	Dictionary of Ming Biography. Goodrich, L. C. and Chaoying Fang, eds. 1976
ECCP	Eminent Chinese of the Ching Period. Hummel, Arthur W. (ed.) 1943–44
EFEO	École française d'Extrême-Orient
f° (ff°)	folio (folios)

FO	Foreign Office (United Kingdom)
IOOC	India Office & Oriental Collections (British Library, London)
MJ	McLeod Journal
MLC	Moeng Lü Chronicle
MLC-LV1	Moeng Lü Chronicle, long version 1 Li Fuyi 1947a
MLC-LV2	Moeng Lü Chronicle, long version 2. Department of Culture and History 1963, see Grabowsky/Liew-Herres Collection
MLC-SV1	Moeng Lü Chronicle, short version 1. Li Fuyi 1947b
MLC-SV2	Moeng Lü Chronicle, short version 2. Gao Lishi 1984
MS	Manuscript
MSG	*Mingshi gao*
MSL	*Ming shilu*
NC	Nan Chronicle
NC-PMN-W	Nan Chronicle, *Phün müang nan*, Wyatt version Wyatt, David K. 1994
NC-PMN-WPK	Nan Chronicle, *Phün müang nan*, Wat Phra Koet version Saraswadee Ongsakul 1996b
NT	Northern Thai
P.	Pali
PP	*Prachum phongsawadan*
PRO	Public Record Office (London)
s.	section
Skt.	Sanskrit
SRI	Social Research Institute (Chiang Mai)
Th.	Thai (Siamese)
Tr.	Transcription from Tai Lü or Tai Yuan script (following Udom 1991)

The following signs have been used:

//	Phonemic transcription
()	Authors' explanations
[]	Additions to the text by the authors
{}	Deletions suggested by the authors
+	Additional month in an intercalary year

Authors’ Note

The Romanisation of Thai (Siamese) words in this volume follows the system outlined by the Royal Institute, with a few exceptions. For example, we prefer to differentiate between the consonants จ and ช by Romanising them *c* and *ch* respectively.

Tai Lü words are generally transcribed into modern Thai script according to their original orthography, thus keeping, for example, the consonant ฅ, which has become obsolete in modern Thai orthography. Since we consider Tai Lü to be a language in its own right, we apply a system of Romanisation which strictly follows Tai Lü phonology. The abbreviation “Tr.” indicates the transcription of a Tai Lü term into modern Thai script while preserving the original Tai Lü orthography. For example, the term *phai thai* (Tr. ไภ่ไท), “commoners”, is pronounced *phrai thai* in Thai and spelled ไพร่ไทย, thus differing from Tai Lü with regard to both phonology and orthography. However, in cases where the Thai cognate is spelled exactly the same—though written in different script—we indicate this by using the abbreviation “Th.”, as in *tao phaya* (Th. ท้าวพระยา), pronounced *thao phraya* in Thai.

On first glance, the reader might also be confused by the mixing of *müang* and *moeng*, two variant spellings for the traditional Tai polity. We have decided to follow the preferred local usage. Thus polities in the Tai Lü speaking area are called “Moeng” (such as Moeng Sing, Moeng La, etc.) whereas Müang Luang Nam Tha and Müang Nan, etc., are used for Lao and Tai Yuan polities. Whenever a Tai polity in the more general sense is meant, *müang* is given preference. In a few cases we used an internationally accepted spelling that deviates from the system elaborated above. Thus *chiang* (a walled city which is a ruler’s seat) is used instead of *ciang* (Tai Lü pronunciation) or *siang* (Lao pronunciation).

The Romanisation of Chinese names and special terms follows the Pinyin system.

Map 1: The Upper Mekong Region, with Present-Day Borders

Map 2: Dai (Tai) Settlements in Yunnan

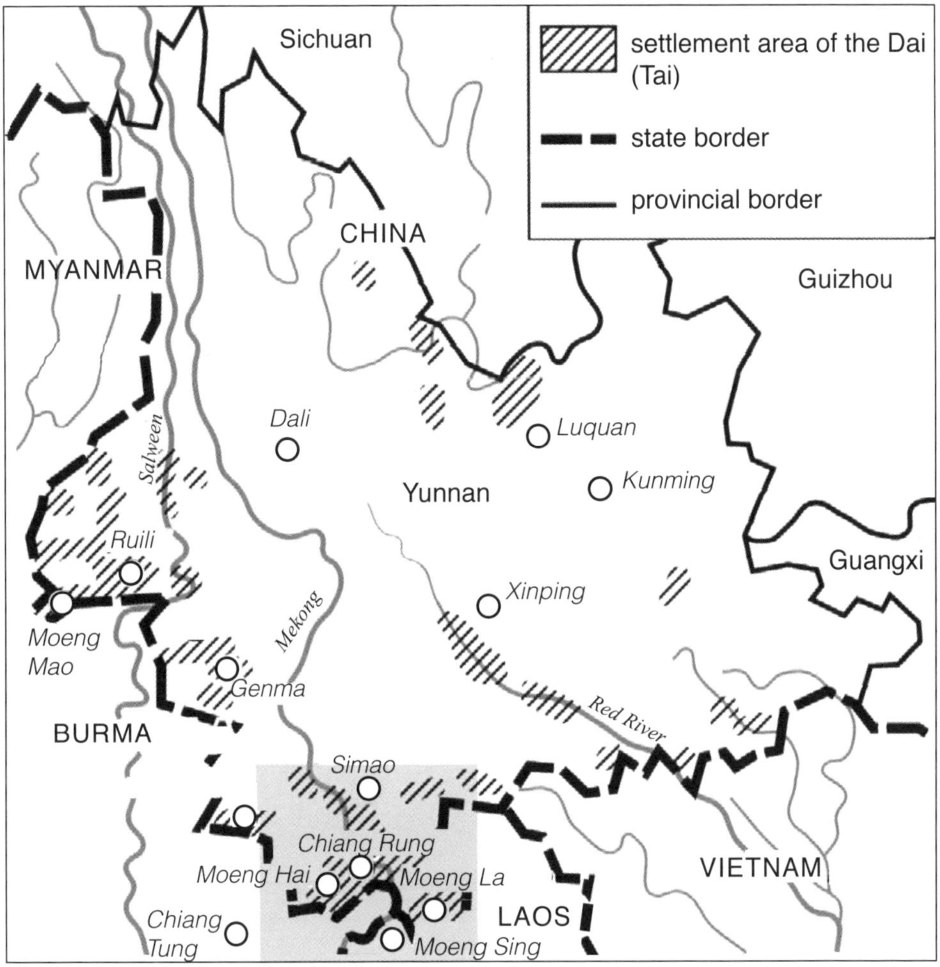

Map 3: Sipsòng Panna in the Late Eighteenth Century

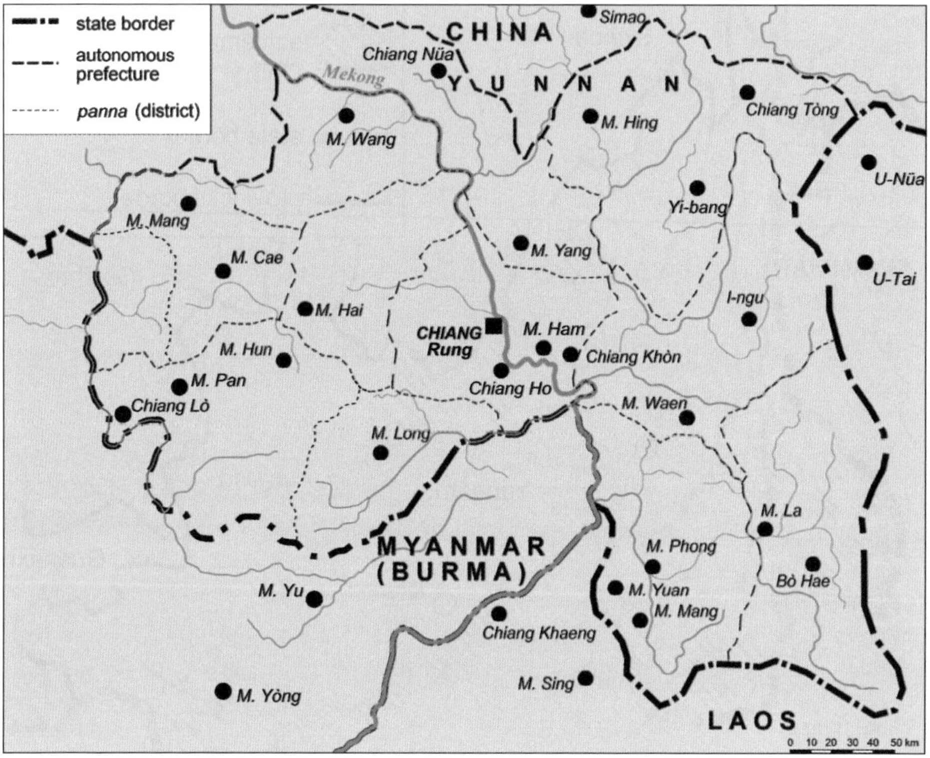

Map 4: District of Moeng Laem, Yunnan Province

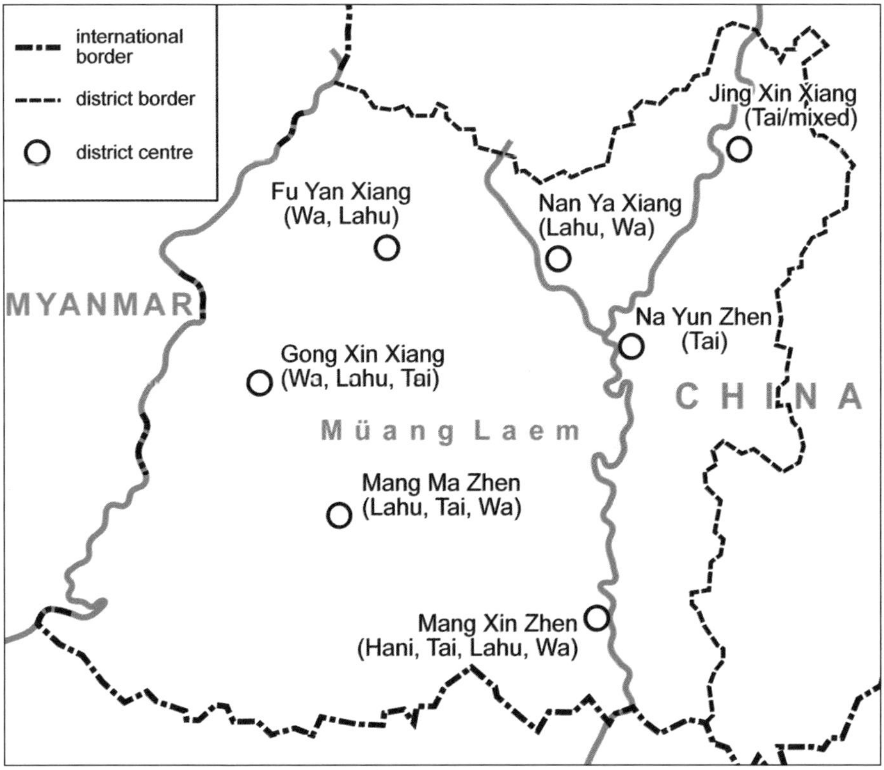

Map 5: British Map of the Upper Mekong Region (1895)

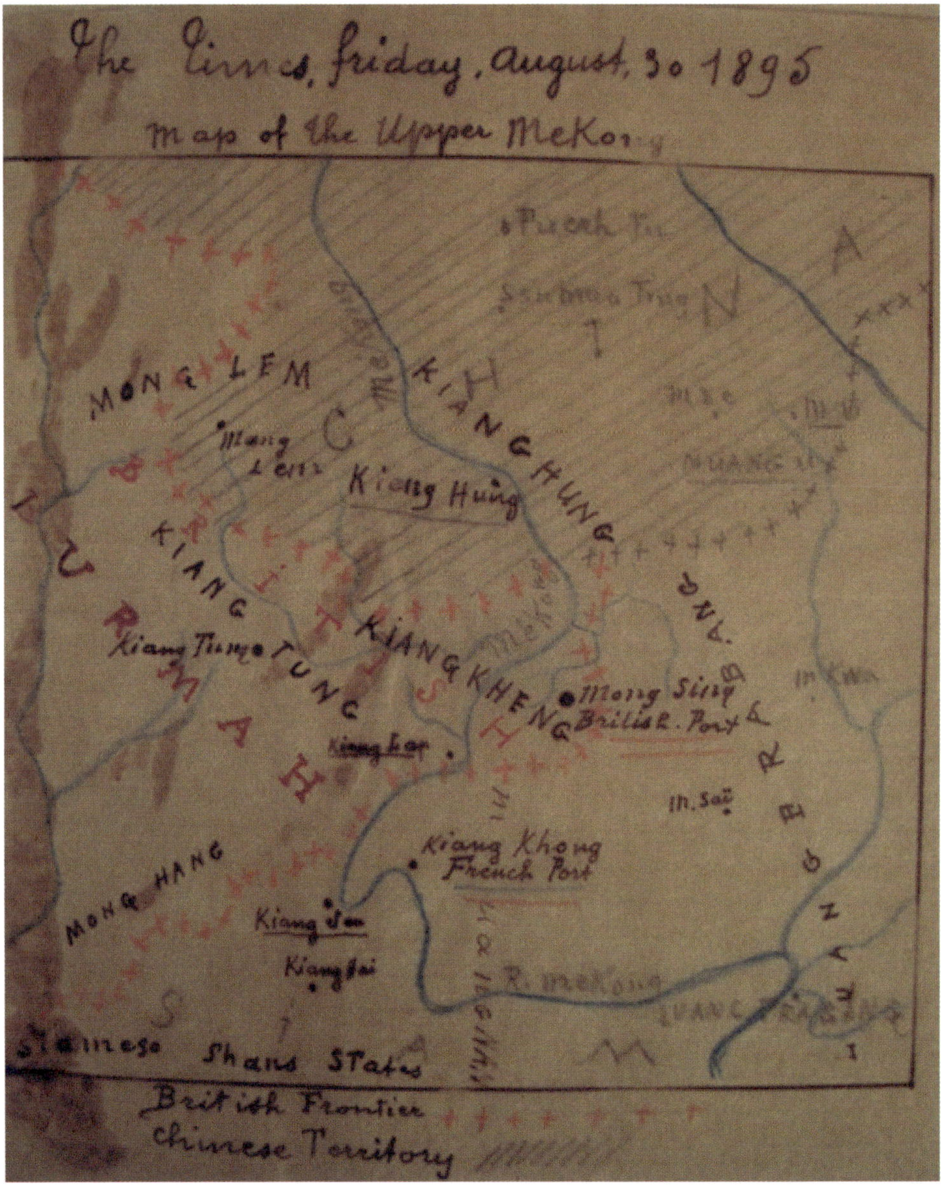

British map of the Upper Mekong region (1895). The whole territory of Chiang Khaeng (including Moeng Sing) is claimed as part of British Burma

SOURCE: Centre des Archives d'Outre Mer (Aix-en-Provence), Gouvernement Général de l'Indochine, Cabinet du Gouvernement Général, no. 20161: Affaire des Sib Song Pan Na

Map 6: French Map of the Upper Mekong Region

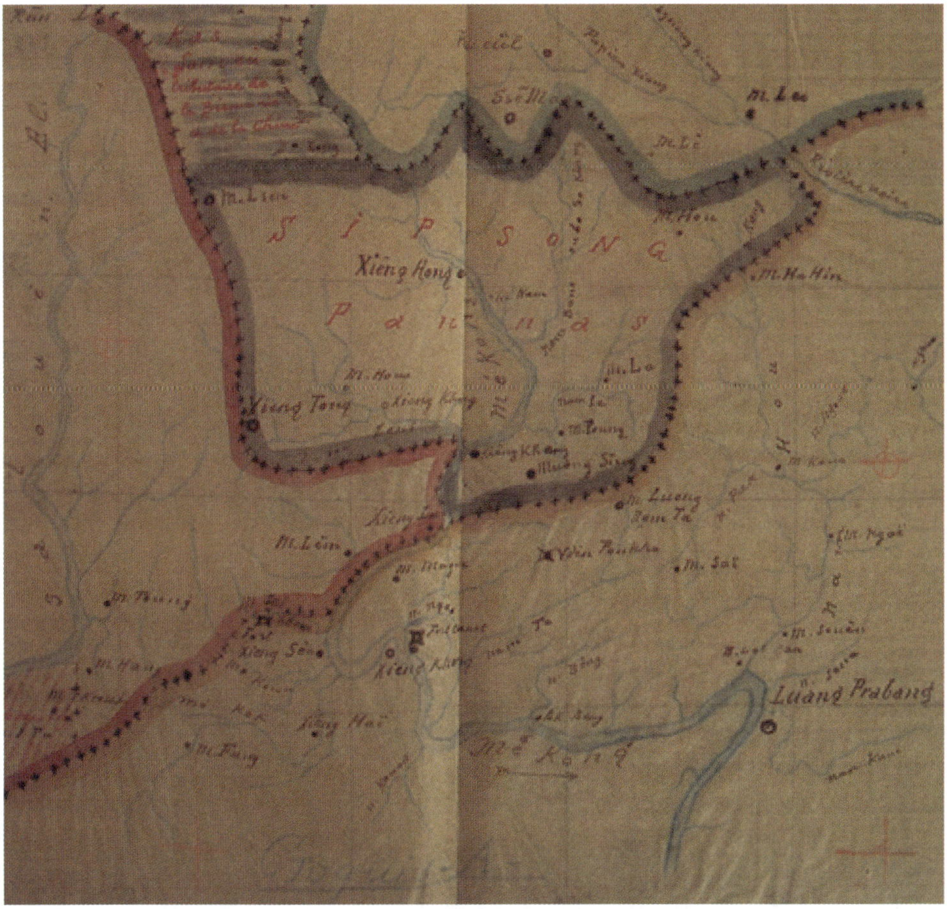

Source: Centre des Archives d'Outre Mer (Aix-en-Provence), Gouvernement Général de l'Indochine, Cabinet du Gouvernement Général, no. 20161: Affaire des Sib Song Pan Na

Map 7: Yunnan and Adjacent Regions in the Seventeenth Century

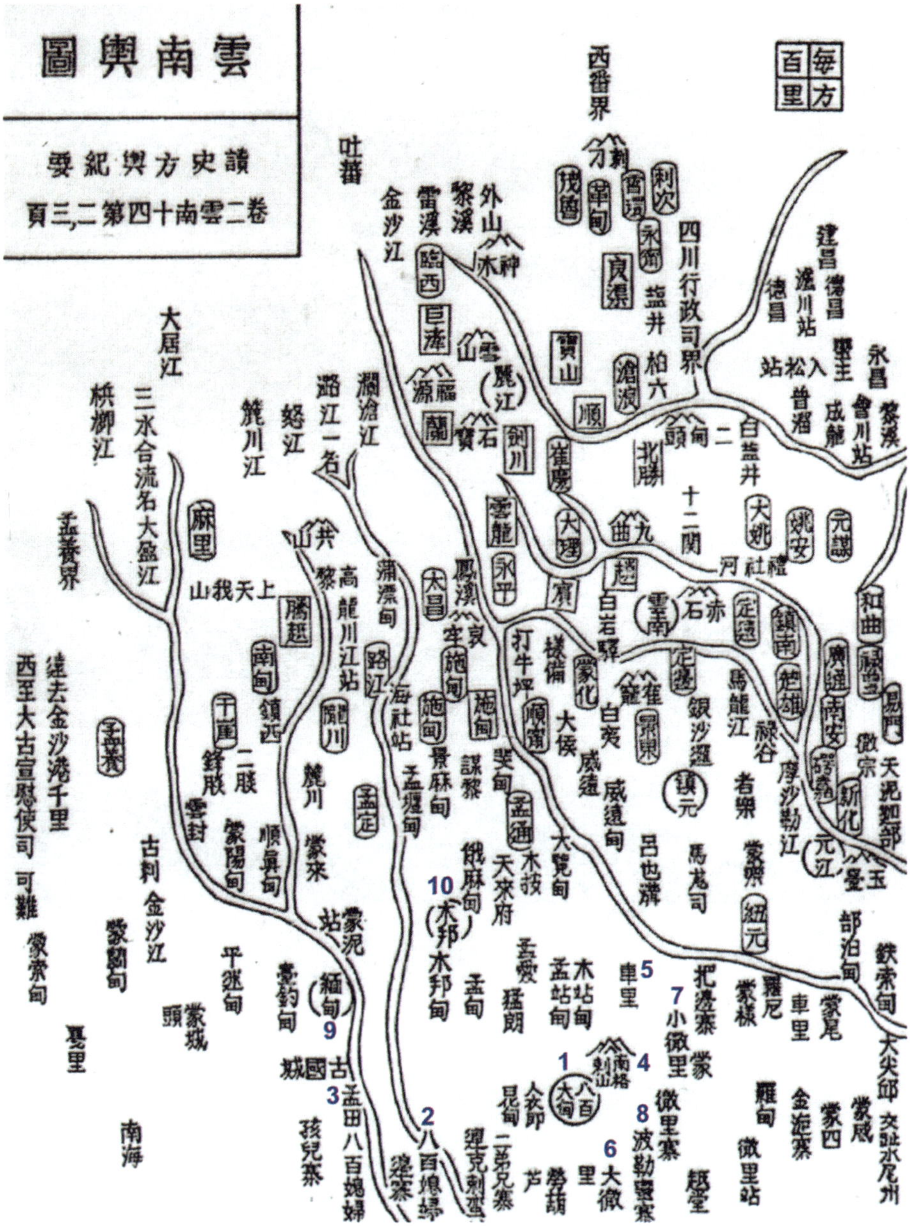

1. Babai-dadian
2. Babai-xifu
3. Mengtian Babai-xifu
4. Nan Gelashan
5. Cheli
6. Greater Cheli
7. Lesser Cheli
8. Bole man zhai
9. Miandian
10. Mubang

Source: Gu Zuyu, *Dushi fangyu jiyao*, ch. 40, Yunnan, ch. 2, 2–3 (numbers and key added by authors)

Map 8: Eighteen Aboriginal Commissions in the Early Nineteenth Century

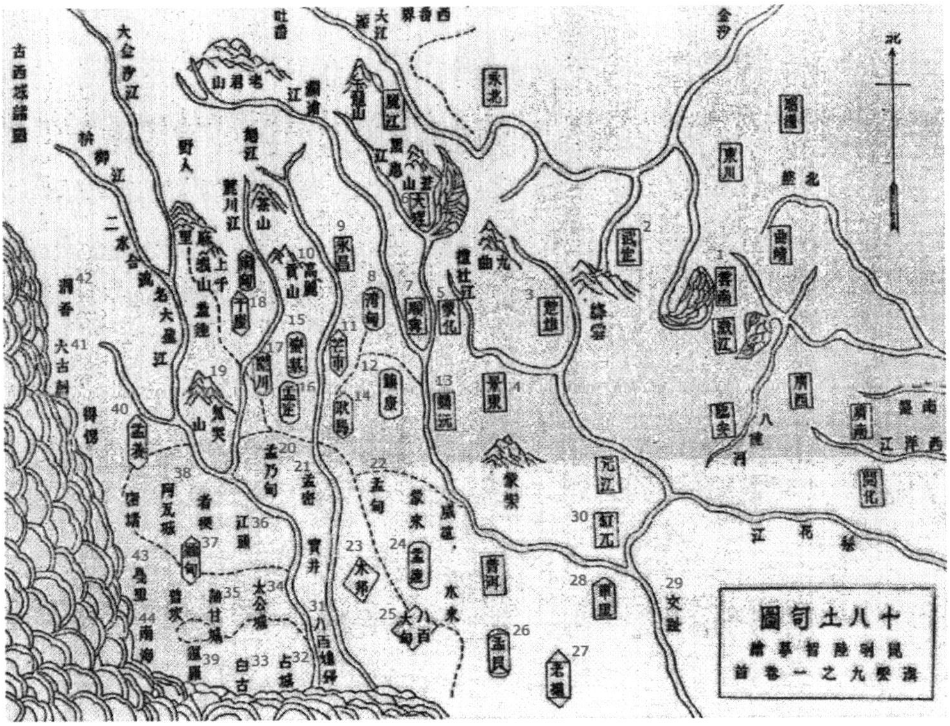

1. Yunnan or Kunming
2. Wuding
3. Chuqiong
4. Jingdong
5. Menghua
6. Dali
7. Shunning
8. Wandian
9. Yongchang
10. Gaoligong shan
11. Mangshi
12. Zhenkang
13. Zhenyuan
14. Gengma
15. Wianmu
16. Wiengding
17. Longchuan
18. Ganya
19. Gui ku shan
20. Mengnai dian
21. Mengmi
22. Menglian
23. Mubang
24. Menglian
25. Babai dadian
26. Menggen
27. Laowo
28. Cheli
29. Jiaozhi, Annam
30. Niuwu
31. Babai xifu
32. Zhancheng
33. Baigu
34. Taigong cheng
35. Pugan cheng
36. Jiangtou
37. Miandian
38. Awa cheng
39. Xianluo, Siam
40. Mengyang
41. Dagula
42. Dongwu
43. Jiali
44. Nanhai

SOURCE: *Dianxi* (1808 ed.), 9, by Shi Fan.

Map 9: Site of Wiang Phakhang, Chiang Rung

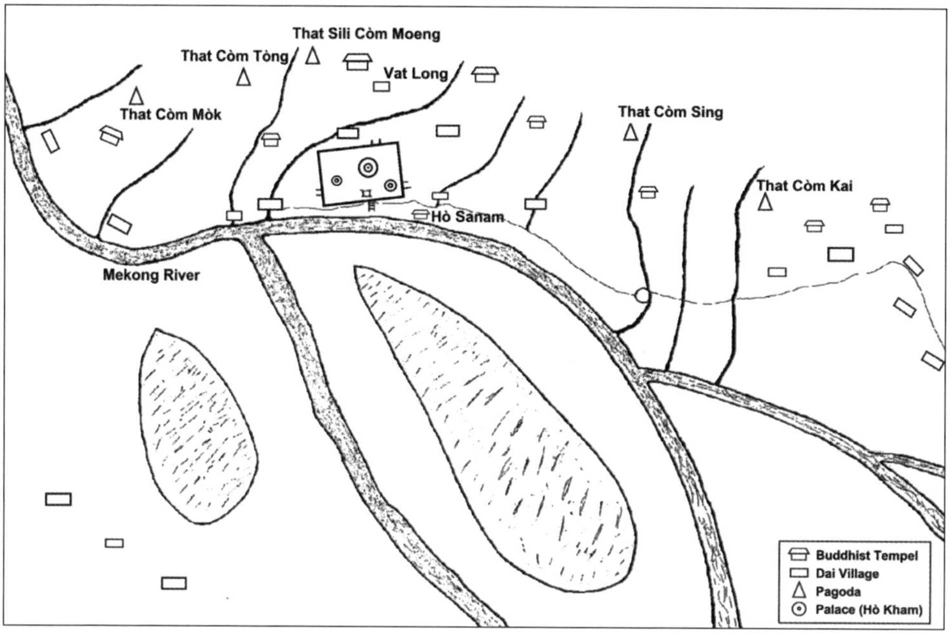

SOURCE: Redrawn by Thinagon Dechadanuwong based on a sketch provided by Hasegawa Kiyoshi.

Preface and Acknowledgements

The present work contains the annotated translations of four versions of the Moeng Lü Chronicles. According to these chronicles, the ancient kingdom of the Tai Lü called Moeng Lü, later Sipsòng Panna, by the local Tai peoples, was founded in the late twelfth century (i.e., in 1180) by King Coeng (Cüang) in the Upper Mekong basin. The capital of the kingdom was called Chiang Rung เชียงรุ่ง (lit., "city of dawn"), which was renamed Chiang Yung เชียงยูง (lit., "city of peacocks"), in the late sixteenth century. Most of the domain of the pristine Tai Lü kingdom lies in the southern tip of today's Yunnan in the People's Republic of China. Moeng Lü with her unique culture and glorious history survived on the periphery of imperial China of the successive dynasties (viz., Southern Song, Yuan, Ming, and Qing) down to the Republic of China (1912–1949).[1] In 1953, not long after the founding of the People's Republic of China, Cheli 車里, hitherto the Chinese rendering of Sipsòng Panna, was reorganised and the Xishuang banna daizu zizhi zhou 西雙版納傣族自治州, translated into English as "Sipsòng Panna Tai Autonomous Prefecture", was established in its stead.[2] Chiang Rung, or Jinghong 景

1. In 1949 Mao Zedong 毛澤東 (1893–1976) and his Chinese Communist Party ousted the government of the Republic of China (Zhonghua minguo 中華民國) under the Nationalist Party (Guomin dang 國民黨). Chiang Kai-shek 蔣介石 (1887–1975) and his Nationalist Party fled to Taiwan. The People's Republic of China (Zhonghua renmin gongheguo 中華人民共和國) under Mao Zedong was founded in October 1949.

2. The administrative divisions of China under the a *sheng* 省 (province) were normally divided into *fu* 府 (prefecture), *zhou* 州 (sub-prefecture), and *xian* 縣 (county) during the time of the Ming dynasty (1368–1644), the Qing dynasty (1644–1911), and the Republic of China (1912–1949). These administrative divisions have been mostly taken over by the People's Republic of China (1949–) with some rearrangements. In 1953, Sipsòng Panna was officially granted the *zizhi zhou* 自治州 (autonomous sub-prefecture) status, not a *zizhi fu* 自治府 (autonomous prefecture), which is a level higher. Although Moeng Lü and other Tai tribal kingdoms, such as Luchuan-Pingmian 麓川平緬 (now *Dehong daizu zizhi zhou* 德宏傣族自治州) in Yunnan during the Ming period were granted the status of a *junmin xuanwei shisi* 軍民宣慰使司 (military-cum-civilian pacification commission), which is an aboriginal commission (*tusi* 土司) normally established in a tribal domain roughly the size of a Chinese *fu* (prefecture). Nevertheless, "Sipsòng Panna Tai

洪 in Chinese is now a modern and bustling city with roughly 200,000 inhabitants, the majority of them are Han Chinese.

Moeng Lü or Sipsòng Panna, known as Cheli 車里 in contemporary Chinese sources, was first mentioned in the *History of the Yuan Dynasty* (*Yuanshi*) in 1284, when the Mongol commander Bu-lu-he-da 步魯合答 pacified Cheli on his way to conquer Babai-xifu 八百媳婦 (Lan Na). Cheli surrendered and pledged allegiance to China under the Mongol emperor. Since then the successive rulers of Moeng Lü became a sort of aboriginal official (*tuguan* 土官) of China. Nevertheless, the Tai Lü kingdom on the southern fringes of China survived as an autonomous, at times semi-independent, polity until the last ruler of Sipsòng Panna, Cao Mòm Kham Lü, who was formally enthroned in 1947 as a youth, abdicated in 1950. According to Tai Lü sources translated in this work, the ruling house of Moeng Lü had a total of forty-four rulers and ruled uninterrupted for almost eight centuries.

Most probably the Council of Nobles (*noe sanam*) in Chiang Rung, who formed the central government of the traditional Tai Lü polity, had historiographers and scribes who were responsible for recording all important events, such as disputes over succession, fratricidal wars, and invasions of neighbouring polities, and kept records of the genealogy of the ruling house. However, the Tai Lü chronicles are not contemporary sources but cumulative records, updated periodically, copied and recopied repeatedly over generations by historians and scribes working for the Tai Lü nobility. Owing to the decentralised political system of Sipsòng Panna, several major *müang* (pronounced moeng in Tai Lü)—such as Moeng Long, Moeng Hai, and Moeng La—have their own historiography. The chronicles of these *müang* deal mostly with local political events and socio-economic structures, paying less attention to wider regional affairs. Thus our emphasis is placed on the dynastic chronicle of Moeng Lü with the focus on the capital Chiang Rung and the events pertaining to the polity of Sipsòng Panna as such.

There are mainly two types of the dynastic Chronicle of Moeng Lü or Sipsòng Panna which we conveniently call the "long version" and the "short version". The long versions provide not only the genealogical records of the ruling dynasty of Phaya Coeng (Cüang) but also contains details of important events of that reign. The short versions mainly contain the genealogies of the various Tai Lü rulers, giving details such as the date of the death of a ruler, the name of his successor, and the names of the legal princes. The extant manuscripts and manuscript copies3 of these chronicles that we have collected are not very old because most of the older manuscripts or copies were lost during the successive wars and foreign invasions during the eighteenth and nineteenth centuries. The destructive "Great Cultural Revolution" (1966–1976) in China

Autonomous Prefecture" has become the standard English translation of "Xishuang banna zizhi zhou". The development of Cheli from a pacification commission of highest rank to a *zizhi zhou* of Sipsòng Panna is a topic that deserves a special study.

3. Here we would like to stress that the extant Tai Lü manuscripts do not represent an *urtext* (original text), but are copies of (probably lost) "original" manuscripts.

also contributed to the disappearance of many precious manuscripts. Since the late 1970s, under a relatively liberal political climate, Tai Lü scholars have taken up the task of recompiling their own chronicles, translating them into Chinese, and publishing them.

To the best of our knowledge, the two oldest Tai Lü manuscripts, one from Moeng Hai and one from Moeng Khün (Chiang Tung), forming the "long version 1" of the Moeng Lü Chronicle on which Li Fuyi's 1947 *Leshi* 泐史 (cited as MLC-LV1) is based, were lost sometime between 1944 and 1946/47.[4] Fortunately, they have been transmitted to us in Li Fuyi's pioneering translation, albeit only in Chinese. The oldest Tai Lü manuscript of the "short version" of the Moeng Lü Chronicle (cited as MLC-SV1) is the one printed alongside Li Fuyi's Chinese translation of the genealogy of the *cao phaendin* of Moeng Lü or Sipsòng Panna, also published in 1947, and thus transmitted to us. For this study we have translated two long versions, i.e., MLC-LV1, and the 1963 Tai Lü chronicle (cited as MLC-LV2), and two short versions, i.e., MLC-SV1 and MLC-SV2. This is the first time that an English translation of the Moeng Lü Chronicle has been made available.

Part I and part 2 of the MLC-LV1 present the Tai Lü chronicle proper. Li Fuyi numbers the sections chronologically from 1 to 32. The division into subsections, numbered 1.1, 1.2, etc., and the subtitles are ours. The content of part 3, completely different from that of part 1 and 2, is divided into sixteen unnumbered topics, probably by Li Fuyi. Since it is part 3 of *Leshi*, we have added the numbers, 3.1, 3.2, and so on. We have also added numbers, titles, and subtitles to the various paragraphs, sections, and subsections of the other three versions of the Moeng Lü Chronicle.

The volume begins with a two-part introduction to the annotated translations of the four versions of the Moeng Lü Chronicle. Part 1 provides a comprehensive introduction to the history of Sipsòng Panna based on indigenous Tai Lü sources, supplemented by Chinese and other sources. It also touches upon the political systems, society and customs, tributary relations between China and Burma, and their respective political relations with neighbouring Tai polities. Part 2 situates and evaluates the historical importance of the four translated versions of the Moeng Lü Chronicle. Corroborative Tai Lü manuscripts are mentioned and various philological problems encountered during the translation are discussed, along with special features of the Tai Lü language and script.

Since MLC-LV1 is only transmitted to us in Li Fuyi's 1947 edition of *Leshi* in Chinese translation--the original Tai Lü manuscript is lost--the transcriptions of the numerous Tai Lü personal names, toponym, and special terms in our English translation as a rule follow that of the MLC-LV2. However, not all the names mentioned in MLC-LV1 can be found in MLC-LV2. In this case, we have done our best to render them as closely as possible to the Tai Lü pronunciation. We have done the same with the several Burmese names found only in MLC-LV1. While the contents of the two long versions of the Moeng Lü Chronicle in many parts are rather similar, yet differ in certain details due to

4. As to how Li Fuyi lost his two Tai Lü manuscripts, see the introduction, part 2, n. 14.

their differing age and source, no attempt has been made to resolve the disparities. The study of textual disparities between MLC-LV1 and MLC-LV2 is beyond the scope this book and requires special study.

A number of people have contributed to the publication of this work. We are indebted to Yan Han (alias Ai Kham), a Tai Lü scholar-official working at the Cultural Bureau of the Political Council of the Prefecture of Sipsòng Panna (Zhou Zhengxie 州政協) in Jinghong, for kindly giving us a copy of the rare 1963 Tai Lü manuscript of the long version of the Moeng Lü Chronicle (MLC-LV2). Cao Maha Khanthawong, a retired Tai Lü scholar in Jinghong, very generously allowed us to inspect and copy several manuscripts in his private collection. These two respected scholars were very helpful during our two field studies in Sipsòng Panna (in 2002 and 2005). They shared with us their profound knowledge of Tai Lü culture, history, and literature. During our field trips in Sipsòng Panna and Dehong in March 2002 we received the kind assistance of Yang Guangyuan, Dao Chenghua, Ai Wenlong, and Zhao Hongyun.

Special thanks are due to the kind old Cao Mòm Kham Lü (Dao Shixun), the last ruler (*cao fa*) of Sipsòng Panna, for granting Foon Ming Liew-Herres and Volker Grabowsky an audience at his villa in Kunming in March 2002. Moreover, Liew-Herres would like to thank Li Fuyi 李拂一 (1901–2010) for giving her an interview in his apartment in Taibei in November 2008 and inviting her to a delicious lunch in a Yunnan Restaurant of Taibei. When asked, Li Fuyi, who is still in relatively good physical and mental health, told her how he had lost the two Tai Lü manuscripts, on which his pioneering translation of the Moeng Lü Chronicle, namely *Leshi* (History of the Moeng Lü), was based.

Liew-Herres would like to thank Geoff Wade in Singapore and Cheng Wen-chin in Taibei for helping to make arrangements for her to see Li Fuyi. She also thanks Chen Qinzhuang 陳欽莊 from the former Hangzhou University, who copied the original edition of *Leshi* for her in 2000, as well as Huang Yuan-chüan 黃淵泉 and Huang Mei-chih 黃美智, both from the National Central Library of Taibei, for their time and effort in searching for and finding the original edition of *Leshi* and another publication of Li Fuyi in 1947 (MLC-SV1) in the library's storage. Gratitude also goes to Gao Lishi 高立士, a Tai scholar in Yunnan, who sent her his Chinese publications on Sipsòng Panna. Among them was the valuable Tai Lü manuscript of the Moeng Lü Chronicle, namely the short version (MCL-SV2), which was published together with his 1982 Chinese translation. Our thanks are due to the Director General Dr. Shiba Yoshinobu 斯波義信 of the Tōyō Bunko (Oriental Library) and Ms. Hirose Yōko 廣瀨洋子 (retired librarian of the Tōyō Bunko) for the photocopies of some pages of the valuable rare Ming works. We are also grateful to Dr. Kato Kumiko and Mr. Isra Yanatan for kindly providing us with copies of several mulberry paper manuscripts from their private collections.

Furthermore, we would like to thank Prasert na Nagara, Khamsèn Chayavong, Ratanaporn Setthakul, Cia Yaencòng (alias Yanyong Ciranakhòn), Aroonrut Wichienkeeo, Bounleuth Sengsoulin, Jan Dreßler, Michel Lorrillard, François Lagirarde, John Hartmann, and Oskar von Hinüber, for their many helpful comments or other forms of support. Charles Sanft and Amanda Katherine Rath assisted in fine tuning and editing the English of our manuscript, and Amanda's critical comments on the introductory parts are also appreciated. Claudia Schroer and Thinagorn Dechadanuwong skilfully prepared the maps. We are most grateful to Uta Gärtner who gave us the benefit of her linguistic expertise in Burmese. We would like to thank Trasvin Jittidecharak and Susan Offner of Silkworm Books for their patience with us and their fine work in dealing with the publication of this complicated book. Finally, we would like to express our gratitude to the German Research Foundation (DFG) for the generous financial support of our present research under the "Traditional Polities of the Tai" project during the years 2001 to 2006.

INTRODUCTION

Contents

INTRODUCTION

I. History and Society of Sipsòng Panna: An Overview

The Sipsòng Panna Tai (Dai) Autonomous Prefecture (Xishuang banna daizu zizhi zhou) was founded in 1953, four years after the proclamation of the People's Republic of China. It is located in southern Yunnan, in the northeast of Burma (Myanmar) and northwest of Laos, covering an area of 19,700 square kilometres with slightly more than one million inhabitants. Though Sipsòng Panna is almost as large as the northern Thai province of Chiang Mai, it has only two-thirds of the latter's population. The average population density in Sipsòng Panna (about fifty persons per square kilometre) is indeed one of the lowest in Yunnan but 95.1 per cent of the autonomous prefecture's territory is covered by mountains and less than one-third of the population, predominantly members of various "hill tribes" such as Hani, Lahu, and Bulang, live in mountainous areas. The vast majority of the population settles in the agriculturally productive plains which make up for only 4.9 per cent of the territory. The thirty plains (*tong*, Th. ทุ่ง), comprising 978 square kilometres, vary in size. The largest plain is that of Moeng Cae, a fertile rice-growing area of 160 square kilometres, followed by the plains of Moeng Long, Moeng Ham, Moeng La, and Chiang Rung, each of which comprise 70–80 square kilometres. The size of most other plains, however, is much smaller, averaging between 20 and 40 square kilometres. The elevation of the river basins ranges between 500 and 1,100 metres. The mountains are approximately 1,000 to 2,300 metres above sea level. The Mekong River, called Lancang jiang 瀾滄江 by the Chinese, flows across Sipsòng Panna in a northwest-southeast direction, dividing the region into almost two equal halves.[1]

Sipsòng Panna is a Tai word which means "twelve districts". The administrative division into twelve districts or *panna* (Th. พันนา) was introduced in the second half of the sixteenth century. Before that time the region was known under its original name, Moeng Lü, literally meaning "the polity/domain of the [Tai] Lü". The Tai Lü had been the politically dominant group since the founding of Moeng Lü in the late twelfth century. Chinese sources generally refer to the region as Cheli (徹里 or 車里). The origin of the toponym Cheli is very old and certainly is derived from the phonetic rendering of the

1. Cia (alias Yanyong) 2005, 259–60; Yanyong and Ratanaporn 2001, 197.

indigenous Tai language.[2] We suspect that most probably it refers to Chiang Lü (Th. เชียงลื้อ), "royal capital of the [Tai] Lü".[3] The term "Cheli" was used by the Chinese until the mid-twentieth century to designate both the Tai Lü polity of Sipsòng Panna as a whole and its capital Chiang Rung (Jinghong) in particular.[4]

To the best of our knowledge, the first six kings of Moeng Lü[5] mentioned in the Moeng Lü Chronicle (Ch. *Leshi*) are not recorded in Chinese sources prior to the Yuan dynasty (1280–1368). Thus, we know nothing about the nature of the relationship between Moeng Lü and China during the Southern Song period (1127–1279). The name Cheli first appeared in the Chinese sources of the History of the Yuan Dynasty (*Yuanshi*) only in AD 1284.[6] Falling under Burmese suzerainty in 1570, Moeng Lü was divided into twelve administrative units (*panna*), the composition and borders of which fluctuated over the centuries (for details, see section 4.3, below).

The pristine domain of Moeng Lü was much larger than that of the present-day autonomous prefecture of Sipsòng Panna in southern Yunnan. Its borders began to shrink by at least the mid-nineteenth century with the advent of treaties with European powers. The Sino-French treaty, for example, was signed in September 1895, and in 1896 one important *panna*, comprising Moeng U-Nüa and Moeng U-Tai, was formally ceded to French Indochina. In 1916, the French established their "Cinquième Territoire Militaire" in these two *müang*, which later became the Lao province of Phong Saly.[7] In addition, in 1913, the southern part of the present day Simao district, with its seat at Puer (Moeng Maen), changed hands from Sipsòng Panna to the province of Yunnan, which was part of China proper.

2. This is Fang Guoyi's hypothesis. See his preface to MLC-LV1. On the derivation of the toponym Cheli, see Li Fuyi 1942, 31–37 and 2003a, 197–200.

3. *Chiang* (เชียง) means a walled town that was the seat of royalty or of the aristocracy. For details, see n. 36.

4. See, for example, the account of Smith and Clark (1954) on the infiltration during World War II of Allied and Seri Thai agents from Kunming into Siam via Chiang Rung, which they call "Cheli".

5. They are Phaya Coeng, Sam Khai Noeng, Ai Kung, Tao Hung Kaen Cai, Tao Haeng Long, and Tao Puwak. See MLC-LV1 and MLC-LV2.

6. *Yuanshi*, chapter 132, 3208. (Memoir of Bu-lu-he-da). See Liew-Herres et al. 2008, 79.

7. See Lacroze 1994, 7–9. A confidential British report on British policies in the Upper Mekong valley doubts the legality of the Franco-Chinese Convention of 1 March 1894. The report points out that the Chinese justified the cession of Moeng U-Tai and Moeng U-Nüa by advancing two contradictory contentions. On the one hand, the Chinese argued that the two Moeng U were not part of Sipsòng Panna but belonged to Yunnan proper. On the other hand, it was claimed that the Burmese Treaty of 1894 referred only to the cis-Mekong part of Chiang Rung but did not extend to those territories situated on the eastern bank of the Mekong River. Morevover, both claims were "inconsistent with the justification [...] advanced by the French, viz., that Moeng U is an old dependency of Annam." See "Siam, France, and China", 1895, 1 [PRO, FO 881/6699].

1. POPULATION

The Tai Lü are traditionally the predominant ethnic group in Sipsòng Panna, which they consider to be their heartland. The Tai Lü refer to themselves as such only when they want to distinguish their own group from other Tai peoples.[8] Otherwise, the Tai Lü of Sipsòng Panna call themselves simply "Tai". The Tai Lü, along with the Tai Nüa of the Dehong Autonomous Prefecture and several smaller Tai groups, such as the Tai Ya, are recognised by the Chinese under the nationality "Dai 傣" (the Chinese rendering of "Tai"). The "Dai" is one of the fifty-six officially recognised nationalities (*minzu* 民族) among the politically motivated constructs of Chinese ethnographers. As a category, however, "Dai" has failed to provide any meaningful basis of self-identification for members of the ethnic Dai who would consider themselves as Tai Nüa, Tai Ya, Tai Laem, or Tai Lü.

For many centuries the Tai maintained their pre-eminent status in the spheres of politics, culture, and economy, while also dominating in their relationships with other ethnic groups in Sipsòng Panna. Almost all Tai Lü have established their villages in the river valleys. They are wet-rice farmers who originally cultivated and consumed only glutinous rice.[9] Ordinary rice is primarily produced for the urban ethnic Chinese population. The Tai Lü are devout believers of Theravada Buddhism which was introduced via Lan Na in the late fourteenth or early fifteenth century. The Tai Nüa are also Buddhists, whereas the Tai Ya adhere to animism. Though having adopted Theravada Buddhism as the state religion many centuries ago, the Tai Lü still practice multifarious aspects of their traditional religion. Local guardian spirits, for instance, are worshipped by each village and *moeng* (*müang*).[10]

According to Yanyong Ciranakhòn (Cia Yaencòng), a leading expert of Tai culture and history, there are 750 Tai villages in Sipsòng Panna of which 714 are inhabited by Tai Lü, 19 by Tai Nüa, and 17 by Tai Ya.[11] Many of the Tai Nüa and Tai Ya villages are situated in the northern districts of Moeng Yang Nòi and Moeng Hing.[12] The ancestors of the Tai Nüa once migrated from Moeng Kla and Moeng Bò, areas to the north of

8. The *Chronicle of Sipsòng Panna*, Moeng Long version (f° 1/17–22), distinguishes between nine Tai groups in the Upper Mekong region, 1. Tai Lü (ไทลื้อ) 2. Tai Nüa (ไทเหนือ), 3. Tai Ya (ไทหย่า), 4. Tai Khae (ไทแค), 5. Tai Ka (ไทกล้า), 6. Tai Khün (ไทขึน), 7. Tai Pan (ไทพั่น), 8. Tai Yuan (ไทยวน), 9. Tai Dam (ไทดำ).

9. There is extensive ethnographic literature on the Tai Lü. A classic is Michael Mormann's seminal paper "Ethnic Identification in a Complex Civilization: Who are the Lue?" (1965). More recent ethno-historical studies are Lemoine 1987; Hsieh 1989; Hasegawa 2000; Ratanaporn 2000a; and Davis 2005.

10. For a good overview of the different Tai groups currently settling in Yunnan and their presumed places of origin, see Liu Yan 1999.

11. Cia (alias Yanyong) 2005, 259.

12. In 2005, 7 of 16 villages in Moeng Yang Nòi, situated to the northeast of Chiang Rung, were Tai Ya (Tai Bò) villages. See field notes of the authors, March–April 2005.

Simao, and the Tai Ya originate from Moeng Ya and Moeng Cung in the Red River valley. Roughly 350,000 Tai Lü live in Sipsòng Panna at the present time. They are related to the Tai speaking population in the "Shan" state of Chiang Tung (Keng Tung) in eastern Burma—a mixture of Tai Khün and Tai Lü—and maintain close cultural and economic ties with the Tai Lü in Müang (Moeng) Sing in Laos.[13] There are no reliable data available on the number of Tai Lü in Burma. However, it can be estimated that at present a total of 200,000 to 300,000 Tai Lü have settled in the eastern part of Burmese Shan State. According to the results of the most recent census conducted in 2005, the Tai Lü population in Laos amounts to 150,000, with the largest concentrations in the northwestern border provinces of Luang Nam Tha and Bò Kaeo where they make up slightly less than 20 per cent of the total population. In addition, more than 400,000 Tai Lü live in northern Thailand, notably in the provinces of Lamphun, Chiang Mai, Chiang Rai, and Nan. The majority of them are descendants of war captives who were forcibly resettled from areas in Sipsòng Panna (especially Moeng La and Moeng Phong) and the eastern Shan states (in particular Moeng Yòng and Chiang Tung) in the first half of the nineteenth century.[14] In contrast to their kin in China, Burma, and Laos, the Tai Lü in northern Thailand have been largely assimilated, both linguistically and culturally, into the local Tai Yuan mainstream.

Apart from the Han Chinese, the Tai Lü are the only ethnic group in Sipsòng Panna that has a written language. The Tai Lü script, a variant of the Dhamma script which was once widely used among Tai peoples of the Upper Mekong region, was introduced as an official script in 1955, though in a simplified form.[15] At present, the Tai comprise one-third of the total population in the autonomous prefecture. The second largest ethnic group are the Chinese who started to migrate in substantial numbers during the Republican period (1912–1949) and today make up almost 26–28 per cent of the population. Whereas the Tai Lü settle predominantly in the villages of the river basins, the Chinese constitute the dominant urban element. In the capital of Chiang Rung, for example, two-thirds of the 150,000 inhabitants are ethnic Chinese, while the Tai Lü count for only one-fifth.[16] A significant rural Chinese population exists only in the sparsely populated eastern tea-growing districts of I-ngu (Yiwu) and I-pang (Yibang).

---

13. As to the Tai Lü of Moeng Sing and the historical development of their polity, the principality of Chiang Khaeng, see Grabowsky 1999b and Grabowsky and Renoo 2008.

14. The forced resettlements of Tai Lü and other Tai groups to northern Thailand in the late eighteenth and early nineteenth centuries is discussed by Grabowsky 1999a.

15. For details, see the introduction, part 2, section 8 of this volume.

16. The remaining one-tenth of the population in the capital are members of other ethnic groups. We obtained the demographic data from Dao Xinhua, a former mayor of Chiang Rung who is the younger half-brother of Cao Mòm Kham Lü, the last ruler (*cao fa*) of Sipsòng Panna. Interview with Dao Xinhua in Chiang Rung, 22 March 2002.

Table 1: Ethnic Groups in Sipsòng Panna, Census of 1990

Nationality (*minzu*)	Absolute	Percentage
Dai (Tai)	270,192	34.04
Han (Chinese)	209,615	26.41
Hani	149,089	18.78
Yi	33,569	4.30
Lahu	46,207	5.82
Bulang (Pulang)	33,723	4.25
Jinuo	17,287	2.18
Yao	14,772	1.86
Hui (Chinese Muslims)	3,097	0.39
Wa	1,781	0.22
Others	11,509	1.45
Total	793,684	100.00

SOURCES: *Jinghong xianzhi* 2000: 108; *Menghai xianzhi* 1997: 100; *Mengla xianzhi* 1994: 76

Table 2: Census of the Eight Districts Taken in 1913 based on *Pusi yanbian zhilüe* (A concise treatise on Pusi and the frontier regions)

County	Households	Males	Females	Total
Cheli (Chiang Rung)	6,952	18,417	17,421	35,838
Moeng Cae	5,899	12,123	11,112	23,235
Moeng Hai	5,445	13,797	13,808	27,605
Moeng Long (Luang)	3,077	5,468	5,390	10,858
Moeng La,	3,812	7,056	8,139	15,195
Yibang (I-pang)/Yiwu (I-ngu)	3,916	8,187	7,116	15,303
Puwen (Moeng Hing)	1,705	3,913	3,766	7,679
Liushun (Chiang Nüa)	7,450	16,875	16,519	33,394
Total	38, 256	85,836	83,271	169,107

SOURCE: Li Fuyi 1949; 1984, 410–11.

The Hani (or Akha) are the third largest ethnic group (19 per cent) and, like the less numerous Lahu and Jinuo, belong to the Tibeto-Burman linguistic family. All three groups migrated to Sipsòng Panna after the Tai Lü had already settled and founded their polities there. Among the many smaller ethnic minorities, the Bulang (Pulang) enjoy a special status. The Mon-Khmer speaking Bulang (4–5 per cent) are recognised as the original inhabitants of Sipsòng Panna and have thus attained a higher status than the other hill tribes who are considered "latecomers".[17]

The earliest modern census in Sipsòng Panna was carried out in 1913 (see table 2). The results of that 1913 census reveal that the total population was only about 170,000, far less than previous estimates. The American missionary Clifton Dodd (1857–1919), a minister in the Presbyterian church touring the region extensively in 1913, arrived at the conclusion that the Tai population alone was around 350,000. However, he based his estimation on the obviously inflated figure of 70,000 tax-paying households in Sipsòng Panna and on the assumption of five persons per household.[18]

It is nearly impossible to extrapolate these figures back into the second half of the nineteenth century, as our knowledge about basic demographic data—fertility, mortality, and migration—during that period remains vague. One element that confounds any determining data is the continuous influx of Tai Lü from Sipsòng Panna into territories that now belong to Burma, Laos, and Thailand. This migration was stimulated by several factors, such as political turmoil in the wake of succession disputes, shortage of rice land, and contact with Tai Lü communities of previous generations of migrants. At any rate, Tai Lü out-migration was substantial and contributed to a demographic stagnation or even decline throughout the nineteenth century. The results of the 1923 and 1933 censuses show that the population of Sipsòng Panna in the 1920s and 1930s stagnated at around 165,000 to 175,000 persons, despite the numbers of Chinese immigration which totalled up to 17–18 per cent in 1933.[19] The Sino-Japanese war (1937–1945) also resulted in a decrease of population as many soldiers and civilians on the Burma-China border were killed, and the spread of malaria caused the death of many Chinese settlers. At the time of "liberation" by the Chinese People's Liberation Army in 1950, the population of Sipsòng Panna was slightly over 200,000.

Beginning in the 1950s, the population steadily increased. Higher birth rates, declining mortality, and an increasing migration of ethnic Chinese contributed to a demographic recovery. In 1956 Sipsòng Panna had a population of 250,000 inhabitants, of which slightly more than 50 per cent were Tai Lü. After the failure of the "Great Leap Forward" (1958/59), many Chinese from Hunan, Kweichou (i.e., Guizhou), and other poor provinces in southern China, migrated to Sipsòng Panna where they worked on

17. Hsieh 1989, 54–56. For details, see the subsequent section 3 on Tai-Kha relations.

18. Dodd [1923] 1996, 185. Dodd's highly influential book *The Tai Race: Elder Brother of the Chinese* is largely based on ethnographic fieldwork in the Tai speaking areas of Yunnan (Sipsòng Panna, Dehong) and the eastern Shan states.

19. See Li Fuyi 1933, 31.

the rubber plantations. A second, mostly urban, wave of Chinese migrants arrived in 1970/71; however, some of them left Sipsòng Panna immediately after the abolition of the people's communes in 1978. Within a quarter of a century the population of the autonomous prefecture of Sipsòng Panna had more than doubled, and by 1982 had increased to some 640,000 inhabitants, of which the Tai Lü made up just one-third (35 per cent). In the same period, the proportion of ethnic Chinese increased from 7 per cent to more than 28 per cent (reaching a peak of 36 per cent in 1977/78).[20] Chinese immigration has slowed down since the early 1990s, and, since the family policy of the Communist Party of China that favours non-Han ethnic groups allows them to have more than one child per family, the proportion of ethnic Chinese in the area seems to have slightly declined over the last decade.[21] However, according to official statistics the population of Sipsòng Panna still increased almost 2.3 per cent per annum, which is about twice as high as the average in China. This indicates a relatively high natural increase of population, especially among Tai Lü and other non-Han minorities.

2. THE TAI POLITY

The origin and ethnogenesis of the Tai peoples was a subject of scholarly controversies over the last century; these disputes even had repercussions on the nationalist historiography of Thailand and Laos. Based on the works of the French sinologist Terrien de Lacouperie and other Western scholars, it was argued that the original homeland of the Tai was somewhere in northern and central China. All these speculations have been rejected on the basis of recent linguistic, historical, and ethnographic evidence which support the theory that the proto-Tai language emerged more than two thousand years ago in the border regions of upper Tonkin and southeastern China (with Guangxi as its core) and that several ethnic groups and cultures had contributed to the birth of Proto-Tai.[22]

2.1 EARLY TAI MIGRATIONS

The expansion of the Tai into their present areas of settlement resulted from several migration waves. The general direction of expansion was from east to west; it changed to a northeast-southwest and north-south direction after the end of the eleventh century. Like other historical migrations of people, such as the "Barbarian Invasions"

20. See Thongthaem 1989, 51–65.

21. Interview with Dao Xinhua, Chiang Rung, on 22 March 2002.

22. As one of the first Western historians of the Tai, Terwiel (1978) critically examined the conflicting theories about the origins and the original homesteads (Urheimat) of the Tai peoples. The latest review of literature is discussed in two conference papers by Placzek (1999) and Diller (2000) from a historical-anthropological and a linguistic perspective respectively. A critique of the theories and hypotheses put forward over the last four or five decades—in continuation of Terwiel's article—is provided by Baker (2002).

of the early European middle ages (the so-called migration period or *Völkerwanderung*), the ancestors of present-day Tai did not completely abandon their ancient homeland. Peoples seldom migrated as a whole, rather mobile groups of aristocrats and their retinue made their way to explore new potential settlement areas.

Uncertainty still remains about the reasons for and the dynamics of the Tai expansions between the seventh and fourteenth centuries. Was it scarcity of land and natural disasters in their homeland or was it the overpowering pressure of the Mongols in connection with continuous political instability within the Tai *müang* that caused the Tai to leave their ancestral homes? Most probably a combination of several factors was responsible for the dynamics of Tai migrations. A firm and efficient military organisation as well as knowledge of advanced irrigation techniques gave the migrating Tai groups an edge over the autochthonous populations.[23]

Though many Thai and some Western scholars, who once considered the kingdom of Nanzhao (728–902) and its successor state, the Dali Kingdom (937–1253), as ancient Tai states, propagated the idea of Sipsòng Panna as a cradle of Tai civilisation and the Tai Lü as "original Thai" (*thai dangdoem* ไทย ดั้งเดิม), there is hardly any doubt that the Tai Lü were not the first human settlers in the region. Ancient legends confirm that the ancestors of the Tai Lü once migrated from a place further to the north called Moeng Lü Long (Luang), which some oral traditions located in the Chinese province of Guizhou. The aboriginal inhabitants of Sipsòng Panna, some of which may have been organised into totemistic societies,[24] were subjugated by military conquest of politically better organised aristocratic Tai groups.

The Tai appear under different ethnic designations in Chinese historical sources. We find, for instance, terms such as "Golden-Teeth-Barbarians" (*jinchi man* 金齒蠻) and "Black-Teeth-Barbarians" (*heichi man* 黑齒蠻)[25] or "Tattooed-Feet-Barbarians" (*xiujiao man* 繡腳蠻) and "Tattooed-Face-Barbarians" (*xiumian man* 繡面蠻) in the

23. See Baker 2002, 18–19.

24. Echoes of totemism are still discernible in ancient Tai Lü legends. A chronicle from Moeng Long, for example, provides interesting insights into the pre-history of Chiang Rung (Pali: Āravī). It says that very few people lived in the region of Arawi, as many inhabitants had fallen victim to the yakṣa or ogres. But then a miracle happened. A "spontaneous or apparitional rebirth" (opapātika) of human beings from the stems of trees occurred. Female tigers, bears, monkeys, frogs, deer, hog deer, and rabbits also gave birth to human babies. When yakṣa women mated with yakṣa men [they conceived and] bore human children, and when the yakṣa died their corpses became stones, rocks, and hills. The same thing happened with the wild animals. The corpses of their human children became rocks in the shape of tigers, bears, monkeys, and deer. Numerous people were now born and the population increased considerably. The people born from the yakṣa and the various wild animals lived in [separate] villages [according to their parentage]. The "children of deer" (*luk kwang*) wore clothes resembling [the skin of] deer, and so on. See "The Chronicle of Sipsòng Panna: A Tai Lü Chronicle on Five *Chiang*—i.e., Chiang Rung, Chiang Tung, Chiang Saen, Chiang Rai, and Chiang Mai—nine lakes and twelve gates", f° 10/1–21.

25. The custom of making the teeth black by chewing betel is still widespread among many Tai peoples.

seventh and eighth century sources.[26] Until the end of the fourteenth century, the term *baiyi* 百夷 (lit., "hundred/numerous barbarians"), or *baiyi* 擺夷 (the barbarians performing the *bai* ceremony), was used as a generic term for a large number of Tai peoples in Yunnan and adjacent regions. Yet, already during the Yuan period (1280–1368), Chinese sources began to differentiate the Tai polities terminologically.[27] To give a few examples: Moeng Lü was called "Cheli" 車里 (or "Cheli" 徹里) both under the Yuan and the Ming rulers, Lan Na was known under the names "Babai-xifu" 八百媳婦 (in Yuan times) or "Babai-dadian" 八百大甸 (in Ming times),[28] and the Lao kingdom of Lan Sang, founded in 1353, is called either "Laowo" 老撾 (Laos) or "Nanzhang" 南掌 (Lan Sang) in contemporary Chinese sources.

2.2 THE *MÜANG*

The original term used to designate the political and social organisation of the Tai is *müang*, pronounced *moeng* in several Tai languages, such as in Tai Lü, and *meng* 猛 in Chinese. It is an ambiguous and elastic term which may carry different meanings depending on the specific social and linguistic context in which it is used. Sometimes it is very difficult, if not impossible, to determine the intended meaning. The territorial dimension of the term *müang* is rather vague. *Müang* refers to the administrative, "urban" centre of a polity, but at the same time it also includes the rural hinterland and can even designate the polity as a whole. Siamese chronicles, for instance, refer to "Müang Ayutthaya" whenever either the capital or the Kingdom of Siam is meant. In several cases the name of a *müang* was retained after the transfer of the capital to a new location. Chiang Rung, the political centre of Sipsòng Panna, was rebuilt several times at different sites, each one situated not far from the others. Each new site was named "Chiang Rung" besides its own local name.

Although the *müang* has its natural border zones, such as watersheds and mountain ranges, it has no clear border lines that would satisfy the modern European understanding of frontier. It can also comprise many smaller units, such as the "subordinate *müang*" (*müang khün*) or "satellite *müang*" (*müang bòriwan*), which represent a replica of the superior *müang*. Thus, the polity as a whole is defined as a *müang* and at the same time as a "confederation of *müang*".[29] The inherent hierarchical structure of the *müang* can best be exemplified by the polity of Müang (Moeng) Mao. From its core area in present-day Dehong, an autonomous prefecture of the Tai Nüa and Kachin (Jingpo) in southwestern Yunnan, Müang Mao expanded under its charismatic ruler Soe Khan Fa at the end of the Yuan dynasty. Under Soe Khan Fa's successors, Müang Mao lost its influence over many of the satellite *müang*, some of which even joined other Tai confederations.

26. See Luce 1961, 43.

27. Liew-Herres 2003a, 145; Daniels 2000, 54–58.

28. As for an analysis of the Chinese sources referring to Babai-xifu or Babai-dadian, see Liew-Herres et al. 2008; Winai 1996.

29. Rujaya 1984, 49.

Müang Mao regained strength at the beginning of the fifteenth century, though only for a relatively short period.[30] This suggests that the *müang* were not always politically stable. In this regard, Yos Santasombat aptly remarks concerning the whole of the Tai-inhabited frontier region between Yunnan and Burma: "Small autonomous political units had often tended to aggregate into larger systems; large-scale feudal hierarchies had fragmented into smaller ones. There had also been violent and rapid shifts in the overall distribution of political power."[31]

The American social anthropologist Stanley Tambiah defines *müang* as a "centre-orientated space".[32] Yet, beyond the purely geographical space, a *müang* comprises above all the population that lives within its territorial borders and is politically organised on the basis of political rule.[33] Hence, it is understandable that even market towns and larger villages could be labelled *müang*, provided that they were the seats of the ruling elites capable of politically dominating nearby rural settlements. The division of the Tai society into aristocracy and commoners is reflected in the polarity between *müang* and village. Though even the smallest Tai *müang* included villages surrounding the administrative centre, it is doubtful whether the village (*ban*) constituted the basic political unit in the polities of the Tai,[34] because political rule was exclusively exercised on the *müang* level. Whereas the village represents the politically unorganised population at large, the *müang* is represented by its ruling class. Under the leadership of the *cao müang* (lit., "lord of the *müang*") the aristocracy alone controls the socio-economic system of the Tai, which is based on wet-rice cultivation and a sophisticated coordination of irrigation in larger territorial spaces, mainly in river basins.[35] The military security was also an obligation of the *müang*. Its capital or main settlement was usually surrounded by a wall or palisade and a moat. These fortified settlements, called *wiang* or *chiang*,[36] also provided shelter for the inhabitants of the neighbouring villages in the wake of imminent attacks by enemies.

---

30. As to the fall and rise of the Shan confederation of Müang Mao, see Liew (1996) on the Luchuan-Pingmian Campaigns (1538–1449). A good overview of the dynamics of territorial expansion and contraction in the "Tai Frontier Zone" along the Chinese-Burmese borderlands during the period 1382–1454 is provided by Fernquest 2006.

31. Yos 2001, 86–87.

32. Tambiah 1976, 74.

33. The Russian linguist Afanassieva (1998) points to the usage of the terms *müang khon* or *müang manut* to denote the human domain in contrast to the spirit world (*müang phi*) and the paradise or heaven (*müang sawan*).

34. This is suggested by Keyes (1987, 28) who states: "In the Tai system, the basic unit of political life was the village (*ban*), and villages were grouped together in larger political entities known as *muang*."

35. Lemoine (1987 and 1997) shows this through the example of the Tai polities in southwestern China and northern Vietnam.

36. Cia Yaencòng (2005, 91) explains the term *chiang* as follows: "A *chiang* is a town or city which is an administrative centre and in most cases the residence of the aristocracy (*cao nai*),

Only a few *müang* centres, such as Chiang Rung and Moeng Hai, possessed a distinctively urban character. These differed from normal villages with regard to the physical presence of an aristocracy and its administrative apparatus. Large tracts of garden land and other agricultural productive areas were enclosed by the "city" walls. Thus one might call these fortified settlements "agricultural towns" rather than "cities". In the political thinking of the Tai there was no place for autonomous villages outside and independent from the *müang* structures.[37] Unlike European medieval towns, the Tai *müang* centres did not possess town ordinances and privileges that distinguished them from the surrounding countryside.

3. TAI-KHA RELATIONSHIP

Almost all Tai myths of origin reflect the political and military conflicts as well as the social and ethnic interaction between invaders and autochthones. The latter are called by various names. Besides the generic term "Kha" and the more neutral term *kha mòn* (ข้าม่อน), "hill people", Tai chronicles use the derogatory ethnonyms "Thamila" and "Milakkhu".[38] The *Tamnan Lü sipsòng pang* (Chronicle of the [Tai] Lü of the Twelve Districts), which deals with the history prior to the founding of Moeng Lü by Phaya Coeng (Cüang) in 1180, reports that the first seven Tai Lü villages in Moeng Alawi (Ālavī), an old name for Chiang Rung, had to defend themselves against the overwhelming power of the Thamila, who are recognised as the original population of Moeng Alawi. Whereas the Tai surrounded their villages with palisades, the much more numerous Thamila did not fortify their settlements. The chronicle portrays a polity in which the Tai and Thamila coexisted peacefully under the leadership of their respective nobility (*khun*). Nonetheless, harmony was frequently interrupted by violent disputes over the control of agricultural resources. The Thamila, accused of "paganism" (*micchādiṭṭhi*), finally succumbed to the militarily superior Tai and became their vassals. The result was an economic division of labour with the Tai cultivating wet rice in the plains and

according to the saying 'Water which is in the sky is rain, people who reside in the *chiang* are the rulers' (น้ำอยู่ฟ้าเป็นฝน คนอยู่เชียงเป็นเจ้า). [...] *Chiang* is a Chinese loanword pronounced *cheng* 城 (เฉิง) in Mandarin but in the Chinese dialect of Kwangtung (Guangdong), which has kept the ancient pronunciation, it is pronounced *seng* (เส่ง). In Lao [the word] is pronounced *siang* (-PC) and in Tai Lü *ceng* (เจง)." In ancient Chinese the term means "wall". Later its meaning was extended and denoted walled cities.

37. Grabowsky 2004, 8.

38. *Pap pün moeng sisip cin cao panna moeng hai*, f° 4r/7. Thamila (Damiḷa) derives from the Indian ethnonym Tamil. The Tamils are a people speaking a Dravidian language; they live mostly in the Indian state of Tamil Nadu and in the north and northeast of Sri Lanka. Cit Phumisak (1976, 377–80) points out that both Thamila and Milakkhu/Milakkha (Pali-ised form of the Sanskrit word Mleccha, lit., "barbarian") are derogatory terms used by the Aryans to designate the autochthonous Dravidian and Austroasiatic population of the Indian subcontinent.

the Thamila practicing slash and burn agriculture on the slopes of forested mountains. The Tai Lü saying *thoen kha na tai* (Tr. เถิ่นข้านาไท), "the forest [belongs to] the Kha, the rice fields [belong to] the Tai" is a most telling reflection of this ethnic-based division of labour.[39] The chronicles of Chiang Tung,[40] Moeng (Müang) Yòng,[41] Moeng Laem,[42] Moeng La,[43] and many other Tai polities represent the historical relations between Tai and Kha in a quite similar manner. One Thamila leader who receives special mention in the *Tamnan lü sipsòng pang* is Cao Coeng (Cüang) Han, who was feared and respected by the Tai because of his bravery. This legendary hero figures prominently in Tai Lü folk-tales, mostly praising him as the founding king of Chiang Coeng (Cüang) who was endowed with supernatural powers. In at least one of the versions of the Moeng Lü Chronicle (MLC-SV2) Cao Coeng Han and the founder of the kingdom of Moeng Lü, Phaya Coeng, merge into one and the same person, thereby reflecting the close inter-ethnic relationship between Tai and Kha.

As lowlanders and rice farmers, the Tai feared the jungle but at the same time they were interested in exploiting its products, such as various kinds of undomesticated animals and, above all, the precious ivory. Hence, the Tai rulers were interested in integrating the "uncivilised" peoples of the forest into their lowland-based political domains. In a kind of "social symbiosis", the Kha became a "patronage people" (*Gefolgsvolk*), a people under the surveillance of the Tai aristocracy. As the German anthropologist Wilhelm Mühlmann has observed with regard to the Sinhalese-Wedda

---

39. See also the more elaborate saying "The inundated fields belong to the Tai, the forests that are reached by forest fires belong to the Kha Si Saen Mòn Ma" (Th. ทุ่งที่น้ำท่วมถึงเป็นของคนไท เถื่อนที่ไฟป่าไหม้ถึงเป็นของข้าสี่แสนหมอนม้า); quoted from Wimon 2000, 35.

40. Sāimöng 1981, 224–28.

41. According to the Müang Yòng Chronicle (Thawi 1984, 24–27, ff° 1–6), the region of Müang Yòng (Mahiyaṅga) was first settled by a group called "Thamin" (ทมิฬ) who founded seven large villages. These Thamin became wealthy and productive farmers (Th. เอาสร้างสวนไร่นา) and succeeded in expanding their sphere of influence in all directions. To the north their polity reached the borders of Moeng Cae and Chiang Rung in present-day Sipsòng Panna. The *cao fa* of Chiang Rung, fearing the powerful "Thamin" of Moeng Yòng, sent his son Prince Sunanta (Sunantakuman) as a secret spy to Moeng Yòng where he defeated the "Thamin" ruler by a ruse. After his victory, Prince Sunanta ruled Moeng Yòng—the subjugated "Thamin" as well as the Tai Lü settlers from Sipsòng Panna—according to the principles of a "just king" (*ratchatham sip prakan* ราชธรรมสิบประการ).

42. Moeng Laem Chronicle, ff° 13–17. The Moeng Laem Chronicle abounds with references to clashes between forces loyal to the *cao hò kham* and Lahu rebels. Tao Fai Son (Suan), the seventeenth ruler of Moeng Laem, was murdered (in 1683) in his own palace by a Musoe commando who wanted to rescue a "Musoe" (Lahu) girl that the Tai ruler had abducted and made his mistress (ff° 40/2–41/9). In 1847/48 a power struggle between two princely brothers also broke out. The Lahu, supporting one of the contending parties, pillaged numerous villages. Peace was restored with the help of Wa troops "who arrived in large numbers to support our Moeng Laem" (f° 44/4–9).

43. The Chronicle of Moeng La (Sòi Sahan or Tao Cang Phuang version) mentions the "Phu Kò"—a derogative expression designating the Akha or Hani people—as the first settlers of Moeng La and Moeng Pong. A Phu Kò officer was even able to seize power and become—though only temporarily—ruler of Moeng La (see ff° 4–7).

relationship in Sri Lanka, the inter-ethnic contact between "civilised lowlanders" and the "people of the forests" created an ethnic dichotomy within the latter group. Those "tamed" highlanders who lived on the fringes of the lowlands and had the most intensive contact with the lowlanders were considered ritually as equals.[44] The various Kha peoples (Lua/Lawa, Wa, Bulang, etc.) in the Tai polities possessed ritual functions as lords of the territorial guardian spirits.

As liaison for the Tai in procuring forest goods, the Kha held a strong economic position as they controlled access to precious forest products, such as ivory, rhinoceros horn, incense, honey, opium, and cardamom, which were then sent as tribute to royal courts in exchange for cloth, knives, pottery, and other consumer goods. They also controlled the cattle trade. The "Chronicle of Moeng Cae" (*cotmaihet moeng cae*) reports that there were nineteen hill villages that were under the jurisdiction of Moeng Cae. These villages were obliged to send yearly tributes to the ruler of Moeng Cae. These tributes consisted of products such as cotton (20 or 30 *chang* ชั่ง = 24–36 kg), beans (30 *chang* = 36 kg), ivory (30 *chang*), vegetables (15 pieces of each kind), bamboo (2–5 sprouts), firewood (2 *wa* or roughly 4 metres), bamboo mats (2 pieces), and many other items.[45] Henry Yule, who was a secretary to Arthur Phayre's mission to Ava in 1855, calls the "Láwas" of the highlands "good cultivators, growing indigo, sugar-cane, and cotton" but also as manufacturers of iron and "good smiths, making dhás[46] and even matchlocks." He notes that the Chinese traders of Chiang Tung, Chiang Rung and adjoining areas relied much on goods produced by the "Láwas".[47] The administration of the hill regions in Moeng Laem resembled that of Sipsòng Panna, where the hill people were organised into twelve *khwaen* (แคว่น, see MLC-LV1, s. 3.15). The nine *khwaen* in Moeng Laem were divided into three "inner districts" (*khwaen nai*), closer under the surveillance of the Tai authorities, and six "outer districts" (*khwaen nòk*) on the periphery.[48] Western reports of the late nineteenth century emphasised the economic importance, particularly of the mineral-rich Wa districts of Moeng Laem.[49]

Despite their political and economic integration into the Tai polities, the autochthonous highlanders were able to preserve a high degree of autonomy. To a certain extent, the Tai-Kha relationship reflected tributary relations which the Tai *müang* maintained with Imperial China. Their sense of cultural superiority notwithstanding, the Tai rulers regarded their Kha subjects as an integral and essential component of

44. Mühlmann 1964, 196–97. The German anthropologist von Eickstedt, quoted by Mühlmann, reports that in the eastern part of Sri Lanka the Sinhalese district chief, dressed in a beautiful sarong, had to take orders while standing whereas the shabbily clothed Wedda was kindly asked by the prince to take a seat.

45. Yanyong and Ratanaporn 2001, 185–86.

46. A Burmese word (ဓား) meaning knife, chopper or sword.

47. Yule 1968, 294.

48. Moeng Laem Chronicle, f° 55, listing the names of the nine *khwaen*.

49. See Warry's confidential report, dated of 23 March 1891, 4–5, in W. Warry 1888–1895 [British Library, IOOC].

their *müang* and appreciated their loyalty in times of common threat. An example of the latter is described in the Moeng Lü Chronicle, according to which at the end of the fourteenth century Cao Khan Moeng (Ch. Dao Kan 刀坎), the then ruler of Chiang Rung, was able to fight off superior Ming troops with the support of the "Lua" tribe until he was finally forced to recognise Chinese suzerainty in 1382.[50] Cao Khan Moeng even married a Lua girl and made her his queen (*nang tewi*). Though the marriage ended shortly after the birth of crown prince Tao Sida Kham (Ch. Dao Xianda 刀暹答), the Lua continued to have certain privileges. Cao Khan Moeng also allowed the young prince to spend the first few years of his life with his mother and grandfather in the mountains. In the neighbouring Tai polity of Moeng Laem, similarly the Tai forged a close military alliance with the local Wa population. Support of the Wa proved crucial to the *cao fa* when the Lahu (Musoe), who had migrated to Moeng Laem later than the Wa and the Tai, launched an uprising against the Tai authorities. As the Moeng Laem Chronicle stresses, "Tai and Wa love each other like brothers and sisters".[51]

In some cases, hill peoples played a crucial role as allies of contending factions in fratricidal conflicts. This was the case when Tao Sunwu (r. 1802–1833) mobilised Lua and Lahu troops to rebuke his uncle Tao Thai Khang (Cao Mòm Maha Wang) with whom he had a dispute. The hill tribe/tribal troops, however, were not able to rescue the *cao fa* who fled to Simao.[52] During the reign of his successor, Cao Mòm Suca Wanna or Tao Coen Cong (Dao Zhengzong 刀正綜) (r. 1834–1864), the ruler's uncle, Cao Maha Khanan, and his two sons conspired to usurp the throne but their coup d'état failed. One of Cao Maha Khanan's sons, Cao Nò Kham, managed to flee and hide in the forests from where he made his way to Moeng Küng Ma (Gengma).[53]

4. TAI LÜ SOCIETY AND ITS ADMINISTRATIVE SYSTEMS

4.1 RULERS AND NOBILITY

The Tai Lü *cao fa* (lit., "lords of heaven") ruled their polities as absolute monarchs, endowed with power over life and death of their subjects.[54] According to the British social anthropologist Edmund Leach, who conducted extensive field research during

50. See MLC-LV1, s. 8, and MLC-LV2, s. 9. Two years later, in 1384, the Cheli Pacification Commission (*xuanwei si*) was established.

51. Moeng Laem Chronicle, f° 16/3. The Wa living near Moeng Laem had a reputation as fierce fighters. Yule (1968, 294) remarks that "[t]he largest, most savage, and most independent bodies of the Láwas are found in the country northward of Muang-Lem."

52. MLC-LV1, s. 31.14 and s. 32.7; MLC-LV2, s. 38.5 and s. 39.6.

53. MLC-LV1, s. 32.7; MLC-LV2, s. 39.6. On fratricidal conflicts, see Liew-Herres 2007.

54. The role of the *cao fa* as the highest judicial authority is reflected in the title Cao Maha Ciwit (Lao: *sivit*), "lord over the great life". The Lao king had this official title until the abolition of the monarchy in December 1975.

the 1930s in the highlands of northern Burma, the *cao fa* led a luxurious life in the reclusiveness of his palace and in isolation from the outside world, surrounded only by his numerous wives and concubines.[55] A good *cao fa*, however, was a man who avoided debauchery and kept in check the greed of his officials.[56] The alleged excessive life-style of Tai princes is put into perspective by early Western travelogues that were totally unimpressed by the splendour of the *cao fa*'s palaces. The palace of the ruler of Chiang Rung, for instance, is called by Captain William Couperus McLeod in 1837, the first European who ever visited Sipsòng Panna, as a "miserable place", and he himself "could never have fancied an inhabited place [...] in such a wretched state."[57] Though the wealth which the Tai *cao fa* was able to display could not even be remotely compared with that of the Chinese imperial court, there was nevertheless a distinct difference between the *cao fa* and his subjects whose houses had to differ in size, décor, and furniture from the "golden palaces" (*hò kham*) of the *cao fa*. No one was allowed to ride in front of the back door of the royal residence; neither animal cadavers nor human corpses could pass the compound of the *hò kham*.[58]

A strict succession law did not exist in Sipsòng Panna.[59] Indeed, in most cases the eldest son born to the *cao fa*'s principal wife (*maha tewi*) would succeed his father to the throne. However, this was not an unalterable rule. Of the forty-four *cao fa*[60] who ruled in Chiang Rung from 1180 until 1950, one half (nineteen) were not the predecessor's sons. The succession from elder to younger brother, from uncle to nephew, or from cousin to cousin was relatively common. Such a succession occurred for the first time when Cao Ai (r. 1287–1347) succeeded his uncle Tao Puwak (r. 1273–1287) who died "without an heir".[61] While in Sipsòng Panna it was an absolute requirement that the new *cao fa* could prove direct descent from Phaya Coeng (r. 1180–1192), the progenitor of the ruling dynasty,[62] this was not necessarily the case in other Tai polities, in which it did happen that charismatic personalities belonging to neither the ruling family nor to the commoners class assumed leadership in popular uprisings against despotic, weak, and corrupt rulers to establish new dynasties. This happened, for example, in the Burmese Shan state of Hsaenwi in 1885.[63]

55. Leach 1954, 215–16.

56. Yos 2001, 88.

57. *McLeod Journal* (MJ), 25 February 1837, Grabowsky and Turton 2003, 351.

58. Scott and Hardiman 1900, 408.

59. For more on succession, see section 6.3.

60. This is according to MLC-LV2. Other versions recognise only forty or forty-one *cao fa*.

61. MLC-LV1, s. 7.1 and MLC-LV2, s. 6.4; s.7.1.

62. A similar rule of succession existed in Lan Na during the period of the Mangrai dynasty (1296–1564). Though lacking a rule of primogeniture, there did exist an unwritten law in Lan Na that only direct descendants of King Mangrai, the founder of Chiang Mai, could be elected king. See Grabowsky 2004, 95.

63. Collis 1938, 251–53, quoted from Yos 2001, 89.

In ruling their kingdoms, the *cao fa* had to rely on the provincial rulers and governors, called *cao müang* or *cao panna*. They were mostly close, in some cases more distant, relatives of the *cao fa* who bestowed them with *müang* or *panna* as fiefs. Though in practice many of the provincial rulers would hand their fiefdoms down to their descendants, formal consent of the *cao fa* was needed for such a transfer of power. Only in rare instances would the *cao fa* reject the succession of a late governor's descendant and appoint a successor of his own choosing instead.[64]

The fragmentation of Sipsòng Panna into thirty river basins of differing sizes favoured centrifugal tendencies of governance; all the more as several *panna* (each of which comprised between one and seven river basins) possessed richer agricultural resources than did the capital, Chiang Rung. Moeng Cae, situated on the west bank of the Mekong River, was well-known as the country's rice bowl and its "forty thousand rice fields" (*si mün na moeng cae*);[65] while the neighbouring Moeng Hai was renowned as an important and wealthy centre of the tea trade.[66] The primacy of the capital, its central geographical position being an asset, was by no means uncontested. Much of its political stability depended on the skills of the *cao fa* to appoint *tao khun* (officials) to appropriate positions both in the royal core domain and in outlying *panna* and *müang*. The *tao khun*, for instance, were required to make an annual journey to the capital to take the oath of allegiance in the presence of the *cao fa*. The oath was sworn by "drinking the water of loyalty".[67] At the oath-taking ceremony, carried out in one of the most prominent Buddhist monasteries in Chiang Rung, the guardian spirits (*thewada*) of the country were invoked to be present as eye-witnesses (*thamma-sakkhi*).[68]

From the above, we can see that the political power base of the *cao fa* of Sipsòng Panna was fragile. However, Shih-Chung Hsieh rejects Tanabe's opinion that the *cao fa*'s political control was restricted to his "home *panna*" of Chiang Rung.[69] Though the *cao fa* usually did not interfere in the internal affairs of each *müang*, this does not imply that he lacked "the real power to do it." Hsieh surmises that the people knew very well

64. The chronicles of Moeng La, Moeng Hai, and Moeng Ham provide lists of governors (*cao müang* or *cao panna*) who apparently all came from noble families with local roots. For sources, see the introduction, part 2, section 5 of this volume.

65. Kato (1994, 31) notes that as the largest *müang*, Moeng Cae had about 1.7 times more land than did Chiang Rung. "If we compare the total amount of land, we can see that the capital *müang* was not in a superior position as regards land."

66. Yanyong and Ratanaporn 2001, 39. The fertility of the plain of Moeng Cae is confirmed, among others, by Dodd (1996 [1923], 188–89) who visited the region shortly before the outbreak of World War I. The Moeng Ham Chronicle, according to the version of Khanan Nakkasen, Ban Suan Mòn (f° 12), claims that Moeng Ham produced abundant amounts of paddy and that fish was very cheap.

67. Tai Lü: *kham satca* (ข่ามสัจจา); Th. *thü nam phra phiphat sattaya* (ถือน้ำพระพิพัฒน์สัตยา).

68. Yanyong and Ratanaporn 2001, 41. For such oath-taking ceremonies, see also MLC-LV2, s. 17.4 and 39.11; MLC-LV1, s. 13.4 and s. 32.11.

69. Tanabe 1988.

that among all the aristocratic leaders to whom they paid land taxes or contributed corvée labour and domestic services, the *cao fa* in his capacity as *cao phaendin* holding the highest rank/most superior in rank/was their sovereign.[70] Moreover, in the *sakdina* system of Sipsòng Panna, the *cao phaendin* possessed the exclusive right to transfer rice fields to high-ranking officials, who were allowed to exploit these "fiefs" economically only as long as they held office. These officials were called *kin na* or "consuming rice fields", as the Tai Lü called the bestowment of fiefs, with the term *na* (rice field) becoming part of their rank. The *upalaca* or viceroy (vice-*saenwi fa*) held the rank *na saen long* (*saen* = 100,000), other close relatives of the *cao fa* the rank of *na mün long* (*mün* = 10,000), and the rank held by the lowest-ranking officials was *na ha* (*ha* = 5).[71]

How did the *cao fa* organise the administration of his country? On what institutions did he rely? What were the tasks and duties of these institutions? The most important institutions of the central government were the *noe sanam nai* and the *noe sanam nòk*:[72]

1. *Noe (nüa) sanam nai* (Inner Council of Nobles). This institution was directly subordinate to the *cao fa*. The members of the *noe sanam nai* remained permanently at the royal court, although their responsibilities and duties were by no means restricted to the court. They were responsible for the defence of the country, the collection of taxes, and the supervision of the provinces. Several officials were in charge of purely ceremonial matters, such as the reception and entertainment of foreign guests or the organising of state rituals. The areas of authority of each of the twenty-eight members of the *noe sanam nai* were not always well-defined as there was much overlapping of responsibilities. The Cao Long Na Kot (Cao Luang Na Kuat) served as a chief of protocol at the royal court when provincial governors or guests from foreign lands arrived. But the Cao Long Khan Kham, who oversaw the court servants, also participated in the reception of guests. As his title indicates, the Cao Long Na Cang (Cao Luang Na Chang) took care of the *cao phaendin*'s war elephants officially enrolled for duty, but he also looked after the royal uniforms and once every three years organised the ritual offerings for the "elephant god" (*tewada cang*). An important task was given to the Phaya Nawa or Phaya Them Nai Hoe (Rüa), the official in charge of the ruler's small navy. Besides his main duty, he was also to ensure that all royal barques were properly repaired prior to the Buddhist New Year. The Phaya Nawa played a prominent role during the royal consecration ceremony as well. Many other examples of multiple and sometimes not directly related duties could be mentioned. The most crucial political functions, however, were taken over by the following four leading members of the *noe sanam nai*:

- Cao Mòm Upalaca (Uparacha): viceroy, deputy of the *cao fa* in charge of military affairs;

---

70. Hsieh 1989, 106.

71. As to details of the *kin na* system in ancient Sipsòng Panna, see Cia (Yanyong) 2005, 291–95.

72. In the following the authors rely, if not stated otherwise, on Yanyong and Ratanaporn 2001, 45–55; Cia (alias Yanyong) 2005, 283–90.

- Cao Long Phasat (Luang Prasat): minister in charge of the security of the palace (*hò kham*);
- Cao Long Na Paen: minister in charge of the *cao fa*'s work, his official duties, schedule, and itinerary and responsible for important state ceremonies;
- Cao Long Na Khwa (lit., "great *cao* of the right-hand rice fields"): minister in charge of the ruler's bodyguard and the reception of foreign guests; exercising control over activities in the countryside.

The mobilisation of soldiers in times of war, for which the Cao Long Na Khwa held main responsibility, was also carried out by two other members of the *noe sanam nai*, namely the Cao Long Na Sai (lit., "great *cao* of the left-hand rice fields") and the Cao Long Coeng Han.

2. *Noe (nüa) sanam nòk* (Outer Council of Nobles). The *cao fa* did not interfere in the daily affairs of this institution, but representatives of the *noe sanam nai* were usually present when the *noe sanam nòk* convened, while it was usually not the case that members of the *noe sanam nòk* participated in meetings of the *noe sanam nai*. The president of the *noe sanam nòk* bore the title Cao Chiang Ha because the *cao müang* of Chiang Ha (a village situated a few kilometres to the south of Chiang Rung) had once given crucial military support to the *cao fa*. The Cao Chiang Ha was expected to mediate conflicts between members of the aristocratic elite (aristocracy) and during the Republican period (1912–1949) he also was the key person in dealings with Chinese state officials.[73] Along with three other senior officials (*sena*), the Cao Chiang Ha belonged to the "four chief ministers" (*si khacoeng*), forming the inner core of the *noe sanam nòk*. The titles of the other three *khacoeng* were:

- the Cao Hòi Dang Ban Òt, sometimes called Tu Long Kao (Thu Luang Khao): vice-president of the *noe sanam nòk* and minister of finance;
- the Cao Hòi Dang Ban Khum: minister responsible for census-taking and judicial affairs;
- the Cao Hòi Dang Còm Wang: minister in charge of the recruitment of able-bodied men (*chai chakan* ชายฉกรรจ์) for corvée labour and military service.

Another high-ranking official of the *noe sanam nòk* was the Cao Na Kat, also called Cao Hòi Dang Kat. As he was responsible for financial matters and the organisation of the markets (*kat*, Tr. กาด, Th. *talat* ตลาด), he was a kind of minister of finance and economy. Below the five abovementioned top positions the *noe sanam nòk* also comprised numerous subordinate officials, including provincial governors. Whereas the *noe sanam nai* convened regularly, the *noe sanam nòk* did so only twice a year, namely in the ninth month of the Tai Lü calendrical year (July, start of the Buddhist lent) and in the twelfth month (October, end of the Buddhist lent). The responsibilities of the *noe sanam nòk* were:

73. Bunchuai 2004 [1954], 63.

- defining territorial borders and responsibilities;
- appointing or dismissing the king or main ruler (*cao fa* or *cao phaendin*) and provincial rulers (*cao müang*);
- mediating disputes between different *müang* or *panna*;
- discussing various matters submitted by a *müang* (or *panna*) for final decision;
- stipulating or improving the system of local administration;
- decision-making on war with other states;
- deciding whether to send tribute to greater powers like China and Burma;
- discussing of activities about which the ruler had asked for advice.[74]

The outer aulic council formed the core of the central government. As minister of finance in charge of the collection of taxes, the Cao Hòi Dang Ban Òt was the most powerful high-ranking official, though all meetings of the council were chaired by the Cao Chiang Ha. The Cao Hòi Dang Ban Òt's political pre-eminence is underlined by the large amount of rice fields bestowed upon him as a fief. Until the early 1950s he had 5,700 *na* or roughly 570 *rai* of rice fields at his disposal (10 *na* = c. 1 *rai* or 0.16 ha) and he could demand 2,310 *hap* (1 *hap* = 60 kg) of paddy from the tillers of his lands. The Cao Hòi Dang Còm Wang "consumed" 4,070 *na* of rice fields from which he could expect 840 *hap* of paddy. In comparison, the Cao Long Phasat, who was the second-highest ranking member of the *noe sanam nòk*—next to the *upalaca*—received only 3,120 *na* of rice fields and a proportionally smaller amount of paddy. Though the head of the *noe sanam nòk*, the Cao Chiang Ha, was bestowed a relatively smaller number of rice fields (1,340 *na*) he was entitled to collect large amounts of taxes in kind, such as bamboo, honey, and beeswax, from various hill-tribe villages in Chiang Rung, Moeng Ham and Moeng Yang.[75] It is noteworthy that while all four *khacoeng* held the rank of *na hòi* (lit., "rice field" and "one hundred") the three chief ministers of the *noe sanam nai*—next to the *upalaca*—held the lower rank of *na sao* (lit., "rice field" and "twenty")[76] although, as Shi-Chung Hsieh points out, they "were much closer to the royal family".[77]

On the local level, the implementation of decisions taken by the *noe sanam* required persons who had gained the confidence of the villagers. These liaison people were called *pò lam*. *Pò* (in Siamese pronounced *phò*) means "father" in all Tai languages and dialects; *lam* is used in modern Thai mainly for "translator" (i.e., as a noun); its primary meaning "to tie (with a rope)" is still known in modern Thai but is the general meaning in Tai Lü and other Tai dialects.[78] According to Cia Yaencòng (alias Yanyong Ciranakhòn), the institution of *pò lam* was originally created to exercise tighter political control over the

74. Yanyong and Ratanaporn 2001, 53.

75. Cia (alias Yanyong) 2005, 294–95.

76. Ibid., 291.

77. Hsieh 1989, 107.

78. Cia (alias Yanyong) 2005, 68.

ethnically and culturally heterogeneous highland populations. In a later period, the *pò lam* system was also expanded to the Tai in the lowlands. Until the traditional Tai Lü system of rule ended through the Communist seizure of power in Yunnan (1950), three categories of *pò lam* were distinguished from one another:[79]

- *Pò lam müang*. These officials, elected from the poll of the *tao khun* members of the *noe sanam nòk*, were the representatives of the *cao fa* and his government in the more than 30 *müang* of the country.
- *Pò lam ban*. They represented the government at the village level and closely cooperated with the village elders.
- *Pò lam khwaen* or *pò lam mòn*. These officials, who in general were Tai Lü , were assigned to supervise the highland villages that were divided into twelve districts (*khwaen*), to give a voice to the non-Tai ethnic groups in the *noe sanam*.

The *müang* and villages (*ban*) of which a *pò lam* was the representative were called *luk lam*; *luk* means "child" or "offspring" in all Tai languages. Apart from the rice fields bestowed upon him according to the *kin na* system (see discussion above), the *pò lam* could also use manpower of his *luk lam* for his own benefit. Several high-ranking officials, such as the Cao Chiang Ha and the Cao Long Na Paen, took a large number of *müang* and villages as their *luk lam*. Although the *pò lam* drew economic benefit from the *luk lam* to which they were entrusted, they did not rule them. That was the task of governors and village headmen.[80] Hence, as Cia Yaencòng argues, the institution of *pò lam* as a mediating voice contributed decisively to the political stability of Sipsòng Panna:

> The *pò lam-luk lam* system which has been passed on since ancient times demonstrates that Sipsòng Panna was a society of cooperation between different social classes and ethnic groups who took over responsibility for each other. Though contradictions did occur all the time they could be solved. An aspect deserving a special study is the reason why the *pò lam-luk lam* system could exist for a long period of time without meeting violent resistance from the lower classes.[81]

The system of local government in Sipsòng Panna diverged so significantly in the various *panna* that generalised statements are almost impossible. The *panna*, at least, had a local administrative council of its own called *noe kwan* (Th. เหนือกว้าน); its chief, the *cao noe kwan* (Th. เจ้าเหนือกว้าน) was the main councillor of *cao panna*.[82] The administrative units below the *müang* level were called *ho sip* (*hua sip*) and *mòn*, integrating the groups of villages in the plains and highlands respectively. Though its literal meaning *ho sip*

79. Yanyong and Ratanaporn 2001, 66–67.

80. Cia (alias Yanyong) 2005, 296–99.

81. Ibid., 300.

82. See for example the frequent mention of this term in the chronicle *Pap pün moeng sisip cin cao panna moeng hai*.

(lit., "head" and "ten") implies that a *ho sip* comprised ideally ten villages, this number was more of symbolic value. According to the Ban Foei Lung version of the Moeng Long Chronicle, none of the more than twenty *ho sip* established in the *panna* of Moeng Long reached the ideal (maximum) number of ten villages. One *ho sip* consisted of five villages, a second one of three villages, two *ho sip* comprised two villages each, but the remaining *ho sip* seemed to have consisted of only one single, probably larger, village.[83] Each *ho sip* was governed by a *cao ho sip* holding the rank of *khun*.[84] A special administrative unit which existed separately from the *ho sip* was the *long* (*luang*). Its existence, however, is only accounted for in the two *panna* of Chiang Rung and Moeng Long.[85] Furthermore, there is scattered evidence in local chronicles, such as those of Moeng Ham and Moeng Long, of the existence of an administrative unit called *bok* (*buak*). The name of one *bok* in Moeng Long, Bok Na Sai (lit., "the *bok* of the left-hand rice fields"),[86] confirms Ai Kham's view that a *bok* was linked with the traditional irrigation system.[87] By the 1930s, when Bunchuai Sisawat, the former governor of Chiang Rai, visited Sipsòng Panna, the distinctions between *ho sip* and *bok* seem to have blurred as Bunchuai Sisawat uses both terms interchangeably in the sense of *tambon* (ตำบล) which is the modern Thai term for commune or sub-district.[88] The extant versions of the Moeng Lü Chronicle provide no clues pertaining to the existence and functioning of the abovementioned administrative units.

4.2 ORGANISATION OF MANPOWER AND SOCIAL STRATIFICATION

The society of Sipsòng Panna, like that of other Tai polities, was divided into four major social classes, namely the hereditary aristocracy (Th. *chüa cao* เชื้อเจ้า), the lower nobility and officials (*tao khun*, Th. ท้าวขุน or *tao phaya*, Th. ท้าวพระยา), the commoners, and the serfs or "slaves" (Tr. *khòi* ข้อย). The administrative elite were recruited from the first two classes. The lowest social class, the serfs or "slaves", were of minor significance if compared to the conception of "slavery" in traditional Siamese society. Mostly over-

83. Yanyong and Ratanaporn 2001, 61–64; Interview with Cao Maha Khanthawong, a senior Tai Lü scholar who lives in Chiang Rung, 9 April 2005. As to the organisation of the *ho sip* in the *panna* of Moeng Long, see the Moeng Long Chronicle, Ban Foei Lung version, ff° 2–4. For the composition of the four *ho sip* in Moeng La in the 1930s see Bunchuai 2004 [1954], 228.

84. Moeng Long Chronicle, Ban Foei Lung version, ff° 9/1–2.

85. Interview with Cao Maha Khanthawong, 9 April 2005. Before 1950, Chiang Rung had four *long/luang* (ten villages + twenty villages) and three *ho sip* (ten villages + nine villages + seven to eight villages). The chiefs of these units were called Phaya Long and Phaya Ho Sip respectively.

86. Moeng Long Chronicle, Ban Foei Lung version, f° 13/11.

87. Interview with Ai Kham, 8 April 2005. Cao Maha Khanthawong, on the other hand, holds the opinion that *bok* (*buak*) signifies outlying areas and was a term rarely used in Sipsòng Panna (interview with Cao Maha Khanthawong, 9 April 2005). Cao Maha Khanthawong's view corresponds with the peripheral location of *bok* in the region of Moeng Sing in today's northwestern Laos. Frequently mentioned in local sources, the *bok* there were situated on the periphery, not in the plain of Moeng Sing. See Grabowsky and Renoo 2008, 17.

88. Bunchuai [1954] 2004, 64.

indebted persons and their descendants, the *khòi* did not carry any significant numerical weight. Focussing on the political history of Sipsòng Panna from the perspective of the ruling dynasty and the aristocratic elite, the Moeng Lü Chronicle provides little information on the living conditions of the non-aristocratic population called either *phai tai* (Tr. ไภ่ไท) or *tai moeng* (Tr. ไทเมิง). This class of commoners, however, did not constitute a uniform block, but was divided into various sub-groups:[89]

1. *Tai moeng* (Tr. ไทเมิง, lit., "freemen of the polity"). They were considered the descendants of the orginal Tai settlers. Their villages were the oldest in the regions and comprised the most extensive rice fields, which the *cao fa* in his capacity as *cao phaendin* (lit., "lord of the land") handed over to them for permanent use. In return, they were obliged to perform corvée labour and to pay military service. As a Tai Lü saying stipulated, "if one tills the rice fields [of the village] one has to perform corvée labour [in return]" (*het na pa wiak*, Tr. เฮ็ดนา พาเวียก). As for these public services, also called *kan moeng* (the affairs of the *müang*), the *tai moeng* had a major share.[90] These services encompassed the construction of roads and bridges as well as the maintenance of dams and canals needed for irrigating the fields.[91]

A significant portion of the rice fields tilled by the *tai moeng* belonged to the village community (*na ban*) and was allocated to individual families according to their needs. Such rice fields were not allowed to be sold or alienated, as they were considered "common land" (*na tanglai*, Tr. นาทังหลาย). If a *tai moeng* decided to abandon his rice field he had to inform the village chief, the person in charge of levying rice taxes.[92]

2. *Lek nòi* (Th. เลกน้อย, petty bondsmen). They were under the control of aristocratic lords and made up the latter's retinue. Therefore, they were also called *khon hoen* (*hüan*) *cao* (persons attached to the household of a lord). Their ancestors were not original settlers but had migrated from other Tai areas, for example, as war captives. The villages of the *lek nòi* were obliged to do regular private services for the *cao fa* and other aristocrats.[93] Their manifold services included the breeding of horses and the domestication of elephants, the collection of firewood, the boiling of salt, the spinning of cotton thread, the repairing of buildings of the nobility, and the participation in public processions. Their labour was called *kan nai hoen cao* (Tr. การในเรินเจ้า, services in the master's household).[94] The *lek nòi* also worked on rice fields belonging to the aristocrats (*na cao*). However, unlike the *tai moeng*, they had no access to common land.

89. See Yanyong and Ratanaporn 2001, 173–77, cf. Kato 1994, 28.

90. Kato 1994, 28.

91. Yanyong and Ratanaporn 2001, 178

92. Wimon 2000, 33.

93. The *cao phaendin* of Sipsòng Panna, i.e., the *cao panna* of Moeng Chiang Rung, was obviously supported by villagers whose task was to cut and "prepare" grass (make hay) for the ruler's elephants and horses. The households who worked for the viceroy (*upalaca*) were divided in two clusters of one hundred households (*pak lang* ปากหลัง) that were associated with the North and the South respectively. See *Moeng Long Chronicle*, Ban Foei Lung version, f° 4/6–8.

94. See Kato 1994, 28.

The Moeng Lü Chronicle reports one interesting case of how newly acquired villages were integrated as *lek nòi* settlements into the social structure of Moeng Lü by their being placed under the direct supervision of the *cao fa*. In 1453, during the reign of Soe Long Fa (r. 1428–1457), several areas originally subordinate to Moeng Maen (Puer) were transferred under the direct jurisdiction of Chiang Rung. The villages in these areas had to render service, such as delivering armed horsemen and protecting the city walls of Chiang Rung, to the *cao fa*. Exempted from providing local labour, they were considered the ruler's *lek nòi*.[95]

3. *Hòn hai* (Th. *ròn rai* ร่อนร่าย, vagabonds). They were direct dependents of their aristocratic lord. The genesis of this numerically insignificant category is not entirely clear. Most convincing is the hypothesis put forward by Yanyong Ciranakhòn and Ratanaporn Sethakul that the *hòn hai* were later migrants from more distant regions who were given rice fields of the *cao fa* and other aristocrats since other land was no longer available.[96] Their plots of land were smaller than those of the first two groups. Therefore, they had to rent fields from neighbouring villages. It is estimated that at the beginning of the Communist rule less than 10 per cent of the rice fields tilled by *hòn hai* was privately owned or belonged to the village community. Together with the *lek nòi*, the *hòn hai* formed the category of *khon nai hoen cao*, "the people in the master's household".

4. *Luk lan tao phaya* (Th. ลูกหลานท้าวพระยา, descendants of the nobility). In most cases they were distant relatives of aristocratic families who had moved from the capital to the countryside and lost their former status as *chüa cao* or *tao phaya*. The *luk lan tao phaya*, who were also known as *cao còm* or *luk khun* (offspring of nobles), were by far the smallest group of commoners. Due to their aristocratic descent, they were preferably recruited for the *cao fa*'s bodyguard.

The group endowed with the most political rights were the *tai moeng*, who formed the backbone of the state. The *tai moeng* constituted a majority of the population in almost all *panna*, except in the *panna* of Chiang Rung, the seat of the *cao fa*, in which the *lek nòi* were dominant. A village consisted in general only of members of one of the four groups. Intermarriage between members of different groups was not allowed.[97] The

---

95. MLC-LV1, s. 12.11 and s. 12.12 does not mention details of the kind of labour which the villagers had to perform. The MLC-LV2, s. 16.21 provides more information: During Soe Long Fa's reign, the *müang* formerly subordinate to Moeng Maen were incorporated into one *panna* (though the *panna* system was formed more than one century later) and counted as ten units of *na ma* (horse fields) and *na kong* (bow fields). "[T]hey had to deliver ten horses and ten horsemen armed with bows and arrows to protect Cao Moeng Lü. They were sent to look for Chinese carpenters to build a wall. They were to be held responsible for the cost of labour and materials. They were sent to serve in the palace of the *saenwi fa*, [performing duties] such as blowing the long horns, beating the drums, and watching the city walls." This is also recorded in Gao Lishi 1984, 111 (reign of Soe Long Fa).

96. As evidence for their hypothesis, Yanyong and Ratanaporn (2001, 175) point out that of the ten *hòn hai* villages that existed in the *panna* of Chiang Rung in 1953, there were four villages of Tai Nüa whose ancestors had a catastrophe (*phai phibat* ภัยพิบัติ) in Chiang Ku.

97. Kato 1994, 28.

last census carried out shortly before the land reform in Sipsòng Panna (1953) showed that in the plain of Chiang Rung only seventeen villages with 777 households and 4,066 persons (29 per cent) belonged to the category of *tai moeng*. However, there were forty-two villages of *lek nòi*, comprising 1,398 households and 7,084 persons (52.2 per cent). Of these villages eighteen served the *cao fa*'s court and the remaining twenty-four high-ranking nobles of the *noe sanam* and the *pò lam*.[98] In the sixteen villages of the *ròn rai*, 403 households with 1,921 persons (14.1 per cent) were recorded, while the six remaining villages belonged to the category of *luk lan tao phaya*, comprising ninety-six families with 486 persons (3.5 per cent).

4.3 THE *PANNA* SYSTEM

In 1564, almost four centuries after the founding of Moeng Lü by Phaya Coeng, the country fell under Burmese suzerainty. Six years later, the over thirty *müang* of the Tai Lü country were divided into twelve *panna*, each of which comprised between one and five *müang*. The term consists of two words: *pan* (Th. พัน), meaning "one thousand", and *na* (นา), meaning "rice field". The term *panna* (Th. พันนา), thus, could be rendered as "one thousand rice fields". However, though the word invokes a connection with wet-rice agriculture, it should not be understood too literally as an area comprising exactly one thousand *rai* (c. 167 hectare). Rather it should be interpreted as an intermediate administrative unit between the *müang* and the state level, and, therefore, it is usually rendered as "district" in Western literature.

The origins of the *panna* system in Moeng Lü are unknown but it most certainly predates the sixteenth century. The first mention of the term *panna* in the Moeng Lü Chronicle relates to the reign of Ai Kung in the first half of the thirteenth century. The chronicle states that the *cao fa*'s younger brother Yi Peng (Piang) was appointed lord of three districts, namely the *panna* of Moeng Hun, Moeng Hai, and Moeng Cae.[99] The territorial limits of these *panna* are not mentioned. During the reign of Tao Sida Kham (first half of the fifteenth century), the three *panna* were given to the *cao fa*'s nephew and adopted son, Soe Long Fa, as a fief on the occasion of the wedding of Soe Long Fa and Tao Sida Kham's eldest daughter, Nang Lun Koei. Later, when Soe Long Fa (r. 1428–1457) had become ruler of Moeng Lü, he ceded a so-called "semi-*panna*" (*küng panna*, Th. กึ่งพันนา), along with two other areas, as dowry to the Lao kingdom of Lan Sang when his second daughter married the Lao king, Phaya Cai Sòngkham.[100]

As one of the present authors has shown, the *panna* system existed in Lan Na already during the time of King Mangrai (r. 1261–1311) and presumably originated in Phayao

98. Yanyong and Ratanaporn 2001, 180.

99. MLC-LV2, s. 3.2; MLC-LV1, s. 2.2. Both versions mention Yi Peng's later revolt and failed attempt to usurp his elder brother's throne.

100. See MLC-LV1, s. 9.9 and s. 12.6; MLC-LV2, s. 11.4 and s. 16.15. This was probably King Sainyacakkaphat Phaen Phaeo (r. 1442–1479/80) whose reign ended a long period of political instability in Lan Sang.

at the end of the eleventh century. In fifteenth-century Lan Na, the *panna* had become the basic administrative unit between the *müang* and the village level, though vague epigraphic evidence suggests the existence of a *pakna* (lit., "one hundred rice fields") as an intermediate unit between *panna* and village (*ban*).[101] Whereas the *müang* represents the older concept, which consisted of old family organisations and units based on villages and urban settlements, the *panna* was obviously a later structure imposed on the network of *müang*. The new *panna* structure facilitated the political and economic penetration of the country by the royal centre.

Whereas in Lan Na the *panna* system seems to have become obsolete since the eighteenth century, it was so firmly and systematically implemented in Moeng Lü in 1570 that the polity became known to the outside world simply as Sipsòng Panna, "[the country] of the twelve *panna*". Six of the twelve *panna* were situated on the west bank of the Mekong, the other six on the east bank of the river. The tributaries of the Mekong partitioned the various *panna* from one another.[102] According to MLC-LV1 (s. 19.15), the administrative division of *panna* was as follows:

Table 3: Administrative Divisions of Sipsòng Panna in 1570

Panna	*Constituent moeng/müang*	*Right/left bank of the Mekong*
Chiang Rung (Jinghong)	Chiang Rung, Moeng Ham, Moeng Nun, Moeng Sung (Song)	right and left bank
Moeng Cae (Mengzhe)	Chiang Cae, Chiang Lu, Moeng Òng	right bank
Moeng Long (Menglong)	Moeng Long	right bank
Moeng Hun (Menghun)	Moeng Hun, Moeng Pan	right bank
Chiang Coeng (Jingzhen)	Chiang Coeng, Moeng Hai, Moeng Ngat	right bank
Chiang Lò (Jingluo)	Chiang Lò, Moeng Mang, Moeng Ngam, Moeng Lang Nüa, Moeng Khòn	right bank
Moeng La (Mengla)	Moeng La, Moeng Ban	left bank
Moeng Hing (Mengling/ Puteng)	Moeng Hing (Puteng), Moeng Bang	left bank
Moeng La (Simao and Liushun)	Moeng La (Simao and Liushun), Moeng Wang	left bank
Moeng Phong (Meng-peng)	Moeng Phong, Moeng Yuan, Moeng Mang	left bank
Moeng U (Mengwu ne)	Moeng U-Nüa, Moeng U-Tai	left bank
Chiang Tòng (Zheng-dong)	Chiang Tòng, Bò La (Yibang), I-ngu (Yiwu)	left bank

SOURCE: MLC-LV1, s. 19.15, by Li Fuyi

101. Grabowsky 2005, 19–20.

102. Thongthaem 1989.

Two centuries later, following a period of political unrest and increased Chinese-Burmese rivalry, the administrative divisions were reorganised. On the fourth waxing of the seventh month in the *dap sai* year CS 1147 (Wednesday, 27 April 1785), the head of the Council of Nobles (*noe sanam*), the Cao Chiang Ha, summoned the nobles and officials from all over the country to discuss political reform. As the result Sipsòng Panna was re-divided as follows:

Table 4: Administrative Divisions of Sipsòng Panna in 1785

Panna	*Constituent moeng/müang*	*Right/left bank of the Mekong*
Moeng La	Moeng La, Moeng Pan	left bank
Moeng La [Hò]	Moeng La Hò (Simao), Moeng La Tai (Liushun)	left bank
Chiang Tòng (Zhengdong)	Chiang Thòng	left bank
Moeng Hing (Mengling or Puteng)	Moeng Hing	left bank
Moeng U (Mengwu)	Moeng U-Nüa, Moeng U-Tai	left bank
Moeng Ham (Menghan or Ganlanba)	Moeng Ham	left bank
Moeng Cae (Mengzhe)	Moeng Cae	right bank
Moeng Hun (Menghun)	Moeng Hun	right bank
Moeng Long (Menglong)	Moeng Long	right bank
Moeng Phong (Mengpeng)*	Moeng Phong, Moeng Yuan, Moeng Mang	left bank
Moeng Hai (Menghai)*	Moeng Hai, Moeng Ngat, Moeng Khòn, Kang Chiang	right bank
Chiang Coeng (Jingzhen)*	Chiang Coeng, Moeng Waen, Moeng Hem, Moeng Yang Nòi	right bank

Source: MLC-LV1, s. 3.11, by Li Fuyi

* Called "lesser *panna*", while the other nine *panna* are termed "large *panna*".

Unfortunately, Tai Lü sources tell us nothing about the reasons for this administrative reform, such as why several *panna*, such as Moeng Long, Moeng La, Moeng Phong, and Moeng U, were hardly affected by the reorganisation while others were. Of greatest significance was the division of Moeng Cae into two *panna*, its former eastern half—Moeng Hai—becoming a new *panna* enlarged by several smaller *müang*. It is interesting to note that the *panna* of Chiang Rung, ruled by the *cao fa* himself, is missing in the list above. It appears, however, on a list provided by Thongthaem Nartchamnong in his overview of the history and ethnography of Sipsòng Panna (1989). The administrative division stipulated in 1785 changed during the nineteenth century.[103]

103. See for example, the list of *panna* which J. G. Scott, British super-intendent in the Shan

In spite of all the territorial and administrative changes that occurred over the centuries, the division of the Moeng Lü polity into six "left bank" *panna* and an equal number of "right bank" *panna* does not seem to have changed. Only Chiang Rung, though usually counted as "right bank" *panna* due to the location of its capital, comprised both banks of the Mekong. However, it was not the largest, most fertile and populous *panna*. In terms of rice production and density of population, Chiang Rung was surpassed by Moeng Cae but, due to its strategic location in the centre of Sipsòng Panna, Chiang Rung remained the leading *panna* throughout the centuries. Chiang Rung was a major crossroads of trade routes. One important route, the so-called "salt caravan route", went from Chiang Rung to the south. The route started from Simao, passed through Moeng Sing, turned east towards Chiang Tung, and from there to Chiang Mai. The eastern route from Chiang Tung to Moeng U via Chiang Rung took ten days; from Moeng U it took another seven days to reach Chiang Mai via Nan. The land route back from Chiang Mai to Chiang Rung passed through Chiang Rai; from there the journey was continued by boat, stopping at Moeng Len, Chiang Lap, Chiang Kok, Müang Nang, Müang Lòng, and Moeng Sing before finally arriving at Chiang Rung.[104]

The *cao fa* resided in a capital, the location of which had changed frequently during the nineteenth century. When W. C. McLeod visited Chiang Rung in March 1837— the first European to have done so—he found the capital of Chiang Rung, called Chiang Yung (lit., "city of peacocks") since the late sixteenth century, "on the western face of a range of hills running north and south" not far from the confluence of the Mae Ha and Mekong Rivers. When fully occupied, the town would contain about 400 houses but McLeod observed that "not above 250" were occupied. Portions of the town were "entirely deserted by the inhabitants". Chiang Yung stood at about 21° 58' north latitude and 100° 39' east longitude.[105] The British diplomat-explorer gives a quite disappointing view of the capital's "splendour":

> This place is not fortified; there is one wide road running from one end of it to the other, and along this there are a great many houses belonging to the Chinese, very poor in their appearance; the streets are narrow, scarcely better than pathways, running up the sides of the hills, without any regularity, and along which terraces had been cut to admit of houses being built. The palace is a conspicuous building standing on the high ground at the foot of the hills, at the northern extremity of the town. The only other objects to be noticed are two or three monasteries, some small pagodas on the face of the hills, and a few banyan

States, obtained during his stay in Moeng Phong in the late 1880s. See Scott 1891, 36 [British Library, IOOC].

104. For ancient trade routes passing Sipsòng Panna, see Kato 1999; Yanyong and Ratanaporn 2001, 206–15.

105. MJ, 9 March and 19–22 March 1837, quoted from Grabowsky and Turton 2003, 370–71, 393.

> trees here and there. With the exception of the valley of the Mé Há the country around is hilly and extremely barren in appearance. [...][106]

When the French expedition led by Francis Garnier arrived at Chiang Rung thirty years later, Chiang Yung was found completely destroyed, only the ruins were left. Since its destruction by Mahacai, the governor of Moeng Phong, "the town of Xieng Hong had been reconstructed to the north of the confluence of the Nam Ha". Though the plain of Chiang Rung was relatively densely populated, the new capital had still attracted very few inhabitants. "It was still a market town rather than a population center", remarked Garnier in 1869.[107] Twenty years later, James G. Scott, British "Officiating Superintendent" in the Shan states, found the new capital of Wiang Phakhang and the plain of Chiang Rung as a whole "equally and remarkably disappointing":

> The capital of a State, which is nearly as large, and is certainly more wealthy, than Kyaingtôn (Chiang Tung), is smaller than any one of its own Panna towns, which I have seen. The plain is not so large as that of Maingthat (Moeng Sat), or of Meung Hsîng (Moeng Sing), or Meung Hpung (Moeng Phong), to say nothing of Meung Sè (Moeng Cae), and a very considerable portion of it is not cultivated. The town stands on a hill face, overlooking the junction of the Nam Ha with the Mekhong, and the 50–60 houses there are scattered about at wide intervals in niches, or on reasonably level features of the slope. [...] Though the site of the town was changed comparatively so recently, the Burmese erected a court-house of brick. All but the base is now in ruins and on this is erected the exceedingly ill-thatched, tumble-down bamboo shed which represents the *haw* (*hò kham*), the residence, of the Sao Kamom (Cao Khamòm).[108]

Wealthier than the plain of Chiang Rung was the fairly large plain of Moeng Ham and Moeng Khòn running up on the east bank of the Mekong which belonged to the *panna* of Chiang Rung. This fertile plain, with a length of 20 to 30 miles and a breadth averaging five miles, produced "vast quantities of paddy". Scott describes Moeng Ham as "the most populous district" he had seen so far in the Shan and Tai Lü areas. Numerous villages scattered along the river and "in addition to extensive rice-fields" the plain was "richly supplied with orchards and groves of coconut, areca palms, and betel vines", and even animal livestock was "procurable in any quantity".[109]

---

106. MJ, 9 March 1837, quoted from Grabowsky and Turton 2003, 371.

107. Garnier 1996, 85.

108. Scott 1891, 30 [British Library, IOOC]. See also the description of Wiang Phakhang, in 1913, by the American missionary William Clifton Dodd (1996, 183). Bunchuai Sisawat, a former governor of the Thai province of Chiang Rai who visited Chiang Rung before the Communist victory of 1949/50, also deplores the miserable state of the *hò kham*. See Bunchuai 2004 [1954], 114.

109. Scott 1891, 29–30 [British Library, IOOC].

Although Sipsòng Panna is a small country in terms of territorial extent and population size, it was geographically and politically always rather fragmented. Chiang Rung's central location on both banks of the Mekong River and on the crossroads of major routes of communication made it a natural choice for becoming a political centre. Nonetheless, the limited agricultural resources, directly controlled by the *cao phaendin,* and the wealth of several larger provincial *müang* always posed restrictions on a pre-eminent role of the capital. Moreover, even with regard to trade, places other than Chiang Rung were of crucial importance.

5. TRADE AND ECONOMY

As has been pointed out in the preceding section, the pre-modern state of Sipsòng Panna was situated on important trading routes which linked southwestern China with Burma and northern Thailand. The Japanese historian Kumiko Kato has reconstructed these trade networks in an impressive study based on extensive interviews with elderly people in Sipsòng Panna who had experiences and memories of trade activities prior to the Communist revolution. She points out that the most important ancient overland trade route started from Kunming going through the Chinese market towns of Puer and Simao, before changing course in a southwesterly direction via Moeng Wang and Moeng Ngat to Moeng Hai. From there, the route proceeded via Moeng Hun and Moeng Pan to Ta Lò (Chiang Lò), a town situated directly on the border to Chiang Tung. One branch of this trade route led from Moeng Ngat to Moeng Cae and from there the shortest way—via Moeng Hun—to Ta Lò. After leaving Ta Lò, the route went to Chiang Tung and from there to Upper Burma.[110] However, the main route passing through Moeng Hai and Moeng Hun seems, according to Kato, to have been the most frequented. Not incidentally, this route was taken by McLeod and his retinue on their way from Chiang Tung to Chiang Rung.[111]

The traders were mostly Chinese Muslims called Hò or Hò Phasi (lit., "Persian Chinese") by the Tai Lü. In large pony caravans they brought clothes, silk, iron products, and a variety of consumer goods from inner China to Sipsòng Panna. There, the Chinese traders bought tea, opium, cotton, and camphor, which they sold either in China or in Burma.[112]

110. In contrast, the present-day trade route leads south to Moeng Hing (Puwen) in the northernmost part of Sipsòng Panna. From there the route continues via Moeng Yang to Chiang Rung, then turns west to Moeng Hai and thereafter changes its course to a southwesterly direction passing Moeng Hun, Moeng Pan until it reaches Ta Lò (Chiang Lò) and finally Chiang Tung. However, Kato does not exclude the possibility that at certain times the present-day route could have been the main route prior to 1950. See Kato 1999, especially maps 2 and 4 on pages 220 and 222.

111. See Grabowsky and Turton 2003, 361–400. McLeod mis-spells M. Hum for M. Hám.

112. See McLeod's desciption of a Chinese caravan that he met halfway between Chiang Tung and Ta Lò, Grabowsky and Turton 2003, 369.

Until the twentieth century, the trade route that ran from Moeng Hai to Chiang Tung and Burma was simply called the "Tea Road" (*senthang baicha* เส้นทางใบชา).[113]A large number of tea plantations existed in Moeng Hai but the most extensive plantations were in the eastern districts of I-ngu and I-pang where thousands of Han Chinese labourers were hired for planting tea.[114] Tea was also the most important of tribute goods sent from Sipsòng Panna to the Qing court, running up to as much as 65,000 *cang* (Tr. ชั่ง, c. 130 tons) each year according to one source.[115]

Even more important than the long-distance trade was the impact of local trade on the regional economy. This was not only trade among various *panna* and *müang* of Sipsòng Panna but also between them and neighbouring Tai polities such as Moeng Laem, Nan, and Luang Prabang. The local trade was carried out mainly by Tai Lü and other Tai merchants of pack oxen, and pack horses or mules. As farmers in many parts of Sipsòng Panna suffered from chronic shortages of rice,[116] they were forced to buy supplementary rice from surplus areas in exchange for a wide variety of local products, including tea, camphor (*karabun* การบูร), opium, seal wax, and salt. Opium from I-pang was exchanged for cotton from Luang Prabang and Nan.[117] Salt was another important commodity. Four rock salt mines (*bò klüa sinthao* บ่อเกลือสินเธาว์) in the southeastern district of Moeng La, situated near the borders to Nan and Luang Prabang, supplied large parts of Sipsòng Panna with this precious and much-needed item. Salt from these mines was also exported to Moeng Sing, Chiang Tung, and Chiang Mai.[118] The governor of Moeng La made "a great deal of money from these salt-mines."[119] As Sun Laichen points out, salt had been transported from Sipsòng Panna to Lan Na from at least the mid-nineteenth century.[120] Apart from salt, cattle were another important export

113. Yanyong and Ratanaporn 2001, 139.

114. See Archer 1891a, 6 [British Library, IOOC]; MJ, 19–22 March 1837, quoted from Grabowsky and Turton 2003, 391.

115. Yanyong and Ratanaporn 2001, 208.

116. Yanyong and Ratanaporn (2001, 212) report that a survey in 1939 revealed that three villages situated near the capital of Chiang Rung had to cover between 20 and 40 per cent of their needs by importing rice from elsewhere. In a fourth village the rate was even up to 88 per cent.

117. Yanyong and Ratanaporn 2001, 139.

118. Archer who travelled to Moeng La in 1887 reports: "These salt districts of Bô Hë, Bô Luang, Bô Ten, and Sang-yong (as well as Müang Ban), though in the administrative district of Müang La, pay revenue directly to Chienghung, and are therefore sometimes said to be not under Müang La, but directly under Chienghung. [...] A good number of hill people from the surrounding country come to these wells for their supplies of salt, but there is, besides, a considerable export as far as the north-eastern provinces of Chiengmai." Archer 1891a, 8 [British Library, IOOC]. See also Archer 1893, 72 [PRO, FO 881/6459].

119. Scott 1891, 26.

120. Sun Laichen 2000, 160.

commodity. Cows and bullocks were abundant in Sipsòng Panna, and the cattle trade thrived throughout the nineteenth century.[121]

The Moeng Lü Chronicle provides very little information about trade and commerce in more ancient times. However, there are some clues showing that Sipsòng Panna was once also rich in gold, silver, copper, and iron. Gold and silver utensils were regularly sent by the *cao fa* of Chiang Rung as tribute to the Ming court.[122] Thus, one can imagine that these mines were actively exploited, at least, during the Ming period. A Tai Lü source, translated by Gao Lishi (1988) into Chinese, points to the mining of gold and silver during the late sixteenth and seventeenth centuries in Nam Kham River in Moeng Long.[123] In the mid-nineteenth century, silver and iron were still found in the territory of Sipsòng Panna, "but the former so small in quantity that the mines are not worked."[124] The Chinese source *Tianxia junguo libing shu* by Gu Yanwu (1613–1682), completed in 1662, mentions the following goods from the Tai states in the Upper Mekong region: perfumed woods from Sipsòng Panna; pepper from the Shan region; benzoic and sandalwood from Lan Na; cowry shells and perfumes from Lan Sang; and jade from Moeng Yang in the Tai Khün state of Chiang Tung. In the earlier part of its history, Sipsòng Panna was able to export goods, such as tools made of iron and looms, which other Tai states were not yet able to produce.[125]

6. THE *TUSI* SYSTEM: TRIBUTARY RELATIONS WITH CHINA

6.1 THE *TUSI* SYSTEM

The Sino-Tai relations should be viewed from the perspective of the unique *tusi* 土司 (aboriginal office/commission) establishments created in late imperial China primarily to rule the non-Han Chinese living in China. Later, during the Ming period (1368–1644) *tusi* were also established in the southern borderlands beyond the southern frontiers of today's China. The non-Han Chinese living in South China were generally referred to as *man* 蠻 or *manyi* 蠻夷, which can be rendered as "barbarians or foreign tribes". These peoples, although living in the domain of China from time immemorial, had their own kings and chieftains. Their social customs differed from those of the Han Chinese,

121. MJ, 18 March 1837, quoted from Grabowsky and Turton 2003, 383.

122. See table 1, "Tribute missions from Cheli (1283–1485) to the Ming Court", in Grabowsky 2008, 56–59.

123. See Gao Lishi, *Meng Long difang zhi yizhu* 猛龍地方志譯註 (Annotated translation of *Nangsü pün moeng long*), 1988, 156–57, quoted by Sun Laichen 2000, 160. According to Gao Lishi (1988), a businessman having his land in Nam Kham (golden river) offered in tribute each year 5 *bat* of golden dusk. Later the gold mine was exhausted and cotton was offered in tribute. A silver mine is not mentioned, but silver was offered as tribute. Iron ore is mentioned as well.

124. MJ, 24 March 1837, quoted from Grabowsky and Turton 2003, 390.

125. The above information is based on Yanyong and Ratanaporn 2001, 136–37.

and they spoke their native tongue, which the Chinese officials from the central government could not understand. However, the regions in which they lived remained under the suzerainty of imperial China in the successive dynasty. In order to rule them, a special system had to be created and this was the *tusi* system. The origin of *tusi* can be traced back to the "prefectures under loose reins" (*jimi fuzhou* 羈縻府州), which were established during the Tang (618–907) and Song (960–1279) periods in regions inhabited predominantly by non-Han Chinese, and not yet assimilated into the great Han cultures. Most of these tribal prefectures were to become the later *tusi* regions.[126]

The *tusi* of the Ming period (1368–1644) were established in five southern provinces of China. These were the two inland provinces (Guizhou and Huguang), and three border provinces (Sichuan, Yunnan, and Guangxi), the homelands of the various groups of "aboriginal peoples" (*turen* 土人), including the Tai in Guangxi, Yunnan, and northern mainland Southeast Asia. The chieftains of these tribal peoples were appointed "aboriginal officials" (*tuguan* 土官), whose posts were hereditary. In the eyes of the imperial court of China the chieftains were just "aboriginal officials"; in the eyes of the tribal peoples they were, in the case of the Tai, the *cao fa* (lord of heaven). The *tuguan* were entrusted to rule their own peoples according to their own customs and laws under the emperor of China. Through the *tusi* system, China secured an indirect rule over the tribal regions. Though some *tusi* were already introduced during the Yuan period, the system was perfected during the Ming period (1368–1644) and adopted by the Qing court (1644–1911), and was still in use until 1949–1950. It is through this *tusi* system that regular tribute missions of the southern tribal lords were sent to the imperial court of China. A wealth of documents was recorded and has been transmitted to us in the form of imperial edicts and memorials submitted by these tribal lords via their tribute missions.[127]

The imperial court of China adopted the method of gradual assimilation or politics of sinicisation to rule these peoples. No troops were sent, if the "aboriginal officials" served the interests of the Chinese court well and did not engage in armed rebellion. The influx of Chinese settlers and thus of taxpaying populations in the remote border areas, as well as the founding of Chinese schools to educate the sons of the aboriginal nobility in Chinese culture, mainly Confucian ethics, and in Chinese language, furthered

126. Liew 1998 (vol. 1), 64 and Liew-Herres 2003a, 147.

127. Detailed stipulations about the delivery of tributes to the Ming court are recorded in the "Collected Statues of the Great Ming" (*Da Ming Huidian*, photographic reprint of the 1587 edition in 1976). The Chinese tribute system under the Qing dynasty is described in Fairbank 1941. The Sino-Siamese tribute relations of the period 1282–1853 are analysed in-depth by Suebsaeng 1971. To the best of our knowledge the tribute relations between the Ming court and the various Tai polities is a subject which has not yet been studied adequately. It is interesting to note that even in the first half of the nineteenth century, strangers who wanted to travel from Chiang Rung to Yunnan proper needed "a reference" to the Chinese governor in Kunming. See MJ, 12 March 1837, in Grabowsky and Turton 2003, 376.

the progressive dissolution of many of the *tusi* organisations.[128] Exposed to continuous sinicisation, many of the 272 *tusi* that had been established during the founding and consolidation of the Ming empire, viz. from the reign of Hongwu to Yongle (1368–1424),[129] were transformed into regular Chinese counties (*xian*) or prefectures (*fu*). This policy of assimilation is called *gaitu guiliu* 改土歸流, which can be rendered as "changing local native offices to regular civil service appointments", i.e., replacing the hereditary aboriginal officials (*tuguan* 土官) with regular or circulating officials (*liuguan* 流官).[130] The *gaitu guiliu* was not only carried out through peaceful means and gradual assimilation; the demotion and abolition of a *tusi*, sometimes by a trial and error method to enforce *gaitu guiliu*, took place throughout the Ming period.[131] The *gaitu guiliu* policy was taken over by the Qing dynasty (1644–1911) and implemented systematically throughout the Qing empire. Nonetheless, the *tusi* system survived—with some modifications and shrinking of territory—through the Republican period (1912–1949), until the *tusi* were finally "liberated" in the 1950s. A case in point is the pristine *tusi* in today's Sipsòng Panna, called Cheli *junmin xuanwei shisi* 車里軍民宣慰使司 (Chiang Lü Military-cum-Civilian Pacification Commission).[132] During the Qing period *gaitu guiliu* was attempted in Cheli (Moeng Lü or Sipsòng Panna) but without much practical result

128. As Mote (1999, 705) observes, "[t]he Ming *tusi* were absorbed into the Chinese system more readily where the in-migration of Chinese settlers occurred the most rapidly. [...] The native peoples were reduced in status, were absorbed into the Chinese population, or were driven out to occupy less desirable hill regions or more remote border areas. It was a centuries-long process of continued Chinese movement [...]." In 1395 an edict was issued to establish Confucian schools in the autochthonous regions in Yunnan and Sichuan. See Liew 1998 (vol. 1), 65, n. 58; *Taizu shilu*, ch. 239, 3475 (Hongwu 28, 6. m., *renchen* day: 27 June 1395).

129. The aboriginal offices (*tusi*) established in the Ming empire are documented in Liew 1998 (vol. 2), 239–332. There were a total of 272 aboriginal offices. The year of establishment and the location are given.

130. The *tuguan* were hereditary posts, whereas the *liuguan* were non-hereditary posts and *liuguan* were not allowed to serve in their native places. They were transferred to another place after serving the term of office. For *gaitu guiliu*, see Liew 1998 (vol. 1), 65; Liew-Herres 2003a, 147; Mote 1999, 705.

131. For instance, Menglian *zhangguan si* (Moeng Laem chieftaincy), established in 1406 and abolished during the Jiajing reign (1522–1566) due to wars, was reinstated in 1585; Yunyuan (lit., "distant cloud") Prefecture was established in Moeng Ying (in Upper Burma) in 1382, renamed Mengyang Prefecture, two years later, reorganised into an aboriginal office, called Mengyang *junmin xuanwei shisi* (Moeng Ying Military-cum-Civilian Pacification Commission), in 1404, was abolished in 1449. See Liew 1998 (vol. 2), 289–96, nos. 62, 69, and 73. There are ample examples documented in Liew 1998 (vol. 2).

132. One of the oldest mentions of this name in the work of a Western scholar is found in Pierre Lefèvre-Pontalis' study of ancient Tai polities in the Indochinese Peninsula. Lefèvre-Pontalis (1900, 66) states: "Muong-Lu (Moeng Lü) is the ethnographic designation of a region, which the Chinese call Tcheli (Cheli) or, more precisely, Tcheli Ssouen-ou-sse (Cheli xuanwei shisi), the capital of which is Xieng-Hung (Chiang Rung). When they want to reproduce the Chinese name, the Lus themselves call this country Muong Sêne-vi-fa (Moeng Saenwi Fa), but in general

until 1953. It was then reorganised into an "autonomous prefecture" (*zizhi zhou* 自治州) of the Tai peoples with a domain much smaller than before.

As mentioned above, in dealing with the "southern barbarians", known as *man* or *yi*, the Ming emperors contented themselves with an indirect rule as long as the native rulers did not challenge the Chinese authorities. In strategically important regions, garrisons (*weisuo*) were established in regions predominantly inhabited by Chinese or by already sinicised tribal peoples. They were located in the vicinity of tribal regions, such as Tengchong and Yongchang in Southwestern Yunnan, in order to strengthen military and political control over the tribal peoples, such as the Tai.[133] However, as a rule, no Chinese troops were permanently stationed in tribal regions until the powerful Emperor Qianlong (r. 1736–1795) of the Qing period. In 1773, troops were ordered to garrison in Cheli (Chiang Lü/Moeng Lü) after the thirty-fourth ruler of Cheli, Dao Weiping (Tao Wui Phin) was dismissed.[134]

There were two categories of *tusi* in Yunnan, one established in inland regions and one on the quasi border or beyond the border regions. The inland *tusi* were under Chinese suzerainty, but the imperial court allowed the chieftains a certain amount of freedom to rule their own peoples according to their own customs. The second category of *tusi* under Yunnan was established beyond the southern frontiers of today's Yunnan. Although the tribal domains under these *tusi* were nominally under Chinese suzerainty, areas such as Lan Na (Babai-dadian) and Lan Sang (Laowo) were largely independent vassal states. Generally, four types of *tusi* were organised: i) the *xuanwei si* 宣慰司, translated into "pacification commission" (highest in rank); ii) *xuanfu si* 宣撫司, translated into "pacification commission" (second in rank); iii) *anfu si* 安撫司, also translated into "pacification commission" (third in rank); and iv) *zhangguan si* 長官司, translated into "chieftain command" or "chieftaincy" (lowest in rank). The tribal rulers were appointed *xuanwei shi* 宣慰使, *xuanfu shi* 宣撫使, *anfu shi* 安撫使, and *zhangguan* 長官 respectively. In general, a tribal polity under a more powerful ruler, having a domain roughly the size of a Chinese prefecture or larger, the pacification commission of the highest rank, viz. *xuanwei si*, was established and the chieftain or the lord of the land was appointed pacification commissioner, viz. *xuanwei shi* (or *saenwi fa*).[135]

they give it the name Sip-song-pan-na, which means in their language 'the twelve thousand rice fields'" [translation by Grabowsky].

133. *Weisuo* 衛所 is a general reference to the almost one thousand major and minor garrisons organised in the Ming empire. For more details, see Liew 1998 (vol. 1), 69–73, and table 11 (364). The *weisuo* garrisons were not established directly in tribal territories where *tusi* were established. For example, the Tengchong Garrison and Jinchi Garrison (in Baoshan), organised on the northern frontiers of Luchuan, were to defend Yunnan proper against the Shan or Tai Nüa and the Burmese. For more on the *weisuo* garrisons in Yunnan, see Liew 1998 (vol. 2), 98–99.

134. See *Gaozong shilu*, ch. 940, 28–29 (Qianlong 38, eighth month, *gengzi* day: 29 Sept. 1773); Dao Yongming 1989, 693–94; 954ff.

135. For more on the *tusi* system of the Ming period, see Liew 1998 (vol. 1), 63–68; on the *tusi* organised in Yunnan, see Liew 1998 (vol. 2), 248–51, 278–99.

Cheli (Chiang Lü, i.e., Moeng Lü) was one of the six such pacification commissions, called *xuanwei si*, established by the Ming court in Hongwu 17 (1384).[136] Menggen (Moeng Khün or Chiang Tung) was not an aboriginal office (*tusi*); it was organised as a "tribal prefecture" (*yuyi fu* 禦夷府), lit., "prefecture for defending the foreigners".[137] The Menggen *yuyi fu* was established in Yongle 3 (1405) during the Ming period and was first placed under the direct command of the Yunnan Regional Military Commission. It was later transferred under the direct administration of the provincial government of Yunnan, i.e., under civil control, perhaps with the intention to make the Tai Khün country a part of Yunnan. Menglian (Moeng Laem), previously subordinate to the Luchuan-Pingmian Pacification Commission (*xuanwei si*), was established as a separate "chieftainship" of the lowest rank (*zhangguan si*) in 1406.[138] During the early Ming period, a pacification commission of the highest rank, called Miandian *junmin xuanwei shisi* (military-cum-civilian pacification commission), was established in modern Burma (Myanmar).[139]

The geographical fragmentation of the Tai-inhabited areas into many small and isolated river basins favoured rivalries among the local rulers, which the imperial court was able to skilfully manipulate to its own advantage by the method of "divide and rule" to attain a "balance of powers" among them. The consequent application of the traditional Chinese method "to fight the barabarians with the help of the barbarians" (*yi man zhi man* 以蠻治蠻 or *yi yi zhi yi* 以夷治夷) in the mid-fifteenth century to curb the power of a too powerful tribal king, Soe Ngam Fa, as in the case of Moeng Mao, resulted in the disintegration of the Tai Nüa polities in today's Dehong region. The descendants of the Mao Shan king, Soe Ngam Pha, eventually moved to Moeng Ying.[140]

Sun Laichen notes that Ming China's political expansion in the northern part of mainland Southeast Asia, buttressed by its advanced military technology, far exceeded that of Mongol China: "China's influence in this region was indeed tremendous."[141] Indigenous records also acknowledge China's superiority and tributary relationship, though with some reluctance.

The *tusi* system was adopted by Emperor Shunzhi (r. 1644–1661), the first Manchu emperor of Qing China. The *cao fa* of Moeng Lü or Sipsòng Panna of the Qing period

136. The Cheli of the Ming period was the northern neighbour of the Lan Na kingdom. For a brief history of the establishment of the Cheli Military-cum-Civilian Pacification Commission, see Liew 1998 (vol. 2), 286–87.

137. See "Treatise on Geography", *Mingshi*, ch. 46, 1194.

138. *Taizong shilu*, ch. 53, 793 (Yongle 4, fourth month, *wuyin* day). For more on the Menglian *zhangguang si*, see Liew 1998 (vol. 2), 296–97.

139. See Liew 1998 (vol. 2), 287–89.

140. See Liew 1998 (vol. 1), 63. This policy is best demonstrated in the abovementioned Luchuan-Pingmian campaigns, in which the Ming court persuaded Mubang (Moeng Pòng) to send troops to help capture the ruler of Müang Mao, Soe Ngam Pha (Ch. Si Ren Fa), and extradite him to the Chinese authorities. See Liew 1996.

141. Sun Laichen 2000, 104.

recognised the Manchu ruler of China as his overlord in the same way as the preceding *cao fa* had recognised the successive Ming emperors. In 1729 (Yongzheng 7, seventh month), the Qing court became directly involved for the first time in the internal affairs of Sipsòng Panna when Chinese officials were sent to collect taxes in the tea producing area of Yiolò, as well as in the salt mine (*bò klüa* บ่อเกลือ) regions of Chiang Tòng and Moeng U (see also following section).[142] In 1773 (Qianlong 38), the *cao fa* of Chiang Rung fled to Burma prompting the Chinese to proclaim the abolition of the *xuanwei si* system and to depose the *cao fa*. However, the Chinese had to return to the old system only four years later, as all the *müang* in Sipsòng Panna resisted the Chinese policy of direct involvement.[143]

6.2 TRIBUTE MISSIONS

In return for protection against internal rivals and external threats the Chinese imperial court expected the Tai rulers to send regular tribute missions. These missions were not limited to political rituals; they were of economic importance as well. Whereas the *tusi* delegations sent horses, elephants, precious metals such as gold and silver, gems (rubies and jade) as well as forest products such as ivory, honey, bees-wax, resin, and spices to the capital Nanjing (1368–1420) and Beijing (after 1421), they were given in return luxury goods such as silk, brocade, gauzes, clothings, and Chinese paper money.[144] The *Mingshi gao* (Draft of the History of the Ming Dynasty) reports the first tribute mission from Cheli to the Ming court in Nanjing in 1383:

> In the year Hongwu 16, third month, on *xinyou* day (20 April 1382), Dao Kan 刀 坎 (Cao Khan Moeng) sent his nephew, Feng Lu 豐 祿, to offer in tribute elephants and local products. An imperial decree was issued to grant Feng Lu one suit of [official] clothes and ten *ding* (spindles or strings) of paper money. Not long after Dao Kan and Feng Lu were granted nine bolts of variegated silks woven with gold threads (*zhijin wenqi*) and the same amount of silks, eighty [*ding*] of paper money, and fifty suits of clothes, [a favour shown] as it was the first time they offered tribute to the [Ming] court.[145]

142. *Shizong shilu*, ch. 84, 22–23; Dao Yongming 1989, 833.

143. See *Gaozong shilu*, ch. 935, 24–26 (Qianlong 38, fifth month); ch. 940, 28–29 (Qianlong 38, eight month); ch. 1005, 33–34 (Qianlong 41, third month). The Chinese deposed the *cao fa*, Dao Saowen (Tao Sao Wün), and his son Dao Weiping (Tao Wui Phin) absconded. See also MLC-LV2, s. 33.2, and Gao Lishi 1984, s. 33.2.

144. MSG, ch. 189, 29b; *Taizu shilu*, ch. 153, 2393–94 (Hongwu 16, third month, *xinyou* day).

145. See Liew-Herres 2003a, 149. As to the different kinds of tribute goods which the *tusi* missions from Yunnan and neighbouring regions sent to China, see *Da Ming Huidian* (Collected Statutes of the Great Ming), chapter 108, 16. The tribute comprises such varied goods as horses, elephants, rhinoceros horns, peacock feathers, ivory, howdahs, gold and silver utensils, green and red rubies and jades.

During the following two and a half centuries, more than forty such tribute missions from Cheli arrived at the imperial court, particularly during the period 1391–1485 (thirty-two missions). Tribute missions from Chiang Tung and Moeng Laem were far less frequent. Only the Babai-dadian Pacification Commission (*xuanwei si*), i.e., Lan Na, equalled Cheli with regard to the number of tribute missions (thirty missions in the period 1391–1485) and the quantity of goods delivered to the imperial court.[146]

The most precious tribute goods which China received from Cheli and other Tai *tusi* were gold and silverware, but elephants and horses suitable for military purposes were also highly appreciated. During the entire Ming period, China's vassal states in upper mainland Southeast Asia delivered yearly specified amounts of silver and gold, in addition to the regular tribute to the imperial court.[147]

Diplomatic relations were not only vigourously cultivated between Ming China and her "aboriginal officials" in mainland Southeast Asia, but they were also fostered among the Tai polities of the Upper Mekong region. In the second half of the thirteenth century, Sipsòng Panna, for instance, received from Lan Na elephant howdahs, golden trays, and cotton wool blankets, while Lan Na received horses, cattle, knives, and one hundred mule-loads of salt produced in the salt mines of Moeng Lao in return.[148] During the reign of Soe Long Fa (1428–1457), Lan Na, Chiang Tung, and Moeng Laem sent tribute gifts to Chiang Rung.[149] As late as the first half of the twentieth century, salt from Sipsòng Panna was still being exported to Laowo (Lan Sang) and Chiang Tung. Moreover, Sipsòng Panna was famous for its production of cowries. Many sources indicate that the region was an important trade route, especially for cowries and salt.[150] Apart from these gifts, according to a Tai Lü source, the mining of gold and silver remained a very important business in the late sixteenth and early seventeenth centuries. Sipsòng Panna was indeed rich in gold, silver, copper, and iron, in addition to salt.

---

146. For tribute relations between Lan Na (Babai) and Ming China, see Liew-Herres et al. 2008, 28–37.

147. Without mentioning the respective periods of time, Sun Laichen (2000, 90–91) provides details on the annual delivery of gold and silver: from Cheli (Sipsòng Panna), 50 *liang* of gold; Mubang (Hsaenwi), 1.400 *liang* of silver; Luchuan (Moeng Mao), 6.900 *liang* of silver; Mengyang (Moeng Yang), 750 *liang* of silver; Mengding, 600 *liang* of silver; Menggen (Chiang Tung), 60 *liang* of gold "in the early period" and 16 *liang* in the "later period"; Nandian, 100 *liang* of silver [...]; Man Mo (Bhamo), 1.000 *liang* of silver; Mangshi (Moeng Khòn/Ruili), 100 *liang* of silver; Menglian (Moeng Laem), 200 *liang* of silver.

148. MLC-LV1, s. 4.6–4.7.

149. MLC-LV1, s. 12.11. The sending of tribute from Chiang Tung to the court in Chiang Rung at any time in the fifteenth century, however, is not confirmed by the Chiang Tung Chronicle. See CTC-PMCT, Thawi 1990, 39–40; CTC-JSC, Sāimöng 1981, 239–41.

150. Sun Laichen 2000, 160.

6.3 SEALS

Seals (*yin* 印) also played a vital role in the Sino-Tai relations, and they are frequently mentioned in the Moeng Lü Chronicle. Apart from other credentials and tally coupons, official seals were issued to local rulers who had been appointed as aboriginal officials (*tuguan* 土官) of China. Each post was clearly engraved on the seal, such as the seal of the *noe sanam* (Council of Nobles) of Moeng Lü engraved with the characters *Cheli xuanweisi yishiting* 車里宣慰司議事庭.

Letters or memorials sent to the Chinese authorities in Yunnan or submitted directly to the imperial court by tribute envoys had to bear the chop of the seal to authenticate the documents. The seal of an aboriginal official was used to authenticate his letters and memorials sent to China, standing as the authorised signature of an "aboriginal official".[151] The official seals issued by imperial China to the aboriginal officials were the coveted objects of seizure in time of tribal armed conflicts and invasions. When, for example, in 1403–4, the *cao fa* of Chiang Rung, Dao Xianda (Tao Sida Kham), invaded Weiyuan Prefecture (Moeng Bò in today's Jinggu), he captured the prefect as well as a number of inhabitants, and took away the prefect's seal. He was forced to surrender the seal and credential which he had taken and sent his brother to the Ming court to apologise so as to avoid a punitive campaign.[152] When a tribal king "serving" as an aboriginal official was forced to flee, such as in the case of Tao Kham Tet and Tao Sunwu, he took with him the most important thing of his office—the seal.[153] When Tao Kham Tet fled with the golden seal adorned with a tiger head to China, the Ming court ordered Soe Long Fa to pay a ransom for it.[154]

The seals were made of various kinds of materials, such as gold, silver, ivory, and wood, depending on the status of the aboriginal officials and the favour he received from the imperial court. When an aboriginal official, namely a tribal ruler, passed away, his successor inherited his post and the seal, but he had to send envoys to inform China and to receive approval. When there was a change in dynasty or a new emperor ascended the throne, new seals bearing the reign of the new emperor were cast and issued to all the aboriginal officials. This is exemplified in the case of Wu Sangui (1612–1678). When Wu Sangui founded his short-lived kingdom of Zhou (1678–1681) in Hengzhou, Hunan, he immediately confiscated the official seal of the *cao phaendin* of Sipsòng Panna, issued by Emperor Shunzhi (r. 1644–1661) of the Qing dynasty in Beijing, and cast a new seal of his reign and issued it to Cao Nò Moeng.[155]

---

151. As to the various types of seals issued to tribal rulers holding the post of *tusi* in Yunnan during various periods, see Xiao Minghua and Zou Yongqiong 1989.

152. See MSG, ch. 189, 30a; *Taizong shilu*, ch. 23, 424–25 (Yongle 1, ninth month, *jiawu* day: 5 October 1403); and MSG, ch. 189, 30a; *Taizong shilu*, ch. 30, 548 (Yongle 2, fourth month, *bingxu* day: 24 May 1404).

153. See MLC-LV1, s. 11.6 and 31.14 respectively.

154. See MLC-LV1, s. 12.3.

155. See MLC-LV1, s. 23.2. In fact it should have been the seal issued by Emperor Kangxi (r. 1662–1722).

In the Moeng Lü Chronicles, the seal issued by the imperial court to the *cao fa* is called *lai cum* (ลายจุ้ม);[156] but when referred together with a paper document, *lai cia* (ลายเจี้ย), it is known as *lai cum lai cia* (ลายจุ้มลายเจี้ย), i.e., a seal along with a paper document. They were kept in the so-called *hò cia kham lüang* (หอเจี้ยคำเหลือง) or "golden libraries" in Kunming or at the palace of the *cao fa*.[157]

When an aboriginal office was abolished, the seal issued was to be returned to the Ming court, as in the case of Jing'an Pacification Commission.[158] If an aboriginal official lost his seal and credential he would petition to the Ming court for replacements, as in the case of Laowo.[159] The official seal of a recalcitrant *tusi* ruler would be confiscated as in the case of Tao Wui Phin (Dao Weiping), the twenty-eighth ruler of Moeng Lü (r. 1767–1777).[160] It is interesting to note that in the Shan states, the Shan *cao fa* used seals to issue official letters. They often entrusted their principal wives to keep the seals and to stamp documents with these seals. The owner or keeper of such seals were called "lord of the seal" (*cao cum* เจ้าจุ้ม) and exercised considerable political influence.[161]

As Chiang Rung was the gateway to Simao through which envoys from other pacification commissions had to pass, its *cao fa* held a privileged position. The author(s) of the Moeng Lü Chronicle boasts of Moeng Lü's privileged position granted by China after Soe Long Fa (1428–1457) aided China in arresting an official of Moeng Mao who had fled to his land. The tribute missions from Lan Na, Chiang Tung, and Moeng Laem had to gain permission from Chiang Rung to continue their journey to China: "If they had no [travel documents] stamped with the seal of Cao Moeng Lü they were not permitted to proceed."[162] It is doubtful whether this had been a general practice or instead reflects the political strength of Moeng Lü during that time.

From a Chinese perspective all *tusi* were under the control of the imperial court, and their territories were all but parts of China. Ming sources therefore do not mention Lan Na, Lan Sang, and Ava (Burma) as external vassal states but as *tusi* under the administration of Yunnan. It seems that this assumption is deeply rooted in imperial

---

156. In Chinese it is called *yin* 印. This suggests that *cum* is not a Chinese loanword but rather a genuine Tai lexeme. In Tai Lü sources, such as *Leshi*, the term *cum yin* (จุ้มหยิ่น)—combining the Tai with the Chinese word—is frequently used for "seal".

157. The importance of sealed documents issed by the Chinese emperor and handed over to the king of Chiang Mai, see a lengthy episode recorded in the *Chiang Mai Chronicle* (Wyatt and Aroonrut 1995: 100). For an analysis of this episode see Liew-Herres et al. 2008, 41–42.

158. See MSG, ch. 189, 31b; *Xuanzong shilu*, ch. 113, 2549–50 (Xuande 9, tenth month, *dingsi* day: 14 November 1434).

159. See *Shenzong shilu*, ch. 493, 9279–80 (Wanli 40, third month, *xinchou* day: 7 April 1412).

160. See MLC-LV1, s. 29.1.

161. In several Shan principalities the principal queen held the position of *nang cum*, i.e., "the queen who keeps the seal" issued by the Chinese emperor. Somphong (2001, 240) reports that in the Shan state of Hsaenwi the governors of subordinate *müang* had to pay obeisance to the *nang cum* when sending tribute to the court of the *cao fa*.

162. MLC-LV2, s. 16.18; see also MLC-LV1, s. 12.10–12.12.

Chinese political thought. It is even reflected in modern Chinese historiography.[163] Sun Laichen perceptively remarks that the claim of the *tusi* as Chinese territory is a typical sino-centric perspective but does not reflect reality. The acceptance of Chinese seals by the *tusi* rulers did not mean that their polities were "ruled" or "controlled" by the Chinese central authorities.[164] China's sphere of intervention had its limits, as is confirmed by the result of a Chinese punitive expedition against Babai-dadian (Lan Na) in 1405, which was not at all impressive.[165] Although Lan Na formally recognised Chinese overlordship and sent not less than eight tribute missions to Beijing during the following decade, the kings of Chiang Mai regarded themselves as rulers *sui generis* and not as recipients of orders from Beijing. Their self-confidence is most clearly expressed in the Chiang Mai Chronicle, reporting the reception of a Chinese delegation by King Tilokarat after the latter's triumphal victory over the Vietnamese in 1480.[166]

The Tai ruler appointed as "aboriginal official" (*tuguan*) of however small a *tusi* by China would be addressed as *cao fa* (lord of heaven) by his subjects. The fact that the Tai rulers never called themselves "aboriginal officials" shows their strong self-confidence and self-respect. In Tai Lü chronicles the ruler of Sipsòng Panna is, as a rule, addressed as *cao phaendin* (lord of the land), but, at times, called *cao saenwi fa* or just *saenwi fa. Saenwi* is clearly the Tai phonetic rendering of the Chinese word *xuanwei* 宣慰, but *fa* (ฟ้า) is a genuine Tai word, meaning "sky", rather than a Tai rendering of the phonetically quite different Chinese word *shi* 使 (commissioners). In other words, *saenwi fa* is an interesting hybrid neologism. It allowed the Tai Lü to subtly render the Chinese official title into their own language without offending China and yet without lowering the status of their *cao phaendin.* In the Chinese translations of the Moeng Lü Chronicle, such as that by Gao Lishi (1984), the official title of the Tai Lü ruler, namely *cao saenwi* or *saenwi fa*, is always rendered as *xuanwei shi.* It is interesting to note how the Tai Lü explained the term *saenwi* (*xuanwei*) in their own context. Whether or not they did it deliberately in a most humorous way by playing with the words to resist the Chinese title enforced on their *cao phaendin* we do not know. In the 1963 Moeng Lü

163. After the end of World War II, a Chinese historian wrote about the history of Chinese-Burmese relations that "[w]hen Burma submitted to our country, Yunnan was our interior land, and Burma then was our external vassal, and so each inch of land [of] Burma belonged to our country. [...]" Liu Boqui 1946, 1; quoted in Sun Laichen 2000, 93. However, this might not be a general conception of Chinese historians of Liu Boqiu's time. Chinese historians of the 1940s, like Li Fuyi (b. 1911) considered the double Moeng U, now in Laos, as Chinese soil, but not Burma. There might have been some unsolved border conflicts between British-Burma, on the one side, and Qing (1644–1911) and Republican China (1912–1949) on the other.

164. Sun Laichen 2000, 94. We would like to point out that there were two types of *tusi* established in Ming China, viz. the inland *tusi* and the frontier *tusi*. Sun Laichen might be talking about the *tusi* established in today's mainland Southeast Asia.

165. For details see Grabowsky 2004, 97–98.

166. See CMC-HP, Wyatt and Aroonrut 1995, 100; CMC-N, Notton 1932, 140–41; CMC-TPCM, Udom et al. 1995, 80–82.

Chronicle we find this interesting explanation of how Moeng Lü became Moeng Saenwi: *Saen* in Tai Lü means "one hundred thousand" and *wi*, which means "bush" or "bundle" is a classifier for bananas. This is made explicit in the following anecdote about Phaya Coeng (Cüang), the first ruler of Moeng Lü.

> Whenever [the lord of] a *müang* came to pay homage to Phaya Coeng, he offered one bunch (*wi*) of bananas to him. [Phaya Coeng] received one hundred thousand bunches of bananas, and thus subsequently Moeng Lü was called Moeng Saenwi.[167]

This story is missing, not surprisingly, from Gao Lishi's (1984) otherwise rather faithful translation of the Tai Lü original. Gao as a Chinese official might have considered the local folklore as "politically incorrect" or may have been afraid that his translations might not go through the censorship of the authorities. To be on the safe side the story was better disregarded.

According to another local tradition, recorded in various versions of the Chiang Khaeng Chronicle, the origins of the term *saenwi fa* is explained against the background of the dual tributary relationship which bound the *cao fa* of Chiang Rung or Āravīraṭha to his Chinese and Burmese overlords. The ruler of Āravīraṭha, the story goes, was endowed with supernatural powers because he was able to walk in the air like the Burmese king (*cao fa man* เจ้าฟ้าม่าน) and the Chinese emperor (*cao fa wòng* เจ้าฟ้าว้อง). One day all the three rulers decided to go into the air to pay the god Indra (Phaya In) a visit. Upon reaching Tāvatiṃsa heaven Indra noticed the smell of fresh meat. Thus he asked the three rulers who among them had already eaten fresh meat. Knowing that this was a kind of meal reserved exclusively for devatā and other celestial beings they vehemently denied doing so, opened their mouths and vomited so that Indra would be convinced of their innocence. However, when the *cao fa* of Chiang Rung vomited, a piece of meat fell out of his mouth. The ruler of Chiang Rung had indeed eaten fresh meat, because on the way to heaven he saw a big, beautiful cow and just wondered how delicious its meat would taste. Having lost face in front of Indra, he fled from Tāvatiṃsa heaven and returned to earth while the Chinese emperor and the Burmese king were continuing their audience with Indra. Since then the Chiang Rung ruler has been referred to by the name *cao saenwi fa* (เจ้าแสนหวีฟ้า) or *cao sani fa* (เจ้าสนีฟ้า), "the ruler who fled from heaven". The name was finally changed to *cao saenwi fa,* which continued to be the official title of the Chiang Rung–Sipsòng Panna rulers until the mid-twentieth century.[168]

167. MLC-LV2, s. 1.4.

168. Grabowsky and Renoo 2008, 22. Bunchuai ([1954] 2004, 28) reports a very similar version of this folk tale which adds two interesting details. First, the Burmese king and the *cao fa* of Chiang Rung were the middle and the youngest sons of the Chinese emperor. The eldest son had become his father's heir. This reflects the paramount supremacy of China in the triangular relationship among China, Burma, and Sipsòng Panna. Secondly, Lord Indra ordered the Chinese

This folk etymology underscores that the Tai Lü regarded their small principality as a polity in its own right. For its survival the ruling elite had to manoeuvre between two powerful empires which possessed "divine blessings", namely China and Burma.

7. TRIBUTARY RELATIONS WITH BURMA

Burma became a major regional power in the second half of the sixteenth century, and the balance of power in the northern part of mainland Southeast Asia changed to the disadvantage of China. Within a few years, King Bayinnaung (r. 1551–1581), ruler of the small kingdom of Toungoo in central Burma, accomplished "the gathering of the Burmese lands". Important steps to accomplishing this objective were the subjugation of the Mon kingdom of Pegu in the south (1551), the conquest of Ava in the north (1555), and the subjugation of the Shan areas to the west of the Salween River (1556).[169] The expansionist policies of Bayinnaung, who considered himself a Buddhist world conqueror (*cakravartin*), did not end with these conquests. In 1558 Chiang Mai, the capital of the kingdom of Lan Na, surrendered following a short siege by a Burmese army containing strong Shan contingents. In the following year, Chiang Saen, an important trading centre situated at a strategically crucial location on the western bank of the Mekong River where remnants of the Lan Na troops had organised stiff resistance, fell into Bayinnaung's hands.[170] All obstacles for a Burmese domination of the Upper Mekong basin were now removed; China had to concentrate even more of her military resources on the defence of her northern frontiers, especially in the northeast, with the rise of the Manchu tribes.

The rise of Burma in the sixteenth century coincided with the weakening of control of the Ming court over the Tai kingdoms on its southern frontiers. Sipsòng Panna was completely under the control of Ava-Burma in the early seventeenth century. The twenty-second ruler of Moeng Lü, Cao In Moeng (r. 1569–1598/1569–1578), was offered a Burmese princess as his queen consort. The Burmese king interfered directly in the appointment of *Saenwi Fa* of Sipsòng Panna. The *saenwi fa* of Sipsòng Panna, after being appointed by China, were required to send envoys to Burma to ask for the consent of the Burmese king. In such circumstances, it is perhaps understandable why the loyalties of the ruling house of Sipsòng Panna were split between China and Burma. Ambitious uncles or cousins offered their allegiance to Burma to strengthen their own power. At one point, there were two Tai Lü *saenwi fa*, one recognised by China and the other by

---

emperor to mop up the vomit of his youngest brother. As a token of gratitude the *cao fa* of Chiang Rung had to pay his eldest brother regular tribute.

169. See Hall 1981, 289; Lieberman 2003, 151–152.

170. The capture of Chiang Mai triggered a confrontation with Lan Sang because the Lao king Setthathilat (1546–1547), temporarily also king of Lan Na, had never fully forfeited his claims to the throne of Chiang Mai. For details, see Grabowsky 2004, 149–50.

Burma.[171] Moeng Lü paid tribute to China and to Burma (for details, see section 8) and learned to survive under the "protection" of two foreign overlords. The supreme rulers of Moeng Lü of this period who owed allegiance to the Burmese king were conferred Burmese titles. They also had Tai Lü and sinicised names.[172]

Whereas Burmese rule over Siam (Ayutthaya) and Laos (Lan Sang) was only temporary, Ava's overlordship over the Tai polities in the basins of the Salween and Mekong Rivers proved more stable. In these regions, the Chinese de facto abolished the *tusi* system. Mubang (Hsipaw), Mengmi (Moeng Mit), Mengyang (Moeng Ying/ Lashio), and Babai (Lan Na) no longer entertained tributary relations with China. Yet, the Chinese influence remained strong in some other Tai areas that were temporarily occupied by Burmese troops. These areas included Menglian (Moeng Laem) and Cheli (Sipsòng Panna), which had surrendered to the victorious Burmese in 1564.

The subdued Tai polities now began sending tribute to Pegu, the Burmese capital until 1634, and to Ava, where the Burmese kings resided thereafter. One of the first missions which the *cao fa* of Sipsòng Panna sent to his Burmese overlord is recorded in the Moeng Lü Chronicle. When the *cao fa*'s Burmese wife asked for permission to visit her father, the king of Burma, Cao In Moeng offered as tribute to his father-in-law a variety of gifts:

> Chiang Rung (1), Moeng Ham (2), Moeng Nun (3), and Moeng Song (4), [forming] the *panna* under the direct administration of the *saenwi fa*, [offered] one golden ring of weight six *bat*; one silver ring of weight six *bat*;[173] six golden flowers, each weighing one *bat*; six silver flowers, each weighing one *bat*; a pair of candles, [the wax] wrapped in gold weighing one *pan*; two bolts of broad satin (*hae long*); four bolts of narrow satin; four bolts of *nan* (probably dark blue dyed cotton); four bags of salt; four [bamboo] tubes of tea, each tube contains five balls [of tea]; and one horse (of unspecified colour). The golden things were not necessarily of the purest gold.[174]

The other eleven *panna* were obligated to deliver similar gifts as tribute, though in smaller quantities. The ruler of Chiang Rung, the *cao saenwi fa*, collected all gifts to be offered in tribute to the king of Burma. The tributary gifts were put into twelve boxes, one for each *panna*.

The letter addressed to the Burmese king, which the *cao saenwi fa* handed over to the envoys, reveals a religious and cosmological dimension unknown to the tributary

171. See Liew-Herres 2007, 88–89. In 1818, Tao Thai Khang led the *cao moeng* from the east and west of the Mekong to Burma, and he returned to Chiang Rung as the Burmese *saenwi fa* at the same time that his nephew, Tao Sunwu, was the Chinese *saenwi fa*. See MLC-LV1, 35, s. 31.7.

172. See Liew-Herres 2007, 89.

173. According to MLC-LV1, 23, s. 19.15, they were golden and silver jars instead of rings.

174. MLC-LV2, s. 24.12.

relationship with Ming China. The Burmese king is praised as a *cakravartin*,[175] a Buddhist world conqueror who guarantees the blossoming of the Buddhist religion (*sāsana*) in all the countries under his benevolent rule.[176]

It is evident that by the time Sipsòng Panna had submitted to Burmese overlordship, the Tai Lü, at least in their majority, were already adherents of Theravāda Buddhism. Yanyong Ciranakhòn and Ratanaporn Sethakul suggest that the Buddhist religion came to the region not earlier than the late fourteenth or early fifteenth century.[177] Due to close political relations and kinship bonds, Buddhism most likely spread from Chiang Mai via Chiang Tung to Sipsòng Panna. During the reign of Tilokarat (Tilok) (1441/42–1487), Lan Na exerted considerable influence on Sipsòng Panna.[178] Though Tai Lü sources refute the claim of the Chiang Mai Chronicle that Tilokarat's armies subdued the whole of Sipsòng Panna making it a vassal state of Lan Na,[179] Buddhism became more firmly entrenched in Tai Lü culture during the second half of the fifteenth and first half of the sixteenth centuries. The use of the Dhamma script, which originates from Lan Na, among the Tai Khün of Chiang Tung and the Tai Lü of Sipsòng Panna might be a clear indicator of the diffusion of Theravāda Buddhism into the Upper Mekong region in the century prior to the establishment of Burmese hegemony.

Moeng Laem, situated off the main route from Chiang Tung to Chiang Rung, was a different case. This polity had largely been untouched by Buddhism before the arrival of the Burmese. The Moeng Laem Chronicle describes the enforcement of Burmese overlordship and the spread of Theravāda Buddhism as parallel processes. During the reign of Tao Fai Yòt, the seventh ruler of Moeng Laem, there were yet no monasteries in the country and "a script did not exist" (*to lik to lai bò mi*, Tr. ตัวลิ่กตัวลายบ่มี).[180] His successor Tao Fai Sin, son of a princess from Chiang Rung, brought the religion from

175. The *cakravartin* ideal of "universal monarch", exhibited by these kings, was closely related to the concepts of the "ten royal virtues" (Th. *totsa barami* ทศบารมี *dasa pāramī*) and the "righteous king" (*dharmarāja*). As to details of the *cakravartin* ideology, see Sunait 1990.

176. As to the content of the letter, see MLC-LV2, s. 24.14. A similar letter is translated in MLC-LV1, 24–25, s. 19.16. The letter is also translated in Dao Shuren 1989, 238–49 (the twenty-fourth ruler). All three letters are similar in content but vary in wording. Gao Lishi 1984, 118 (the twenty-fourth ruler) did not take the trouble to translate the letter.

177. Yonyong and Ratanaporn 2001, 239.

178. CMC-HP, Wyatt and Aroonrut 1995, 83–84; CMC-N, Notton 1932, 115; CMC-TPMC, Udom et al. 1995, 67.

179. All versions of the Moeng Lü Chronicle insist that Tilok's siege of Chiang Rung failed. See the MLC-LV2, s. 18.5 and MLC-LV1, s. 13.7. The latter version states: "The chieftain (i.e., lord) of Lan Na (i.e., Phaya Tilaka) marched to attack Chiang Rung, but after one month and twenty days still had not captured it. [Thus he] pulled his troops back to attack Moeng Cae. On arrival he found that the moat around the fortifications was three *jing* deep (lit., "three necks' deep"). He besieged and attacked [Moeng Cae], but after one month and twenty days he could not capture it either. Hence, he withdrew his troops silently."

180. Moeng Laem Chronicle, f° 19/12.

"Moeng Kham Angwa" (Ava-Burma) to Moeng Laem where it has flourished since that time. The chronicle also reports that in the year CS 843 (AD 1481/82) a diplomatic mission was sent to the Burmese court at Ava. The Tai envoys took a letter, four swords, four bolts of "big" silk, twelve bolts of "small" silk, two pairs of large silver candles, two pairs of gilded candles, three rifles, two pairs of shoes made of silk, twelve red carpets, and four horses of which one was wearing gilded saddlery. All these goods were sent to the "great king of the golden city of Ava" (*cao mahu khusat wiang kham Angwa*) to ask him for religious support. The Burmese king was highly delighted. He sent to Moeng Laem two elephants—one male and one female—along with a copy of the *Tipitaka*, four Buddha images, two gilded parasols, four white parasols, four red parasols, and one golden cup. The royal decree (*ameindaw*) of the Burmese king also appointed the ruler of Moeng Laem to the rank of *cao hò kham* (the ruler of the golden palace) of Moeng Laem Pekkharaṭha Mahā Jeyya Pavarasadhamma.[181]

Fearing the increase of Burmese infuence in the region, the Chinese authorities in Yunnan now intervened and demanded a kind of power-sharing arrangement with the Burmese. The chronicle mentions that Chinese officials (*khun khaek*) appeared in Moeng Laem. They brought with them the seal of Moeng Khae (i.e., of the imperial court), which they presented to the ruler (*cao*) of Moeng Laem. The Burmese official (*khun man*) also presented the seal of the king of Burma to the local ruler. Thereafter, military equipment such as lances, swords, rifles, and cross-bows were offered. In addition, the *tao khun noe* (*nüa*) *sanam kham* (i.e., the members of the Royal Council) and members of the local nobility presented various kinds of gifts to the *cao hò kham* of Moeng Laem.[182]

8. SIPSÒNG PANNA AS A CHINESE-BURMESE CONDOMINIUM

In territories where the spheres of influence of China and Burma overlapped, such as in Moeng Laem, Chinese-Burmese condominiums were established, and vassal states with double loyalties emerged. This pattern prevailed until the late nineteenth century and is felicitously expressed in the following Tai metaphor: *Hò pen pò man pen mae*, which means "The Chinese (*hò*) are [our] father, the Burmese (*man*) [our] mother."[183] This was a stock diplomatic phrase in both Chiang Rung and Moeng Laem.[184] The enthronement of a new *cao fa* in Sipsòng Panna had to be officially recognised by both the Chinese emperor and the Burmese king. However, it was not easy for the Chinese imperial court to share dual overlordship in Sipsòng Panna with Burma because China regarded not

181. Ibid, ff° 20/12–22/5.

182. Ibid., f° 25/5–12.

183. The metaphor is placed more in-depth within a wider historical perspective by Yanyong and Ratanaporn 2001, 109–13. This is also recorded in MLC-LV1, s. 19.6.

184. See confidential report of W. Warry, dated 23 March 1891, 3, in Warry 1888–1895 [British Library, IOOC].

only Sipsòng Panna as her vassal state but also Burma, as demonstrated in the Ava-Burma Pacification Superintendency that had been established in 1403.[185] The political and military power of China in its efforts to effectively curb the Burmese influence in the Upper Mekong region was still limited at that time. Therefore, the Chinese tolerated Burmese influence in the region, provided that Burma recognised China's ritual superiority. The latter was symbolised by associating Chinese representatives in Sipsòng Panna with the more prestigious "right hand" and the Burmese envoys with the "left hand".[186] When shortly after ascending the throne in Chiang Rung, Cao In Moeng (r. 1569–1578) married a daughter of Burmese king Bayinnaung in order to strengthen the tributary relations with his overlord in the west, the presence of high-ranking Chinese officials at the coronation ceremony was considered necessary for legitimating Cao In Moeng's rule. As the Moeng Lü Chronicle states:

> [Consequently], the Chinese authorities at Moeng Sae (Kunming) ordered senior officials (*khun long*) of Moeng La (Simao) and Moeng Maen (Puer) to go to Chiang Yung (i.e., Chiang Rung). At that time [the representatives of] the two courts of China and of Burma held friendly negotiations and an agreement was reached. They jointly proclaimed and invested Cao In Moeng as *saenwi fa*. Cao In Moeng paid respect to the Heavenly Court as father and the Burmese court as mother (*hò pen pò man pen mae*) [...].[187]

The Moeng Lü Chronicle contains many more references to such joint Chinese-Burmese investitures of Tai Lü *cao fa*.[188] For example, the chronicle reports the ascension to the throne of Cao Mòm Kham Lü (r. 1621–1634), saying that the new ruler "had succeeded to the throne, and the Heavenly Court (*cao hò*) had conferred on him

185. *Ming shilu* (Veritable Records of the Ming Dynasty), 27 October 1403. See http://epress.nus.edu.sg/msl.

186. According to the Chinese, the left is higher than the right; see MLC-LV1, s. 19.6: "The emissary of the Heavenly Court holding the left hand of the *saenwi fa* and the emissary of the Burmese side holding his right hand, they led him to ascend the throne." To deal with Chinese and Burmese authorities, the court at Chiang Rung appointed two high-ranking diplomatic officials called *pò khaek hò* (Th. พ่อแขกฮ่อ) and *pò khaek man* (Th. พ่อแขกม่าน) respectively. The former was responsible for the Chinese guests (*khaek hò*) and always sat on the *cao fa*'s right-hand side, the latter took care of the Burmese guests (*khaek man*) and sat on the *cao fa*'s left-hand side. See Yanyong and Ratanaporn 2001, 114.

187. According to MLC-LV2, s. 24.6, the emissary of the Heavenly Court held the right hand of the *saenwi fa* and the emissary of the Burmese side held his left hand. The same is recorded in Gao Lishi 1984, 116; but MLC-LV1, s. 19.6, states just the opposite. See n. 186 above.

188. See, for example, the sections in MLC-LV2 on Cao Sili Suthamma (r. 1603–1620), Cao Mòm Kham Lü (r. 1621–1634), Cao Mòm Tao (r. 1634–1641), Cao Nò Moeng (r. 1642–1655), Cao Moeng Tao (r. 1655–1668/69), Cao Paeng Moeng (r. 1670–1697/98), Tao Sao Wün (r. 1707–1730), and Cao Mòm Suwan (r. 1746–1763).

[the title *saenwi fa*], he again sent [a delegation of] officials (*khun*) with tributary gifts to report to the king [of Burma], who also bestowed on him [the title] *saenwi fa*."[189]

Apart from joint participation in coronation ceremonies, the dual Chinese-Burmese overlordship was also reflected in the issuing of seals by the Burmese king to the *cao fa* of Chiang Rung in addition to those given by the Chinese emperor. King Bayinnaung's seal was made of ivory and had a diameter of three inches. Mount Meru was depicted in relief, surrounded by seven mountain chains. Below Mount Meru the seal showed an ocean in which two *ānanda* fish were swimming, while above the mountain there was the image of a palace, the sun and the moon. The *cao fa*'s office kept this Burmese seal along with the seal issued by the Chinese emperor until the Communist victory in 1950.[190]

The intensity of the Burmese and Chinese influence in their Tai condominiums fluctuated over the centuries. Roughly speaking, Burmese influence prevailed in the early Konbaung period (1752–1819), during which time the Ava militarily intervened at least six times in support of rival factions in Sipsòng Panna. After the defeat of Burma in the first Anglo-Burmese war (1824–1826), the political influence of the court of Ava in Sipsòng Panna began to decline. Since the early 1850s, the Chinese were again the dominant regional power. At times, the Mekong River demarcated the Chinese and Burmese spheres of influence, as the *Mingshi gao* (Draft of the History of the Ming Dynasty), published in 1723, indirectly acknowledges. According to this source, after the recognition of Burmese suzerainty by Cao Nò Moeng (r. 1530–1568), the Cheli Pacification Commission disintegrated into two different polities:

> In the year Jiajing 11 (1532), the Burmese bandit, Mang Yingli 莽應裏 (sic) (Nandabayin, r. 1581–1599),[191] occupied Baigu 擺古 (Pegu) and annexed [the lands of] the various barbarians one after another, like silkworms nibbling mulberry leaves. [The chieftains of] most of the aboriginal commissions (*tusi*), being threatened by Mang Yingli, served as his guides. At that time the Cheli pacification commissioner, Dao Nuomeng 刀糯猛 (Cao Nò Moeng, r. 1530–1568), also submitted to Burma. Hence, there were two Cheli, the Greater Cheli and Lesser Cheli. The Greater Cheli owed its allegiance to Burma, while the Lesser Cheli to the Han (China).[192]

189. MLC-LV2, s. 27.2.

190. Yanyong and Ratanaporn 2001, 109–10.

191. It could not have been Mang Yingli who conquered Pegu in 1532, but was probably Mang Ruiti (Tabinshwehti, r. 1531–1550) or Mang Yinglong (Bayinnaung, r. 1551–1581).

192. MSG, ch. 189, 32b; Liew-Herres 2003b. See also *Ming shilu*, 28 May 1627 (http://epress.nus.edu.sg/msl). The statement on the Greater and Lesser Cheli cannot be traced in *Shizong shilu*, ch. 134–145 (Jiajing 11). In Tianqi *Dian zhi*, ch. 30, 34 on Cheli, it states: "In the reign of Jiajing (1522–66), [Cheli] was subordinate to Burma. In the year Wanli 11 (1584), the government troops attacked Burma. The pacification commissioner (*xuanwei*) Dao Nuomeng (Cao Nò Moeng) sent envoys to offer in tribute elephant(s) and local products. The elder brother stayed in the Greater

When the Chinese government in 1729 suppressed a rebellion in the six districts situated on the east bank of the Mekong, these districts were placed under the newly founded prefecture of Puer for several decades.[193] During that time the sphere of influence of the *cao fa* was limited to his core area around Chiang Rung and the five districts situated on the west bank.[194] The Tai Lü principality of Chiang Khaeng that extended over both banks of the Mekong was also divided into a Burmese and a Chinese sphere of influence during the seventeenth and eighteenth centuries. A special military zone, controlled by Burmese troops, was limited to the west bank territories of Chiang Khaeng.[195] Moeng Laem, which was a powerful *müang* outside Sipsòng Panna that supported the Chinese government, was rewarded by being granted the right to govern parts of the hill areas formerly under the control of Sipsòng Panna.[196]

Burmese political as well as cultural influence finds expression in the Tai Lü literary language as well. The Moeng Lü Chronicle, the earliest extant version composed not long after 1864 or 1875 (see page 78), documents a fairly large number of Burmese loanwords in the field of politics and administration. Burmese terms such as *ahmu-gyi* (အမှူးကြီး envoy), *ameindaw/amintò* (အမိန့်တော် royal decree), *asouya* (အစိုးရ government), and *kantò* (ကန်တော့ tribute, state gift) ought to be mentioned in this context. In contrast to Burmese, Chinese loanwords are less apparent in this chronicle. Apart from the official title of the *cao fa*, *xuanwei shi*, there are terms like *xinfu* (tally credentials).

When the British diplomat and explorer W. C. McLeod arrived in Chiang Rung in March 1837, Sipsòng Panna was still the classic paradigm of a *müang sòng fai fa* (lit., "a *müang/moeng* [underneath] both parts of heaven"). With this expression, the Tai

---

Cheli and offered his allegiance to Burmese envoys; the younger brother stayed in the Lesser Cheli and offered his allegiance to Chinese envoys." The Greater and Lesser Cheli is also mentioned in Min Hong-xue's memorial recorded in *Xizong shilu*, ch. 83, 4033 (Tianqi 7, fourth month, *gengxu*: 28 May 1627); see also *Yunnan tongzhi* 244, on *tusi* 4. This is also confirmed in *Leshi*: In CS 930 (Longqing 2: 1568 AD) when the king of Dagon (Moeng Dagon) from Burma appointed general Mahatan 麻哈坦 (Maha Tham) to command an army to conquer Jingyong (Chiang Yung), Dao Nuomeng (Cao Nò Moeng) became a vassal of the king of Burma. He commanded his aboriginal military corps and followed the king of Burma, bearing the title *fasutuo tanma luoshe* 法穌妥坦麻邏闍 (Fa Suttho Thammalaca), namely Mang Yinglong 莽應龍 (Bayinnaung, r. 1551–1581), to conquer Ayutuo (Ayutthaya) and Jingmai (Chiang Mai). See MLC-LV1, s. 17.2.

193. See Bourne (1885, 22 [PRO, FO 97/484]) stating that "[i]t was only in 1730 that this prefecture (Puer Fu) was established and the country was brought under the direct rule of China. It had previously formed a part of the territory of a people referred to in Chinese history as the Chin-ch'ih golden teeth-being also called Ch'an-li or Ch'ê-li, the name of their country." See also O'Conor 1895, 43 [PRO, FO 422/4].

194. Warry Report dated 15 June 1891, 16, in Warry 1886–1895 [British Library, IOOC]. Kato (1997) discusses in-depth the reasons for the rebellion which she sees in excessive payments of tribute, notably in the form of silver. She also discusses the course and consequences of the rebellion.

195. See Grabowsky 2003a, 52; Grabowsky and Renoo 2008, 43–44.

196. Kato 1997, 4.

used to designate the status of their polities as vassal states with two overlords. The governor of Moeng Long, one of the twelve districts (*panna*), gave McLeod insightful information about the tribute to be paid to Burma and China. The *cao fa* of Chiang Rung, for example, sent an annual tribute of 65½ *viss*[197] of gold to China, in addition to rice and tea, especially the famous Puer tea[198] that was planted in the northeast of Sipsòng Panna. To Ava, the Burmese capital, each of the twelve "petty Tsòbua (*cao fa*)" had to present, once every three years:

A gold cup, weighing	2½	ticals
Tinsel cloth	1	piece
Silk cloth	1	piece
Shoes	1	pair
Salt	1	cake
Tea	1	viss.
Candles covered with gold leaf	1	viss.
Candles covered with silver leaf	1	viss.
Candles covered with gold flowers	1	viss.
Candles covered with silver flowers	1	viss.[199]

McLeod reports that the *xuanwei shi*, i.e., the *cao fa* of Chiang Rung, presented the same amount as the other eleven *cao fa* but with "the addition of two ponies and the gold cup, weighing 7½ ticals."[200] In a similar way that the ruler of Sipsòng Panna paid tribute to the Burmese king, he himself received from "[e]ach of the petty Tsóbua (i.e., the provincial governors) [...] the same annually to the Tsen Wi fuá (i.e., *saenwi fa*) as they do triennially to Ava."[201] Thereby the *cao phaendin*'s authority vis-à-vis the provincial rulers was reinforced. The system of tribute payments could be adjusted quite flexibly to changing requirements.[202]

The network of relations between Chiang Rung and its two powerful overlords determined the amount and size of the tribute. David Richardson, a British diplomat and explorer who visited the Tai regions at the same time as McLeod, observed that Chiang Tung, a Tai principality solely dependent on Burma, sent annual tribute to Ava. However, Moeng Laem and Chiang Rung, vassals of both China and Burma, delivered tribute to Ava in between longer intervals: Moeng Laem sent tribute every eighteen

197. A *viss*—also written *vis*, *bis* or *bisse*—was a unit of measurement used in India and Burma. One *viss* was the equivalent of 1.417 kg in Madras, 1.512 kg in Bengal, and 1.656 kg in Burma (Kahnt and Knorr 1987, 339).

198. See Natcha 1998, 37.

199. MJ, 24 March 1837, quoted from Grabowsky and Turton 2003, 394.

200. Ibid.

201. Ibid.

202. Ibid.

months, Chiang Rung only every three years.[203] In other words, at the beginning of the second third of the nineteenth century, tributary relations with Beijing had already gained more importance than similar relations with the Burmese court.[204]

Richardson's statement about Moeng Laem is largely confirmed by McLeod: "That state is tributary both to China and to Ava; it pays, annually, tribute to the former, and triennially to the latter."[205] Other examples for "vassal states with two overlords" in the first half of the nineteenth century were, according to the two British diplomats, the Lao kingdoms of Vientiane and Luang Prabang. Vientiane "was at the time of its destruction (1828) tributary to Siam, but paid a triennial tribute to Cochin China (i.e., Vietnam)."[206] Although Luang Prabang was a Siamese vassal state, it paid triennial tribute to the Vietnamese imperial court at Hué. We also learn that Luang Prabang even tried to embrace China: "It likewise sends two elephants every eight years, as a mark of submission to China."[207]

By the time of McLeod's and Richardson's missions to the Tai states in the Upper Mekong and Salween regions, Chiang Tung was no longer sending tribute to China. Scott explains the absence of formal relations between China and Chiang Tung mainly by the "fairly strong" Burmese presence in that state.[208] The Tai Khün state paid tribute to Burma annually, sending gold and silver flowers and other tribute gifts (*bannakan* บรรณาการ). In case of war, Chiang Tung was expected to furnish 5,000 troops to Ava.[209] Yet, even without formal tributary relations, the trade between Chiang Tung and Yunnan remained important. Goods imported from China included silk, iron pots, salt, honey, and straw hats; exports to China comprised tea, ivory, rhinoceros horns, birds' wings and feathers, and cotton. In most cases, the Chinese merchants exchanged their goods for cotton and other local merchandise.[210]

---

203. *Richardson Journal*, 24 March 1837, quoted from ibid., 505. Three years was the usual frequency of sending tribute to China for more distant lands, according to the Ming Statutes.

204. This is clearly reflected in Scott's notes on the political situation in the Burma-China frontier regions at the end of the nineteenth century. Scott concludes that until the British conquest of Upper Burma (1885) "Moeng Lem and Kēng Hung appear to have paid tribute to both Burma and China, though the latter country no doubt exercised by far the greater influence in these two States." Scott 1896, 2 [British Library, IOOC, Eur F 278/90].

205. MJ, 27 February 1837, quoted from ibid., 358.

206. MJ, 23 January 1837 quoted from ibid., 315.

207. Ibid.; cf. Scott (1900, 401) who makes a similar statement, probably quoting McLeod without mentioning him explicitly. At this juncture the question is raised whether certain aspects of Lao foreign policy can only be understood against the background of a multiple tributary relationship with its three competing neighbours, i.e., Siam, Vietnam, and China.

208. Scott 1900, 401.

209. MJ, 27 February 1837, quoted from ibid., 358. That figure indicates a population of 25,000 or 35,000 persons in the core area, if one accepts as a reasonable estimate a ratio of five to seven persons per household.

210. Detailed lists of goods and their prices—both purchase prices in China and selling prices

The status of the Tai polities as Chinese-Burmese condominiums had the advantage of playing "father" (China) and "mother" (Burma) against each other and of gaining a maximum of autonomy, if not de facto independence, through skilful manoeuvring. This happened, however, only in exceptional situations. On the whole, the disadvantages prevailed. Since a strict rule of primogeniture did not exist in the Tai *müang*, dynastic disputes within the ruling houses frequently flared up. In the course of dynastic strife the rival parties sought military support from different overlords. This was the case in Sipsòng Panna, where between 1818 and 1857 a series of bloody fratricidal wars plunged the country into turmoil. The rival factions of the ruling house of Chiang Rung turned to China or Burma for political backing and military support, and from 1849 Siam also joined in the power struggle in Sipsòng Panna.[211] The result for the people in the affected areas was disastrous: there was flight, deportation, and disease, and hunger left deep marks.[212] Since the Burmese used Chiang Tung, where they maintained a strong military presence, as their main basis for moving troops to Sipsòng Panna, a sense of distrust grew between Chiang Tung and the pro-Chinese loyalists in Chiang Rung.[213] Although the wars gave several *panna*, such as Moeng La and Moeng Phong in the southeast, the possibility of temporarily increasing their political autonomy, the long-term disruptions to the economy and society certainly outweighed the short-term advantages.

At least in the nineteenth century, China and Burma tried to avoid direct confrontation between their armies and to keep the "proxy wars" in Sipsòng Panna at a low level. In 1838, the Chinese "father" and the Burmese "mother" reached an agreement to force the contending parties—Chiang Rung, Chiang Tung, and Moeng Laem (supporting the Chiang Rung loyalists)—to accept a peace accord. This agreement was sealed by an oath-taking ceremony that reveals much of the traditional worldview of the Tai, which is rooted in Buddhism and spirit cults.[214]

The agreement did not hold for long, and fighting resumed only a few years later. The Chinese-Burmese condominium over Sipsòng Panna came to an end in 1885 with the British conquest of Upper Burma. While it would be interesting to discuss which of the

in Chiang Tung—are provided by McLeod. See MJ, 25 February 1837, ibid., 353–54.

211. The Siamese involvement in the internal affairs of Sipsòng Panna is, for example, reflected in an eyewitness report called *Phongsawadan müang chiang rung* (1964).

212. For details of this episode, see Grabowsky 2004, 296–303.

213. The Chiang Tung Chronicle records several previous cases in which the Burmese used Chiang Tung as their operational base against the Tai Lü of Sipsòng Panna. Such was the case in 1625 (directed against a Tai Lü uprising recorded in the Moeng Lü Chronicle for 1627) and in 1785. See CTC-PMCT, Thawi 1990, 52 and 59.

214. For a vivid account of that ceremony where not only the "three gems" (Buddha, Dhamma, and Sangha) but also "the deities, Lord Indra, Lord Brahma, the Garuda, the dragons (*nak* นาค), the lords of all the four worlds, the princess of the earth (*nang thòlani* นางธรณี), and the guardian spirits of the three great cities (*maha nakhòn* มหานคร)" were invoked as witnesses, see MLC-LV2, s. 39.11. Similar is recorded in MLC-LV1, s. 32.11.

two overlords was considered more benign or the least harmful, a satisfactory answer would require a thorough analysis of warfare in the Tai borderlands since the sixteenth century, which is beyond the scope of this book. A cursory overview, however, suggests that Chinese military interventions, at least in Sipsòng Panna, were less frequent and less destructive than those of the Burmese. For instance, in the half-century between 1763 and 1812 Burmese troops attacked Sipsòng Panna not fewer than six times. During the 1763–1767 period, troops from Chiang Tung, Chiang Khaeng, and Moeng Yòng collaborated with Burmese forces to seize numerous people from Sipsòng Panna with the aim of resettling them in other regions. There were no comparable large-scale deportations carried out by the Chinese. Sipsòng Panna suffered from a substantial loss of population when a Burmese invading force deported numerous people from the west bank *panna* to Ava, following the suppression of a Tai Lü uprising in 1627.[215] Li Fuyi's version of the Moeng Lü Chronicle states:

> In the *moeng mao* year, CS 989 (Tianqi 7, AD 1627), the king of Burma ordered his general(s) (*jiang*) to launch an attack on Moeng Lü. They were victorious, and the *saenwi fa* Cao Ong Moeng (sic), the chieftain (sic) of Moeng Cae, Cao Si Mün Na Inta Rao (Zhao Simen Na Yida Lao 詔四悶納尹打勞), and the inhabitants of the various places (*müang*) on the west bank of the river (Mekong) were captured and deported to Ava. Only very few people were left [in the various *moeng* after the devastation].[216]

By 1728, Sipsòng Panna had not yet recovered from the demographic disaster which Burmese king Thalun's campaign of 1627 had caused, with large tracts of land in Sipsòng Panna still laid to waste. The scarcity of population forced the Chinese government to drastically reduce the amount of rice and other tribute the *cao fa*'s court had to deliver to China.[217] Not only had the population in the plains decreased tremendously, but also the population of the twelve *khwaen* in the mountainous regions was reduced. "The land was in chaos, the scope of the *panna* shrank."[218]

215. The Chiang Tung Chronicle records this uprising for the year 1625. See CTC-PMCT, Thawi 1990, 52 and Saimöng 1981, 250.

216. MLC-LV1, s. 20.2. This campaign is not recorded in MLC-LV2 or in Gao Lishi 1984. Chinese sources confirm the disastrous consequences of the Burmese punitive campaign adding interesting details on the background of the conflict between Ava and Chiang Rung. See MSG, ch. 189, 32b. See Liew-Herres 2003b.

217. Sun Laichen 2000, 306.

218. Dao Yongming, *Cheli xuanwei shi*, 339, quoted from Sun Laichen 2000, 297.

9. RELATIONS WITH NEIGHBOURING POLITIES

The relationship between Sipsòng Panna and the other Tai states were mostly based on kinship relations. Aristocratic groups founded new *müang* and married women from other local elites. Most rulers of Moeng Lü used their daughters to establish loyalties with governors of important *müang* or rulers of neighbouring polities.

9.1 RELATIONSHIP BETWEEN MOENG LÜ (CHELI) AND LAN NA (*BABAI*)

In 1298, a powerful army from Lan Na attacked "Greater Cheli" (i.e., the west bank territories including Chiang Rung), an ally of the Burmese. "Lesser Cheli" (i.e., the east bank territories), an ally of China, ganged up with Lan Na. That was the reason for a Chinese punitive campaign against Lan Na in 1301 that, nonetheless, failed. The *Zhaobu zonglu* 招捕總錄 (General records of pacifying and arresting the tribal peoples),[219] a rather important, rare, Yuan-China source on the Tai polities in the Upper Mekong valley, provides interesting details of King Mangrai's campaign against Chiang Rung which are not recorded in historical sources on Lan Na and Sipsòng Panna:

> In the year Dade 2 (1298), the Kingdom of Babai-xifu, enticed by Hu Long 胡弄 of the Lesser Cheli, sent 50,000 soldiers to fight for lands with the aboriginal official of the Meng hulong dian 夢胡龍甸 (fortified village/town of Moeng Khun Long) and with the son of Hu Nian 胡念 of the Greater Cheli, Han Gang 漢綱, killing one another. Moreover, [Babai] sent his subordinate Hun Gan 渾干 (Khun Kham)[220] to lead 100,000 men to invade Mengyang 蒙樣 (Moeng Yang) and other places.[221]

The war between the imperial troops of the Mongol and the Lan Na forces dragged on for several years. Fighting was particularly fierce in 1301 and 1302. More Mongol soldiers, however, succumbed to malaria, which was endemic in the subtropical region, than died on the battlefield. The military and political pressure from China continued for another ten years until China, under the Mongols, finally gained the upper hand. Chinese sources report that in 1312 tribute missions from Babai-xifu (Lan Na), Greater Cheli, and Lesser Cheli were sent to the Yuan imperial court.[222]

At times, the ruler of Chiang Rung had to flee to a neighbouring Tai polity to ask the friendly rulers for political support. In the late seventeenth century Cao Paeng Moeng (r. 1670–1697/98) was unable to resist attacks of hill-tribe rebels, the so-called "white-

219. This work by an unknown Yuan author was edited by Qian Xizuo 錢熙祚 in 1844 and reprinted in the 1889 collectanea, *Shoushange congshu* 守山閣叢書.

220. Hun Gan is most probably the phonetic rendering of Khun Kham, the shortened name of Mangrai's second son and successor, Cai Songkham/Chai Songkhram (ชัยสงคราม).

221. *Zhaobu zonglu*, 10 (Babai-dadian), in Liew-Herres et al. 2008, 80.

222. *Yuanshi* 24, 553, see Liew-Herres et al. 2008, 83. The emperor of China at that time was a Mongol and the troops were predominantly Mongol.

headed bandits" (*kha ho khao*, Th. ข้าหัวขาว). Together with his family and followers, the Tai Lü king escaped to Lan Sang where he was given asylum by King Suriyavongsa.[223]

Internal strife in Sipsòng Panna enabled other Tai states to intervene. In 1459/60, during the reign of Tao Sam Pò Lütai, Tao Còm Pha of Moeng Long and Tao Ut of Moeng Hun were dissatisfied with the ruler of Chiang Rung and tried to topple him. They asked King Tilokarat (called "Phaya Tilaka" in the Moeng Lü Chronicle, which is the Pali variant of his name) of Lan Na to support their cause. "Phaya Kalòm of Lan Na–Chiang Saen Luang" sent a force but the attack failed and the Lan Na forces suffered heavy casualties.[224] After a siege of one month and twenty days, King Tilokarat pulled his troops back to attack Moeng Cae. He then besieged and attacked Moeng Cae, but again after one month and twenty days, he failed to capture it as well. He quietly withdrew his troops. Tilokarat stopped at Moeng Yòng for a long time before he dared to travel back to Chiang Mai of Lan Na. The Chiang Mai Chronicle reports only briefly the military campaign against Sipsòng Panna in 1455–1457, in the course of which Moeng Wang and Ban Cae were conquered. The campaign was only partially successful. During the first invasion in the *dap kai* year (1455–1456), the Lan Na forces failed to take the strategically important village of Ban Cae. One year later, a second assault on Ban Cae succeeded, but before reaching Chiang Rung the Lan Na forces withdrew, as they feared a Siamese attack (*sük ayutthaya* ศึกอยุธยา) from the rear.[225]

In the defence of their country the Tai Lü had received support from neighbouring Chiang Tung. The Phaya Moeng Khün (lord of Chiang Tung), Sili Suthammalaca, led his troops to give Tao Sam Pò Lütai reinforcements. Thus after the war, Tao Sam Pò Lütai rewarded him by ceding Moeng Ma and Moeng La Tip to the ruler of Chiang Tung.[226] The support of Chiang Tung for the besieged Tai Lü forces is only mentioned in the Moeng Lü Chronicle. Neither the chronicles of Chiang Tung and Chiang Mai nor contemporary Chinese sources, such as the *Ming shilu*, provide corroborative evidence. The Chiang Tung Chronicle reports even a tribute mission sent by the incumbent ruler of Chiang Tung, Phaya Candapuṇṇarāja, to Chiang Mai in response to the gifts which King Tilokarat had given him on the occasion of his coronation.[227] Such

223. MLC-LV2, s. 31.3. Though MLC-LV1, does not mention this incident, it is recorded in the Lao chronicle of Khun Bulom. There it is stated: "At that time, Kālā Yuga had occurred in Meuang Sanī Fā, because Hoh Hua Khav attacked Meuang Sanī Fā. So Chau Indra Kumāra, ruler of Meuang Sanī Fā, together with his younger sister Nang Chanda Kumārī and his people fled to ask for the aid of Phrayā Suriya Vongsā at Viang Chan" (Souneth 1996, 293).

224. MLC-LV2, s. 18.2; see also MLC-LV1, s. 13.5. The Chiang Mai Chronicle confirms the defeat of the Tai Yuan invasion forces: "So King Tilokarat took his forces up to attack the Lü domains. He was unable to take M[üang] Phrong (Phong), and withdrew." CMC-HP, Wyatt and Aroonrut 1995, 88.

225. CMC-HP, Wyatt and Aroonrut 1995, 83–84; CMC-TPCM, Udom et al. 1995, 67; CMC-N, Notton 1932, 115.

226. MLC-LV1, s. 13.8; MLC-LV2, s. 18.6. See also Renoo 2001, 63.

227. CTC-JSC, Saimong 1981, 240; CTC-PMCT, Thawi 1990, 40.

a display of harmony between suzerain (King Tilokarat of Lan Na) and vassal (Phaya Candapuṇṇarāja of Chiang Tung) hardly conforms with military clashes between both sides at around the same time, neither must it be ruled out completely.

Most decisive for the successful defence against the invading Lan Na forces was, however, support from hill peoples. Tao Sam Pò Lütai appointed an official named Mün Nòn Long (Luang), whose title was *lam kha kao* (Th. ล่ามข้าเก่า), "the supreme official in charge of the Kha",[228] to recruit his followers (the so-called *kha kao*) to attack the Lan Na forces. Mün Nòn Long enlisted 4,000 men; they proved quite successful. The invaders lost a great number of elephants and horses and many people were killed or wounded. King Tilok returned to Lan Na. The lord of Moeng Long, Tao Còm Pha, and the lord of Moeng Hun, Tao Ut, defected from their own lands.[229]

In the year CS 824 (AD 1462), the lord of Moeng Ngat and Moeng Khang, Tao Cet (i.e., Tao Som, Soe Long Fa's seventh son), sought help from King Tilok of Lan Na who entrusted the lords of Chiang Saen and of Chiang Rai to recruit 40,000 soldiers to escort Tao Cet from Moeng Lü to Lan Na.[230] At that time Moeng Yòng had been desolate for already more than a decade, as many of the local population had fled the oppression of its "cruel and tyrannical" ruler in 1451.[231] So Tao Cet and his men were resettled in Moeng Yòng. Since then Moeng Yòng was subordinate to Lan Na. Moeng Ngat and Moeng Khang were depopulated because the people followed Tao Cet to Moeng Yòng.

The internal unrest in Moeng Lü and the fight for the throne as well as the military intervention of Lan Na troops are clearly recorded in contemporary Chinese sources. The *Ming shilu*, for example, reports:

> In the year Tianshun 1, second month, on *gengshen* day (21 March 1457), the regional commander (*zong bingguan*) of Yunnan-cum-the vice-commissioner-in-chief (*dudu tongzhi*), Mu Lin 沐 璘, submitted a joint memorial: "The pacification commissioner (*xuanwei shi*) of the Cheli (Moeng Lü) Military-cum-Civilian Pacification Commission, Dao Baxian 刀 霸 羡 (Tao Phasaeng), had committed suicide. The younger brothers, Banya Zhong 板 雅 忠 (Phaya Còm) and others, have already elected their elder brother, San Bao Lidai 三 寶 歷 代 (Tao Sam Pò Lütai), to rule the land on their behalf. Now Banya Zhong is again creating unrest and banding together with Babai (Lan Na). He is borrowing men and horses [from Babai] and killing out of vengeance (blood feuds). We intend to transfer government troops to pacify and quell [the revolt] but the warm spring is approaching and the epidemic attributed to miasma is flourishing. We should not yet mobilise the troops and march on

228. According to MLC-LV1, 14, s. 13.9, "*lanjia*" (*lam kha kao*) was the speaker or the representative stationed at the capital, i.e., Chiang Rung.

229. MLC-LV1, s. 13.9; MLC-LV2, s. 18.7.

230. MLC-LV1, s. 13.10; MLC-LV2, s. 18.8.

231. MLC-LV1, s. 12.13; MLC-LV2, s. 16.22. There is no mention of a tyrannical ruler whose actions provoked the mass exodus of his subjects in the fifteenth century, or even later. See Müang Yòng Chronicle, Thawi 1984.

> recklessly." The emperor replied: "San Bao Lidai, a son of a concubine (*shunie*), has usurped [the post] of the son of a legal consort (*di*) and murdered (*mouhai*) Dao Baxian, prompting Banya Zhong to borrow troops [from Babai] to attack and kill [him]. [Mu] Lin and others should send suitable officials to pacify and instruct Banya Zhong (Phaya Còm) et al., and make an investigation to find out who is the legal heir to the post of the pacification commissioner (*xuanwei shi*). The causes of the succession conflict are to be reported and they should be ordered to withdraw their forces and settle their conflicts.[232]

In 1485, King Tilok tried to subdue Sipsòng Panna a second time. This time the Lan Na monarch adopted a different strategy. Instead of launching a direct attack on Chiang Rung, the weaker polities at the periphery, such as Moeng Ngat, were subdued. The ruler of Moeng Ngat then re-settled at Moeng Yòng, which at that time was deserted. The Chiang Mai Chronicle portrays the campaign as a victory—Chiang Rung was "plundered"[233]—although the casualties on the Lan Na side seemed to be quite high according to Tai Lü sources.[234]

After the reign of King Müang Kaeo (1495–1526), which is generally considered the "Golden Age of Lan Na" because of the many religious donations and the height of literary productivity during that period, the influence of Chiang Mai in the Upper Mekong region declined. The de facto political split of Lan Na into a western part with Chiang Mai as its centre and an eastern part under the predominance of Chiang Saen had already emerged in the second quarter of the sixteenth century and further deepened after the conquest of Chiang Mai by Burmese troops (in 1558) when the whole of Lan Na fell under the political hegemony of Burma. For more than two centuries Chiang Mai almost disappeared from the Tai Lü world.[235] At the beginning of the eighteenth century Chiang Saen became the main political and military centre from which the Burmese exercised control over the entire Upper Mekong valley, and it is therefore not surprising that Chiang Saen is frequently mentioned in the Moeng

232. *Yingzong shilu*, ch. 275, 5860 (Tianshun 1, second month, *gengshen* day), see Liew-Herres 2003b. More on intra-dynastic conflicts that involved invitation of help from neighbouring Tai polities, see Liew-Herres 2007.

233. CMC-HP, Wyatt and Aroonrut 1995, 102; CMC-TPCM, Udom et al. 1995, 82; CMC-N, Notton 1932, 142.

234. See MLC-LV2, s. 18.7.

235. Since the 1630s Chiang Mai had lost much of its former influence in the Upper Mekong region. After the Burmese established their regional headquarters in Chiang Saen (in 1701), Chiang Mai became only a local centre, among many others, in a politically fragmented "southern Lan Na". Therefore, it is no wonder that the Moeng Lü Chronicle and other Tai chronicles—such as those of Chiang Saen, Chiang Rai, and Chiang Khaeng—pay less and less attention to Chiang Mai with regard to the political situation from the mid-sixteenth to the late eighteenth centuries. For changing power relations in Lan Na during that period see Grabowsky 2004, 149–60, and Grabowsky 2005.

Lü Chronicle pertaining to events of the sixteenth to eighteenth centuries. Chiang Mai comes to the fore again only in the early years of the nineteenth century when King Kawila of Chiang Mai (r. 1782–1816) initiated his scheme of forced resettlements affecting the areas north of Chiang Saen. Thousands of people, including Tai Lü from Sipsòng Panna, were evacuated by invading Tai Yuan troops to the southern part of Lan Na. The social disruption caused by these campaigns left a deep mark on the collective memory of the Tai Lü and other populations in the Upper Mekong valley (for details, see section 10).

9.2 RELATIONS WITH SMALLER TAI POLITIES

In 1406, Tao Sida Kham purged several smaller neighbouring polities that dared to challenge Chinese power. Full of gratitude, the Chinese emperor bestowed on Chiang Rung the authority to rule Moeng Hing, Moeng La (Simao), and Moeng Lusun (Liushun). The power of Sipsòng Panna increased considerably, and "the chieftains from various places came to offer tribute" to Tao Sida Kham, whose domain expanded to Moeng Maen (present-day Puer). So boasts the 1990 version of the Moeng Lü Chronicle.[236] Neighbouring Tai polities, such as Lan Sang, Moeng Laem, and Moeng Khün (Chiang Tung) came to fear the king of Chiang Rung. To allay their concerns, Tao Sida Kham forged marriage alliances with the ruling dynasties in these states. He himself married a princess from Chiang Tung. His younger brother, Peo Fai Fa, took the daughter of the Moeng Laem ruler as his wife.[237] The marriage alliances between the royal courts of Chiang Rung, Chiang Tung, and Moeng Laem continued for many generations. For example, in 1470 the younger brother of the ruler of Chiang Tung married Tao Sam Pò Lütai's daughter, Nang Khò Moeng.[238] This marriage took place a couple of years after Tai Khün auxiliary troops had joined in the defence of Chiang Rung in warding off an attack from Lan Na. Kinship ties between the ruling houses of the three Tai polities could contribute to long-term political stability in the region but also could encourage military interventions in fratricidal wars.

The Tai Lü kings and princes practised polygamy. As a rule they took the princesses of neighbouring Tai or Shan polities, such as Chiang Tung and Moeng Laem, as their consorts. The Moeng Lü princesses were also married to the princes of the surrounding Tai or Shan polities. So the family ties of the ruling house extended to the peripheral lands

236. Tao Kòng Saeng and Ai Kham (1990), 34; see also Renoo Wichasin 2001, 77. However, in the 1987 Chinese edition of the Moeng Lü Chronicle (MLC) revised and collated by Thao Khwang Saeng and Ai Kham, on which their 1990 Tai Lü version of MLC is based, the above statement is not mentioned. Neither is it stated in the contemporary Chinese sources, the MSG and the MSL. See Liew-Herres 2003b. Over the years of our study of the various versions of the MLC we stumbled across several discrepancies between the Tai Lü versions and their Chinese translations, and vice versa. However, it is not within the scope of this study to go into more detail on this topic.

237. MLC-LV1, s. 9.4.

238. MLC-LV1, s. 13.19.

of Moeng Lü. In times of fighting for the throne, troops from maternal grandparents or fathers-in-law were sought. The Tai Lü kings were also allowed to marry their cousins or their deceased cousin's wives to strengthen their position or claim to the throne, such as in the case of Soe Long Fa, one of the grandsons of Cao Khan Moeng. This makes the relationships of the ruling house very complicated.

The members of the ruling house, invested as *cao moeng*, split into factions in times of dispute over succession to the throne. The ambitious uncles of the crown prince also posed a great threat to the throne, in particular when the crown prince was still not of age on the death of his father, as in the case of Tao Sunwu (Cao Maha Nòi) (r. 1802–1833) and his uncle Tao Thai Khang (Cao Mòm Maha Wang). The Moeng Lü Chronicle is replete with killings and civil wars. Recorded in the two long versions of Moeng Lü Chronicle translated here are three cases of fratricide and three rather long fratricidal wars fought for the throne of the *saenwi fa*. As the chronicles of many reigns are very brief, there were probably more unrecorded violent conflicts among the ruling class.[239]

In the fifteenth century Burma and China exercised joint control over the region. However, in 1582, Burma ordered Chiang Tung, Sipsòng Panna, Moeng Laem, and Lan Na to send a joint force to attack Moeng Saenwi (Hsaenwi/Moeng Pòng) in the northern Shan region as this polity had rebelled against Burma. In 1625, the Burmese ordered Chiang Tung and several smaller Tai *müang* to punish Sipsòng Panna where "the Tai Lü had rebelled against Mangthra (i.e., the Burmese king)".[240] Whenever a Tai state rebelled against Burma, the Burmese tried to use forces from other Tai states to punish the recalcitrant state, either alone or together with Burmese troops.

In the mid-sixteenth century Burma considerably expanded her sphere of influence in the Upper Mekong valley. Having already conquered fifty-one Tai *müang,* King Bayinnaung (Pha Mahakasat Fa Suttho Thammalaca), attacked Sipsòng Panna in CS 925 (AD 1563/64) and subdued the Tai Lü polity. The Tai Lü ruler, Cao Un Moeng, later supported the Burmese king in the campaigns against Lan Sang and Ayutthaya. As the frontiers between the Tai states in the region were sometimes disputed, the Burmese king, now the highest sovereign in the region, had to settle the territorial disputes among his vassals. The Sipsòng Panna ruler assisted him in this task, thereby gaining some advantages for himself. For example, Müang Sai was formerly a *müang* claimed by both Sipsòng Panna and Luang Prabang. Bayinnaung decided to divide Müang Sai into two halves called "Lü Müang Sai" and "Lao Müang Sai" respectively. Therefore, Müang Sai became a "*müang* with two overlords" (*müang sòng fai fa* เมืองสองฝ่ายฟ้า).[241]

239. For more on fratricides and armed struggles for the throne of the *saenwi fa*, see Liew-Herres 2007.

240. CTC-PMCT, Thawi 1990, 52; see also CTC-JSC, Saimöng 1981, 250.

241. MLC-LV2, s. 22.3.

In Müang Luang Nam Tha the borders of three *müang* had to be defined: Sipsòng Panna, Lan Na, and Lan Sang. The Lao king was not content with the strip of land he received and demanded a revision of the border with Sipsòng Panna. Bayinnaung thus asked the three parties to engage in a stupa-building contest. The representatives from three sides had "equal" merit (*puñña*) in building the stupa, thus the Burmese king ordered the demarcation of Müang Luang Nam Tha and a Bodhi tree was planted in the centre of the fortified city to mark the boundary. The *müang* which came under the influence of Sipsòng Panna were: Moeng Sing, Moeng Long (Luang) Pukha, Chiang Khaeng, Moeng Moeng, Moeng Khang, Müang Lòng, and Chiang Kok.[242] Thereafter, the border at Chiang Rai and Chiang Saen was fixed.[243] The Chronicle of Sipsòng Panna says that Moeng Yòng, Moeng Phayak, and Moeng Palaeo, which were stipulated to depend on Chiang Tung, "had formerly belonged to Sipsòng Panna." The author of the chronicle further complains: "Fa Suttho of Ava came to take a lot of land from Sipsòng Panna."[244]

10. FORCED RESETTLEMENTS

Under the reign of Phaya Coeng in the late twelfth century, the domain of Sipsòng Panna was still an independent polity comprising numerous smaller and larger *müang*. Its population was supposed to be numerous, if we believe the hyperbolic figure mentioned in the Moeng Lü Chronicle that in the times of King Coeng "one hundred thousand small and large *müang*" were subordinate to Moeng Lü.[245] According to Sun Laichen, between 1497 and 1523, the old capital of Moeng Lü comprised more than 10,000 households and the total population of the capital and its surroundings would have been around 50,000.[246]

242. All these *müang* belong to the principality of Chiang Khaeng, which maintained close political relations with Moeng Lü in the fifteenth and sixteenth centuries. During that time, this small Tai Lü principality regularly sent tribute to Chiang Rung. However, it is doubtful whether this tributary relationship was continued during the seventeenth century. See Grabowsky and Renoo 2008, 28–32.

243. On demarcating the borders of Moeng Lü, Moeng Lao, and Lan Na, see MLC-LV2, s. 22.4–22.5. This is also recorded in Gao Lishi 1984, 115 (s. 22.5).

244. Yanyong and Ratanaporn 2001, 109.

245. MLC-LV2, s. 1.3. Cf. the likewise hyperbolic figure of 8,440,000 inhabitants of Chiang Tung (Khemmarat) reported in the same chronicle (s. 1.2). The number of *ho (hua) mün* (lit., "heads of 10,000", "myriad commanders") or 844, which obviously forms the basis of the above population figure, might be more realistic but the supposition that one *ho mün* commanded an average of 10,000 persons appears highly questionable. However, according to MLC-LV1 (s. 1.4), and Gao Lishi (1984, 105), it was Moeng Lü, instead of Chiang Tung, which had a total of 8,440,000 subjects at Phaya Coeng's time.

246. See Sun Laichen 2000, 258. The author does not disclose the sources on which this figure is based. His argument that the name of old Chiang Rung, Chiang Tai (rendered Jingde in Chinese),

This figure appears inflated, and a modest maximum number of 3,000 households or 15,000 inhabitants looks more realistic. But even this figure is remarkable as the city of Chiang Rung had only 2,654 households and 14,623 people in 1923. At any rate we may suggest that the population density in Sipsòng Panna before the political and social upheavals of the early seventeenth century was relatively high. The Tai Lü country suffered from a substantial loss of population when in 1627 a Burmese invading force deported numerous people from the west bank *panna* to Ava.[247]

By 1728, Sipsòng Panna had not yet recovered from the demographic disaster that Burmese king Thalun's campaign of 1627 had caused; large tracts of land in Sipsòng Panna still lay fallow due to a scarcity of population. This circumstance forced the Chinese government to drastically reduce the amount of rice and other tribute the *cao fa*'s court had to deliver to China.[248] Not only had the population in the plains decreased drastically, but also the population of the twelve *khwaen* in the mountainous zone was reduced. In short, after the Burmese campaign against it, "the land was in chaos, the scope of the *panna* shrank."[249]

Possible increases of population in the second half of the eighteenth century, had no sustainable effect. In the first two decades of the nineteenth century troops from Lan Na launched several campaigns against Sipsòng Panna to pull the region into the Siamese orbit of influence. The Moeng Lü Chronicle says that "in the *ka kai* year CS 1165 (AD 1803/4) Kawila of Chiang Mai (r. 1782–1816) conquered and annexed Phrae and Nan" before marching his troops to Moeng Ta Lò (Daluo). This is misleading as the Northern Thai principalities of Phrae and Nan were not dependencies of Chiang Mai; all three principalities maintained, independently from each other, tributary relations with Bangkok. Phrae and Nan voluntarily supported King Kawila's military campaigns against Chiang Tung and other Shan *müang* in the Salween region in 1802–1803. One year later, the joint forces from Chiang Mai and Lampang, led by Kawila's brother, viceroy Thammalangka, as well as troops from Nan, Vientiane, and Bangkok, launched a decisive attack against Chiang Saen, the last fortress that the Burmese still possessed in the Upper Mekong region at that time. The fall of Chiang Saen paved the way for a further expansion northwards. Following a widespread pattern of warfare in pre-colonial Southeast Asia, the military campaigns of Chiang Mai and its ally Nan were not in order to annex land but primarily to ensure the political loyalty of the subjugated *müang*, all former dependencies of Burma, and to deport large segments of the conquered populations to the devastated rice-growing areas in the south of Lan Na.[250]

means "city (*chiang*) of the ten thousand (*tai*) households" is wrong, because *mün* is the word for ten thousand in Tai Lü language.

247. See discussion in section 8 above.

248. Sun Laichen 2000, 306.

249. Dao Yongming, *Cheli xuanwei shi*, 339, quoted from Sun Laichen 2000, 297.

250. The policies of forced population movements in northern Thailand during the Early Bangkok period are extensively discussed in Grabowsky 1999a and 2004.

Kawila's campaign against Chiang Rung in 1806 was a failure. Burmese troops were stationed in the capital of Sipsòng Panna and kept the *cao fa*, Tao Yung Khò (Dao Yonghe, or Cao Fa Can) in custody at Moeng Laem. Though Tao Yung Khò managed to escape from his Burmese guards and made his way to Ta Lò to join the Lan Na troops, most of Sipsòng Panna, including the capital, remained in Burmese hands. Tao Yung Khò persuaded members of his extended family to visit him at Kawila's camp and together they were escorted into exile in Nan where the *cao fa* died childless.[251] Even so, Sipsòng Panna did not come to peace. The 1963 version of the Moeng Lü Chronicle states without giving further details: "At that time Kawila deported large numbers of the population of Sipsòng Panna to Phrae, Nan, and Chiang Mai."[252] The oldest extant version of the Moeng Lü Chronicle translated by Li Fuyi (MLC–LV1) is much more specific. This version speaks of a bloody war that "Kawila of Siam" (i.e., the Chiang Mai army) led against the Burmese troops. "Those who could not flee [in time]" were captured and deported for resettlement in Chiang Mai and Nan. "Consequently the region around Chiang Yung (Chiang Rung) was depopulated and became desolate." [253]

Northern Thai sources confirm the military campaign of 1807–1808. Troops from Lampang led by the Cao Wang Na attacked Sipsòng Panna again and deported a number of Lü families from that region to Lampang and Chiang Mai:

> On Thursday, the eighth waning of the seventh month in the *müang mao* year, CS 1169 (30 April 1807), the *sala* of the *phrabat* (in Lampang) was inaugurated. The *cao wang na* (i.e., viceroy) of Lampang attacked Sipsòng Panna, the country of the [Tai] Lü. [...] He brought the [Tai] Lü families down [to Lampang] and delivered them to the king.[254]

The version of the Moeng Lü Chronicle, revised by Tao Kwang Saeng and Ai Kham in 1989, reports that in 1812 Kawila launched a third attack but was repulsed by Chinese troops. Kawila withdrew with his forces to Moeng La and Moeng Phong where he gathered many people whom he resettled in Moeng U-Nüa and Moeng U-Tai.[255] However, this seems doubtful, as these two *müang* never belonged to Kawila's sphere of influence. This episode is not mentioned in any of the versions translated in this volume and seems to be incorporated from other sources, probably even including Northern Thai chronicles, by Tao Kwang Saeng and Ai Kham. The event mentioned here refers to the Nan attack of 1812 on Sipsòng Panna, which is recorded in the Nan Chronicle as well.[256]

251. MLC-LV2, s. 37.4.

252. MLC-LV2, s. 37.5.

253. MLC-LV1, s. 31.4.

254. *Cotmaihet lan na*, ff° 26/2–27/1, in: Sarassawadee 1993, 25.

255. Renoo 2001, 675.

256. In fact, the Chiang Mai Chronicle reports that Northern Thai forces, led by Kawila's younger brother and viceroy, Thammalangka, were led against areas on the west bank of the Mekong, such as Moeng Yòng, Phayak, and Moeng Len where "all people" were "rounded up"

In the course of that large military campaign, thousands of people from Moeng La, Moeng Phong, and Moeng Long Pukha were deported to Nan. Altogether, six thousand people were resettled in Nan at that time.[257] A connection of these forced resettlements with the construction of additional irrigation canals only two years later seems most plausible.[258] The building of a new capital two kilometres to the north of the old one, in 1817–18, might have benefited from the influx of war captives as well. In fact, Nan had close ties with the Tai Lü *müang* in the southeastern part of Sipsòng Panna, such as Moeng La and Moeng Phong. In 1846, Nan intervened in favour of their close allies in Sipsòng Panna and even sent these allied Tai Lü nobles to Bangkok.

Forced resettlements had a strong impact on the Tai Lü polities throughout the eighteenth and nineteenth centuries, especially during the so-called "Burmese wars" (*sük man* ศึกม่าน). Tai Lü sources, such as the Moeng Lü Chronicle, call this whole period the "Kawila era" (*yuk kawila* ยุคกาวิละ). It is evident that in Tai Lü usage "Kawila" does not just mean the historical king of Chiang Mai, who ruled from 1782 to 1816, but rather refers generically to his policy of *kep phak sai sa kep kha sai müang* (เก็บผักใส่ซ้า เก็บข้าใส่เมือง, lit., "Gather vegetables and put them into baskets; gather people and put them into *müang*"), which is an old Northern Thai (Tai Yuan) metaphor for forced relocations of populations,[259] notably from Tai-speaking areas in the Upper Mekong and Salween regions to various places in Lan Na. This policy was pursued not only by King Kawila of Chiang Mai but also by the rulers of Nan and other smaller principalities. Tens of thousand of Tai Lü, Tai Khün, and other ethnic groups found new homesteads in Lan Na during the late eighteenth and early nineteenth centuries. In Nan Province a total of fifty-eight new Tai Lü villages can be identified. Their ancestors had migrated from various Tai Lü *müang*, both inside and outside Sipsòng Panna, such as: Moeng La, Chiang Rung, Moeng Phong, Moeng Yòng, Moeng Len, Moeng Long Pukha, Chiang Hòn, Chiang Lom, and Moeng Ngoen.

The impact of forced population movements on the spread of Tai Lü settlements throughout the Upper Mekong region can be illustrated by the following striking example: The inhabitants of Ban Huai Meng in Chiang Khòng District, Chiang Rai Province, are

---

(CKC-HP, Wyatt and Aroonrut 1995, 180). The remaining population fled to the jungle and had not yet returned by 1813, as MLC-LV1, s. 31.4 and 31.5 indicate.

257. NC-PMN, SRI 82.107.05.043–043: "Pün wongsa mahakhasat tanglai", ff° 169/4–170/1; NC-PMN-W, Wyatt 1994, 104–5; NC-PMN-WPK, Sarassawadee 1996b, 46 (f° 3). The NC (Wyatt 1994, 105) stresses that in the third month (Mārgaśīrṣa) of the year CS 1174 (Tai Yuan calendar), i.e., in December 1812, the victorious army had already left the area of operation to deport "6,000 prisoners from Müang La, Müang P[h]ong, Chiang Khaeng, and Müang Long Pukha to Nan. "In the *ka lao* year, CS 1175, he left his army and went to Nan, arriving in the eighth month."

258. Ten thousand able-bodied men were conscripted for these extensive public works. The same number of conscripts was used in March 1816 when it turned out that the Samun Dam was not stable enough. See NC-PMN, SRI 82.107.05.043–043: *Pün wongsa mahakhasat tanglai*, ff° 170/4–171/1; NC-PMN-W, Wyatt 1994, 105; NC-PMN-WPK, Saraswadee 1996b, 25 (f° 4).

259. For a discussion of the meaning and origin of this metaphoric saying, see Grabowsky 2001.

originally Tai Lü, whose ancestors had migrated from Ban Bò, Ban Khum and Ban Ngai in Moeng U (Sipsòng Panna) to escape Chinese oppression. Thus they decided in 1885 to settle in Moeng Sing. A few years later (i.e., in c. 1889), troops from Nan had arrived in Moeng Sing, and the Tai Lü settlers moved to the south along with the retreating Nan forces, finally founding new homesteads in *tambon* Wiang, *amphoe* Chiang Khòng. Roughly fifteen hundred families were resettled on the banks of the Mekong River to the north of *amphoe* Chiang Khòng. They named one of their new villages Ban Huai Meng.[260]

11. SIPSÒNG PANNA UNDER CHINESE RULE (1912–1950)

While Li Fuyi's MLC-LV1 ends in 1864, the MCL-LV2 and other versions, such as Dao Shuren (1989) and Gao Lishi (1984), have updated it by including the reigns of the last five *saenwi fa*. Only the reigns of the last three *cao fa* of Chiang Rung fall, fully or partially, into the so-called Republican period (1912–1949) of China. These are the reigns of Cao Mòm Kham Lü (1884–1924), alias Dao Cheng'en, Cao Mòm Suwanna Phakhang (1927–1943), and Cao Mòm Kham Lü (1947–1950). Though the last two reigns were relatively close to the year of re-editing and compiling the 1963 version of the Moeng Lü Chronicle (i.e., MLC-LV2), surprisingly, no details of the political events of the first half of the twentieth century are included, despite the abundant historical sources of this period found in the Veritable Records of the Qing Dynasty and other works on Yunnan.

The Kuomintang (Chinese Nationalist Party) toppled the Qing dynasty on 10 October 1911. The year before, a serious disruption in the relations between Sipsòng Panna and the Chinese authorities occurred when the ruler of Moeng Cae rebelled. The reason for the crisis was the aspiration of the ruler of Moeng Cae to establish himself as the supreme ruler of all *panna* situated on the western bank of the Mekong River. The event that eventually brought the souring relations between Moeng Cae and Chiang Rung to a flashpoint was a trivial one. A compensation that a subordinate of the ruler of Moeng Cae had to pay for a damaged "cow's cushion" (*mòn wua*) was the last straw. The armed conflict that severely affected the stability in the western parts of Sipsòng Panna is therefore colloquially called the "Cow's Cushion War" (*sük mòn wua* ศึกหมอนวัว).

The conflict started in 1908 when Cao Ya Tao (also called Cao Kòng Kaeo), the ruler of Moeng Hai, died. The late ruler had two sons from different wives. His eldest son, Cao Ya Hong, was born to the principal wife, who was a princess from Moeng Cae, while his second son, Cao Ya Mai, was the son of a minor wife from Moeng Hun. Cao Ya Hong, who succeeded his father, died only one year later, in October 1909. Cao Ya Mai became the new ruler of Moeng Cae, according to the explicit wishes of his elder half-brother shortly before he passed away. Cao Ya Hong's sons Cao In Moeng, Cao Kòng, and Cao La were unhappy with their father's decision and turned to their maternal

260. Yanyong and Ratanaporn 2001, 152.

uncle, Cao Ya Long of Moeng Cae, for political and military support. The conspiracy was detected at an early stage and Cao Ya Mai forced his three nephews to drink the "water of allegiance" in front of all nobles and senior monks of Moeng Ham. Both sides took an oath of eternal loyalty towards each other. This oath, however, did not last for long.[261]

At the end of 1908, Cao La went to trade salt with a cow caravan after the end of the harvest time. He borrowed a cow's cushion from Ca Kap Kham (Tr. จ่ากาบคำ), a noble from Ban Hin (บ้านหิน). Ca Kap Kham had borrowed the cushion from a military commander or *saen pon* (Th. แสนพล), a noble from Ban Laeng (บ้านแลง). In early 1909, after the end of the salt trade, Cao La returned the cow's cushion to the *saen pon*. But as the cushion was damaged, Saen Pon refused to take it back and demanded compensation from Cao La which the latter refused to pay. To make things worse, Cao La used his power to demand money from the *saen pon,* who turned to the *cao müang* of Chiang Hai, who was Cao La's uncle. In his capacity of ruler, Cao Ya Mai decided that Ca Kap Kham of Ban Hin had to pay compensation for the damaged cushion, but Ca Kap Kham, who had the support of Cao La, argued that the *cao müang* was taking the *saen pon*'s side. The conflict between the two village nobles escalated to a bitter conflict between the two villages. Cao Ya Mai then sent troops to punish Ca Kap Kham, who could count on the support of the three brothers, who were the sons of the late *cao müang* of Moeng Hai. As the forces of the latter were too weak, they turned to Cao Ya Long Sikhat, the ruler of Moeng Cae, their maternal uncle (*lung fai manda*, Th. ลุงฝ่ายมารดา). The Moeng Cae troops defeated Cao Ya Mai who fled to Moeng Hun.[262]

Now the *cao fa* of Chiang Rung tried to mediate and force the ruler of Moeng Cae to make a compromise but the latter refused. Thus Chiang Rung and Moeng Cae reached the brink of war. Mediation efforts of the Chinese authorities at Puer (Moeng Maen) also failed. The Chinese therefore came to view Moeng Cae as a rebellious township in Sipsòng Panna and decided to quell the uprising. A force of seven hundred soldiers from Moeng Hai and Chiang Rung attacked the Moeng Cae forces that took powerful positions of defence at Chiang Coeng. The 1963 version of the Moeng Lü Chronicle does not provide details on the course of the war and only states that the Moeng Cae forces were able to organise stiff resistance for quite a long time:

> The ruler of Moeng Cae then established his camps at the fortified town (*wiang*) of Chiang Coeng. The troops of Sipsòng Panna [and the Chinese troops] attacked Moeng Cae. They fought for three years, but neither [side] could gain a victory. [...][263]

Dao Shuren's version, however, provides a fascinating, detailed account of the conflict, in the course of which even the Shan state of Chiang Tung (Keng Tung/Moeng

---

261. *Pap pün moeng sisip cin cao panna moeng hai*, f° 38r/4–8.

262. Ibid., f° 38r/9–13.

263. MLC-LV2, s. 42.11.

Khün), then already a British protectorate, became involved as a supporter of the Moeng Cae rebels. In June 1910, the Chinese authorities decided to mobilise additional forces. Soldiers from Simao and Puer were recruited and reinforced by troops from Moeng Laem. Finally, both sides gathered large forces. The troops of the Chiang Rung side numbered thousands of soldiers whereas the ruler of Moeng Cae commanded strong forces, including Lahu (Musoe) auxiliary troops. However, the attackers were mostly untrained and unmotivated men; hence, they failed to overrun Chiang Coeng, which at that time was only a small *müang* of just seven villages.[264] Only when the Chinese authorities sent three hundred elite border troops under the command of Ke Shuxun 柯樹勳 (1862–1926) to Chiang Coeng could the rebel army be defeated. The ruler of Moeng Cae tried to escape; he disguised himself as an ordinary civilian but was betrayed by one of his attendants. He was caught and executed. His head was delivered to the *cao phaendin* in Chiang Rung.[265] Others, such as the governor of Chiang Coeng, were taken into permanent custody in Puer. The military commander of the rebels, Phaya Kham Daeng managed to escape to Chiang Tung. The last fighting ended in September 1910. As a result of the war many rice fields in the fertile lands of Moeng Cae, Moeng Ham, and Chiang Coeng were laid to waste, and people fled even to Moeng Yòng in Burma in search for food.[266] After the end of the Cow's Cushion War, the Chinese became more and more directly involved in the internal affairs of Sipsòng Panna.[267]

As a reaction to the unrest in Sipsòng Panna, the Chinese authorities decided to put Moeng Cae, Moeng Hai, Chiang Coeng, Moeng Hun, and Moeng Ngat under the supervision of Chinese officials and the five *müang* were transformed into five districts, which were later reorganised into three districts. The Kuomintang policy aimed at changing the local government into one dominated by outsiders, which was in fact in accordance with the imperial *gaitu guiliu* 改土歸流 (lit., "to replace the aboriginal official by a circulating official") policy, which was implemented as early as during the late Ming period. The Chinese resident commissioner Ke Shuxun of Sipsòng Panna demanded from the British authorities in Chiang Tung the extradition of Phaya Kham Daeng but the British refused. In 1912, Ke Shuxun (Khò Su Sin) modified his policy in Sipsòng Panna again and restored a local ruler in the areas west of the Mekong River. The new policy was called "to appoint outsiders in order not to change the local rule" (which resembles the *gaitu guiliu* policy.

In 1913, the Chinese established the border zone administrative department of Pusoe (called Pusi *yanbian xingzheng zongju* 普思沿邊行政總局, a combination

264. *Pap pün moeng sisip cin cao panna moeng hai*, f° 42v/–43v; see also Yanyong and Ratanaporn 2001, 258–59.

265. *Pap pün moeng sisip cin cao panna moeng hai*, f° 45v/–46r.

266. Ibid., f° 47r.

267. Yanyong and Ratanaporn 2001, 259. See also Dao Shuren's version of the Moeng Lü Chronicle (Dao Shuren 1989, 477–78), translated in MCL-LV2, as an appendix.

of Puer and Simao).[268] The twenty-six *müang* and eleven remaining *panna* of Sipsòng Panna were divided into eight numbered administrative areas, called *qu* 區 (district), i.e., (1) Chiang Rung, (2) Moeng Cae, (3) Moeng Hun, (4) Moeng Long (Luang), (5) Moeng La, (6) Moeng I-ngu, (7) Moeng Hing, and (8) Chiang Nüa. Some of these districts comprised one to two *müang*, others three to four *müang*. They were administered by Chinese officials who worked alongside the Tai Lü officials appointed by the *cao fa* of Chiang Rung. The Chinese side consisted of clerks, interpreters, policemen and lawyers. In 1917, the administrative centre of the fifth district was moved from Moeng La to Moeng Phong, from where communications to Moeng Sing in Laos were much easier. In 1921, district no. 4, which consisted only of Moeng Long, was incorporated into district no. 1 (Chiang Rung). Moeng Ngat and Moeng Khang of district no. 2 and Moeng Wua of district no. 8 were put together to form the new district no. 4 with Moeng Ngat as its centre.[269]

The Chinese resident commissioner, Ke Shuxun, had as his power base a border security force of 300 men. Many soldiers and officers were natives from Guangxi, Ke Shuxun's home province. Due to his suppression of the Moeng Cae rebellion, he had enormous prestige. Many of his retired soldiers and officers settled down in Sipsòng Panna and became engaged in various trades and agricultural activities. Several of Ke Shuxun's own relatives held key positions in the administration of Sipsòng Panna, such as his son-in-law, Li Fuyi (b. 13 Nov. 1901). The commander of the independent battalion no. 1 was Ke Yunsen 柯運森 (Khoe Yin Soen), Ke Shuxun's grandnephew. By 1923, authorities in Puer and Kunming increasingly feared that Ke Shuxun was becoming a warlord whose activities no one in Puer could control any longer. In order to curb Ke Shuxun's influence, the authorities in Puer discussed the situation with Cao Mòm Suwanna Phakhang, the then *cao fa* of Sipsòng Panna. It was decided to set up a permanent military security force of 30 men in each of the eight districts, amounting to a total of 240 men. To finance this force, each household in Sipsòng Panna had to pay 0.4 Yunnanese rupees (1 Yunnanese rupee was equivalent to ½ Indian rupee).

The political situation since the late 1920s became more and more complicated. In 1949, Sipsòng Panna was divided into six districts (*xian*) and one zone (*ju*), i.e., Cheli (with its seat in Chiang Rung), Nanqiao (in Moeng Cae), Fohai (in Moeng Hai), Zhenyue (in I-ngu), Liushun (in Chiang Nüa), and Simao (in Moeng La), as well as the zone of Ningjiang (in Moeng Wang).[270]

This does not mean that some resistance against Chinese rule did not occur. In 1912, for example, rumours occurred that in a Tai Lü village in Moeng Yòng (in British Burma) a black hen was able to sing a strange song in the Tai Lü language. The content of the song was directed against the Chinese rule in Sipsòng Panna. The two owners of

268. See Liew and Grabowsky 2004, 157.

269. Yanyong and Ratanaporn 2001, 261–62.

270. See the map of Sipsòng Panna taken from Li Fuyi 1949, ix.

the black hen, Ai Na and I Canda, transcribed the song into Tai Lü script and distributed leaflets in the adjacent district of Moeng Long. Under the leadership of Ai Cai San, 600 to 700 people in Moeng Long gathered to resist the Chinese power. Ke Shuxun quelled the rebellion and many people died, but Ai Cai San escaped to Moeng Yòng. In 1918, the Lahu people staged a rebellion against the Chinese. Ting Pa Li, the rebel leader, claimed to be the reincarnation of a god. Some Tai Lü people joined the rebels. At a ferry crossing of the Mekong Tai Lü gathered to attack Chinese merchants, killing eighty people.[271]

During Word War II Yunnan remained under the control of the Kuomintang government, which confronted Japanese troops in the south as large parts of the Southeast Asian mainland were occupied by Japan from 1942 until 1945. As a frontier zone bordering the Shan state of Chiang Tung that came under Japanese control in 1942, Sipsòng Panna was considered of vital strategic importance by the Chongqing government of Chiang Kai-shek. Kuomintang troops were stationed in almost all districts of Sipsòng Panna and the local population suffered during the war, as did the whole of China. In 1943, at the height of the war, Cao Mòm Suwanna Phakhang passed away. The late ruler had two sons, Cao Mòm In Moeng and Cao Mòm Mahacai, born to his third wife, who were presumably still very young. Thus the throne was offered to his nephew and adopted son, Cao Mòm Kham Lü (alias Dao Shixun 刀世勳),[272] at that time a student in Chongqing. The nephew succeeded his uncle in 1944 but did not return to Chiang Rung until 1947, when he was officially enthroned under his royal name Cao Mòm Kham Lü.

In March 2002, Volker Grabowsky and Foon Ming Liew-Herres had the privilege of meeting Cao Mòm Kham Lü at his private villa in Kunming. In a residential quarter of the Chinese nomenclature he leads a quiet life together with his Chinese wife. In a one-hour interview, the last *cao fa* of Sipsòng Panna, an elderly well-educated, friendly and humble man, who appeared in good health, told us of his eventful and turbulent life during the war. Cao Mòm Kham Lü said that only one year after his enthronement he returned to Kunming to continue his studies. That was during the final phase of the Chinese civil war. As Cao Mòm Kham Lü's father, Cao Mòm Saeng Moeng (Tao Tung Thin), who acted as regent, was in charge of the day-to-day administration in Chiang Rung, he was very close to the Republican regime. He therefore joined the Kuomintang troops when the latter retreated to Burma following the "liberation" of Sipsòng Panna by the Chinese People's Liberation Army in early 1950.[273] Shortly thereafter the Chinese communists took over the control of Yunnan. Sipsòng Panna was reorganised into an "autonomous prefecture" in 1953 and the throne of the *cao fa* and the autonomous institution of *noe sanam* (Council of Nobles) were abolished. With the loss of the throne

271. Yanyong and Ratanaporn 2001, 277–78.

272. He was the son of Cao Mòm Suwanna Phakhang's sixth brother, Cao Mòm Saeng Moeng (alias Dao Dongting).

273. Interview of Foon Ming Liew-Herres and Volker Grabowsky with Cao Mòm Kham Lü in Kunming, 20 March 2002.

and the crucial institution of *cao fa,* the pristine polity of Moeng Lü, with all its ups and downs, sank into oblivion.

The Moeng Lü Chronicle ends with the regretful words: "From the times of Phaya Coeng [to the end of the dynasty], there were altogether forty-four rulers in the dynasty and more than eight hundred years have passed."[274]

274. MLC-LV2, s. 44.1.

II. Manuscripts of the Moeng Lü Chronicle

On the final day of his sojourn in Chiang Rung, 25 March 1837, the British diplomat-explorer Lieutenant William Couperous McLeod, the first European to have visited the area, asked the chief minister of Sipsòng Panna for "the history of the place", i.e., for a copy of the official chronicle of Chiang Rung and Sipsòng Panna (Moeng Lü). The minister "looked serious" when confronted with the foreigner's request. As McLeod writes: "[A]fter considering a short time he asked me whether I wished he should lose his head; that there was but one copy, and that lodged in the palace, and though he afterwards promised to have extracts made for me from it, he never did so."[1] This entry in McLeod's published diary is the earliest confirmation of the existence of the Moeng Lü Chronicle. This manuscript was possibly a draft of the oldest extant version of the chronicle, which was most likely composed sometime after 1864 or 1875 (see page 78), not long after the death of Cao Mòm Suca Wanna (r. 1834–1864), the incumbent king (or *saenwi fa*) of Sipsòng Panna at the time of McLeod's visit. There is little doubt that the European envoy's request embarrassed the minister, who might have considered the ruling dynasty's official history a state secret, especially in such politically turbulent times of intra-dynastic conflicts. It is due to the efforts of a local Chinese official in Puer, Li Fuyi 李拂一, that this oldest version of the Moeng Lü Chronicle has survived, albeit in Chinese translation.

1. MJ, 25 March 1837, Grabowsky and Turton 2003, 397.

1. HISTORY OF MOENG LÜ, THE OLDEST EXTANT VERSION (MLC-LV1)

The History of Moeng Lü, or *Nangsü Pün Moeng Lü*, hereafter *Leshi* 泐史, translated from two Tai Lü manuscripts by Li Fuyi 李拂一 into Chinese in 1943, is the oldest extant version of the Moeng Lü Chronicle. Li Fuyi, born in Puer (Moeng Maen) in 1901, grew up in poverty after his father's early death. He most probably had contact with the Tai Lü in Puer when he was young and later learned their language. At that time Puer, located in the north of Chiang Rung, was predominately inhabited by Tai Lü. Li Fuyi later became a Chinese official and was the first Chinese official of the Republican period (1912–1949) to show interest in the indigenous Tai Lü sources.[2]

Li Fuyi is the son-in-law of the powerful late Qing official in Southern Yunnan, the late governor of Pusi, Ke Shuxun 柯樹勳 (1862–1926).[3] It is perhaps due to this connection with Ke Shuxun that he served at different periods as the district magistrate of Fohai 佛海 (Moeng Hai) and Cheli 車里 (Chiang Rung) counties. Shortly before Sipsòng Panna's "liberation" by the communist forces, Li Fuyi left mainland China for Taiwan, where he continued his research on Sipsòng Panna. During his long career, he authored several important works pertaining to historical sources on Sipsòng Panna and the Tai Lü.[4]

Li Fuyi first heard of the Moeng Lü Chronicle in the winter of 1923 when he visited Sipsòng Panna. He writes in his preface to *Leshi*:

> In the winter of the twelfth year of the Republican period (1923), during my sojourn in Sipsòng Panna, I heard the name of the "History of Moeng Lü" (*Nangsü pün moeng lü* or *Nangsü pün moeng sipsòng panna*), which is revered by the aboriginal tribes (i.e., Tai Lü) as their national history. I heard that a rare copy was preserved at the pacification commission (i.e., Council of Nobles or *noe sanam* in Chiang Rung). Moreover, some [manuscript copies] were held by lesser tribal chiefs (i.e., *cao mòm*) of various *müang* (polities) and the families of important personalities. These families keep their copies secret from [outsiders] and

2. Li Fuyi's ancestral home, however, is in Guilin, the provincial capital of Guangxi. One of the present writers, Foon Ming Liew-Herres, had the privilege of meeting with Li Fuyi at his Taibei home in November 2008.

3. Ke Shuxun was sent to pacify the unrest in Moeng Cae of Sipsòng Panna in 1910 (see the introduction, part 1, section 11 of this volume). In 1912, after the death of Li Zhaoyuan 黎肇元, Ke Shuxun became the assistant governor of the Simao office 思茅廳. One year later, Ke Shuxun was promoted to be the governor of the administrative headquarters of the Pusi frontier region (*Pusi yanbian xingzheng zongju* 普思沿邊行政總局).

4. *Dianbian shidi Menggen tusi zhi kaocha* (A study of the lost territory of Moeng Khün Aboriginal Commission on Yunnan frontier) 1912; *Cheli* (Sipsòng Panna) 1933; *Leshi* (History of Moeng Lü), i.e., MLC-LV1 (reprinted in 1983 and 2008); *Cheli xuanwei shixi kaoding* (Recension of the Genealogy of the Saenwi Fa of Sipsòng Panna), including the translation of the Moeng Lü Chronicle into Chinese, i.e., MLC-SV1 (reprinted in 1983 and in 2008); *Shier banna jinian* (Chronicles of Sipsòng Panna) 1949; *Shier banna zhi* (Treatise on Sipsòng Panna) 1955; and *Zhenyue xian xinzhi gao* (Draft of the new treatise on Zhenyue County) 1984.

> are reluctant to show us. After a long time [spent in enquiring], I managed to procure the middle and lower end chapters (i.e., parts 2 and 3) [of the *History of Moeng Lü*] from the tribal squad leader of Menghai (i.e., Cao Moeng Hai), Mr. Dao Zonghan 刀宗漢 (Tao Còm Kham),[5] and read them. I was told that they were copied from the manuscript preserved at the pacification commission [in Chiang Rung]. Therefore, I had an extra copy made [for myself].[6]

We can deduce from the above that this was sometime in the late 1930s, after Li Fuyi had gained the trust and friendship of the then Cao Moeng Hai who let him read and make a duplicate of the Tai Lü manuscript of the Moeng Lü Chronicle. It is upon this chronicle that parts 2 and 3 of his ground-breaking translations called *Leshi* are based.

The Tai Lü records of the thirteen ancient *cao phaendin* (lit., "lord of the land", i.e., the king) of Moeng Lü, on which part 1 of Li Fuyi's *Leshi* is based, was not obtained in Sipsòng Panna. Li Fuyi writes about the unusual circumstances by which they were obtained in his preface to *Leshi*:

> In the summer of the twenty-ninth year (1940), on my journey back from India, I made a stopover at Menggen (Moeng Khün, i.e., Chiang Tung). I was a guest of a Baiyi (i.e., Tai Khün) family in Moeng Khün. One day while I was glancing over the collection of storybooks, songbooks, and other books, [in my host's house], the Upper Chapter (i.e., part 1) of the *History of Moeng Lü* that I had been searching in vain for all these years lay in front of me. I immediately talked [with my host, and] wanted him to lend it to me in order to make a copy. My host told me that he was interested in neither history nor geography; moreover the copy was given [to him] by a visitor from Sipsòng Panna. He therefore generously allowed [me] to have it. [However, at that time I] had not yet translated [it].[7]

Chiang Tung (Keng Tung) was at that time still under British rule. Li Fuyi surely had his reasons not to reveal the identity of the man who had generously provided him with part 1 of the Moeng Lü Chronicle. After obtaining the two Tai Lü manuscripts, which form the three parts of MLC-LV1, Li Fuyi started translating them into Chinese in 1943. Describing the difficult circumstances under which he translated the chronicles, Li states:

---

5. Dao Zonghan (Tao Còm Kham, 1903–1944) succeeded to the post of chieftaincy of Menghai in 1919, assuming the title Cao Moeng Hai. See *Menghai xian zhi* (Local Gazetteer of Moeng Hai County) 1997, 869–70.

6. See the preface to MLC-LV1, 2, by Li Fuyi. During that time the aboriginal offices (*tusi*) were not yet abolished, although the *gaitu guiliu* (replacing aboriginal officials by circulating officials) policy had been partly implemented in Sipsòng Panna. Therefore, from the perspective of Li Fuyi the seat of Sipsòng Panna, the *noe sanam* (Council of Nobles), was the pacification commission (*xuanwei si*) and the *cao phaendin* (lord of the land) was the pacification commissioner (*xuanwei shi*).

7. See the preface to MLC-LV1, 2, by Li Fuyi.

> In January of the thirty-second year (1943), when Daluo (Moeng Ta Lò) was occupied by the enemy (the Japanese), I was forced to move all the important reference works and maps on the history and geography of Sipsòng Panna that I had collected over all the years to Simao (Moeng La) for safe-keeping. A year later, Changsha was lost [to the enemy], followed by Hengyang (both in Hunan Province). The Thai enemy, active at the border region, also sought to collaborate [with the Japanese]. At that time I happened to travel from Kunming to Simao (Moeng La). I deeply felt that if [the sources] were scattered and lost again, it would not be an easy task to collect them once more; it would also be difficult to safeguard them. Moreover, since the development of aerial warfare, the lives of people are at risk at all times and places. Hence, [I had the manuscript] translated as a matter of urgency. [...] They are copied in small booklets in a handy format for carrying along.

In his preface to *Leshi*, Li Fuyi does not mention who assisted him in translating the three parts of the Tai Lü manuscripts into Chinese that would constitute his *Leshi*. He remains rather vague concerning the translator; he first wrote in the preface, *ran wei de yiyi ye* 然未得迻譯也 (lit., "However, [it] was not yet translated"). Later he wrote *nai ji wei yi chu* 乃亟為譯出(lit., "Hence, [it was] translated as a matter of urgency"). Even if Li Fuyi could speak and read Tai Lü, he must have had local Tai Lü scholars who could read old Tai Lü, Pali, Sanskrit, and Burmese, to help him in his translations.[8]

Part 1 of *Leshi* deals with the chronicles of the first thirteen ancient rulers of Moeng Lü. It begins with the reign of Phaya Coeng (r. 1180–1192), its legendary dynastic founder, and ends with the reign of Tao Sam Po Lütai (r. 1457–1497). The chronicles of these thirteen rulers vary in length, from quite brief to lengthy expositions. The chronicles of Soe Luang Fa (r. 1428–1457) and Tao Sam Pò Lütai are the longest; whereas those of Phaya Coeng, Tao Hung Kaen Cai (r. 1234–1257), Cao Khan Moeng (r. 1347–1391), Tao Sida Kham (r. 1391–1413); Tao Kü Moeng (r. 1413–1415), and Tao Kham Tet (r. 1415–1428) are of medium length; the rest are very brief. The extant complete manuscript of the Moeng Lü Chronicle is by no means based on contemporary records; it is a cumulative work, compiled posthumously, updated and revised, and copied and recopied periodically. They were mostly written on mulberry paper; none of the extant versions of the Moeng Lü Chronicle had ever been published until Li Fuyi's *Leshi* and a short version of the genealogy in 1947 [i.e., MLC-SV1]. One of the reasons for the extremely varied lengths of the entries for the thirteen ancient rulers may be ascribed to historical sources at hand for the royal historiographer or scribe. The reason for the quite short entries could be a lack of written records for a particular reign, due to events such as civil wars or foreign invasions. It could also be that the author deliberately ignored the records for personal reasons, such as rivalry between and among loyal

8. Liew-Herres met Li Fuyi in Taibei in November 2008. When asked how he translated *Leshi* Li Fuyi explained that, except for those passages that he could not understand and required the assistance of a monk, he translated the manuscript comepletely by himself. He added that although he reads Tai Lü, Gao Lishi's ability is better than his.

clans. The original chroniclers of the reigns of Soe Long Fa and Tao Sam Pò Lütai most likely lived closer to the events and had more records at hand.

Part 2 of *Leshi* begins with the reign of Cao Nò Moeng (r. 1530–1568) and ends with the assassination of Dao Zhengzong (i.e., Cao Mòm Suca Wanna, r. 1834–1864).

The chronicles of the three rulers between Tao Sam Pò Lütai and Cao Nò Moeng, viz. Sam Khai Noeng (r. 1497–1502), Cao Khan Moeng (r. 1502–1523) and Cao Sali Sompan (r. 1523–1530), are not recorded in either Li Fuyi's Moeng Khün or in his Moeng Hai manuscripts on which his translation of *Leshi* (i.e, MLC-LV1) are based. They are, however, recorded in MLC-SV1, namely the Genealogy of the *Cao Phaendin* of Moeng Lü or Sipsòng Panna compiled most probably by Dao Zhengzong (Tao Coen Cong or Cao Mòm Suca Wanna). As Li Fuyi explains in his preface to *Leshi*:

> The historical events of the three rulers, from the fourteenth to sixteenth reigns, that are missing in the original text of part 1, have been cursorily supplemented on the basis of the *Cheli xuanwei shixi* (Genealogy of the Cheli pacification commission) so as to make [the chronology] complete.[9]

In fact, the very brief chronicles of the three rulers after Tao Sam Pò Lütai in part 1 of *Leshi* are collated from the *Cheli xuanwei shixi kaoding* 車里宣慰世系考訂 (Recension of the Genealogy of the *Saenwi Fa* of Sipsòng Panna), which is the short version of the Moeng Lü Chronicle revised and edited by Li Fuyi, instead of taken directly from the short version of the Moeng Lü Chronicle composed by Dao Zhengzong (Tao Coen Cong or Cao Mòm Suca Wanna) and translated into Chinese by Li Fuyi (1947b).[10]

In part 1 the capital city of Moeng Lü is called Jinglong 景 曨 (Chiang Rung), which means "city of dawn". In parts 2 and 3, after Cao Nò Moeng (r. 1530–1568) had offered his allegiance to the Burmese king, both the capital of Moeng Lü and the country as a whole are referred to as Jingyong 景 永 (Chiang Yung), "city of peacocks" and the "kingdom of peacocks". However, the Burmese called Moeng Lü the great Chiang Yung-gyi or "kingdom of peacocks".[11] It was during the reign of Cao Nò Moeng (r. 1530–1568) that the Burmese king began to expand eastwards and invaded Moeng Lü. The name of Sipsòng Panna was first used in the reign of Cao In Moeng (r. 1569–1598), who was offered the Burmese princess, Nang Bo Kham (golden lotus princess) in marriage.[12] Fixed amount of gifts were collected from the lords of the twelve *panna* and offered to Cao In Moeng's Burmese father-in-law. Since then, Moeng Lü was called Sipsòng Panna.

9. See preface to MLC-LV1 by Li Fuyi, 3.

10. For the annotation of the two works see Liew and Grabowsky 2004, no. 4, 166–67. The brief chronicles of the three rulers are taken from MLC-SV1, 19–21. This short version of the Moeng Lü Chronicle, printed along with Li Fuyi's (1947b) translation, 44–63, has been translated into English in the present work.

11. See preface to MLC-LV1 by Li Fuyi, 3; see also MLC-LV1, s. 17.1.

12. See MLC-LV1, 21, line 4 (s. 19.5).

Part 3 of *Leshi* deals with the miscellaneous territorial records, such as lands ceded as dowries when Tai Lü princesses were married to the lords of the adjacent polities, land taxes commuted to silver raised by the Chinese authorities from the twelve *panna*, Burmese invasions, the *müang* under the twelve *panna*, procedures for inheriting the post of *saenwi fa*, defence of the strategic passes, the twelve *ho* (*hua*) *khwaen* of the *saenwi fa*, and the domain and frontiers of Moeng Lü. Such valuable information in part 3 is not given in Gao Lishi (1984) or in the 1963 version of the Moeng Lü Chronicle (i.e., MLC-LV2).

The last dates mentioned in the three parts of *Leshi* are CS 859 (AD 1497), the year Tao Sam Pò Lütai passed away; CS 1226 (AD 1864), the year Cao Mòm Suca Wanna (Tao Coen Cong) was assassinated; and CS 1237 (AD 1875), the year Tao Cin An (Cao Mòn Sò) was escorted by Phaya Long Panya Nakang and others to Moeng La (Simao). The date of the manuscript in part 1 of the *Leshi* remains unclear. It must have been based on a pre-1940 manuscript. Given the last dates mentioned in parts 2 and 3, these manuscripts were most likely produced in the late nineteenth or early twentieth century.

Concerning the authorship of the Tai Lü manuscripts and the Chinese translations of *Leshi*, Li Fuyi writes in his preface:

> In the translation, care is taken to preserve [as close as possible] the style of the original text. [...] The style of writing in part 1 is clear and precise and many ancient words are used (i.e., Pali, Sanskrit, and Burmese). Moreover, from the beginning to the end it is consistent and seems to have been written by one hand. It is indeed invaluable. In parts 2 and 3 the styles of writing are inconsistent. They must have been written by a number of amateurs lacking proper training. All the three parts lack attribution to authorship.[13]

Leshi was first published by Wenjian Publishers in February of 1947, the eighth in the series of *Xinan yanjiu congshu* (Collectanea of Southwest Studies) of the National Yunnan University in Kunming. It contains the translator's acknowledgements, as well as a preface by Fang Guoyu (1903–1983), a specialist on Yunnan history and sources pertaining to Yunnan, a preface by Li Fuyi written in Kunming and dated 13 November 1946, and a table of contents, followed by the translations of all three parts. The appendix contains a glossary of personal and geographic names and special terms in Chinese and Romanised Tai Lü transcriptions. Unfortunately, the two Tai Lü manuscripts on which Li Fuyi's translations are based are not published together with the *Leshi*. It is said they were lost during the war.[14]

13. See preface to MLC-LV1, p. 2, line 14 and p. 3, lines 6–7, by Li Fuyi.

14. In November 2008, Liew-Herres met Li Fuyi, then 107 years old, in his Taibei apartment where he lives with his grandson and granddaughter-in-law. When asked how he lost the Tai Lü manuscripts on which his *Leshi* (MLC-LV1) was based, he answered that his student Cao Maha Wong had borrowed them from him. In 1946, when Li was about to go to Kunming for a meeting he could not find his student. It was during war time. Later he heard that his student had died in Burma. Li noted that *Leshi* was translated mainly in 1943.

More than three decades after the first edition, Li Fuyi revised *Leshi* and had it reprinted by Taibei: Furen Publishers in 1983, together with a short version of the chronicle (MLC-SV2).[15] In the postscript to his revised edition, Li Fuyi writes that the draft of the translation of *Leshi* was completed during the resistance movement of the war period, at a time when people were fleeing the conflict. At that time, the translations were based solely on the original texts with the aim of preserving the precious historical sources on the seven-century history of the frontier region in their original form that had hitherto been neglected. As such, erroneous dates and historical events were translated as given.[16] Here Li Fuyi meant that the 1947 edition of *Leshi* was translated directly from the Tai Lü manuscrips together with their errors. However, Li Fuyi does not state on which primary or modern Tai Lü sources his 1983 revised edition of *Leshi* was based.[17] The 1947 edition of *Leshi* is more interesting to us in this regard. Liew-Herres's translation is based solely on the 1947 edition of *Leshi*. The Tai Lü transcriptions of personal and geographic names, as well as special terms, have been improved, based on the translation of the 1963 Moeng Lü Chronicle (i.e., MLC-LV2). The transcriptions given in the appendix of the 1947 edition of *Leshi* are not taken into account as they are rather basic, if not outdated, and thus cannot be taken as standard transliterations. As the three original Tai Lü manuscripts on which *Leshi* is based are lost, Li Fuyi's *Leshi* is perhaps the oldest surviving Tai Lü document, albeit in Chinese, on the history of Moeng Lü.

2. CHRONICLE OF THE FORTY-FOUR *CAO PHAENDIN* OF SIPSÒNG PANNA (MLC-LV2)

In 1963, on the occasion of the tenth anniversary of the founding of the autonomous prefecture of Sipsòng Panna, original manuscripts of the chronicles of the forty-four *cao phaendin* of Sipsòng Panna, written in old Tai Lü script, were stencilled and mimeographed by the Department of Culture and History of Nationalities of the Prefectural Government (i.e., MLC-LV2, hereafter the 1963 Moeng Lü Chronicle). Copies of this 1963 Moeng Lü Chronicle, which was then the "official chronicle" of Sipsòng Panna, were distributed to various *cao moeng* in the newly created prefecture. However, not long after, the "Great Cultural Revolution" broke out. This so-called "Great Cultural Revolution" turned out to be a nationwide human disaster for the Chinese and the minority peoples in China. In comparison, its repercussions on the field of culture were

15. In November 2008, when Liew-Herres visited Li Fuyi she obtained the third edition of *Leshi* from the author, published by Taibei: Furen Publishers in October 2008 and signed personally by the author. This is the reprint of the 1983 edition of *Leshi*.

16. See Li Fuyi 1983a, 106, i.e., the reprint of MLC-LV1.

17. Textual comparison between the MLC-LV1 and its revised edition, i.e., Li Fuyi 1983a (reprinted in 2008) is beyond the scope of this study.

greater in minority regions, including Sipsòng Panna, than elsewhere, as much of the cultural heritage, including manuscripts, was lost forever. Monastic education declined and was nearly brought to a halt for many years. Buddhist temples were destroyed and numerous old documents—both palm-leaf and mulberry paper manuscripts—were burned or lost during the decade-long persecution of local heritage. Moreover, during the 1960s and 1970s the old Tai Lü script was banned from public use, and the Chinese authorities propagated the exclusive use of a newly created simplified script, which is easier to handle for printing newspapers but unsuitable for the copying of religious and other traditional texts (for details, see section 8 below). A whole generation of young Tai Lü grew up without the ability to read and write the old script and, therefore, with no direct access to their ancestors' rich literary heritage.[18]

The situation began to gradually improve in the early 1980s when the government in Beijing adopted a more liberal rule and began giving more cultural autonomy to ethnic minorities.[19] The cultural and religious revival in Sipsòng Panna also brought about a renewed interest in regional literature. Local scholars began copying manuscripts of the Tai Lü chronicles which had survived the vandalism of the Cultural Revolution, and even used traditional mulberry paper as writing material. In several instances these scholars simply copied the 1963 Moeng Lü Chronicle, albeit with minor amendments. A mulberry paper manuscript copied in 1984 by a man called Cao Solawong from Chiang Long in Moeng Hai, is a prime example. Unfortunately, the scribe does not mention from which older manuscript he copied his text, but a word-by-word comparison with the 1963 version shows that both texts are nearly identical. Even the incorrect calculation of Gregorian calendar dates, traditionally given in *cūlasakarāja* (lit., "little era"), are the same. There can be hardly any doubt that Cao Solawong's Moeng Hai manuscript was directly copied from a manuscript copy of the 1963 Moeng Lü Chronicle.

In 1984, Gao Lishi published his Chinese translation of a long version of the Chronicle of the Forty-Four *Cao Phaendin* of Sipsòng Panna, under the title *Xishuang Banna zhao pianling sishisi shi shimo* 西雙版納召片領四十四世始末.[20] Gao Lishi explains very clearly in the preface to his 1984 translation of the Moeng Lü Chronicle:

18. The younger generation of the Han Chinese are only taught the "simplified characters". Most of them are unable to read the classical Chinese written in "complex characters", in which the rich Chinese literature, history, culture, and so forth of over two thousand years have been transmitted.

19. Sarah Davis (2005, 58) quotes the Japanese historian Kiyoshi Hasegawa who reports "that in the 1950s there were 574 temples in Sipsongpanna and 6,449 monks and novices. After the Cultural Revolution, in 1981, this number was down to 145 temples and 655 novices. In 1997, Wat Pajay (the most prominent monastery in Chiang Rung) housed about seventy-five monks between the ages of seven and forty from all over the region. Three years later, there were 560 village temples and over 7,000 monks and novices in Sipsongpanna. Most villages had their local temples, and Wat Pajay supervised them."

20. See Liew and Grabowsky 2004, no. 20, 179. Gao Lishi's (1984) Chinese translation cited above was translated into English by Liew-Herres in 2003.

> The original document of this translation is kept in the Archive of the Prefectural Government (i.e., in Chiang Rung). There is also a copy in the Provincial Museum [of Yunnan]. In the year 1963, on the tenth anniversary of the founding of Sipsòng Panna Tai Autonomous Prefecture, the local government had the original document stencilled, mimeographed and distributed. [The stencilled copies] can be found in various *müang* (polity) and the circulation [of these stencilled manuscript copies] is rather wide.[21]

From the above, it is clear that Gao Lishi's translation is in fact based on the 1963 Moeng Lü Chronicle. Gao Lishi maintains that his work is a faithful translation of the original Tai Lü text. He writes in the preface to his 1984 translation:

> The title of the book and the contents are as they are in the original document. The [present] translator only makes the paragraphs and adds the punctuation. For convenience of readers, the necessary notes are given in the parentheses. Originally [I] intended to publish the Tai Lü texts alongside the Chinese translation. However, due to problems arising in printing (typesetting) [I] could not accomplish it. [...]. For difficult vocabulary and Burmese terms that I had problems translating I sought help from my comrades Dao Shixun (Cao Mòm Kham Lü) and Zhao Weiyang, who gave me their warm advice.[22]

Although Gao Lishi's translation can be considered quite reliable, and the names of the forty-four *cao phaendin* and the dates given match exactly those in the 1963 Moeng Lü Chronicle, there are a number of obvious textual discrepancies which cannot simply be considered inaccurate translations. A number of sections in Gao Lishi's translations are not found in the "official" 1963 Moeng Lü Chronicle. We may speculate from this that Gao Lishi has taken these additional sections from other sources. For example, the final paragraph of the chronicle of Cao Khan Moeng's reign (the twentieth ruler of Moeng Lü, r. 1496–1518), which deals with the early history of Moeng Sing, appears only in Gao Lishi's translation (p. 114); it is not recorded in the "official" 1963 Moeng Lü Chronicle or in any other extant version of the chronicle that we know of. Therefore, this early history of Moeng Sing has been added as an annotated source in our English translation of the 1963 Moeng Lü Chronicle (see section 20.2).

The 1963 Moeng Lü Chronicle records the forty-four successive rulers from Phaya Coeng (Paya Zhen 帕雅真, r. 1159–1180) to Cao Mòm Kham Lü (Dao Shixun 刀世勛, r. 1947–1950), covering a period of almost eight centuries of dynastic history. The 1947 *Leshi* covers the period from the reign of Phaya Coeng (r. 1180–1192) to the reign of Cao Mòm Suca Wanna or Dao Zhengzong (r. 1834–1864). All together, the chronicles of thirty-seven rulers have been included. The contents of the 1963 Moeng Lü Chronicle are in many ways rather similar to those of Li Fuyi's 1947 *Leshi* (i.e., MLC-LV1).[23] However,

21. See Gao Lishi 1984, 103.

22. Ibid.

23. The texts of Li Fuyi's MLC-LV1 are also in many ways similar to those of Gao Lishi's 1984 edition of the forty-four *cao phaendin* of Sipsòng Panna. However, textual comparison of these

both texts differ in a number of important details. Apart from the serious discrepancies in dates and some slight differences in the rulers' names, a crucial difference pertains to the total number of rulers (i.e., *cao phaendin*) in the dynasty founded by Phaya Coeng.[24] The 1963 Moeng Lü Chronicle, and hence that of Gao Lishi (1984), includes five rival rulers not listed in Li Fuyi's 1947 *Leshi*. By this, we can surmise that they were perhaps not recognised as legitimate rulers of Moeng Lü by the compilers of the dynastic chronicles on which Li Fuyi's translations are based. These five are Cao Yi Peng Lak Sai (the seventh ruler, r. 1270–1271), Tao Kumman (the eleventh ruler, r. 1430–1432), Tao Bakòng (the fourteenth ruler, r. 1439–1441), Cao Moeng Tao (the thirtieth ruler, r. 1655–1669),[25] and Cao Fa Can or Tao Yung Khò (the thirty-seventh ruler, 1770–1779). Whereas Li Fuyi's 1947 *Leshi* lists Dao Shengwu or Cao Maha Nòi (r. 1802–1833) as the legitimate ruler of Sipsòng Panna and his uncle Tao Thai Khang (Cao Mòm Maha Wang) as regent (LV1: r. 1802–1817; LV2: r. 1780–1785), in the 1963 Moeng Lü Chronicle and Gao Lishi (1984) Tao Thai Khang is listed as the thirty-eighth ruler, reigning from 1786 to 1809.

Moreover, the 1963 Moeng Lü Chronicle (section 16.4) records how Tao Sam Pò Lütai's two elder brothers, Tao Bakòng and Tao Sòng Moeng, were sent into exile by their uncle-cum-stepfather Soe Long Fa, and the later founding of Chiang Khaeng, a Tai Lü principality situated to the south of Sipsòng Panna (in present-day Laos and Burma), by Tao Bakòng (see sections 16.5–16.10). Li Fuyi's 1947 *Leshi* only states that the two brothers escaped down the Mekong on a raft (section 12.2), but mentions nothing about their exile and the eventual founding of Chiang Khaeng. While both the 1963 Moeng Lü Chronicle and Li Fuyi's 1947 *Leshi* acknowledge Soe Long Fa's political influence on the Upper Mekong region, only the 1963 chronicle mentions the incorporation of Moeng Maen (Puer) into the polity of Moeng Lü with the explicit consent of the Chinese emperor, who took back the official seal that had been issued to Moeng Maen and conferred it upon Soe Long Fa of Chiang Rung (section 16.21). Furthermore, the unrest caused by the so-called "White-Headed Rebellion" (*soek ho khao*) in 1728, which provoked a Chinese military intervention and resulted in substantial territorial losses for Sipsòng Panna, is also not mentioned in Li Fuyi's 1947 *Leshi,* but is at least briefly recorded—though it is chronologically confusing—in the 1963 Moeng Lü Chronicle (see MLC-LV2, s. 31.3). Finally, Li Fuyi's 1947 *Leshi* ends with the reign of Cao Mòm Suca Wanna (Tao Coen Cong; in Pinyin, Dao Zhengzong) who was killed by Ma Biao in 1864 (see section 32.37). The 1963 Moeng Lü Chronicle continues from the death of Cao Mòm

---

two versions is beyond this study. It is a pity that we were unable to obtain a copy of the Tai Lü manuscript of the Moeng Lü Chronicle on which Gao Lishi's translation is based.

24. Here we can only take the lineage from Phaya Coeng to Cao Mòm Suca Wanna (Dao Zhengzong), as MLC-LV1 gives records up to Cao Mòm Suca Wanna, who corresponds to the thirty-ninth ruler of the MLC-LV2 and of Gao Lishi 1984.

25. Li Fuyi (MLC-LV1) has mixed up the name of Cao Moeng Tao with his father's name, Cao Mòm Tao (r. 1634–1641), a mistake rectified in revised editions. See Li Fuyi 1983b and 2008b.

Suca Wanna (the thirty-ninth ruler) to Cao Mòm Kham Lü or Tao Sü Sin (the forty-fourth ruler). In other words, the 1963 chronicle has been updated to the Communist takeover of Yunnan in 1950, with a total of forty-four Tai Lü rulers. Textual disparities do exist between the 1963 Moeng Lü Chronicle and the no longer extant Tai Lü manuscripts on which parts 1 and 2 of Li Fuyi's 1947 *Leshi* are based. Nonetheless, the two versions of the dynastic chronicles that we have translated and annotated tell us much about the history of Moeng Lü over seven centuries.

The 1963 Moeng Lü Chronicle can be roughly divided into four parts. The *first part* comprises the reigns of the first eight rulers of Moeng Lü, starting with a relatively detailed account of Phaya Coeng (Cüang), the founder of the Tai Lü polity. However, this account is more a eulogy of the ruler's prowess rather than a record of the actual political events that happened during this reign. Phaya Coeng's three elder sons were sent to rule over neighbouring Tai polities, namely Lan Na, Moeng Lai (Upper Tonkin), and Lan Sang, whereas his youngest son was heir to the throne of Moeng Lü. This narrative is a typical ancient myth, which is also told in other Tai chronicles, whereby the sons of the founder of a dynasty were sent to rule over neighbouring states except one son, usually the youngest, who succeeded his father to the throne. The accounts of the next seven reigns, from Sam Khai Noeng (LV2: r. 1180–1201; LV1: 1192–1211) to Cao Ai (LV2: r. 1271–1311; LV1: 1287–1347) are, however, very brief. In most cases only the relationship of the new *cao fa* with his predecessor (for example, father vs. son, elder brother vs. younger brother), the year of his ascension to the throne, the year of death, the age at death, and the names of the ruler's sons are recorded. It seems that the main purpose of these brief accounts is to ensure a continuous genealogy of the ruling house. More detailed historical events of these reigns recorded and kept at the Council of Nobles of Chiang Rung or elsewhere were not at hand, probably lost due to civil wars. The account of the reign of Cao Ai, the eighth ruler, is particularly brief. Apart from the years of ascension to the throne and of death we learn that he passed away at the age of fifty-seven after a reign of forty-one years and that his only son, Cao Khan Moeng, was his successor. The long reign of Cao Ai, however, was by no means uneventful. We know from Chinese sources, such as *Yuanshi* (History of the Yuan Dynasty), that there was much unrest in Moeng Lü and adjacent regions during the last decade of the thirteenth century. The *Yuanshi* (chapter 61, 1484) records that in 1294 the "chieftain of Meng'ai 孟爱 (Moeng Ai) of the Golden Teeth (a term referring to Tai peoples), who submitted recently, sent his son to offer tribute." Two years later, in the winter of 1296/97, the Military-cum-Civilian Route Command of Cheli (Moeng Lü) was established.[26] It seems that the Moeng Ai of the Golden Teeth meant the Tai Lü polity (*moeng/müang*) ruled by Cao Ai of Chiang Rung.

The *second part* of the chronicle begins with the reign of Cao Ai's son, Cao Khan Moeng

26. According to *Jingtai Yunnan tujing zhishu*, the military-cum-civilian route command of Cheli was established in Zhiyuan 11, *jiaxu* (1274). Taxes in gold and silver were to be raised annually. In *Zhengde Yunnan zhi* it is stated that the military-cum-civilian route command of Cheli was

(LV2: r. 1312–1350; LV1: 1347–1391), the ninth ruler, and ends with Cao Sili Sompan (LV2: r. 1518–1539; LV1: 1523–1530), the twenty-first ruler. The accounts of the ancient rulers of Moeng Lü given in Li Fuyi's 1947 *Leshi*, namely part 1, end here (as has been mentioned, the last three rulers in part 1 have been collated by Li Fuyi).

It is not until the account of the reign of Cao Khan Moeng that more political events, which can be partially verified by contemporary Chinese sources, are recorded. Though the date of his ascension to the throne and the year of his death are obviously incorrect—in contrast to Li Fuyi's 1947 *Leshi*—there is no doubt that the main theme of Cao Khan Moeng's turbulent reign, i.e., military resistance against Chinese state power, is based on historical fact.

Cao Khan Moeng, known in Ming sources as Dao Kan 刀坎, is the first Tai Lü *cao fa* mentioned in the *Taizu shilu*, i.e., the veritable records of the founder of the Ming dynasty (1368–1644); thus also recorded in the official History of the Ming Dynasty (*Mingshi*) and its predecessor, the Draft of the History of the Ming Dynasty (*Mingshi gao*). Contemporary Chinese sources dated 7 April 1382, confirms the capitulation of the "tribal chieftain" (*manzhang*) Dao Kan 刀坎 (Cao Khan Moeng).[27] Two years later, the record dated 27 August 1384 states that the Cheli Military-cum-Civilian Pacification Commission (*junmin xuanwei si*) was organised and Cao Khan Moeng appointed the pacification commissioner (*xuanwei shi*).[28] Thereafter, Moeng Lü maintained uninterrupted tributary relations with the Ming court. Until the mid-sixteenth century China was the only major power besides Lan Na that Moeng Lü had to reckon with. For a short period in the late fifteenth century Lan Na, under King Tilok (r. 1442–1487), failed twice to conquer Chiang Rung. Among the thirteen rulers recorded in the second part, two figures, namely Soe Long Fa (LV2: r. 1446–1466; LV1: 1428–1457), the sixteenth ruler, and Tao Sam Pò Lütai (LV2: r. 1467–1490; LV1: 1457-1497), the eighteenth ruler, are outstanding because of the very detailed accounts given. Moeng Lü was replete with decades of fratricidal wars. One is tempted to speculate that the author(s) of chronicles of these two reigns could have relied on contemporary records or other special records. Other reigns, however, are recorded in far less detail.

The reign of Cao Un (Ong) Moeng (LV2: r. 1539–1567), i.e., Cao Nò Moeng (LVI: r. 1430–1568), the twenty-second ruler, marks the beginning of the *third part* of the 1963 Moeng Lü Chronicle, and this part coincides with the beginning of part 2 of Li Fuyi's 1947 *Leshi*. It ends with the reign of Cao Mòm Suca Wanna or Tao Coen Cong (LV2: r. 1788–1818; LV1: 1834–1864), the thirty-ninth ruler, which also corresponds with the end of part 2 of Li Fuyi's 1947 *Leshi*. The reigns of these eighteen rulers cover a period of roughly three centuries, a time when Moeng Lü was under the dual overlordship of China and Burma. Special attention is given to Cao In Moeng under whose reign a major

established in the Zhiyuan reign (1265–1294) and subordinate to it were six *dian* (villages/ polities).

27. See *Taizu shilu*, ch. 143, 2246–47 (Hongwu 15, second month+, *guimao* day).

28. MSG, ch. 189, 29b; *Taizu shilu*, ch. 164, 2535 (Hongwu 17, eighth month, *bingzi* day).

administrative reform was carried out. In 1570, Moeng Lü was divided into twelve districts called *panna*; hence, the change in the county's name from Moeng Lü to Sipsòng Panna. The account of Cao In Moeng's reign also contains a meticulous inventory of gifts sent from Sipsòng Panna to the Chinese and Burmese courts. Of special interest is the detailed narrative of events during the fratricidal wars which brought Sipsòng Panna almost to the brink of destruction in the first half of the nineteenth century (according to Li Fuyi's 1947 *Leshi*), namely the reign of Tao Coen Cong or Cao Mòm Suca Wanna (LV2: section 39; LV1: section 32).

Though the contents of the 1963 Moeng Lü Chronicle do not differ substantially from that of Li Fuyi's 1947 *Leshi*, the dates recorded in the 1963 chronicle are highly controversial. Starting with the reign of Cao Sili Suthamma (LV2: r. 1603–1620; LV1: 1628–1639), the dates given in Li Fuyi's 1947 *Leshi*, which seems to be more reliable, are almost two decades later than those given in the 1963 chronicle (for details, see section below).[29] Until the reign of Cao Mòm Suca Wanna (LV2: r. 1788–1818; LV1: 1834–1864), this gap amounts to forty-six years.

The *fourth part* of the chronicle, not recorded in Li Fuyi's 1947 *Leshi*, begins with the reign of Cao Mòm Sò (LV2: r. 1863–1879), the fortieth ruler. The chronicle states that the new *cao fa* succeeded his uncle-cum-adoptive father, Cao Mòm Suca Wanna, to the throne in CS 1225 (AD 1863/64), without explaining how this was possible if the previous ruler had already passed away in CS 1180 (AD 1818/1819). There was a lapse of forty-five years between the two reigns. We can deduce that the fourth part of the 1963 Moeng Lü Chronicle, namely the chronicles of the last five rulers of Sipsòng Panna, is not based on the same manuscript as the first three parts. It is compiled from a different one. The author(s) of the 1963 Moeng Lü Chronicle did not endeavour to adjust the dates of the two reigns so as to suggest a continuity of succession. Among the few political events recorded in the fourth part of the chronicles, the revolt of Moeng Cae in 1909/10 deserves special mention as it paved the way for more direct Chinese involvement in the internal affairs of Sipsòng Panna. The short reign of Cao Mòm Kham Lü (sinicised name: Dao Shixun, r. 1947–1950) ends the eight centuries of dynastic history of Moeng Lü or Sipsòng Panna.

All the long versions of the Moeng Lü Chronicle, including Li Fuyi's 1947 *Leshi* and the 1963 chronicle, focus on the dynastic and political history of Sipsòng Panna. There are brief mentions of state rituals, but other cultural aspects, including Buddhism, are not discussed in the chronicle. Unlike other political chronicles of the Tai, such as the Chiang Mai Chronicle or the Chiang Tung Chronicle, almost nothing is said of the spread of Buddhism or the relationship between the Buddhist *sangha* and the political order.

29. Certain clues suggest that most likely Li Fuyi adjusted the dates with the help of contemporary Chinese sources. The year Tao Sida Kham succeeded his father, Cao Khan Moeng, to the throne (see section 9.1) and the year Cao Paeng Moeng died (see section 25.3), for instance, tally with the dates recorded in Chinese sources.

3. GENEALOGY OF THE *CAO PHAENDIN* OF MOENG LÜ OR SIPSÒNG PANNA (MLC-SV1)

Li Fuyi first translated the short version of the Moeng Lü Chronicles into Chinese and published it in 1933 in *Minzhong shenghuo* 民眾生活, but the original Tai Lü manuscript and its translation were not at hand when he made a recension and translated the short version of the genealogy of the rulers (i.e., *saenwi fa* or *cao phaendin*) of Moeng Lü [namely MLC-SV1 by Li Fuyi].[30]

Li Fuyi's MLC-SV1 belongs to one of the many short versions of the Moeng Lü Chronicle. The Tai Lü text is printed along with Li Fuyi's Chinese translation in part 2 of Li Fuyi's *Cheli xuanwei shixi kaoding* (Recension of the Genealogy of the *Saenwi Fa* of Sipsòng Panna), published by Wenjian Publishers in Kunming in April 1947 (pp. 44–63). The original Tai Lü manuscript on which the text is based was kept in Chiang Rung and copied in 1943 by Luo Zeguang 羅澤光 on Li Fuyi's request.[31] It is most probably the oldest extant Tai Lü manuscript of the genealogy of the rulers of Moeng Lü. It records the genealogies of thirty-eight rulers, from the reign of Cao Phaya Coeng and his death in 1180 down to the reign of Cao Mòm Long Khòng Kham (r. 1926–1943), alias Cao Mòm Suwanna Phakhang (see MLC-LV2, s. 43). In Li Fuyi's translation from Tai Lü into Chinese (p. 59), Li points out that the authorship of the Tai Lü manuscript is probably ascribed to Dao Zhengzong (Cao Mòm Suca Wanna). His conclusion is drawn from the statement: "When Tao [Khamòm] Suwan was the ruler, he had three sons: the eldest son, namely [my] elder paternal uncle Tao Thai Pin, died early without an heir."[32] It is intriguing to note that in the section on Cao Maha Nòi (r. 1817–1833), predecessor of Cao Mòm Suca Wanna (r. 1837–1865), the narration changes from a third-person to a first-person perspective. The narrator states that "my uncle" (*pò lung khacao*, Th. พ่อลุงข้าเจ้า) adopted "me" (*khacao*, Th. ข้าเจ้า) and made "me" heir to the throne.[33] Therefore, the second part, which covers the last four reigns, is considered a later addendum and the narrator from the royal house was obviously Tao Coen Cong (Cao Mòm Suca Wanna). It seems that Li Fuyi did not try to change or rectify the dates of this short chronicle despite its high historiographical value.

The Tai Lü text has been transcribed into modern Thai script by Thawi Sawang-panyangkun and cross-checked by Prasert na Nagara.[34] However, the Thai transcription

30. See the preface to MLC-SV1, 1, written by Li Fuyi on 2 September 1944.

31. Ibid.

32. See MLC-SV1, 58–59, s. 32, referring to the reign of Tao Thai Khò.

33. See MLC-SV1, 58–63. Another example is "my father Tao Thai Khang (Cao Mòm Maha Wang)".

34. It was published in the journal *Ruam botkhwam prawattisat* (Collected Articles on History, vol. 15, 1993, 1–11), which is the yearbook of the Historical Society under the Royal Patronage of H.R.H. Princess Mahachakri Sirindhorn.

is not based on Li Fuyi 1947b (i.e., MLC-SV1), but on Li Fuyi 1983, the revised edition, which has been updated to include the reign of Cao Mòm Kham Lü (r. 1947–1950).

4. GENEALOGY OF THE RULERS OF SIPSÒNG PANNA (MLC-SV2)

Another translation from a short version of the Moeng Lü Chronicle is included in this volume. It is based on a mulberry paper manuscript preserved in the Provincial Museum of Yunnan. Gao Lishi's Chinese translation[35] is printed alongside the Tai Lü text, which was copied (handwritten) from the original manuscript, but only the first two folios are reproduced in facsimile. The first folio states: "This leporello manuscript comprises three parts" (หน้าทับพายเคล้า พับหน่วยนี้ค่าวในมันเปนค่าวสิพพาบท ๓ ถ้านแล). Then follows the sentence: "Copied/ composed on the second waxing of the first month of AD 1965 (๑៩๖๕ ตัว เดือน ๑ โลก ออก ๒ ค่ำ แต่งแมแล), i.e., on Monday, 4 January 1965. Finally, we are informed of the scribe's name: Tao Saeng Kwang (ผู้แต่งแม เท่าแซ้งควาง). The second folio, running over 15 lines, is divided into two sections. The first section (lines 1–9) is an address of the author to his readers. In a very traditional style he pays his respect to the elders of the entire country. The second section (lines 9–15) comprises the initial part of the chronicle.[36]

The chronicle itself can be divided into three parts. Part 1 records the reigns of thirty-two rulers and the brief dynastic history of 602 years, from Phaya Coeng Han (r. before 1180) to Tao Sao Wün (r. 1729–1782). Part 2 is a short supplement dealing with miscellaneous records, such as tribute, seal, and credentials conferred by the Chinese emperor on various *cao fa* of Sipsòng Panna. It seems that this part has been culled from Chinese sources. Part 3 contains a brief description of the boundaries of the domain of Moeng Lü and a list of the twelve territorial units (*khwaen*) inhabited by non-Tai ethnic groups (*kha*).

---

35. Gao Lishi's work, entitled *Xishuang banna zhao pianling shixi zhuyi* 西雙版納召片領世系註譯 (Annotated translation of the genealogy of *cao phaendin* of Sipsòng Panna), was published in 1982 in the *Journal of Nationalities* (*Minzu xuebao*) of the Institute of Nationalities of Yunnan (*Yunnan minzu yanjiu suo*), 81–91.

36. A detailed description of the Tai Lü manuscript on which Gao Lishi's translation is based is also given in the preface to MLC-SV2, 81. Gao states that the original title of the book is *Sixa but sam than (Sikha but sam than).* On the cover page the serial number is 255 (1–129), in all forty pages. The section on the genealogy of the *cao phaendin* is taken from pp. 16–22. As the original manuscript is old and the margins of the book are tattered, it was re-edited and copied by Dao Jianguang 刀 建 光 (Tao Saeng Kwang) in 1965. See Liew and Grabowsky 2004, 178–179, no. 19). Gao Lishi maintains that his Chinese translation, apart from inserting these paragraphs, is faithful to the original text. Liew-Herres has translated it into English for her co-authors to cross-check against the original Tai Lü text.

5. CORROBORATIVE TAI LÜ SOURCES

For the annotations of the four versions of the Moeng Lü Chronicle discussed above, as well as for the History of Sipsòng Panna (see the introduction, part 1 of this volume), a wide range of primary sources from both Sipsòng Panna and beyond were used. Among the various corroborative Tai Lü sources, eleven texts deserve special mention.

TEXT 1: CÜA KRÜA CAO SAENWI SIPSÒNG PANNA (DYNASTIC HISTORY OF THE RULERS OF SIPSÒNG PANNA)

This long version of the Moeng Lü Chronicle was compiled by the two Tai Lü scholars Tao Kwang Saeng (Dao Guangxiang 刀光祥) and Ai Kham (Yan Han 岩罕), and was published in Kunming in 1990. The text is written in Tai Lü language and printed in old Tai script.[37]

The work is neither a critical edition of an old manuscript nor the reconstruction of an original text. In fact, it is a modern synthesis based on a wide range of Tai Lü chronicles and other sources, including Chinese ones. The two compilers, highly reputed scholars from Chiang Rung, explain their methods in the introduction (pp. 1–18). In 1983, thirty years after the founding of Sipsòng Panna Tai Autonomous Prefecture, the local authorities decided to revise the "official history" of Sipsòng Panna, which was edited and stencilled in 1963 (i.e., MLC-LV2). For this purpose the Historical Commission of Sipsòng Panna appointed a team of scholars who collected eleven other manuscripts in order to verify and "purify" (Th. *chamra* ชำระ) the 1963 Moeng Lü Chronicle. Unfortunately, the compilers do not mention the exact titles and locations of each of the twelve texts forming the basis of the "revised edition" of "The genealogies of the forty-four rulers [of Sipsòng Panna]". In March of 1985, more than twenty Tai Lü scholars held a symposium to discuss the extant Tai Lü manuscripts of the various versions of the Moeng Lü Chronicle and to decide on the draft of a "purified" new version. This draft was then translated into Chinese and supplemented by contemporary Chinese sources, such as the Veritable Records of the Ming and of the Qing dynasties. A collated Chinese version of a Concise History of Sipsòng Panna was completed in June 1986. The Concise History was distributed half a year later to various government departments and important officials [in Sipsòng Panna and Kunming] for review and final approval. The official Chinese edition of the Concise History, entitled *Cheli xuanwei shixi jianshi* (Concise History of the Genealogies of the *Saenwi* of Sipsòng Panna), was published in April 1987. Thereafter, the Tai Lü edition was revised by integrating the Concise History, notably only those amendments which were based on the Chinese sources, into the draft of the "purified" Tai Lü text of March 1985. Although Tao Kwang Saeng and Ai Kham assure the reader that they tried to keep the wording of

37. A Chinese version of the same text was published earlier, in April 1987, as no. 1 of the series *Banna wenshi ziliao xuanji* 版納文史資料選輯 (Selected Collections of Source Material of Literature and History of Sipsòng Panna. See Liew and Grabowsky 2004, 167–69, no. 5.

that text whenever it was considered reliable, numerous additions and omissions were made whenever that seemed not to be the case. None of these changes are indicated in footnotes or annotations, making it rather difficult to use this work as a primary source for the study of the Moeng Lü Chronicle.

TEXT 2: PAP PÜN KHAO CÜA KHÚA CAO SAENWI FA SIPSÒNG PANNA (GENEALOGY OF THE FORTY-FOUR RULERS OF THE DYNASTY)

The text by unknown authorship is based on a manuscript preserved by Cao Phaya Long (Zhao Paya Long 召帕雅龍), the father of Dao Xiaozhong 刀孝忠 from Moeng Hai.[38] It records the successive rulers of Sipsòng Panna, from the founder-king Cao Phaya Coeng (r. 1180–1212) to the forty-fourth ruler Cao Mòm Kham Lü (Dao Shixun, r. 1947–1950). This record deviates in certain details both from Li Fuyi's 1947 *Leshi* (MLC-LV1) and the 1963 Moeng Lü Chronicle (MLC-LV2) discussed above. The years of the various reigns differ as well. Of particular interest is a very detailed account of the so-called "Cow's Cushion War" fought between Moeng Cae and Chiang Rung in 1908–1910. This war is not recorded in most of the extant versions of the Moeng Lü Chronicle but, for example, in The Chronicle of the Forty Rulers of Panna Moeng Hai (see text 8 below). We therefore have integrated it into our translation of the 1963 Moeng Lü Chronicle (MLC-LV2).

The text has been transcribed into modern Thai script and used as the basic primary source by Wimon Khetta in his master's thesis, the Moeng Lü/Sipsòng Panna Chronicle (Silpakorn University 2000). According to Wimon, the text was "revised" (*chamra*) by a local Tai Lü scholar called Khanan Còm.

TEXT 3: CAO PHAENDIN SIPSÒNG PANNA (CHRONICLE OF THE RULERS OF SIPSÒNG PANNA)

The text (53 ff°), copied by Cao Maha Khanthawong (Chiang Rung) from an unknown Tai Lü manuscript, is a collection of legends associated with the twelve *cao fa* who ruled Sipsòng Panna before the ascension to the throne of Cao Phaya Coeng. This important historical document states that the first Tai Lü ruler arrived at Moeng Arawi (original name of Chiang Rung) where he founded seven stockade villages. The lands on the east and west of the Mekong were not yet cultivated at that time. The Tai Lü fought against the indigenous people living in the region for control of the land.

38. This long version of the Moeng Lü Chronicle was translated into Chinese by Dao Shuren 刀述仁 in the volume *Cheli xuanwei shi shixi jijie* 車里宣慰使世系集解 (Kunming: Yunnan minzu chubanshe, 1989, 218–82). The original Tai Lü text bears the title พับพื้นเคล้า เชื้อเคือเจ้าแสวนหวีฟ้า ๑๒ พันนา ทุติยะ ตั้งชั่วภยาเจิงถึงเจ้าคำลือน้อย ชื่อห้อเท้าลื้อซิ้น ตามชื่อนามเสียงมี ๔๔ ได้เปนเจ้านั่งแท่น ตามสุภาสิตตา สืบตามมา มี ๔๑ ชิ่นเจ้าแล, which is printed (unfortunately not in facsimile) in the same publication (377–480). See Liew and Grabowsky 2004, no. 15.

TEXT 4: TAMNAN PHÜN MÜANG SIPSÒNG PANNA (CHRONICLE OF SIPSÒNG PANNA)

This text has been transcribed into modern Thai and edited by Thawi Sawangpanyangkun (1986). The editor obtained the original manuscript in the early 1980s from Phra In Kaeo Aphithammo (Abhidhammo), a Tai Lü monk who fled from Sipsòng Panna to Burma and also helped with the transcription. Thawi states in the preface to his book that for comparative reasons he used two other versions of the Sipsòng Panna Chronicle. One version was provided by Phra Khruba Saengla Thammasiri (Dhammasiri) and the other by Cao Khammun Nòkham, the former governor (*cao müang*) of Moeng Cae. Thawi's *Tamnan phün müang sipsòng panna* is not a coherent text with a single narrative but a collation of different stories. The first part of the manuscript (ff° 1/1–4/6) deals with the early history of the regions prior to the founding of Chiang Rung and is similar to text 3, but also includes elements of the "Chronicle of the Servants of the 400,000 Horse Cushions" (*Khao nithan kha si saen mòn ma*). Only the second part (ff° 4/7–9/8) pertains to the dynastic history of forty-four rulers of Sipsòng Panna. The final part (ff° 9/8–13/7) is a miscellaneous collection of historical records from different periods.

TEXT 5: PAP PÜN SIPSÒNG PANNA SAENWI FA PEN PÜN TAI LÜ HAO LAE (CHRONICLE OF THE PACIFICATION COMMISSIONERS OF SIPSÒNG PANNA: A TAI LÜ CHRONICLE)

The mulberry paper manuscript of 57 folios, each comprising 20–21 lines, was composed in CS 1363 (AD 1991) by a former monk from Moeng Long. The author's name is mentioned at the beginning of the manuscript: "My name is Ai Khan Kaeo. When I grew up I was called Khantha; this was my name as a novice (sāmaṇera). When I left monkhood, I was called Pò Ai Ton (f° 1/1–2)." The author emphasises his modest social background: "I am of commoner origin; I am not from a family belonging to the Council of Nobles" (f° 1/7). As to the motives of writing the chronicle, Ai Khan Kaeo states: "As I fear that the young generation will no longer know about the traditions and customs of the country, I feel obliged to write this chronicle. I [began to] write it on the thirteenth waxing day of the eighth month in the *ruang met* year CS 1353, a Monday or a *ruang kai* day as the Tai say (Monday, 10 June 1991)."

The subtitle of the chronicle connects the history of Sipsòng Panna with the other Tai polities in the Upper Mekong region: "There are five *ciang* (*chiang*): Chiang Rung, Chiang Tung, Chiang Saen, Chiang Rai, Chiang Mai, and there are nine lakes (*nòng*) and twelve gates (*patu*)." The chronicle can be divided into four parts. In the first part (ff° 1/17–2/17) the author gives a rough overview of the different ethnic groups in the Tai speaking world and the origins of humankind. Before starting with the second part, the author writes: "I [continue to] write on the second waning day of the ninth month in the *ruang met* year CS 1353, a *kot sai* day as the Tai say (Friday, 28 June 1991), at the auspicious constellation 23 (f° 2/18–20)." Part 2 (ff° 3/1–35/10) deals with the mythical history of Moeng Lü prior to its founding by Phaya Coeng. The confrontation between the Tai Lü, who migrated from (a mythical) Moeng Mithila or Moeng Sae in the north, and the aboriginal inhabitants of Sipsòng Panna is also reflected in this legendary part. Part 3 (ff° 35/11–50/22) is an concise version of the Moeng Lü Chronicle covering the dynastic history until the Communist victory in 1950. The final part (ff° 51/1–57/20) is a miscellaneous collection of information which the author considered worth recording: the resettlement campaigns of the Lan Na rulers during the first half of the nineteenth century (*soek kalòm*), the legend of Cao Fa Dek (Lek) Nòi, the Burmese expansion in the Upper Mekong region during the second half of the sixteenth century, a list of important *müang* in the region with their Tai and Pali names, and, finally, the author's conclusion of his own chronicle.

TEXT 6: PÜN MOENG LONG (MOENG LONG CHRONICLE), BAN FOEI LUNG VERSION

The undated mulberry paper manuscript, which was probably copied from an older one in the 1980s or 1990s, comprises 43 folios, each of which has 14 lines. This chronicle is of particular interest because in its initial part (ff° 1–4) it provides a precise description of the local administration of Moeng Long, a *panna* bordering the Burmese Shan state of Chiang Tung. The genealogy of provincial governors (*cao panna*) in the second section of the manuscript (ff° 5–19) places political developments in the southern periphery of Sipsòng Panna in the context of events at the royal court in Chiang Rung. Thus we learn a great deal about the local perspective of the fratricidal wars which affected Sipsòng Panna in the first half of the nineteenth century. The final part of the chronicle (ff° 20–43) deals primarily with traditional rituals and customs in Moeng Long.

TEXT 7: PÜN MOENG HAM (MOENG HAM CHRONICLE), KHANAN NAKKASEN VERSION

The mulberry paper manuscript of unknown authorship comprises 23 folios, each of which consists of between 13 and 14 lines. As to the provenance of the manuscript, the colophon at the end of the text states: "This legendary chronicle (*tamnan nithan niyai*) was copied by Cao Maha Khanthawong from a manuscript of the Moeng Ham Chronicle, which is in the possession of Khanan Nakkasen from Ban Son Mòn in Moeng Ham, on the eighth waxing of the second month, CS 1358 (18 December 1996)." The structure of the text resembles that of text 6. The first part (ff° 1/1–10/2) describes the borders and the territorial divisions of Moeng Ham, a rich and fertile *müang* under the jurisdiction of *panna* Chiang Rung. The second part (ff° 10/2–12/10) comprises a short genealogy of twelve governors (*cao moeng*) of Moeng Ham. The final part of the chronicle is a collection of legends pertaining to Buddhist reliquaries and saints.

TEXT 8: PAP PÜN MOENG SISIP CIN CAO PANNA MOENG HAI (CHRONICLE OF THE FORTY RULERS OF PANNA MOENG HAI), CAO SOLAWONG MAHA BUNTAN VERSION

The mulberry paper manuscript, which is in the possession of Maha Còm and Khanan In from Ban Kat (near Moeng Hai), comprises 48 folios, each of which consists of between

15 and 17 lines. According to the colophon: "Cao Solawong Maha Buntan of Chiang Long composed or copied (*taem*) [this text] in the *poek yi* year, CS 1360, on the twelfth waning of the fourth month (Saturday, 13 February 1999)." Apart from the first five folios, in which an overview of the administrative system and ethnography of Moeng Hai is given, the manuscript records the reigns of altogether forty rulers of Moeng Hai, which was one of the largest *panna* on the west bank of the Mekong River. Though the *panna* system was introduced to Moeng Lü only in the second half of the sixteenth century, all rulers of Moeng Ham are addressed as *cao panna* (lords of the *panna*). The origins of the ruling house are traced back to the seventh century, and it seems that at least the first dozen rulers are legendary characters. The narrative becomes more focussed on political developments when the Burmese political expansion in the late sixteenth century is discussed. A long section is devoted to the so-called "Cow's Cushion War" between Moeng Cae and Chiang Rung in 1908–1910 (also mentioned in text 2). This most detailed account covers almost one-fifth of the whole manuscript (ff° 35–43). It seems that it was based on an eyewitness report.

TEXT 9: PÜN MOENG LAEM (MOENG LAEM CHRONICLE), LONG NGO PAN-BAN YANG VERSION

Though Moeng Laem was never a part of Sipsòng Panna, this small Tai principality to the west of Moeng Cae maintained close political, economic, and cultural relations with its larger neighbour. More than once Moeng Laem provided a kind of safe haven for high-ranking Tai Lü nobles who fled from the political turmoil in Chiang Rung. The paper manuscript, dated CS 1353 (AD 1991), comprises 63 pages, each of which consists of 12 lines. The front page states:

> Composed by monk (*bhikkhu*) Luang Ngua (Long Ngo) Pan, from Ban Yang in Moeng Laem, a person having studied astrology. He recorded [the history of Moeng Laem] for posterity so that future generations (*cao luk khun lan*) can comprehend the customs of the country[39] in the past. [This chronicle] is composed in the year CS 1353, AD 1991, BE 2535, still remaining 2465 years.[40]

The manuscript is an interesting combination of traditional historiography and modern scholarship. The first section (pp. 1–7) contains detailed lists of districts, sub-districts and villages in Moeng Laem. This section is followed by a dynastic chronicle of twenty-eight rulers of Moeng Laem since its founding in the early twelfth century down to the Communist victory in 1949 (pp. 8–54). The final section (pp. 55–63) comprises lists of traditional ranks and a list of deaths—in China as well as in other warring nations—during the two world wars. The second part, which makes up the bulk of the

39. This term is expressed in the following Tai Lü idiom: *han hit poeng moeng* (หันหิด/ฮีตเปิงเมิง); *han* means "to see", *poeng* is derived from a Shan word, which means "rule" or "pattern".

40. According to a wide-spread Buddhist belief, the religion (*sāsanā*) of Buddha Gautama comes to an end after a period of five thousand years.

manuscript, provides valuable information pertaining to Moeng Laem's relationship to neighbouring Tai polities, including Sipsòng Panna. They can be used for cross-checking the Moeng Lü Chronicle.

6. THE CHRONOLOGY OF THE MOENG LÜ CHRONICLE

In Sipsòng Panna, as in other Tai speaking regions, dates are usually given in the so-called "little era" (*cūlasakarāja*), the first year of which corresponds to AD 638 in the Gregorian calendar. In addition to the *cūlasakarāja* year, in Tai historical records a second system of naming the years is used which is thought to derive from China. This system employs a set of ten words (which refer to the position of a specific year within the current *cūlasakarāja* decade) in combination with a set of twelve words (which indicate the corresponding animal year) to produce a sixty-year cycle (for details, see section below). The two short versions of the Moeng Lü Chronicle (MLC-SV1 and MLC-SV2) use both systems for dating the years, in many cases (MLC-SV1) including the mention of the corresponding Chinese reign years. This allows for a cross-checking comparison of both dates and thereby the detection of scribal errors. The 1963 chronicle (i.e., MLC-LV2), on the other hand, does not employ the sixty-year cycle but gives dates only in the *cūlasakarāja* year by adding the corresponding *Anno Domini* year (AD) in round brackets. This is a clear indication that the two short versions represent an older, more archaic layer of Tai Lü historiography.

In Li Fuyi's *Leshi* (MLC-LV1) the dates are first given in *cūlasakarāja* (CS), with the Chinese sixty cyclic years. These are then converted into the Chinese reign year with the corresponding year of the Christian era. For example, Phaya Coeng was enthroned as the ruler of Moeng Lü in CS 542, a *gengzi* year (Song Chunxi 7, AD 1180). Li Fuyi was familiar with the Chinese sources. Although Li Fuyi states that he translated *Leshi* from the Tai Lü manuscripts, faithfully including the errors contained in the original text, clues can be found in *Leshi* that at least a few dates were adjusted to accommodate those given in the Chinese sources.

The conversion to Chinese reign years and the *Anno Domini* dating system in parenthesis is obviously ascribed to Li Fuyi. This hypothesis can be substantiated by pointing out six cases where Li Fuyi's sleight of hand appears most clearly.

1. The last time Dao Kan (Cao Khan Moeng, r. 1347–1391) offered tribute to China was in 1387.[41] Hence Cao Khan Moeng passed away between 1387 and 1391. According to *Mingshi gao*, Dao Xianda (Tao Sida Kham, r. 1391–1413) succeeded his father in the year Hongwu 24 (AD 1391) and he sent his younger brother Dao San Pala (Tao Sam Phaya) to offer tribute to China.[42] This is the first time Tao Sida Kham is mentioned in contemporary Chinese sources. However, in other Tai Lü sources, such as the 1963

41. See *Taizu shilu*, ch. 183, 2756 (Hongwu 20, seventh month, *bingxu* day: 22 August 1387).

42. See MSG, ch. 189, 29a; taken from *Taizu shilu*, ch. 213, 3148 (Hongwu 24, tenth month, *jiwei* day: 2 November 1391).

chronicle, Tao Sida Kham reigned between 1350 and 1430, which is a gap of forty years. As the *Mingshi gao*, based on the dates of the *Ming shilu* (Veritable Records of the Ming Dynasty), are quite accurate, Li Fuyi (MLC-LV1) most probably has adjusted the year given in the Tai Lü manuscript on which his translation is based to accommodate the year recorded in Chinese sources.

In 1413, the emperor sent the palace eunuch Hong Zaisheng 洪仔生 to take an imperial decree to Dao Xianda (Tao Sida Kham). However, Dao Xianda had already passed away before the imperial envoy arrived.[43] According to the 1963 version (cf. Gao Lishi 1984: 108), Tao Sida Kham passed away in CS 793 (AD 1430; Xuande 5 of the Ming period). This is a clear indication that Li Fuyi must have altered the dates of the Tai Lü manuscripts on which his 1947 *Leshi* is based (see MLC-LV1, s. 9).

2. According to the 1963 Moeng Lü Chronicle (section 31.1), Cao Paeng Moeng (r. 1670–1698) was on the throne twenty-seven years, lived to the age of thirty-nine years, and died in CS 1060 (AD 1698). The same is recorded in Gao Lishi (1984: 120). Yet, the Veritable Records of the Qing Dynasty, a contemporary Chinese source that is very precise in dates, gives the following account:

> In the year Yongzheng 4, ninth month, *bingshen* day (2 October 1726), the grand co-ordinator of Yunnan cum supreme commander of Yunnan and Guizhou, O-er-tai (1680–1745), submitted a memorial reporting that Dao Zhao Bianmeng (Cao Paeng Moeng) had passed away and petitioned to allow his son Dao Zhao Jinbao (Tao Cao Cin Pao) to succeed.[44]

Therefore, Cao Paeng Moeng could not have passed away in CS 1060 (AD 1698), twenty-eight years earlier than O-er-tai's report. Cao Paeng Moeng passed away not long before O-er-tai's report. The year CS 1086 (Yongzheng 2, 1724) given in Li Fuyi's MLC-LV1 (section 25.3) is surprisingly close to that in contemporary sources, another indication that the dates of the 1947 *Leshi* have been altered.

3. In the year Yongzheng 8, twelfth month, *renyin* day (15 January 1731; CS 1092), the supreme commander of Yunnan and Guizhou, O-er-tai (1680–1745), submitted a memorial reporting that the *saenwi fa* of Cheli under Puer in Yunnan, Dao Jinbao (Tao Cin Pao), had passed away. His sons were still young. He asked for permission to appoint his younger brother Dao Xi Men Na (Cao Si Mün Na) as regent, who would care for the orphans.[45] According to the 1963 Moeng Lü Chronicle (section 32.1) and Gao Lishi (1984: 121), Tao Cin Pao died in CS 1069 (AD 1707). This does not agree with the Chinese sources. However, according to Li Fuyi's 1947 *Leshi*, Dao Jinbao reigned from 1724–1729. Again, the year of Dao Jinbao's death (Yongzheng 7: 1729) given in Li Fuyi's MLC-LV1 is surprisingly close to that given in contemporary Chinese sources.

---

43. See MSG, ch. 189, 31; *Taizong shilu*, ch. 145, 1717 (Yongle 11, eleventh month, *wuxu* day: 15 December 1413).

44. See *Shizong shilu*, ch. 48, 5.

45. See *Shizong shilu*, ch. 101, 3.

4. According to the 1963 Moeng Lü Chronicle (section 33.1) and Gao Lishi (1984: 121), Tao Sao Wün was twenty-five years old when he ascended the throne in CS 1069 (AD 1707). But according to the Veritable Records of the Qing Dynasty, Dao Shaowen was fifteen years old in the year Yongzheng 12, eighth month, *jisi* (23 September 1734).[46] The age (15) and the year (Yongzheng 7: 1729) given in Li Fuyi's 1947 *Leshi* (MLC-LV1, s. 27.1) are as stated in the contemporary Chinese sources. It is hard to believe that Li Fuyi has not adjusted the age and the year in his translation to comply with the Chinese sources

5. The 1947 *Leshi* records (section 27.1) that Dao Shaowen had been dismissed in CS 1129, a *moeng kai* year (Qianlong 32, AD 1767), after the Heavenly Court accused him of incompetence in managing affairs. According to the Veritable Records of the Qing Dynasty, the "stupid" and "cowardly" *saenwi fa* of Cheli, Dao Shaowen, was deposed in Qianlong 31, twelfth month, *bingwu* day (10 January 1767).[47]

6. In Li Fuyi's 1947 *Leshi* (section 28.3), it is stated that "in CS 1135, a *ka sai* year (Qianlong 38, AD 1773), [the Qing court] dispatched officials to investigate [the matter]. [Tao] Suwan and [Tao] Wui Phin were arrested one after the other and brought to Moeng Maen (Ninger), where they were escorted to Moeng Sae Long (Kunming). [Tao] Wui Phin and [Tao] Cao Then (Thian) were removed from their posts." According to the Veritable Records of the Qing Dynasty, Dao Weiping was deposed in Qianlong 37, sixth month, *xinwei* day (7 July 1772).[48]

Given the above evidence, it is hard to believe that Li Fuyi has not adjusted the dates of the Tai Lü manuscripts on which his 1947 *Leshi* is based.

7. THE TRANSLATION OF OFFICIAL TAI LÜ TITLES AND OTHER SPECIAL TERMS INTO CHINESE

Among the salient points in Li Fuyi's Chinese translation, *Leshi,* are his choice of proper words and terms. The translation of Tai Lü titles into Chinese is not an easy task. The Tai call their rulers *cao* (lord), *cao fa* (lit., "lord of heaven") or *phaya* (king). These words reflect the pride and self-esteem of the Tai ruling dynasty. From a Chinese perspective, the Tai *cao fa* were subordinate rulers of petty principalities who certainly do not deserve forms of address reserved for royalty. For example, Li Fuyi renders "Phaya Moeng Kaeo" into Chinese as "Mengjiao qiu" (chieftain of Moeng Kaeo), and "Phaya Chiang Rung" is rendered similarly into Chinese as "Jinglong qiu" (chieftain of Chiang Rung). Thus *qiu* 酋 (chieftain) is Li Fuyi's translation of *phaya.* Phaya Coeng is rendered "supreme chief" (*da shouling* 大首領), whereas *cao phaendin,* which means "lord of the land", is rendered *xuanwei shi* (*saenwi fa*). However, Gao Lishi (1984) transcribes *cao phaendin*, which means "lord of the land", as *zhaopian ling* 召片領. In some cases, Li Fuyi

46. See *Shizong shilu*, ch. 146, 13 [the report of Yongzheng 12, eight month, *jisi* day (23 September 1734)].

47. See *Gaozong shilu*, ch. 774, 10–11.

48. See *Gaozong shilu*, ch. 910, 8.

transcribes the Tai Lü titles and terms into Chinese instead of looking for appropriate Chinese equivalents. *Phaya* into *ba* 叭 or *banya* 版雅; *cao* or *tao* into *zhao* 詔, *dao* 刀, or *tao* 匋; *ban* (village) into *man* 蠻; and *moeng* into *meng* 猛, in particular Burmese terms, are examples. It is interesting to note that the Tai Lü title *tao* or *cao*, transcribed as *dao* 刀, was taken by the Chinese authorities as the surname of the *cao fa* and *cao moeng* (see MLC-LV1, section 5.1). Until today many of the descendants of the Tai Lü nobility have the surname Dao.

Tianchao 天朝 (Heavenly Court), or *tianchao huangdi* 天朝皇帝 (emperor of the Heavenly Court), is Li Fuyi's renderings of *phaya hò* or *cao lum fa*. In Chinese *shicai* 食采 and *shiyi* 食邑 both mean "to take up the fief(s)". Thus being sent or invested as the lord of Lan Na is rendered "to take up the fief of Lan Na".

As for the death of sixteen ancient Tai Lü kings recorded in part 1, Li Fuyi uses the word *hong* 薨, a word used for the death of a prince, except for the usurpers Dao Gengmeng (Tao Kü Moeng), Dao Dian (Tao Kham Tet) and She Longfa (Soe Long Fa), for whom Li Fuyi used the word *si* 死, a word used for the death of an ordinary man. In part 2 of *Leshi*, for the death of the Tai Lü rulers who had submitted to the Burmese king, Li Fuyi no longer uses the word *hong*. He chose the word *si* or *zu* 卒, which means "death", but not the word signifying the death of a prince. We do not know the exact Tai Lü words used for the death of their *cao phaendin* in *Leshi* because the Tai Lü texts were not printed alongside the translations, and the two Tai Lü manuscripts are now lost (see page 79). However, in Li Fuyi (MLC-SV1), the short version of the chronicle, the Tai Lü text is printed together with the translations. The following words indicating the death of the Tai Lü rulers can be traced: *mòranna sia* (มรณะเสีย), *cutti* (จุติ), *cutti tai* (จุติตาย), *sang bun* (สร้างบุญ), and *sang bun pai* (สร้างบุญไป). In Tai Lü *sia* means "to lose", and *mòrana*, which is derived from Pali *maraṇa*, means "death". The Tai Lü word *cutti*, which is derived from the Pali *cuti* (Skt. *cyuti*), means "vanishes, passes away". The use of this word indicates the high status of the deceased person. *Sang bun* means "having acquired merit" and *sang bun pai* means "to pass after having acquired merit". Both latter terms reflect Buddhist ethics, as a ruler was expected to rule according to the prescriptions of a just monarch. The original word for the death of the first thirteen *cao phaendin* of Moeng Lü was most probably *cuti tai*, which Li Fuyi rendered into Chinese as *hong*.

In Chinese there are four words for death: *beng* 崩 (lit., "collapse like a mountain") is used exclusively for the death of a sovereign or emperor/empress, *hong* 薨 (the upper part of the character refers to a dream and the lower part is the word "to die") refers solely to the death of a feudal lord or a prince, or a high official, and *si* 死 or *zu* 卒 (died) refer to the death of a non-royal person. In the mid-1940s when Li Fuyi was translating the Moeng Lü Chronicle (i.e., *Leshi*), the *cao phaendin* of Moeng Lü were still recognised as legitimate feudal lords or aboriginal officials (*tuguan*), or specifically *xuanwei shi*, (pacification commissioners), rendered into Tai Lü as *saenwi fa*. Here the original Tai Lü is probably *cutti* (see MLC-SV1).[49]

49. In part 1 of MLC-LV1 Li Fuyi used *hong*; in part 2 he used *zu* or *si*.

According to the 1963 Moeng Lü Chronicle (section 1.2), they all invested Phaya Coeng as *cao saenwi fa* (*xuanwei shi*), the supreme chief of the [domain] of Sipsòng Panna (cf. MLC-LV1 by Li Fuyi and Gao Lishi 1984: 105). However, during the reign of Phaya Coeng the term *saenwi fa* was not yet known to the Tai Lü and Moeng Lü was not yet called Sipsòng Panna. This anachronism provides a clue that the 1963 version was a revised manuscript of the Moeng Lü Chronicle. In Li Fuyi's *Leshi* the terms *xuanwei shi* (*saenwi fa*) and Xishuang Banna (Sipsòng Panna) are only used in part 2. The term *saenwi fa* first appears in the reign of Cao Nò Moeng (see MLC-LV1, section 17.1), and "Sipsòng Panna" first appears in the reign of Cao In Moeng (see MLC-LV1, section 19.5) as the twelve *panna* were established no earlier than 1570, almost four centuries after the death of Phaya Coeng.

It is interesting to note that the term *xuanwei shi* 宣慰使, rendered into Tai Lü as *saenwi fa*, is used only in part 2 of Li Fuyi's *Leshi*. In the 1963 version of the Moeng Lü Chronicle and Gao Lishi (1984) the term *saenwi fa* (obviously derived from the Chinese *xuanwei shi*, translated into English as pacification commissioner) appears in the reign of Phaya Coeng. This shows that part 1 of Li Fuyi's *Leshi* is based on a Tai Lü manuscript which was not subjected to revision in the 1960s as were the 1963 Moeng Lü Chronicle and Gao Lishi (1984).

In Li Fuyi's *Leshi* the transcriptions of the rulers' names, such as Dao Kan, Dao Xianda, Dao Gengmeng, Dao Baxian, Dao Dian, Dao Bagong, Dao Shuangmeng, and Dao Shiwan exactly follow those of the Chinese sources: *Ming shilu*, *Mingshi gao*, *Mingshi*, *Qing shilu*, etc. The later translators, such as Gao Lishi (1984), Dao Shuren (1989), and others, created their own, sometimes idiosyncratic, systems of transcription. The Tai Lü names were transcribed so closely by the translation office of the Ming court (*Siyi guan*) that we have no problems in identifying them.

As for the *müang* conferred on the Tai Lü princes, Li Fuyi renders this term into Chinese as *caiyi* (land set apart for feudal lords) or *shicai* 食采, (lit., "eat the fief"). In fact *shicai* or *shiyi* (lit., "eat the conferred land") in Chinese means "fief". The *cao phaendin* of Moeng Lü granted principalities in outer *müang* and even in "foreign" lands, such as Moeng Kaeo, Moeng Lao, or Lan Na, to those of their sons who were not made crown prince. These grants, in turn, could be passed on to their descendants. They were the lords or viceroys of the principalities, known as *cao mòm* (Tr. เจ้าหม่อม, transcribed into Chinese as *taomeng* 陶孟 or *toumu* 頭目). The term *taomeng* appears rather often in the Ming sources and the Ming officials understood it to refer to a tribal envoy (see MSG, ch. 189, 29a).

As a rule, the Tai Lü princes were invested as the lords of the outer *müang* when they came of age, such as *shicai yu Menglong* 食采于猛籠 (lit., "eat the fief in Moeng Long"). They were the governor of the *müang*. However, in Li Fuyi's perspective the *moeng* or *müang* governed by the Tai Lü princes were the *caiyi* 采邑 (fief) granted to them.

8. CHARACTERISTICS OF TAI LÜ LANGUAGE AND SCRIPT

Tai Lü is one of the many dialects of the Tai language family. The maximum area in which the Tai language family is spoken stretches from southern China (chiefly Guangxi, Guizhou, and Yunnan), to Thailand, Laos, and the northern part of the Malay Peninsula, and to the northern sections of Burma and Upper Assam in India. The heartland of the Tai Lü is in the present-day Sipsòng Panna Tai Autonomous Prefecture, situated in the southernmost part of Yunnan. Sipsòng Panna, with the capital in Chiang Rung (Jinghong), is still widely known by its ancient name Moeng Lü, which means the "land" or "polity" of the Tai Lü people. There are clusters of Tai Lü settlements in the adjacent Lao provinces of Phong Sali (which until 1895 belonged to Sipsòng Panna) and Luang Nam Tha (in the districts of Moeng Sing and Moeng Long) as well as in the Burmese Shan state of Chiang Tung (Keng Tung), notably around Moeng Yòng and Moeng Luai. Owing to forced resettlements and voluntary migrations in the eighteenth and nineteenth centuries, today the Tai Lü have spread throughout the region and are found in northern Laos and northern Thailand. At present, slightly more than one million speakers of the Tai Lü language are living in the Upper Mekong region.[50]

The Tai Lü language, which has six distinctive tones,[51] is divided into several dialects, as described by Gedney (1999 [1964]), Li Fang Kuei (1964), and Hartmann (1984). The "standard" Tai Lü is spoken in the capital Chiang Rung as well as in the southern and eastern districts or *panna* (Moeng Long, Moeng La, and Moeng Phong), whereas the dialects spoken in the western *panna* of Moeng Cae and Moeng Hai show some Shan influences. Hartmann demonstrates that tonal contours for corresponding tones in the Tai Khün language of Chiang Tung and the Tai Lü dialect of Moeng Yòng are "nearly identical".[52] The dialects of Moeng Sing and other Tai Lü–inhabited areas in northern Laos have not yet been the subject of a serious linguistic study. However, according to our own observations, the Tai Lü dialect of Moeng Sing seems to be closer to the Chiang Rung dialect, especially with regard to vowel length contrasts. Furthermore, the low class initial consonant /ñ/ (written ᨿ or ᨬ) has lost its palatalisation in the Chiang Rung dialect as well as in the other dialects of Sipsòng Panna and is pronounced /y/ as in Siamese, whereas the Moeng Yòng dialect has preserved the original palatalisation.[53] In initial position, the proto-Tai voiced unaspirated stops are pronounced in Tai

50. As to Tai Lü demographics, see details in the introduction, part 1, section 1 of this volume.

51. Li Fang Kuei 1977, 17–18, characterises these tones as: a. the high level tone 55 (slightly rising before a pause); b. the falling tone 31; c. the high rising tone (starting at a point slightly below the middle pitch, and rising up to high 25; d. the mid level tone 33; e. the low rising or low level tone 13 or 11 (variants appearing under different phonological environments); and f. the mid-low level tone 22. See also Hartmann's phonological description of the Tai Lü language in comparison with neighbouring Tai languages (Hartmann 1984, 17–40).

52. Hartmann 1984, 21.

53. Ibid., 34.

Lü—as in Tai Yuan and Tai Khün—as voiceless unaspirated sounds and not voiceless aspirated sounds as in the Siamese language. The low class initials *g, *j, *d, and *b are pronounced /kh/, /ch/, /th/, and /ph/ in Siamese but /k/, /c/, /t/, and /p/ in Tai Lü. Our system of Romanisation of Tai Lü words follows Tai Lü, not Siamese phonology. For example, the Tai Lü cognate of the Siamese word for "one thousand" is Romanised as *pan*, not *phan*, but transcribed พัน. The reader, therefore, should be aware that the Romanisation of Tai Lü expressions transcribed into Siamese (marked "Tr.") differ from that of genuine Siamese terms. Among the few exceptions to this rule are words like *chiang*, pronounced *ciang*, whose widely-used orthography has been maintained.

The Tai Lü script is a variant of the Dhamma script (*tua aksòn tham*), which was probably developed from the ancient Mon alphabet of Hariphunchai. Though the diffusion of this script in the Upper Mekong region has still to be studied thoroughly, we may assume, based on our present state of knowledge, that the script spread from Lan Na to Chiang Rung and other parts of Sipsòng Panna no later than the mid-fifteenth century, probably during the reign of King Tilok when Lan Na expanded politically and culturally into the Tai Lü speaking areas. The Lao, Lan Na, and Tai Lü versions of the Dhamma script are very similar to one another, and the lexemes of the Lao, Lan Na, and Tai Lü languages are to a very high degree identical.[54] Manuscripts in these languages and scripts from Laos, Northern or Northeast Thailand, and Sipsòng Panna can be read and, to a certain extent, understood by anyone literate in any one of them.

A major orthographical reform of the Tai Lü script occurred in 1953, when the new rulers in Beijing established, as part of Simao Prefecture, "Sipsòng Panna Tai Autonomous Prefecture". To facilitate the learning of the Tai Lü language and script, particularly among non-Tai ethnic groups, including a growing number of Chinese immigrants, the Chinese authorities set up a commission of local scholars and bureaucrats to design a completely new Tai Lü alphabet that was officially introduced in 1955. The simplified alphabet abolished the Pali consonants, banned the use of ligatures, which are typical for the Dhamma script, and "simplified" the shape of the remaining consonant and vowel graphemes, as well as lined up consonants, vowels, and tone markers in one single line. Since then, the younger generation has been educated exclusively in the new script, which is also used for the typesetting of vernacular books and newspapers, such as the *Xishuang Banna baozhi* (Sipsòng Panna Newspaper), founded in 1957.[55] As suggested above, script reforms constituted a radical break with the past; those acquainted only with the new alphabet are unable to read texts written

54. This can bring about incorrect classifications of Tai manuscripts by researchers not sufficiently familiar with the regional variations of the Dhamma script. For example, almost all manuscripts listed by Wenk (1975) in his catalogue of Lao manuscripts in Germany are in fact Lan Na manuscripts.

55. Isra 2001, 461; Aphiradi 2003, 9.

in the traditional Tai Lü Dhamma script, which was probably one of the goals of the simplification.[56]

While the old Tai Lü script was practically forbidden during the period of the Cultural Revolution, it has been experiencing a revival since the late 1980s. It is now taught at the monasteries, which have been gradually reopened since then. In addition, the old script has been used for re-editing religious and traditional secular literature over the last two decades.

8.1 TAI LÜ ORTHOGRAPHY

Tai Lü orthography is similar to that of other scripts belonging to the Dhamma group of scripts, such as Tai Yuan or Lan Na, Tai Khün, and Dhamma-Isan or Dhamma-Lao scripts.[57] As the Tai Lü phonetic system bears certain characteristics, the written language attested to in old Tai Lü manuscripts differs from that of other Tai ethnic groups. Students encounter various difficulties in interpreting Tai Lü texts. Although Tai languages of the Upper Mekong region share a common basic vocabulary with each other, each language has borrowed numerous words from neighbouring languages, both Tai and non-Tai, such as Chinese, Burmese, Shan, Lao, and Thai (Siamese).

Although in general the phonemes in Tai Lü differ from those in central Thai (Siamese) and the Tai language of Lan Na (Kam Müang), the orthography used in the manuscripts under study is mostly written according to the rules for Tai Lü script. The differences in phoneme refer to vowels and diphthongs rather than to consonants. The most important phonetic changes that had occurred in Tai Lü, probably prior to the early nineteenth century, will be explained in the following section by comparing phonemes in Kam Müang and Tai Lü cognates.

Vowels

1. The (Kam Müang) phoneme /e/ or /e:/ is pronounced /i/ or /i:/, for example:

ติม (เต็ม)	to be full
ปิน (เป็น)	to be
ข่มหิง (เหง)	to abuse, mistreat

2. The (Kam Müang) phoneme /o/ or /o:/ is pronounced /u/ or /u:/, for example:

ริพูร (ริพล)	military forces, troops
หูน (หน)	direction; road, way
ลุง (ลง)	to descend

56. Simplified Chinese characters were also introduced at the same time in China. As a result, young Han Chinese are only taught the simplified Chinese characters in school, and newspapers and books are printed in simplified characters. They are unable to write and read the traditional, more complex Chinese characters.

57. Sai Kam Mong's (2004) recent monograph "The History and Development of the Shan Script" includes the Tai Khün variant of the Dhamma script but fails to mention the Tai Lü script.

3. In many syllables the (Kam Müang) phoneme /a/ is pronounced /ɛ/, for example:

แส่น (สั่น)	to tremble, to vibrate
แถุนด (ถนัด)	to be skilful, adroit, good at
แทด (ทัด)	to be accurate, correct

Note: As a rule, the cases 1 and 2 appear only when the final consonant is a nasal but case 3 also is valid when the syllable ends with a stop consonant.

Diphthongs

Nowadays the Tai Lü no longer use diphthongs (Th. *sara prasom*) in their spoken language. The written language, however, has preserved an archaic orthography that maintains diphthongs which are pronounced as simple vowels or monophthongs. This is the case for the diphthongs /i:a/ and /u:a/, now pronounced /e/ and /o/ respectively.

Note: As for the diphthong /ʉ:a/, pronounced /ə:/ in Tai Lü, the graphemes that once represented the original diphthong are no longer used.

1. Words (syllables) containing the diphthong /i:a/ in Thai are pronounced with /e:/, for example:

เม (เมีย)	wife
เสง (เสียง)	voice, sound; noise
เส (เสีย)	to have to be abandoned, thrown away or discarded (a term implying imperativeness and expressing loss)

2. Words (syllables) containing the diphthong /u:a/ are pronounced with /o:/ in Thai, for example:

โห (หัว)	head
โม (มัว)	to be dim, obscure, cloudy
โหลง (หลวง)	main; royal

3. Words (syllables) containing the diphthong /ʉ:a/ are pronounced with /ə:/ in Thai, for example:

เมิง (เมือง)	polity, principality; realm (*müang/moeng*)
เคริ่ง (เครื่อง)	object; utensil; accessory
เฺิน (เรือน)	house

8.2 OVERCORRECTION

It is well-known that many people in Thailand have difficulty in differentiating between the consonants /r/ and /l/, with the phoneme /r/ quite often pronounced as /l/ in colloquial speech. Some people who may be afraid of being considered ignorant of or insensitive to the complexities of their own mother tongue would say /r/ instead of /l/ more often than necessary only to be on the "safe side". This phenomenon of "overcorrection" (Th. *kae koen het* แก้เกินเหตุ) is also known in the context of Tai Lü written language. As has already been mentioned, the Tai Lü script has been derived from the Dhamma script of Lan Na. Spoken Kam Müang does have diphthongs, and they are therefore expressed in Lan Na orthography. As spoken Tai Lü does not have—or, at least no longer has—diphthongs, modern Tai Lü scribes feel uncertain how to write words which historically were once pronounced with a diphthong. Thus we find the Tai Lü word *ho*, "head" sometimes written โห according to modern pronunciation, but sometimes written หัว (*hua*) like its Kam Müang cognate. Similarly, the word *leng*, "to look after, to feed", would be written either เล้ง or เลี้ยง (*liang*). However, if a scribe lacks philological training and basic knowledge of historical linguistics he might be tempted to "overcorrect" the spelling of words incorrectly. Thus the word *lok* (โลก, Skt./P. loka = world) is often written ลวก (*luak*) with the contention that this is the historical orthography, which is not the case. Other typical examples of such over corrections are สามเณียร (*samanian*) instead of สามเณร (*samanen*, P. samanera = novice), รบ (*hop*) instead of รูป (*hup*, Skt./P. rūpa = form), and เทียด (*tiat*) instead of เทศ (*tet*, Skt. deśa = country, land), such as in the name of Tao Kham Tet, the fifteenth ruler of Moeng Lü.[58]

8.3 LOANWORDS

From the documents we have analysed, it is evident that the Tai Lü language has a lot of influences from languages of other Tai groups as well as from foreign languages, such as Chinese, Burmese, Pali, Sanskrit, and Khmer. Pali words used in the manuscripts are, for example, *netta* (eye), *hattha* (hand), and *buddhābhiseka* (consecration of the Buddha). As topics related to Buddhism do not feature prominently in the Moeng Lü Chronicle, the number of terms of Pali or Sanskrit origin is rather limited. Moreover, some loanwords are used along with semantically related Tai Lü words. For example, the term ซากถวาย (*sak thawai*) combines the Burmese word ဆက် /sɛ:'/, "to offer respectfully", with the Khmer-derived Tai Lü word *thawai*, having the same meaning (see MLC-LV2, f° 34). Of greatest importance and most numerous, however, are the Chinese loanwords, followed by words of Burmese origin. Most of these loanwords are related to administrative issues which reflect the long-term political tributary relations of Sipsòng Panna with these two major regional powers.

58. For examples of the widespread phenomenon of overcorrection in the orthography of Tai Lü manuscripts, often reflecting the scribe's "pseudo-eruditeness", see Aphiradi Techasiriwan's master's thesis (2003) on the "Development of Tai Lü scripts and orthography".

Table 5: Chinese Loanwords in the Moeng Lü Chronicle

Thai transcription	Romanised form	Chinese	English translation
คายฝ้าง	*kai fang*	*kai fang* 開放	to release, to let go
ต่ายควาน	*tai kwan*	*dai guan* 代管	regent, or represent (same as *dai li*)
ต่ายลี	*tai li*	*dai li* 代理	to represent, as a regent
ชุงป่าน	*cung pan*	zong ban 總辦	general-administration, refers to the post of Chinese resident commissioner Ke Shuxun
พี้แน้	*pi nae*	*pi ye* 畢業	graduated; accomplished
แซวกุ่ง	*saeo kung*	*xiaogong* 小貢	"small" tribute/tax
ต้ากุ่ง	*ta kung*	*dagong* 大貢	"big" tribute/tax
จิ้มกุ่ง	*cim kung*	*jin gong* 進貢	to offer tribute
หว่าน	*wan*	*wan* 碗	bowl
ธู้ง	*thung*	*tong* 桶	bucket, pail
แหล่น	*laen*	*lian* 練	to train soldiers
ถุ่ย	*thui*	*tui* 退	to draw back, to retreat
แค่ว	*kaeo*	*jiao* 交 / 繳	to send, to hand over
ต่ายลีฟู	*tai li fu*	*daili* 代理 *fu* 副	[to rule as] regent; [to be] an assistant
ชุงตู้	*sung tu*	*zongdu* 總督	commander-in-chief
แหล่นพิ่น	*laen pin*	*lianbing* 練兵	to train soldiers
อ่าน	*an*	*ancha* 安插	to appoint, to install
จิ้มก้อง	*cim kòng*	*jin gong* 進貢	to send/deliver tribute
แสนหวี	*saenwi*	*xuanwei* 宣慰	pacification
หยิ่น	*yin*	*yin* 印	Seal. In Tai Lü *yin* is always preceded by the word *cum* (จุ้ม), which also means "seal": *cum yin* (จุ้มหยิ่น).
คว่านลิแว่นชาง คือคอนแซ่งควิน หย้ามืน	*kwan li waen cang kü kòn saeng kwin ya mün* (from MLC-SV1)	*Yuanjiang zongguan xingsheng yamen* 元江總管行省衙門	an official title conferred by the Chinese emperor on Soe Long Fa. Though there are various interpretations of this title, the most probable rendering is "route commander of Moeng Cung".

Table 6: Burmese Loanwords in the Moeng Lü Chronicle

Thai transcription	Romanised form	Burmese	English translation
อมิงต่อ	*amingtò*	/əmeiŋ'do/ အမိန့်တော်	royal decree
อมุคี	*amuki*	/əmaˀ`ci/ အမတ်ကြီး/ θaŋəmaˀ`ci/ သံအမတ်ကြီး	a high-ranking court official; ambassador, envoy
ผัด	*phat*	/phaˀ/ ဖတ်	to read
ชะคาย/ชิกคาย	*cakai / cikkai*	/siˀ`ke/ စစ်ကဲ	a (Burmese) second-in-command of a military unit
ชิกโป่	*sikpo*	/siˀbou/ စစ်ဗိုလ်	military chief or officer
มูซา / มุยซา	*musa / muisa*	/myou"`sa/ မြို့စား	governor
มังซาม	*mangsam*	/`miŋ`ða/ မင်းသား	prince
ธุงจ่าน	*thungcan*	/`thouŋzaŋ/ ထုံးစံ	custom, tradition
กั่นทอ	*kantò*	/gədo'/ ကန်တော့	to pay obeisance with one's hands clasped palm to palm and raised to touch one's forehead; to present a gift in respect and gratitude
พุงต่อ	*pungtò*	/`phouŋdo/ ဘုန်းတော်	power, charisma, virtue
อะหย่องต่อ	*ayóngtò*	/əyauŋdo/ အရောင်တော်	royal splendour
อะหย่าต่อ	*ayatò*	/əyado/ အရာတော်	royal property
อะมูต่อ	*amutò*	/ðhmu'do/ အမှုတော် ဝတ်တော် ?	royal duty
ธาม	*tham*	/`thaŋ/ ထမ်း	to carry on the shoulder
แมงซา	*maengsa*	/`miŋ`ða/ မင်းသား	prince
แย	*yae*	/`ye/ ရဲ	police

CHRONICLE OF SIPSÒNG PANNA

Annotated Translations of Four Versions of the Moeng Lü Chronicles

Contents

CHRONICLE OF SIPSÒNG PANNA

IV. Genealogy of the *Cao Phaendin* of Sipsòng Panna (MLC-SV2)

I. History of Moeng Lü (*Leshi*) by Li Fuyi (MLC-LV1)

PART ONE (1180–1530)

1. PHAYA COENG (BA ZHEN 叭真), R. 1180–1192

1.1 THE FIRST RULER; CAO LUM FA GRANTS PHAYA COENG A GOLDEN SEAL

In *culasakarāja* (hereafter CS) 542, a *kot cai* year (AD 1180), Phaya Coeng came to Moeng Lü to be the ruler. His father conferred on him [royal] insignia, weapons, clothing, ornaments, and many other things. Cao Lum Fa, [known] by the name of Pothiyan,[1] cast a golden seal [adorned with] a tiger head for [Phaya Coeng], and nominated him as the [supreme] ruler of the region. Consequently [Phaya Coeng] was enthroned as the most reverent Buddhist ruler of the Moeng Chiang Rung Hò Kham.[2]

1.2 FOUNDING OF CHIANG LAN

In CS 552, a *kot set* year (AD 1190), on the tenth waxing day of the sixth month, a *dap pao* [day], Saturday (sic), at dawn, [Phaya Coeng] founded his capital at Chiang Lan.[3] Previously there was a local official (sic) called Ai Lan [living] in that place; therefore [the capital] was named after him.[4]

1. *Cao lum fa* is a generic term for the emperor of China, but the Cao Lum Fa Pothiyan mentioned here probably referred to Duan Zhixing (r. 1173–1200), the ruler of the kingdom of Later Dali (1096–1253) in Yunnan, instead of Emperor Guangzong (r. 1190–1194) of the Southern Song dynasty (1127–1279).

2. A rather similar account is given in Gao Lishi 1984, 105, s. 1.1; MLC-LV2, s. 0.1 and 1.1; Dao Shuren 1989, 220.

3. We are not sure whether "Saturday" is Li Fuyi's own interpretation or stated in his original Tai Lü manuscript from Moeng Khün. But according to Dao and Kang (1989b), Phaya Coeng moved to Wiang Chiang Lan at dawn, on Friday, the tenth waxing day of the sixth month, CS 552, a *kot set* year (summer of 1190), eleven years after he had been enthroned as the ruler of Moeng Lü.

4. Li Fuyi (MLC-LV1, 1) uses the term *diguan* 地官 (local official). In Gao Lishi and other sources, Ai Lan was the Lua (Lawa) chieftain (*khun lua*). In Gao Lishi 1984, 105, s. 1.1, it states: "Previously

1.3 PHAYA COENG BECOMES THE OVERLORD OF THE TAI

After Phaya Coeng had defeated various lands in the north, [the polities of] Lan Na, Moeng Kaeo,[5] and of Moeng Lao[6] were ruled by him. At that time the emperor of the Heavenly Court (sic)[7] was the overlord.[8] Phaya Moeng Kaeo[9] by the name of Nara Phiramma, Phaya Chiang Rung by the name of Mung Moeng, and Phaya Lan Na by the name of Pothi Latcalot,[10] as well as Phaya Lawaek,[11] Chin Chan (Jin-zhan),[12] Yok Yai

---

Chiang Lan was called Ban Ai Lan because there was a Lua (Lawa) chieftain (i.e., Phaya Lua) called Ai Lan living there. Later, when Phaya Coeng became the great [ruler] after subduing the various *müang*, he founded the capital city there. Since then [the place] was called Chiang Lan." A very similar account is given in MLC-LV2, s. 0.1; Dao Shuren 1989, 220. This information tells us that the indigenous people of Moeng Lü of the pre-Phaya Coeng era were not Tai Lü. The Lawa chieftain might have helped Cao Phaya Coeng to subdue the indigenous peoples in Chiang Lan and the polities (*müang*) to the east and west of the Mekong. According to MLC-LV1, index, 1, Chiang Lan, the old capital of Moeng Lü was located about 3 *li* (1½ km) in the east of Chiang Rung.

5. Probably Moeng Kaeo does not refer to Moeng Kaeo Luang (i.e., the polity of Jiaozhi or Chiao-chih in Annam and Tonkin), but to Moeng Lai (Laizhou or Laichou) in Northern Vietnam, on the border of Yunnan.

6. Moeng Lao refers to the kingdom of Lan Sang (1353–1707/13), founded by Fa Ngum (1353–1373/74), the grandson of Suvanna Khamphong (r. 1316–1344?). According to the table of the kings of Lan Cang (Lan Xang or Lan Sang) from the Phraya dynasty there were three rulers prior to Fa Ngum, i.e., Phraya Lang (1271–1316?), Suvanna Khamphong, and Khamhiao (1344?–1353). See Stuart-Fox 1998, 147.

7. Here Li Fuyi (MLC-LV1, 1) uses the term *tianchao wangdi* 天朝皇帝 (lit., "emperor of the Heavenly Court"). In the original Tai Lü manuscript this is most likely Phaya Hò (ruler of China), called Cao Lum Fa Pothiyan. *Cao lum fa* is the Tai Lü rendering for the emperor of China. See the MLC-LV2, s. 1.2 and Gao Lishi 1984, 105. s. 1.3. The Phaya Hò cannot actually refer to the emperor of the Southern Song dynasty (1127–1279) since Yunnan was incorporated into China only during the Yuan dynasty (1280–1368).

8. Li Fuyi (MLC-LV1, 1) uses the word *gong zhu* 共主 (lit., "common lord", i.e., overlord). In AD 1180, the Song emperor was preoccupied with defending his northern frontiers and empire against the Jin (Ruzhen) and the Mongols. The "overlord" here probably referred to Duan Zhixing 段智興 (r. 1173–1200), the ruler of the Later Dali, not Emperor Xiaozong (r. 1163–1189), the Southern Song emperor.

9. In Li Fuyi (MLC-LV1, 1), he was called *Mengjiao qiu* 猛交酋 (chieftain of Moeng Kaeo). In MLC-LV2, s. 1.2 and Gao Lishi 1984, 105, s. 1.3, he was Phaya Kaeo (lord of the Kaeo). Thus "chieftain of Moeng Kaeo" in Li Fuyi means Phaya Kaeo.

10. According to MLC-LV2, s. 1.2 and Gao Lishi 1984, 105, s. 1.3, Pothi Latcalot was Phaya Lan Sang, i.e., the monarch of the Lao kingdom of Lan Sang.

11. According to Gao Lishi 1984, 105, s. 1.3 and MLC-LV2, s. 1.2, he was Phaya Moeng Khün, called Phaya Lawaek.

12. Jin Zhan 金占 is interpreted by Li Fuyi 1983a, 82 as two places: Jin (Chin), refering to China, and Zhan (Cham) or Zhanpo (Champa).

(Yoyai),[13] to the south (*tai la*)[14] and around the banks (*fak nam*)[15] of the Khün River, and of Khün Khiam (Khem),[16] etc. conferred with one another. They all persuaded [Phaya Coeng] to ascend the throne. [Consequently], the dripping water ceremony[17] was performed and Phaya Coeng was enthroned as the supreme chief (sic).[18]

1.4 THE CORONATION OF PHAYA COENG

[They] brought along one *phasat* (i.e., palace), height thirty-five *wa*, and one golden jar, which was three by three *sòk* and three *sòk* in height,[19] weighing 7,400,000 (sic) *kham*,[20] and adorned with seven kinds of gems. Furthermore, there were seventy-seven parasols,[21] and [a total of] 12,000 consorts and ladies-in-waiting. The queen was called Nang Akka Mahesi.[22] [Among the foreign emissaries] participating in the coronation were the Hò,[23] Yok Yai (Yoyai),[24] Chin Chan (Jinzhan),[25] Kula (Indians or Pegu),[26] Phasi

13. Not yet identified.

14. According to Li Fuyi 1983a, index, 82, Daila 埭臘 (Tae Klak) (sic) refers to an exotic land in the south, but we believe that *tai la* (*dai la*) means "in the south" and is not a place-name.

15. According to Li Fuyi 1983a, index, 82, 法湳 (Fak Nam) (sic) is a place in overseas; however, *fang nam* means "river bank" and is not a place-name.

16. According to MLC-LV1, index, 2, Kongke 崆岢 (Khung Kgyd) (sic) is the ancient designation of Menggen (Moeng Khün), now known as Chiang Tung (Keng Tung).

17. The "dripping water ceremony" is the ceremony of enthronement.

18. Both in MLC-LV1, 1 and Gao Lishi 1984, 105, s. 1.3, the term *da shouling* 大首領 (supreme chief) is used. This means that Phaya Coeng was enthroned as the *cao phaendin*, i.e., *somdet pha pen cao*, which means the sovereign of Moeng Lü. According to MLC-LV2, s. 1.2, they all invested (*ussaratchaphiset*) Phaya Coeng as *cao saenwi fa*, the supreme chief of the [domain] of Sipsòng Panna.

19. One standard *wa* or *wa luang* (วาหลวง) is an ancient Tai measure of length equal to 2 m or about 80 inches. In the Tai Lü and Shan areas a *wa* was less than 2 m, varying between 1.7 and 2.0 m. One *wa* is always equal to four *sòk*. One *sòk* is considered to be the distance from the tip of the middle finger to the elbow joint; as the length of a *sòk* depends on the *wa*, it fluctuates between 42 and 50 cm.

20. The weight of the golden pitcher or jar was five *lan* and four *saen* (540,000 units of gold]. See Gao Lishi 1984, 105, s. 1.4; MLC-LV2, s. 1.2. In the revised edition, Li Fuyi 1983a, 2, argues that the weight of the golden water pitcher was 5,400,000 *kham*. In Tai Lü script the numbers 7 and 5 look very similar.

21. There were seventy-seven white parasols. See Gao Lishi 1984, 105, s. 1.4; MLC-LV2, s. 1.2.

22. The Nang Tewi (the principal queen) was called Nang Ramma. See the MLC-LV2, s. 1.2. According to Gao Lishi 1984, 105, s. 1.4, the Nang Maha Laca (Raja) Tewi was called Nang Ramma. In MLC-SV1, 45, s.1, the queen's name is Maha Tewi Rammanni. *Nang* means Mrs. or Miss; and Akkha Mahesi, derived from Pali, is the Tai way of addressing the queen.

23. Here Hò, which sounds close to *hua* 華, means the Chinese.

24. Not yet identified.

25. Not yet identified.

26. Kala (Tr. กลา) is the Burmese word for foreigners (/kə`la/ ကုလား), notably natives of India. It is

(Paxi),[27] to the south (*tai la*) and around the banks (*fak nam*) of the Khün River, and from Khün Khiam (Khem) and various other lands. [In the polity] there were 8,440,000 subjects, 9,000 white elephants, and 97,000 horses.[28]

1.5 THE FOUR SONS OF PHAYA COENG

Phaya Coeng had four sons: The eldest, named Tao Pung Hoeng (Roeng), was invested as the lord of Lan Na; the second son, named Tao Ai Paeng, was invested as the lord of Moeng Kaeo; the third son, named Tao Yi Kham Hoeng (Roeng), was invested as the lord of Moeng Lao (i.e., Lan Sang); and the fourth son, named Tao Khai Noeng, later succeeded his father [to the throne] as Most Dignified Buddhist Ruler of Moeng Chiang Rung Hò Kham (the Golden Palace Kingdom of Chiang Rung).[29]

1.6 PHAYA COENG PASSES AWAY

Phaya Coeng was on the throne twelve years. He passed away (*hong*)[30] in the *tao cai* year, CS 554 (Shaoxi 3, AD 1192), at the age of seventy-three. He was the founder [of Chiang Rung], the first generation ruler [of Moeng Lü].

often written *kula* (Tr. กุลา). Later on, the word was misapplied to English and other Westerners who were sometimes called *kala/kula khao*, "white strangers". According to Ming sources, in Yongle 4, seventh month, *renwu* day (7 September 1406), the Great Gula Pacification Commission (Pegu) was established. See *Guoque*, ch. 14, 973; *Taizong shilu*, ch. 55, 818.

27. Phasi (Tr. ผาสี) derives from Persia, but in the Tai Lü context the term signifies the Hui or Chinese Muslims, sometimes also called *hò phasi* (Tr. ห้อผาสี) in contrast to the Han or *hò long* (Tr. ห้อหลวง), as the Hui in Yunnan are indeed mostly of Turkish and Persian origin.

28. A similar account is given in MLC-LV2, s. 1.2 and Gao Lishi 1984, 105, s. 1.4. But unlike MLC-LV1, 1, the eleplants were not white.

29. Here MLC-LV1, 2, used the term *shicai* 食采, lit., "to eat the fief". As a rule, the Tai Lü princes were invested as the lords of the outer *müang* when they were of age. They became the governors of these *müang*. Li Fuyi renders it as *shicai* and the principality to Li Fuyi is *caiyi* 采邑 (fief). A similar account is given in MLC-LV2, s. 1.5 and Gao Lishi 1984, 105, s. 1.5. It was only in the reign of Phaya Coeng that the right of primogeniture was not followed. After the reign of Tao Khai Noeng, the Tai Lü kings practised the right of primogeniture.

30. In Chinese *beng* 崩 (collapse like a mountain) is used exclusively for the death of an emperor or empress; *hong* 薨 (the upper part of the character means "dream" and the lower part means "die") refers solely to the death of a feudal lord, a prince, or a high official. In the mid-1940s when Li Fuyi was translating the MLC-LV1, the ancient rulers of Moeng Lü were recognised as feudal lords or high aboriginal officials. Here the original Tai Lü is probably *cutti* (vanished, passed away).

2. TAO KHAI NOENG (TAO KANG LENG 匋釭冷), R. 1192–1211

2.1 THE SECOND RULER; A TRIBUTARY LAND OF CHINA

In CS 554, a *tao cai* year (AD 1192), Tao Khai Noeng[31] succeeded his father Phaya Coeng to the throne, and became Most Revered Buddhist Ruler of Moeng Chiang Rung Hò Kham (the Golden Palace Kingdom of Chiang Rung). He owed allegiance to the Heavenly Court (*tianchao*),[32] called *Gua Jingtai yuannian* (sic).[33] The emperor of the Heavenly Court (*tianchao huangdi*) (sic) (i.e., Phaya Hò Cao Lum Fa)[34] established the tradition for offering tribute: One major tribute was to be offered every nine years, followed by one minor tribute every five years. He was invested as the king of Chiang Rung.[35]

2.2 THE TWO SONS OF TAO KHAI NOENG

Tao Khai Noeng had two sons: the eldest, named Tao Pung (Kung),[36] was [invested as] crown prince; the second was named Ai Yi Peng (abbreviated as Yi Peng).[37] The eldest son Tao Pung succeeded his father to the throne as the ruler; the second son Ai Yi Peng was invested as the lord of the three *panna*, Moeng Hun, Moeng Hai, and [Moeng Cae].[38]

---

31. His full name was probably Tao Sam Khai Noeng. In Gao Lishi 1984, 105 and MLC-LV2, the second ruler was called Sam Khai Noeng (r. 1180–1201). His name is similar to the third son of Tao Sam Pò Lütai (r. 1457–1497), Sam Khai Noeng (r. 1497–1502), the seventeenth ruler, according to MLC-LV1, 17, s. 14.1; but according to Gao Lishi 1984, 114, s. 19.1, and MLC-LV2, s. 19.1, he was the nineteenth ruler and reigned between 1491 and 1495.

32. Here Li Fuyi (MLC-LV1, 2) renders it as *tiancao* 天朝 (lit., "Heavenly Court"). But in MLC-LV2, s. 2.1, it is *cao wòng*, which is a combination of the Tai *cao* (lord) and the Chinese *wang* 王 or *huang* 皇, which mean "king" and "emperor" respectively.

33. In MLC-LV2, s. 2.1, it says, *Min Sao Cin Phaen*, but in MLC-SV1, 45, s. 2, it is *kin thawai waennaen* (Tr. กินถวายแว่นแน่น), which, in Pinyin, sounds like *Jingtai yuan nian* 景泰元年 (i.e., Jingtai 1). If it means *Jiatai yuan nian* 嘉泰元年, then it corresponds to AD 1201. However, MLC-LV1, 2, renders it as *Gua Jingtai yuannian* 寡景泰元年, namely "Jingtai 1 of the Ming dynasty", which corresponds to AD 1450. In Chinese *gua* 寡 (few, unworthy) is a term of depreciation, a humble way for fuedal lords to address themselves. Here Li Fuyi meant Emperor Jingtai. This date is definitely wrong. The error is obviously ascribed to Tai Lü scribes/historiographers, who were not well versed in the various reigns of imperial China.

34. In MLC-LV2, s. 2.2 and Gao Lishi 1984, 105, s. 2.2, it is *phaya hò cao lum fa* (Tr. พระยาห้อเจ้าลุ่มฟ้า), which means "ruler" or "lord" of China. Li Fuyi (MLC-LV1, 2) renders it as *tianchao huangdi* 天朝皇帝 (emperor of the Heavenly Court).

35. Li Fuyi (MLC-LV1, 2) renders it as Jiujiang Wang 九江王 (lit., "king of Jiujiang"). Jiujiang refers to the Jiulong Jiang 九龍江 (lit., "nine dragon river"), which flows through Chiang Rung. Hence Jiujiang Wang means "king of Chiang Rung".

36. He was also known as Ai Pung (Ai Kung). See section 3.1. below and MLC-LV2, s. 2.3 and s. 3.1.

37. The parenthesis should be ascribed to Li Fuyi (MLC-LV1, 2).

38. The three *panna* were in Moeng Hun, Moeng Hai, and Moeng Cae. See MLC-LV2, s. 3.2; Gao Lishi 1984, 106, s. 3.2; Dao Shuren 1989, 221. The term *panna*, an administrative division for levying tribute taxes, is first used here.

2.3 TAO KHAI NOENG PASSES AWAY

Tao Khai Noeng (also known as Khai Noeng)[39] was on the throne nineteen years. He passed away (*hong*) at the age of sixty-eight in the *hong met* year, CS 573 (Jiading 4, AD 1211). He was the second generation [ruler] (the second ruler).

3. TAO PUNG (TAO BENG 匋怦), R. 1211–1234

3.1 THE THIRD RULER; THE FIRST FRATRICIDAL WAR

Tao Khai Noeng's eldest son Tao Pung (also known as Ai Pung)[40] succeeded his father to the throne in CS 573, a *hong met* year (AD 1211). His younger brother, [Ai] Yi Peng, revolted and attempted to usurp the throne. Later, he was killed by his elder brother Tao Pung. After his death he became a *soe moeng* (i.e., *phi moeng*) [the designation of a type of spirit or deity, roughly the same as *she* (*soe*)].[41] Hence, oblations have to be offered at a certain time of the year, and it is observed to the present day.

3.2 TAO PUNG (AI KUNG) PRAYS FOR A SON; THE BIRTH OF TAO HUNG (RUNG) KAEN CAI

The lord Tao Pung (Ai Kung) had no son. Hence he ordered Tao U-Nge (Tao Wu-e) to pray for a son at the ants' nest. [The queen] became pregnant one night later. When the son was born, he was therefore called Tao U-Nge. [The boy] grew up to be very competent and another name, that of Tao Hung (Rung) Kaen Cai was bestowed on him.[42]

3.3 TAO PUNG (AI KUNG) PASSES AWAY

Tao Pung (Ai Kung) was on the throne twenty-three years and passed away (*hong*) at the age of seventy years in a *kap sanga* year, CS 596 (Duanping 1, AD 1234). He was the third ruler [of Moeng Lü].

---

39. The parenthesis should be ascribed to Li Fuyi (MLC-LV1, 2).

40. Ditto.

41. The above parentheses should be ascribed to MLC-LC1, 3. The Tai Lü people believe in spirits or deities (*phi*). When a lord of a *müang* (polity), i.e., *cao mòm*, passes away he is worshipped as the sprit of the polity, called *soe moeng*, transcribed into Chinese by Li Fuyi as *she meng*. In Gao Lishi 1984, 106, s. 3.2, it is *phi moeng*, which is the same as in MLC-LV2, s. 3.2.

42. The story of the birth of Tao Hung (Rung) Kaen Cai is not recorded in MLC-LV2, s. 3.1–3.2 or Gao Lishi 1984, 106. Probably it has been deleted during the revision.

4. TAO HUNG (RUNG) KAEN CAI (TAO LONG JIAN ZAI 匋隴建仔), R. 1234–1257

4.1 THE FOURTH RULER AND HIS TWO CHILDREN

Tao Hung (Rung) Kaen Cai, the son of Tao Pung (Kung) (or Ai Pung), succeeded in his father's stead as the ruler in CS 596, a *kap sanga* year (AD 1234). He had one son and one daughter. The son was called Tao Haeng Long and the daughter was called O (Ua) Ming Còm Moeng when she was young (i.e., still an infant).[43] When she was [at the age of] learning to walk (a toddler) she was named Nang O (Ua) Paeng.[44] When she reached [the age of] womanhood she was renamed Nang Kham Kai.[45]

4.2 NANG KHAM KAI MARRIES THE KING OF LAN NA

Later in the year CS 599 (AD 1237), she was married to Phaya Lao of Lan Na. Phaya Lao loved and indulged her very much. One night she dreamt that the Tianlang star [Dao Phakai][46] fell from the south and plunged into her belly. When she was awake she told Phaya Lao what she had dreamt. Consequently, on the following day Phaya Lao invited a [*mò*] *acan* (i.e., soothsayer or diviner) to consult him about the omen of the dream. The soothsayer (*acan*) Phammana (Ba Mana) told [him that] the queen was going to have a very capable crown prince who later was going to defeat the various kingdoms in the south.[47]

---

43. According to Gao Lishi 1984, 106, s. 3.2 and MLC-LV2, s. 3.2, Ai Pung (Kung) had one son called Tao Hung (Rung) Kaen Cai and a daughter called Nang O (Ua) Ming Khai Fa. But in MLC-LV1, O (Ua) Ming Còm Moeng was Tao Hung (Rung) Kaen Cai's daughter and Tao Haeng Long's sister. She was the mother of King Mangrai. In MLC-SV1, 45, s. 4, Nang O Ming Khai Fa was also Tao Hung (Rung) Kaen Cai's daughter, not his younger sister.

44. At this time she was called Nang Ok Aen. See MLC-SV1, 45, s. 4; MLC-LV2, s. 4.2; Gao Lishi 1984, 106, s. 4.2.

45. According to the Chiang Mai Chronicle, Thao Rung Kaen Chai (i.e., Tao Hung Kaen Cai) bestowed on his daughter the name Lady Theppha Kham Khrai (i.e., Nang Kham Kai) when she married Cao Lao Meng. Cao Lao Meng at the age of thirty-five years became king in his father's place and made Lady Theppha Kham Khrai his primary queen. See CMC-HP, Wyatt and Aroonrut 1995, 14–15; CMC-N, Notton 1932, 20; CMC-TPCM, Udom et al. 1995, 11.

46. According to MLC-LV1, 3, it was the *tianlang xing* 天狼星 (lit., "heavenly wolf star") that entered Nang Kham Kai's belly. According to MLC-LV2, s. 4.2, it was *dao phakai* (a shooting star) flying from the south that plunged into her belly. According to Gao Lishi 1984, 106, 4.2, it was a comet or shooting star (*liuxing* 流星) coming from the east (sic) that plunged into her belly. According to the Chiang Mai Chronicle, it was Venus, the morning star. See CMC-HP, Wyatt and Aroonrut 1995, 15; CMC-N, Notton 1932, 20. In any case, it was a star that caused Mangrai's mother to conceive her famous son. See also MLC-LV2, s. 4.3, n. 37.

47. Similar content is given in Gao Lishi 1984, 106, s. 4.2 and MLC-LV2, s. 4.2.

4.3 BIRTH OF PRINCE MANGRAI

The queen's belly grew bigger gradually and ten months later, in CS 601, a *kat kai* year (Jiaxi 3, AD 1239), in the sixth month, on an auspicious day, [the queen] gave birth to a baby boy.[48]

One full month after [the birth] the ruler of Moeng Lü, Tao Hung (Rung) Kaen Cai, accompanied by his queen, went to celebrate the first month ceremony for his grandson, and to perform the ritual of "tying the thread" (i.e., the *su khwan* ceremony) for him.[49] When they arrived at Chiang Rai, a person called Kumman was named Mangkala Nalai.[50] After Tao Hung Kaen Cai had returned to Moeng Lü, the people began to call his grandson, i.e., the son of Nang Kham Kai, Tao Mangrai.

4.4 GIFTS FROM MANGRAI'S GRANDFATHER

Later, Tao Hung (Rung) Kaen Cai had a golden top (*mak khang*) cast and gave the toy to his grandson. Again later, the people (i.e., attendants) told him that his grandson had grown up and loved to play the flute. Hence, Tao Hung (Rung) Kaen Cai gave him a golden flute.[51]

4.5 MANGRAI, RULER OF CHIANG RAI

After Tao Mangrai[52] had reached adulthood he succeeded his father as ruler of Chiang Rai. Indeed [he] fought and conquered Chiang Mai-Lan Na, and other places.[53]

---

48. The Tai Lü sources confirm that the prince was born in the sixth month. However, the year in which the prince was born is rather controversial. Gao Lishi 1984 and Dao Shuren 1989: born in CS 572 (AD 1210); Dao and Kang 1989b: born in CS 601 (1239 AD); Dao and Wu 1983: born in CS 602 (AD 1240). However, according to the CMC-HP (Wyatt/Aroonrut 1995, 15), Mangrai was born "in the *poek set* year—one chronicle says the *kat kai* year, on the ninth waning of the first month, a Sunday, near dawn, in the eighth lunar mansion". Wyatt and Aroonrut remark that "the chronological data work out *almost* perfectly for Sunday, 2 October 1238, which was in the *poek set* year 600, not the *kat kai* year 601".

49. Here Li Fuyi (MLC-LV1, 3) renders the *su khwan* ceremony as *shuanxian li* 拴線禮 (lit., "tying the thread ceremony"). The *su khwan* ceremony is performed in many occasions, such as when a newborn baby is a month old. In this case, in the ceremony the baby would be bathed and given a name.

50. The translation in MLC-LV1, 3, is ambiguous. *Kumman* (P. kumāra) means a baby, a son or an infant. Here it means a one-month-old baby. Thus the translation should say that the baby was named Mangkala Nalai. However, according to MLC-LV2, s. 4.3 and Gao Lishi 1984, 106, s. 4.3, it was Tao Hung Kaen Cai who named his nephew (sic) at the one-month ceremony Mangkala Nalai.

51. A similar account is given in MLC-LV2, s. 4.3; Gao Lishi 1984, 106, s. 4.3.

52. Mangrai (born in 1238, accession to the throne in 1259/60) was named after his father Cao Lao Meng and his maternal grandfather Thao Rung Kaen Chai, signifying that he was the son of Thao Meng and grandson of Thao Rung. See CMC-HP, Wyatt and Aroonrut 1995, 16; CMC-N, Notton 1932, 21; CMC-TPCM, Udom et al. 1995, 12. This folk etymology that "Mang" derives from "Meng" is, however, quite doubtful. In fact, *mang* (มัง) — from Burmese *ming* (မင်း) — is a prefix of Mon origin which originally signified royalty.

53. This probably refers to the later conquest of Hariphunchai by King Mangrai in 1292 (according

4.6 MANGRAI'S GIFTS FOR HIS GRANDFATHER

Thereupon, a piece of land was assigned to his maternal grandparents, solely for them to take hot baths [there]. Moreover, every year elephant howdahs were made. One howdah was for bearing the golden imperial insignia and one howdah was for bearing the silver insigna. Royal insignia were also placed in a golden tray. Furthermore, pure gold was used to cast a bottle-gourd, which was to be used as a jar for drinking water. Again twenty mattresses and twenty cotton wool blankets were made and presented to the ruler of Moeng Lü.

4.7 TAO HUNG (RUNG) KAEN CAI'S GIFTS FOR HIS GRANDSON

In return, his maternal grandfather, Tao Hung (Rung) Kaen Cai, gave his grandson every year twenty horses, twenty cows, twenty donkeys, twenty felt blankets, twenty steel knives, and one hundred loads of salt produced from Bò Hoek (Moxie 磨歇).[54]

4.8 TAO HUNG (RUNG) KAEN CAI PASSES AWAY

Tao Hung (Rung) Kaen Cai was on the throne twenty-three years. He passed away (*hong*) at the age of sixty-two in a *moeng sai* year, CS 619 (Baoyou 5, AD 1257). This was the fourth generation [ruler of Moeng Lü].

5. TAO HAENG LONG (DAO LIANG LONG 刀兩龍), R. 1257–1273

5.1 THE FIFTH RULER; CONFERMENT OF THE SURNAME DAO (TAO) ON TAI LÜ LORD

Tao Haeng Long, the son of Tao Hung (Rung) Kaen Cai, succeeded his father to the throne in CS 619, the *moeng sai* year (AD 1257). Only then did the Heavenly Court (i.e., Moeng Hò)[55] bestow on him the surname Dao (Tao or Cao) and thus he was called Tao Haeng Long.[56]

---

to the Jinakālamālīpakaraṇaṃ) or 1281 (according to the Chiang Mai Chronicle). See Ratanapañña 1968, 112; CMC-HP, Wyatt and Aroonrut 1995, 31–33. See also Sarassawadee 2005, 55.

54. Moxie or Mohei 磨黑 (Bò Hoek or Bò Khoe) is located in the south of Zhenyue County (Moeng La) where salt was produced.

55. AD 1257 corresponds to Baoyou 5 of the Southern Song period (1127–1279). The Mongols conquered the Later Dali (1096–1253) in 1253. The Heavenly Court or Moeng Hò could not have referred to the Southern Song court (1127–1279). Thus the Moeng Hò most probably referred to the Yunnan court (Moeng Mithila?) at Kunming (in Tai, Moeng Sae Luang 猛熙).

56. The same is recorded in the MLC-LV2, s. 5.2 and Gao Lishi 1984, 106, s. 5.2. *Dao* 刀 (knife) is the Chinese rendering of the Tai *tao/thao* or *chao/cao* (lord, ruler), which is not a surname but a royal title. The Tai Lü people did not have surnames, so the Chinese took their title for their surname. If the information in the text here is true, the "surname" Dao/Tao for the Tai rulers in Moeng Lü was conferred around the mid-thirteenth century by the Mongol ruler of China. In today's Yunnan, some Tai peoples have the family name Dao and they are usually the descendants of the Tai nobility.

5.2 TAO HAENG LONG'S TWO SONS

[Tao Haeng Long] had two sons: the elder one was named Ai Puwak[57] and the second one was called Yi [Peng/Piang] Lak Sai.[58]

5.3 CAO MOENG FÒNG ADOPTS YI PENG LAK SAI

As the incumbent lord of Moeng Fòng (Pòng) (i.e., Cao Moeng Fòng/Pòng) of that time, Fa Kham Kòng, had no son, he asked Tao Haeng Long to give him his second son Yi [Peng/Piang] Lak Sai to be his heir.[59] Hence, Tao Haeng Long sent his second son, escorted by attendants and others on twenty horses, to become the heir of the lord of Moeng Fòng. Later the lord of Moeng Fòng (Pòng) died and Yi [Peng/Piang] Lak Sai succeeded his adoptive father to the throne [of Moeng Fòng].[60]

5.4 TAO HAENG LONG PASSES AWAY

Tao Haeng Long became the ruler at the age of thirty-eight and was on the throne sixteen years. He passed away (*hong*) at the age of fifty-four in the *ka lao* year, CS 635 (Xianchun 9, AD 1273). This was the fifth generation [ruler of Moeng Lü].

6. TAO PUWAK (DAO BUWA 刀補瓦), R. 1273–1287

6.1 THE SIXTH RULER

Tao Haeng Long's son Tao Puwak succeeded his father to the throne in the *ka lao* year, CS 635 (AD 1273). His younger brother Yi [Peng/Piang] Lak Sai was then the ruler of Moeng Fòng.

6.2 YI PENG (PIANG) LAK SAI ATTACKS HIS ELDER BROTHER

In the third year (AD 1275), when Tao Puwak was on the throne, Yi [Peng/Piang] Lak Sai suddenly led the people of Moeng Fòng and the troops of Moeng Mao Long[61] to

57. In MLC-SV1, 47, s. 6, he is also called Tao Putok; in MLC-LV2, s 5.3 and Gao Lishi 1984, 106, s. 6.1, he was called Tao Puwak.

58. In MLC-SV1, 47, s. 5 and MLC-LV2, s. 5.3, he is called Yi Peng (Piang) Lak Sai.

59. Moeng Fòng (Pòng), i.e., the Tai Pòng. Fa Kham Kòng was the chieftain of Mubang (Moeng Fòng/Pòng, i.e., Hsaenwi), in today's Hsaenwi-Hsipaw (Sipò), in Burma.

60. According to MLC-LV2, s. 6.3 and Gao Lishi 1984, 107, s. 6.3, Moeng Fòng began to be called Moeng Saenwi because the younger brother of the *cao saenwi fa* of Sipsòng Panna had succeeded to the throne of Moeng Fòng (Pòng). Moeng Fòng (Pòng), in Chinese Mubang 木邦, is known as Hsaenwi in Western literature. This name is derived from the Chinese *xuanwei shi* 宣慰使 (pacification commissioner), which has been rendered into Tai as *saenwi fa*.

61. Moeng Mao Luang, in today's Ruili, in Dehong Autonomous Prefecture, Yunnan, was the Luchuan-Pingmian Pacification Commission of the Ming period. In 1275 AD, the ruler of Moeng Mao Luang was Si Ke Fa 思可發 (Soe Khan Fa, died in 1370), also transliterated derogatorily into Si Ke Fa 死可伐 (lit., "death and can be extirpated"). On the Luchuan-Pingmian Campaign, see Liew 1996.

attack his elder brother. The battle was fought at Moeng Cae (Mengzhe 猛遮).[62] [As Yi Peng Lak Sai] could not gain a victory he withdrew.[63]

6.3 TAO PUWAK PASSES AWAY

Tao Puwak was on the throne fourteen years when he passed away (*hong*) at the age of fifty-two in the *moeng kai* year, CS 649 (Zhiyuan 24, AD 1287) without an heir. This was the sixth generation ruler (sixth ruler of Moeng Lü).

6.4 YI PENG (PIANG) LAK SAI RETURNS TO MOENG LÜ AS THE SEVENTH RULER

{Yi Peng Lak Sai returned to succeed his elder brother to the throne, but died in less than a year, in the *moeng pao* year, CS 639 (AD 1277). This is the sixth generation ruler (seventh ruler of Moeng Lü).}[64]

7. CAO AI (DAO AI 刀愛), R. 1287–1347

7.1 THE EIGHTH RULER ASCENDS THE THRONE

In CS 649, a *moeng kai* year (AD 1287), Cao Ai, the son of Yi [Peng/Piang] Lak Sai, succeeded [his elder uncle] Tao Puwak (sic) as the ruler at the age of twenty. He was on the throne sixty years and passed away (*hong*) at the age of eighty in the *moeng kai* year, CS 709 (Zhizheng 7, AD 1347). This was the seventh generation [the eighth ruler of Moeng Lü].[65]

7.2 CAO AI'S SON

[Cao Ai's] son Cao Khan [Moeng] (Dao Kan) succeeded [his father].[66]

---

62. Moeng Cae is located at the seat of the precious Nanqiao County 南嶠縣 (in today's Moeng Hai), on the west of the Mekong.

63. But according to MLC-LV2, s. 6.2 and Gao Lishi 1984, 107, s. 6.2, it was Moeng Mao Luang that sent troops to attack Chiang Rung, not Yi Peng Lak Sai.

64. The above account is taken from MLC-SV1, 47, s. 7. That Yi Peng Lak Sai returned to Moeng Lü as ruler is confirmed in other Tai Lü sources. See MLC-LV2, s. 7.1; Gao Lishi 1984, 107, s. 6.4; Dao Shuren 1989, 387; Renoo 2001, 37.

65. According to other sources, Yi Peng Lak Sai was the seventh ruler of Moeng Lü (the sixth generation ruler) and Cao Ai was the eighth ruler of Moeng Lü (the seventh generation ruler).

66. In the MSG, MSL, and *Mingshi*, he is known as Dao Kan 刀坎 (Cao Khan Moeng). Dao Kan was first mentioned in Hongwu 15 (1382). In Gao Lishi 1984, 107, s. 9.1 and in MLC-LV2, s. 8.2, he is called Cao Khan Moeng. Li Fuyi might have adjusted his name according to Chinese sources.

8. CAO KHAN MOENG (DAO KAN 刀坎), R. 1347–1391

8.1 THE NINTH RULER ASCENDS THE THRONE

In the *moeng kai* year, CS 709 (1347 AD), Cao Khan [Moeng] succeeded his father Cao Ai to the throne at the age of thirty-nine. Cao Khan [Moeng] was clever and talented.

8.2 CAO KHAN MOENG'S RETREAT TO THE NAM LAM RIVER

When [Cao Khan Moeng] heard that the troops of the Heavenly Court (i.e., Moeng Hò) were approaching, [he] marched [his soldiers] from Chiang Lan to Chiang Rung where he garrisoned. [Thereupon he] declared that he was going to resist the Heavenly Court. Immediately afterwards, the troops of the Heavenly Court arrived, exactly as expected. The forces were quite large.[67] Hence, Cao Khan [Moeng] retreated to Wiang Pha Daeng (lit., "red-cliff city") at Moeng Cae (Mengzhe), but he was still frightened. He retreated further to the hills and following the river Nam Lam he sought refuge around the upper reaches of the river.

8.3 CHINESE TROOPS THREATEN CAO KHAN MOENG

At that time the troops of the Heavenly Court had already deployed all over Moeng Cae. [The Chinese officials] ordered the local people to go to look for Cao Khan [Moeng]. Cao Khan [Moeng] deceived them by saying that Cao Khan [Moeng] had already gone to Moeng Lao (i.e., Lan Sang or Laos). The [officials of] the Heavenly Court replied that if Cao Khan [Moeng] had really moved to Moeng Lao, then Moeng Lü would be deserted and would have fallen into ruin. [The Chinese officials] continued that the troops of the Heavenly Court would absolutely not allow Cao Khan [Moeng] to defy the emperor of the Heavenly Court (i.e., Cao Lum Fa). Whoever dared to resist was destined to be killed; [however], if he would surrender [and pay allegiance to China], the troops of the Heavenly Court would certainly withdraw.

8.4 CAO KHAN MOENG CAPITULATES AND TAKES OATH OF ALLEGIANCE

Consequently, Cao Khan [Moeng] capitulated as he felt that he was unable to repulse [the Chinese troops].[68] He buried stones (*mak hin*)[69] in [three places] in the form of a triangle [as evidence] of taking the oath [of allegiance]: one piece [of stone] was buried

---

67. In the year Hongwu 14 (1381), under the command of Fu Youde 傅友德 (committed suicide in 1394), Lan Yu 藍玉 (executed in 1393), and Mu Ying 沐英 (committed suicide in 1393) the combined Ming forces of 300,000 men marched south to conquer Yunnan, which was pacified in Hongwu 15 (1382). For the conquest of Yunnan, see MSG, ch. 187, 1–2; *Taizu shilu* (Hongwu 15); CHC 7 (1988), 143–46.

68. According to Chinese sources, Dao Kan came to offer his capitulation in Hongwu 15, second month+. The Route Command of the Yuan was reorganised into Cheli Military-cum-Civilian Prefecture and Dao Kan was appointed the tribal prefect of Cheli. See *Taizu shilu*, ch. 143, 2246–47 (Hongwu 15, second month+, *guimao*: 7 April 1382); MSG, ch. 189, 29.

69. In Tai Lü it is *mak hin*. See MLC-LV2, s. 9.4.

at the pass of Khü Wiang in Moeng Cae, one piece was buried by the bank of Nam Ha Nòi (Little Liusha River), located to the east of the fortified town of Moeng Cae,[70] and one piece was buried at Chiang Kham.[71] The stones were one *wa* (fathom) and one *sòk* long. After the great military forces of the Heavenly Court had retreated, Cao Khan [Moeng] then returned to Chiang Lan.[72] At that time [it was] a *tao set* year, CS 744 (i.e., Hongwu 13 (sic), AD 1382).[73]

8.5 CAO KHAN MOENG MARRIES THE LAWA GIRL HÒI SAM CIK

Previously, there was a Lawa (Lua) lass,[74] who found a precious thing called a three-pronged conch shell (*hòi sam cik*).[75] She took it to the market at Chiang Lan. Incidentally Cao Khan [Moeng] was on a tour in town and saw the Lawa lass. He became totally besotted with the girl, married her and made her his queen (*nang tewi*).[76] He loved her very much.

8.6 BIRTH OF TAO SIDA KHAM

However, after a long time the queen still had not given [birth to a baby]. Therefore she told Cao Khan [Moeng]:

> My lord, probably because my parents are living in the hills I have no son. [I] want to ask [my lord] to make a cradle adorned all over with gold and give it to [my] foster-father (i.e., Cao Khan Moeng's father-in-law) to call for the soul of a son [for me].[77]

---

70. Nam Ha Nòi (Ch. Liusha xiaohe 流沙小河) is in Menghai (Moeng Hai) County (previously Nanqian and Fohai).

71. All sources consulted confirm that the third stone or pile of stones was buried at Chiang Kham. The three places where the stones were buried form the shape of a triangle.

72. Chiang Lan is located 3 *li* (c. 1.5 km) to the east of Cheli (Chiang Rung).

73. CS 744 corresponds to AD 1382 and this was Hongwu 15. Yunnan was conquered by the Ming troops under the command of Fu Youde 傅友德 (committed suicide in 1394) and others in Hongwu 15 (1382), not in Hongwu 13 (1380), as indicated by Li Fuyi. According to MSG (ch. 189, 29b), Dao Kan 刀坎, who surrendered in Hongwu 15, was appointed the prefect of Cheli Military-cum-Civilian Prefecture (i.e., Moeng Lü). In the same year, third lunar month, Dao Kan sent his nephew Feng Lu 豐祿 to offer tribute to the Ming court. In Hongwu 17, eighth lunar month (1384) Dao Kan's son, Dao Sifu 刀思拂, paid tribute; consequently in the following month, the Ming court reorganised the prefecture into the military-cum-civilian commission of the *saenwi fa* of Cheli and Dao Kan was appointed the *saenwi fa*.

74. See MLC-LV2, s. 9.5 and Gao Lishi 1984, 107, s. 9.5. She possibly belonged to the Ji-nuo tribe 基諾族.

75. See MLC-LV2, s. 9.5.

76. Ditto.

77. By the tradition of Lawa (Lua) who lived in the hills, they had to make a cradle adorned all over with gold to seek the soul of a son. See MLC-LV2, s. 9.5–6 and Gao Lishi 1984, 107, s. 9.6.

Cao Khan [Moeng] followed her request and had a cradle that was covered completely with gold made promptly. It was given to her to bring to Ban Dòi (lit., "hill village"), where his parents-in-law were living, to pray for [the soul of] a son. Not long after, she indeed gave birth to a very beautiful son and hence he was named Tao Sida Kham (Dao Xianda).

8.7 THE LAWA QUEEN LOSES HER THREE-PRONGED CONCH SHELL

One day when the queen went to a balcony [to warm herself in the sun][78] and incidentally she took out the three-pronged conch shell (*hòi sam cik*). Suddenly it fell from her hands downstairs. A pig with a spotted forehead, which happened to pass by, swallowed the three-pronged conch shell.[79] Since then Cao Khan [Moeng] found his queen (Nang Lawa)[80] disgusting.

8.8 THE LAWA QUEEN AND HER SON ARE SENT BACK TO BAN DÒI

[Cao Khan Moeng] sent her back to Ban Dòi to live with his parents-in-law and told the villagers to look after his son well. They were to live by cultivating the hill lands. The villagers were exempted from paying tribute and performing miscellaneous labour services. However, they were not allowed to leave the hills. Not until Tao Sida Kham was five years old did his father bring him back to live with him.[81]

8.9 THE THREE SONS OF CAO KHAN MOENG

Cao Khan [Moeng] had three sons: The eldest, Tao Sida Kham, was invested as crown prince; the second son Tao Kumman was invested as the lord of Na Mün Long.[82] The younger brother of Tao Kumman, Peo (Piao) Fai Fa,[83] was invested the lord of Na Saen at Chiang Lan.[84]

---

78. According to MLC-LV2, s. 9.7, Dao Shuren 1989, 391, and Renoo 2001, 51, she went to the balcony to warm herself in the sun.

79. According MLC-LV2, s. 9.7, a spotted neck pig bit and broke it into pieces.

80. See ibid.

81. See MLC-LV2, s. 9.7 and Gao Lishi 1984, 108, s. 9.7.

82. Na Mün Long (lit., "ten thousand rice fields") is located in Moeng Cae.

83. According to Dao Shuren 1989, 226, Peo (Piao) Fai Fa means "Peo of the heavenly fire" (*Tianhuo Biao* 天火彪).

84. According to MSG (ch. 189, 29b–30a), Dao Kan 刀坎 (Cao Khan Moeng) had another son called Dao Sifu 刀思拂 (Cao Soe Fa), whom he sent to offer tribute to the Ming court in Hongwu 17, seventh month (1384). Dao Xianda 刀暹荅 (Tao Sida Kham) had another younger brother called Dao San Pala 刀三怕剌 (Tao Sam Phaya), who was sent to pay tribute to the Ming court in Hongwu 24 (1391). In Hongwu 28 (1395), Dao Xianda sent another younger brother, Dao Wu 刀吾 (Tao Ut), to the Ming court to express thanks and offer tribute. In Yongle 1 (1403), Dao Xianda sent another younger brother called Dao La 刀臘 to offer tribute to the Ming court. Thus Dao Kan had more than three sons—at least seven—unless there was a misunderstanding between the Tai Lü envoys and the Ming court.

8.10 CAO KHAN MOENG PASSES AWAY

As Cao Khan [Moeng] grew older he gradually felt that he could no longer cope with warfare and dealing with the local affairs. Later he passed away in the *hong met* year, CS 753 (Hongwu 24, AD 1391)[85] at the age of eighty-three after being on the throne forty-four years. He was the eighth generation (the ninth ruler of Moeng Lü).[86]

9. TAO SIDA KHAM (DAO XIANDA 刀暹答), R. 1391–1413

9.1 THE TENTH RULER MARRIES A PRINCESS OF MOENG KHÜN

Tao Sida Kham succeeded his father to the throne in the *hong met* year, CS 753 (AD 1391).[87] Phaya [Moeng] Khün—the lord of Moeng Khün—[88] by the name of Ai Òn[89] married his younger sister Nang Pòng Samoe[90] to [the *suenwi fa*] Tao Sida Kham as his queen.

9.2 TAO SIDA KHAM'S CHILDREN

The queen had a son, called Tao Kü Moeng, and a daughter, called Nang Lun Koei.[91] Tao Sida Kham had another son called Tao Kham Daeng (probably he was Dao Dian, see

---

85. According to MSG, Dao Xianda (Tao Sida Kham) succeeded his father in the year Hongwu 24 (AD 1391). The last time Dao Kan (Cao Khan Moeng) offered tribute to China was in 1387. See *Taizu shilu*, ch. 183, 2756 (Hongwu 20, seventh month, *bingxu*: 22 August 1387). Hence Dao Kan passed away between 1387 and 1391, probably in CS 753 (1391). However, other translated Tai Lü sources give much earlier years. Most likely Li Fuyi has changed the year given in the Tai Lü manuscript to accommodate the year given in contemporary Chinese sources. See MSG (ch. 189, 29) taken from the *Taizu shilu*, ch. 213, 3148 (Hongwu 24, tenth month, *jiwei* day: 2 November 1391).

86. Although the year in which Cao Khan Moeng was enthroned and the year he passed away given in different sources are controversial, all sources consulted confirm that he surrendered under the military forces of China and he had three sons.

87. According to MSG, Tao Sida Kham succeeded his father Dao Kan (Cao Khan Moeng) in Hongwu 24 (1391) and he sent his younger brother Dao San Pala (Tao Sam Phaya) to offer tribute to China. See MSG, ch. 189, 29a. However, the Veritable Records mentions that Tao Sida Kham sent his younger brother to offer tribute, and that he was Dao Kan's son. See *Taizu shilu*, ch. 213, 3148 (Hongwu 24, tenth month, *jiwei* day: 2 November 1391). This is the first time Tao Sida Kham is mentioned in contemporary Chinese sources. Most probably Li Fuyi (MLC-LV1) has adjusted the year given in the Tai Lü manuscript, on which his translation is based, to correspond with the year recorded in Chinese sources.

88. This insertion should be ascribed to Li Fuyi (MLC-LV1, 7). Phaya Moeng Khün is the title of the lord of Moeng Khün (Chiang Tung).

89. In MLC-LV2, s. 10.2 and Gao Lishi 1984, 108, he was Phaya Moeng Khün, called Òn Ai.

90. According MLC-LV2, s. 10.2; Gao Lishi 1984, 108; and Dao Shuren 1989, 227, she was called Nang Samoe.

91. Nang Lun Koei later married his cousin Soe Long Fa (Süa Luang Fa), see s. 9.9 below.

below)[92] who was invested as the lord of Na Mün Paen. He had another son called [Tao] Saen Nang who was invested as the lord of Moeng Hing (Mengling 猛嶺, i.e., Puteng).[93]

9.3 TAO KUMMAN, THE LORD OF NA MÜN LONG (LUANG)

Tao Kumman, the younger brother of Tao Sida Kham, had one son,[94] who inherited the principality of Na Mün Long (Luang)[95] after the death of Tao Kumman.[96]

9.4 PEO FAI FA, HIS MOENG LAEM CONSORT, AND THEIR THREE SONS

His third younger brother, Peo (Piao) Fai Fa, took Nang Paeng Kham Daeng, who was the daughter of Cao Moeng Laem, Phaya Sòng Fa (Ba Shuang Fa),[97] as his consort. Nang Paeng Kham Daeng bore Peo Fai Fa three sons: The eldest son was called Daet Ham Ya [Pò Tai],[98] who, after the death of Peo Fai Fa, inherited his father's principality in Na Saen at Chiang Lan. The second son, called Ngei Ka,[99] died young. The third son was named Soe Long Fa (or Süa Luang Fa).[100]

92. This parenthesis should be ascribed to Li Fuyi. See MLC-LV1, 7. The man called Dao Dian in contemporary Chinese sources was probably Tao Kham Tet (Tiat). See below, s. 9.5.

93. Most probably Tao Sida Kham had three sons: Tao Kü Moeng, Tao Kham Tet, and Tao Saen Nang (the lord of Meng Hing).

94. According to MLC-LV2, s. 11.2 and Gao Lishi 1984, 108, Tao Kumman had two sons, namely Cao Ai and Cao Yi.

95. Na Mün Long (lit., "ten thousand large rice fields"), located in Moeng Cae, was later called Si Mün Na Mün Long (i.e., forty thousand large rice fields) of Moeng Cae, which means extensive lands. See Dao Shuren 1989, 232.

96. According to MLC-LV1, Tao Kumman did not succeed his elder brother, Tao Sida Kham, to the throne. However, in other sources Tao Kumman was on the throne about a year before being ousted by his nephew, Tao Kham Tet (Tiat).

97. Could this Cao Moeng Laem, called Phaya Sòng Fa, be the same Cao Moeng Laem, called Phaya Hom Fa or Phaya Phai Hom Fa? See below MLC-LV1, 9, s. 11.3 and s. 11.4.

98. According to MLC-LV2, s. 10.4; Gao Lishi 1984, 108; and Dao Shuren 1989, 227, he was called Daet Ham Ya Pò Tai, which, according to Dao Shuren, means "bright sun shining on grassland".

99. According to the MLC-LV2, s. 10.4; Gao Lishi 1984, 108; and Dao Shuren 1989, 227, he was called Thaloem Ka, which, according to Dao Shuren, means "glint of a sword".

100. All the *cao phaendin* of Moeng Lü (Sipsòng Panna) were addressed as Phaya, Tao, or Cao, except Soe Long Fa. Soe Long Fa's name is rather similar to that of the king of Moeng Mao. *Soe* (Th. *süa*) means "tiger"; *fa* (*pha*) means "sky". He was the contemporary of Si Ren Fa (Soe Ngam Pha, d. 1446) and Si Ji Fa (Soe Ki Pha, d. 1454). Soe Long Fa's mother was the princess of Moeng Laem and the ruler of Moeng Laem was related to the ruling house of Moeng Mao. Soe Long Fa was probably related to the rulers of Moeng Mao Luang.

9.5 TAO KHAM TET (TIAT) AND HIS UNKNOWN SON

Tao Kham Tet (Tiat) (Dao Dian),[101] the second son of Tao Sida Kham, had a son. As he was good-for-nothing, he had no name (was unknown).

9.6 TAO SAEN NANG AND HIS TWO SONS

The third son [of Tao Sida Kham], [Tao] Saen Nang, had two sons: the elder was named Cao Ai and the second called Cao Yi.[102] The two brothers were both enfeoffed the principality of Moeng Hing (Mengling 猛嶺).[103]

9.7 APPOINTING SOE LONG FA THE LORD OF MOENG PHONG

Soe Long Fa, the third son of Peo Fai Fa, was intelligent, resourceful, and brave. Tao Sida Kham had adopted him when he was young and brought him up as his own son. [He] was granted Moeng Phong (Mengpeng 猛捧)[104] as his principality[105] and appointed military commander,[106] concurrently entrusted with the task of managing all the local affairs.

9.8 SOE LONG FA'S AFFAIR WITH TAO SIDA KHAM'S CONCUBINE

Later, because [Soe Long Fa] had a licentious affair with a [lesser] consort (*fei* 妃) of Tao Sida Kham, he was banished as [the affair] was discovered by Tao Sida Kham. After beging expelled he roamed about without anyone to turn to. He earned his living as a hawker for three years.[107]

---

101. Tao Kham Tet (Tiat) is most probably another name for Tao Kham Daeng. According to contemporary Chinese sources, Tao Sida Kham (Dao Xianda) sent his son Dao Dian (sinicised name of Tao Kham Tet) to the National University (*guozi jian*) in Nanjing as hostage after the Moeng Lü frontier guards had prevented the natives of Yuanjiang (Moeng Cung) from entering Moeng Lü. The natives were transporting military provisions while Tao Sida Kham was fighting against Lan Na. For more details see MSG, ch. 189, 30b; *Taizong shilu*, ch. 53, 793–94 (Yongle 4, fourth month, *wuyin* day: 6 May 1406).

102. According to MLC-LV2, s. 11.2; Gao Lishi 1984, 108; and Dao Shuren 1989, 228, Cao Ai and Cao Yi, the two lords of Moeng Hing, were the sons of Tao Kumman. In this case Cao Ai and Cai Yi were Tao Saen Nang's cousins.

103. Moeng Hing (Mengling, in Chinese, Puwen 普文, previously Puteng 普騰), is located between Chiang Rung and Simao 思茅 (Moeng La).

104. Located in the former Zhenyue County 鎮越縣, now Mengla County 猛臘縣, to the east of the Mekong.

105. This means Soe Long Fa was invested as the lord (or governor) of Moeng Phong.

106. *Cao pon soek* (Tr. เจ้าพลเสิก). Both Li Fuyi (MLC-LV1, 7) and Gao Lishi 1984, 108, render it as *dai bingguan* 帶兵官 (military commander). In MLC-LV2, s. 11.3, it is *cao pon soek* (military commander).

107. Similar accounts are given in MLC-LV2, s. 11.3; and Gao Lishi 1984, 108. But according to Dao Shuren 1989, 227–28, Soe Long Fa was thrown out of the palace and banished to a small remote village. He received an order that for three years he was only allowed to earn his living as a peddler and was not allowed to take other jobs.

9.9 SOE LONG FA MARRIES NANG LUN KOEI

Thereafter, because of lack of people to handle the administration of the local affairs, Tao Sida Kham finally called him back and married his daughter Nang Lun Koei[108] to him. Moreover, Moeng Hun (Menghun), Moeng Hai (Menghai), etc., [a total of] three *panna*,[109] were conferred on him as his principality.[110] He was, as before, appointed military commander. His maternal grandparents were then living in the distant Moeng Laem.

9.10 SOE LONG FA'S JUST RULE

Soe Long Fa managed matters concerning local development and passing sentences on criminals, as well as those relating to the people cultivating land, systematically and fairly. Therefore, peace prevailed in the land and there was no hardship caused by war. The people were happy and enthusiastic. The lords (*tao phaya*) from various places (*müang*)[111] came to offer tribute [and submission]. The domain [of Moeng Lü] expanded to Moeng Maen [Nao].[112]

9.11 TAO SIDA KHAM PASSES AWAY

Tao Sida Kham was on the throne twenty-two years and passed away (*hong*) at the age of sixty-two in CS 775, a *ka sai* year (Yongle 11, AD 1413).[113] He was the ninth generation [the tenth ruler of Moeng Lü].[114]

---

108. According to MLC-LV2, s. 11.4, she was the daughter of the princess of Chiang Tung.

109. A similar account is recorded in MLC-LV2, s. 11.4 and in Gao Lishi 1984, 108. According to Dao Shuren 1989, 228, the three *panna* were Moeng Hun, Moeng Hai, and Moeng Ngat.

110. This means Soe Long Fa, the adopted son and son-in-law of Tao Sida Kham, was the ruler or governor of the three *panna*.

111. According to MLC-LV2, s. 11.5, they were *tao phaya*, i.e., provincial rulers.

112. Moeng Maen is the Tai name of the Chinese town of Puer 普 洱, which was previously called Ninger 寧 洱, located c. 60 km north of Simao (Moeng La). It corresponds to the present-day autonomous county of Puer for the Hani and the Yi nationalities.

113. In 1413, the emperor sent palace eunuch Hong Zaisheng 洪 仔 生 to bring an imperial decree to Dao Xianda (i.e., Tao Sida Kham). Before the arrival [of the imperial envoy] Dao Xianda had already passed away. See MSG, ch. 189, 31; *Taizong shilu*, ch. 145, 1717 (Yongle 11, eleventh month, *wuxu* day: 15 December 1413). According to MLC-LV2 and Gao Lishi 1984, 108, Tao Sida Kham passed away in CS 793 (i.e., AD 1430; Xuande 5 of the Ming period). This is a piece of evidence showing that Li Fuyi must have altered the dates of the Tai Lü manuscripts on which his translation of *Leshi* is based.

114. In MSG several important events that took place during the reign of Dao Xianda (i.e., Tao Sida Kham) are recorded, such as Moeng Lü requested the Ming court to send troops to attack Lan Na, the Marquis of Pacifying the West, Mu Sheng 沐 晟, commanded troops, reinforced by the troops of Moeng Lü and Hsaenwi, to attack Lan Na; and Dao Xianda repeatedly sent his younger brothers and sons to offer tribute to the Ming court, and so forth. See MSG, ch. 189, 29a–31b (Liew-Herres 2003b).

10. TAO KÜ MOENG (DAO GENGMENG 刀更孟), R. 1413–1415

10.1 THE ELEVENTH RULER AND HIS QUEEN NANG AEN KÒM

In the year CS 775 (AD 1413), Tao Kü Moeng proclaimed himself (*zili*)[115] as ruler and succeeded his father [to the throne as *saenwi fa*].[116] He married the daughter of Tao Hin Pan, named Nang Aen Kòm, and made her his queen consort.

10.2 TAO KÜ MOENG'S THREE SONS

The queen bore three sons: the eldest was named Tao Bakòng (Dao Bagong 刀霸供), the second son was named Tao Sòng Moeng (Dao Shuangmeng 刀雙孟), and the third son was named [Tao] Sam Pò Lütai (San Bao Lidai 三寶歷代).[117]

10.3 THE RULER'S CRUELTY

Tao Kü Moeng was a cruel and unscrupulous ruler. He favoured strange punishments and invented the methods of crushing [criminals] with a mangle,[118] hanging criminals on a cowherd's pole by an iron hook into the spine; and slicing off a piece of flesh per day, a punishment of slow dismemberment of prolonged death. When someone committed a crime, his siblings and relatives would be incriminated. He neither followed the ancestral injunctions nor listened to the advice of [his cousin] Soe Long Fa. As Soe Long Fa was afraid that he would be the [next] victim, he sought refuge at Ban Ca in Moeng Hun.[119]

---

115. Li Fuyi uses the term *zili* 自立 (proclaiming oneself) implying that there was an internal fight for the throne in the ruling house. According to other Tai Lü manuscripts, after the death of Tao Sida Kham his younger brother Tao Kumman, instead of his son Tao Kü Moeng, ascended the throne of *cao phaendin/saenwi fa* and reigned about three years. See MLC-SV1, 49; MLC-LV2, s. 11.1; Gao Lishi 1984, 108; Dao Shuren 1989, 228. According to Li Fuyi (MLC-SV1), Tao Kumman was deposed by his nephew Tao Kham Tet. Tao Kham Tet was on the throne only a year before he was attacked by his cousin Soe Long Fa.

116. In 1413, [...] On arrival [of the imperial envoy] Dao Xianda (Tao Sida Kham) had passed away and his eldest son Dao Gengmeng (Tao Kü Moeng) proclaimed himself [ruler]. He, who was arrogant and cruel, could not gain the hearts of his people. He died not long thereafter. See MSG, ch. 189, 31; *Taizong shilu*, ch. 145, 1717 (Yongle 11, eleventh month, *wuxu* day: 15 December 1413); Liew-Herres 2003b.

117. In Li Fuyi's *Leshi* the transcriptions of these names follow exactly those of the Chinese sources: MSL, MSG, *Mingshi*, etc. The later translators, such as Gao Lishi 1984, Dao Shuren 1989, and others create their own transcriptions.

118. According to MLC-LV2, s. 12.3, this was a pressing tool (mangle); according to Dao Shuren 1989, 229, it was a sugarcane mangle.

119. According to Li Fuyi (MLC-LV1, index, 5), Ban Ca is in Moeng Hun, previously Fohai County 佛海縣. The village is in the south of today's Menghai County (Moeng Hai). According to MLC-LV2, s. 12.4 and Gao Lishi 1984, 109, Soe Long Fa sought refuge in Moeng Cae and Moeng Hun.

10.4 DEPORTING TAO KÜ MOENG TO CHIANG FÒNG

In the third year of the reign of Tao Kü Moeng (CS 777, Yongle 13, AD 1415), Tao Kham Tet (Dao Dian 刀典), afraid that he would be killed by him (his elder brother Tao Kü Moeng) for no reason, revolted and banished him to Chiang Fòng (Jingfeng 景逢)—a distant land at the edge of the world.[120]

10.5 TAO KÜ MOENG'S VIOLENT DEATH AT MOENG KHÒN

The people of Chiang Fòng, afraid that on his arrival the inhabitants would flee in all directions, had a secret discussion. They deceived him by saying that he would merely be resettled at Moeng Nun (Menglun 猛崙).[121] They forced Tao Kü Moeng on to the back of an elephant and transported him to Moeng Khòn (Mengkuan 猛寬),[122] where he was strangled to death. After the death of Tao Kü Moeng, he became the deity of the *müang* (*soe moeng* or *phi moeng*)[123] and so until the present day, oblations have to be offered to him yearly. It was in CS 777, a *dap met* year (AD 1415). He was the tenth generation [the eleventh ruler of Moeng Lü].

11. TAO SÒNG MOENG (DAO SHUANGMENG 刀雙孟) AND TAO KHAM TET (DAO DIAN 刀典), R. 1415–1428[124]

11.1 THE TWELFTH AND THIRTEENTH RULERS

After Tao Kü Moeng had been banished and killed, [his] second son Tao Sòng Moeng was enthroned.[125] Meanwhile [his] eldest son Tao Bakòng had already taken up his principality (*shiyi*) in Moeng Phong (Mengpeng 猛捧)[126] for three years when he heard

120. This phrase "a distant land at the edge of the world" given in parenthesis in MLC-LV1, 8, should be ascribed to Li Fuyi (MLC-LV1). According to MLC-LV2, s. 12.5, Tao Kü Moeng was ousted and sent by Tao Kham Tet to live in Fak Thoe and then to Chiang Fòng, in today's Ban Chiang Pòm. According to Gao Lishi 1984, 109, Tao Kham Tet ousted Tao Kü Moeng and sent him to live in Ban Chiang Pòm in Chiang Rung.

121. Also known as Xiao Menglun 小猛崙 (Lesser Moeng Nun), now a part of Zhenyue County. According to Dao and Kang 1989b, 328, in the year CS 785 (AD 1433), Tao Kham Tet banished Tao Kü Moeng to Fade 法德 (in lower Ban Fa 曼法 of Moeng Ham 猛罕) and nominated Tao Sòng Moeng, the four-year-old second son of Tao Kü Moeng, to succeed his father.

122. In the southeast of Ganlanba 橄欖壩 (i.e., Moeng Ham), south of Chiang Rung.

123. He became a *phi moeng* after his death. See MLC-LV2, s. 12.6; Gao Lishi 1984, 109.

124. In the original subheading of Li Fuyi (MLC-LV1), this is just Dao Dian 刀典 (Tao Kham Tet). Tao Sòng Moeng is added, albeit he was on the throne less than three months.

125. According to MLC-LV2, s. 13.1 and Gao Lishi 1984, 109, Tao Sòng Moeng was thirteen years old when he succeeded his father to the throne.

126. This means Tao Bakòng was the lord/governor of Moeng Phong. Moeng Phong is located c. 36 km west of Moeng La and on the east bank of the Mekong.

that Tao Sòng Moeng had been enthroned. Tao Bakòng and his mother had a private discussion and said:

> According to the right [of primogeniture], the eldest son should succeed [his father]. Tao Bakòng is the elder. But for what reason, instead of Tao Bakòng, has Tao Sòng Moeng been enthroned [as ruler]?

[They] were upset.

11.2 TAO KHAM TET USURPS HIS NEPHEW'S THRONE

Tao Sòng Moeng was enthroned in [his elder brother's] stead, [but was on the throne for only] two months and fifteen days before being ousted by [his uncle] Tao Kham Tet (Tiat).[127] As the people found what Tao Kham Tet had done unjust, they drove him away not long afterwards.

11.3 FRATRICIDAL WAR BETWEEN THE TWO COUSINS TAO KHAM TET AND SOE LONG FA

Tao Kham Tet (Tiat) sought support from Soe Long Fa. [But] Soe Long Fa said:

> Until now nobody has informed me about the matter concerning dethroning [Tao Sòng Moeng and Tao Bakòng] and enthroning [Tao Kham Tet]. When my father, the king (i.e., Tao Sida Kham), was on the throne, all local matters were placed under my administration.[128] To my astonishment, immediately after the death of my father, the king, you guys have created a state of confusion in the land. It is as dark as if there were no sun in the sky (i.e., lawlessness). Moreover, [you guys] put pressure on me, but I cannot be partial to the left or to the right.[129]

127. According to MLC-LV2, s. 13.2 and Gao Lishi 1984, 109, s. 13.2, Tao Sòng Moeng had succeeded to the throne three months and fifteen days before Tao Bakòng returned to Chiang Rung. However, Tao Sòng Moeng is mentioned in contemporary Ming sources (i.e., MSL) between 22 December 1416 and 22 January 1429, as still alive. During those thirteen years the nephew of Tao Sida Kham, namely Soe Long Fa (rendered into Chinese as Dao Long or Dao Si Long), and the grandson of Tao Sida Kham, namely Tao Sòng Moeng, fought against each other. According to a memorial of Mu Sheng (1368–1439) recorded on 1 August 1431 (Xuande 6, sixth month, *bingchen* day), both Dao Long and Tao Sòng Moeng had passed away, and Tao Bakòng ascended to the throne. Tao Bakòng's name appears in contemporary Ming sources between 1 August 1431 and 14 November 1434 (Xuande 9, tenth month, *dingsi* day). See Liew-Herres 2003b.

128. Soe Long Fa was adopted by his uncle Tao Sida Kham when he was young. Later he married Tao Sida Kham's daughter, Nang Lun Koei. Soe Long Fa, being Tao Sida Kham's adopted son and son-in-law, was aiming for the throne.

129. This implies that he could not screen his cousin (Tao Kham Tet) or his nephews (Tao Bakòng and Tao Sòng Moeng). In MLC-LV2, s.15.2, the last sentence says: "[...] and you want me to go and pay you homage. Even after my death, my spirit (*preta*) would not go to pay you homage." The wording in Gao Lishi 1984, 109 (s. 15.2), is slightly different: "[You] intend to proclaim yourself king

Tao Kham Tet was dissatisfied. Eventually, he went to the river yonder (*jiang wai*)[130] to muster soldiers and men (*bing ding*) to launch an attack on Soe Long Fa.[131]

11.4 SOE LONG FA SEEKS MILITARY SUPPORT FROM CAO MOENG LAEM

During this time, Soe Long Fa was still stationed at Ban Ca (Manjie 蠻結) of Moeng Hun (Menghun 猛湣)[132] and took no heed of it. He declared that he was going to lie down and wait for the sword to come (i.e., wait for his cousin's attack);[133] but on the other hand he sought help from his maternal grandparents (sic) in Moeng Laem, [Phaya Phai Hom Fa].[134] Consequently, the lord of Moeng Laem, Phaya [Phai] Hom Fa, sent his younger brother, called Kham Ham Fa,[135] [to rescue his grandson]. [Kham Ham Fa] commanded the troops of Moeng Laem and marched to [Moeng Hun] to reinforce [Soe Long Fa].

11.5 TAO KHAM TET'S DEFEAT AT MOENG HUN

In CS 790, a *poek san* year (Xuande 3, AD 1428), they fought at Moeng Hun.[136] Defeated, Tao Kham Tet fled to the couch grass (*mao cao*)[137] in the field. Kham Ham Fa was wounded by seven arrows. Soe Long Fa captured one elephant and pursued [the enemy] to Chiang Lan (Jinglan 景蘭).[138] Consequently, all the places (i.e., *müang* and *ban*) capitulated. Tao

---

and succeed to the throne; yet you want my support and me to go to pay you homage. [You indulge yourself] in vain hope."

130. Here Li Fuyi (MLC-LV1, 9) explains in parenthesis that this refers to the region to the east of the Mekong River, which is known as "within the river" (*jiang nei* 江内).

131. According to MLC-LV2, s. 15.3 and Gao Lishi 1984, 109, Tao Kham Tet rallied the *cao mòm* of the various *müang* [along the banks of the] Mekong [and told them to send troops] to attack Ban Ca at Moeng Hun.

132. Moeng Hun, in modern Menghai County, previously known as Fohai County 佛海.

133. Li Fuyi (MLC-LV1, 9), translated it into *wo dai dao zhi* 臥待刀至 (lit., "lie down to wait for the sword"); whereas Gao Lishi 1984, 109, s. 15.3, translated it into *zuo yi dai bi* 坐以待斃 (sit down to wait for the death). In MLC-LV2, s.15.3, it says, "Naturally Soe Long Fa would not just sit and wait for the sword".

134. The same is given in Dao and Kang 1989b, 329. But the maternal grandfather of Soe Long Fa was Cao Moeng Laem, called Phaya Sòng Fa. See above MLC-LV1, 7, s. 9.4; Dao and Kang 1989b, 327; MLC-LV2, s. 10.4; Gao Lishi 1984, 108 (s. 10.4). According to MLC-LV2, s. 15.3 and Gao Lishi 1984, 109 (s. 15.3), Soe Long Fa sought help from his father-in-law Cao Moeng Laem, Phaya Phai Hom Fa.

135. He later became the husband of Soe Long Fa's eldest daughter Nang O (Ua) Ming Khai Foei. See below s. 12.1.

136. The battle was fought at Hae Na Kha, according to MLC-LV2, s. 15.4, and Gao Lishi 1984, 109 (s. 15.4).

137. In Malay it is *lalang* grass.

138. Located 3 *li* (c. 1 ½ km) to the east of Cheli (Chiang Rung).

Kham Tet fled to a hillock in Chiang Ha.[139] This place was thus known as *Còm Süa* by the people.

11.6 TAO KHAM TET FLEES WITH SEAL AND DIES

Not long after, [Tao Kham Tet] took the golden seal [adorned] with a tiger head and fled for the Heavenly Court (i.e., Cao Lum Fa).[140] En route he stopped at Moeng Nam Thai Fan (Pan), where he died.[141] Tao Kham Tet was on the throne eleven years.[142] He was the eleventh generation (sic) tenth generation [the thirteenth ruler of Moeng Lü].

12. SOE LONG FA (SHE LONG FA 奢隴法), R. 1428–1457, AND TAO PHASAENG (DAO BAXIAN 刀霸羨), R. 1457[143]

12.1 THE FOURTEENTH RULER AND HIS SON-IN-LAW KHAM HAM FA FROM MOENG LAEM

Soe Long Fa[144] ascended the throne in CS 790, the *poek san* year (AD 1428). When Kham Ham Fa[145] was about to withdraw to Moeng Laem, Soe Long Fa said:

> In this military campaign you have gained more merit. Moeng Laem is just a small land. The domain of Moeng Lü[146] is several times larger than Moeng Laem.

Hence [Soe Long Fa] bestowed Na Mün Long[147] on Kham Ham Fa to be his principality

139. Located to the south of Cheli (Chiang Rung).

140. In practice he could have only fled to Simao (Moeng La) or at the farthest Kunming (Moeng Sae Luang), where he had to wait for the approval of the Chinese authorities and be escorted to the Ming capital, then in Beijing.

141. According to Li Fuyi (1983a, 11 and 87), Moeng Nam Thai in Tai means Nanjing (1368–1421), the southern capital of the Ming dynasty. But according to MLC-SV1, 49, s. 12, and Dao Shuren 1989, 231, Tao Kham Tet died at Nam Ngai Sai Kham (lit., "golden sand river" or the Irrawaddy?). According to MLC-LV2, s. 15.5 and Gao Lishi 1984, 109, s. 15.1., he died by the banks of the Nam Thai River.

142. According to the MLC-LV2, s. 15.1, Tao Kham Tet (Tiat) reigned only three years.

143. The original subheading in Li Fuyi (MLC-LV1, 9) gives only Soe Long Fa. Tao Phasaeng succeeded Soe Long Fa and reigned for two months. The subheading is revised to reflect this.

144. Soe Long Fa was the third son of Peo Fai Fa, thus was Tao Sida Kham's nephew. His mother was the princess of Moeng Laem, Nang Paeng Kham Daeng. Soe Long Fa was probably Dao Long (Tao Long) 刀弄 or Dao Si Long 刀思弄 (Tao Soe Long), mentioned in the Ming sources

145. Kham Ham Fa was the younger brother of the ruler of Moeng Laem, Phaya Phai Hom Fa.

146. In MLC-LV2, s. 16.2 it is Moeng Lü *saenwi fa*.

147. According to MLC-LV2, s. 16.2 and Gao Lishi 1984, 110, s. 16.2, *na mün luang (long)* means a large piece of rice fields of ten thousand units in size.

and married his [eldest] daughter Nang O (Ua) Ming Khai Foei to him. Kham Ham Fa then stayed [in Moeng Lü].

12.2 SOE LONG FA MARRIES NANG AEN KÒM; THE FATE OF HER THREE SONS

Soe Long Fa took the mother of Tao Bakòng and Tao Sòng Moeng, called Nang Aen Kòm,[148] as his consort, but soon promoted her to be the queen (*nang tewi* or *nang moeng*). As the two brothers, Tao Bakòng and Tao Sòng Moeng, were afraid that perhaps the people would support Soe Long Fa in harming them, they boarded a [bamboo] raft and fled down the Mekong River. At that time Tao Sam Pò Lütai was still young.[149] Soe Long Fa wanted to kill him, but his mother, Nang Aen Kòm, protested and said:

> My two elder sons have been murdered.[150] My present situation is indeed extremely sad. If [Your Lord] must kill all the brothers, then I am no longer willing to be [your] queen. I will use a sharp knife to poke into my throat and kill myself. It would be better to die than to live.[151]

As a result, Tao Sam Pò Lütai's life was spared.

12.3 SOE LONG FA RANSOMS THE GOLDEN SEAL

The golden seal [adorned] with a tiger head was taken away by Tao Kham Tet [and brought] to Nam Thai Fan (Pan).[152] The emperor of the Heavenly Court (i.e., Cao Lum

148. Soe Long Fa had at least three wives. He first married his cousin Nang Lun Koei and later married his deceased cousin Tao Kü Moeng's wife Nang Aen Kòm, probably to strengthen his claim to the throne. According to MLC-LV2, s. 15.3 and Gao Lishi 1984, 109 (s. 15.3), he had a father-in-law in Moeng Laem, Cao Moeng Laem, Phaya Phai Hom Fa. So he must have a princess of Moeng Laem as his wife. Nang Aen Kòm, daughter of Tao Hin Pan, was the queen of Tao Kü Moeng (r. 1413–1415). According to *Yingzong shilu* (ch. 292; Tianshun 2, sixth month, *renshen* day: 26 July 1458), after the death of Tao Kü Moeng, his wife remarried the ruler of Cheli, Dao Si Long 刀思弄 (Tao Soe Long, viz. Soe Long Fa). After the death of Dao Si Long, his son Tao Phasaeng succeeded him to the post. Hence, Dao Si Long, not Dao Long, was probably Soe Long Fa. See Liew-Herres 2003b.

149. Acording to MLC-LV2, s. 16.11 and Gao Lishi 1984, 110 (s. 16.11), he was just a toddler.

150. The fates of the two brothers given in various sources vary slightly. Tao Bakòng (age nineteen) and Tao Sòng Moeng (age sixteen) were sent by his uncle-cum-stepfather into exile for misconduct including stealing cows. They were put on bamboo rafts together with fifteen young male attendants (*bao tai*) and twelve young male serfs (*bao kha*) and sailed down the Mekong. Later the elder brother founded Chiang Khaeng and the rest of his followers many villages. See MLC-LV2, s. 16.4–16.10; Gao Lishi 1984, 110 (s. 16.4–16.10); Dao Shuren 1989, 230–31. For the founding of Chiang Khaeng, see Grabowsky 2003b. According to contemporary Chinese sources the two brothers were not murdered. They were actually appointed *saenwi fa* by the Ming court. See Liew-Herres 2003b.

151. MLC-LV2, s.16.11 varies slightly: "My two sons have been sent away by you on a raft. It is like [you] have killed them. [...] Death would be more dignified than staying alive."

152. According to MLC-LV2, s. 16.12, it is Nam Ngai Sai Kham. But in the same chronicle, s. 15.5, it is Nam Thai Fan.

Fa) ordered Soe Long Fa to come and ransom it. Hence, Soe Long Fa presented one *saen* of gold and one *saen* of silver[153] to the emperor in exchange [for the seal and thus the right] to defend (sic) (i.e., rule) the land [of Moeng Lü].[154]

12.4 KHAM HAM FA LEAVES NA MÜN LONG FOR MOENG CAE

Kham Ham Fa [of Moeng Laem] did not live in Na Mün Long very long before he abandoned the land. On the pretext of wanting to be near Moeng Laem, he moved to Moeng Cae and took Moeng Cae as his principality. He constructed a Buddhist temple and a pagoda on the summit of Moeng Cae and called it hill fort (i.e., Mòn Wiang). He called himself Mün Long Saen Lò.

12.5 THE NINE SONS OF SOE LONG FA

Soe Long Fa had nine sons: the eldest [son] Tao Phasaeng was the crown prince; the second [son] Tao Còm Pha[155] was granted Moeng Long as his principality; the third son Tao Saeo [was conferred the lord of Na Mün Long]; the fourth son Tao Yòt [was conferred the lord of Müang Luang Nam Tha (in Laos)]; the fifth son Tao Kham [was conferred the lord of Moeng U-Nüa (in Laos)], and the sixth son Tao Ut was granted Moeng Hun as his principality; the seventh son Tao Som (namely Tao Cet)[156] was granted Moeng Ngat and Moeng Khang as his principality. The above seven sons were born to the same mother. The eighth son Tao Fa Nòi [was conferred the lord of Na Mün Long][157] and the ninth son Tao Sòt Sòi [was conferred the lord of Chiang Lu].

12.6 SOE LONG FA'S SIX DAUGHTERS AND THEIR CONSORTS

[Soe Long Fa] also had altogether six daughters: The eldest daughter [Nang O (Ua) Ming Khai Foei] was married to Mün Long Saen Lò (namely Kham Ham Fa).[158] Another daughter, by the name of Nang Ok Kham Foei, was married to the lord of Lan Sang

---

153. According to Dao and Wu 1983, 4, one *saen* is 200 *jin* (catty). But according to Dao and Kang 1989b, 330, one *saen* is 3,330 *liang* (taels). One Chinese *jin* is 16 *liang*. According to MLC-LV2, s. 16.12, Soe Long Fa paid one *mün* of [pure] silver and one *saen* of [pure] gold to ransom the golden seal.

154. From the Ming court's point of vew, the *saenwi fa* of Moeng Lü was their aboriginal officials (*tuguan*). They were allowed to rule their land and defend the frontier lands for China. Li Fuyi was a Chinese official, so he translated it into *liu zhen di fang* 留 鎮 地 方 (lit., "stay to defend the land"). See MLC-LV1, 10). The same is translated in Gao Lishi 1984, 110. In MLC-LV2, s. 16.12, it is "[He was] still [permitted] to stay within the land [to rule]".

155. He was most likely Banya Zhong (Phaya Còm) mentioned in MSG (ch. 189. 32a; on Cheli) in Tianshun 2, sixth month (1458). See also the *Yingzong shilu*, ch. 292, 6242 (Tianshun 2, sixth month, *renshen* day). See Liew-Herres 2003b.

156. This parenthesis is probably added by Li Fuyi (MLC-LV1, 10).

157. He died in Moeng Nim. See MLC-LV2, s. 16.14 and Gao Lishi 1984, 111, s. 16.4.

158. According to MLC-LV2, s. 16.15, he was Saen Moeng Cae (i.e., Kham Ham Fa). They had a son called Laca. See also Gao Lishi 1984, 111, s. 16.15.

(i.e., Phaya Lan Sang), Phaya Cai Sòngkham.[159] These two daughters were born to Nang Lun Koei.[160] There was another daughter (third daughter) called Nang Ai Mun who was married to [the lord of] Moeng Cung (i.e., Yuanjiang).[161] There was another daughter (fourth daughter) called Nang Üai Lao who was married to Saen Dao Yat of Chiang Ha. The two daughters (fifth and sixth daughter), Nang Kòng Kham and Nang Aen Wang, were both married to Saen Kham (sic).[162]

12.7 THE FOUR SONS OF MÜN LONG SAEN LÒ AND NANG O (UA) MING KHAI FOEI

Mün Long Saen Lò (i.e., Kham Ham Fa) and Nang O (Ua) Ming Khai Foei (the eldest daughter of Soe Long Fa) had four sons. The eldest son, called Saen Kham Daeng, was granted Chiang Kham as his principality; the second son, called Tao O, was granted Na Mün Cae as his principality; the third son, named Tao Kham, was granted Na Chiang Cae as his principality; the fourth son, named Tao Kòng Kham, was granted Na Chiang Yang as his principality. They had three daughters but names were not yet given to them.[163]

12.8 TAO SAM PÒ LÜTAI MARRIES THE THREE DAUGHTERS OF SAEN LÒ

Tao Sam Pò Lütai gradually grew older. When he was sixteen years old, [he showed himself] to be very intelligent and capable. Soe Long Fa therefore adopted him, granted him Moeng Phong[164] as his principality, and appointed him military commander. [Tao Sam Pò Lütai] married the three daughters of [Mün Long] Saen Lò (i.e., Kham Ham Fa) as his principal and secondary consorts.[165]

12.9 REVOLT OF SOE NGAM FA OF MOENG MAO LONG

Later, the lord of Moeng Fòng (Pòng) (i.e., Phaya Moeng Fòng) by the name of Soe

---

159. According to MLC-LV2, s. 16.15, he was the Phaya of Moeng Luang Prabang of Laos. More information on the land ceded to Phaya Lan Cang (Sang) as dowry in CS 823 (AD 1461) is given in MLC-LV2, s. 16.15. A similar account is given in Gao Lishi 1984, 111, s. 16.15.

160. She was the eldest daughter of Tao Sida Kham.

161. MLC-LV2, s. 16.15, explains that the Tai peoples of Moeng Cung were called Tai Ya and Tai Khae. The Tai Ya (Tr. ไทหย่า) and Tai Khae (Tr. ไทแค) are two smaller Tai groups in Sipsòng Panna. Unlike the Tai Lü they are not Buddhists but adhere to their ancient ancestor worship. Gao Lishi 1984, 111, 16.15, adds that "Moeng Thalang is Mojiang, Moeng Lae is Jiangcheng County and Moeng Ti is the plain of Mojiang. At that time those were regions inhabited by Tai Lü, Tai Ya, and Tai Khae."

162. Saen Kham was namely Saen Kham Daeng. According to MLC-LV2, s. 16.15 and Gao Lishi 1984, 111, s. 16.15, the last two daughters married Saen Wang of Chiang Kham.

163. The above information is not given in other Tai Lü chronicles. According to MLC-LV2, s. 16.15 and s. 18.10; Gao Lishi 1984, 111, s. 16.15; and Dao Shuren 1989, 232, they had only one son called Tao (Cao) Laca.

164. In the south of Zhenyue County, at modern Ninger.

165. They were the granddaughters of Soe Luang Fa. According to MLC-LV2, s. 16.16 and Gao Lishi 1984, 111, 16.16, Sam Pò Lütai married the third daughter of Saen Lò of Moeng Cae, instead of all three daughters.

Ngam Fa (She An Fa)[166] living in Moeng Mao Long, who was known as Cae Lan Chiang Saen,[167] rebelled against the Heavenly Court (i.e., Cao Lum Fa) with all his might. The emperor of the Heavenly Court (i.e., Cao Lum Fa) sent the high commissioner (*khun yai*)[168] Shang Qiu 商球 (sic), commanding a contingent of troops, to attack him.[169] This was in CS 808, the *lai yi* year (Zhengtong 11, 1446 AD).

12.10 SOE LONG FA DELIVERS THE HEAD OF ONE OF SOE NGAM FA'S COURTIERS TO THE HEAVENLY COURT

Soe (Süa) Ngam Fa could not repulse the imperial troops and fled to Ava (Th. Angwa).[170] His superintendent (*zongli*)[171] retreated to Moeng Lü. Soe Long Fa killed him and delivered his head to the emperor of the Heavenly Court (i.e., Cao Lum Fa). Thus he gained great respect and favour [from Cao Lum Fa] and was called, "*Bashou tianzi jinmen zhi nengzhe* 把守天了金門之能者" (lit., "capable one guarding the golden gate for the son of heaven").[172] He was invested with greater authority than any other aboriginal commissioners (*tusi*) (i.e., *cao fa* or *cao moeng*) [of the region].[173]

12.11 SOE LONG FA BECOMES THE REGIONAL OVERLORD

Consequently, the lords (*phaya*) of Moeng Cha (Mengzha 猛乍), Moeng Yuan (Mengrun 猛潤) (i.e., the Tai Yuan kingdom of Lan Na), Moeng Khün (Menggen 猛艮) (i.e., Chiang Tung), Moeng Laem, and of other [*müang*], offered in tribute the gifts prepared and sent their envoys to Moeng Lü. They would think it dishonourable if they

---

166. She An Fa (Soe Ngam Pha or Cao Ngam Pha) is known in Chinese sources as Si Renfa 思任發, the ruler of Luchuan-Pingmian, i.e., Moeng Mao.

167. *Cae lan* (Tr. แจ้ล้าน) in Tai means "city of one million", which here refers to the capital city of Moeng Mao. In MLC-LV2, s. 16.17 it is called *Ce Ciang (Chiang) Saen.*

168. According to MLC-LV2, s. 16.17, it is *khun yai* (high-ranking official).

169. Li Fuyi suspects that Shang Qiu 商球 was in fact Zhang Hong 張洪 (1364–1447), the author of *Shi Mian Lu* 使緬錄 (Record of an envoy to Burma). On Zhang Hong, see DMB I.85–88. However, according to Ming sources, in Zhengtong 11 (1446) Si Renfa (Soe Ngam Fa), the chieftain of Luchuan-Pingmian, was handed over to Wang Zheng 王政, the chiliad (*qianhu*) of the Ming army. The commanders-in-chief of the third Luchuan-Pingmian campaign in 1443 (Zhengtong 8) were Wang Ji 王驥 (1378–1460) and Jiang Gui 蔣貴 (1380–1449). See Liew 1996, 185–86.

170. On the successive punitive military campaigns launched against Moeng Mao, see Liew 1996.

171. In MLC-LV2, s. 16.18 it is "one of his courtiers (*amat*)". In MLC-SV2, 111, s. 16.18, it is "an important comrade" (*tonghuo* 同伙) under Soe Ngam Fa. Li Fuyi (MLC-LV1, 11) translates *amat* as *zongli* 總理 (superintendent).

172. MLC-LV2, s. 16.18 states: *Kwan li waen thang ki ya min*, interpreted by Gao Lishi 1984, 111, s. 16.18, as *Guanli yuanzhang ju yamen* 管理元章居衙門, which means "great heroes guarding the national main gate (*patu moeng*) of Cao Lum Fa". If *waen thang* is the Tai rendering of Yuanjiang 元江 (i.e., Moeng Cung), then Soe Long Fa was promoted to be the governor of Moeng Cung as well.

173. From the perspective of Li Fuyi, in the 1940s the lords of various *müang* were the aboriginal officials (*tuguan*) of China.

did not receive the letters of conferment from Moeng Lü. It is recorded that Moeng Cha presented one elephant nine *sòk* tall. Moeng Yuan (Lan Na) presented one golden tray [with feet] for sacrificial fruits weighing 700 taels (*liang*).[174] Moeng Khün presented 1,000 taels of silver.[175] Moeng Laem presented twenty taels of silver.[176] In return Soe Long Fa granted each of them one *panna* of land taxes, ten men for general service, ten horsemen,[177] and several musicians to blow horns and beat drums.

12.12 THE POWERFUL RULER OF MOENG MAEN (PUER)

At that time Moeng Maen (i.e., Puer 普洱) was the most powerful *müang* (polity) of all the *müang*.[178] The seal and credential (*yinxin*) granted [to Moeng Maen] by the emperor of the Heavenly Court (i.e., Cao Lum Fa) was larger than that given to Moeng Laem. The official documents of various *müang* had to bear the seals of the lord of Moeng Maen and of Soe Long Fa before they could be considered valid and be dispatched. Moeng Tae, Moeng Saeng, Bò Hoek, Khwaen Siao, Na Kot Si Thung, Òi Loeng and other [*müang*] all had to render their service to Soe Long Fa.[179]

12.13 THE TYRANT RULER OF MOENG YÒNG

There was [a man] by the name of Mün Mu, who was the lord of Moeng Yòng (Mengyong 猛勇). His disposition was cruel and tyrannical. When the people could no longer endure his oppression they rebelled against him. In the *hong met* year, CS 813 (Jingtai 2, AD 1451), the people fled in all directions. Soe Long Fa arrested Mün Mu and banished him to Na Cae Ua. Consequently, Moeng Yòng was deserted and depopulated. Nam Luai [River] was taken as the boundary [between Moeng Lü and Moeng Yòng].[180]

12.14 THE COUNTRY PALACES OF SOE LONG FA

During the reign of Soe Long Fa the land was very peaceful. Hence, he toured various places and wherever he went he had a country palace built. [To the west of the Mekong

174. In MLC-LV2, s. 16.20, the weight is given as: 24 *hòng* and 5 *the* (700 units). In Gao Lishi 1984, 111, s. 16.20, it is 7 *hòng*, i.e., 24.5 taels.

175. In MLC-LV2, s. 16.20, the gift was 1,000 [units] of silver, i.e., 35 *hòng*. In Gao Lishi 1984, 111, s. 16.20, it is 35 taels.

176. MLC-LV2, s. 16.20 gives 20 *hòng* of silver; Gao Lishi 1984, 111, s. 16.20, gives 20 taels.

177. According to MLC-LV2, s. 16.21, this is *na ma* (lit., "horse rice fields"). Gao Lishi 1984, 111, s. 16.21, translates *na ma* and *na kong* into "horse fields" and "bow fields" respectively.

178. Moeng Maen was regarded as the leading *müang* (i.e., *mae moeng*, which means "mother *müang*"). See MLC-LV2, s. 16.19.

179. According to MLC-LV2, s. 16.21, they had to cultivate the wet rice fields (*na nai hoen*, นาในเฮิน) for the *saenwi fa*, Soe Long Fa.

180. In MLC-LV2, s. 16.22 it is stated: "They allied with Moeng Fòng to go against Mün Mu, the ruler of Moeng Yòng. Eventually Mün Mu was arrested and killed. A similar account is given in Gao Lishi 1984, 112, s. 16.22. See also Dao Shuren 1989, 234.

River were]: one [country palace] at Ban Tung, one at [Ban] Còm Wang, one at Chiang Kang, one at Moeng Hun,[181] one at Son Khwan, one in the town of Moeng Cae, one at Tung Khai,[182] one at Nòng Ban, one at Kho Khae (Luqie), and one [at Dòn Coeng] on the pasture of Moeng Hai. To the east of the river [Mekong] were: one at Moeng Nun,[183] one at Moeng Yang, one at Moeng Hing (i.e., Puwen), and one at Moeng Maen (i.e., Puer). In each country palace one royal concubine (*feizi*) was installed. One year he travelled east of the [Mekong] River and the next west of the [Mekong] River.

12.15 MOENG PAN AND MOENG BÒ ARE OFFERED TO SOE LONG FA

In the *ka lao* year, CS 815 (Jingtai 4, AD 1453), when [Soe Long Fa] was on tour in Moeng Pan and Moeng Bò (in Jinggu), [the lords] of these two places offered their lands to [Soe Long Fa] and became his subjects.[184]

12.16 CAO AI AND CAO YI

Consequently, Soe Long Fa ordered the lord of Moeng Hing, Cao Ai, to take up his principality in Moeng Pan and Moeng Bò (in Jinggu 景谷); Cao Yi was to take up his principality in Panna Moeng Hun[185]—Cao Ai and Cao Yi were [Tao] Saen Nang's sons.[186]

12.17 SOE LONG FA PASSES AWAY

Soe Long Fa was on the throne thirty years and died (*si*)[187] at the age of eighty in the *moeng pao* year, CS 819 (Tianshun 1, AD 1457).

12.18 THE FIFTEENTH RULER, TAO PHASAENG, COMMITS SUICIDE AT MOENG HING

Tao Phasaeng (Dao Baxian) succeeded [his father] to the throne in the same year and

181. According to MLC-LV2, s. 16.23 and Gao Lishi 1984, 112, 16.23, "one at Chiang Kang of Moeng Hun".

182. Tung Khai is not given in MLC-LV2, s. 16.23, and Gao Lishi 1984, 112.

183. According to MLC-LV2, s. 16.23 and Gao Lishi 1984, 112, s. 16.23, "one at Chiang Fòng".

184. According to MLC-LV2, s. 16.24; Gao Lishi 1984, 112, s. 16.24; and Dao Shuren 1989, 235, Soe Long Fa incorporated Moeng Kla (Ka), Moeng Bò, and Moeng Pan into the domain of Sipsòng Panna. The three *müang* are in today's Jinggu County 景谷, in the north of Puer 普洱 (Moeng Maen).

185. According to MLC-LV2, s. 16.24 and Gao Lishi 1984, 112, Cao Yi was appointed to be the governor of Moeng Hing (i.e., Puwen).

186. This final phrase should probably be ascribed to Li Fuyi (MLC-LV1, 12). According to MLC-LV1, 7, s. 9.6, Cao Ai and Cao Yi were Tao Saen Nang's sons and Tao Saeng Nang was the third son of Tao Sida Kham. However, according to MLC-LV2-1963, s. 11.2; Gao Lishi 1984, 108, s. 11.2; and Dao Shuren 1989, 228, Cao Ai and Cao Yi, both invested as lords of Moeng Hing, were Tao Kumman's sons.

187. Unlike the death of other *cao phaendin* (or *saenwi fa*), here Li Fuyi (MLC-LV1, 12), uses the word *si* 死, which means "die", instead of *hong* 薨, a euphemism for the death of a feudal lord or prince. We have no way to cross-check with the original Tai Lü manuscript as it was lost. So we do not know if it is the word choice of Li Fuyi, or of the scribe of the Tai Lü manuscript.

was ousted just two months later because the people refused to submit to him.[188] Tao Phasaeng fled to the Heavenly Court (sic) (Cao Hò).[189] En route he suddenly committed suicide, cutting his throat at Moeng Hing (Mengling 猛嶺, i.e., Puwen 普文).[190] He was the twelfth generation (sic) eleventh [the fifteenth ruler of Moeng Lü].

13. TAO SAM PÒ LÜTAI (SAN BAO LIDAI 三寶歷代), R. 1457–1497

13.1 THE TAI LÜ PEOPLE ELECT THEIR SIXTEENTH RULER

After Tao Phasaeng had committed suicide by cutting his throat, the people looked for an [appropriate] ruler but could not find one. Therefore, [messengers] were sent to various *müang* (polities) to announce that the people ought to have freedom [to elect their ruler]. [The case] of Tao Phasaeng was to be established as a precedent. Whoever was not needed would be ousted; whoever was needed would be supported as the ruler [and led to the throne].

The announcement states:

> When a candidate's name is nominated [and chanted], those who agree shall harmonise with [the chant]; those who disagree shall remain silent. The election is carried out by announcing the name of each candidate.[191] The names of all the proposed candidates, one after another, will be called out and chanted. Shall we first propose Tao Còm Pha[192] as ruler and chant his name?

188. According to Dao and Wu 1983, 6, Tao Phasaeng succeeded his father in the year CS 817 (1455 AD) and was on the throne only five months before being deposed. The same is given in MLC-LV2 (DCH 1963, s. 17.1) and Gao Lishi 1984, 112, 17.1. But according to Dao Shuren 1989, 235, Tao Pasaeng succeeded his father in the year CS 828 (1466 AD) and was deposed seven months later.

189. In the mid-fifteeth century, the Ming court was in Beijing. The text here probably refers to Kunming (Moeng Sae), the seat of the Mu clan, hereditary rulers of Yunnan. The first emperor of Ming appointed his adopted (most probably illegitimate) son Mu Ying (1345–7 June 1392) to rule Yunnan. He and his sons and descendants ruled Yunnan until the fall of the Ming empire, the last duke of Qianguo being Mu Tianbo (d. 1661).

190. See also MLC-LV2, s. 17.1. According to MSG (ch. 189, 31b), in Xuande 7, ninth month (1432), the tribal clan member (*tushe*) of Cheli, Tao Phasaeng, dispatched a tribal headman (*toumu*, i.e., *cao mòm*), Cao Ai, to pay tribute and petitioned for succeeding to the post. It was approved. [...] A memorial of the regional commander of Yunnan dated Tianshun 1, second month (1457) reported he had committed suicide. See Liew-Herres 2003b.

191. Li Fuyi (MLC-LV1, 12–13), translates it into *chang ming tuixuan* 唱名推選, lit., "election by chanting the names". Gao Lishi 1984, 112, also translates it *chang ming*, "chant the name". A similar method is recorded in MLC-LV2, s. 17.2.

192. He was the second son Soe Long Fa, the lord of Moeng Long.

13.2 SOE LONG FA'S SONS ARE VOTED DOWN BY THE PEOPLE

[The election lasted] from early in the morning until sunset; the beating of the evening drums had already been sent out from the court to outside the gate but not a single man harmonised with the chanting [of Tao Còm Pha's name] (i.e., seconded the nomination). Following that, the names of all Soe Long Fa's sons were called out one after another in order [of seniority], but not even a single man from among the people harmonised with the chanting [of their names].

13.3 TAO SAM PÒ LÜTAI'S NOMINATION

Later, as the name of Tao Sam Pò Lütai was announced [and chanted], all agreed unanimously and applauded in support of him. They cheered and celebrated for three days.[193] A chief headman (sic) (*tao phaya*)[194] said:

> All the people have elected my elder brother to be the ruler. This is quite good. Be it hill land or wet paddy fields, just grant me enough for my clothing and food (i.e., livelihood) and let me be a commoner and cultivate my own food to be self-reliant. I will be satisfied with just this.[195]

13.4 THE CORONATION CEREMONY

After [the *cao phaendin*] had been elected, they proceeded to the Buddhist temple. Facing the Buddha statue, the Buddhist scriptures (*sutra*), and the three symbols of Buddhism (the three gems), they took the oath.[196] The oath was then engraved in the temple [in two places], one pasted with gold and the other with silver.[197] After the [oath-taking] ceremony all the people returned to their respective lands (*müang*) where they lived in peace.

193. That Tao Sam Pò Lütai was elected to be the *cao phaendin*, is confirmed in Chinese sources. In the year Tianshun 1, second month (March 1457), Tao Phasaeng committed suicide. His younger brother, Phaya Còm (i.e., the second son Tao Còm Pha), and others nominated his elder brother, Tao Sam Pò Lütai, to succeed to the post. But then Phaya Còm again created unrest and banded together with Babai (Lan Na) to kill and take revenge. For details, see MSG, ch. 189, 32a; *Yingzong shilu*, ch. 275, 5860 (Tianshun 1, second month, *gengshen* day: 21 March 1457). See Liew-Herres 2003b.

194. Here Li Fuyi (MLC-LV1, 13) added a parenthesis: "Probably he was the Banya Zhong 板雅忠 in *Mingshi*." Banya Zhong (Phaya Còm) was Tao Phasaeng's younger brother Tao Còm Pha, who banded with Lan Na against Sam Pò Lütai. See *Mingshi*, ch. 315, 8157 (MSG, ch. 189, 32a); *Yingzong shilu*, ch. 275, 5860 (Tianshun 1, second month, *gengshen* day: 21 March 1457).

195. A very similar account is recorded in MLC-LV2, s. 17.3 and in Gao Lishi 1984, 112, s. 17.3.

196. According to the MLC-LV2, s. 17.4, Gao Lishi 1984, 112, s. 17.3, and Dao Shuren 1989, 236, it is: "Facing the three gems (i.e., the Buddha, the Dharma, and the Sangha) they took the oath."

197. "The oath was engraved on a silver and a golden plate. See Gao Lishi 1984, 112, s. 17.3. But according to MLC-LV2, s. 17.4, it is: "The silver and golden chisels were used in the oath-taking ritual as well."

13.5 OUTBREAK OF FRATRICIDAL WARS AMONG COUSINS

In CS 820, a *poek yi* year (Tianshun 2, AD 1458), the lord of Moeng Long (Tao Còm Pha) and the lord of Moeng Hun (Tao Ut) hatched a plot.[198] They went to invite Cao Lan Na, Phaya Tilaka,[199] to join forces with them to attack Tao Sam Pò Lütai. Hence, Sam Pò Lütai abandoned *Wiang* Chiang Lan and chose Chiang Rung as his capital.[200] Phaya Tilaka commanded a force of 200,000 soldiers and taking the lord of Moeng Long, Tao Còm Pha, as his guide, [he] advanced to Moeng Cae [with his troops]. On the pretext that Tao Sam Pò Lütai had become the son-in-law of Saen Lò (i.e., Mün Long Saen Lò)[201] of Moeng Cae [and that Saen Lò] used his power to suppress the people, Cao Lan Na marched straight to attack Moeng Cae.

13.6 SAEN LÒ OF MOENG CAE OUTWITS PHAYA TILAKA

At that time Moeng Cae was not at all prepared [for an attack]; the town was not enclosed with a single stake or stick. In a great hurry bamboo poles were used as palisades to enclose [the town], and blankets, white cloths, and other materials were hung over [the bamboo poles] to give the appearance of fortifications. At the same time, Saen Lò cheated Cao Lan Na and said:

> The old Saen Lò has gone to Chiang Rung to beg for mercy for the people. If Your Lord (i.e., Cao Lan Na) could defeat Chiang Rung, we all will be your subjects and servants forthwith.

Cao Lan Na agreed and so transferred his soldiers to attack Chiang Rung. Saen Ló took the opportunity to fortify the town with palisades, working day and night. The thickness of the palisades was four to five *kam*; the elephant palisades (i.e., thicker stakes) were eight *kam* around (40 inches).[202] In twenty days they had completed building the fortifications.

13.7 PHAYA TILAKA FAILS TO CAPTURE CHIANG RUNG AND MOENG CAE

Cao Lan Na (i.e., Phaya Tilaka) marched to attack Chiang Rung, but after one month and twenty days [he] still had not captured it. [Thus he] pulled his troops back to attack Moeng Cae. On arrival he found that the moat around the fortifications was three necks'

198. They were the second and seventh sons of Soe Long Fa.

199. King Tilok (r. 1441–1487) was a son of Sam Fang Kaen (1402–1441) and grandson of Saen Moeng Ma (r. 1385–1401).

200. According to MLC-LV2, s. 18.2, and Gao Lishi 1984, 113, s. 18.2, Sam Pò Lütai was forced to abandon Chiang Lan and went to build Wiang Chiang Mu.

201. Saen Lò was namely Kham Ham Fa, the younger brother of Phaya Phai Hom Fa, the lord of Moeng Laem.

202. One *kam* is the circumference of the thumb and index finger put together, i.e., approximately five inches.

deep. He besieged and attacked [Moeng Cae], but after one month and twenty days he could not capture it either. Hence, he withdrew his troops quietly.[203]

13.8 CESSION OF MOENG MA AND MOENG LA TIP TO CHIANG TUNG; PHAYA TILAKA RETURNS TO CHIANG MAI

At that time the Phaya Moeng Khün by the name of [Cao] Sili Suthammalaca led his troops to give [Moeng Lü] reinforcements. After the war Tao Sam Pò Lütai ceded Moeng Ma and Moeng La [Tip] to reward [Phaya] Moeng Khün. The lord of Lan Na, Phaya Tilaka, retreated. But when he reached Moeng Yòng he delayed proceeding further, as he felt ashamed to meet the elders (i.e., nobles) and the people because of his defeat. After a long time, [he] finally made a detour, led by his guide, from Pak Yòng[204] to Moeng Phong. Then, taking a small path, they travelled back to Chiang Mai [of Lan Na].[205]

13.9 TAO SAM PÒ LÜTAI RECRUITS TROOPS TO ATTACK LAN NA

Tao Sam Pò Lütai then appointed a man called Mün Nòn Long, who was the *lam kha* [*kao*] (*lanjia*) (representatives stationing at the capital)[206] to recruit his former peoples (*kha kao*). He enlisted four thousand men to attack Lan Na. [As a result] Lan Na lost a great number of elephants and horses; many people were killed or wounded. [Phaya Tilaka returned to his land].[207] Consequently, the lord of Moeng Long, Tao Còm Pha, and lord of Moeng Hun, Tao Ut, defected from their lands.[208]

13.10 TAO CET SEEKS MILITARY HELP FROM LAN NA AND RESETTLES HIS FOLLOWERS IN MOENG YÒNG

In CS 824, a *tao sanga* year (Tianshun 6, AD 1462), Tao Cet (i.e., Tao Som), who was the lord of Moeng Ngat and Moeng Khang, sent men (envoys) to request from the lord of Lan Na, Phaya Tilaka, as well as from the lord of Chiang Saen and the lord of Chiang Rai to send a total of forty thousand soldiers to escort [him] to leave Moeng Lü for

203. A similar account is given in MLC-LV2, s. 18.4–5 and in Gao Lishi 1984, 113, s. 18.4–18.5.

204. This means the estuary of the Yòng River.

205. A similar account is given in MLC-LV2, s. 18.6–7, and in Gao Lishi 1984, 113, s. 18.6–7. The Chiang Mai Chronicle confirms Tilok's military campaign against the Tai Lü in 1459/60, at a time when Chiang Mai was battling with Ayutthaya over the control of the Sukhothai region. "So King Tilokarat took his forces up to attack the Lü domains. He was unable to take M. Phrong (Moeng Phong), and withdrew." The chronicle, however, does no confirm military operations further north up to Chiang Rung and Moeng Cae. See CMC-HP, Wyatt and Aroonrut 1995, 88; CMC-N, Notton 1932, 122; CMC-TPCM, Udom et al. 1995, 71.

206. This parenthesis is ascribed to Li Fuyi. See MLC-LV1, 14. But according to MLC-LV2, s. 18.7 and Gao Lishi 1984, 113, Mün Nòn Luang was the [*pò*] *lam* of the *Kha Kao*.

207. See MLC-LV2, s. 18.7 and Gao Lishi 1984, 113.

208. Li Fuyi (MLC-LV1, 14) translates this as *qiguo* 棄國, meaning "deserted one's country". But in MLC-LV2, s. 18.8 and in Gao Lishi 1984, 113, it is stated: "Later, Cao Moeng Hun (i.e., Tao Ut) and Cao Moeng Long (Tao Còm Pha) continued to go against Sam Pò Lütai."

Lan Na.[209] [On the way they] stopped at Moeng Yòng. When Tao Cet saw that [Moeng Yòng] was desolate and uninhabited he petitioned for letting all the soldiers and people resettle there to cultivate the land. [This was granted.] Consequently, the inhabitants of Moeng Yòng increased gradually. Since then Moeng Yòng was subordinate to Lan Na.[210] However, Moeng Ngat and Moeng Khang were depopulated and left desolate because the people had followed Tao Cet and migrated [to Moeng Yòng].

13.11 SAEN KHAM DAENG AND HIS SON TAO LACA

The son of Saen Lò, called [Saen] Kham Daeng, was granted Na Saen (Na Xian) of Chiang Lan as his principality by Tao Sam Pò Lütai; therefore he was called Saen Kham Daeng.[211] Saen Kham Daeng had a son, called Tao Laca, who was born to Soe Long Fa's daughter, Nang Kòng Kham.[212]

13.12 SAEN LÒ ATTACKS HIS BROTHER IN MOENG LAEM

In CS 827, a *dap lao* year (Chenghua 1, AD 1465), Saen Lò marched to attack Moeng Laem. His elder brother, Phaya Phai Hom Fa (Cao Moeng Laem), commanded all able-bodied males from Moeng Cae to go [and repulse the attacker]. Both sides suffered heavy casualties and [Saen Lò] could not capture [Moeng Laem]. So, he turned back and led his troops to attack Moeng Nim.[213] Saen Lò ordered Soe Long Fa's son, Tao Fa Nòi,[214] to go and attack [Moeng Nim]. Tao Fa Nòi was killed when his troops were defeated. The two men, Mün Long and Mün Cae, barricaded themselves in the fortified Kio Nim (Jiuning) of Moeng Cae.[215] Defeated, they fled to Moeng Hun. Only four hundred odd able-bodied males from Moeng Cae survived. Hence they followed Saen Lò and were stranded at Moeng Hun.[216]

209. A similar account is recorded in MLC-LV2, s. 18.8 and in Gao Lishi 1984, 113.

210. Since then Moeng Yòng has been subordinate to Chiang Saen Luang [of Lan Na]. See MLC-LV2, s. 18.9; the same is recorded in Gao Lishi 1984, 113.

211. Saen Kham Daeng, the son-in-law of Soe Long Fa, was called Panna Kham Daeng. See MLC-LV1, s. 13.18.

212. On Tao Laca see also MLC-LV2, s. 18.10. Nang Kòng Kham was the fifth daughter of Soe Long Fa.

213. Moeng Nim (Mengying 猛 穎) is the variant name of Moeng Yuan (Mengyun 猛 允, i.e., Lan Na). See MLC-LV1, index, 9.

214. Tao Fa Nòi was the eighth son of Soe Long Fa.

215. Kio Nim, or Kio Ku Wiang Moeng Cae, is located in the vicinity of the fortifications of the previous Nanqiao County, in today's Moeng Hai County, to the west of the Mekong. See MLC-LV1, index, 9.

216. The above event is not recorded in MLC-LV2; Gao Lishi 1984; or Dao Shuren 1989. Saen Lò or Mün Luang Saen Lò, named Kham Ham Fa, was the lord of Moeng Cae.

13.13 DEATH OF SAEN LÒ; SAEN KHAM DAENG BECOMES RULER OF MOENG CAE

In the *poek cai* year, CS 830 (Chenghua 4, AD 1468), Saen Lò passed away. Saen Kham Daeng inherited his father's principality in Moeng Cae.[217] Saen Kham Daeng was by nature a kind-hearted (sympathetic) man and the people were happy under him. All the people from the east of the river [Mekong] came to offer their submission. As a result Moeng Cae became prosperous and well-populated as before.

13.14 REBULIDING MOENG NGAT AND MOENG KHANG

Later in the *kot yi* year, CS 832 (AD 1470), [Saen Kham Daeng] sent his son Tao Laca (Raja) to Moeng Ngat to cultivate the land, and another son to Moeng Khang to cultivate the land there. Since then the population of Moeng Ngat and Moeng Khang increased gradually.[218]

13.15 THE SIX SONS OF TAO SAM PÒ LÜTAI

Tao Sam Pò Lütai had six sons and four daughters: The eldest son, called Tao Yi, was the crown prince; the second son was Cao Moeng [Khak];[219] and the third son, Sam Khai Noeng, was appointed military commander[220] and granted Moeng U [-Nüa] as his principality.[221] The fourth son Cao Am was granted Moeng Nun as his principality. The fifth son Cao Ai and the sixth son Cao Khan Moeng were still young. They were not yet granted any principality.[222]

---

217. Saen Kham Daeng was also the lord of Na Saen of Chiang Lan, and had been invested by Tao Sam Pò Lütai.

218. Here Li Fuyi (MLC-LV1) uses the term *tunken* 屯 墾 (lit., "to station", "to cultivate"). The term derives from the ancient system of *tuntian* 屯 田 (farming colony), in which soldiers, civilians, and salt merchants were sent to what were usually border regions to reclaim land and organise farming colonies. For the system of *tuntian* farming, see Liew 1984. However, we do not think that *tuntian* farming was implemented by the Tai Lü peoples. Here it probably means that Saen Kham Daeng sent one son to Moeng Ngat and another to Moeng Khang to be the lords of these two *müang* to recruit people to resettle and cultivate the land, namely to rebuild Moeng Ngat and Moeng Khang. See MLC-LV2, s. 18.10.

219. According to MLC-LV2, s. 18.11, he was called Cao Moeng Khak, but according to Gao Lishi 1984, 113, s. 18.11, he was called Cao Am and was granted Moeng Khak as his principality and therefore was called Cao Moeng Khak. He is not to be confused with the younger brother of Phaya Khün, called Cao Moeng Khak, who married Nang Khò Moeng, the third daughter of Tao Sam Pò Lütai. See below, s. 13.19.

220. The Tai for "military commander" is *cao pon soek* (Tr. เจ้าพลเสิก). See MLC-LV2, s. 18.11.

221. It is namely Moeng U-Nüa, which was formally ceded to French Indochina in 1896. Together with Moeng U-Tai they form the bulk of Phong Sali Province of Laos where the ethnic Lü still make up the majority of the Tai-speaking ethnic groups.

222. According to MLC-LV2, s. 18.11 and Gao Lishi 1984, 113, Tao Sam Pò Lütai had five sons and six daughters. The eldest son was Tao Yi, the second Cao Moeng Khak (i.e., Cao Am), the third Sam Khai Noeng, the fourth Cao Ai, and the fifth was still young. Cao Am had a son called Cao Kham Moeng.

13.16 THE FOUR DAUGHTERS OF TAO SAM PÒ LÜTAI

The eldest daughter Cao Nang was married to Panna Kham Daeng. The second daughter Nang Aen Fòng was married to Mün Long's son, Tao Saeo (sic).[223] Tao Saeo and Nang Aen Fòng had two sons: the elder was named Han Kòng and the second was called Chiang Klat. The third daughter [of Tao Sam Pò Lütai], called Nang Khò Moeng,[224] and the fourth daughter, called Cao Nge, had just reached the age of putting on hairpins.[225]

13.17 TAO SAM PÒ LÜTAI ATTACKS HIS COUSIN TAO UT AT MOENG HUN

In the *poek cai* year, [CS 830] (AD 1468), Tao Sam Pò Lütai attacked Moeng Hun because the lord of Moeng Hun, Tao Ut,[226] had colluded with Lan Na and created trouble. Tao Ut fled to his elder brother in Moeng Long.[227] Therefore, Tao Sam Pò Lütai sent his men to persuade the scattered refugees [to return to their homes]. But the people of Moeng Hun built their huts (shelters) in the fields and refused to return to their own houses. [Tao Sam Pò Lütai] could do nothing. The people of Moeng Hun invited Tao Ut back to Moeng Hun to be the ruler.

13.18 DEATH OF TAO UT; DEPORTATION OF THE PEOPLE OF MOENG HUN

In CS 831, a *kat pao* year (Chenghua 5, AD 1469), [Tao Ut revolted again.] Panna Kham Daeng (i.e., Saen Kham Daeng) launched another attack on Moeng Hun, killed Tao Ut, and presented his head to Tao Sam Pò Lütai. Tao Sam Pò Lütai had the people of Moeng Hun deported because they should not have had invited Tao Ut back. One group was deported to Chiang Rung and another group to Moeng Cae. Thus, Moeng Hun was left desolate and without inhabitants.

13.19 TAI KHÜN PRINCE CAO MOENG KHAK MARRIES NANG KHÒ MOENG

In CS 832, a *kot yi* year (Chenghua 6, AD 1470), the younger brother of Phaya Khün—the lord of Moeng Khün[228]—by the name of Cao Moeng Khak, married Tao Sam Pò Lütai's daughter Nang Khò Moeng.[229] Therefore he was asked to stay and serve Tao Sam Pò Lütai.

---

223. But Tao Saeo was Soe Long Fa's third son, the lord of Na Mün Long. According to MLC-LV2, s. 18.11 and Gao Lishi 1984, 113 (s. 18.11), Sam Pò Lütai's eldest daughter was married to Tao Saeo's son Mün Long, i.e., a grandson of Soe Long Fa.

224. She married the younger brother of Phaya Khün (i.e., Cao Moeng Khün), called Cao Moeng Khak. See below s. 13.19.

225. As for the six daughters of Sam Pò Lütai, see MLC-LV2, s. 18.11; Gao Lishi 1984, 113; and Dao Shuren 1989, 238–39. According to Chinese custom, girls at the age of fifteen *sui* 歲 (i.e., 14) were allowed to have their hair done up and to wear hairpins.

226. He was the sixth son of Soe Long Fa.

227. Tao Còm Pha, the second son of Soe Long Fa, was Cao Moeng Long.

228. The parenthesis should probably be ascribed to Li Fuyi.

229. According to MLC-LV2, s. 18.14 and Gao Lishi 1984, 113, Phaya Moeng Khün, by the name of Cao Moeng Khak, married the fifth daughter of Tao Sam Pò Lütai, Nang Khò Moeng.

13.20 THE CONFLICT BETWEEN THE CROWN PRINCE TAO YI AND CAO MOENG KHAK

Cao Moeng Khak was a fussy man. He had audiences with [his royal father-in-law] several times per day. Every time he came he brought with him cushions to sit or lay upon.[230] Tao Yi said:

> I am the crown prince, yet dare not be so ostentatious; [moreover], there is no such etiquette for having an audience with a ruler. Who has ever seen anyone bringing his luggage to an audience? From his behaviour we can deduce that if one day [my] royal father passes away, he surely has his schemes.

Hence the two attacked and ridiculed each other. Tao Sam Pò Lütai stopped them and told [his son]:

> This is my beloved son-in-law. You should not quarrel with him.

13.21 TAO YI INVITES CAO MOENG KHAK TO A FEAST

Consequently, Tao Yi prepared a feast[231] and invited a large number of guests to entertain Cao Moeng Khak in the hope of clearing up the previous grudge. Cao Moeng Khak said:

> He only wants to lure me there to kill me.

He refused to go. Greatly exasperated, Tao Yi then told the young men whom he had invited to finish up drinking the wine and eating the meat before adjourning to attack Cao Moeng Khak. Cao Moeng Khak fled and hid himself in the room of Tao Sam Pò Lütai.[232]

13.22 THE QUEEN PLOTS AGAINST TAO YI

As the queen (the natural mother of Cao Ai and Cao Khan Moeng)[233] wanted to set up her own son [as crown prince] and remove Cao Mòm Luk (means the crown prince, namely Tao Yi),[234] she slandered [the prince royal] to Tao Sam Pò Lütai:

> The crown prince intends to commit regicide and establish himself [as the ruler].

230. According to other sources he had cushions and pillows brought to an audience. See MLC-LV2, s. 18.14; Gao Lishi 1984, 113; Dao Shuren 1989, 239; Dao and Kang 1989b, 336.

231. Li Fuyi (MLC-LV1, 16) used the phrase *zhu jiu peng niu* 煮 酒 烹 牛, lit., "boil the wine and cook cow", i.e., prepare a feast.

232. A similar account is recorded in MLC-LV2, s. 18.16–17.

233. The parenthesis should probably be ascribed to Li Fuyi (MLC-LV1, 16).

234. Ibid.

Tao Sam Pò Lütai believed her and ordered Mün Long[235] to attack Cao Mòm Luk. However, Mün Long defied the order on the grounds that Cao Mòm Luk was innocent. Consequently, the queen (*nang tewi*) took 1,200 taels (*liang*) of pure silver (*bai yin*)[236] to bribe Panna Kham Daeng, and confided to him her plot to remove [the prince royal] so as to establish her own [son as crown prince]. Panna Kham Daeng and Nang Moeng (i.e., the queen) were siblings. Moreover, Panna Kham Daeng harboured an old grudge against Cao Mòm Luk (i.e., Tao Yi). The reason was that Panna Kham Daeng had a beautiful scroll of brocade.[237] Tao Sam Pò Lütai[238] once asked for it but [Panna] Kham Daeng refused because he was a niggard. Cao Mòm Luk ridiculed him by saying,

> It is not made of red gold but merely of red copper.

In fact *kham daeng* means red gold, whereas red copper is *tòng daeng*. As a result, [Panna Kham Daeng] hated [Cao Mòm Luk] and kept aloof from [him]. After receiving the bribe from [his sister] the queen, [he] attacked Cao Mòm Luk on the hill behind the palace in Chiang Rung but was defeated.[239]

13.23 TAO SAM PÒ LÜTAI ATTACKS HIS SON TAO YI

Hence, [Tao] Sam Pò Lütai personally [led men] to help him (i.e., Panna Kham Daeng) attack [his own son]. When Cao Mòm Luk saw that his father was coming to attack him he said:

> According to ritual, a son does not fight with his father.

Therefore, he fled to Moeng Phong.[240]

---

235. According to Li Fuyi (MLC-LV1, 15, s. 13.16), the second daughter of Tao Sam Pò Lütai, Nang Aen Fòng, married Mün Long's son Tao Saeo (see above s. 13.16). But according to MLC-LV2, s. 18.11, the eldest daughter of Sam Pò Lütai, Cao Nang, was married to Tao Saeo's son called Mün Long. According to Gao Lishi 1984, 113, s. 18.11, Mün Long was Soe Long Fa's grandson. But Tao Saeo was Soe Long Fa's third son, the lord of Na Mün Long. In any case Sam Pò Lütai sought help from his son-in-law Mün Long or Tao Saeo to fight his eldest son.

236. One tael (*liang*) is 37.3 gm (1.3 ounces). 1,200 taels = 44,760 gm = 44.76 kg. *Baiyin* (lit., "white silver") means pure silver. It was 2,200 taels as given in Gao Lishi 1984, 114, s. 18.17. According to MLC-LV2, s. 18.17, the amount of pure silver was also 2,200 *cang*.

237. In MLC-LV2, s. 18.17, it was a beautiful golden embroidered coat; according to Gao Lishi 1984, 114, it was a beautiful embroidered belt; according to Dao Shuren 1989, 240 and Dao and Kang 1989b, 337, it was a golden buffalo (*jin shuiniu* 金水牛), an antique.

238. According to MLC-LV2-1963, s. 18.17; Gao Lishi 1984; Dao Shuren 1989; and Dao and Kang 1989b, it was the crown prince Tao Yi who wanted to have it, not Sam Pò Lütai.

239. According to MLC-LV2, s. 18.17, they fought at Kòng Hua Kum near Chiang Rung.

240. See MLC-LV2, s. 18.18; Gao Lishi 1984, 114.

13.24 CAO MOENG KHAK IS DRIVEN BACK TO MOENG KHÜN

The people were dissatisfied with [Tao] Sam Pò Lütai. All of them said that the local unrest was caused by that *lao* (namely Cao Moeng Khak).[241] The people rose against Cao Moeng Khak. Tao Sam Pò Lütai hid him in various *ho pha pong*.[242] The people concentrated on attacking him day and night with guns, crossbows, and firearms. As Cao Moeng Khak could no longer hide himself, he fled [upstream] along the Mekong River, via Moeng Wang, Moeng Khang, Moeng Cae,[243] [whence he] returned to Moeng Khün (Chiang Tung). The people of Moeng Khang escorted Nang Khò Moeng to Moeng Khün and gave her to Cao Moeng Khak. Cao Moeng Khak and his wife blamed his elder brother, Phaya Khün, for not [sending troops] to help them. [Hence, Cao Moeng Khak] killed him (Phaya Khün) and then fled to *kongmen*.[244] Later he died as well.

13.25 THE DEATH OF CROWN PRINCE TAO YI

In the *hong mao* year, CS 833 (Chenghua 7, 1471 AD), Cao Mòm Luk (i.e., Tao Yi) was living in Moeng Phong. One day after drinking [rice wine] at Ban Khai, he rode on an elephant up the hill Dòi Nòi (i.e., Dòi Mòn Haeng Hap) where he committed suicide with his spear.[245] Panna Kham Daeng no longer dared to live at Na Saen in Chiang Lan.[246] He sought refuge in Moeng Cae.

13.26 CAO AI BECOMES RULER OF MOENG BÒ AND MOENG PAN

At first Cao Ai was conferred Moeng Bò and Moeng Pan (both in today's Jinggu) as his principality. After [Panna] Kham Daeng had fled, Na Saen of Chiang Lan was granted to him as his principality. The people called him Saen Bò because he came from Moeng Bò.[247]

241. The parenthesis is most probably ascribed to Li Fuyi. Li Fuyi (MLC-LV1, 16) used the word *ci lao* 此 狫, which can be interpreted as "this fellow" or "this Lao man".

242. *Ho pha pong* (*he pa beng* 和 爬 繃) probably means "inner quarters of the palace". According to MLC-LV2, s. 18.19, Sam Pò Lütai had his son-in-law hidden in the house of the spirits of the royal family, but according to Gao Lishi 1984, 114, Tao Sam Pò Lütai hid his son-in-law in the house of royal relatives.

243. These three *müang* were located in the former Ningjiang Department and Nanqiao County, now Menghai County to the west of the Mekong.

244. Li Fuyi (MLC-LV1) renders it as *kongmen* 空 門 (lit., "empty gate"). Here, Li Fuyi probably means a Buddhist temple. According to MLC-LV2, s. 18.19 and Gao Lishi 1984, 114, Cao Moeng Khak returned to Moeng Khün.

245. A rather similar account is recorded in MLC-LV2, s. 18.20 and in Gao Lishi 1984, 114. Tao Yi was probably murdered by the agent of the queen or by Panna Kham Daeng.

246. Chiang Lan is located about 3 *li* (1 ½ km) to the east of Chiang Rung.

247. Concerning Cao Ai's death, see MLC-LV2, s. 16.24 and Gao Lishi 1984, 112, s. 16.24.

13.27 TAO SAM PÒ LÜTAI PASSES AWAY

[Tao] Sam Pò Lütai succeeded to the throne in the *moeng pao* year, CS 819 (AD 1457), at the age of forty-two. He reigned forty years and passed away (*hong*) at eighty-two in the *moeng sai* year, CS 859 (Hongzhi 10, AD 1497). This was the thirteenth (sic) eleventh generation [the sixteenth ruler of Moeng Lü].[248]

14. TAO SAM KHAI NOENG (SAN KAI LENG 三凱冷), R. 1497–1502

14.1 THE SEVENTEENTH RULER

[Tao] Sam Khai Noeng succeeded his father [Tao] Sam Pò Lütai to the throne in the year CS 859 (AD 1497) at the age of forty-five. He ruled five years and passed away (*hong*) at the age of fifty in the *tao set* year, CS 864 (Hongzhi 15, AD 1502). He, who had no heir, was the fourteenth (sic) twelfth generation [the nineteenth ruler of Moeng Lü]. As his fourth and fifth younger brothers, C̄ao Am and C̄ao Ai, both died young, he was succeeded by his sixth younger brother Cao Khan Moeng.[249]

> Li Fuyi (MLC-SV1), Tai Lü: [Tao Sam] Pò Lütai had four sons: the eldest son was called Tao Yi, the second son was Sam Khai Noeng, the third son was Cao Am, and the youngest son was Tao Ai. Tao Yi died before he could succeed to the throne and had no son. [Hence], Sam Khai Noeng succeeded his father to the throne in the year *moeng sai*, CS 859 (AD 1497), at the age of fifteen. He was on the throne five years and passed away (*cuti tai*) at the age of twenty in the *tao set* year, CS 864 (AD 1502), without an heir. This is the twelfth generation ruler (the seventeenth ruler of Moeng Lü).

15. CAO KHAN MOENG (ZHAO KAN 詔侃), R. 1502–1523

15.1 THE EIGHTEENTH RULER

Cao Khan Moeng succeeded his elder brother Sam Khai Noeng in CS 864, a *tao set* year (AD 1502), as the ruler at the age of forty-six. He was on the throne twenty-one years and passed away (*hong*) at sixty-seven in CS 855, a *ka met* year (Jiajing 2, AD 1523). This

248. Part 1 of MLC-LV1 ends here. Two other Tai Lü chronicles, "Historical records of the various generations after Phaya Coeng" and "Genealogy of the late kings", translated into Chinese by Dao and Wu 1983 and by Dao and Kang 1989b respectively, also end with Tao Sam Pò Lütai without the following three reigns. See Liew and Grabowsky 2004 (documents no. 2 and no. 22 respectively).

249. According to the preface to MLC-LV1, 3, by Li Fuyi, the following three reigns are not recorded in part 1 of the original Tai Lü manuscript, on which his translation is based. They are supplemented by MLC-SV1. According to Liew-Herres' investigation, however, Li Fuyi took the three reigns from his *Cheli xuanwei shixi kaoding* (Li Fuyi, 1947c, 19–21), instead of from MLC-SV1, 53 of the same book, which is translated directly from the Tai Lü manuscript. The three reigns translated from the Tai Lü text in MLC-SV1 by Li Fuyi are thus added below for comparison.

was the fifteenth (sic) generation [the eighteenth ruler of Moeng Lü]. Cao Khan Moeng had a son called Cao Sili (Sali) Sompan.

> Li Fuyi (MLC-SV1), Tai Lü: The third son of [Tao] Sam Pò Lütai, Cao Am, died (*mòranna sia*) before he could succeed to the throne and had no heir. The fourth son Cao Ai also could not succeed [to the throne]. [He] had a son by the name of Cao Khan [Moeng], who succeeded to the throne as ruler in the *tao set* year, CS 864 (AD 1502), at the age of sixty-four. He was on the throne twenty-one years and passed away (*cuti tai*) at the age of eighty-five in the *ka met* year, CS 885 (AD 1523). This is the thirteenth generation ruler [the eighteenth ruler of Moeng Lü].

16. CAO SILI (SALI) SOMPAN (ZHAO SHILI SONGBAN 詔室利崧版), R. 1523–1530

16.1 THE NINETEENTH RULER

[Cao] Sili (Sali) Sompan succeeded his father Cao Khan Moeng as ruler in CS 885, the *ka met* year (AD 1523), at the age of twenty-six. He was on the throne seven years and passed away (*hong*) at the age of thirty-three in CS 892, the *kot yi* year (Jiajing 9, AD 1530). This was the sixteenth (sic) generation [the nineteenth ruler of Moeng Lü]. His son Cao Nò (Un) Moeng[250] (sic) succeeded him.

> Li Fuyi (MLC-SV1), Tai Lü: Cao Khan [Moeng] had one son called Cao Sali Sompan who succeeded his father to the throne in the *ka met* year, CS 885 (AD 1523), [at the age of thirty]. He was on the throne thirty-seven years and passed away (*cuti tai*) in the *kot san* year, CS 922 (AD 1560), [at the age of sixty-seven]. This is the fourteenth (sic) generation [the nineteenth ruler of Moeng Lü].

250. According to other sources, Cao Sili (Sali) Sompan's son was called Cao Un/Ong Moeng. See MLC-SV1, 53, s. 19; MLC-LV2, s. 21.1; MLC-SV2, 86, s. 22; Gao Lishi 1984, 115, s. 21.1; Dao and Kang 1989a, 288; Dao Shuren 1989, 242.

PART TWO (1530–1864)

17. CAO NÒ MOENG (DAO NUOMENG 刀糯猛), R. 1530–1568

17.1 THE TWENTIETH RULER

Cao Sili (Sali) Sompan died (*si*) in the *kot yi* year, CS 892 (Jiajing 9, AD 1530). He had one son by the name of Cao Nò Moeng (sic).[251] The Heavenly Court (i.e., the Ming court) appointed him the *saenwi fa* (*xuanwei shi*).[252] Until that time Chiang Yung (i.e., Cheli)[253] was not a vassal of Mian (Burma).[254]

17.2 FA SUTTHO THAMMALACA CONQUERS CHIANG YUNG

In the *poek si* year, CS 930 (Longqing 2, AD 1568), the king of Dagon (Yangon)[255] of Burma appointed general Maha Tham to command an army to conquer Chiang Yung. Only then did Cao Nò Moeng (sic) submit to His Majesty, the king of [Ava-] Burma.[256]

251. Cao Nò Moeng's (Dao Nuomeng 刀糯猛) name first appears in Ming sources in Jiajing 11 (1532) and then in Wanli 13, fifth month (1585), in Wanli 14, sixth month (1586), and in Wanli 18, third month (1590). But Cao Ong Moeng's (Dao Yunmeng 刀韞猛) name first appears in Ming sources in Tianqi 7, fourth month (1627). See MSG, ch. 189, 32. Li Fuyi had consulted the Ming sources when he transcribed the names of the Tai Lü *saenwi fa* into Chinese. The Chinese renderings of the Tai Lü personal names of the *saenwi fa* in MLC-LV1 and MLC-SV1 by Li Fuyi are exactly the same as those used in *Mingshi*, MSG and MSL, as well as those used in the Qing sources. But according to Li Fuyi (MLC-SV1) the incumbent *saenwi fa* was Cao Ong Moeng (Dao Yunmeng), r. from 1560 to 1588. In MLC-LV2, s. 22.1–11; Gao Lishi 1984, 115; and Dao Shuren 1989, the incumbent *saenwi fa* was Cao Un (Ong) Moeng, r. 1539–1567.

252. The term *xuanwei shi* 宣慰使, rendered into Tai Lü as *saenwi fa*, is used only in part 2 of MLC-LV1, by Li Fuyi. In MLC-LV2 and Gao Lishi 1984 the term *saenwi fa* (obviously derived from the Chinese *xuanwei shi*, translated into English as pacification commissioner) appears in the reign of Phaya Coeng. This shows that part 2 of MLC-LV1 is based on a Tai Lü manuscript, which was not subjected to revision in the 1960s as in MLC-LV2 and Gao Lishi 1984.

253. The parenthesis is apparently ascribed to Li Fuyi. Cheli 車里 is the Chinese rendering of Chiang Lü or Moeng Lü. On the origin of the name Cheli, see Li Fuyi 1979, 31–37, 197–200.

254. Moeng Lü because a vassal of Burma (now called Myanmar) began in the reign of Cao Nò Moeng. Chiang Rung (lit., "city of dawn") was then renamed Chiang Yung (lit., "city of peacocks"). Thus in part 2 of MLC-LV1, Chiang Rung is called Chiang Yung.

255. Dagon was the capital of Toungoo (Taungu) dynasty, also known as the Second Burmese Empire, 1486–1752 or 1531–1752. When King Alaungpaya (r. 1752–1760), who founded the Konbaung dynasty (1752–1885), conquered Southern Burma in the mid-1750s, he developed Dagon as a port and renamed it Yangon (Rangoon), which means "end of strife".

256. The expansion of Burmese power to the east is rather well documented in contemporary Chinese sources. According to MSG, in Jiajing 11 (1532), the Burmese bandit, Mang Yingli (sic) (Nandabayin, r. 1581–1599) occupied Pegou (Pegu) and annexed [the lands of] various barbarians one after another, like silkworms nibbling mulberry leaves. [The chieftains of] most of the aboriginal commissions (*tusi*) were threatened by Mang Yingli (sic) and served as his guides. At that time the pacification commissioner of Cheli, Dao Nuomeng (Cao Nò Moeng) (sic), submitted to

17.3 CAO NÒ MOENG DIES AT MOENG PHAYAK

He commanded his aboriginal troops (sic)[257] and followed the king of [Ava-] Burma, Fa Suttho Thammalaca (Mang Yinglong),[258] to conquer Ayutthaya and Chiang Mai.[259] During the victorious march back at Moeng Phayak[260] the *saenwi fa* Cao Nò Moeng (sic) fell ill and died (*bing si*).[261]

18. CAO SILI (SALI) SUNANTA (ZHAO SHILI SUNANDA 詔室利穌赧打), R. 1568

18.1 THE TWENTY-FIRST RULER AND CAO NÒ MOENG'S TWO SONS

Cao Nò Moeng (sic) had two sons: the eldest was named Cao Sili (Sali) Sunanta and the second was called Cao In Moeng. After the death (*si*) of Cao Nò Moeng (sic) the Heavenly Court (Ming court) appointed his eldest son Cao Sili (Sali) Sunanta as the *saenwi fa*.[262]

Burma. Hence, there were two Cheli. The Greater Cheli (to the right of the Mekong) owed allegiance to Burma, while the Lesser Cheli (to the left of the Mekong), to China. See MSG, ch. 189, 32b; Liew-Herres 2003b. On Greater and Lesser Cheli, see Li Fuyi 1979, 203–6. It could not have been Mang Yingli who conquered Pegou in 1532. It was probably Mang Ruiti (Tabinshwehti, r. 1531–1550) or Mang Yinglong (Bayinnaung, r. 1551–1581).

257. From the perspective of a Chinese official, Li Fuyi (MLC-LV1, 19) renders "Tai Lü troops" as *tulian* 土練, by which he probably meant "native/local militia" (*lian* being the abbreviation of *lianyong* 練勇).

258. Here Li Fuyi (MLC-LV1, 19) adds in the parenthesis that he was namely Mang Yinglong 莽應龍. Burennaung or Bayinnaung or Pha Mahakasat Fa Suttho Thammalaca (r. 1551–1581) is known as Mang Yinglong in Chinese sources. In Gao Lishi 1984, 115, s. 22.2, the king of Ava was called Phaya Mahakasat Pun.

259. According to the Chiang Mai Chronicle (Wyatt and Aroonrut 1995, 122), King Mae Ku of Chiang Mai rebelled against King Poeng Phawa Min Taya (i.e., Bayinnaung) of Pegu in CS 926 (1564/65).

260. Moeng Phayak is located in the southeast of Chiang Tung (Keng Tung) in Burma.

261. Here Li Fuyi (MLC-LV1, 19) used the word *bing si* 病死 (died from illness), instead of *hong* 薨 (death of a lord). In part 2 of MLC-LV1 the more respectable word *hong* is no longer used for the death of the *saenwi fa*. More information is given in other versions of the Moeng Lü Chronicle, recording how the Burmese general Fa Suttho commanded Cao Un Moeng to Moeng Sai (i.e., Xinping 新平, Yunnan) to delimit the boundaries, planted a Bodhi tree in Müang Luang Nam Tha (Laos) at the convergent point of the three frontiers, and then went to Chiang Rai to negotiate with Cao Chiang Rai about demarcating the frontiers. See MLC-LV2, s. 22.3–8; and Gao Lishi 1984, 115, s. 22.3. Either Li Fuyi failed to translate it, which is not likely because he stated in the preface that his translation is faithful to the original Tai Lü manuscripts, or the scribes of the later Tai Lü manuscripts of this reign have collated it with sources of other manuscripts.

262. The chronicle of this reign is very short in all versions consulted. Cao Sili (Sali) Sunanta reigned only six months. It could have been that he was murdered by the pro-Burmese faction.

19. CAO IN MOENG (DAO YINGMENG 刀應猛), R. 1569–1598

19.1 THE TWENTY-SECOND RULER

Cao Sili (Sali) Sunanta ruled six months before he died (*zu*). The Heavenly Court (sic) then appointed his younger brother Cao In Moeng as the *saenwi fa*.

19.2 ESCORTING FA SUTTHO THAMMALACA BACK TO AVA

Cao In Moeng dispatched four officials (i.e., Tai Lü lords)—one selected from the east of the river (Mekong), one from the west of the river, and two from the capital Chiang Yung (Chiang Rung)—to escort the king of Burma [Fa Suttho Thammalaca][263] to Angwa (Ava) of the Golden Land (Moeng Kham). This was in CS 931, [a *kat sai* year] (Longqing 3, *jisi* year AD 1569).

19.3 CAO IN MOENG SUBMITS TO THE KING OF BURMA AND MARRIES PRINCESS NANG BO KHAM

In view of the *saenwi fa* Cao In Moeng had submitted to the suzerainty of the Burmese Court, the king of Burma issued a special decree and invested the *saenwi fa* with [the title] Coti Nakkala (Nagara) Maha Caiya Pawala Suthammalaca[264] and gave the princess Nang Bo Kham to the *saenwi fa* in marriage. She was known as the Golden Lotus Queen.[265] An ivory seal was bestowed [on the *saenwi fa* Cao In Moeng]. The seal is three fingers wide, engraved in the middle with the "sacred Mount Meru" (Khao Sanero),[266] which is surrounded by seven hills (i.e., Khao Sattaphan), below which is the sea. There are three [supporting] pillars and a pair of turtles (*anon* fish),[267] on which is a pagoda with a sun and a moon.[268]

---

263. According to MLC-LV2, s. 24.2 and Gao Lishi 1984, 116, s. 24.2, the Burmese king was Fa Suttho Thammalaca.

264. According to Gao Lishi 1984, 116, 24.2, the Cao Angwa, Phaya Mahakasat (lit., "lord of Ava, the great king", i.e., the Burmese monarch), granted Cao In Moeng sugar (*phòi tò*) and the honourable title, Coti Nakkala (Nagara) Maha Caiya Pawala Suthammalaca. Li Fuyi (MLC-LV1, 19), translated it into: *Zuodi guo da zizhu fulu zhishan wang* 左 磾 國 大 自 主 福 祿 至 善 王 (lit., "great sovereign of the blessed and most virtuous king of the Coti land"). Coti Nakkala means "bright capital", as the Burmese called Sipsòng Panna after her capitulation.

265. Li Fuyi (MLC-LV1, 20) translated it into *Jinlian wanghou* 金 蓮 王 后, which means "golden lotus queen", Nang Bo Kham. According to MLC-LV2, s. 24.3, she was called Nang Suwanna Patumma Bo Kham.

266. Li Fuyi (MLC-LV1, 20) translates Khao Sattaphan as *xumi shenshan* 須 彌 神 山 (lit., "sacred Mount Meru"), which is the famous sacred Buddhist mountain, the abode of gods and deities.

267. According to MLC-LV2, s. 24.2, it is *anon* fish. But both MLC-LV1, 20 and Gao Lishi 1984, 116, s. 24.2 render it as *ao yu* 鰲 魚 (turtle fish).

268. A similar account is recorded in MLC-LV2, s. 24.2 and in Gao Lishi 1984, 116, s. 24.2.

19.4 THE DOWRY OF THE BURMESE PRINCESS

In addition the following gifts were given as dowry:

1) Four elephants, male and female each one pair, six arms' length *sòk* (*zhou*) in height;
2) a pair of golden trays (*bian*), {each weighing seven *khan* and seven *cap*},[269] both with twelve corners, the edges inlaid with precious stones (gems);
3) a pair of golden bowls, {each weighing one *khan* and one and a half *cap*};[270]
4) a pair of *pinang* containers,[271] namely the boxes for putting the lime, {each weighing seven and a half *cap*};[272]
5) a pair of small golden lions (*tep sing*), {each weighing five *cap*};[273]
6) a case for the golden warm-pot, engraved with one peacock head and inlaid with precious stones (gems);[274]
7) one golden bottle [for storing] hair oil, engraved with double peacocks and inlaid with precious stones (gems);[275]
8) one golden spoon (ladle) for scooping rice, {weighing one/two and a half *cap*};[276]
9) one golden crown inlaid with precious stones, {weighing four *khan*} and edged with twenty-four golden flowers;[277]
10) twenty-five golden *pinang* (betel nut) plates;[278]
11) one golden carriage (sedan chair);[279]
12) one golden water jar inlaid with gems, {weighing five *khan*};
13) one golden lid for a water jug, inlaid with gems, {weighing two *khan*};
14) a golden spittoon, {weighing five *khan*};

269. The weight is given in MLC-LV2, s. 24.3 and in Gao Lishi 1984, 116, s. 24.3.

270. Ditto.

271. *Pinang* is a kind of areca nut or betel nut, chewed together with lime and leaves of betel plant by some Asian peoples.

272. The weight is given in the MLC-LV2-1963, s. 24.3 and in Gao Lishi 1984, 116, s. 24.3.

273. Ditto.

274. According to MLC-LV2-1963, s. 24.3, 6, it is one golden box [containing] fermented tea, engraved with a one-headed swan (*hangsa* or *haṃsa*) and inlaid with red gems, weighing two *khan* and two and a half *cap*.

275. According to MLC-LV2, s. 24.3, it is one golden box [containing] a razor, engraved with a double-headed swan and inlaid with red gems, weighing six *cap*. But according to Gao Lishi 1984, 116, s. 24.3, it is one bottle for hair oil, engraved with one peacock and inlaid with gems, weighing two *khan* and seven and a half *cap*.

276. See MLC-LV2, s. 24.3, 8; the same is given in Gao Lishi 1984, 116, s. 24.3.

277. According to MLC-LV2, s. 24.3, 9, the top of the crown is adorned with twenty-four golden flowers; but according to Gao Lishi 1984, 116, 24.3, the edge of the crown is adorned with twenty-four golden flowers with five rows of borders.

278. According to MLC-LV2, s. 24.3, 10, it is twenty-five small golden cups.

279. According to MLC-LV2, s. 24.3, 11, it is one canopied palanquin.

15) ten long knives (swords) wrapped in golden foil (or ten gold-plated long knives);
16) two golden long knives (swords) inlaid with three rows of rubies;
17) a pair of long knives (swords/pikes) with ivory hilts;
18) a pair of *tangba* (sic);[280]
19) sixteen gold-plated spears and sixteen silver-plated spears;[281]
20) a pair of white parasols. The parasols were divided into three layers, each of which was decorated with twelve golden Bodhi leaves, altogether thirty-six golden Bodhi leaves;
21) a pair of single layer parasols;
22) a pair of ceremonial headgear pasted with golden [foil];
23) twelve pairs of golden umbrellas;
24) a pair of hatchets (axes);
25) a pair of *buzhang* 篰杖;[282]
26) a pair of sun-shaped insignia;
27) a pair of bone-clusters (*ci gu duo* 刺骨朵);[283]
28) a pair of palm-leaf fans stuck with golden [foil];
29) a pair of golden sandals;
30) twelve golden caps (headgears);
31) a pair of walking sticks wrapped with golden [foil];
32) a pair of red painted walking stucks made of tin;
33) one big gong (*meng*) pasted with gold with a diameter of five *cap* (*zha*);[284]
34) a pair of cymbals pasted with gold;
35) one tiny waist drum;
36) a set of nine-tone drums, nine in all;[285]
37) one *dingning* drum (丁寧鼓);
38) one *jili* drum (嘰哩鼓);[286]
39) a set of silver flutes (a kind of short pipe);[287]

280. Li Fuyi (MLC-LV1, 20, line 7) renders it as *tangba* 鎲鈀 (pikes?), which is a type of ancient weapon, like a crescent spear with a handle. According to Gao Lishi 1984, 116s. 24.3, it was a pair of spears or pikes (*mao* 矛). In MLC-LV2, 18, s. 24.3, this is a pair of *naraka* spears.

281. The same is recorded in Gao Lishi 1984, 116, s. 24.3. But according to MLC-LV2, 18, s. 24.3, it is sixteen spears decorated with golden and silver tassels.

282. Unclear meaning; probably a kind of fan.

283. Unclear meaning.

284. One *cap* (*zha*) is the width between the thumb and the index-finger or middle finger stretched out, giving the minor and major *cap* respectively. Thus the Tai *cap* is similar to a span (the length between the thumb and little finger). One *cap* is about five inches.

285. Each drum gives a different tone.

286. It is not clear what Li Fuyi means by *dingning* drum and *jili* drum.

287. The parenthesis should be ascribed to Li Fuyi.

40) one big silver flute;
41) a pair of military bugles/trumpets;
42) two sets of elephant howdahs pasted with gold;
43) two big copper cannons;
44) a pair of ceremonial insignia in the shape of a hand;
45) twelve insignia for dancing;
46) twelve square parasols edged with lotus;
47) a model of two-story official residence with twelve rooms, the roof of which was covered with tiles and the four pillars of which were pasted with golden foil;
48) a throne covered with golden [foil], height three *sòk* (*zhou*) and length four *sòk*, decorated with flowers made of oil-ash, inlaid with sky blue, on both front corners of the throne a protecting Buddha was erected, [each] holding a long knife to protect the throne; and there were two pictures;
49) one piece of scroll adorned with golden leaves;
50) one wrap skirt (sarong) woven with golden thread;
51) one suit of ceremonial coat (namely an overcoat) ;[288] and
52) one red golden woollen ceremonial coat, edged with embroidered ribbons of a width of three fingers.[289]

The official residence, the throne, clothing and the insignia of the *saenwi fa* were permitted to take these (i.e., the above) as the standard.[290]

19.5 THE BURMESE PRINCESS AND HER ENTOURAGE ARRIVE AT CHIANG RUNG

The above-listed gifts and the princess were brought to [Moeng Lü], escorted by the emissaries sent by the Burmese king, bearing an edict, who followed the tribute envoys of the *saenwi fa* to Chiang Yung (Chiang Rung).[291] When the news [of their arrival] reached the *saenwi fa*, he was very delighted. Therefore, he dispatched the officials of Sipsòng Panna[292] to welcome [the Burmese princess] at the outskirts [of Chiang Rung].

288. Ibid.

289. This numbering is inserted by the present translator for easy reading. Similar lists of dowries are recorded in other versions of the Moeng Lü Chronicle, albeit the gifts given vary slightly. See MLC-LV2, s. 24.3; Gao Lishi 1984, 116; Dao Shuren 1989, 245.

290. The official residence of the Tai lord in Moeng Ti (i.e., Nandian *xuanfusi* in today's Dehong) and that in Moeng Laem (i.e., Menglian *xuanfusi*) have been well-preserved. Both are very grand and can be considered as palaces.

291. A rather similar account is recorded in Gao Lishi 1984, 116, s. 24.4: "Cao Angwa dispatched emissaries, *ahmu-gyi* and *ahmu-mat*, to escort the princess and *saenwi fa* Cao In Moeng to Chiang Rung. It was in CS 932, a *kot sanga* year (AD 1570). Since then Chiang Rung (lit., "city of dawn") was renamed Chiang Yung (lit., "city of peacocks"). Lan Na came to offer submission as well. An edict was issued bestowing [the title] Nakkala (Nagara) Hò Kham on the *saenwi fa*. See also MLC-LV2, s. 24.4.

292. Moeng Lü is first called Sipsòng Panna (Xishuang banna) during the reign of Cao In Moeng, in part 2 of MLC-LV1, 21, line 4.

[The princess and her entourage] swarmed into the fortified-town of Chiang Yung (Wiang Chiang Rung). Various kinds of stage-plays were performed and they had a great celebration.

19.6 INVESTMENT OF CAO IN MOENG AS CHINESE AND BURMESE *SAENWI FA*

The news [of the marriage] reached the Heavenly Court (sic)[293] [The matter] was redirected to the senior official of Moeng Sae [Long] (Kunming)[294] who ordered the senior officials of Ninger (Moeng Maen) and of Simao (Moeng La)[295] to travel to Chiang Yung. [The emissaries] of both sides, the Heavenly Court and the Burmese [court], were in complete harmony. The *saenwi fa* was very grateful for the generous treatment. Therefore, he paid his respect to the Heavenly Court as a father and to the Burmese court as a mother. The emissary of the Heavenly Court holding the left hand[296] of the *saenwi fa* and the emissary of the Burmese side holding his right hand, they led him to ascend the throne. [Cao In Moeng] was invested as the *saenwi fa* by both sides and the ceremony of sprinkling the sacred water was performed.

19.7 HONOURS TO QUEEN NANG SUWANNA PATUMMA

During the [ceremony of] sprinkling water *Nang Suwanna Patumma Tewi* was promoted and the honourable title, Nang Maha Suwanna Patumma Akka Mahesi Tewi, was conferred on her.[297]

19.8 CEREMONY OF RECEIVING AN IMPERIAL EDICT

For the ceremony of receiving the imperial edict, one mat made of the stems of *kan tòng* grass, a piece of red and a piece of white cloth, eight pairs of candles, one pot for

293. Here *tianchao* refers to the Ming court in Beijing. In CS 931 (1569 AD) it was the court of Emperor Longqing.

294. Kunming, the provincial capital of Yunnan is known to the Tai as Moeng Sae Long. The parenthesis should be ascribed to Li Fuyi.

295. In Gao Lishi 1984, 116, 24.6, the officials were from Moeng Maen (Puer 普洱) and Moeng La (Simao 思茅). In the original Tai Lü manuscript, on which Li Fuyi's MLC-LV1 is based, they are most probably not Ninger 寧洱 and Simao 思茅 but Moeng Maen and Moeng La. Ninger is located in Puer, in the north of Simao. At that time it was usual that the high officials in Kunming did not go to Sipsòng Panna personally. Kunming depended on the local officials in Simao and Puer, the two southern Chinese outposts, to deal with the Tai Lü *saenwi fa* directly. The information gathered by these officials was reported to Kunming.

296. According to the Chinese custom of the time, left was higher in rank than right.

297. Similar accounts are given in MLC-LV2-1963, s. 24.6 and Gao Lishi 1984, 116, s. 24.6.

drinking water, and one *hòi* (1 *hòi* = 3.3 taels)[298] of mercury of the ninth grade of purity were needed.[299]

After the imperial edict had been received, the official responsible for managing general affairs[300] would be commanded to safeguard it. On an auspicious day, the *saenwi fa* would put the imperial edict in a golden bowl which was placed on the silver tray. A piece of red cloth was used to cover the golden bowl. The secretary-official[301] would carry the imperial edict to the great hall of the government building and read it aloud. After the imperial edict had been read, the edict, the golden bowl, the silver tray, and the red cloth would be given to the *saenwi fa* for safekeeping.

19.9 OATH-TAKING CEREMONY

After the imperial edict had been read, the *saenwi fa* summoned all the chieftains and vice-chieftains (sic) of the various polities in Sipsòng Panna[302] for a meeting to make a decision. Accompanied by the emissaries of Burma and others they proceeded to the Buddhist temple. Facing the Buddha statue, the sutras, and the ceremonial representative of the three Buddhas (sic), they performed the oath-taking ceremony with utmost sincerity.[303] After the ceremony, when the Burmese emissaries were going to return to Burma to report to [His Majesty], the [Tai Lü] *saenwi fa* bestowed on [them] the following gifts.

298. Here the long parenthesis in the main text of MLC-LV1, 21, added by Li Fuyi, is transferred to this footnote. Li explains: *hòi* is a unit of Tai weights: ten *hòi* is one *bat*, ten *bat* is one *mün*, ten *mün* is one *saen*; below *hòi* the units are *hong*, *tie (the)*, and *fen*. Ten *fen* is one *tie*, ten *tie* is one *hong*, thirty-three *hong* is one *pan*, and one *hòi* is equivalent to the standard Chinese weight three *liang* and three *qian* (i.e., 3.3 taels). According to Gao Lishi 1984, 131, one Tai *bat* is 0.33 tael, one *hòi* is 3.3 taels, and one *pan* is 33 taels. As to the Chinese weights: one *jin* (catty) is about 1 1/3 pounds, 16 *liang* (taels) is one *jin*, and 10 *qian* is one *liang*. One *liang* is about 1.3 ounces. Hence, one hòi (*huai*) is about 4.29 ounces.

299. Most probably Li Fuyi has made a mistake here. According to MLC-LV2, s. 24.7, it is one water pot made of silver of ninth grade of purity weighing two *hòi*.

300. Li Fuyi (MLC-LV1, 21) renders it as *zong shuwu guan* 總庶務官, which is translated as above. But according to MLC-LV2, s. 24.7 and Gao Lishi 1984, 116, s. 24.7, Panna Bao Cai was entrusted to guard the royal decree. The term "Panna Bao Cai" is explained in MLC-LV1, 55, s. 3.11, by Li Fuyi. They were the three lesser *panna* located to the west of the Mekong (namely Lesser Cheli).

301. Li Fuyi (MLC-LV1, 21) renders it as *shuji guan* 書記官, which is translated as above. But according to MLC-LV2, s. 24.7 and Gao Lishi 1984, 116, s. 24.7, it is the *khun khaek*, which means "secretarial official" (*shuji guan*) as explained by Gao Lishi.

302. According to MLC-LV2, s. 24.7, and Gao Lishi 1984, 116, s. 24.7, they were the civil and military officials of Sipsòng Panna.

303. According to MLC-LV2, s. 24.7, they took the oath of drinking the water of loyalty to the Chinese and Burmese courts, facing the three Buddhist jewels (*sòng phanet kaeo cao sam pakan*). See also Gao Lishi 1984, 117, 24.7.

19.10 GIFTS BESTOWED ON THE BURMESE EMISSARIES

In all, the Burmese chief emissary (*dashi*)[304] was bestowed one *pan* of silver of ninth grade of purity (as is true in the following),[305] the vice-emissary (*fushi*) eight *hòi* of silver, the third-rank emissary six *hòi* of silver, and the fourth-rank emissary four *hòi* of silver. Each of the four mahouts and each of the fourteen soldiers (sic) in the retinue[306] was granted one *hòi* of silver. The chief headman (*da toumu*) of Moeng Khün[307] was granted eight *bat* of silver of ninth grade of purity (as is true in the following);[308] and the vice-headman (*er toumu*) six *bat* of silver. Since then the quantity of gifts conferred on emissaries sent on the occasion of betrothal was to take this as the standard.

19.11 GIFTS BESTOWED ON THE CHINESE OFFICIALS

In addition, the chief official (*shouguan*)[309] of the Heavenly Court was bestowed one *pan* and one *hòi* of silver of the ninth grade of purity, the second-rank official (*ciguan*) one *pan* of silver of the ninth grade of purity, the third-rank emissary (*shiquan*) eight *hòi* of silver of the ninth grade of purity, and the fourth-rank emissary six *hòi* of silver of the ninth grade of purity. The first-rank escort of the retinue (*suiyuan*) was bestowed one *hòi* of silver of the ninth grade of purity and the second-rank escort of the retinue five *bat* of silver of the ninth grade of purity. Thereafter, [this amount of gifts given] was to be taken as the standard. Then, the body of officials (*guanyuan*) and emissaries (*shijie*) from China and Burma returned to their respective lands.

19.12 GIFTS BESTOWED ON BURMESE EMISSARIES ON BUDDHIST FESTIVALS

This year was an intercalary year (i.e., CS 931, AD 1569) and there were two ninth months.[310] The Burmese king dispatched emissaries to congratulate the *saenwi fa* on the

304. In MLC-LV2, s. 24.8 it is the chief emissary, *amuki* (*ahmu-gyi*).

305. The parenthesis is probably ascribed to Li Fuyi (MLC-LV1, 22). Here it means that lesser envoys were also given silver with 90 per cent of silver content.

306. According to Gao Lishi 1984, 117, s. 24.8 and MLC-LV2, s. 24.8, they were the fourteen escorts in the retinue. Li Fuyi (MLC-LV1, 22) renders it as *sui-cong bing-ding* 隨從兵丁, which is translated as above. In fact in olden times, *bing-ding* normally referred to "private soldiers" of a powerful clan.

307. Both Li Fuyi (MLC-LV1, 22) and Gao Lishi 1984, 117 render it as *da toumu* 大頭目 (lit., "chief headman"), by which they probably mean "chief *cao mòm*". According to MLC-LV2, s. 24.8, he was the *nai kao* of Moeng Khün (i.e., Chiang Tung).

308. Here the parenthesis added by Li Fuyi in the main text of MLC-LV1, 22 is transferred to this footnote: Burmese weights: four *bat* is one *cap*, ten *cap* is one *khan*, ten *khan* is one *còi* or *ku*, one *còi* is namely one Burmese catty (*jin*), which is about forty-four Chinese taels (*liang*). According to Gao Lishi 1984, 131, one Tai *cap* is 0.44 tael, one *khan* is 4.4 taels, and one *còi* is 44 taels.

309. Probably here the "chief official" or "leading official" means the imperial envoy from Kunming (Moeng Sae), not from the Ming court in Beijing.

310. According to Gao Lishi 1984, 117, s. 24.9, it was on the full moon day of the second ninth month.

summer festivals (*shouxia jie*).[311] The *saenwi fa* presented a mat made of *kan tòng* grass stems, a piece of red and a piece of white cloth, four pairs of wax candles, one pot for drinking water, and eight *bat* of mercury (sic)[312] of the ninth grade of purity [to the Burmese emissaries]. A secretarial official (*shuji guan*) was entrusted [to receive the edict]. He placed the edict from the Burmese king on a silver tray and carried it [with two hands] to the hall of the official residence (sic)[313] where he read [it] aloud. After the ceremony of [reading the edict] had been performed, the [Tai Lü] *saenwi fa* gave the chief official (*shouguan*) of the body of emissaries from Burma six *hòi* of silver of the ninth grade of purity and the secondary official (*ciguan*) five *hòi* of silver of the ninth grade of purity. Each of the four escorting soldiers (*gending*) was given one *hòi* of silver of the ninth grade of purity, which made a total of four *hòi*. In addition, the chief headman (*da toumu*) of Moeng Khün was given six *bat* of silver of the ninth grade of purity and the secondary headman four *bat* of silver of the ninth grade of purity. Thereafter, all the emissaries coming to offer their congratulations on the occasion of the summer festival (*shouxia jie*) were to be given gifts according to this same standard.[314]

19.13 QUEEN SUWANNA PATUMMA BO KHAM GIVES BIRTH TO A SON

In the *kot sanga* year, CS 932 (Longqing 4, 1570 AD),[315] the Golden Lotus Queen (i.e., Nang Suwanna Patumma Laca Tewi) bore a son and he was named Cao Ong Moeng (sic).[316] The queen and the ruler had a huge Buddhist temple built. The temple was located in the western part of Wiang Chiang Yung. A Buddha statue[317] was cast and

---

311. The summer festivals, rendered as *shouxia jie* 守 夏 節 by Li Fuyi (MLC-LV1, 22), refer to the Tai Lü, *khao watsa* (Tr. เข้าวัสสา) and *òk watsa* (Tr. ออกวัสสา). The corresponding Thai names are *khao phansa* (เข้าพรรษา) and *òk phansa* (ออกพรรษา), meaning "entering the rainy season" and "leaving the rainy season" respectively. The two Buddhist festivals are celebrated to mark the beginning and the end of the Buddhist lent retreat which lasts from mid-July to mid-October. It is customary for Buddhist monks to remain at their monastery and to observe the lent retreat during the rainy season for a period of three months. See Doré and Premchit 1992, 258–66.

312. In MLC-LV1, 22, it is *shuiyin* 水 銀, which means mercury; but in Gao Lishi 1984, 117, s. 24.9, it is two *hòi* of pure silver (*baiyin* 白 銀).

313. Li Fuyi (MLC-LV1, 22), translates it into *guanxie litang* 官 廨 禮 堂, which means "the hall of the official residence". From Li Fuyi's perspective the palace of the *cao phaendin* was the "official residence of the *saenwi fa*". Gao Lishi renders it as "the palace of the *saenwi fa*". See Gao Lishi 1984, 117, s. 24.9.

314. This is not recorded in MLC-LV2 but a similar account is given in Gao Lishi 1984, 117, s. 24.9.

315. According to MLC-LV2, s. 24.10, it was in the year CS 934. The same is given in Gao Lishi 1984, 117, s. 24.10. CS 934 corresponds to AD 1572 and Longqing 6.

316. According to other Tai Lü chronicles the son of Cao In Moeng and Nang Suwanna Patumma Tewi was called Cao Nò Moeng (or Cao Nò Kham), instead of Cao Ong Moeng (Dao Yunmeng 刀 韞 猛. See MLC-SV1, 53; MLC-LV2, s. 24.10; and 24.18; Gao Lishi 1984, 119; Dao Shuren 1989, 247. Cao In Moeng also had a daughter who was married to Cao Lan Sang. See part 3, section 3.4 below.

317. According to MLC-LV2, s. 24.10 and Gao Lishi 1984, 117, s. 24.10, the statue of the Buddha was seven *sòk* high.

placed on the precious throne with his face looking in the direction of the city of Angwa (Ava) of the great Burmese kingdom. It was named the Temple of Golden Lotus, in Tai Lü called Wat Bo Kham, which also means the Golden Lotus Temple.[318]

19.14 THE QUEEN'S HOMESICKNESS

During the three years when the queen was in Chiang Yung the [paddy] grains had ripened four times.[319] [The queen] had a longing [to see her] parents and asked the *saenwi fa* for permission to return to Burma to visit her relatives. Therefore the *saenwi fa* commanded the various subordinate aboriginal commissions (sic) of Sipsòng Panna[320] to dispatch men to escort the Golden Lotus Queen to Angwa (Ava). Moreover, gifts were collected from [the various *panna* of] Sipsòng Panna to offer to the Burmese king.

19.15 TRIBUTE GIFTS COLLECTED FROM THE TWELVE *PANNA*

[The *müang* forming the twelve *panna* and the tribute gifts offered are] as listed in the following:[321]

I) [Moeng] Chiang Rung (1), Moeng Ham (2), [and two] other [*müang*][322] under the direct jurisdiction of the *saenwi fa* forming one *panna*, offered in tribute [to the Burmese king] one golden jar weighing six *bat*; six golden flowers, each weighing one *bat*; six silver flowers, weighing altogether six *bat*; a pair of wax candles wrapped with gold weighing one *pan*; two bolts of satin; four bolts of narrow satin; four bolts of lake-crepe (*huzhou*);[323] four bags of salt; four bamboo tubes of tea, five balls in each tube; and one horse of unspecified colour of hair/skin, either wild or tame; it was also not allowed to change. The [grade of the gold] of the golden jar and golden flowers was disregarded.[324]

---

318. The monastery under the royal patronage (*wat long*) was named Suwanna Patumma Ārāma, which means Golden Lotus Temple. See MLC-LV2, s. 24.10 and Gao Lishi 1984, 117.

319. According to MLC-LV2, s. 24.11, it was "three or four years later". But in Gao Lishi 1984, 117, s. 23.11, it is stated that "paddy had ripened four times, namely three years later, ...".

320. Here Li Fuyi (MLC-LV1, 23) renders it as *ge shu tusi* 各屬土司 (lit., "various subordinate aboriginal commissions/offices"), which actually means the thirty *müang* (*moeng*) and twelve *panna* listed in s. 19.15. Each *panna* was responsible for sending a fixed quantity of gifts to Burma. Since then Moeng Lü has popularly been called Sipsòng Panna.

321. The numbers given to each panna below have been added by the present translator.

322. Chiang Rung, Moeng Ham, Moeng Nun, and Moeng Song, forming one *panna*, were under the direct jurisdiction of the *saenwi fa*. See MLC-LV2, s. 24.12 and Gao Lishi 1984, 117.

323. *Huzhou* 湖縐, lit., "lake-crepe", was probably produced in China. But according to MLC-LV2, s. 24.12; Gao Lishi 1984, 117; and Dao Shuren 1989, 248, this was *nan* (dark blue cotton). Gao Lishi explains that *nan* is *huzhou*.

324. In MLC-LV1, 23 by Li Fuyi it is stated: 金瓶金花不計成色, which is translated as above. Here Li Fuyi probably means the quality of the gold of the golden jar and the golden flowers is not taken into account.

II) Moeng Cae (3), Chiang Lu (4), and Moeng Òng (5), forming one *panna*, offered in tribute [to the Burmese king] one golden jar weighing eight *the*, one silver jar weighing eight *the*, two bolts of narrow satin, and two bolts of lake-crepe (or dark blue cotton).

III) Moeng Long (6), forming one *panna*, offered in tribute [to the Burmese king] one golden jar weighing eight *the*, one silver jar weighing eight *the*, two bolts of narrow satin, and two bolts of lake-crepe (or dark blue cotton).

IV) Moeng Hun (7) and Moeng Pan (8), forming one *panna*, offered in tribute [to the Burmese king] one golden jar weighing eight *the*, one silver jar weighing eight *the*, two bolts of narrow satin, and two bolts of lake-crepe (dark blue cotton).

V) Chiang Coeng (9), Moeng Hai (10), and Moeng Ngat (11), forming one *panna*, offered in tribute [to the Burmese king] one golden jar weighing eight *the*, one silver jar weighing eight *the*, two bolts of narrow satin, and two bolts of lake-crepe (dark blue cotton).

VI) Chiang Lò (12), Moeng Mang (13), Moeng Ngam (14), [Moeng] Lang Nüa (15), and Moeng Khòn (16), forming one *panna*, offered in tribute [to the Burmese king] one golden jar weighing eight *the*, one silver jar weighing eight *the*, two bolts of narrow satin, and two bolts of lake-crepe (dark blue cotton).

The above were the gifts offered in tribute by the six *panna* located in the west of the [Mekong] River.[325]

VII) Moeng La (17) and Moeng Ban (18),[326] forming one *panna*, offered in tribute [to the Burmese king] one golden jar weighing four *bat*, one silver jar weighing four *bat*, two bolts of narrow satin and two bolts of lake-crepe (dark blue cotton).

VIII) Moeng Hing (i.e., Puteng)[327] (19), Moeng Bang (20),[328] forming one *panna*, offered in tribute [to the Burmese king] one golden jar weighing eight *the*, one silver jar weighing eight *the*, two bolts of narrow satin, and two bolts of lake-crepe (dark blue cotton).

IX) Moeng La (i.e., Simao and Liushun),[329] (21) and Moeng Wang (22),[330] forming one *panna*, offered in tribute [to Burma] one golden jar weighing eight *the*, one silver jar weighing eight *the*, two bolts of narrow satin, and two bolts of lake-crepe (dark blue cotton).

---

325. The above western *panna* is the so-called "Greater Cheli". See the introduction, part 1, section 8, n. 192 of this volume.

326. In Mengla County (previously Zhenyue County).

327. Moeng Hing to the Chinese officials was Puteng 普 騰. The parenthesis is probably added by Li Fuyi.

328. Mengwang 猛 旺, under Simao, is in the northern part of Chiang Rung County, including southern Simao City.

329. Moeng La to the Chinese officials was Simao 思 茅 and Liushun 六 順.

330. Mengwang 猛 往 is the seat of Jiangning County 江 寧 縣. See MLC-LV1, index, 10.

X) Moeng Phong (23), Moeng Yuan (24), and Moeng Mang (25),[331] forming one *panna*, offered in tribute [to Burma] one golden jar weighing eight *the*, one silver jar weighing eight *the*, two bolts of narrow satin, and two bolts of lake-crepe (dark blue cotton).

XI) Moeng U-Nüa (26) and Moeng U-Tai (27),[332] forming one *panna*, offered in tribute [to Burma] one golden jar weighing eight *the*, one silver jar weighing eight *the*, two bolts of narrow satin, and two bolts of lake-crepe (dark blue cotton).

XII) Chiang Tòng (28), Bò La (Yibang) (29), I-ngu (Yiwu) (30), forming one *panna*, offered in tribute [to Burma] one golden jar weighing eight *the*, one silver jar weighing eight *the*, two bolts of narrow satin, and two bolts of lake-crepe (dark blue cotton).

The above were the tribute gifts offered by the six *panna* located to the east of the [Mekong] River.[333]

19.16 LETTER AND TRIBUTE GIFTS PRESENTED TO THE BURMESE KING

The above tribute gifts [collected] from Sipsòng Panna were transported to Angwa (Ava). They were then wrapped up carefully with paper and packed separately in twelve boxes (one box for each *panna*). Together with a letter (memorial) they were presented to the Burmese king. The letter reads:

> [I],[334] Maha Caiya Pawala (Bòwòra) Suthammalaca,[335] the king (*wang*)[336] of this humble land Chiang Yung (i.e., Chiang Rung), [called] Coti Nakkala (Nagara),[337] pay my respect and prostrate myself before Your Majesty (*dianxia*),[338] the Most Blessed Great

331. These three *müang*, Mengpeng 猛捧, Mengrun 猛潤, Mengmang 猛漭, are located in the south of Mengla County (previously Zhenyue County 鎮越縣), on the border of Laos.

332. These two *müang*, now Phong Sali Province of Laos, were officially ceded to French Indochina in 1896.

333. This is so-called "Lesser Cheli". In AD 1570 the domain of Sipsòng Panna was divided into twelve administrative districts called *panna* for the purposes of levying tribute taxes, comprising a total of thirty-two *müang*. Nevertheless, according MLC-LV2, s. 24.12, there were thirty-five *müang* under the twelve *panna*; Gao Lishi (1984, 117–18) gives thirty-six *müang* and Dao Shuren (1989, 248), only thirty-one *müang*.

334. In MLC-LV2, s. 24.14, it is *kha pha bat*, which means "servant of the king's feet".

335. In MLC-LV1, 24, Li Fuyi renders it as *da zizhu fulu zhishan wang* 大自主福祿至善王, lit., "great autonomous, blessed, and kindest king". In MLC-LV1, index, 11, the Tai Lü name is transcribed into Maha Jaeyia Pavara Suhdamma Raja (sic), i.e., Coti Nakkala (Nagara) Maha Caiya Pawala Suthammalaca. See MLC-LV2, s. 24.14.

336. In Chinese *wang* 王 means king or prince.

337. According to MLC-LV1, index, 11, the Burmese called Cheli (i.e., Sipsòng Panna) "Coti Nakkala" (Nagara).

338. Here Li Fuyi (MLC-LV1, 24) uses the term *dianxian* 殿下 (lit., "below the steps of the palace"), which is the respectful way of addressing the emperor, feudal lords, or the crown prince.

Emperor[339] and offer the tribute gifts. Your Lord (*zhu*)[340] is the sovereign of all nations in this world.[341] Your Lord is the lord of the white (albino) elephants, the lord (*zhu*) of the red elephants, the lord of good elephants and horses, the lord of the Golden Hills and the Silver Hills, the lord of the Precious Liuli Glass Hills,[342] and the lord of the ships and ferries (or harbours). Your Majesty has seven previous things. Your Majesty is the greatest pillar of the world. Your Lord is the lord of the Moon Palace,[343] so bright and shining and beautiful as the sun. Your Lord is comparable to the beautiful moon, the golden lilies and all kinds of flowers, glittering like gold, unmatched. Your Lord has five kinds of precious things that are the heirlooms of the state. Your Lord is the great protector of the Buddhist law. Your Lord is endowed with the blessed kindness brought from a previous life. Your Lord commands the Buddhist precepts, and is endowed with perfect wisdom and perfect ability. Your Lord knows the ten official admonitions and possesses the seven virtues (valour, a sense of shame, integrity, propriety, trustworthiness, wisdom, and righteousness)[344]. Your Lord's merits are sufficient to be the ruler of various lands in the world. [I] respectfully offer in tribute the golden flowers and silver flowers, golden jar(s) and silver jar(s), satin and crepe silks, and others [things]. In future this precedent will always be observed. [I have given] a special order [entrusting] the lords [of the various *müang*] of my humble land Sipsòng Panna to send their envoys as representatives and to prepare with respect the wax sticks/candles, which together with [the tribute gifts] are to be offered to Your Majesty, the Great Emperor. My humble land with [all] respect recognises Your Majesty, the Great Emperor, as [our] lord. [My land and the people of] Sipsòng Panna are willing to be your subjects and servants forever, and will bear the responsibility for paying every kind of land taxes and rendering corvée. With utmost respect, [I] wish [Your Majesty] an abundant harvest of grains of all sorts and that everything may turn out as [Your Majesty] wishes. [I] prostrate myself before [Your Majesty and beg for Your Majesty's] perusal and enlightened advice.[345]

339. Li Fuyi (MLC-LV1, 24) renders it as *zhi fu da huangdi* 至福大皇帝, which is translated literally as above. In MLC-LV2, s. 24.14, his title is "Sali Suwanna Wala Bat Cak Kham Ekalaca Phawala Ong Long".

340. Here Li Fuyi (MLC-LV1, 24) uses the word *zhu* 主, which means lord or ruler.

341. Li Fuyi (MLC-LV1, 24) translates it into *shijie wanguo zhi zhu* 世界萬國之主, which is translated as above. In the MLC-LV2, s. 24.14, it is "conqueror of all kingdoms of the earth".

342. Li Fuyi (MLC-LV1, 25) renders it as *liuli baoshan* 琉璃寶山. In MLC-LV2, s. 24.14, it is the "Red Jewel Mountain".

343. Li Fuyi (MLC-LV1, 25) renders it as *qionglou yuyu* 瓊樓玉宇, which is interpreted as above.

344. The parenthesis is most probably ascribed to Li Fuyi (MLC-LV1, 25).

345. This letter, rather similar in wording and content as that in MLC-LV2, s. 24.14, is not translated in Gao Lishi 1984, 118. Similar letter is translated by Dao Shuren (1989, 248–49).

19.17 LETTERS AND GIFTS FOR THE BURMESE HIGH OFFICIALS

After submitting the memorial [to the Burmese king], several letters were composed. One was presented to the crown prince,[346] one to the chief of the council of state,[347] one to the field marshal (*cao po mu*),[348] one to the representative stationed in the capital of Burma (Ava), one to the Council [of Nobles] of Moeng Nai,[349] and one to the Mayor,[350] asking for advice and help. Moreover, gifts were presented to the officials of the Burmese court and these are listed as follows:

1. [The gifts] presented to the Field Marshal[351] included five *pan* of golden thread, making a total of one hundred; ten sheets of red felt; one set of leather clothes; ten bags of needles; ten pairs of shoes; two [bamboo] tubes of tea; one golden bowl weighing five *cap* (2.2 taels); one silver bowl, engraved with flowers, weighing eight *cap* (3.52 taels); one silver knife; and one bolt of broad satin.

2. [The gifts] presented to the two crown princes[352] included a total of two bolts of broad satin, two bolts of narrow satin, two bolts of lake-crepe (*nan* or dark blue cotton), two pairs of shoes, four bags of needles, and twenty strings of golden thread.

3. The four ministers[353] were given a total of four bolts of broad satin, four bolts of narrow satin, four bolts of lake-crepe (*nan* or dark blue cotton), four pairs of shoes, four bags of needles, and forty strings of golden needles.

4. The four secretaries[354] were given a total of four bolts of broad satin, four bolts of

346. According to MLC-LV2, s. 24.15, it is *maengsa* (prince); Gao Lishi (1984, 118) renders *maengsa* as marquis (*hou*).

347. Li Fuyi (MLC-LV1, 25) renders it as *guohui zongli* 國 會 總 理, which is translated as above. Here Li probably means head of the *hlut-daw*, the Council of Ministers in pre-colonial Burma. As to structure and the responsibilities of the hlut-daw, see Lieberman 1984.

348. Li Fuyi (MLC-LV1, 25) renders it as *da yuanshuai* 大 元 帥, i.e., field marshal or commander-in-chief. The parenthesis (*zhao beng mu* 詔 綳 牧) should be ascribed to Li Fuyi. According to MLC-LV2, s. 24.16, it is Po Mu Maha Khasat, i.e., commander-in-chief or marshal, but according to Gao Lishi 1984, 118, *cao po mu* means "prime minister" (*chengxiang*).

349. Li Fuyi (MLC-LV1, 25) renders it as *mengnai huiyi* 猛 乃 會 議, which is translated as above. But according to MLC-LV2, s. 24.15 and Gao Lishi 1984, 118, this is the *Yung Tung* of Moeng Nai (i.e., the ruler of Moeng Nai).

350. Li Fuyi (MLC-LV1, 25) renders it as *shizhang* 市 長, i.e., Mayor. According to MLC-LV2, s. 24.15 and Gao Lishi 1984, 118, this was Cao Chiang Tung, i.e., the lord of Chiang Tung.

351. Li Fuyi (MLC-LV1, 25) renders it as *da yuanshuai* 大 元 帥, i.e., field marshal or commander-in-chief. According to MLC-LV2, s. 24.16 and Gao Lishi 1984, 118, s. 24.15, he was *po mu maha khasat*, lit., "military commander, great warrior".

352. According to Gao Lishi 1984, 118, it is *miao sha* (*myo-sa* or *maengsa*), i.e., marquis.

353. According to Gao Lishi 1984, 118, it is *miao ji* (*maengki*), i.e., *guowang dachen* 國 王 大 臣, king's senior official or minister.

354. Li Fuyi (MLC-LV1, 25) renders it as *mishu* 秘 書, secretary. According to Gao Lishi 1984, 118, it is *wu duan wen*, i.e., *shangshu* (minister).

narrow satin, four bolts of lake-crepe (*nan* or dark blue cotton), four pairs of shoes, four bags of needles, and twenty strings of golden thread.

5. The four Circuit Intendants[355] were given a total of four bolts of broad satin, four bolts of narrow satin, four bolts of lake-crepe (*nan* or dark blue cotton), four pairs of shoes, four bags of needles, and eight strings of golden thread.

6. The four officials in charge of dispatching documents (or letters) of the royal house[356] were given a total of four bolts of narrow satin, four bolts of lake-crepe (*nan* or dark blue cotton), four pairs of shoes, four bags of needles, and eight strings of golden thread.

7. The four secretarial officials (*zha ye ji*)[357] were given a total of four bolts of narrow satin, four bolts of lake-crepe (*nan* or dark blue cotton), four pairs of shoes, four bags of needles, and eight strings of golden thread.

8. The four officials in charge of miscellaneous matters (*ao shuang yao*)[358] were given a total of four bolts of narrow satin, four bolts of lake-crepe (*nan* or dark blue cotton), four pairs of shoes, four bags of needles, and eight strings of golden thread.

9. The four officials in charge of receiving documents for the royal house[359] were given [a total of] four bolts of narrow satin, four bolts of lake-crepe (*nan* or dark blue cotton), four pairs of shoes, four bags of needles, and eight strings of golden thread.

10. The secretary (*zhaye*)[360] was given one bolt of narrow satin, one bolt of lake-crepe (*nan* or dark blue cotton), one pair of shoes, one bag of needles, and two strings of golden thread.

355. Li Fuyi (MLC-LV1, 25) renders it as *daoyuan* 道員. According to Hucker (1985), it means "Circuit Intendants", officials in charge of Circuits (*dao*) in the hierarchy of territorial administration. But according to Gao Lishi 1984, 118, they were the four *nakang suiji* (Burmese: *nakhan daw*, "royal reporters"), rendered by Gao Lishi into *wangshi neiwu shuguan* 王室內務庶官, inner secretary of royal house.

356. Li Fuyi (MLC-LV1, 26) renders it as *wangshi fawen guan* 王室發文官, i.e., officials in charge of dispatching letters and documents of the royal house. In Gao Lishi 1984, 118, the royal secretary is called *shang-sui-xiang*.

357. The parenthesis should be ascribed to Li Fuyi (MLC-LV1, 26). *Zha ye ji* 鮓也己 (*sa-yei [daw] gyi*) is translated into *shuji guan* 書記官 (secretarial official). It is a Burmese official title for the chief secretary or secretary. Gao Lishi 1984, 118 translates *sha ye ji* as "recorder".

358. The parenthesis should be ascribed to Li Fuyi (MLC-LV1, 26). Li Fuyi translates *ao shuang yao* 傲雙堯, which is the title of a Burmese official, into *shu wu guan* 庶務官 (official in charge of miscellaneous matters, i.e., secretary).

359. Li Fuyi (MLC-LV1, 26) renders it as *wangshi shouwen guan* 王室收文 (i.e., officials in charge of receiving documents and letters for the royal house). According to Gao Lishi 1984, 118, it is *shang duo kang*, which Gao also translates as *wangshi shouwen guan*.

360. The parenthesis is ascribed to Li Fuyi (MLC-LV1, 26). Li Fuyi renders *zha ye* 鮓也 (*sa-yei*) as *shuji* 書記 (secretary). According to Gao Lishi 1984, 118, it is *la song sha ye*, which Gao translates as *shuji guan* (secretarial official).

11. The special representative stationed at the Headquarters of the Marshal (*lam po mu*)[361] was given one bolt of narrow satin, one bolt of lake-crepe (*nan* or dark blue cotton), one pair of shoes, one bag of needles, and two strings of golden thread.

12. The special representative stationed at the parliament (*lam lob tou*)[362] was given one bolt of narrow satin, one bolt of lake-crepe (*nan* or dark blue cotton), one pair of shoes, one bag of needles, and two strings of golden thread.

19.18 THE TRIBUTE EMISSARIES AND THEIR TRAVELLING ALLOWANCES

Four tribute emissaries were dispatched by the *saenwi fa* [to deliver the gifts]: One chieftain (sic)[363] from the east of the river, one chieftain (sic) from the west of the river, one senior official from the capital,[364] and one secretarial official.

The senior official from the capital was issued one *sòk* of fine silver[365] for travelling expenses and one horse, [which is] worth five *khan* [of silver].[366] The secretarial official was issued seven *khan* and one *cap* of fine silver for travelling expenses and one horse, [which is] worth five *khan* [of silver]. The chieftain (sic) (i.e., *cao mòm*) from the west of the river was issued seven *khan* and five *cap* of fine silver for travelling expenses and one horse, [which is] worth five *khan* [of silver]. The chieftain (sic) from the east of the river was issued seven *khan* and five *cap* of fine silver for travelling expenses, one horse, [which is] worth five *khan* [of silver]. Each emissary brought along with him three soldiers [as his personal attendants], in all, twelve soldiers. Each soldier was issued three *khan* of fine silver for travelling expenses. Altogether four pack horses were provided for official use.

19.19 MOENG LÜ EMISSARIES ARRIVE AT THE BURMESE COURT, 1572

In CS 934, a *tao san* year (Longqing 6, 1572 AD), the various officials of Sipsòng Panna offered in tribute the gifts that they had brought along to the Burmese king. In addition, [the Tai Lü emissaries] distributed the gifts to the crown prince, the prime minister

---

361. The parenthesis should be ascribed to Li Fuyi (MLC-LV1, 26). Li Fuyi renders *lang beng mu* 朗綳牧 (*lam po mu*) as *zhu yuanshuaifu daibiao* 駐元帥府代表 and it is translated as above. But according to Gao Lishi 1984, 119, he was *la-song nan-po mu*, which means "royal guard".

362. The parenthesis should be ascribed to Li Fuyi (MLC-LV1, 26). Li Fuyi translates *lang luo duo* 朗裸墮 (*lam lob tou*) into *zhu guohui daibiao* 駐國會代表. Thus it is translated as above.

363. Li Fuyi (MLC-LV1, 26) renders it as *zhangguan* 長官, lit., "senior official" or "chieftain". Li probably means the *cao moeng*, or the lord of the *müang*.

364. According to Gao Lishi 1984, 119, he was the senior chieftain of Chiang Rung. Li Fuyi probably means the emissary was a member of the Council of Nobles in Chiang Rung.

365. *Wenyin* 紋銀 is a horseshoe-shaped silver ingot with the highest percentage of fine silver.

366. According to Gao Lishi 1984, 119, the senior official of Chiang Rung was issued one *còi* (44 taels) of fine silver for travelling expenses, one horse, and five *khan* (one *khan*: 4.4 taels) of silver for transportation.

(namely the president of the parliament)[367] and to various officials of the Burmese side, before returning [home].

19.20 GIFTS BESTOWED BY THE KING OF BURMA

When the various [Tai Lü] emissaries were going to return, the king of Burma gave them gifts [to be brought back and bestowed on the *saenwi fa* and other nobles in Sipsòng Panna]:

The *saenwi fa* (viz. Cao Phaendin Cao In Moeng) was given two pieces of brocade curtain, one piece of cloth woven with golden thread, four pieces of cloth for wrap-skirts (or sarong), four bolts [of cloth for] headdresses (each bolt was twenty spans in length),[368] four scarves (*yi*), four pieces of yellow cloth, four pieces of *nanbian* (*nam ban*) cloth,[369] two *pan*[370] of purple sandalwood (*can daeng*), two *pan* of white sandalwood (*can khao*),[371] two *pan* of "black medicine" (*hei yao*),[372] two *pan* of *a-wei* (asafoetida or *ferula scorodosma*),[373] two *pan* of pepper (*phik nòi*); two *pan* of *zhongkui* fruits,[374] and two *pan* of white sugar (*küa wan*).

Cao Moeng Paeng (the aboriginal commissioner of Moeng La)[375] received: one wrap-skirt (sarong), one piece [of cloth for] headgear, one *pan* of purple sandalwood, one *pan* of white sandalwood, two scarves, two pieces of yellow cloth, two pieces of *nanbian* cloth (*nan* or dark blue cotton), one *pan* of white sugar, and one *pan* of *zhongkui* fruits (i.e., *mak pai nam*, see above).

367. The parenthesis should be ascribed to Li Fuyi (MLC-LV1, 26). According to Gao Lishi 1984, 119, they were *miaosha* (*maengsa*), *miaoji* (*maeng-gyi*), and *ajia maha xina* (*akka maha sina*) (civil and military high officials).

368. The parenthesis should be ascribed to Li Fuyi (MLC-LV1, 27).

369. In MLC-LV2, s. 24.17, it is four *ho* (bolts) of *nam ban* (variegated cloth); Gao Lishi 1984, 119, transcribes this as *nan-ban* (Tai: *nam ban*), which means yarns of ramie or flax (*masha* 麻紗), a kind of dark blue cotton.

370. One *pan* is about 33 taels and one tael is about 31 grams.

371. In MLC-LV2, s. 24.17, it is "two *pan* of red sandalwood (*can daeng*) and two *pan* of white sandalwood (*can khao*)". The same is given in Gao Lishi 1984, 119.

372. According MLC-LV2, s. 24.17, it is *ya dam*, which is probably opium or black curcuma.

373. Asafoetida is a bad-smelling gum resin obtained from various Asiatic plants of the parsley family. It was used to treat some illnesses or, in folk medicine, to repel disease. Despite its odour, asafoetida is also used in cooking.

374. According to MLC-LV2, s. 24.17, it is *mak pai nam*, the fruits of the *bòraphet* tree (*phak ho nam*). According to Gao Lishi 1984, 119, it is *mak pai nam* powder/flour.

375. The parenthesis should probably be ascribed to Li Fuyi (MLC-LV1, 27). The same is given in Gao Lishi 1984, 119. Cao Moeng Paen was the lord of Moeng La.

The superintendent, Phaya Saen Chiang Ha[376] was given one scarf, one headgear, one piece of yellow cloth, one piece of *nanpian* cloth (cloth woven from yarns of ramie or flax), five *hòi*[377] of purple sandalwood, five *hòi* of white sandalwood, five *hòi* of white sugar, five *hòi* of pepper, and five *hòi* of *zhongkui* fruits (i.e., *mak pai nam*).

The four officials of the Council[378] each received one scarf, one headgear, five *hòi* of purple sandalwood, five *hòi* of white sandalwood, five *hòi* of black pepper, five *hòi* of white sugar, and five *hòi* of *zhongkui* seeds (i.e., *mak pai nam*).

The various [aboriginal officials] of the aboriginal offices (tusi) (sic) of Sipsòng Panna[379] were given two pieces [of cloth for] headgear, two pieces of *nanpian* cloth (*nan* or dark blue cotton), two scarves, two pieces of yellow cloth, five *hòi* of purple sandalwood, five *hòi* of white sandalwood, five *hòi* of pepper, and five *hòi* of white sugar. Altogether there were twelve sets [of these gifts].

In addition, the four tribute envoys each received one piece of woollen cloth, one bolt of foreign cloth twenty spans long, and one piece of cloth woven with golden threads. In all there were four sets and each [envoy] received one set [of gifts]. In the future, even if the numbers of tribute envoys is increased to ten, nevertheless the gifts will still be limited to four sets.

19.21 CAO IN MOENG PASSES AWAY

[In CS] 960, a *poek set* year (Wanli 26, AD 1598), Cao In Moeng died (*zu*).

20. CAO ONG MOENG (DAO YUNMENG 刀韞猛), R. 1598–1628

20.1 THE TWENTY-THIRD RULER AS VASSAL OF TWO OVERLORDS

In the *poek set* year, CS 960 (Wanli 26, AD 1598), the Heavenly Court appointed Cao Ong Moeng (sic)[380] to be the *saenwi fa*. Cao Ong Moeng (sic) also dispatched his prime minister (sic)[381] to present a letter to the king of Burma and report the event. The

376. According to MLC-LV2, s. 24.17, they were the senior officials (*khun luang*) of the Council of Nobles (*noe sanam*). In Gao Lishi 1984, 119 (s. 24.17), he was Phaya Saen Chiang Ha, i.e., the president of the Council of Nobles, Cao Chiang Ha. See the introduction, part 1, section 4.1 of this volume.

377. One *hòi* = c. 3.3 taels.

378. Li Fuyi (MLC-LV1, 27) renders it as *geyuan* 閣員, which means "officials of the Inner Cabinet" (*neige* 内閣). Most likely Li Fuyi means the senior officials of the Inner Council of Nobles (*noe sanam nai*).

379. Li Fuyi (MLC-LV1, 27), as a Chinese official, regards the Tai *cao mòm* as aboriginal officials of the *tusi* 土司 (aboriginal offices). Here it means the *cao mòm* (lords) of the various *müang* in Sipsòng Panna. See Gao Lishi 1984, 119.

380. In other Tai Lü sources it was the reign of Cao Nò Moeng (Dao Nuomeng 刀糯猛), also called Cao Nò Kham. See MLC-SV1, 52–53, s. 21; MLC-LV2, s. 25.1–2; Gao Lishi 1984, 119; Dao Shuren 1989, 250.

381. Li Fuyi (MLC-LV1, 27) translates it into *chengxiang* 丞相, which means "prime minister". Here Li Fuyi probably means the speaker or head of the Council of Nobles (*noe sanam*), generally

Burmese king consented and recognised him as the lord of Sipsòng Panna to succeed his father [Cao In Moeng] to the throne.

20.2 BURMESE PUNITIVE CAMPAIGN AGAINST MOENG LÜ, 1627

In the *moeng mao* year, CS 989 (Tianqi 7, AD 1627), the king of Burma ordered his commander-in-chief to launch an attack on Moeng Lü. He gained a victory and captured the *saenwi fa* Cao Ong Moeng (sic), the chieftain (sic) of Moeng Cae, Cao Si Mün Na Inta Rao, and the inhabitants of the various places (*müang*) on the west bank of the river (Mekong) and deported them to Angwa (Ava). Only very few people were left [in the various *müang* after the devastation].[382]

20.3 RETURN OF ABSCONDED WAR CAPTIVES TO MOENG LÜ; THE FOUNDING OF AVA

In the following year, only a small number of people managed to escape and return. [Hence], the Han Baiyi (i.e., Tai Nüa)[383] from the region in Moeng Kla[384] were recruited to open up and cultivate the deserted land. All local organisations and customs remained unchanged. After this, the king of Burma, Fa Suttho Thammalaca[385] built his capital in Ava and lived there. He no longer travelled to [Moeng] Dagon Hongsa.[386] A palace and houses were constructed and officials and lesser officials were appointed. All the ceremonial rites and [political] systems were to follow the old ones.[387]

21. CAO SILI (SALI) SUTHAMMA (ZHAO SHILI SUTANMA 詔室利穌坦瑪), R. 1628–1639

21.1 THE TWENTY-FOURTH RULER AS VASSAL OF TWO OVERLORDS

In CS 990, a *poek si* year (Chongzhen 1, AD 1628), Cao Ong Moeng (sic) (Cao Nò Moeng) died (*zu*). He had one son by the name of Cao Sili (Sali) Suthamma. The Heavenly Court

---

known as Cao Chiang Ha or Huai Lang Long Sa. But according to MLC-LV2, s. 25.2 and Gao Lishi 1984, 119, Cao Nò Kham sent emissaries (*amat*) to the king of Burma.

382. This piece of information is not recorded in MLC-LV2 or in Gao Lishi 1984.

383. According to Li Fuyi's explanation the Han Baiyi 漢擺夷 were the Tai Nüa, offspring of the mixed marriages between Chinese men and Tai Lü women. See MLC-LV1, index, 14.

384. Mengjia 猛戛 (Moeng Kla/Ka) is in Jinggu County (Moeng Bò), north of Puer.

385. This Burmese king was probably Anaukpetlun (r. 1606–1628).

386. According to Li Fuyi, Moeng Dagon Hongsa is Yangon (Rangoon). See MLC-LV1, index, 14. When King Alaungpaya (who founded the last dynasty of Myanmar kings) conquered Southern Myanmar in the mid-1750s, he developed Dagon as a port and renamed it Yangon (Rangoon), which means "end of strife".

387. Information on the reign of Cao Nò Moeng (r. 1584–1602) is very scanty. The above information on deporting the Tai Lü people is not recorded in MLC-LV2, s. 25.1–2 or Gao Lishi 1984, 119.

(under Emperor Chongzhen)[388] appointed him as the *saenwi fa*. He also dispatched officials to deliver a letter to the king of Burma and report [the event]. The king of Burma appointed Cao Sili (Sali) Suthamma as the *saenwi fa* of the Burmese side (court).

21.2 CAO SILI (SALI) SUTHAMMA'S TWO SONS

In CS 1001, a *kat mao* year (Chongzhen 12, AD 1639), Cao Sili (Sali) Suthamma died (*zu*) at the age of forty-seven. He had two sons: the elder son was Cao [Mòm] Kham Lü[389] and the younger was Cao Mòm Tao.[390]

22. CAO [MÒM] KHAM LÜ (ZHAO KANG LE 詔鈧勒), R. 1639–1669

22.1 THE TWENTY-FIFTH RULER AS VASSAL OF TWO OVERLORDS

In the *kat mao* year, CS 1001 (AD 1639), Cao Sili (Sali) Suthamma died (*zu*). The Heavenly Court (under Emperor Chongzhen) appointed his son Cao [Mòm] Kham Lü as the *saenwi fa*. He also dispatched his officials to deliver a lettter to the king of Burma and report [the event]. The king of Burma approved and appointed Cao [Mòm] Kham Lü as the *saenwi fa* of the Burmese side (court). This was in the *kot si* year, CS 1102 (Chongzhen 13, AD 1640) and he was then twenty-two years old.[391]

22.2 THE FALL OF THE MING AND CAO MÒM KHAM LÜ SUBMITS TO THE QING COURT

Later, [Emperor] Shizu[392] of the Manchu dynasty of the Qing (1644–1911) defeated the Ming dynasty (1368–1644). He ascended the great throne and became the ruler of the Heavenly Court. The Ming dynasty fell. Hence, Cao [Mòm] Kham Lü presented gold[393] and submitted to[394] the Manchu [court in Beijing].[395]

---

388. This was the last emperor of the Ming dynasty (1368–1644). Emperor Chongzhen (r. 1628–1644) committed suicide together with a faithful palace eunuch at the Coal Hill behind the palace in Beijing when the troops of rebel leader Li Zicheng marched to Beijing.

389. According to Gao Lishi 1984, 120 and MLC-LV2, s. 27.1–3, he is Cao Mòm Kham Lü (r. 1621–1634). However, this Cao Mòm Kham Lü is not to be mixed up with the forty-second Tai Lü king, called Tao Soen Oen (Dao Cheng'en 刀承恩), whose Tai Lü name is also Cao Mòm Kham Lü (r. 1878–1922). See Gao Lishi 1984, 128 (the forty-second ruler); MLC-LV2, s. 42.1–15; MLC-SV1, 63.

390. Cao Mòm Tao is not to be mixed up with his son's name Cao Moeng Tao, also transcribed into Chinese by Li Fuyi (MLC-LV1, 29) as Dao Mudao.

391. In this case Cao Mòm Kham Lü was born in AD 1618.

392. This was Fu Lin (1638–1661), the Emperor Shunzhi (r. 1644–1661), the ninth son of Abahai.

393. *Xianjin* 獻金 (lit., "offering gold") means "offered in tribute money in the form of gold".

394. *Guishun* 歸順 means "to yield" or "to submit", signifying pledging allegiance and offering tribute.

395. This statement is not recorded in other Tai Lü sources, such as MLC-LV2; Gao Lishi 1984; Dao Shuren 1989. According to the Veritable Records of the Qing Dynasty, in Shunzhi 17, eighth month,

In the *hong pao* year, CS 1023 (Shunzhi 18, AD 1661), the Heavenly Court bestowed an official seal and letter of appointment[396] on Tao Cao Kham Lü (i.e., Cao Mòm Kham Lü) and appointed him as the *saenwi fa*. His dominions extended to Moeng Cung (Yuanjiang).[397] Tao Cao Kham Lü was in office thirty years and died (*zu*) at the age of fifty-two in the *kat lao* year, CS 1031 (Kangxi 8, AD 1669).

22.3 THE TWO SONS OF CAO MÒM KHAM LÜ

Cao [Mòm] Kham Lü had two sons: The elder son [Cao] Saeng Moeng[398] died early. The second son Cao Nò Moeng was still young.[399]

22.4 CAO MÒM TAO, THE TWENTY-SIXTH RULER, R. 1642–1666

{In the *tao sanga* year, CS 1004 (Chongzhen 15, AD 1642) Cao Mòm Tao succeeded his elder brother Cao [Mòm] Kham Lü as *saenwi fa* at the age of seventeen. Later Emperor Shizu (i.e., Shunzhi, r. 1644–1661) of the Manchu Qing [dynasty] became the ruler of the Heavenly Court and ascended the throne. The Ming dynasty was defeated. Cao Mòm Tao presented gold (i.e., offered tribute) and submitted. In the year Shunzhi 18 (the *hong pao* year, CS 1023 AD 1661), the Heavenly Court issued seal, letter patent, and credential and appointed Cao Mòm Tao as *saenwi fa*. The domain [of Sipsòng Panna] extended to Yuanjiang (Moeng Cung). Five years later Cao Mòm Tao passed away. He was in office (sic) a total of twenty-four years and was forty-one years old. It was in the *lai sanga* year, CS 1028 (Kangxi 5, AD 1666). He was the nineteenth (sic) generation [ruler]. He had a son called Cao Moeng Tao. After the death of Cao Mòm Tao, his elder brother's son Cao Nò Moeng succeeded [him to the throne]}.[400]

---

bingshen (CS 1022; 17 September 1660) the *saenwi fa* Dao Mudao (Cao Moeng Tao) surrendered. See also *Qing shilu*, ch. 139, 12. It is possible that Li Fuyi has added this record in his translation.

396. Li Fuyi (MLC-LV1, 28) renders it as *yinxin guafeng zhaozhi* 印信掛封照紙, which is translated as above.

397. The above information on the expansion of the domain of Sipsòng Panna is not recorded in MLC-LV2 or in Gao Lishi 1984. Yuanjiang 元江 (in Tai: Moeng Cung), located in the northeast of Sipsòng Panna and north of Laos, covers the eastern part of the modern Simao District, inhabited by the Hani and the Yi tribes.

398. According to MLC-SV1, 55, s. 24, his full name is Cao Mòm Saeng Moeng. According to MLC-LV2, s. 27.3 and Gao Lishi 1984, 120 (the twenty-seventh ruler), his name is Cao Saeng Moeng.

399. The two sons were still young when their father passed away. Not long after, the eldest son Cao Saeng Moeng also passed away before he could succeed his father. See MLC-SV1, 55, s. 24; MLC-LV2, s. 27.3; Gao Lishi 1984, 120; Dao Shuren 1989, 251.

400. This section is taken from Li Fuyi 1983a, 35–36, the revised edition of MLC-LV1. Li Fuyi does not mention on which manuscript his revised edition of MLC-LV1 is based. The reign of Cao Mòm Tao is recorded in MLC-LV2, s. 28.1–3, as well as in Gao Lishi 1984, 120, (the twenty-eighth ruler) and Tao Shuren 1989, 252 (the twenty-eighth ruler).

23. CAO NÒ MOENG (DAO NUOMENG 刀懦猛), R. 1669–1681

23.1 THE TWENTY-SEVENTH RULER AND THE REGENT

In the *kat lao* year, CS 1031 (AD 1669), Cao Nò Moeng[401] was [nominated] as *saenwi fa*. As he was still young the Heavenly Court appointed his uncle Cao Mòm Tao as regent [to rule the region].[402]

23.2 WU SANGUI'S SHORT-LIVED KINGDOM

In the *ka pao* year, CS 1035 (Kangxi 12, AD 1673 AD), Wu Sangui rebelled against the Qing court, declared independence and proclaimed himself emperor.[403] The official seal and credential issued by [Emperor] Shunzhi (r. 1644–1661) were surrendered [to Wu Sangui]. A new seal [of office] was bestowed on Cao Nò Moeng who, as before, was [entrusted] to administer local affairs jointly with Cao Mòm Tao.[404]

23.3 CAO NÒ MOENG DIES WITHOUT AN HEIR

Cao Nò Moeng was in office twelve years and died (*zu*) at the age of twenty-five, without an heir, in the *hong lao* year, CS 1043 (Kangxi 20, AD 1681).

24. CAO MOENG TAO (DAO MUDAO 刀穆禱), R. 1681–1684

24.1 THE TWENTY-EIGHTH RULER; WU SANGUI'S REVOLT IS CRUSHED

In the *hong lao* year, CS 1043 (AD 1681), Cao Moeng Tao succeeded [his cousin to the throne] as the *saenwi fa*. In that year the revolt led by Wu Sangui (1612–1678) was pacified.[405]

---

401. His name is similar to Cao Nò Moeng (Dao Nuomeng 刀糯猛) (see above s. 17.1–2), the son of Cao Sili Sompan. But according to MLC-LV2, s. 25.1–2, he was also called Cao Nò Moeng (r. 1584–1602), who was Cao In Moeng's son. See also Gao Lishi 1984, 120.

402. He was the second son of Cao Sili Suthamma. According to MLC-LV1, s. 28.3 and Gao Lishi 1984, 120 (the twenty-eighth ruler), Cao Mòm Tao had a son called Cao Moeng Tao (the thirtieth ruler). Cao Mòm Tao adopted his elder brother Cao Mòm Kham Lü's second son Cao Nò Moeng (the twenty-ninth ruler) when he was on the throne.

403. Wu Sangui (1612–2 October 1678) was an erstwhile general of the defunct Ming dynasty. He was a native of Liaodong, which first surrendered to the Manchus and then revolted. Between 1657 and 1661 Generalissimo Wu was militarily active in Yunnan before he founded the short-lived Kingdom of Zhou (1678–1681) in Hengzhou, Hunan. See ECCP II, 877–80; Chu Hsi-tsu 1932; A. Hsi 1975.

404. This account is not recorded in MLC-LV2, 29.1–2 or in Gao Lishi 1984, 120 (the twentieth ruler).

405. Though Wu Sangui died in 1678 (Kangxi 17), his grandson continued the rebellion until 1681 (Kangxi 20), when he was finally crushed.

24.2 CAO MOENG TAO BECOMES THE CHINESE *SAENWI FA*

Cao Moeng Tao offered tribute [to the Qing court and so] the Heavenly Court conferred on [him] the seal and credentials and appointed [him] as the *saenwi fa*.[406]

24.3 CAO MOENG TAO *BECOMES* THE BURMESE *SAENWI FA*

Cao Moeng Tao sent emissaries to deliver a letter to the king of Burma and report [the event]. The king of Burma granted his approval and appointed Cao Moeng Tao as the *saenwi fa* of the Burmese side (court).

24.4 CAO MOENG TAO'S SON

In the *kap cai* year, CS 1046 (Kangxi 23, AD 1684), Cao Moeng Tao died (*zu*) at the age of fifty-one. He left one son by the name of Cao Paeng Moeng.

25. CAO PAENG MOENG (ZHAO BIANMENG 詔匾猛), R. 1684–1724

25.1 THE TWENTY-NINTH RULER AS THE *SAENWI FA* OF TWO OVERLORDS

In the *kap cai* year, CS 1046 (AD 1684), the Heavenly Court appointed Cao Paeng Moeng as the *saenwi fa*. Hence, he sent emissaries to deliver a letter to the king of Burma and report [the event]. The king of Burma consented and appointed him the *saenwi fa* of the Burmese side (court).

25.2 NANG TEWI RULES AS REGENT, R. 1684–1702

At that time Cao Paeng Moeng was only four years old,[407] [so] Nang Tewi (the queen dowager),[408] became regent. At that time Nang Tewi was forty-four years old; [she ruled as regent] until the *tao sanga* year, CS 1064 (Kangxi 41, AD 1702). When Cao Paeng

406. This Cao Moeng Tao is not to be confused with the name of his father Cao Mòm Tao, the second son of Cao Sali Suthamma. Cao Moeng Tao was the son of Cao Mòm Tao and a grandson of Cao Sali Suthamma. But contemporary Chinese sources give the following accounts: In the year Shunzhi 17, eighth month, *bingshen* day (17 September 1660), the *saenwi fa* of Cheli in Yunnan Dao Mudao 刀木禱 (Cao Mòm Tao or his son Cao Moeng Tao) surrendered. See *Shizu shilu*, ch. 139, 12. In the year Shunzhi 17, twelfth month, *jiawu* day (13 January 1661), a mink [coat], bolts of satin, and horse-saddles were conferred on the aboriginal commissioner of Cheli, Dao Mudao. See *Shizu shilu*, ch. 143, 9. In the year Shunzhi 17, twelfth month, *guimao* day (22 January 1661), the [official] seal was cast and issued to the *saenwi fa* of Cheli. See *Shizu shilu*, ch. 143, 14. Dao Mudao is mentioned again in the *Qing shilu* in Kangxi 1, tenth month, *jiwei* day (29 November 1662). He reported that the bogus prince of Jin, Li Dingguo 李定國 (d. 7 August 1662) had fled to Chiang Saen, where he died of illness. See *Shengzu shilu*, ch. 7, 16–17. This Dao Mudao was probably the father of Cao Moeng Tao.

407. According to MLC-LV2, s. 31.1, Cao Paeng Moeng was twelve years old. See also Gao Lishi 1984, 120, s. 31.1.

408. The parentheses should be ascribed to Li Fuyi (MLC-LV1, 30).

Moeng was twenty-two years old, Nang Tewi handed the power over to him. In the *ka sai* year, CS 1075 (Kangxi 52, AD 1713), Nang Tewi died (*zu*) at the age of seventy-three.

25.3 CAO PAENG MOENG PASSES AWAY; THE RULER'S TWO SONS

Cao Paeng Moeng was in office (sic) forty years before he died (*zu*) at the age forty-four in CS 1086, a *kap si* year (Yongzhen 2, AD 1724).[409] Cao Paeng Moeng had two sons: the elder was Tao Cin Pao (Dao Jinbao) and the second Tao Sao Wün (Dao Shaowen).[410]

26. TAO CIN PAO (DAO JINBAO 刀金寶), R. 1724–1729

26.1 THE THIRTIETH RULER AS *SAENWI FA* OF TWO OVERLORDS

In the *ka si* year, CS 1086 (AD 1724), the Heavenly Court appointed Tao Cin Pao as the *saenwi fa*. At that time he was sixteen years old.[411] Hence, Tao Cin Pao sent envoys to deliver a letter to the king of Burma and report [the event]. The king of Burma consented and appointed Tao Cin Pao as the *saenwi fa* of the Burmese side (court).

26.2 THE DEATH OF TAO CIN PAO AND HIS SON AND FIVE GRANDSONS

In the *kat lao* year, CS 1091 (Yongzheng 7, AD 1729), Tao Cin Pao died (*zu*).[412] He had

409. According to MLC-LV2, s. 31.1, Cao Paeng Moeng was on the throne twenty-seven years, lived to the age of thirty-nine years, and died in CS 1060 (i.e., AD 1698). The same is recorded in Gao Lishi 1984, 120, 31.1. However, contemporary Chinese sources, which are very precise in dates, give the following account: "In the year Yongzheng 4, ninth month, *bingshen* day (2 October 1726), the grand co-ordinator of Yunnan and supreme commander of Yunnan and Guizhou, O-er-tai (1680–1745), submitted a memorial reporting that Dao Zhao Bianmeng (i.e., Tao Cao Paeng Moeng) had passed away and petitioned to allow his son Dao Zhao Jinbao (i.e., Tao Cao Cin Pao) to succeed [to the post/throne]". See *Shizong shilu*, ch. 48, 5. Thus Cao Paeng Moeng could not have passed away in CS 1060 (AD 1698), twenty-eight years earlier than O-er-tai's report. Cao Paeng Moeng passed away not long before O-er-tai's report. Thus the year given in Li Fuyi (MLC-LV1, 30) is plausible. Most probably Li Fuyi has adjusted the date.

410. Cao Paeng Moeng also had two daughters; one was married to Cao Moeng Bò and one to Cao Moeng Pan (see below s. 3.5 and s. 3.6). According to MLC-LV2, s. 31.3–4 and Gao Lishi 1984, 121 (s. 31-2–3), during the reign of Cao Paeng Moeng the "white-headed bandit" (*kha ho khao*) created unrest. These sources confirm that Cao Paeng Moeng had two daughters, one married Cao Moeng Bò and the other Cao Moeng Pan. The same is given in Dao Shuren 1989, 254, but not in MLC-LV1.

411. According to MLC-LV2, s. 32.1 and Gao Lishi 1984, 121, s. 32.1, he was twenty-two years old on accession to the throne.

412. In the year Yongzheng 8, twelfth month, *renyin* day (15 January 1731), the supreme commander of Yunnan and Guizhou, O-er-tai (1680–1745), submitted a memorial reporting that the *saenwi fa* of Cheli under Puer in Yunnan, Dao Jinbao (Tao Cin Pao), had passed away. His sons were still young. He asked for permission to appoint his younger brother Dao Xi Men Na (Cao Si Mün Na) as regent, who would care for the orphans. See *Shizong shilu*, ch. 101, 3. But according to MLC-

one son, who had a stammer and could not speak properly. The people nicknamed him Cao Thao Hu Nok (i.e., Tao Cao Thao). Cao Thao Hu Nok's son was Cao Moe (sic) and Cao Moe's (sic)[413] sons were Cao Kang, Cao Sü, Cao Saeng (died early), Cao Mahacai, Cao Kham La, and others.[414] [As for this lineage], the Heavenly Court (*cao hò*) appointed none of them [as *saenwi fa*]. This was a subsequent matter.[415]

27. TAO SAO WÜN (DAO SHAOWEN 刀紹文), R. 1729–1767

27.1 THE QING COURT DEPOSES THE THIRTY-FIRST RULER

In the *kat lao* year, CS 1091 (AD 1729), the Heavenly Court appointed Tao Sao Wün[416] as the *saenwi fa*. He was then fifteen years old.[417] Tao Sao Wün sent emissaries to deliver a letter to the king of Burma and report [the event]. The king of Burma appointed [Cao] Mòm Tao (his Tai name), whose [Chinese name] is Tao Sao Wün, as the *saenwi fa* of the Burmese side (court).[418] In the *moeng kai* year, CS 1129 (Qianlong 32, AD 1767), the Heavenly Court accused him of being incompetent in managing the affairs and dismissed him.[419]

LV2, s. 32.1 and Gao Lishi 1984, 121, s. 32.1, Tao Cin Pao died in CS 1069 (AD. 1707). This date is not in accord with the Chinese sources. In Yongzheng 12, eighth month, *jisi* (23 September 1734), the supreme commander of Yunnan and Guizhou, Yin Jishan (1696–1771) memorialised the *saenwi fa* of Cheli under Puer Prefecture in Yunnan, Dao Jinbao, who passed away in Yongzheng 7 (1729). As his son (sic) Dao Shaowen was still young, his succession was suspended. As he was then fifteen years old, he requested to succeed [to the post] according to rules. See *Shizong shilu*, ch. 146, 13. Note that according to MLC-LV1, Dao Shaowen was Dao Jinbao's younger brother.

413. The same is given in Li Fuyi 1983a, 38, the revised edition of MLC-LV1. But according to MLC-LV2, s. 33.4, the people called Cao Thao Hu Nok because he was deaf and he stammered. However, Cao Moe is not mentioned in Gao Lishi 1984, 121, s. 33.4 or in Dao Shuren 1989, 255.

414. According to other sources, the stammering prince had five sons: Cao Kang, Cao Sü, Cao Saeng (died young), Cao Mahacai, and Cao Kham La. See MLC-LV2, s. 33.4; Gao Lishi 1984, 121, s. 33.4; Dao Shuren 1989, 255. Here Li Fuyi (MLC-LV1, 30) could have mixed up the names of the sons of the stammering prince.

415. Li Fuyi (MLC-LV1, 30) renders it as *ci shi hou shi* 此是後事 (lit., "This was a subsequent matter"). Probably Li means "This was a later decision of the Qing court."

416. He was the younger brother of Tao Cin Pao.

417. According to MLC-LV2, s. 33.1 and Gao Lishi 1984, 121, s. 33.1, Tao Sao Wün was twenty-five years old on accession in CS 1069 (AD 1707). But according to the Veritable Records of the Qing Dynasty, Dao Shaowen was fifteen years old in the year Yongzheng 12, eighth month, *jisi* (23 September 1734). See *Shizong shilu*, ch. 146, 13. The year given in MLC-LV1, 30, is so close to that given in contemporary Chinese sources. It is hard to believe that Li Fuyi did not adjust the year in his translation to match the year given in Chinese sources.

418. The parenthesis should be ascribed to Li Fuyi (MLC-LV1, 31). Cao Mòm Tao's sinicised name is Dao Shaowen (Tao Sao Wün).

419. The Veritable Records of the Qing Dynasty state that the stupid and cowardly *saenwi fa* of

27.2 TAO SAO WÜN'S SONS AND GRANDSONS

Tao Sao Wün had six sons and many grandchildren and great-grandchildren. They are listed in as follows:

The eldest son was Tao Wui Phin (Dao Weiping). Tao Wui Phin had one son called Tao Yung Khò (Dao Yonghe), whose Tai name is Cao [Fa] Can (Zhao Zhan).[420]

The second son was Tao Cao Then (Thian) (Dao Zhaoding).[421] Tao Cao Then (Thian) had two sons: The eldest son was Cao Maha Phom (Zhao Maha Peng). Cao Maha Phom had [a son called] Cao Maha Sang (Maha Sang). The second son was Cao Maha Khanan (Zhao Maha Nankan).[422] Cao Maha Khanan had [two sons]: Cao Nò Kham (Zhao Nuokang) and Cao Phom (Zhao Peng).

The third son, [Tao] Cao Paeng (Zhao Bian),[423] died young and had no heir.

The fourth son Tao [Cao] Suwan (Dao Shiwan)[424] had three sons: The eldest Tao Thai Phin (Dao Taiping), [whose Tai name was] Cao Kumman (Zhao Gongman),[425] died young. The second son was Tao Thai Khò (Dao Taihe), [whose Tai name was] Cao Mòm Maha Wong (Zhao Mahaweng); Tao Thai Khò had a son called Tao Sunwu (Dao Shengwu), [whose Tai name was] Cao Maha Nòi (Zhao Maha Lei). The third son was Tao Thai Khang (Dao Taikang), [whose Tai name was] Cao [Mòm] Maha Wang (Zhao Maha Wang). Tao Thai Khang had [two sons]: Tao Coen Cong (Dao Zhengzong), [whose Tai name was] Cao Mòm Suca Wanna (Zhao Suzha Wanna), and Tao Soen Cong (Dao Chengzong), [whose Tai name was] Cao Lamma Awuttha (Langma Awuta).[426]

The fifth son [Tao] Cao Saeng (Zhao Xiang)[427] died young and had no heir.

The sixth son, [Tao] Cao Cai (Zhao Zai),[428] had two sons. The eldest was Cao Maha Phom

---

Cheli, Dao Shaowen, was deposed in Qianlong 31, twelfth month, *bingwu* (10 January 1767). See *Gaozong shilu*, ch. 774, 10–11.

420. See MLC-LV2, s. 34.2. According to Gao Lishi 1984, 123, s. 34.2, his Tai Lü name is Cao Fa Can (Zhao Fa Jian), i.e., Cao Can, and his sinicised name is Dao Yuhe. These are just variant transcriptions of Tao Yung Khò (Dao Yonghe).

421. Tao Cao Thian was the vice-king or the vice-*saenwi fa*, the *upalaca* or *cao upalaca* or *maha upalaca*. See MLC-LV2, s. 34.2; Gao Lishi 1984, 122, s. 34.2; Dao Shuren 1989, 255–56.

422. See MLC-LV2, s. 35.4. According to Gao Lishi 1984, 122, s. 35.5, he was Cao Mòm Maha Khanan (Zhao Meng Maha Kanglang), Cao Mòm being his title.

423. Cao Paeng was Tao Cao Paeng. See MLC-SV1, 57, s. 29; MLC-LV2, s. 33.3; Gao Lishi 1984, 121, s.33.3; Dao Shuren 1989, 255.

424. He is also known as Tao Cao Suwan. See MLC-LV2, s. 33.3 and Gao Lishi 1984, 121, s. 33.3.

425. According to MLC-LV2, s. 35.2, his Tai name, apart from Cao Kumman, is Cao Mòm Mahasang. The same is given in Gao Lishi 1984, 122, s. 35.2.

426. See MLC-LV2, s. 38.8–39.1; Gao Lishi 1984, 124, s. 38.10.

427. See MLC-LV2, s. 33.3; Gao Lishi 1984, 121, s. 33.3.

428. See MLC-SV1, 57; MLC-LV2, s. 33.3; Gao Lishi 1984, 121, s. 33.3.

(Pung) (Zhao Maha Peng) and the second son was Cao Kha Then (Thian) (Zhao Kading), (died young). [Tao Cao Cai] had one daughter, still young when Tao Cao Cai died.[429]

28. TAO WUI PHIN (DAO WEIPING 刀維屏), R. 1767–1777

28.1 THE THIRTY-SECOND RULER AND HIS YOUNGER BROTHER, THE *UPALACA*

In CS 1129 (AD 1767), the Heavenly Court appointed Tao Wui Phin as the *saenwi fa*. Tao Wui Phin sent emissaries to deliver a letter to the king of Burma and report [the event]. The king of Burma consented and appointed Tao Wui Phin as *saenwi fa* of the Burmese side (court). His younger brother Tao Cao Then (Thian) was appointed the vice-*saenwi fa* (*upalaca*) of the Burmese side (court).

28.2 THE RULER AND THE *UPALACA*'S DEFECTION TO MOENG YÒNG

In the following year, [Tao] Wui Phin and his younger brother [Tao] Cao Then (Thian) listened to the dissent sown by his son-in-law Cao Moeng Nai (Zhao Mengnai) and Cao Kòng (Zhao Guang) of Moeng Yòng (Mengyong) and so resented the Heavenly Court. Consequently, [they] transported their personal belongings, took their relatives, and defected to Moeng Yòng. Later they returned to the seat [of the *saenwi fa* in Chiang Rung], but the Heavenly Court distrusted them.[430]

28.3 ARREST AND DEPOSITION OF THE *SAENWI FA* AND THE *UPALACA*

In the *ka sai* year, CS 1135 (Qianlong 38, AD 1773), [the Qing court] dispatched officials to investigate [the matter]. [Tao] Suwan and [Tao] Wui Phin were arrested one after another and brought to Moeng Maen (Ninger), where they were escorted to Moeng Sae Long (Kunming). [Tao] Wui Phin and [Tao] Cao Then (Thian) were removed from their posts.[431]

28.4 PROHIBITION OF THE DEPOSED RULERS' SONS TO BECOME *SAENWI FA*

The Heavenly Court prohibited [Tao] Wui Phin's son Cao [Fa] Can (i.e., Tao Yung Khò), and [Tao] Cao Then's sons, Cao Maha Phom (Zhao Maha Peng) and Cao Maha Khanan (Zhao Maha Kannan), to succeed to [the post of *saenwi fa*].

429. According to Gao Lishi 1984, 122, s. 35.6, Tao Cao Cai had three sons and four daughters, and their names are recorded. The same is stated in MLC-LV2, s. 35.4, but their names are not recorded.

430. This incident is also recorded in MLC-SV1, 57, s. 30 (Tao Wui Phin); MLC-LV2, s. 34.2 and s. 36.4; Gao Lishi 1984, 122, s. 34.2 and 36.3.

431. According to the Veritable Records of the Qing Dynasty, Dao Weiping was deposed in Qianlong 37, sixth month, *xinwei* (7 July 1772). See *Gaozong shilu*, ch. 910, 8.

29. TAO SUWAN (DAO SHIWAN 刀士宛), R. 1777–1796

29.1 RETURN OF TAO SUWAN AS THE THIRTY-THIRD RULER

In the *moeng lao* year, [CS] 1139 (Qianlong 42, AD 1777), the Heavenly Court confiscated the seal and credential[432] of the military-cum-civilian commission of the *saenwi fa* of Cheli (i.e., *Cheli junmin xuanwei shi*)[433] from [Tao] Wui Phin (Dao Weiping) and gave them to his younger brother [Tao] Suwan (Dao Shiwan). [Tao Suwan] was ordered to return to Sipsòng Panna to succeed his elder brother to the throne (post).

29.2 DEATH OF TAO WUI PHIN IN MOENG SAE LONG

Nevertheless, [Tao] Wui Phin was detained [in Kunming]. In the *hong pao* year, CS 1143 (Qianlong 46, AD 1781), [Tao] Wui Phin died (*si*) at the age of forty-five in Moeng Sae Long (Kunming).[434]

29.3 TAO SUWAN IS APPOINTED AS THE BURMESE *SAENWI FA*

In the *kot set* year, [CS] 1152 (Qianlong 55, AD 1790), the commander-in-chief of the Horse Bureau concurrently in charge of the cavalry troops of Burma was appointed the supreme commander of Moeng Nai. He dispatched the messenger Dopung Yanjo Tewa (Duobeng Yanzuo Diewa) to deliver an edict summoning Tao Suwan to Burma to succeed to [the post] and to collect the seal and credential (*yinxin*). [Tao] Suwan was delighted and sent Cao Ong (Zhao Yun) to Burma to request permission from the king of Burma to appoint Tao Suwan as the *saenwi fa* of the Burmese side (court). The king of Burma approved the request and issued the letter of conferment [to him].[435]

29.4 DEATH OF TAO SUWAN; THE RULER'S OFFSPRING

In the *lai si* year, CS 1158 (Jiaqing 1, AD 1796), on the fourth waxing day of the fifth month,[436] Tao Suwan (Dao Shiwan) died (*zu*). He had three sons: the eldest Tao Thai

---

432. According to MLC-LV2, s. 34.3, n. 250, it was *cum yin* (i.e., "seal") and *pu ca kao ci*. In MLC-SV1, 60–61 (s. 34, n. 88), Li Fuyi translated it as *guafeng zhaozhi* 掛封照紙, which means letter of conferment.

433. According to MLC-LV2, s. 34.3, it is the official seal (*cum yin*) and the letter of conferment (*pu ca kao ci*) of the *Coeli swaenwi sisü*, which is the Tai Lü rendering of *Cheli junmim xuanwei shi* 車里軍民宣慰使, an official title granted to Tai Lü king.

434. According to MLC-LV2, s. 34.3, Tao Wui Phin lived in Moeng Sae (Kunming) three years before dying of illness. But according to Dao Shuren (1989), 30.2, the *cao hò* (ruler of China) arrested and killed him in Moeng Sae (Kunming).

435. The above account is neither recorded in MLC-LV2-1963 nor in Gao Lishi 1984.

436. 1158 Phalguna 4 or Wednesday, 1 March 1797.

Phin (Dao Taiping)[437] died young and had no heir, the second was [Tao] Thai Khò (Dao Taihe),[438] and the third [Tao] Thai Khang (Dao Taikang).[439]

He had four daughters: the eldest was Nang Paeng Moeng Long (Luang), the second Nang Kang, the third daughter Nang Saeng Pin, and the fourth daughter Nang Kòi Fòng. The eldest daughter was married to the *saenfu* [*fa*] of Moeng Laem (i.e., Cao Moeng Laem);[440] the second daughter was betrothed to a tribal military officer (sic) of Moeng U-Nüa (i.e., Cao Moeng U-Nüa),[441] the third daughter was betrothed to the *cao fa* of Moeng Phong;[442] and the fourth daughter was betrothed to a tribal military officer (sic) of Puteng (i. e., the lord of Moeng Hing).[443]

30. TAO THAI KHÒ (DAO TAIHE 刀太和) VIZ. CAO MÒM MAHA WONG, R. 1797–1802

30.1 THE THIRTY-FOURTH RULER IS REJECTED BY THE KING OF BURMA

In the *moeng sai* year, CS 1159 (Jiaqing 2, AD 1797), the Heavenly Court appointed Tao Thai Khò (Dao Taihe)[444] as the *saenwi fa*. Tao Thai Khó dispatched envoys to Burma to ask the king of Burma to confer on him an additional appointment. The Burmese authorities disapproved because Tao Thai Khò was [too] young.

---

437. His childhood name was Cao Kumman, and his Tai Lü name Cao Mòm Mahasang. See MLC-LV2, s. 35.2; Gao Lishi 1984, 122 (thirty-fifth ruler Tao Suwan).

438. His Tai Lü name was Cao Mòm Maha Wong. See MLC-LV2, s. 35.2; Gao Lishi 1984, 122.

439. His Tai Lü name was Cao Mòm Maha Wang. See MLC-LV2, s. 35.2; but according to Gao Lishi 1984, 122, his Tai Lü name was Cao Mòm Maha Cae, which might be a mistake.

440. Li Fuyi (MLC-LV1, 32) renders "Cao Moeng Laem" as "Menglian *xuanfu* 孟璉宣撫". Cao Moeng Laem, during the Ming period and later Qing period, was conferred the title *xuanfu shi* 宣撫使, so *saenfu fa*, which is a grade lower in rank than *xuanwei shi* (Tai: *saenwi fa*). According to Gao Lishi 1984, 122, s. 35.3, Moeng Ping and Moeng Lam were granted as her dowry. Since then the two *müang*, Moeng Ping and Moeng Lam, have been under the jurisdiction of Cao Moeng Laem and were no longer under Sipsòng Panna. See also MLC-LV2, s. 35.3. This is mentioned in MLC-LV1, 56, s. 3.1.

441. "Cao Moeng U-Nüa" is rendered as Mengwu *tubian* 猛烏土弁 by Li Fuyi (MLC-LV1, 32). The term *bian* 弁 refers to "low-ranking military officer". From Li Fuyi's perspective at that time Cao Moeng U was a low-ranking tribal military officer of China. Moeng U-Nüa was officially ceded to French Indochina in 1896.

442. According to Gao Lishi 1984, 122 (the thirty-fifth ruler), the third daughter was married to Cao Sü and they were childless. Cao Sü was the second son of Cao Moeng Thao Hu Nok. See Gao Lishi 1984, 121 (the thirty-third ruler). A rather similar account is given in MLC-LV2-1963, s. 35.3.

443. According to MLC-LV2, s. 35.3 and Gao Lishi 1984, 122, s. 35.3, the fourth daughter Nang Kòi Fòng married the ruler of Moeng Phong. She bore two sons: the eldest son was called Cao Mahacai and the second son was called Cao Paka Kumman.

444. He was the second son of Cao Mòm Suwan (Dao Shiwan) and his Tai name is Cao Mòm Maha Wong.

30.2 SUPPORTED BY CHINA AND BURMA, UNCLE AND NEPHEW BOTH BECOME *SAENWI FA*

[The king of Burma] immediately dispatched Yie La (Yela) with a letter summoning Tao Cao Then (Thian) to Burma to state that he agreed to be the subject and servant (i.e., to be a vassal) of both the Heavenly (China) and the Burmese [courts]. Thus, Tao Cao Then (Thian) dispatched Phaya Long Khoen from Moeng Cae and Phaya U-ten (U-tian) from Chiang Rung to Burma to make a request on his behalf. The king of Burma consented and appointed Tao Cao Then (Thian) the *saenwi fa* of the Burmese side (court). [As a result] the Heavenly Court appointed Tao Thai Khò and the Burmese court appointed [Tao] Cao Then (Thian). The elder uncle (Tao Cao Then) and the nephew (Tao Thai Khò) were both appointed *saenwi fa*.[445]

30.3 TAO CAO THEN REBELS AGAINST BURMA AND IS DEFEATED

A year [later], Tao Cao Then (Thian), incited by Cao Kòng from Moeng Yòng, defied the imperial order of the king of Burma Bodaw[-hpaya].[446] In an armed confrontation with the Burmese, [Tao Cao Then] was defeated and fled into hiding. The Burmese marched into [Tao] Cao Then's camp, arrested Cao Kòng and killed him. His head together with his daughter Nang Tip were delivered under escort to the king of Burma. The Burmese troops marched back to Chiang Yung and camped there. [Tao] Cao Then hid in the hills and refused to come out. Hence, the Burmese troops had the official residence (sic) of [Tao] Cao Then at Chiang Dòn Long[447] burnt down before they broke camp and withdrew to Ava. [Tao] Cao Then died (*zu*) in the *kot san* year, CS 1162 (Jiaqing 5, AD 1800).[448]

30.4 THE TWO SONS OF TAO CAO THEN (THIAN)

[Tao] Cao Then (Thian) had two sons. The elder was Cao Maha Phom and the second Cao Maha Khanan. Neither of them was appointed as [*saenwi fa*] because both the Heavenly [court] and the Burmese side disapproved of them.[449]

445. See also MLC-LV2, s. 36.3; Gao Lishi 1984, 122, s. 36.2. This means the Burmese authorities refused to recognise Tao Thai Khò as the rightful *saenwi fa* and appointed Tao Cao Then (Thian), his elder uncle, as the *saenwi fa* of Sipsòng Panna. This sowed the seeds of the later fratricidal conflicts and succession disputes between Cao Maha Khanan and his son Cao Nò Kham, and the two grandsons of Cao Mòm Suwan, Cao Mòm Suca Wanna (Tao Coen Cong, i.e., Dao Zhengzong) and Cao Lamma Awuttha (Tao Soen Cong, i.e., Dao Chengzong). See Liew-Herres 2007.

446. The Burmese king here is probably Bodaw-hpaya (r. 1782–1819), son of Alaungpaya (r. 1752–1760) of the Konbaung dynasty (1752–1885).

447. Li Fuyi (MLC-LV, 33) renders "the palace" of Tao Cao Then as *guandi* 官邸 (official residence). In MLC-LV1, 33, it is Jing Luanlong 景鑾龍 (Chiang Dòn Luang), as in MLC-LV2, s. 36.4. But in Gao Lishi 1984, 122, s. 36, s. 36.3, the place is Ban Dòn Luang (Man Nuan Long 曼暖龍).

448. A rather similar account is recorded in MLC-LV2, s. 36.4 and in Gao Lishi 1984, 123, s. 36.3, but according to these two chronicles, Tao Cao Then (Thian) died in the year CS 1130 (AD 1768).

449. See MLC-LV2, s. 35.4. According to Gao Lishi 1984, 122, s. 35.4, Tao Cao Then's eldest son Cao

30.5 TAO THAI KHÒ'S PREMATURE DEATH

In the same year (AD 1800), Tao Thai Khò (i.e., Cao Mòm Maha Wong) dispatched Phaya Long Kheo Kham Paen [from Chiang Rung and Cao] Laca Cai from Moeng Cae to Burma to present a memorial to the king, requesting permission to succeed [to the throne].[450] The king of Burma consented and appointed Tao Thai Khò the *saenwi fa* of the Burmese side. The emissary of Burma brought the letter of conferment [to Tao Thai Khò]. However, [when the Burmese emissary] arrived at Chiang Tung (i.e., Moeng Khün), [he received the news that] Tao Thai Khò had died of illness. So there was nobody to whom the letter of conferment could be delivered. That was in CS 1164, a *tao set* year (Jiaqing 7, AD 1802).[451]

30.6 TAO YUNG KHÒ IS APPOINTED BY BURMA BUT REJECTED BY CHINA

Tao Thai Khò (i.e., Cao Mòm Maha Wong) had a son, [called Tao Sunwu (Dao Shengwu), whose Tai name was Cao Maha Nòi].[452] He was just two years old (sic), too young to be entrusted to manage affairs.[453] Thus the [nobles of] Sipsòng Panna had a meeting and decided to go to Moeng Long to invite Tao Yung Khò, whose [Tai name] was Cao [Fa] Can,[454] to be the ruler. But the Heavenly Court disapproved. Nevertheless, Tao Yung Khò still dispatched Cao Tham of Moeng Hai and [Cao] Laca Cai of Moeng Long to Angwa (Ava) to request permission for succession. They followed the envoys sent by Burma to Ava. The king of Burma therefore appointed Tao Yung Khò the *saenwi fa* of the Burmese side (court).

Maha Phom had two sons and four daughters. His two sons died young. Of his four daughters, the eldest daughter married Cao Moeng Khaeng, the second daughter married Cao Moeng Nun, and the third daughter married Cao Mahacai of Moeng Phong. Whom the fourth daughter married is unclear. Tao Cao Then's second son Cao Mòm Mahakhanan had two wives. The principal consort was the elder sister of Phaya Sing Kham. She had a daughter called Nang Can Kham, who married Cao Maha Nòi and had a son. The secondary consort had a daughter called Nang Po Kham, who married Cao Mòm U-Nüa.

450. They were Phaya Long Kheo Kham Paen from Chiang Rung and Cao Laca Cai from Moeng Cae. See Gao Lishi 1984, 123, s. 36.4. In MLC-LV2, s. 36.5, it is just recorded that *cao saenwi fa* Maha Wong Tao Thai Khò sent officials (*khun*) to Burma with tribute to offer to the king of Burma.

451. A rather similar account is recorded in Gao Lishi 1984, 123 (the thirty-sixth ruler), and in MLC-LV2, s. 36.5.

452. The parenthesis is added by the present translator. On Tao Thai Khò's son, see MLC-LV1, 31, s. 27.2.

453. Li Fuyi (MLC-LV1, 33) renders it as *buneng renshi* 不 能 任 事, which means "cannot be entrusted to manage affairs". This is from the perspective of a Chinese official. In fact Li Fuyi means that "Tao Sunwu was too young to be appointed as the *saenwi fa* to rule Sipsòng Panna". According to Gao Lishi 1984, 123, s. 36.5 and MLC-LV2, s. 36.6, Cao Maha Nòi (Tao Sunwu) was only two months old when his father passed away.

454. His Tai Lü name is Cao Fa Can or Cao Can. See MLC-LV2, s. 34.2 and 37.1; Gao Lishi 1984, 123, s. 37.1; Dao Shuren 1989. He was the son of the late *saenwi fa* Tao Wui Phin (Dao Weiping), see above s. 28.1–3.

30.7 DIVIDED ALLEGIANCE IN SIPSÒNG PANNA; TAO YUNG KHÒ, DEFEATED, FLEES TO CHIANG TUNG

Later, Tao Yung Khò (Dao Yonghe, viz. Cao Fa Can) was not on friendly terms with Cao Maha Phom.[455] Thus Tao Yung Khò hastily sent his bodyguards[456] to kill Cao Maha Phom at Chiang Lò.[457] As the six *panna* located to the east of the river (Mekong) had always supported Cao Maha Phom they refused to submit. Under the leadership of the Cao Fa of Moeng Phong they commanded troops to attack Tao Yung Khò. The six *panna* located to the west of the river could not triumph over [the six *panna* in the east]. Tao Yung Khò brought his wives and children [to Chiang Tung (Moeng Khün)] and sought refuge from the chieftain (sic) of Chiang Tung (Cao Chiang Tung). [They] lodged at Ban Mai Tòi.[458]

30.8 TAO YUNG KHÒ (CAO FA CAN) OFFERS WESTERN SIPSÒNG PANNA TO BURMA

Not long afterwards, Tao Yung Khò (Cao Fa Can) travelled to Ava to ask the king of Burma to send troops to help him return to Sipsòng Panna. He was willing to present the six *panna* to the west of the river (Mekong) to Burma, while the six *panna* east of the river were, as before, to be under the suzerainty of the Heavenly Court (Cao Hò). The [Mekong] river was to be the boundary. The king of Burma could not be persuaded, as there was no such precedent; moreover, Tao Yung Khò's [ulterior] motive was instigating a war. He sent Tao Yung Khò to prison. A year later [Tao Yung Khò] was handed over to the supreme commander Satò, who banished him to Moeng Nai.[459]

31. TAO SUNWU (DAO SHENGWU 刀繩武), VIZ. CAO MAHA NÒI, R. 1802–1833

31.1 THE THIRTY-FIFTH RULER AND THE REGENT TAO THAI KHANG (CAO MAHA WANG)

In the *tao set* year, [CS] 1164 (Jiaqing 7, AD 1802), Tao Sunwu (whose Tai name was

455. He was the eldest son of Tao Cao Then (Thian). Thus Tao Yung Khò (Cao Can or Cao Fa Can) and Cao Maha Phom were cousins.

456. Li Fuyi (MLC-LV1, 33) renders it as *yiwei* 翊衛, which the present translator interprets as "bodyguard". According to Hucker (1985), *yiwei* refers to "standby guard", a military unit at the dynastic capital. In MLC-LV2, s. 37.2, it is *kaeo-han* (soldiers). In Gao Lishi 1984, 123, s. 37.2, it is *gun-ge* 滾課 (khun-khaek), which means *yuwei* 御衛 (imperial guards).

457. Located in the southwest of the previous Fohai County (now Moeng Hai), on Burmese border.

458. See MLC-LV2, s. 37.3; Gao Lishi 1984, 123, s. 37.3. According to MLC-LV1, index, 16, Ban Mai Tòi (Man Mai Dui 蠻邁兌) is in Chiang Tung (Moeng Khün).

459. Li Fuyi (MLC-LV1, 34) renders it as *zongdu saduo* 總督薩舵, which is translated as above. According to MLC-LV2, s. 37.3 and Gao Lishi 1984, 123, s. 37.3, Cao Fa Can was handed over to Maengki Satò (*myo-gyi sa-taw*) and was banished to Moeng Nai for a year.

Cao Maha Nòi) succeeded [his father] as the *saenwi fa* at the age of just two years.[460] Hence, the Heavenly Court (i.e., the Qing court) made his uncle Tao Thai Khang (whose Tai name was Cao Mòm Maha Wang) regent and conferred on him the seal and credential, as well as the letter of conferment, allowing him to administer (rule) Sipsòng Panna.

31.2 ANNEXATION OF MOENG PHRAE AND NAN; KAWILA MENACES SIPSÒNG PANNA

In the *ka kai* year, [CS] 1165 (Jiaqing 8, AD 1803), Kawila[461] of Chiang Mai conquered and annexed Moeng Phrae and Moeng Nan. [He then marched north and] stationed his troops at [Moeng] Ta Lò.[462] At that time [all the *cao fa* and *cao moeng*] to the east of the Lu [River] (Nam Khong)[463] had submitted to Kawila except Tao Yung Khò (Cao Fa Can) alone.[464]

31.3 TAO YUNG KHÒ DEFECTS TO CHIANG MAI AND DIES AT MOENG NAN

In the *lai yi* year, [CS] 1168 (Jiaqing 11, AD 1806), Ngon Moang Moeng (Yun Meng Meng), supreme commander of Moeng Nai, ordered Tao Yung Khò (Cao Fa Can) to lead his troops and follow the Burmese commander-in-chief Sayachuo Na-nao (Sayazuo Nanuo) to attack [Kawila]. They were stationed at Moeng Laem and [then] marched together to Moeng Cae. [But], Tao Yung Khò was disgruntled at having been arrested and imprisoned by Burma (see above s. 30.8); moreover, he hoped to make use of the troops of Kawila to reoccupy Sipsòng Panna so that he could be the *saenwi fa* again. So he secretly presented silks[465] to Kawila at Moeng Ta Lò and persuaded Kawila to move

---

460. Tao Sunwu was the grandson of Cao Mòm Suwan, thus Tao Thai Khang's nephew. Tao Sunwu's reign is mentioned under his uncle Tao Thai Khang (Cao Maha Wang) in Gao Lishi 1984 and MLC-LV2 (the thirty-eighth ruler).

461. King Kawila of Chiang Mai (r. 1782–1816) played a major role in expelling the Burmese from Lan Na territory. His policy of forced resettlement campaigns in the Upper Mekong and Salween regions, which aimed at weakening Burmese supply lines and augmenting the manpower in his own core area, were also pursued by his close Tai Yuan allies, notably the principality of Nan in eastern Lan Na. The sentence above makes implicitly clear that "Kawila" does not solely mean a particular person—King Kawila—but generically refers to Tai Yuan rulers in general who implemented the policy of *kep phak sai sa kep kha sai müang* (เก็บผักใส่ซ้า เก็บข้าใส่เมือง, lit., "Gather vegetables and put them into baskets, gather people and put them into *müang*"). For details, see the introduction, part 1, section 10 of this volume.

462. Moeng Ta Lò (Daluo 大洛), located in Fohai County, is a border town on the eastern bank of Nam Lam River, only 5 km to Burma.

463. Lujiang 潞江 or Nujiang 怒江 is the Chinese rendering of the Tai "Nam Khong", which is called "Salween" in the West.

464. This event is mentioned in MLC-LV2, s. 37.4. A similar account is given in Gao Lishi 1984, 123, s. 37.4. The date given is "in the following year", i.e., 1780 AD.

465. In olden times *bipo* 幣帛, i.e, silks, which were valuable goods, were offered as gifts. According to Gao Lishi 1984, 123, s. 37.4, it was "silver and money". Here, Li Fuyi means money was used to bribe the Tai Yuan military commander.

his camps to Nòng Wat, the octagon pagoda [in] Chiang Coeng.[466] As a result, Tao Yung Khò submitted to Kawila and became a turncoat. He secretly brought his wives and children to the camps of Kawila. Later, he followed Kawila and defected to Chiang Mai where he passed away without an heir [in Moeng Nan].[467]

31.4 WARS BETWEEN BURMA AND CHIANG MAI; DEPORTATION OF WAR CAPTIVES TO CHIANG MAI AND NAN

In the years from [CS] 1168 to 1170 (Jiaqing 13, a *poek si* year, AD 1808), the Burmese commander-in-chief Sayachuo Na-nao fought a violent and bloody war with Kawila of Siam (sic). Various places, [such as] Chiang Tung (Moeng Khün), Chiang Yung (Chiang Rung), Moeng Laem, Chiang Khaeng, and Moeng Yòng were ruined and the villages were made desolate. Numerous officials (nobles) and civilians from various places fled in great confusion to [Moeng] Küng Ma (Gengma),[468] Moeng Kla, Moeng Bò, Moeng Tuo, Moeng Pan, Moeng Kaeo, and Laos (Lan Sang), as well as to Chinese regions (i.e., Moeng Hò) to seek refuge. Those who could not flee [in time] were all captured by Kawila and deported to regions in Chiang Mai and Moeng Nan. Consequently the region around Chiang Yung (Chiang Rung) was depopulated and became desolate.[469]

31.5 ENLISTING REFUGEES TO REBUILD CHIANG YUNG; KAWILA'S BASES AT CHIANG TUNG AND MOENG LAEM

In [CS] 1175 (Jiaqing 18, a *ka lao* year, AD 1813), the Heavenly Court entrusted the Regent Tao Thai Khang (Cao Mòm Maha Wang) to gather together [the refugees]. The officials (nobles) and the civilians, who had fled, were asked to return to Chiang Yung (Chiang Rung) to build [their] stockade-villages. At that time, the inhabitants of Chiang Khaeng and Moeng Yòng had not yet returned [to their home villages]. Kawila then turned back to Chiang Tung and Moeng Laem to develop the region and made long-term plans for stationing there.[470]

---

466. The temple (*wat*), known as Bajiao Ting 八角亭 (lit., "octagon pagoda"), or Nòng Wat, which is still extant, is in Chiang Coeng, located between Moeng Cae and Moeng Hai. According to MLC-LV2, s. 37.4 and Gao Lishi 1984, 123, s. 37.4, the location of the camp is at Nòng Wat lake (fish pond), near Ban Phasat in Chiang Coeng.

467. A rather similar account is given in Gao Lishi 1984, 123, s. 37.4. A condensed version is given in MLC-LV2, s. 37.4.

468. This is located in today's Gengma Tai and Wa Nationalities Autonomous County in Yunnan, in the north of Moeng Laem, quite far away from Chiang Rung.

469. A quite similar account is given in Gao Lishi 1984, 123, s. 37.5. See also MLC-LV2, s. 37.5. A Tai Lü manuscript from Moeng Long claims that a total of 150 families from Moeng Long and Moeng Yòng alone were resettled in Chiang Mai. See *Pap pün sipsòng panna saenwi fa pen pün tai lü hao lae*, f° 51/7–8.

470. A fairly similar account, but differing in detail, is given in Gao Lishi 1984, 123, s. 38.1. See also MLC-LV2, s. 38.1.

31.6 BURMA SUMMONS TAO SUNWU AND HIS UNCLE TAO THAI KHANG TO AVA

In *moeng pao* year, [CS] 1179 (Jiaqing 22, AD 1817), the Heavenly Court formally appointed Tao Sunwu (Dao Shengwu, or Cao Maha Nòi) as *saenwi fa*.[471] At that time the Crown Prince of Burma Maha Ne Myo (Maha Nie Miu) was the supreme commander of Burma.[472] He sent envoys to Chiang Yung (Chiang Rung) to summon Tao Sunwu (Cao Maha Nòi) and Tao Thai Khang (Cao Mòm Maha Wang) to proceed to Burma (Ava). As both of them were unable to leave [Chiang Rung] because of official responsibilities, they appointed Cao Mahacai, Cao Ta Lò,[473] and Phaya Long Khaek Compu to be their representatives. They were to follow the Burmese envoys to Ava. Displeased, the king of Burma said it was unacceptable for Tao Sunwu (Cao Maha Nòi) and Tao Thai Khang (Cao Mòm Maha Wang) to refuse to come in person. [Consequently], another [delegation of] Burmese emissaries, [led by] Miang Lòk Cò Cwa (Mang La Zuo Zhao) and Mòng Kan Taek (Meng Guang Die), was sent. They were to follow the representatives of Chiang Yung (Chiang Rung), Cao Mahacai and Cao Ta Lò, back to Chiang Yung (Chiang Rung) and urge Tao Thai Khang and Tao Sunwu to go to Burma. But as Tao Sunwu was in charge of the seal and credential (seal holder), he was not able to leave.

31.7 TAO THAI KHANG BECOMES THE BURMESE *SAENWI FA*

In the *poek yi* year, [CS] 1180 (Jiaqing 23, AD 1818), the various headmen (i.e., the *cao mòm* or lords of the various *moeng*) from the east and west of the river [Mekong], under the leadership of his (Tao Sunwu's) uncle Tao Thai Khang (Cao Mòm Maha Wang), travelled with the Burmese emissaries to Ava to make obeisance to the king of Burma Bodaw[-hpaya]. The king of Burma was very delighted, and forthwith appointed Tao Thai Khang the Burmese side of the *saenwi fa* [with] the title Coti Nakkala (Nagara) Maha Wongsa Laca.[474] In the same year Tao Thai Khang (Cao Mòm Maha Wang) returned to Chiang Yung (Chiang Rung) to assume the post of the *saenwi fa* of the Burmese side. [Thus], at that time there were two *saenwi fa* (i.e., *cao phaendin*) in Chiang Yung (Chiang Rung): the Heavenly Court recognised Tao Sunwu (Cao Maha Nòi), while the Burmese court recognised [the regent] Tao Thai Khang (Cao Mòm Maha Wang).[475]

---

471. Compare with Gao Lishi 1984, 123, s. 38.2: Cao Mòm Maha Wang succeeded to the post/throne in the year CS 1148, *bingwu* (Qianlong 51 of the Qing, 1786 AD) at the age of thirty-eight. He was on the throne twenty-three years and passed away at the age of sixty-one in the year CS 1171, *jisi* (Jiaqing 14, 1809 AD). At that time many [people from] Chiang Khaeng, Moeng Yòng, Chiang Tung, and Moeng Laem "who had left because of Kawila" (i.e., because of raids from Chiang Mai and Nan) returned to their native land to rebuild their homes. Only then did the Heavenly Court confer the seal and credential on Cao Maha Nòi [and appoint him] ruler. See also MLC-LV2, s. 38.2.

472. At that time *Li-cai Mi-yang* (Burmese crown prince), called Maha Ni Moyue (Maha Ne Myo), was the military commander-in-chief (*tongshuai*) of Moeng Nai. See Gao Lishi 1984, 123, s. 38.3. This is not recorded MLC-LV2, s. 38.3.

473. In MLC-LV2, s. 38.3, it is Cao Mahacai of Ta Lò instead of Cao Mahacai and Cao Ta Lò.

474. A similar account is given in Gao Lishi 1984, 124, s. 38.3 and MLC-LV2, s. 38.3.

475. A similar account is given in Gao Lishi 1984, 124, s. 38.3 and MLC-LV2, s. 38.4. According to

31.8 POWER STRUGGLE BETWEEN UNCLE AND NEPHEW; DIVIDED LOYALTIES IN SIPSÒNG PANNA

Later, because of their power struggle, uncle and nephew were not on friendly terms with each other. Tao Thai Khang was more powerful [than his nephew]. Tao Sunwu, aware that he was of no match for [his uncle], made excuses and sought refuge in Moeng La (Simao). All the officials and people from the east of the river [Mekong] followed him.[476]

31.9 TAO SUNWU BRIBES KAWILA TO ATTACK HIS UNCLE

Later, Tao Sunwu (Cao Maha Nòi), dissatisfied with the Chinese officials [in Simao], secretly sent Cao Khanan from Moeng Òng (Mengwang)[477] to bring silks as gifts to Moeng Pae (Phrae) and Moeng Nan to [bribe and] persuade Kawila to attack Tao Thai Khang (Cao Mòm Maha Wang).[478]

31.10 BURMESE MILITARY INTERVENTION AND THE ARREST OF TAO SUNWU

In CS 1184, a *tao sanga* year (Daoguang 2, AD 1822), they fought at Ganlanba (i.e., Moeng Ham). Kawila, defeated [by Cao Mòm Maha Wang], shifted to plunder Moeng Yò and Moeng Bun.[479] At that time, the Burmese side appointed commander-in-chief (i.e., *khun long*) Suai Ling Tewa (Rui Lin Diewa) to pick one hundred and fifty men for a suicide squad.[480] [They] marched straight to Chiang Yung (Chiang Rung). When Tao Sunwu (Cao Maha Nòi) saw that the Burmese troops were approaching, he dared not return to Moeng La (Simao) because he was afraid that the Chinese officials would increase his crimes. Thus he abandoned his wives and children in Simao (Moeng La), and [fled] to I-pang (Bò La) and hid in the hills.[481] The Burmese commander-in-chief Suai Ling Tewa found out that the unrest caused by Kawila was instigated by Tao Sunwu

---

MLC-LV2 and Gao Lishi 1984, Tao Thai Khang was the thirty-eighth ruler.

476. According to Gao Lishi 1984, the uncle and nephew ruled together a year before they split up. The lords of the five *müang* to the east of the Mekong all supported Cao Maha Nòi. See Gao Lishi 1984, 124, s. 38.4. A rather similar account is given in MLC-LV2, s. 38.4. The de facto division of Sipsòng Panna into two spheres of influence is confirmed by McLeod who visited Chiang Rung in early 1837. "These two chiefs, namely Mahá Noi and Mahá Wang, ruled at the same time, one on the left bank, and the other on the right bank of Mé Khong; but their rule was not peaceful; there was constant warfare carried on between them, and though Mahá Noi obtained the assistance of the states of Muang Luang Phaban (Prabang), and Muang Nan, Mahá Wang proved successful." MJ, 12 March 1837, Grabowsky and Turton 2003, 377.

477. The same is confirmed in Gao Lishi 1984, 124 (the thirty-eighth ruler). But according to MLC-LV2, s. 38.4, Cao Khanan was the ruler of Moeng Bang.

478. A rather similar account is given in Gao Lishi 1984, 124, s. 38.4. See also MLC-LV2, s. 38.4.

479. Previously Moeng Yò and Moeng Bun were in Moeng La (Zhenyue County) under Sipsòng Panna, now in Laos.

480. Li Fuyi (MLC-LV1, 36) renders it as *gansi budui* 敢死部隊 (lit., "dare-to-die corps").

481. I-pang (Bò La) is located at the seat of the earlier Xiangming County, now under Simao (Moeng La).

(Cao Maha Nòi) and learned of [Tao Sunwu's] hiding place. He took a small path into the hills of I-pang (Bò La), arrested [Tao Sunwu], and delivered him under escort to Ava. At the same time the king of Burma summoned Tao Thai Khang (Cao Mòm Maha Wang) to Burma (Ava) to question him.[482]

31.11 TAO SUNWU IS IMPRISONED IN AVA

The result of the investigation was the Burmese found Tao Sunwu (Cao Maha Nòi) guilty and incarcerated him in the royal prison. His uncle Tao Thai Khang (Cao Mòm Maha Wang) had pity on him and begged the king of Burma for his release and return, but [this petition] was rejected. He then asked the king of Burma to allow his nephew Tao Sunwu to serve as a personal attendant of the king of Burma and not to imprison him.[483]

31.12 TAO THAI KHANG'S BURMESE TITLE AND THE PALACE OF THE *SAENWI FA*

The king of Burma conferred an additional title on Tao Thai Khang (Cao Mòm Maha Wang), known as Coti Nakkala (Nagara) Maha Wongsa Pawala Suthammalaca. Moreover, he was entitled to use the throne and insignia. The official residence (palace) of the *saenwi fa* (i.e., *cao phaendin*) was allowed to have twelve rooms, with two floors [above] and one ground floor. The ground floor was open all the way through and not divided into rooms. It was permitted a tile roof. Four of the pillars of the house were allowed gold decorations. He was, as before, to return to Chiang Yung (Chiang Rung) to perform his duty.[484]

31.13 RETURN OF TAO SUNWU FROM AVA AND HIS DETAINMENT AT MOENG LA (SIMAO)

In the *dap lao* year, [CS] 1187 (Daoguang 5, AD 1825), Tao Sunwu (Cao Maha Nòi) was still detained in Ava. Hence the Heavenly Court (the Manchu court) sent envoys to Ava. Taking the road via Ban Mò (Bhamo) and Hua Keo (Hejiu), they travelled to Ava and demanded that Burma deliver Tao Sunwu (Cao Maha Nòi) [to them]. [Tao Sunwu] was first brought to Kunming (Moeng Sae Long), and then was placed in Simao (Moeng La) where he lived [under detention] for six years.[485]

31.14 TAO SUNWU COLLUDES WITH THE HILL TRIBES; DEFEATED TAO SUNWU FLEES TO MOENG SÒ

In the *ka sai* year, [CS] 1195 (Daoguang 13, AD 1833), Tao Sunwu (Cao Maha Nòi) stealthily bribed the Lua (Lawa), Musoe (Luohei), and San Thaen (Sandeng), as well as

482. A rather similar account that deviates in details, is given in Gao Lishi 1984, 124, s. 38.5. See also MLC-LV2, s. 38.4–5.

483. A rather similar account is given in Gao Lishi 1984, 124, s. 38.6; see also MLC-LV2, s. 38.5.

484. The above information not recorded in Gao Lishi 1984, 124 (the thirty-eighth ruler) and MLC-LV2 (the thirty-eighth ruler).

485. A similar account is given in Gao Lishi 1984, 124, s. 38.7 and in MLC-LV2, s. 38.5–6.

the aboriginal officials (i.e., the lords or *cao moeng*) of Moeng La Tai (Liushun), Moeng Hing (Puteng), Moeng Ong (Mengwang), Chiang Tòng (Zhengdong), Moeng U-Nüa (Mengwu), and other [*müang*], [and won their support to launch] a joint attack on Tao Thai Khang (Cao Mòm Maha Wang). Tao Thai Khang marched his troops to the foothills of Dòi Nam Yang (Nanyang), where he defeated the forces of Tao Sunwu (Cao Maha Nòi) and then proceeded to Moeng La (Simao).[486] At that time, Tao Sunwu (Cao Maha Nòi) was still living in Moeng La (Simao), and was apprehensive that the Chinese officials would incriminate him. The Chinese officials ordered him to disband his militia (*lianyong*) but he defied the order. The Chinese officials [in Simao] were exasperated. So they petitioned the governor-general of Yunnan and Guizhou[487] and requested that he be dismissed from office.[488] [They] arrested his wife (wives) and son(s) and brought them under escort to Kunming. Tao Sunwu then took his seal and absconded secretly. Later, he passed away at Moeng Sò on the border of Vietnam.[489]

32. TAO COEN CONG (DAO ZHENGZONG 刀正綜), VIZ. CAO MÒM SUCA WANNA, R. 1834–1864

32.1 THE THIRTY-SEVENTH RULER

In the *kap san* year, CS 1196 (Daoguang 14, AD 1834), Tao Thai Khang (Cao Mòm Maha Wang) petitioned to the Heavenly Court (i.e., the Qing court) to nominate his son Tao Coen Cong (Cao Mòm Suca Wanna)[490] [for the post of] *saenwi fa* (viz. *cao phaendin*) to succeed [him].

32.2 TAO THAI KHANG DIES; THE RULER'S TWO SONS

In the *lai san* year, CS 1198 (Daoguang 16, AD 1836), Tao Thai Khang (Cao Mòm Maha

486. A rather similar account is given in Gao Lishi 1984, 124, s. 38.8. A brief account is given in MLC-LV2, s. 38.5.

487. The seat of the governor-general (*zongdu* 總 督) of Yunnan and Guizhou was in Kunming.

488. Li Fuyi (MLC-LV1, 36) renders it as *ge zhi* 革 職. From the perspective of a Chinese official, Li Fuyi meant to "dismiss Dao Shengwu (Tao Sunwu) from the post of *saenwi fa*".

489. A rather similar account is given in Gao Lishi 1984, 124 (the thirty-eighth ruler); a brief account is given in MLC-LV2, s. 38.6. If Moeng Sò is on the border of Moeng Kaeo, it probably refers to Moeng Thaeng (or Dien Bien Phu) in Sipsòng Chu Thai of Vietnam. However, Li Fuyi (MLC-LV1, index, 17) has located the place in Keng Tung, which is most unlikely because the sphere of influence of Tao Sunwu did not reach west of the Mekong.

490. The parenthesis should be ascribed to Li Fuyi. Tao Coen Cong is the Tai Lü rendering of Dao Zhengzong 刀 正 綜 (in Pinyin). In the original Tai Lü text most probably his Tai Lü name Cao Mòm Suca Wanna is used, instead of Dao Zhengzong. Gao Lishi 1984, 124, s. 39.1 states, "Cao Mòm Suca Wanna, whose Chinese name is Dao Zhengzong, succeeded his father to the throne."

Wang) died (*zu*). Tao Thai Khang had two sons: the eldest was Tao Coen Cong (Dao Zhengzong) and the second was called Tao Soen Cong (Dao Chengzong).[491]

32.3 TAO COEN CONG AND TAO SOEN CONG SEND ENVOYS TO AVA

In the *moeng lao* year, CS 1199 (Daoguang 17, AD 1837), the *saenwi fa* Tao Coen Cong (Cao Mòm Suca Wanna) and his younger brother [Tao Soen Cong] ordered Phaya Long Sai, the aboriginal commissioner (sic) of Moeng Cae (i.e., Phaya Moeng Cae), the aboriginal commissioner (sic) of Puteng (i.e., Cao Moeng Hing), Phaya Phom of Chiang Tòng, and Phaya Pala of Moeng Phong to deliver a memorial to the king of Burma. The king of Burma consented and appointed Tao Coen Cong as the *saenwi fa* of the Burmese side with the honorific title, Coti Nakkala (Nagara) Maha Wongsa Laca. His younger brother Tao Soen Cong [also called Cao Sili (Sali) Wanna][492] was appointed the vice-*saenwi fa* (i.e., *upalaca*). Phaya Long Sai, the [Tai Lü] emissary sent [by Chiang Rung], was ordered to take the letters of conferment back without delay.[493]

32.4 FRATRICIDAL WAR; CAO MAHA KHANAN FIGHTS FOR THE THRONE

In the *poek sanga* year, CS 1200 (Daoguang 18, AD 1838), Cao Maha Khanan,[494] [Tao] Cao Cai,[495] Cao Nò Kham[496], and Cao Phom,[497] who were the leaders, colluded with Phaya Long Cang, Phaya Long Cana Lücai, Phaya Còm Kham, and others. They led three hundred soldiers to Chiang Yung (Chiang Rung) to fight for the succession [of the throne with the two brothers]. They immediately besieged the city (*wiang*) of the *saenwi fa* (i.e., Chiang Yung) and declared that they were going to kill Tao Coen Cong (Cao Mòm Suca Wanna) and his younger brother [Tao Soen Cong] and annihilate the headmen (nobles) of their immediate family and other people [related to them].[498]

---

491. He was Cao Sili (Sali) Wanna Upalaca, also known as Cao Lamma Awuttha [Kumman].

492. The parenthesis should be ascribed to Li Fuyi (MLC-LV1, 37). Tao Soen Cong is the Tai Lü rendering of Dao Chengzong 刀承綜 (in Pinyin). In the original Tai Lü text most probably his name is Cao Sili (Sali) Wanna Upalaca.

493. A very similar account is recored in Gao Lishi 1984, 124, s. 39.2; see also MLC-LV2, s. 39.2.

494. He was the second son of Tao Cao Thian. Thus he was the cousin of Tao Coen Cong's father.

495. Tao Cao Cai was the sixth son of Tao Sao Wün (Dao Shaowen), so Tao Cao Cai was the uncle of Cao Maha Khanan and grand-uncle of the young Tao Coeng Cong (Dao Zhengzong) and Tao Soen Cong (Dao Chengzong).

496. According to MLC-LV1, 31, s. 27.2, Cao Nò Kham was the eldest son of Cao Maha Khanan (second son of Tao Cao Then and a grandson of Tao Sao Wün) and thus was Cao Coen Cong's cousin. But according to Gao Lishi 1984, 122, 35.6, Cao Phom, Cao Cai, and Cao Nò Kham were the three sons of Tao Cao Cai (the sixth son of Tao Sao Wün). Hence they were the uncles of Cao Coen Cong. But Tao Sao Wün's grandsons are not given in MLC-LV2.

497. He was a younger brother of Cao Nò Kham.

498. A similar account is given in MLC-LV2, s. 39.3 and Gao Lishi 1984, 125, s. 39.3. Cao Mòm Suca Wanna (or Dao Zhengzong) and Cao Lamma Awuttha (or Dao Chengzong) were the sons of Cao Mòm Maha Wang (Tao Thai Khang) and grandsons of Cao Mòm Suwan (Dao Shiwan), who was a younger

32.5 CAO CHIANG HA'S RUSE

At that time, Cao Chiang Ha (the speaker of the *noe sanam*)[499] and those [nobles] of Sipsòng Panna who disagreed with Cao Maha Khanan, pretended to surrender to them. However, in the middle of the night they sent the tribal military officer (*tubian*) (sic) of Moeng Phong (Mengpeng)[500] to bring Tao Coen Cong (Cao Mòm Suca Wanna) and his younger brother across the river (Mekong) and have them first hidden at Ban Na Kha, [where they] were escorted to Moeng La (Simao) without delay. After [the two brothers] had gone, Cao Chiang Ha summoned the nobles of Sipsòng Panna for a meeting. They decided to appoint Cao Nò Kham as the *saenwi fa* and proposed promoting Phaya Long Cang, Phaya Long Cana Lücai, and Phaya Còm Kham[501] to be the ministers (*chengxiang*) of the Council of Nobles (*noe sanam*). As the three men were going to the Council of Nobles to assume their posts, soldiers hidden in an ambush set up by the various nobles of Sipsòng Panna suddenly rose and caught the three men and immediately had them killed in the Council of Nobles. Frightened, Cao Nò Kham fled to hide in the hills.[502]

32.6 THE *SAENWI FA* AND THE *UPALACA* FLEE TO SIMAO; CHINESE INVESTIGATION

Only when the Chinese officials in Simao (Moeng La) saw the arrival of the fleeing brothers, Tao Coen Cong (Cao Mòm Suca Wanna) [and Cao Lamma Awuttha], did they send men to Chiang Yung (Chiang Rung) to investigate [the matter]. Following [the investigation, the Simao officials] submitted a report together with the Chinese officials in Puer (Moeng Maen) to the supreme commander (*zongdu*) of Yunnan [in Kunming]. The supreme commander issued an order to instruct Cao Chiang Ha, which said:

---

brother of Tao Cao Thian (Dao Zhaoding). Tao Thai Khang and Cao Maha Khanan were cousins. Cao Nò Kham, supported by his father, was fighting for the throne with his cousins Cao Mòm Suca Wanna and Cao Lamma Awuttha.

499. The parenthesis should be ascribed to Li Fuyi (MLC-LV, 37). The *noe sanam* was an administrative council, where the nobles (*khun*) convened to discuss state affairs. The president of the council was called Cao Chiang Ha. The functioning of the *noe sanam* is discussed in more detail in the introduction, part 1, section 4.1.

500. According to MLC-LV2, s. 39.3, this was Cao Moeng Phong, but Li Fuyi (MLC-LV1, 37) regards him as a *tubian* 土 弁 (petty tribal military officer), since the *cao moeng* in the 1940s were still appointed by China as lesser military officers to guard the frontier lands.

501. According to MLC-LV2, s. 39.4, the three *phaya* were to be promoted to *amat ton phu yai* (i.e., high-ranking officials) [of the *noe sanam*].

502. This account is confirmed in almost all details in the 1852/53 eyewitness report of Mahacai, the ruler of Moeng La who supported Cao Chiang Ha in his struggle against Cao Nò Kham. According to this corroborative source, the president of the Council of Nobles recruited more than three thousand men who easily overwhelmed the forces loyal to Cao Nò Kham. "The population was frightened, and Nai Nò Kham fled to Moeng Ham" (ไพร่บ้านพลเมืองตื่นตกใจ นายหน่อคำหนีไปเมืองรำ). *Phongsawadan müang chiang rụng* 2002, 420.

> Cao Maha Khanan and others[503] go against the law to fight for [the throne/post] and create unrest in the land. Although the three accomplices, Phaya Long Cang, [Phaya Long Cana Lücai, and Phaya Còm Kham] have been killed, the [evil] roots and branches have not yet been eradicated. Cao Chiang Ha is to take the responsibility of eradicating the remnant evildoers. Nobody is allowed to go against the law of the Heavenly Court. Those who violate [the law] shall to be executed.[504]

32.7 CAO NÒ KHAM FLEES TO MOENG KÜNG MA

Cao Nò Kham went into hiding in [the forests of] the hills. [But] when he realised that his father (Cao Maha Khanan), brother (Cao Phom), and clan members had all been killed, he fled from Sipsòng Panna to Moeng Pan (in Jinggu) [and then to Moeng] Küng Ma (Gengma) where he sought refuge. Not long after, he returned to Chiang Yung (Chiang Rung) and mustered the Pha Phüng (hill tribes in Fohai) and Musoe (Luohei) to harass Sipsòng Panna. Defeated, [the tribal troops] dispersed. Later he again hid himself at Pha Phüng.[505]

32.8 CHIANG TUNG TROOPS FETCH CAO NÒ KHAM FROM THE HILL PEOPLES

The chieftain (sic) of Chiang Tung (i.e., Phaya Moeng Khün) sent [his son] Tao Bun Hoeng (Roeng) to lead [a troop of] fifty valorous soldiers[506] to Ban Kha Wa of Chiang Can to fetch Cao Nò Kham and force him to leave the Kha [Kui], the Lua (Lawa), and Musoe (Luohei). At that time, the troops under Cao Chiang Ha were engaged in a bitter and bloody war with the Pha Phüng and Musoe [to capture Cao Nò Kham]. Tao Bun Hoeng (Roeng) got Cao Nò Kham [from the Pha Phüng and Musoe] and brought him away immediately. En route, from Moeng Mang to Moeng Cae, they burnt and looted between eleven and fifteen villages, [including] Ban Ko (Man'guo), Hua Moeng (Hemeng), Ban Kha (Manka), and other [villages]. Going via Kha Yang Ngoen they arrived at Chiang Tung (Keng Tung) and sought refuge from the chieftain (sic) of Chiang Tung (i.e., *cao fa* of Chiang Tung).[507]

---

503. Here it means Cao Maha Khanan, his two sons, and his uncle Tao Cao Cai. See section 32.4 above.

504. A rather similar account, but slightly different wordings, is given in Gao Lishi 1984, 125 (the thirty-ninth ruler) and MLC-LV2, s. 39.5.

505. According to Gao Lishi 1984, 125, s. 39.6, Cao Nò Kham mustered Lua, Kha Kui, and Pha Phüng, and returned to harass Sipsòng Panna. Defeated, he fled to the hills of Kha Kui Pha Phüng. A similar account is given MLC-LV2, s. 39.6.

506. Both Li Fuyi (MLC-LV1, 38) and Gao Lishi 1984, 125, s. 39.7 render it as *yong shi* 勇士 (lit., "valorous soldiers"). Here they probably mean "well-trained soldiers".

507. A rather similar account is given in Gao Lishi 1984, 125, s. 39.7; a condensed account is given in MLC-LV2, s. 39.7.

32.9 CAO NÒ KHAM AND CAO MAHA PHOM ATTACK SIPSÒNG PANNA

In that year (CS 1200; AD 1838), the chieftain (sic) of Chiang Tung incited Cao [Maha] Phom[508] and Cao Nò Kham to launch another attack on Sipsòng Panna and Moeng Laem from the rear. At that time Sipsòng Panna was still fighting a war against the Mosoe.[509] On learning that Cao Nò Kham was leading his troops to attack them, they dispatched a contingent of soldiers to fight against Cao Nò Kham at [Ban] Na Ngòi in Moeng Pan.[510] Cao Nò Kham's troops were defeated. The troops of Sipsòng Panna pursued [their enemies] to Moeng La and Moeng Ma (in Chiang Tung). The disastrous wars went on for a long time and the hostilities had no end.[511]

32.10 CHINESE AND BURMESE ENVOYS SENT TO END THE CIVIL WAR IN CHIANG RUNG

The news reached the Heavenly Court (Manchu court) and the Burmese court, both of which regarded Cao Nò Kham as the sole ringleader of the hostilities. Thus, on the side of the Heavenly Court, the Chinese officials of Moeng La (Simao) dispatched the district magistrate Wei and the district magistrate Shen[512] to Chiang Yung (Chiang Rung) to end the hostilities. The Burmese side also sent high officials, the *pyanki* (official title) Nòratha and the *sitkè* of Chiang Tung,[513] to Chiang Yung (Chiang Rung) to mediate the disputes. [The delegates of] the Heavenly [Court] and of the Burmese [court] convened at Chiang Yung.

The [chief] delegate of Chiang Yung was the commander-in-chief of Sipsòng Panna, [Cao] Puttha Phommawongsa Mangkala Singhalaca of Moeng Chiang Ha.[514] The [chief] delegate of Moeng Laem was the commander-in-chief of Moeng Laem, [Cao] Puttha Phommawongsa Cotikalatha Wòlalaca. The [chief] delegate of Chiang Tung was the commander-in-chief of Moeng Khün, Phaya Long Khaek Compu. As the three [conflicting] parties [Chiang Yung, Moeng Laem, and Chiang Tung] were vassals of the Heavenly Court as well as the Burmese court, they had to obey the agreements

---

508. According to Gao Lishi 1984, 125, s. 39.8 and MLC-LV2, s. 39.8, he was Cao Maha Phom. Cao Maha Phom was the elder brother of Cao Maha Khanan. Hence he was Cao Nò Kham's uncle.

509. According to Gao Lishi 1984, 125, s. 39.8 and MLC-LV2, s. 39.8, they were the Kha Kui.

510. Located in the west of Fohai County.

511. A similar account is given in Gao Lishi 1984, 125 (the thirty-ninth ruler), and MLC-LV2, s. 39.8–9. According to Mahacai's eyewitness report, the troops of Chiang Tung and Cao Nò Kham attacked only the border panna of Chiang Lò where they were defeated by forces loyal to Chiang Rung. See *Phongsawadan müang chiang rung* 2002, 421.

512. Li Fuyi (MLC-LV1, 38) and Gao Lishi 1984, 125, s. 39.9 render it as *da laoye* 大老爺 (lit., "great master/lord"), which is the respectful way of addressing a district magistrate in imperial China.

513. The parenthesis should be ascribed to Li Fuyi (MLC-LV1, 38). *Pyanki* (Tr. ปยู่านคี) is an official title for a senior official. Literally it means "the great [personality who] translates". It derives from Burmese *pyan-gyi* (ပြန်ကြီး); *pyan* (ပြန်) means "to translate" and *gyi* (ကြီး) means "great". *Sitkè* is an official title, comparable to military officer or platoon leader. See MLC-LV1, index, 18. Li Fuyi renders *pyanki* as *zongdu* 總督 (supreme commander).

514. This is the full title of Cao Chiang Ha, the president of the Council of Nobles (*noe sanam*).

reached by the emissaries of the Heavenly and Burmese courts, and accept the terms with sincerity. In particular Chiang Tung had to accept the terms because they had sent troops to support [Cao Nò Kham] against Sipsòng Panna.[515]

32.11 PEACE TREATY WITH CHIANG RUNG, MOENG LAEM, AND CHIANG TUNG

Consequently, an agreement was reached and five copies of the document (peace treaty) were prepared. The delegate of the Heavenly Court kept one copy for their records; the delegate of the Burmese side kept one copy for their records; Chiang Yung kept one copy; and Chiang Tung and Moeng Laem each kept a copy. The [delegates of] the Heavenly Court and the Burmese court together with the [delegates of] the three parties (i.e., Chiang Yung, Moeng Laem, and Chiang Tung) drank the water of the oath of allegiance together in the Wat Yang Pan in [Moeng] Ta Lò. They swore to the Heavenly Emperor, the Dragon King, the Three Gems, and the village deities, and swore on the Buddhist sutras.[516]

After taking the oath, the emissary of the Heavenly Court wanted Chiang Tung to hand Cao Nò Kham over for trial, as he was the man responsible for the years of wars and unrest. The Chiang Tung side requested that he be placed in their custody and not extradited. The Heavenly Court side said that they could agree not to extradite him if [Chiang Tung] could put him under proper custody and guarantee that he would not come out again to harass Sipsòng Panna. Chiang Tung agreed to all these points and promised that if the custody was not done properly and he re-emerged to give the region troubles the Heavenly Court and Burmese would be informed immediately. If there were a breach of promise the Heavenly emperor (*shangdi*) would be the witness. Chiang Tung added a supplementary request:

> If, in future the incumbent *saenwi fa* (Tao Coen Cong, i.e., Cao Mòm Suca Wanna) should pass away without an heir, the five copies [of treaty] that have been made are to be gathered together and Cao Nò Kham shall to be allowed to return to Chiang Yung (Chiang Rung) and succeed to the post (i.e., the throne) of *saenwi fa*.

Consequently five copies of the supplementary treaty were made and each party took one copy for their records. It was in the *kat kai* year, CS 1201, on the second waxing day of the seventh month (Daoguang 19, AD 1839).[517]

---

515. A rather similar account is given in MLC-LV2, s. 39.9–10 and in Gao Lishi 1984, 125, s. 39.9–10.

516. According to MLC-LV2, s. 39.11, "They swore to the Three Gems and the witnesses were the deities, Lord Indra, Lord Brahma, the Garuda, the dragons (*nak*), the lords of all the four worlds (*tao tang si*), the princess of the earth (*nang thòlani*), and the guardian spirits of the three great cities (*maha nakòn*)".

517. 1201 Jyeṣṭha 2 or Wednesday, 15 May 1839. A rather similar account is given in Gao Lishi 1984, 125, s. 39.11–12 and in MLC-LV2, s. 39.11–12.

32.12 CAO NÒ KHAM IS SENT TO AVA

In that year, on the fifth waxing day of the first month,[518] the Cao Fa of Chiang Tung ordered Cao Nò Kham to go to Angwa (Ava) to serve the king of Burma and advised him that [if he complied] it would not be too difficult for him to acquire a fief (sic) in the future.[519] Hence, [Cao Chiang Tung] sent his son, the former minister (sic) Tao Bun Hoeng (Roeng), to escort Cao Nò Kham to Ava to be the attendant of the chief minister and the various officials of the Burmese court.[520]

32.13 TAO COEN CONG SENDS TRIBUTE TO AVA WITHOUT APPEARING IN PERSON

In the *kot cai* year, CS 1202 (Daoguang 20, AD 1840), the king of Burma sent *pyanki* Nòratha to deliver an edict to the *saenwi fa* Tao Coen Cong (Cao Mòm Suca Wanna) summoning him to come to serve in the palace.[521] Because the *saenwi fa* had official obligations to the emperor of the Heavenly Court (Manchu court) he could not leave his post to travel to [Ava]. [So Cao Mòm Suca Wanna] appointed Phaya Long Singhalacacai as head of the official [delegation]. He was to lead Phaya Long Acina Phom, Cao Moeng Hun, Phaya Long Lacawang of [Moeng] Ta Lò (i.e., Chiang Lò), and Phaya Nakkawicai of Moeng La to Ava to offer the tribute gifts. The king of Burma was displeased that the [Tai Lü] *saenwi fa* did not appear personally. He rejected the tribute gifts and refused to let the tribute envoys [from Chiang Rung] enter the palace. The envoys were also not allowed to return; they were detained in Angwa.[522]

32.14 TAO COEN CONG'S DILEMMA

At the same time the king of Burma issued an edict and gave it to the Burmese envoys, Mòng Cuo Ya (Cao)[523] and Mòng Waeng. They were to go with Phaya Long Acina Phom to Chiang Yung (Chiang Rung) and urge the *saenwi fa* again to come to Angwa (Ava). The *saenwi fa*, in a dilemma, was extremely distressed, so he reported the matter to the Heavenly Court. The Heavenly Court sent the vice-magistrate Liao to Chiang Yung to negotiate with the Burmese envoys, maintaining that the *saenwi fa* had official duties and had never left his office without permission. So the *saenwi fa* asked the Burmese envoy Mòng Waeng to return to Angwa (Ava) to ask the king of Burma for permission to

518. 1201 Karttika 5 or Monday, 11 November 1839.

519. Li Fuyi (MLC-LV1, 39) renders it as *shiyi* 食邑, which means "fief" or "principality" granted to a prince or a feudal lord. In fact, Li Fuyi meant that Cao Nò Kham could be appointed the lord of a *müang* if he behaved properly.

520. A rather similar account is given in Gao Lishi 1984, 125–126, s. 39.14. Cf. MLC-LV2, s. 39.14.

521. The king of Burma had a palace built which was called Nansui Hexiang (Nam Sui Hò Saeng). *Nam sui* is Burmese, while *hò saeng* is Tai meaning "diamond palace". [His Majesty] sent an emissary called Pyanki Nòratha, carrying an imperial edict, to go to call the *saenwi fa* Cao Mòm Suca Wanna (i.e. Dao Zhengzong) to go and serve in the imperial palace.

522. A rather similar account is given in Gao Lishi 1984, 126, s. 39.15.

523. He was also known as Mòng Cuo Cao. See Gao Lishi 1984, 126, s. 39.16.

send his younger brother, the vice-*saenwi fa* (*upalaca*) Tao Soen Cong (Cao Sili Wanna), as his representative. If permission were granted, Mòng Waeng would then be sent back to made a report. His younger brother would then immediately proceed [to Angwa] on his behalf. The Burmese envoy Mòng Cuo Yia (Cao) and Nakham Ne Myo of Moeng Nai would stay in Chiang Yung to wait for the news. The time limit agreed upon was two months.[524]

32.15 TAO COEN CONG'S ILLNESS

In the *hong pao* year, CS 1203 (Daoguang 21, AD 1841), the *saenwi fa* Tao Coen Cong (Cao Mòm Suca Wanna) was taken ill. As it was considered better [for him] to move to another place [to avoid the demons of illness], he went to Moeng Ham (Ganlanba). However, the nobility and other [officials] of Sipsòng Panna still remained in the official residence (sic) ⌊of Chiang Rung][525] to entertain the honoured guests from Burma.[526]

32.16 NEWS ABOUT AN IMPENDING ATTACK FROM CHIANG MAI; THE BURMESE LEAVE SIPSÒNG PANNA IN PANIC

At that time there were people from Moeng Yòng who went to Nòng Kwang and Foei Lai to do business.[527] As they saw that there were many people coming from Kawila, they sent letters to inform [Moeng] Chiang Khaeng and Chiang Yung (Chiang Rung) [of this] and told them to strengthen the defence measures. In case of an emergency, they were to share their fortune and misfortune and render mutual help in times of trouble. Sipsòng Panna was to immediately go on the alert, and the guards along the borders were to be reinforced. Chiang Khaeng and Chiang Yung handed over the original letters they received to the Burmese envoys to read. The Burmese envoys, Mòng Cuo Yia (called Mòng Cuo Cao),[528] Nakham Ne Myo, and others were in a panic. They wanted to return to Burma without delay. The officials of Sipsòng Panna tried to persuade them not to go, but it was to no avail. So they had to make ready the packhorses and servants to escort them from Moeng La to Moeng Ma and then to Chiang Tung (Keng Tung).[529]

32.17 THE BURMESE ENVOYS FALSIFY CHARGES AGAINST TAO COEN CONG

After the unrest caused by Kawila (i.e., the ruler of Lan Na) had been quelled, the Burmese envoys were afraid that they would be punished for having taken action on their own accord (i.e., leaving Chiang Yung), without the order of the king of Burma.

524. A similar account is given in Gao Lishi 1984, 126, 39.16–17.

525. Li Fuyi (MLC-LV1, 40) renders it as *yamen* 衙門 (official residence or government office). Here it means the palace of the *saenwi fa*.

526. A similar account is given in Gao Lishi 1984, 126, s. 39.18.

527. These two places were probably located in the south of Moeng Yòng and Chiang Khaeng in the realm of Kawila.

528. The parenthesis should be ascribed to Li Fuyi (MLC-LV1, 40).

529. A similar account is given in Gao Lishi 1984, 126, s. 39.21.

The chieftain (sic) of Chiang Tung (i.e., Cao Fa of Chiang Tung) also wanted to seize the opportunity to reinstate Cao Nò Kham as ruler of Sipsòng Panna. So they colluded with one another to falsify charges against Cao Mòm Suca Wanna (Tao Coen Cong):

> [Cao Mòm Suca Wanna] refuses to come to Burma upon receiving the edict, but seeks refuge at Moeng Ham (Ganlanba) instead. [He] does not live within the city of Chiang Yung, and moves all his inhabitants away. Moreover, [he] constructs forts at various strategic points in Chiang Yung and takes precautions against Burma. [He] kills one Khamu [man] brutally. Moreover, in the Burmese camp [he] has Cao Moeng Phong as a planted agent. [This] is going to put the Burmese envoys and others in a disadvantageous position. Therefore the Burmese envoys are forced to flee and seek refuge in Chiang Tung. Moreover, the *saenwi fa* has quitted the Burmese post; he secretly petitioned to the high-ranking officials of the Heavenly Court for the construction of fortifications and camps to defend against [us] and so on (and so forth).[530]

32.18 THE BURMESE KING REPRIMANDS TAO COEN CONG AND INSTALLS CAO NÒ KHAM AS THE *SAENWI FA*

On receiving the report, the king of Burma was outraged and issued an order to reprimand Cao Mòm Suca Wanna (Tao Coen Cong) and to appoint Cao Nò Kham as the *saenwi fa*, bearing the title Mahacai Laca. [The king of Burma] ordered Cao Moeng Hun and Phaya Long Sing to accompany Cao Nò Kham. Leading 2,000 Burmese troops and 3,000 Khamu [men], altogether a force of 5,000 men, they marched to attack Chiang Yung (Chiang Rung).[531]

32.19 TAO COEN CONG SENDS HIS YOUNGER BROTHER AND MOTHER TO AVA TO PLEAD HIS CASE

After Cao Mòm Suca Wanna (Tao Coen Cong) had pondered over [his situation] again and again, he deemed that Chiang Yung (Chiang Rung), located between two powers (China and Burma), would remain under their control in any case. He was no longer worried about the various fabricated accusations made by the Burmese envoys who colluded with Chiang Tung [against him]. So, he sent his younger brother (the vice-*saenwi fa*)[532] to accompany their mother and younger sister(s), as well as many nobles

530. See also Gao Lishi 1984, 126 (the thirty-ninth ruler).

531. According to Gao Lishi 1984, 126, this Cao Moeng Hun is Phaya Long Sing, not to be confused with the Phaya Long Sing who was later executed by Cao Nò Kham (see below, s. 32.25). Other sources estimate the total strength of the Burmese forces at more than 10,000 soldiers, which might be an exaggerated figure. See *Phongsawadan müang chiang rung* 2002, 422.

532. The parenthesis should be ascribed to Li Fuyi (MLC-LV1, 41). The younger brother of Dao Zhengzong (Tao Coen Cong) was called Dao Chengzong (Tao Soen Cong), but in Tai he was called, Cao Lamma Awuttha or Cao Sili Wanna Upalaca.

from Sipsòng Panna, down to Chiang Tung. There they prepared a statement [and dispatched it to] Moeng Nai, declaring that he had not left [his Burmese post]. When the Burmese side (authorities) received the statement, an order was issued telling Cao Nò Kham, the tribal military officers (*tubian*) (sic), and headmen (*toumu*) (sic)[533] to stay at Moeng Nai for the time being to await orders.[534]

On the second waning day of the eleventh month,[535] the Burmese envoy Mòng Waeng brought the vice-*saenwi fa* and the various chieftains (i.e., nobles or *cao mòm*) of Sipsòng Panna to Moeng Nai. At that time the king of Burma, who was on an imperial inspection tour, had arrived at Moeng Ukalapat at [Moeng] Dagon (Yangon/Rangoon). The *sitkè* Kani Nguan and *sitkè* Maeng Pan Chuo, et al., intended to mediate for them, but it was to no avail. The *pyanki* Nòratha was then to go to [Moeng] Ukalapat to ask the crown prince Pagan Min to solve [the problem] for them.[536]

On the fourth waning day of the first month,[537] the crown prince informed the chief official of the Ahyan Yung Tuo (the Burmese king's country palace),[538] at Moeng Nai and said:

> For the time being Cao Nò Kham should postpone going to Chiang Yung (Chiang Rung). The vice-*saenwi fa* (Cao Sili Wanna Upalaca) and his mother also need not go to Angwa (Ava). Both parties are to be put up in Moeng Nai and given protection.

Later, on returning to Angwa (Ava), the king of Burma learned of the settlement, of which he also approved.[539]

32.20 THE BURMESE URGE TAO COEN CONG TO GO TO AVA

On the fourteenth waning day of the same month,[540] again the two *sitkè long* (i.e., military commanders)[541] of the Burmese side (Kani Nguan and Maeng Pan Chuo)[542] sent

533. Li Fuyi (MLC-LV1, 41) renders it as *tubian* 土弁 (low-ranking military officer) and *toumu* 頭目 (headman). Here they mean "military officers" in the camp. See Gao Lishi 1984, 126, s. 39.23.

534. A rather similar account is given in Gao Lishi 1984, 126, s. 39.23.

535. According to Gao Lishi 1984, 126 (the thirty-ninth ruler) it corresponds to 17 November.

536. A rather similar account is given in Gao Lishi 1984, 126 (the thirty-ninth ruler). Pagan Min (r. 1846–1853) was the ninth king of the Konbaung dynasty (1752–1885).

537. 1203 Karttika 19 or Tuesday, 2 November 1841.

538. The parenthesis should be ascribed to Li Fuyi (MLC-LV1, 41).

539. See also Gao Lishi 1984, 126, s. 39.24.

540. According to Gao Lishi 1984, 126, s. 39.25, it corresponds to 29 January. His calculation is wrong as the first month of the Tai Lü lunar calendar does not fall together with the international solar month of January. The date 1203 Karttika 29 is indeed equivalent to Friday, 12 November 1841.

541. Burmese: *sitkè taw* (စစ်ကဲတော်).

542. The parenthesis should be ascribed to Li Fuyi (MLC-LV1, 41).

Bodaw Ye Suai Tòng Nòratha, *pyanki* Nòratha, and Cao Phommawong of Moeng Cae to Chiang Yung (Chiang Rung) again to summon the *saenwi fa* [to Angwa].[543]

32.21 CHINESE ENVOYS SENT TO AVA VIA CHIANG TUNG

In CS 1204, a *tao yi* year, the sixth month (Daoguang 22, AD 1842), the *saenwi fa* still could not proceed to Burma. The Chinese officials in Puer (Moeng Maen) and Simao (Moeng La) sent the vice-magistrate Liao and the magistrate Zhu to Chiang Yung (Chiang Rung). They, together with the Burmese envoys, Bodaw (General) Ye Suai Tòng Nòratha as well as Cao Moeng U, and Cao Moeng Ngat, Phaya Long Acina Phom, and others, travelled down to Chiang Tung, whence they were going to proceed to Angwa (Ava) to negotiate with the Burmese court. First they wrote a letter and sent it to Moeng Nai, asking Moeng Nai to forward it to Angwa, to which Angwa replied:

> There is no such precedent for the Chinese guests [taking the route] from Chiang Tung via Moeng Nai [to Angwa]. If they must proceed [to Angwa], they ought to take the route from Ban Mò (Bhamo) via Hua Ko (Koe) (northern route) [to Angwa] and then return by the same route.[544] Cao Nò Kham is allowed to proceed to [Chiang Yung]; the vice-*saenwi fa* (*upalaca*) and his mother are permitted to proceed to Angwa (Ava).[545]

32.22 DETAINING TAO SOEN CONG AND HIS MOTHER IN AVA

On the second waxing day of the eighth month,[546] the senior marshal[547] had the vice-*saenwi fa* (Cao Sili Wanna Upalaca) as well as his mother put up at a postal relay station located opposite to his [headquarters].[548]

32.23 BURMESE MILITARY OFFICIALS ESCORT CAO NÒ KHAM TO CHIANG RUNG

In that year (AD 1842), after the Burmese high-ranking official (i.e., *sitkè long*), called

543. See Gao Lishi 1984, 126, s. 39.25.

544. There were fixed routes for the foreign tribute envoys to travel to China. Envoys from Burma had to take the route from Ava to Bhamo (Ban Mò) and entered China via Western Yunnan, probably at Tengchong.

545. A very similar account is given in Gao Lishi 1984, 126–127, s. 39.26. This is an example showing that the Tai Lü texts of Li Fuyi (MLC-LV1) and of Gao Lishi (1984) on which their translations are based are in principle very close to each other.

546. 1203 Jyeṣṭha 2 or Saturday, 22 May 1841.

547. Li Fuyi (MLC-LV1, 42) and Gao Lishi 1984, 127, s. 39.27 render it as *da yuanshua* 大元帥 (i.e., great/senior marshal). Here it probably means the Burmese military commander-in-chief or the Burmese king.

548. According to Gao Lishi, they were put up at the postal relay station located opposite to the headquarters of the senior marshal. See Gao Lishi 1984, 127. But according to MLC-LV2, s. 39.21, they were thrown into the royal guardhouse.

[*Sitkè*] Kani Nguan, had brought Cao Nò Kham and transferred his camp to Chiang Tung, [he] appointed Nakham Mòng (Maung) So and Nakham Ne Myo as commanders-in-chief to lead three thousand soldiers to escort Cao Nò Kham [back] to Chiang Yung (Chiang Rung). [However], the *saenwi fa* Tao Coen Cong (Cao Mòm Suca Wanna), together with the officials and the people, crossed the [Mekong] river to the eastern bank to avoid them. Only two tribal military officials (sic)[549] of Moeng Cae and of Moeng Hun went to welcome [them]. Cao Nò Kham [and the troops] were divided and encamped at Chiang Lan and at the temple Wat Bo Nòi (lit., "small lotus temple") at Chiang Tü.

32.24 THE ABORTIVE CHINESE-BURMESE PEACE NEGOTIATIONS

When the news reached Simao (Moeng La), the Chinese officials there sent the three tribal military officials (sic)—[Cao] Moeng Phong, [Cao] Moeng Long, and [Cao] Moeng Ham (Ganlanba)—as well as Phaya Long Mangkala Paya and Phaya Long Sai [to accompany] the vice-magistrate Liao and his troops [to Chiang Yung]. They were to be brought to the eastern side of the river and to encamp at Ta Kò (at Ban Chiang Laeng). The Chinese and Burmese [delegates] crossed the river [to meet and] negotiate, but after two months no agreement was reached. Hence the Chinese officials returned directly to Kunming (Moeng Sae). All the people in Sipsòng Panna moved to [other places] to avoid [the impending confrontation] when they saw that the Burmese and Chinese were at odds.

32.25 BURMESE-SUPPORTED CAO NÒ KHAM BECOMES THE *SAENWI FA*; OPPONENTS ARE EXECUTED

Taking it for granted that the Heavenly Court and Sipsòng Panna had been defeated and fled because of cowardice, Cao Nò Kham, the Burmese, the Tai Khün [of Chiang Tung], and others mocked them. Consequently, they supported Cao Nò Kham as the *saenwi fa* and had Phaya Long Sing [the headman of Chiang Yung], Phaya Long Sulaye [Paeng] of Moeng Laem, and the president of the Council of Nobles (i.e., *noe sanam*) of Moeng Phong, and other [officials], executed.

32.26 THE BURMESE DEMAND RANSOMS FROM SIPSÒNG PANNA FOR THE RELEASE OF PRISONERS

The vice-*saenwi fa* (*upalaca*) Tao Soen Cong (Cao Sili Wanna or Cao Lamma Awuttha) was detained in Angwa. The Burmese charged the judicial official of Sipsòng Panna to return to get the silver to ransom [them].[550] For a tribal headman (*cao mòm*) one *còi* and two *khan* (ca. 52.8 taels) [of silver] were demanded, and for a soldier six *khan* (26.4 taels).

549. Here again Li Fuyi (MLC-LV1, 42) renders it as *tubian* 土弁, which means "petty tribal military officer". It was a post normally conferred on the *cao* (lord) of smaller *müang*. They were in fact Cao Moeng Cae and Cao Moeng Hun.

550. Li Fuyi (MLC-LV1, 42) renders it as *huishou shuzui yin* 回收贖罪銀, which means "to return to get the silver to atone for the crimes".

These were all paid. Moreover, the Burmese and others robbed the Chinese merchants, some of whom were even killed.[551]

32.27 EXPULSION OF CAO NÒ KHAM AND HIS BURMESE ALLIES

Consequently the Chinese officials in Puer (Moeng Maen) and Simao (Moeng La) ordered the three tribal military officials (sic),[552] of Moeng Phong, Moeng La, and Liushun (Moeng La Tai) to command the aboriginal soldiers (sic)[553] of Sipsòng Panna to drive Cao Nò Kham, together with the Burmese, [the Tai of] Moeng Yang, the [Tai Khün of] Moeng Khün, as well as the Khamu and vagabonds, etc., out of the territory of Sipsòng Panna. [The Tai Lü troops] pursued them as far as Chiang Tung. [From there] an official letter was dispatched to the Burmese court. [As a result] the king of Burma sentenced the vice-*saenwi fa* (Cao Sili Wanna Upalaca) and his mother, as well as the various tribal headmen (sic),[554] to imprisonment in the royal prison.[555]

32.28 ARREST OF THE RINGLEADERS AND ACQUITTAL OF THE *UPALACA* AND HIS MEN

Furthermore, the crown prince (sic) [Mu] Pakhan Maeng[556] was sent to investigate the matter on the spot. He reported:

> The *saenwi fa* Cao Nò Kham did not handle [the matter] appropriately. The Burmese envoys failed to help him to rule properly. Moreover, they killed people recklessly, and oppressed and collected money from them illegally. The local people blame the Burmese and Cao Nò Kham.[557]

551. In Gao Lishi 1984, 127, 39.31, it is stated: "The vice-*saenwi fa* (i.e., *upalaca* Tao Soen Cong) was detained in Angwa. Those whom he sent back to [Chiang Yung] to get money [were also detained by the Burmese troops encamping in Chiang Yung] and silver was needed to ransom them. For one *cao mòm* (headman) two *khan* (8.8 taels) of silver were needed and for one suite 6 *khan* (26.4 taels) of silver. The goods and horses of the Chinese traders doing business in Chiang Yung were robbed by the Burmese; some of the Chinese traders were also killed by the Burmese soldiers." A condensed account is given in MLC-LV2, s. 39.20.

552. Li Fuyi (MLC-LV1, 42) renders it as *tubian* 土弁, which is translated as above. These were in fact the *cao mòm* (lord of a *müang*).

553. Here Li Fuyi (MLC-LV1, 42) renders it as *tubing* 土兵, which is translated as above. From the perspective of Chinese officials at that time, the Tai Lü soldiers of Sipsòng Panna were merely the "aboriginal soldiers" and the *cao phaendin* (lord of the land) was the "aboriginal official".

554. Li Fuyi (MLC-LV1, 42) renders it as *toumu* 頭目 (lit., "headman"). These were the *cao mòm*.

555. A similar account is given in Gao Lishi 1984, 127, s. 39.32 and in MLC-LV2, s. 29.21.

556. According to MLC-LV2, s. 39.22, this was the Burmese military commander Mu Pakhan Maeng. But according to Gao Lishi 1984, 126, s. 39.33, Pakhan Maeng was not a crown prince, but a *cao po mu* (marquis).

557. See also the report of a Burmese officer to the king of Ava stating: "The rulers of Chiang Rung and Müang Phong did not plan an uprising. The reason [for the conflict] was that Nathom Mòng So, a Burmese, and Cao Nò Kham arrested nobles (*khunnang*) of Chiang Rung and killed them.

The king of Burma appointed *sitkè* Mòng (Maung) Kintuk as commander-in-chief and reinforced his troops with two thousand men. In the sixth month of the *ka mao* year, CS 1205 (Daoguang 23, AD 1843),[558] they reached Chiang Tung. An investigation was conducted and the ringleaders of the unrest were uncovered. Hence, [he] had *sitkè* Kani Nguan, Nakham Mòng (Maung) So, Nakham Ne Myo, Nakham Canthabuli,[559] and Mòng Ta Li, et al., arrested and thrown into the prison. The vice-*saenwi fa* (Cao Sili Wanna Upalaca) and his mother as well as the various headmen (sic), were found innocent and acquitted. They were released immediately but were ordered to stay at Angwa (Ava) as before.[560]

32.29 TAO COEN CONG OFFERS TRIBUTE TO AVA

In the year CS 1205 (1843 AD),[561] the *saenwi fa* Tao Coen Cong (Cao Mòm Suca Wanna) dispatched the tribal military officers (sic) of Moeng U-[Nüa], Phaya Long Cuo Su (Ba Long Zuo Shu),[562] Phaya Long Watcila Panya of Moeng Ham (Ganlanba), and Phaya Long Cai Songkham of Moeng Long, et al., as delegates, to offer in tribute one white-eyed black horse, one black-eyed white horse, and two elephants.[563] They set out, taking a route from Moeng Laem, via Mang Loen, Moeng Pòng (Mubang), and Sipò (Hsipaw) to Burma (Ava). The king of Burma sent [his] messenger (sic) to welcome them at Sipò.[564] Unexpectedly, the messenger took a portion of the tribute gifts and travelled by a short cut via Moeng Nai to Chiang Tung. There, he handed [the gifts] over to Cao Nò Kham, who offered the [stolen gifts] in his own name as tribute to the king of Burma. The tribal military officer (sic) of Moeng U-[Nüa][565] arrived at Angwa and handed the

---

The Chinese felt humiliated and ordered Sipsòng Panna to fight against the Burmese army. Cao Alammawutha (i.e., the *upalaca*, Cao Lamma Awuttha) has not committed any mistake. Please release him." See *Phongsawadan müang chiang rung* 2002, 424.

558. The date is not stated in MLC-LV2, s. 39.22. It is the period between 29 April and 28 May 1843. But according to Gao Lishi 1984, 127, s. 39.33, they arrived in Chiang Tung in the eighth month.

559. *Sitkè* and *nakham* are Burmese military titles.

560. "In the third month of the year *maseng saptasok* (February 1846) the Burmese king entrusted a Burmese *ahmu-gyi* and 150 soldiers to send Cao Alammawutha (i.e., Cao Lamma Awuttha), his mother, and his younger sister [back home]." See *Phongsawadan müang chiang rung* 2002, 425.

561. The date is also not stated in MLC-LV2, s. 39.23 or Gao Lishi 1984, 127, s. 39.34.

562. According to Gao Lishi 1984, 127, s. 39.34, he was Cao Moeng U-Nüa [called] Phaya Long Cuo Su. Thus the above translation is rectified.

563. A similar account is given in Gao Lishi 1984, 127, s. 39.34. A condensed account without mentioning the names is given in MLC-LV2, s. 39.23.

564. Here Li Fuyi (MLC-LV1, 43) renders it as *xingren* 行人, which means "messenger". However, in Gao Lishi 1984, 127, s. 39.34, it is "The king of Burma sent an emissary (*shichen* 使臣) to welcome them at Sipò (Hsipaw)." But in MLC-LV2, s. 39.23, it is stated that "the Burmese king sent an *ahmu-gyi* (emissary) to go and fetch the tribute gifts (*kantò*) at Sipò".

565. He was Cao Moeng U-Nüa, namely the ruler of Moeng U. See Gao Lishi 1984, 127, s. 39.34; MLC-LV2, s. 39.24.

remaining portion of the tribute gifts to the vice-*saenwi fa* (*upalaca*) (Cao Sili Wanna) and his mother for them to offer as tribute to [the king]. Sipsòng Panna detained the officials from Angwa. Some of them suggested that another portion of [gifts] should be taken and distributed to the Burmese officials, but the Burmese side refrained from making any comment.[566]

32.30 CAO COEN CONG'S TRIBUTE GIFTS ARE REJECTED; CAO NÒ KHAM IS TO PAY TRIBUTE IN PERSON

In the fourth month of that year (AD 1843/44),[567] the *saenwi fa* (Tao Coen Cong or Cao Mòm Suca Wanna) dispatched another [tribute delegation led by] the tribal military officers (sic) of Chiang Tòng[568] and Phaya Long Khoen of Moeng Cae to bring one red-hare horse, which had a jade top and four white legs,[569] and three common oxen to Chiang Tung (Moeng Khün), intending to offer them to the king of Burma. The king of Burma rejected [the gifts] and ordered that the [animals] be brought back. The king of Burma ordered that the encampments at Chiang Tung be broken and summoned the various officers back to Burma. He also ordered Cao Nò Kham to proceed to Ava to perform the ceremony of presenting tribute gifts.[570]

32.31 CAO NÒ KHAM OFFERS TRIBUTE TO THE BURMESE KING

In the *kap si* year, CS 1206 (Daoguang 24, AD 1844),[571] Cao Nò Kham, as head [of the delegation], led the tribal military officers (sic) of Moeng Cae and of Moeng Hun, as well as Cao Lacawong and Phaya Long Atya of Moeng Hing (Puteng) to Angwa, bringing the tribute gifts with them to offer to the king of Burma. The king of Burma accepted two

566. See Gao Lishi 1984, 127, s. 39.34. A condensed account is given in MLC-LV2, s. 39.23–24.

567. No date is given in Gao Lishi 1984, 127, s. 39.35, and MLC-LV2, s. 39.25. It is the period between 20 January and 17 February 1844.

568. He was Cao Chiang Tòng, namely the ruler of Chiang Tòng. See MLC-LV2, s. 39.25; Gao Lishi 1984, 127, s. 39.35.

569. Li Fuyi (MLC-LV1, 43) and Gao Lishi 1984, 127 render it as *chitu ma* 赤兔馬, lit., "red hare (or rabbit) horse". *Chitu ma* was the name of a horse ridden by Lü Bu 呂布, the famous general during the Three Kingdoms epoch (AD 220–265). It was a type of very good and fast horse probably from the western regions. In MLC-LV2, s. 39.25 it is just "a horse with a yellow head and four white legs".

570. This is also recorded in Gao Lishi 1984, 127, s. 39.35 and MLC-LV2, s. 39.25.

Here we can see that around the mid-nineteenth century, not long before Burma was conquered by the British (British Burma, 1885–1948), the Chinese power in Yunnan was feeble. The power of Ava had reached Chiang Rung. Burma grew so powerful that it no longer paid heed to the *cao phaendin* of Chiang Rung recognised by the Chinese authorities under the Manchu court. Burma chose own *saenwi fa*, Cao Nò Kham, and ignored Cao Mòm Suca Wanna, better known as Dao Zhengzong by the Chinese. China was then preoccupied with the cumulating problems caused by Western political and economic invasions in the coastal frontier regions.

571. No date is stated in Gao Lishi 1984, 127, s. 39.36 or MLC-LV2, s. 39.25.

elephants and then handed them on to the vice-*saenwi fa* (*upalaca*) (Tao Soen Cong or Cao Sili Wanna) and his mother.[572]

32.32 EXECUTION OF THE FOUR CULPRITS

As to *sitkè* Kani Nguan he passed away after one month of imprisonment. The four men, Nakham Mòng (Maung) So, Nakham Ne Myo, Nakham Canthabuli, and Mòng (Maung) Ta Li, et al., were arrested and escorted to Moeng Nai where, on order of the king of Burma, they were executed at the military headquarters[573] for the crime of having gone to Sipsòng Panna to create unrest.[574]

32.33 SIAMESE TROOPS INVADE MOENG PHONG; CAO MAHACAI AND HIS MOTHER ARE ESCORTED TO BANGKOK

In the *hong kai* year, CS 1213 (Xianfeng 1, AD 1851), Cao Nò Kham led the Siamese troops to invade Moeng Phong.[575] The tribal military officer (sic) of Moeng Nòi[576] sent troops to rescue him (Cao Mahacai) but was defeated. (Since Moeng Nòi had been burnt and looted by Siam, it had, at that time, no inhabitants—only a desolate river plain was left.)[577] The tribal military officer (sic) of Moeng Phong, Cao Mahacai,[578] and his mother were arrested and sent to Bangkok under escort.[579]

32.34 TAO SOEN CONG IS DETAINED IN BANGKOK

When [Tao] Soen Cong (i.e., Cao Lamma Awuttha or Cao Sili Wanna), the younger brother of the *saenwi fa* Tao Coen Cong (i.e., Cao Mòm Suca Wanna), learned of [the news], he thought that Cao Mahacai[580] was probably still in the land of Lan Sang (Laos),

572. A rather similar account is given in Gao Lishi 1984, 127, 39.36. A condensed account without mentioning the names is given in MLC-LV2, s. 39.26. Li Fuyi pointed out in his preface to MLC-LV1, 3, that probably the text of the three years, from CS 1206 to 1213, is incomplete, namely MLC-LV1, s. 32.31–32.33.

573. According to MLC-LV1, 44, they were executed at the *xingying* 行營 (lit., "travelling camp") in Moeng Nai. *Xingying* refers to the military headquarters set up at various strategic locations. But according to the MLC-LV2, s. 39.26, the four men were executed at the border of Moeng Nai.

574. A very similar account is given in Gao Lishi 1984, 127, s. 39.37 MLC-LV2, s. 39.26.

575. Moeng Phong is located 35 km west of Moeng La in Zhenyue County, to the east of the Mekong and near the border of Burma. It is interesting to note that the Moeng Lü Chronicle is silent on the events that occurred in the six-year period, 1844–50. For that period see *Phongsawadan müang chiang rung* 2002, 425–31.

576. He was Cao Moeng Nòi, i.e., the governor of Moeng Nòi.

577. The parenthesis should probably be ascribed to Li Fuyi (MLC-LV1, 44).

578. Cao Mahacai was the grandson of Tao Cin Pao (Dao Jinbao) and the son-in-law of Cao Maha Phom; Cao Maha Phom was the eldest son of Tao Cao Then (Thian).

579. The above information is not given in Gao Lishi 1984 or MLC-LV2.

580. Cao Mahacai should be Tao Soen Cong's (Dao Chengzong's) cousin.

[so he] went personally to Moeng U-[Nüa] to rescue him. However, when he arrived, Cao Mahacai had already been extradited to Bangkok. The king of Siam declared that if Tao Soen Cong (Cao Sili Wanna Upalaca) would come in person to Bangkok to negotiate the terms then the tribal military officer (sic) of Moeng Phong could be released. Tao Soen Cong, not aware that this was a ruse, went personally and was detained. Only Cao Mahacai was released. He returned to Chiang Yung (Chiang Rung) to discuss with the *saenwi fa* Tao Coen Cong (Cao Mòm Suca Wanna) for a plan of rescue. It was in the year CS 1213 (AD 1851).[581]

32.35 BANGKOK DEMANDS RANSOM FOR THE RELEASE OF TAO SOEN CONG

The majority of the people (nobles) decided to use gold and silks to ransom him, but the incident had to first be reported to the Heavenly court and the Burmese Court, as Chiang Yung (Chiang Rung) was not allowed to negotiate directly with the Kingdom of Siam. So a man was sent to Angwa (Ava). The king of Burma told Chiang Yung to take one hundred boys and one hundred girls to [Siam] to barter for [the release of] Tao Soen Cong (Cao Sili Wanna Upalaca) and of the mother of Cao Mahacai.[582]

32.36 CHINESE ENVOY SEEKS THE RELEASE OF TAO SOEN CONG FROM BANGKOK

The [Tai Lü] emissary returned to Chiang Yung but the local people considered [the Burmese terms] unacceptable. They still intended to use gold and silks to ransom them. However, some of them held differing opinions. Annoyed, Cao Mahacai returned to Moeng Phong.

Incidentally, at that time, the Heavenly Court had sent an envoy to instruct Chiang Yung on other matters. The envoy [from Moeng Hò] told [Chiang Yung] to let the government (i.e., China) deal with [the case] and let the [Chinese] envoy go to Bangkok to demand from the king of Siam the return of Tao Soen Cong (Cao Sili Wanna Upalaca) and others. Therefore, Chiang Yung prepared the presents and sent Phaya Kham Lü and Phaya Khan Moeng to lead three hundred soldiers to escort the envoy Ma Biao 馬標 (a Muslim who held a military post in the Simao *ting*).[583] Carrying the edict from the Heavenly Court, [Ma Biao and his entourage] first went to Lan Sang, where they were later escorted by two [Lao] men sent by the local chieftain (sic) [to Chiang Mai]. The envoy of the Heavenly Court, his retinue, and soldiers stayed in Chiang Mai while the Siamese officials were bringing the presents to Bangkok. The king of Siam accepted the presents, and Tao Soen Cong (Cao Sili Wanna Upalaca) and the mother of Cao Mahacai

581. This information is not given in Gao Lishi 1984 and MLC-LV2.

582. This information is only given in MLC-LV1, 44.

583. The parenthesis should be ascribed to Li Fuyi (MLC-LV1, 44). Ma Biao was a Muslim from Weiyuan 威遠 (Moeng Bò). See Li Fuyi 2008a, 77, n. 25. Many Muslims (or Hui) in Yunnan have the surname Ma, which means horse. They were the descendants of the Muslim soldiers from western China who followed the Mongols in the conquest of Yunnan in 1253. Simao *ting* 思茅廳 was a bureau or city council established in Simao.

were immediately released. Moreover, all the inhabitants captured previously from various places in Chiang Yung and deported to Siam were released and allowed to go home.[584]

32.37 TAO COEN CONG IS KILLED ON HIS WAY TO MOENG LA

In CS 1226, a *kap cai* year (Tongzhi 3, AD 1864), the *saenwi fa* Tao Coen Cong (Cao Mòm Suca Wanna) mobilised more than six thousand aboriginal militiamen (sic) from Sipsòng Panna to reinforce Moeng La (Simao) and Moeng Maen (Puer). As he proceeded to the foothills of Dòi Ai Haeng Long at Maliping,[585] he was ambushed by Ma Biao, the gang under Du Wenxiu,[586] and was killed. He was in office thirty years and died at the age of forty-two *sui*.[587]

584. This interesting piece of information is not given in MLC-LV2, Gao Lishi 1984, or Dao Shuren 1989.

585. The hills are known as Dalishi Shan 大力士山 (lit., "man of great strength") at Maliping 麻栗坪. Maliping is located in the south of Simao, between Moeng La and Moeng Hing.

586. See *Puer fu zhi* (Gazetteer of Puer Prefecture), quoted in Li Fuyi 2008, 77, n. 25. The Muslim rebels under the leadership of Du Wenxiu 杜文秀 (1828–1873) had occupied Simao and Puer around the mid-nineteenth century. On the Muslim rebellion in Yunnan that broke out in 1856, see *The Cambridge History of China*, vol. 2, *Late Ch'ing*, 1989, 212–213; ECCP II, 743.

587. Part 2 of MLC-LV1 by Li Fuyi ends here. *Sui* is the Chinese way of counting age, adding a year for the gestation time in the womb. This would indicate 1823/24 as the year of his birth. A rather similar account is given in Gao Lishi 1984, 126–127, s. 39.40. But according to Gao Lishi, 127–28, s. 39.38–39.41, the vice-*saenwi fa* (Dao Chengzong) married in Moeng Long on the way back to Chiang Yung. He had a son called Cao Mòm Khung Kham and was later called Cao Mòm Sò (whose Chinese name was Dao Jun'an; in Tai: Tao Cin An). He was adopted by his uncle, Cao Mòm Suca Wanna (i.e., Dao Zhengzong). The deputy *saenwi fa*, i.e., *cao upalaca* (Cao Nò Kham), was killed by the *khun han* (military official) of Moeng Phong. Cao Mòm Suca Wanna had one son called Cao Mòm Saeng. Cao Mòm Suca Wanna was succeeded by his nephew Cao Mòm Sò (Tao Cin An). According to Mahachai's eyewitness report of 1852/53, Cao Mòm Suca Wanna had reached the age of twenty-eight in that year. Thus he would probably have been born in 1824 or late 1823. See *Phongsawadan müang chiang rung* 2002, 419. Cao Mòm Suca Wanna's year of birth was also confirmed by McLeod during his visit to Chiang Rung in March 1837. McLeod describes Maha Wang's son "Chou Phung" (probably Cao Mòm Suca Wanna's personal name) as "a lad of 13 years of age". See MJ, 12 March 1837, Grabowsky and Turton 2003, 377.

PART THREE (1237–1875)[588]

3.1 MOENG LONG PUKHA (MENG LONG PUKA 猛龍埔卡)

In CS 599 (Jiaxi 1 of the Song, a *moeng lao* year, AD 1237), when Tao Hung (Rung) Kaen Cai married his daughter Nang Kham Kai to the chieftain (sic) of Chiang Rai (Phaya Lao of Lan Na),[589] Moeng Long Pukha[590] and Moeng Phayak[591] as well as other lands were granted as her dowry. Since then, Moeng Long Pukha and Moeng Phayak and the other lands were permanently subordinate to Chiang Rai (Hai).[592]

3.2 CHIANG KHAENG (ZHENGQIAN 整欠)

In the past Chiang Khaeng (namely Jingqian)[593] was in fact subordinate to Chiang Yung (Chiang Rung). [The relationship of Chiang Yung and Chiang Khaeng] was reminiscent of that of an uncle and nephew.[594] From the time of the reign of Phaya Lek Nòi (i.e., Cao Fa Dek Nòi) to that of Fa Ya (phaya)[595] [Chiang Khaeng] had owed allegiance to Chiang Yung.

In CS 930, a *poek si* year (Longqing 2, AD 1568), the king of Burma Fa Suttho Thammalaca (Mang Yinglong)[596] defeated Chiang Yung, and the five *müang* (polities) under Lan Na were [then] incorperated into the domain of Burma.

Consequently, the chieftain of Chiang Khaeng sent ten border guards from Nokkiek Pass (Rujie Ai)[597] to escort the king of Burma to the Burmese capital Ava and offered in tribute ten swords. Burma transferred five *müang* under the jurisdiction of Phaya

588. Part 3 of MLC-LV1 is not given in MLC-LV2, Gao Lishi 1984, or in Dao Shuren 1989.

589. The parenthesis is perhaps ascribed to Li Fuyi (MLC-LV1, 47). He was Cao Chiang Rai (Hai), the father of Mangrai.

590. It is located in Moeng Sing in northwestern Laos, at the Golden Triangle.

591. Moeng Phayak is located 51 km to the southeast of Chiang Tung (Keng Tung).

592. Nang Kham Kai (i.e., Nang Ua Ming Còm Moeng) was the daughter of Tao Hung (Rung) Kaen Cai (r. 1234–1257). See above, the reign of Tao Hung Kaen Cai (4.1–4.8); see also CMC-HP, Wyatt and Aroonrut 1995, 14–15; CMC-N, Notton 1932, 20. It was since that time that Moeng Lü lost two *müang* to Lan Na.

593. Jingqian 景欠 is the variant transcription of Jingqian 景千. The parenthesis should be ascribed to Li Fuyi. Jingqian is the Chinese rendering of Chiang Khaeng.

594. This may imply that Chiang Khaeng was founded by Tao Bakòng, the eldest son of Tao Kü Moeng. Tao Bakòng and his younger brother Tao Sòng Moeng were sent into exile down the Mekong by his uncle Soe Long Fa after the death of their father. See above, the reign of Soe Long Fa (s. 12.2). In Gao Lishi 1984, 110, s. 16.5, the founding of Chiang Khaeng is recorded in detail.

595. Cao Chiang Khaeng or Phaya Chiang Khaeng is rendered as the "chieftain of Chiang Khaeng" by Li Fuyi (MLC-LV1, 47); and *fa ya* 法雅 is most probably Li Fuyi's rendering of "Phaya".

596. The parenthesis is added by Li Fuyi (MLC-LV1, 47). Mang Yinglong 莽應龍 is the Chinese rendering of Bayinnaung (r. 1551–1581. 1551). He was styled Pha Mahakasat Fa Suttho Thammalaca. See above, section 17.3.

597. According to MLC-LV1, index, 21, Rujie Ai (pass) is Ai Nokkiek.

[Chiang Khaeng],[598] while the Nokkiek Pass was put under the jurisdiction of the chieftain of Moeng Yu (Mengyu).[599]

3.3 MOENG YÒNG (MENGYONG 猛勇)

Moeng Yòng was in fact the fief (principality) of the son of the *saenwi fa*.[600] Since the time when Cao Sunanta Satulu was invested as the lord of Moeng Yòng,[601] tribute [gifts] were offered to the fatherland Chiang Yung (Chiang Rung) on all the festivals of *khao watsa* and *òk watsa* (i.e., the summer festivals).[602] On all matters, [Cao Moeng Yòng] had to comply with [the decisions of] the *saenwi fa*; [he] had to defer and give absolute support to the *saenwi fa*. Moreover, [he] established a manor in Chiang Lan, which was called Mün Na Yòng.

In the year CS 930 (AD 1568), the king of Burma, Fa Suttho Thammalaca, marched to attack [Moeng Yòng].[603] Frightened, the chieftain (sic) of Moeng Yòng fled and went into hiding. [Cao Moeng Yòng then] sent Saen Sulin (Surin) to lead ten soldiers to go and welcome [Fa Suttho] and escorted the king of Burma back to Ava. Thereupon, the king of Burma appointed Saen Sulin (Surin) the chieftain (sic) of Moeng Yòng and told him to return to be the lord. Every year Saen Sulin (Surin) offered in tribute candles wrapped in golden [foil] to the king of Burma. This [tradition] is observed down to the present day.

3.4 MOENG YÒ (MENGYUE 猛約) AND MOENG BUN (MENGBEN 猛奔)

In the *kap sanga* year, CS 956 (Wanli 22, AD 1594), the *saenwi fa* Cao In Moeng married his daughter to the chieftain of Lan Sang (i.e., Cao Lan Sang) as his queen. Moeng Yò and Moeng Bun were bestowed on his daughter as dowry-principalities. Since then, Moeng Yò and Moeng Bun were under the jurisdiction of Lan Sang.[604]

---

598. Probably they were the five *müang* taken from Lan Na.

599. Moeng Yu is located in the eastern part of Burma's Shan State. In the period c. 1858–1884/86, it was the capital of the principality of Chiang Khaeng. See Grabowsky 1996b.

600. Moeng Yòng is located in the southwest of Moeng Yu in Chiang Tung, Burma. Li Fuyi (MLCLV1, 47) renders it as *shiyi* 食邑 (lit. "eat the fief"). It refers to land granted to a feudal lord as his appanage. In Tai Lu it is probably *kin na* ("consuming the rice fields"). Here it is better to render *shiyi* as "principality".

601. Here Li Fuyi (MLC-LV1, 47) renders it as *shicai* 食采 (lit., "eat the fief"), which means the same as *shiyi*. Here it means Cao Sunanta Satulu became the Lord of Moeng Yòng.

602. They are celebrated at the beginning and at the end of Buddhist lent respectively. This parenthesis should be ascribed to Li Fuyi (MLC-LV1, 47). Li Fuyi renders it as *shou xia jie* 守夏節 (summer festivals). See also section 19.12, n. 311 above.

603. In CS 930, the Burmese king of Dagon (Yangon) sent General Maha Tham to attack Chiang Rung. See above, section 17.2.

604. Cao In Moeng only had one son, born to the Burmese princess. See section 19.13 above.

3.5 MOENG BÒ (MENGBO 猛 博)

In the *ka sai* year, CS 1075 (Kangxi 52 of the Qing, AD 1713), the *saenwi fa* Cao Paeng Moeng married his daughter to the chieftain (sic) of Moeng Bò (i.e., Cao Moeng Bò).[605] Thereupon, Moeng Bò was to be ruled by his son-in-law. Later his son-in-law surrendered to the Heavenly Court (China); thereafter, Moeng Bò was no longer subordinate to Chiang Yung (i.e., Chiang Rung).

3.6 MOENG PAN (MENGBAN 猛 班)

In the *poek sanga* year, CS 1080 (Kangxi 57 of the Qing, AD 1718), the *saenwi fa* Cao Paeng Moeng married his daughter to the chieftain (sic) of Moeng Pan (i.e., Cao Moeng Pan).[606] Thereupon Moeng Pan was handed over to his son-in-law. Later his son-in-law surrendered to the Heavenly Court (China); thereafter, Moeng Pan was no longer subordinate to Chiang Yung (Chiang Rung).

3.7 MONEY AND LAND TAXES (*QIAN-LIANG* 錢 糧)[607]

In the sixth year of Yongzheng [reign] (the *poek san* year, CS 1090; AD 1728),[608] [the lord] of Moeng Cae, Cao Si Mün Na Kang Kong, received an order from the *saenwi fa* that he was also appointed to rule the eight *müang* (polities) west of the river [Mekong].[609] Moreover, [the domains that were under his administration] were extended as far as the sources the of the Nam Lam[610] and Nam Pi[611] Rivers, and to other places.

Since the time after Sipsòng Panna had been wantonly pillaged by the king of Burma (1568 AD), Fa Suttho Thammalaca, the land was desolate and its inhabitants few. [They] did not have the [man] power to deliver the land taxes (*liang*) to the Heavenly Court. Thus, a meeting was held, and it was decided that the [land taxes paid in kind] were to be commuted and paid in silver. According to calculation [the land taxes] that ought to be paid amounted to 1,084 *dan* (picul)[612] of rice grain, commuted and apportioned as follows:

605. Moeng Bò is located in Jinggu County, north of Puer (Moeng Maen).

606. Moeng Pan is also located in Jinggu County.

607. This refers to land taxes levied in kind which were commuted to silver, a prevalent currency in China of that time.

608. In the original Tai Lü text it is probably "In the *poek san* year, CS 1090". Li Fuyi probably has converted the Tai year into the Chinese reign, i.e., Yongzheng 6, *wushen* year.

609. The eight *müang* listed in Li Fuyi 1983a, 59, are: Chiang Coeng (Jingzhen), Moeng Ngat (Meng'a), Moeng Ngam Lang Nüa (Meng'ang Lang'nen), Moeng Khòn (Mengkang), Moeng Hun (Menghun), Moeng Hai (Menghai), Moeng Ta Lò (Daluo), and Moeng Man (Mengman).

610. Nam Lam is flowing along the border of Moeng Cae and Chiang Tung.

611. Not yet identified.

612. One Chinese *dan* or picul is about 132 or 133 pounds.

Domain/Polity	*Land taxes commuted to silver to be paid*
Chiang Rung (Jinglong 景 曨)	593 *liang* (taels), seven *qian*, four *fen*, eight *li*, and two *hao* (593.7482 taels).
Moeng Lang Nüa (Menglang 猛 朗)[613]	464 *liang*, three *qian*, five *fen*, eight *li*, and eight *hao* (464.3588 taels).
The eight *müang* on the west of the river [Mekong]	559 *liang*, six *qian*, nine *fen*, two *li*, and two *hao* (559.6922 taels).
Moeng Long (Menglong 猛 籠)	339 *liang*, one *qian*, one *fen*, eight *li*, and two *hao* (339.1182 taels).
Moeng La (or Simao 思 茅), and Moeng La Tai (Liushun 六 順)	227 *liang*, six *qian*, seven *fen*, four *li*, and eight *hao* (227.6748 taels).
Moeng Wang (Mengwang 猛 往)[614]	20 *liang* (20 taels).
Moeng Pan (Mengpan 猛 伴)[615]	33 *liang*, eight *qian*, seven *fen*, and one *li* (33.871 taels).
Bujiao 補 角 (?)[616]	16 *liang*, nine *qian*, four *fen*, seven *li*, and eight *hao* (16.9478 taels).
I-ngu (Yiwu 易 武)[617]	28 *liang*, one *qian*, seven *fen*, nine *li*, and eight *hao* (28.1798 taels).
Moeng Òng (Mengwang 猛 旺)[618]	48 *liang*, eight *qian*, eight *fen*, two *li*, and four *hao* (48.8824 taels).
Moeng Hing (Miengling 猛 嶺)[619]	19 *liang*, four *qian*, eight *fen*, three *li*, and five *hao* (19.4835 taels).
Bò La 播 剌 (or Yibang 倚 邦)[620]	397 *liang*, eight *qian*, seven *fen*, nine *li*, and eight *hao* (397.8798 taels).
Total	2,749 *liang*, eight *qian*, three *fen*, six *li*, and five *hao* (2,749.8365 taels).

The land taxes in kind commuted to silver raised from the domains from Chiang Rung to I-ngu and other places were to be delivered to Moeng La (Simao); the land taxes in kind commuted to silver raised from Moeng Òng was to be delivered to Moeng Maen (Puer). Whenever silver was to be delivered two workers were needed. Each worker

613. In modern Langcang Lahu Autonomous County, northeast of Moeng Laem.

614. Located at the seat of Jiangning District, northwest of Chiang Rung, on the west of the Mekong.

615. Located in Zhenyue County, north-northeast of Moeng La, near the border of Laos.

616. Located in Zhenyue County, between I-ngu and Moeng Pan, near the border of Laos.

617. At the seat of Zhenyue County.

618. Located in Simao County (Moeng La).

619. Namely Puteng, in Simao (Moeng La).

620. Previously Yibang was located at the seat of Xiangming County, which was later placed under Simao (Moeng La).

was given six taels of silver, with 80 to 90 per cent of silver content.[621] This amounted to twelve taels.

The land taxes in kind commuted to silver (*liangyin* 糧 銀), *tiaoding* 條 丁 (adult males), *huohao* 火 耗 (melting wastage)[622] and other items to be raised from the chiliad commander (*qianzong* 千 總) of Moeng Cae and the various *müang* (polities) in the west of the river are as follows:

The [total] land taxes in kind commuted to silver to be delivered by the various *müang* to the west of the river—including charges [such as] delivery and approval (*jiepi* 解批) commuted to the equivalent (*zheming* 折明?), paper and wrapping (*zhizha* 紙紮), and silver bags (*yindai* 銀袋), etc.: 391 *liang*, two *qian*, and one *fen* (391.21 taels).

Tiaoding 條 丁 (?)	194 *liang*, seven *qian*, and five *fen* (194.75 taels).
Huohao 火 耗 (melting wastage)	38 *liang*, nine *qian*, and five *fen* (38.95 taels).
Buzheng xiang 補 正 項 (subsidising the regular item/ surcharges)	25 *liang*, six *qian*, and five *fen* (25.65 taels).
Total	650 *liang*, five *qian*, and six *fen* (650.56 taels).
Surcharges for the sea and credential (*yinxin jiaojia* 印 信 繳 價)	548 *liang*, seven *qian*, eight *fen*, and five *li* (548.785 taels).
Total	1,190 *liang*, three *qian*, four *fen*, and five *li* (1,190.345 taels).

The ninety-five *heleng* 呵 冷 (*huo-noeng/ho hoen*)—a household unit (*menhu danwei* 門戶單位)[623]—were held responsible for the various items [of taxes] listed above, excluding the surcharges for the seal and credential (*yinxin jiaojia*). These were distributed among [the households] listed, as follows:

Domain	Number of households (in *heleng*)
Moeng Cae (Mengzhe 猛 遮)	34 *heleng*
Moeng Hun (Menghun 猛 混)	16 *heleng*
Moeng Hai (Menghai 猛 海)	14 *heleng*
Moeng Ngat (Meng'a 猛 阿)	10 *heleng*
Moeng Man (Mengman 猛 滿)	7 *heleng*
Chiang Coeng (Jingzhen 景 真)	6 *heleng*
Moeng Ngam Lang Nüa (Meng'ang Lang'nen 猛 昂 朗 嫩)	3 *heleng*
Moeng Chiang Lò (Meng Jingluo 猛 景 洛)	3 *heleng*
Moeng Khòn (Mengkang 猛 康)	2 *heleng*

621. This means six taels of 80 to 90 per cent pure silver.

622. A kind of surcharge.

623. The parenthesis should be ascribed to Li Fuyi (MLC-LV1, 50).

It was decided that the distribution of [the land taxes] was to be calculated according the number of households. Ten households (*ho sip*) of the hill tribe (Kha) were equivalent to five households of the native tribe (Tai Lü). The average [land taxes] to be paid to the Heavenly Court were calculated accordingly. It was like buying water to drink and paying a road toll for walking.

The land taxes in kind to be paid, commuted to silver (*liang yin*), were divided into eight items. The names of each tax and the amount raised from each *heleng* (household unit) are as listed in the following:

Types of Taxes	Paid by each *heleng* (household unit)
1. The regular/amount of land tax commuted to silver (正項糧銀)	2.704 taels
2. Silver for tiaoding (條丁銀)	2.05 taels
3. Silver for melting wastage (火耗銀)	0.41 taels
4. Surcharge on the regular amount of land tax commuted to silver (補正項糧銀)	0.27 taels
5. Silver for delivery and approval (解批銀)	0.574 taels
6. Silver for commutation to equivalent ? (折明銀)	0.44 taels
7. Silver for silver bags (銀袋銀)	0.33 taels
8. Silver for paper and wrapping (紙扎銀)	0.07 taels

According to this calculation, each *heleng* was to deliver a total of 6.848 taels of silver for the regular item of land tax commuted (正項), for *tiaoding* (條丁), for melting wastage (火耗), for surcharges on regular items (補正項), for delivery and approval (解批), for commutation to equivalent (折明), for silver bags (銀袋), and for paper and wrapping (紙扎).

Domain/Polity	No. of households (in *heleng*)	Total silver to be paid
Moeng Cae 猛遮	34	232.832 taels
Moeng Hun 猛滑	16	109.568 taels
Moeng Hai 猛海	14	95.872 taels
Moeng Ngat 猛阿	10	68.48 taels
Moeng Man 猛滿	7	47.936 taels
Chiang Coeng 景真	6	41.088 taels
Moeng Ngam Lang Nüa 猛昂朗嫩	3	20.544 taels
Moeng Chiang Lò 猛景洛	3	20.544 taels
Moeng Khòn 猛康	2	13.696 taels

The total amount of the above land taxes in kind commuted to silver (*qian-liang*) to be paid by Moeng Cae and the eight *müang* under it was 650.056 taels. Furthermore, it was decided that each *müang* was to give 0.1 tael of official silver (*guan-yin* 官銀) to the general secretary (*zong shu-ji* 總書記) of Moeng Cae.

3.8 THE BURMESE INVASION OF MOENG LONG (MENGLONG 猛籠)

In the *kap san* year, CS 1126 (Qianlong 29, AD 1764), the Burmese general Phuo Tin Laca (Bo Ding She 波丁闍) invaded Moeng Long,[624] causing the entire population to flee and disperse to different [places]. In that armed confrontation the tribal military official of Moeng Hun, Cao Phaya, the tribal military official of Moeng Long, Cao Ah Lim, and the tribal military official of Chiang Coeng, Cao Phaya Long Panna, were all killed.

3.9 THE BURMESE INVASION OF MOENG CAE (MENGZHE 猛遮)

In the *dap lao* year, CS 1127 (Qianlong 30, AD 1765), the Burmese invaded [Moeng Cae] and the battle was fought at Nam Kham (Nankan 南坎).[625] One contingent of the Burmese soldiers invaded Moeng Cae.[626] As Moeng Cae could not repulse [the enemy], on the second waning day of the fifth month,[627] under the command of the tribal military officer (sic) Atya Cao Si Mün Na (Aya Zhao Simen Na 阿雅詔四悶那), [whose sinicised] name was Tao Saen Fu (Dao Shoufu 刀守甫),[628] the people fled to Moeng Pan (Mengban 猛班).[629] They began to return only on the ninth waning day of the eleventh month,[630] after the Burmese had retreated. In the *lai set* year, CS 1128 (Qianlong 31, AD 1766), on the third waxing day of the eighth month,[631] [Cao Moeng Cae] returned and stationed [his troops] in the old fortified town.[632]

624. Located c. 55 km south of Chiang Rung, near the border of Burma.

625. Nam Kham, located in the south of Ruili, a border town in Burma, is rather far away from Moeng Cae.

626. In the west of Moeng Hai, north-northeast of Moeng Ta Lò (Daluo), west of the Mekong.

627. 1127 Phalguna 17 or Tuesday, 25 February 1766.

628. According to Li Fuyi (MLC-LV1, index, 21), Dao Shoufu is the Chinese name of the tribal chiliarch commander (*tu qianzong* 土千總) of Moeng Cae. Hence Dao Shoufu was Cao Moeng Cae, the lord of Moeng Cae. *Tu qianzong* was his Chinese official title.

629. Moeng Pan is now the Jinggu Autonomous County of the Tai and Yi Nationalities, the Weiyuan Prefecture of the Ming period, located in the north of Moeng Cae (Mengzhe), now under the jurisdiction of the Simao District.

630. 1128 Bhādrapada 24 or Saturday, 27 September 1766.

631. 1128 Jyeṣṭha 3 or Sunday, 11 May 1766.

632. Thus, the Burmese troops occupied Moeng Cae over five months and the inhabitants of Moeng Cae took nine months to move back to their homes in Moeng Cae.

3.10 THE BURMESE CAPTURE OF MOENG TA LÒ (DALUO 打洛)

The supreme commander, the magistrate Hua 華大人 (i.e., Hua Feng 華封),[633] who was originally stationed to defend Moeng Khün (Menggen), later withdrew [his troops]. The Burmese came to invade again. At that time, the squad leader Han Rong 韓榮[634] commanded two hundred soldiers defending Ta Lò. For twenty days, they fought a fierce and bloody battle against a Burmese force of four thousand men. But the forces stationed at Moeng Hun[635] defied the order to go to rescue them. As a result, Han Rong's troops were destroyed and the squad leader Han Rong was killed. Only four soldiers managed to escape. It was in CS 1129, a *moeng kai* year (Qianlong 32, AD 1767), on the eleventh day in the fifth month, waning. Later, when the Son of Heaven (Emperor Qianlong) learned of the truth after investigation, [His Majesty] had the three Chinese officials (Si Bangzhi 司邦直, Gan Qizhuo 甘其卓 and Quan Shu 權恕) who had defied the order to send reinforcements, executed.[636]

3.11 SIPSÒNG PANNA

In the *dap sai* year, CS 1147 (Qianlong 50, AD 1785), on the fourth waxing day of the seventh month,[637] the president of the Council of Nobles (*noe sanam*),[638] Cao Chiang Ha (Zhao Jingha 詔景哈), summoned the various chief headmen (*da toumu*)[639] of Sipsòng Panna and the various nobles of the aboriginal commissions (*tusi*)[640] for a meeting at the Council of Nobles. [A plan] to divide Sipsòng Panna [into various *panna*] was drafted and submitted to the *saenwi fa* (i.e., *cao phaendin*), who approved it. Sipsòng Panna was divided as follows:

633. According to Li Fuyi (MLC-LV1, index, 21), this was Ghwa Jung-yie (probably referring to Hua Rongjie).

634. According to Li Fuyi (MLC-LV1, index, 21), this was Gan Baojung (probably referring to Han Baorong).

635. In the northeast of Moeng Ta Lò, in previous Fohai County.

636. This incident is mentioned in the Veritable Records of the Qing Dynasty, in *Gaozong shilu*, ch. 782 (Qianlong 32, fourth month). See *Xishuang banna shiliao jilu* (special issue) 1987, 70–71.

637. 1147 Vaiśākha 4 or Tuesday, 12 April 1785.

638. Li Fuyi (MLC-LV, 54) translates this as *shangyiyuan shouxi* 上議院首席, which means "president of the senate or upper house", i.e., *noe sanam*, where the nobles conferred on important political and social matters.

639. Here Li Fuyi means the high-ranking Tai Lü officials in Chiang Rung. There were four ranks of senior officials under the *cao phaendin* in Chiang Rung, namely Du Long Gao (Phaya Long Kao), Du Long Fa Hao (Phaya Long Fa Kao), Du Long Na He (Phaya Long Na Hae), and Du Long Zhang (Phaya Long Cang), in charge of civil affairs. See Li Fuyi 1933, 107–8.

640. Here Li Fuyi means the *cao mòm* of the various *müang*, subordinate to Chiang Rung. The imperial Chinese authority appointed them as *tuguan* (aboriginal official).

1. Moeng La (Mengla 猛臘) and Moeng Pan (Mengban 猛伴)[641] form one large *panna.*
2. Moeng La Hò (Simao 思茅) and Moeng La Tai (Liushun 六順)[642] form one large *panna.*
3. Chiang Tòng (Zhengdong 整董)[643] is [counted as] one large *panna.*
4. Moeng Hing (Mengling 猛嶺, i.e., Puteng 普騰)[644] is [counted as] one large *panna.*
5. Moeng U-Nüa (Mengwu 猛烏) and Moeng U-Tai (Wude 烏得)[645] form one large *panna.*
6. Moeng Ham (Menghan 猛罕, i.e., Ganlanba 橄欖壩)[646] is [counted as] one large *panna.*
7. Moeng Cae (Mengzhe 猛遮)[647] is [counted as] one large *panna.*
8. Moeng Hun (Menghun 猛涽)[648] is [counted as] one large *panna.*
9. Moeng Long (Menglong 猛籠)[649] is [counted as] one large *panna.*

The above nine *panna* were regarded as larger *panna* (*da banna*).

10. Moeng Phong (Mengpeng 猛捧) and Moeng Yuan (Mengrun 猛潤),[650] regarded as a *bao cai panna* (*baozai banna* 報仔版納),[651] form a lesser *panna.*
11. Moeng Hai (Menghai 猛海), Moeng Ngat (Meng'a 猛阿),[652] Moeng Khòn

641. Both *müang* are located in today's southern Mengla County, near the border of Laos.

642. These two northern Tai *müang*, previously belonging to Sipsòng Panna are now part of Simao District situated to the north of Sipsòng Panna.

643. In the northeast of Sipsòng Panna, Previously under Jiangcheng County (Moeng Lae), in the northwest of Moeng U on the border of Laos.

644. This great *panna* is located between Simao and Chiang Rung.

645. Moeng U-Nüa and Moeng U-Tai, in today's Phong Sali Province of Laos, were ceded to French Indochina officially in 1896.

646. This *panna* is located in the south of Chiang Rung, on the Mekong.

647. Located in the west of the Mekong, previously Nanqiao County, in today's western part of Menghai County (Moeng Hai).

648. Located in the south of Moeng Hai/Rai, previously Fohai County, in today's Menghai County, to the west of the Mekong.

649. Located in the south of Chiang Rung, near the border of Burma.

650. These two *müang* are located in the south of the earlier Zhengyue County, in today's southern Mengla County, to the east of the Mekong, on the border of Burma.

651. *Bao cai* is transliterated into *baozai* 報宰, whose duty was to provide standby guards (*yiwei* 翊衛) and perform miscellaneous service. See Li Fuyi 1983a, 78, n. 26.

652. These two *müang* are located to the west of the Mekong in today's Menghai County.

(Mengkuan 猛 寬),[653] and Kang Chiang (Gangjing 岡 景), regarded as a *bao cai panna*, form a lesser *panna*.

12. Chiang Coeng (Jingzhen 景 真),[654] Moeng Waen (Mengyuan 猛 遠),[655] Moeng Hem (Mengxing 猛 醒),[656] and Moeng Yang Nòi (Xiao Mengyang 小 猛 養),[657] regarded as a *bao cai panna*, form a lesser *panna*.

The above three *panna* were regarded as lesser *panna*.

Moeng Mang (Mengman 猛 滿) and Moeng Khang (Mengkang 猛 康) were [counted] as two *lei lang* (*ruai rang/hoi dang*),[658] which served to [provide] *kha he lei ke kang* 卡 和 雷 珂 慷 (?).[659] Moeng Wang (Mengwang 猛 往) and Moeng Nun (Menglun 猛 崙), each [counted] as one *lei lang*, served to [provide] *mengnai* 猛 迺 *wanggang* 枉 岡 *pasha* 帊 廈 (Phasat).[660] Chiang Fa (Jingfa 景 法)—20 units of rice fields is one *na sao* (or *na saw*)—[661]

---

653. Moeng Khòn is located c. 28 km to the east of Moeng Ham (Ganlanba) and 20 km west of Moeng Nun.

654. Located in the previous Nanqiao County, between today's Moeng Hai and Moeng Cae, to the west of the Mekong.

655. In the previous Zhenyue County, today's Mengla County, in the north of Moeng La, to the east of the Mekong.

656. According to Li Fuyi (MLC-LV1, index, 21), Mengxing is located in the south of Zhenyue County (i.e., south of today's Mengla County).

657. Located about 30 km to the northeast of Chiang Rung.

658. *Lei lang* (*hoi dang*) and *na sao* (*na saw*) are units of rice fields, thus, the division of *panna* was based on the wet-rice irrigation system. Twenty units of rice fields (or arable land) are one *na sao*, four *na sao* are one *lei lang* (or *huai lang*) and four *lei lang* are one *panna*. However, the area of each unit of rice field is not clear. *Na Nuai Lang* is also the official title of the senior headmen who received emoluments of 100 units of rice fields. Subordinate to the *saenwi fa* of Chiang Rung were four senior officials called the four *khacoeng*. Cf. the introduction, part 1, section 4.1 of this volume. They received varying amount of emoluments or appanages paid in buckets/loads of rice. See Li Fuyi 1983a/2008a, 78–79, n. 27.

659. In MLC-LV1, 55, Li Fuyi translates it into "served [to provide] *ka he lei ke kang*" (卡 和 雷 珂 康). The original translation of Li Fuyi is not clear. But in Li Fuyi's revised edition of MLC-LV1, Li revises it to: "Moeng Mang and Moeng Kkang, counted as two *lei-lang* (*hoi dang*), served to provide small guns 小 槍 (short spears 短 矛) and golden strips (*gujin* 箍 金) [for weaving things]". See Li Fuyi 1983a/2008a, 67.

660. In Li Fuyi (MLC-LV1, 55) he translated it into *mengnai wanggang pasha* (猛 迺 枉 岡 帕 廈), which is not clear. But in Li Fuyi's revised edition of *Leshi*, he revised it to: "Moeng Wang is counted as one *hoi dang* and Moeng Nun is counted as one *hoi dang*. [They] served as decorating *phasat*." See Li Fuyi 1983a/2008a, 79, n. 28. *Pasha* 帊 廈 or *pasa* 帕 薩 (i.e., *phasat*) is a pagoda made of bamboo and pasted with coloured paper or silk.

661. The parenthesis should be ascribed to Li Fuyi (MLC-LV1, 55).

Moeng Khòn (Mengkuan 猛 寬), Shang Tai (Shangdai 尚 岱),[662] Bò Long (Molong 磨龍),[663] Moeng Chiang Lò (Meng Jingluo 猛 景 洛),[664] Moeng Khoang (Mengkuang 猛 匡), and Ban Ngen (Mangen 蠻 山 艮)—in the plain of Chiang Rung[665]—each [counted] as one *na sao*, and Ban Nòng (Mannong 蠻 弄) and Ban Long (Manlong 蠻 龍)—both are located in Ganlanba (Moeng Ham)[666]—together [counted] as one *na sao*. Four [of these] *na sao* were responsible for [providing] candle wax and lamp oil. Four *na sao* are one *lei lang*, and four *na sao* (sic) *lei lang* constitute one *panna*.[667]

3.12 PANNA PING AND PANNA LAM (BANNA BING-LANG 版納丙朗)

In CS 1156, a *kap yi* year (Qianlong 59, AD 1794), Cao Mòm Suwan (Dao Shiwan) married his daughter, Nang Paeng Moeng Long (Niang Bian Meng Long 孃 扁 猛 龍),[668] to [Cao] Moeng Laem. Panna Ping [and Panna] Lam were given as his daughter's dowry. Since then Panna Ping and Lam were no longer subordinate to Chiang Yung (Chiang Rung).[669]

3.13 INHERITANCE (*CHENGXI* 承襲)

In CS 1237, a *dap kai* year (Guangxu 1, 1875 AD) [waning moon of the sixth month], Tao Cin An (Dao Jun'an 刀 鈞 安),[670] escorted by Phaya Long Panya Nakang (Ba Long Banya Nagang 叭 龍 班 雅 那 槓), Phaya Long Khaek (Ba Long Qian 叭 龍 欠), Phaya Saliwicai Phasat (Ba Xiyuzai Pasha 叭 西 羽 仔 帊 廈), Ban Nòng Tom (Man Nong Dong 蠻 弄 董), and Phaya Cai Nam (Ba Zai Nan 叭 仔 赧), et al, proceeded to Moeng La (Simao), where he was to undergo due formalities of becoming the *saenwi fa* and receive the seal and credential (*yinxin* 印 信), announcement (*bugao* 佈 告), document (*zhazi* 札 子), certificate of appointment (*weipai* 委 牌), and other items. The tribal squad leader (*tu bazong*) (sic) of Moeng La Tai (Liushun) Cao Mòm (Zhao Meng 詔 孟)[671] declared that

662. Most probably it refers to Chiang Tai (景 岱), in the northwest of Moeng Phong, in today's Mengla County, to the east of the Mekong.

663. In southern Mengla County, south of Bò Hoek (or Bò Khoe), on the border of Laos.

664. It corresponds to the Chinese name Daluo, in the previous Fohai County, on the border of Burma.

665. The parenthesis should be ascribed to Li Fuyi (MLC-LV1, 55).

666. Ditto.

667. If one *na sao* is 20 units of rice fields, 4 *na sao*, which is one *lei lang* (*hoi dang*), are 80 units of rice fields. Four *lei lang* is one *panna*. Therefore one *panna* has 320 units of rice fields.

668. She was the eldest daughter Cao Mòm Suwan (Tao Suwan). See section 29.4 above.

669. Panna Ping-Lam refers to Moeng Ping and Moeng Lam. This is also recorded in MLC-LV2, s. 35.3; and Gao Lishi 1984, 122, s. 35.3. However, the year is not given.

670. He was the son of the *upalaca* Tao Soen Cong (Cao Lamma Awuttha) and his Tai name is Cao Mòm Sò, also known as Cao Khamòm Khung Kham. He succeeded his uncle Cao Mòm Suca Wanna (Tao Coen Cong) as the *saenwi fa*. See MLC-LV2, s. 39.27; Gao Lishi 1984, 128, s. 39.8.

671. Here Li Fuyi means the Tai lord of Moeng La Tai. Liushun is the Chinese equivalent of Moeng

5,000 taels (one tael = 1.3 ounces)[672] of silver were needed as a gift for the three men—the second lord 二爺 (Ee Yie), the Ming lord 明公 (Min Kung), and Little Li 小李 (Xiao Li).[673] At the same time, [he said that] all the nobles of Sipsòng Panna, and the tribal military officials (*tubian*) (sic) of the various *müang*[674] ought to get the seals and warrants for the frontier passes (*guanfang wenshu*) from the Chinese officials in Moeng La (Simao). Two copies of a testimonial (*baojie* 保結) bearing the seal of the *saenwi fa* were to be delivered to the Chinese officials in Moeng La (Simao) and two copies were to be submitted to the superintendent (*zongdu*) of Yunnan (in Kunming). Besides, they had to prepare (or provide) ten taels of pure silver (*wenyin* 紋銀). The Council of Nobles (i.e., *noe sanam*) was to receive 3.3 taels and the secretary (*shuji*) and secretary general (*shuji zhang*) each got 3.3 taels. Of the 5,000 taels which were for presenting to the Chinese officials, each *müang* was allowed to retain one tael.[675] Moreover, the participants of the delegation included [the four lords] from Moeng Cae, [namely] Cao Phaya Long Si Mün Na (Zhao Ba Long Simen Na 詔叭龍四悶那),[676] Phaya Long Khung Kham (Ba Long Kong Kang 叭龍空鈧), Phaya Long Khantha-wong (Ba Long Gandaweng 叭龍敢塔蓊), and Phaya Fak Kham (Ba Fa Kang 叭法鈧), as well as Phaya Cai Nam (Ba Zai Nan 叭仔赧) from Moeng Ham (Ganlanba), Phaya Han (Ba Han 叭憨) from Moeng Cha (Mengzha 猛乍), Phaya Ung Kan (Ba Weng Gan 叭蓊幹) from Moeng Long (Menglong 猛籠), and Cao Ho Ruai (Zhao Helei 詔呵雷) from Chiang Pan (Jingban 景班) et al. The two copies of testimonial bearing the seal, one in Chinese and one in Tai Lü, submitted, said:

> The hereditary *saenwi fa* of Cheli (i.e., Sipsòng Panna) Tao Cin An (Cao Mòm Sò) presents this testimonial, which bears the seal to the superior civil and military officials of Simao Prefecture (Moeng La). The tribal military official (*tubian*) (sic), this *tao* (lord), is in fact from the legal lineage of the *saenwi fa*. All the people have passed the resolution [and nominated him] unanimously. [I] present this testimonial and beg Your Excellencies, the Chinese officials, to issue the frontier pass seal and the letter of conferment. [I] entreat you to allow [him] to succeed to the post. [I] request that [he be allowed] to report [on matters] to the various levels [of the bureaucracy] and to the Son of Heaven. Yours very truly.

Moreover, each *müang* was to prepare two copies of the testimonial (*baojie*) and the

---

La Tai.

672. This is 6,500 ounces of silver (or about 406 lb or 184 kg), which was not a small sum of money.

673. The three men were obviously the Chinese officials in Simao.

674. Here Li Fuyi means the *cao mòm* (lords) who were appointed by the Chinese authority as military officials.

675. There were a total of twenty-two *müang* in Sipsòng Panna, thus 22 taels were deducted.

676. According to Li Fuyi (MLC-LV1, index, 22), he was Atya Cao Si Mün Na mentioned in section 3.9 above.

four senior headmen (*da toumu*)[677] of the Council of Nobles (*noe sanam*) were to prepare two copies. The other proper formalities and how they should be performed would be worked out one by one under the oversight and guidance of the tribal squad leader (*tu bazong*) of Moeng La Tai (Liushun).[678]

3.14 STRATEGIC PASSES AND BORDER GUARDS (*GUAN'AI SHOUWEI* 關隘守衛)

The frontier guards of the various passes between Sipsòng Panna and other places are described and listed in the following:

The frontier between Moeng U-Nüa (Mengwu 猛烏) and Moeng Kaeo (Jiaozhi 交阯) [is to be guarded by] Commander Laca Ao (Luoshe Ao 邏闍坳) with 100 soldiers, 60 guns, and 40 spears, stationed at Pang Tui Pass (Bangdui Ai 邦堆隘), which is a journey of four days and three nights from Moeng U and ten days and nine nights from Chiang Yung (i.e., Chiang Rung).

The frontier between Moeng U-Tai (烏得) and Laos (老撾) [is to be guarded by] Commander Laca Panya (Luoshe Banya 邏闍班雅) with 60 soldiers, 40 guns, and 20 spears, stationed at Pang Tòng Pass (Bangdong Ai 邦董隘), which is a journey of one day from Moeng U-Nüa and nine days and eight nights from Chiang Yung.

The frontier between Moeng Pan (Mengban 猛伴)[679] and Laos [is to be guarded by] Commander Phaya Kham Nak (Ba Kang Na 叭鈧那) with 60 soldiers, 40 guns, and 20 spears, stationed at Pu Kang Pass (Bugang Ai 埔岡隘), which is a journey of one day from Moeng Pan and seven days and six nights from Chiang Yung.

The frontier along Moeng La (猛臘, i.e., Zhenyue), Moeng Pae (Mengbie 猛別) and Moeng Nan (Mengnan 猛南)[680] [is to be guarded by] Commander Laca Pha (Luoshe Pa 邏闍帕) with 100 soldiers, 60 guns, and 40 spears, stationed at Luai Gin Pass (Leijin Ai 雷瑾隘), which is a journey of one day from Moeng La and nine days and eight nights from Chiang Yung.

The frontier along Moeng Phong (Mengpeng 猛捧), Chiang Mai (Jingmai 景邁), and Lakòn (Laguan 剌管) [is to be guarded by] Commander Laca Wanglo (Luoshe Wangluo 邏闍輞洛) with 100 soldiers, 60 guns, and 40 spears, stationed at Moeng Yuan (Mengrun 猛潤),[681] which is a journey of one day from Moeng Phong and eight days and seven nights from Chiang Yung.

Moeng Long Pass (Menglong Ai 猛籠隘) is to be guarded by Commander Phaya Lü (Ba Leluo 叭勒洛) with 100 soldiers, 60 guns, and 40 spears, stationed at Nam Yang

677. Here Li Fuyi means the four chief ministers (*khacoeng*) at the Council of Nobles.

678. From this statement we can deduce that the Tai Cao Mòm of Liushun (Moeng La Tai) was well versed in Chinese and the ceremonial procedure for appointing the *cao fa* or *cao phaendin* (Tai sovereign) and the *cao mòm*.

679. In Zhenyue County, near the border of Laos.

680. Both *müang* are located in present-day Thailand.

681. Moeng Yuan on Nam Lam River is located about 14 km downstream from Moeng Phong on the border of Laos.

Pass (Nanyang Ai 南 央 隘), which is a journey of one day from Moeng Long (Menglong 猛 籠) and five days and four nights from Chiang Yung.

Moeng Mang Pass (Mengmang Ai 猛 漭 隘),[682] located on the border of Laos, is to be guarded by Commander Laca Pha Kan (Luoshe Bagan 邏 闍 爬 干) with 60 soldiers, 40 guns, and 20 spears, stationed at Mang Peng Pass (Mangben Ai 漭 本 隘), which is a journey of one day from Moeng Mang (Mengmang 猛 漭) and six days and five nights from Chiang Yung.

Moeng Wang (Mengwang 猛 往),[683] on the border of Musoe Dòi (Luohei Shan 裸 黑 山),[684] is to be guarded by Commander Phaya Phom (Ba Peng 叭 捧) with 60 soldiers, armed with 40 guns, and 20 spears, stationed at Pang Fa Pass (Bangfa Ai 邦 發 隘), which is a journey of one day from Moeng Wang and six days and five nights from Chiang Yung.

From Moeng Long Pass (Menglong Ai 猛 籠 隘) to Chiang Khaeng Pass (Zhengqian Ai 整 欠 隘), it is a journey of three days and two nights.

From Chiang Khaeng Pass to Moeng Phong Pass (Mengpeng Ai 猛 捧 隘), it is a journey of three days and two nights.

From Moeng La Pass (Mengla Ai 猛 臘 隘) to Moeng Pan Pass (Mengban Ai 猛 半 隘), it is a journey of two days and one night.

From Moeng Pan Pass to Moeng U-Tai Pass (Wude Ai 烏 得 隘), it is a journey of four days and three nights.

From Moeng U-Tai Pass to Moeng U-Nüa Pass (Shang Mengwu Ai 上 猛 烏 隘), it is a journey of four days and three nights.

3.15 ESTATES (*ZHUANGYUAN* 莊園)

The designations of the "twelve *ho khwaen* (*he quan* 呵 圈) of the *Kha*" under the direct jurisdiction of the *saenwi fa (khwaen means "estate", kha means "serf", thus the private estates of the saenwi fa)*,[685] are as follows:

1. Khwaen Khòng (Quan Kuang), 2. Khwaen Kham Te (Quan Kang Tao), 3. Khwaen Lòt (Quan Nuo), 4 Khwaen Mang Pha (Quan Mang Ba), 5. Khwaen Sam Sa (Quan Xisa), 6. Khwaen Khoe Kham (Quan Kekan), 7. Khwaen Hu Lang (Quan Lulang), 8. Khwaen

682. In modern Mengman 猛 滿 (Moeng Man), southern Zhenyue County, on Nam Man River, north of Moeng Sing.

683. In Ningjiang 寧 江, northwest of Chiang Rung.

684. In the region Yakou 雅 口, Lancang County.

685. This parenthesis is added by Li Fuyi (MLC-LV1, 59). According to Gao Lishi, "*Ka Xishuang huoquan*" (*kha sipsòng ho khwaen*) is a compound of *kha* (serfs), *sipsòng* (twelve), *ho* (*hua*) (head), *khwaen* (district). *Ho khwaen*, like *panna*, is an administrative district. The *saenwi fa* of Sipsòng Panna dividedthe regions inhabited by the hill tribes into twelve districts, each headed by a *balong* (*phaya luang*), whose responsibilities were to raise taxes and provide labour for the *saenwi fa*. See MLC-SV2, n. 72.

Mò (Quan Mo), 9, Khwaen Dai (Quan Lai), 10. Khwaen Kai (Quan Gai), 11. Khwaen Nòng (Quan Long), and 12. Khwaen Lai (Quan Lai).[686]

In total there are twelve *khwaen*.

3.16 THE DOMAIN AND ITS BORDERS (*JIANGJIE* 疆界)

The domain of Sipsòng Panna and her borders with Burma are recorded explicitly as follows:

To the south, [it starts] from the flow of the river (Mekong) at Pha Sam Sao Nam Khao Hu (i.e., water flowing into the cave of the three-summit hills; pha sam sao means "tripod stones" or "three-summit hills"),[687] passes across to Ton Mi Long (the ridge of the hillock) (*mi long liangzi*),[688] and runs along the ridge to Moeng Long Pukha (Menglong Buka)[689] [and then] to the [hills of] Pu Kok Pagoda (Bu Boda 埔 波 塔). It then passes through the centre of the river plain until reaching the Kòng Hae (Rae) Daeng Hills (Guang Lie Liang Shan 廣 烈 亮 山).[690] Where it is closer to the Lan Sang (Laos) side it is subordinate to Lan Sang and where it is closer to the Chiang Yung side it is under Chiang Yung.[691]

The northern [frontier line] begins at Nòng Tao Lao Sai (*nong dao lao shui* 弄 島 老 水),[692] runs straight to [Hat] Tao Pu Taen Beach (*dao bu dian tan* 島 埔 典 灘), to Nam Kang (Nan Gang 南 槓), Nam Cian (Nan Jin 南 金), and to Nam Tae (Nan Die 南 堞), until reaching Si Thung Wai Leng (Si Tong Huai Leng 西 通 淮 楞), Nam Kot Khwaen Siu (Ge Quan Xie River 戈 圈 秀 河), to Moeng Tae (Mengdie 猛 蝶), Moeng Saeng (Mengxiang

686. The designations of the twelve districts correspond chiefly to those given by Gao Lishi in MLC-SV2, 89, and in Dao and Kang 1989a, 311, albeit in variant Chinese transliterations.

687. Here Li Fuyi (MLC-LV1, 60) explains in the parenthesis that *pha sam sao* means "stone pillars in the form of a tripod" (*san zhu yan* 三 柱 岩), as do Dao and Kang 1989a. According to the annotation in MLC-SV2, 88, *pha sam sao* means "three-legged-stone" (*san jiao shi* 三 腳 石), namely "hills with three summits" (*san feng shan* 三 峰 山). Li Fuyi explains in the parenthesis that *nam khao hu*, which he transcribes into Chinese as *nan hao lu* 南 毫 魯, means "a cave where water falls down" (*luo shui dong* 落 水 洞).

688. Here Li Fuyi (MLC-LV1, 60) transcribes it into *milong liangzi* 米 龍 梁 子 (the ridge of the *Mi Long* [hills]). According to MLC-SV2 it is *ton mi long liangzi* which means "the ridge of the great bear hills", which is the same as Dao and Kang 1989a. This is a lingua franca of Tai Lü and Chinese.

689. In present-day Laos. See Gao Lishi 1982, 88.

690. According to Dao and Kang 1989a the Kòng Hae (Rae) Daeng Hills means "red-stone hills" (*hong shi shan* 紅 石 山). However, according to MLC-SV2, it means "going across the river plain to Kòng Hae (Rae) Daeng, the "pale red stony hills".

691. In MLC-SV2 it is stated: "Going across the river plain to Kòng Hae (Rae) Daeng, the pale red stone hills, which are on the border of Lan Sang (Laos). This is the domain under the *saenwi fa*". In Dao and Kang (1989a) it states: "Going through the centre of the river plain to Kòng Rae Raeng Hills (red stone hills), taking the watershed of the hills as the boundary, where the source of the water flows to Lan Sang it belongs to Lan Sang and where the source of the water flows to the domain under the *saenwi fa* it is under the jurisdiction of the *saenwi fa*."

692. According to MLC-SV2, it is *nòng tao sai* (lit., "sandy turtle pond").

猛香), Moeng Maen (Mengmian 猛緬), Bò Hoek (Mohei 磨黑), Moeng Cung (Mengzhong 猛冢) to Ai Sa Kham Khoe (Aisa Kehuan 愛薩苛緩),[693] to Ngòn Long (Yuanlong 院龍), to Nam Ang (Angbang River 昂蚌河), to Nam Luai (Nanlei 南累),[694] along Nam Luai, either meandering or going straight to the Three Lords (san dao 三島), through the region of the Pu Moan (Pu Manmo 蒲蠻磨). One *tao* (chief) belongs to Chiang Tung (Jingdong 景棟), one *tao* (chief) to Chiang Saen (Jingxian 景線), and one *tao* (chief) to Chiang Yung (Jingyong 景永).[695] From the *tao* (chief) subordinate to Chiang Yung it runs straight to Moeng Phayak (Mengba 猛叭), going around [back] to Pha Sam Sao (three-summit hills) and Nam Khao Hu (water flowing into a cave), until reaching the border of Chiang Yung.[696]

The ancient name of Sipsòng Panna was *Aravirastra* (Aluobi 阿羅毗). In the past the domain extended in the east to Laos, in the south to Chiang Rai (Jinghai 景海), in the west to the Nam Khong (Nan Kong 南孔, i.e., the Salween) and in the north to Moeng Cung (Yuanjiang 元江).[697]

693. In MLC-SV2 it is Ai Sa Kham Khoe.

694. In MLC-SV2 it is Nam Lam.

695. Lit., "three chieftains", a frontier region where Keng Tung, Lan Na, and Sipsòng Panna meet, ruled by three lords and demarcated by the Burmese king Fa Suttho Thammalaca (r. 1551–1581) in 1567/68, during the reign of Cao Ong Moeng. See Gao Lishi 1984, 115, and Dao Shuren 1989, 243–44.

696. In MLC-SV2 it states: "This is the domain and frontier to be guarded and the domain and frontier previously under the *saenwi fa* were these."

697. The domain described corresponds chiefly with that described in MLC-SV2, 88–89, and Dao and Kang 1989a, 310.

II. Chronicle of the Forty-Four Reigns of the *Cao Phaendin* of Sipsòng Panna (MLC-LV2)

0.1 PREAMBLE

Here the past events of the rulers of the ancient land[1] of Sipsóng Panna will be narrated. Phaya Coeng was the [first] ruler of Moeng Lü. He came from the land of Saenwi (original: *swaenwi* แสวนหวี) and established himself in Chiang Lan. Previously there was a Lua (Lawa) chieftain (*khun lua*) called Ai Lan living in Chiang Lan. Thus [the place] was named Ban Chiang Lan. Later, when Phaya Coeng became the great [ruler] after subduing [the various *müang*], [the place] was thus called Chiang Lan (lit., "royal capital of [Ai] Lan") as it was then called after a Lua whose name was Phaya Lan.[2]

1. PHAYA COENG, R. 1159–1180

1.1 THE FIRST RULER

Phaya Coeng was the supreme ruler. In the year CS 521 (AD[3] 1159) the father of Phaya Coeng conferred on [his son] five items of royal insignia. He ascended the throne at the age of thirty-two (sic),[4] was on the throne twenty-one years,[5] and passed away at the age of fifty-three (sic) in the year CS 542 (AD 1181 sic/1180).

---

1. *Bohan maha nakòn* (Th. โบราณมหานคร), from Skt. borāṇa, "ancient", and mahā nagara, "the great city".

2. Many Tai *müang* were founded by non-Tai, mostly Mon-Khmer, rulers who were later subjugated by the Tai immigrants. The rivalries and, quite often, violent conflicts are reflected, for example, in the chronicles of Chiang Tung, Moeng Yòng, and Luang Prabang. See the introduction, part 1, section 3 of this volume.

3. The original has *sakkhat lok* (สักขาดโลก, lit., "international era.")

4. Gao Lishi (1984, 105) points out that he would have been forty-three.

5. If he reigned a total of twenty-one years, he would have been enthroned in CS 521 (AD 1159).

1.2 THE CORONATION OF PHAYA COENG

When Phaya Coeng was invested as the ruler of Moeng Lü, Phaya Hò (ruler of China), called Cao Lum Fa Pothiyan; Phaya Kaeo,[6] called Nara Phiramma; Phaya Chiang Rung, called Mung Moeng; Phaya Lan Sang, called Pothi Latcalot (Bodhi Rāja-raṭha); and Phaya Moeng Khün, called Phaya Lawaek; as well as [the people] from everywhere[7] all invested[8] Phaya Coeng as *cao saenwi fa* (*xuanwei shi*),[9] the supreme chief of the [domain] of Sipsòng Panna.[10] When Phaya Coeng was installed as supreme ruler, a *phasat* (i.e., palace), which had a height of fifteen *wa*,[11] was erected. [There was] a golden jar, the size of which was three *sòk*[12] in length, width, and height, weighing 540,000 [units] of gold and adorned with seven kinds of gems. There were seventy-seven white parasols and [a total of] 12,000 ladies-in-waiting and consorts, headed by Nang Tewi (Maha Rājadevī),[13] called Nang Ramma. Those coming to offer their allegiance were the Hò (Chinese), who

6. Here it means the ruler of Moeng Kaeo. Whether "Moeng Kaeo" refers to the Vietnamese kingdom or rather to smaller Tai polities in Upper Tonkin is still a point of debate.

7. In Gao Lishi (1984, 105) it is stated: "[...] from the source and mouth of the river under heaven and from the basins and hills came to attend the glorious coronation and the various joyous celebrations".

8. *Utsalatcaphiset* (Th. อุสสาราชภิเสด), a Pali compound consisting of the components ussā[ha], "strength, power" + raja, "king" + abhiseka, "consecration, inauguration" (Skt. abhiṣeka).

9. *Xuanwei shi*, commonly translated into "pacification commissioner" and phonetically rendered into Tai Lü as *saenwi fa*, was a title bestowed on so-called tribal rulers in South China. Pacification commissions were only established during and after the Yuan period (1280–1368). See the introduction, part 1, section 6 of this volume.

10. As far as we know, Moeng Lü was not called Sipsòng Panna during the reign of Phaya Coeng. The name Sipsòng Panna was used after Moeng Lü had become a vassal of Burma in the late sixteenth century. This shows that MLC-LV2, is based on a relatively new or revised manuscript copy. In MLC-LV1, the term Sipsòng Panna first appears in the reign of Tao In Moeng (r. 1569–1598).

11. In MLC-LV1, 1, it is 35 *wa* (วา). One standard *wa* or *wa luang* (วาหลวง) is an ancient Tai measure of length equal to 2 m or about 80 English inches. In the Tai Lü and Shan areas a *wa* was less than 2 m, varying between 1.7 and 2.0 m.

12. One *wa* is always equal to four *sòk*. One *sòk* is considered equal to the distance from the tip of the middle finger to the elbow joint; as the length of a *sòk* depends on the *wa*, it fluctuates between 42 and 50 cm.

13. Nang Tewi (นางเทวี, Skt/Pali: devī) means the principal queen, also called *mahesi* (มเหสี). She has to be distinguished from the queen mother called *maha tewi* (lit., "great queen").

talked with the Kaeo (Vietnamese),[14] the Kula (Indians)[15] [and] Phasi (Muslims).[16] The population under the rule of Moeng Khün or Khemmarat comprised a total of 8,440,000 people. There were 844 *hua mün* (lit., "heads of ten thousand" or myriad commander), 9,000 elephants and 97,000 horses.

1.3 MOENG LÜ AND HER DEPENDENCIES

During the reign of Phaya Coeng, the domain of Sipsòng Panna (sic) was not a vassal of Burma or of China. It was an independent *saenwi fa*. In the time of Phaya Coeng one hundred thousand (i.e. numerous) small and large *müang* were subordinate to Sipsòng Panna. [At times] one single village made up a *müang*. There was a total of one hundred thousand *müang*.

1.4 AN EXPLANATION OF THE TERM *SAENWI*

Whenever [the lord of] a *müang* came to pay homage to Phaya Coeng, he offered one bunch (*wi*) of bananas to him. [Phaya Coeng] received one hundred thousand bunches of bananas, and thus subsequently Moeng Lü was called Moeng Saenwi.[17]

1.5 THE FOUR SONS OF PHAYA COENG

Phaya Coeng had four sons: the eldest son was called Lao Yoe Hoeng (Roeng), the second son was called Ai Paeng, the third son Yi Kham Hoeng (Roeng), and the fourth son Sam Khai Noeng. The eldest son, called Lao Yoe Hoeng, was sent to rule[18] Lan

---

14. Kaeo (แกว) is an ethnonym used by the Tai Lü and other Tai peoples, including the Tai Yuan and the Lao, to signify the Vietnamese. It might be a phonetic rendering of Jiao[zhi]. The Chinese called Northern Vietnam Jiaozhi 交趾 (lit., "crossed toes"), which is a very old name. To the best of our knowledge, the land of the Vietnamese was called Jiaozhi, allegedly because the Vietnamese sat crossing their legs.

15. Kala (Th. กลา) is the Burmese word for foreigners (/kə`la/ ကုလား), notably natives of India. It is often written *kula* (Tr. กูลา). Later on, the word was misapplied to English and other Westerners who were sometimes called *kala/kula khao*, "white strangers".

16. Phasi (Th. ผาสี) derives from Persia, but in the Tai Lü context the term signifies the Hui or Chinese Muslims, sometimes also called *hò phasi* (Th. ห้อผาสี) in contrast to the Han or *hò long* (Th. ห้อหลวง), as the Hui in Yunnan were indeed mostly of Turkish and Persian origin.

17. Lit., "the country [whose ruler received] one hundred thousand bunches [of bananas]". This is a Tai Lü rendering of the Chinese title *xuanwei shi*, which can be translated into "pacification commissioner", conferred on the "tribal" rulers. See n. 9 above for *xuanwei shi*, and the introduction, part 1, section 6.3 for Moeng Saenwi.

18. *Bai kin* (Tr. ไพกิน), meaning "to go and/to eat". In MLC-LV1, it is translated as *shi cai* or *shi yi* (lit., "eat the land"), the closest rendering in English is "fief". Here it means "sent to a fief or principality to be the ruler". A son of a Tai Lü king, apart from the prince royal or crown prince, was bestowed sometimes several *panna* of land when he became an adult and was sent there as lord and the lordship was, in general, hereditary. On the *kin moeng* system of the Tai Lü, see Cia (Yanyong) 2005, 291–95; Bunchuai (vol. 1) 2004, 63–64.

Na–Chiang Mai in [present-day North] Thailand;[19] Chiang Mai was one *hò kham*.[20] The second son called Ai Paeng was sent to rule Moeng Kaeo, not Moeng Kaeo Long (Luang) (i.e., Vietnam proper) [but] Moeng Lai (Laichou).[21] Moeng Lai was also regarded as one *hò kham*. Its territory bordered on Moeng Sóng U–Phong Sali, which at that time was part of Sipsòng Panna. Nowadays [Moeng Sòng U–Phong Sali] borders on Chiang Ko (i.e., Zhongguo, or China).

The third son Yi Kham Hoeng was sent to Lan Sang–Vientiane as ruler. This was [another] *hò kham* which was a dependency of Luang Prabang. At that time Laos (Moeng Lao) was called Moeng (Müang) Lan Sang, but nowadays it is called Pathet Lao.[22] Later Laos ceased to be [an independent] country and became a vassal state of Thailand. Its old capital was Luang Prabang. These [first] three sons went to offer their submission to foreign countries.

The fourth son Sam Khai Noeng, who ruled in Sipsòng Panna, succeeded in his father's stead to be the *saenwi fa*.

2. SAM KHAI NOENG, R. 1180–1201

2.1 THE SECOND RULER

Sam Khai Noeng succeeded in his father's stead in the year CS 542 (AD 1182 sic/1180).[23] It was during the reign of the emperor of China (*cao wòng*)[24] Min Sao Cin Phaen.[25] He was twenty-seven years old on succeeding to the throne and reigned

---

19. *Pathet thai* (Tr. ประเทียดไธ = ประเทศไทย). This is not an old Tai Lü term for Thailand or Siam, which is usually called "southern country" (*moeng tai*, Tr. เมิงใต้). The last sentence was probably added by a later scribe.

20. I.e., [a country/polity with] a golden palace.

21. Ch. Laizhou, located c. 110 km south of Jinping (a border town in Yunnan), in northern Vietnam.

22. "Pathet Lao" (lit., "land of the Lao") is a recent term which would not have appeared in old Tai Lü texts where the more flexible Tai term *moeng/ müang*—indicating "city", "principality", "domain", or "country, land", depending on the specific context—would have been preferred to *pathet/ prathet* (Skt/Pali: deśa, "land").

23. The conversion into AD in the Tai Lü text is wrong. It should be AD 1180.

24. The Tai *cao wòng* (Th. เจ้าว้อง) is a combination of the Tai *cao* (lord) and the Chinese *wang* 王 or *huang* 皇, which means "king" and "emperor" respectively. Thus the Tai expression *cao wòng* means emperor of China.

25. Here obviously the Tai Lü scribe has converted the date into the Chinese reign incorrectly; the transcribed syllables "Min Sao Cin Phaen" sound like Ming Chao Jing[tai] 明 朝 景 泰. However, Jingtai 1 of the Ming period corresponds to AD 1450, but AD 1180 corresponds to Chunxi 8 of the Southern Song dynasty.

twenty-one years; he lived to the age of forty-eight and passed away in the year CS 563 (AD 1203 sic/1201).[26]

2.2 A TRIBUTARY LAND OF CHINA

During his reign there was a *phaya hò* (ruler of China), the *cao lum fa*, called Pothiyan (Bodhiñāna), who issued him a golden seal [adorned with] a tiger head and a golden plate [with] inscriptions,[27] and conferred on him the *saenwi fa* of Chiang Rung of Cheli. During that time the *cao hò* said:

> One small tribute in every five years and one big tribute in every nine years are to be offered as the token of submission. The tribute gifts are to be delivered to Moeng Sae-Kunming.[28]

2.3 THE TWO SONS OF SAM KHAI NOENG

Sam Khai Noeng had two sons: the eldest son was called Ai Kung and the second son was called Yi Peng (Piang).[29]

3. AI KUNG, R. 1201–1206

3.1 THE THIRD RULER

The eldest son Ai Kung[30] succeeded to his father's throne in the year CS 563 (AD 1203 sic).[31] He was twenty-seven years old on enthronement, reigned for five years, and passed away at the age of thirty-two in the year CS 568 (AD 1206).

3.2 AI KUNG'S CHILDREN AND THE FIRST FRATRICIDAL WAR

Ai Kung had a son named Tao Hung (Rung) Kaen Cai and a daughter named Nang O (Ua) Ming Khai Fa.[32] The younger brother of Ai Kung, Yi Peng (Piang), was invested

---

26. This should be AD 1201.

27. This was most probably a tally-plate issued by China to the Tai Lü lord, a credential for his emissaries to enter Chinese territory at an appointed town, where they proceeded to the capital to offer tribute. For more on the tribute system of China, see Fairbank 1941.

28. Note that Yunnan was only conquered by the Mongols after the fall of the Later Dali in AD 1253. During the reign of Ai Kung (1201–1206) Yunnan was not yet incorporated into China proper under the Southern Song dynasty (1127–1279).

29. He was called Ai Yi Peng or Yi Peng. See MLC-LV1; MLC-SV1; and Dao Shuren 1989.

30. The original word is "Pung" instead of "Kung", probably a scribal error as the respective initial Tai Lü consonants are very similar to each other.

31. CS 563 corresponds to AD 1201.

32. According to MLC-LV1; MLC-SV1; MLC-SV2; Dao Shuren (1989); and Dao and Kang (1989a); as well as the Chiang Mai Chroncile, it is Ua Ming Còm Moeng, the daughter, not younger sister, of Tao

as the lord of the three *panna*, Moeng Hun, Moeng Hai, [and Moeng Cae]. Because he plotted to usurp his elder brother's throne, he was killed by his elder brother. After his death he became a *phi müang* and every year oblations were offered, which is practised to the present day.[33] During this generation a fratricidal war broke out because of fighting to become the ruler of *saenwi fa* (i.e., for the throne).

4. TAO HUNG KAEN CAI, R. 1206–1227

4.1 THE FOURTH RULER

Tao Hung Kaen Cai succeeded his father to the throne in the year CS 568 (AD 1206). He was fourteen years old at his succession. He was on the throne twenty-one years and passed away at the age of thirty-five in the year CS 589 (AD 1230 sic/1227).[34]

4.2 TAO HUNG KAEN CAI'S YOUNGER SISTER AND HER HUSBAND CAO CHIANG RAI

Tao Hung Kaen Cai had a son named Tao Haeng Long. The younger sister of Tao Hung Kaen Cai, Nang O (Ua) Ming Khai Fa, was renamed Nang Ok Aen when she was a bit older.[35] Later, when the lord of Chiang Rai came to win her hand, and when she was about to get married, she was renamed Nang Kham Kai. She was much loved by Cao Chiang Rai. Not long after, one night the lady dreamt that a shooting star (*dao phakai*) flying from the south plunged into her belly. When the lady (*nang*) awoke from sleep she told the lord of Chiang Rai the details of her dream. On the next day, the *phaya* called for a *phammana acan* (Skt. brāḥmaṇa ācārya, a soothsayer) to interpret the dream. The *acan* said:

> The lady is going to give birth to a great son and when he grows up he is going to conquer and defeat the *tao phaya* (here, rulers or kings) of various lands in the south (dakkhiṇa).

Rung Kaen Cai. Only MLC-LV2, DCH 1963, and Gao Lishi (1984) claims that she was Tao Rung Kaen Cai's younger sister. According to this version, Mangrai was Tao Rung Kaen Cai's nephew instead of grandson.

33. Each *müang* in Sipsòng Panna had its own pantheon of *phi müang* (ผีเมือง), "spirits of the *müang*", which included former heroic kings, like Phaya Coeng, but also renowned nobles who died a tragic death; sometimes the *phi müang* were representatives of ethnic minorities, like the Kha, or are celestial beings. Each *müang* had its rules of how to worship its own *phi müang* for whom special shrines (*hò* หอ) were built. As to the rituals pertaining to the worship of *phi müang* in Sipsòng Panna, see Yangyong and Ratanaporn 2001, 223–38.

34. This should be AD 1227.

35. Most likely when she was a toddler.

4.3 BIRTH OF PRINCE MANGRAI

After a pregnancy of ten months, the lady indeed bore a son. It was in the year CS 572 (AD 1212 sic/1210),[36] in the sixth month.[37] One month after [the prince] was born, the elder brother of the lady, Phaya Moeng Lü, Tao Hung Kaen Cai, accompanied by his wife, went to the city of Chiang Rai to attend his nephew's one-month-old [ceremony] and gave his nephew the name Mangkala Nalai (Maṅgala Nārāya). Phaya Tao Hung Kaen Cai then returned to his land. Later, all the people called him Tao Mangrai, the son of Nang Kham Kai, the nephew of Tao Haeng (sic) Hung Kaen Cai. After that, Tao Hung Kaen Cai sent his confidants (*khon phu di* คนผู้ดี) to visit his nephew every month. The emissary came back and reported [to his lord]:

> Your Lord's nephew is already grown and would love to play *mak khang* (tops).

Forthwith Tao Hung Kaen Cai had a golden top cast and sent it [to the prince]. Later, the emissary again said:

> Your Lord's grandson (sic) would love to play a flute.

The Phaya (i.e., the lord) had a golden flute cast and had it delivered [to the prince]. Tao Mangrai grew up to be a [very] shrewd [man]. He had profound knowledge and wrote his teachings for all the nobles and officials (*tao phaya*) as instructions, which have been observed to the present day.

4.4 TAO HUNG KAEN CAI'S SON

Tao Hung (Rung) Kaen Cai had a son called Tao Haeng Long.

5. TAO HAENG LONG, R. 1228–1254

5.1 THE FIFTH RULER

Tao Haeng Long succeeded his father to the throne in the year CS 590 (AD 1230 sic/1228).[38] He was seventeen years old on succession [to the throne], ruled twenty-six

---

36. This should be AD 1210.

37. According to MLC-LV1, this was on an auspicious day in the sixth month of the year CS 601 (AD 1239). However, according to the CMC-HP (Wyatt and Aroonrut 1995, 15), Mangrai was born "in the *poek set* year—one chronicle says the *kat kai* year, on the ninth waning of the first month, a Sunday, near dawn, in the eighth lunar mansion." Wyatt and Aroonrut remark that "the chronological data work out *almost* perfectly for Sunday, 2 October 1238, which was in the *poek set* year 600, not the *kat kai* year 601". See also MLC-LV1, s. 4.3, nn. 46 and 48.

38. This should be AD 1228.

years, lived to the age of forty-three, and passed away in the year CS 616 (AD 1256 sic/ 1264).[39]

5.2 CONFERMENT OF THE SURNAME DAO (TAO) ON TAI LÜ LORD

During the reign of Tao Haeng Long, the Hò (i.e., China) conferred on [him] the surname Tao (Dao). Since then [the Tai Lü lords] have had the surname Tao and this has been adopted to the present day.[40]

5.3 TAO HAENG LONG'S TWO SONS

Tao Haeng Long had two sons: the eldest son was called Tao Puwak and the second son was called Yi Peng (Piang) Lak Sai.

6. TAO PUWAK, R. 1255–1269

6.1 THE SIXTH RULER

Tao Puwak succeeded his father to the throne in the year CS 617 (AD 1257 sic/1255).[41] He was twenty-two years old when he assumed power,[42] was ruler for fourteen years, lived to the age of thirty-six, and passed away in the year CS 631 (AD 1271 sic/1269).[43]

6.2 INVASION OF MOENG MAO LONG

Tao Puwak had no son. During [Tao Puwak's] reign Moeng Mao Long[44] sent troops to attack on [Chiang Rung]. Defeated by Sipsòng Panna, [they] retreated to their country.

6.3 CAO MOENG FÒNG ADOPTS YI PENG (PIANG) LAK SAI

At that time Cao Moeng Fòng,[45] whose name was Fa Kham Kòng, had no son to succeed him; so [the *cao*] brought Tao Puwak's younger brother Yi Peng Lak Sai [to Moeng Fòng]

---

39. This should be AD 1254. Note that Möngke (also spelled Mangu, r. 1251–1259), the grandson of Genghis Khan (r. 1206–1227), conquered the Later Dali (1096–1253) that had been founded by the House of Duan, in AD 1253. Several Western historians maintain that Möngke's armies, under the command of his brother Kubilai (1215–1294), conquered the Thai kingdom of Nanchao. See *Encyclopaedia Britannica* (1992) 8, 254. This is misleading. Nanchao or Nanzhao (728–902) was a contemporary kingdom of the Tang dynasty (618–907), in present-day Yunnan. Moreover, it was not a Tai kingdom but was dominated by the ancestors of the Lolo, a Tibeto-Burman ethnic group.

40. The Chinese *dao* 刀 (lit., "knife") is obviously derived from the Tai *tao* (Th. ท้าว), which means "lord". Many of the descendants of the Tai Lü lords in today's Sipsòng Panna have the surname Dao (i.e., Tao/Cao).

41. CS 617 corresponds to AD 1255.

42. *Hap moeng* (Tr. รับเมิง) (lit., "to receive the country").

43. CS 631 corresponds to AD 1269.

44. In present-day Ruili (Moeng Khòn), Dehong.

45. Here Fòng is probably a copyist's error for Pòng.

as an adopted son. At that time Yi Peng Lak Sai was already married and had a son call Cao Ai. After coming to Moeng Fòng, he took a Moeng Fòng princess (*nang*) as his consort, who bore him a son. Later, after Cao Moeng Fòng had passed away, Yi Peng Lak Sai was nominated to succeed to his adoptive father's throne in Moeng Fòng. It was then that Moeng Fòng began to be called Moeng Saenwi (i.e., Hsaenwi).[46] Because the younger brother of the *cao saenwi fa* of Sipsòng Panna had succeeded to the throne, [Moeng Fòng] earned the name Saenwi, [which is used] to the present day.[47]

6.4 YI PENG (PIANG) LAK SAI RETURNS TO MOENG LÜ

At the time {[when] the sixth [ruler] Tao Puwak passed away},[48] Sipsòng Panna had no ruler, and it was impossible to find an heir to the throne. [All the nobles, after] conferring with [one another], went to invite Cao Yi Peng Lak Sai, the ruler of Moeng Fòng, to return to [Chiang Rung to be the lord]. The son born to the secondary consort[49] of Moeng Fòng was to remain there to succeed to his [father's] throne; the son born to the Moeng Lü consort was to be brought back to Sipsòng Panna.

7. CAO YI PENG (PIANG) LAK SAI, R. 1270–1271

7.1 THE SEVENTH RULER

Cao Yi Peng Lak Sai succeeded his elder brother to the throne in the year CS 632 (AD 1271 sic/1270). He was age thirty-four at his enthronement, reigned six months, lived to the age of thirty-five, and passed away in the year CS 633 (AD 1272 sic/1271).

7.2 YI PENG (PIANG) LAK SAI'S SON

Yi Peng Lak Sai had one son called Cao Ai.

8. CAO AI, R. 1271–1311

8.1 THE EIGHTH RULER

Cao Ai succeeded his father to the throne in the year CS 633 (AD 1272 sic/1271). At enthronement he was sixteen years old. He reigned forty-one years, lived to the age of fifty-seven, and passed away in the year CS 673 (AD 1313 sic/1311).

---

46. See MLC-LV1, s. 5.3, n. 59.

47. Moeng Fòng is today's Saenwi Sipò (Hsipaw).

48. This sentence is in Gao Lishi (1984, 107). As it does not appear in MLC-LV2, and in Dao Shuren (1989), it is probably Gao Lishi's own addition.

49. In the original Tai Lü text it is *me* (*mia*) (เมีย), which means "wife". The principal queen would be called *mahesi* (มเหสี), a title derived from Pali.

8.2 CAO AI'S SON

Cao Ai had a son called Cao Khan Moeng.

9. CAO KHAN MOENG, R. 1312–1350

9.1 THE NINTH RULER

Cao Khan Moeng succeeded his father to the throne in the year CS 674 (AD 1314, sic).[50] He was twenty-six years old at enthronement, reigned thirty-eight years, lived to the age of sixty-four and passed away in the year CS 712 (AD 1352 sic/1350).

9.2 CAO KHAN MOENG'S RETREAT TO THE NAM LAM RIVER

Cao Khan Moeng was a ruler who staunchly resisted the Hò (i.e., China).[51] He founded Wiang Chiang Rung at Chiang Tü.[52] Eventually, the Chinese indeed came. [Cao Khan Moeng] was defeated and retreated to Wiang Pha Daeng (lit., "red-cliff city") at Moeng Cae; again defeated, [the *cao fa*] withdrew to Pang Pün[53] on the bank of the Nam Lam River.

9.3 CHINESE TROOPS THREATEN CAO KHAN MOENG

The Chinese [court] summoned Cao Moeng Lü {i.e., Cao Khan Moeng}[54] for an audience in person. The people (*phai moeng*) said that Cao Khan Moeng had escaped to Moeng Lao (Laos). [The Chinese officials] answered that the ruler (*cao*) of Moeng Lü was not allowed to go against Cao Lum Fa.[55] If he would continue to defy Cao Lum Fa, he would forthwith be executed. If he would submit, then [the Chinese troops] would be withdrawn.

---

50. CS 674 corresponds to AD 1312.

51. Cao Khan Moeng, rendered into Chinese as Dao Kan, is mentioned seven times in contemporary Ming sources between April 1382 and August 1387 (Hongwu 15 to 20). See Liew-Herres (2003b) translation of contemporary Chinese sources on Cheli, translated from the *Ming shilu* and the *Mingshi gao*. This is a clear indication that the dates of the Tai Lü sources are unreliable.

52. Dao Shuren (1989) says that the Chinese came to found Chiang Rung at Chiang Tü but that Cao Khan Moeng was already there. After the founding of Chiang Rung by the Chinese Cao Khan Moeng fled to Moeng Cae (Wiang Pha Daeng).

53. In Dao Shuren (1989) it is "Kün" (Th. คืน). Again it must be emphasised that the Tai Lü initial consonants which correspond to Siamese พ and ค resemble each other and are therefore easily mistaken.

54. Gao Lishi 1984, 107.

55. Cao Lum Fa (เจ้าลุ่มฟ้า), or "lord under heaven", a Tai designation for the emperor of China or the Heavenly Court.

9.4 CAO KHAN MOENG CAPITULATES AND TAKES OATH OF ALLEGIANCE

Cao Khan Moeng, {aware that he had no power to resist},[56] then took the oath of allegiance to the Chinese [emperor].[57] He buried stones (*mak hin*) as proof (*sakkhi*) [of the oath]. The stones were buried in three places: one [stone] was buried at the pass of the *khü wiang* (i.e., the city wall) in the vicinity of Moeng Cae; one [stone] was buried on the [right] bank of the Nam Ha Nòi (Little Ha River), located to the east of the fortified town of Moeng Cae; and one [stone] was buried at Chiang Kham. The stones were more than one *wa* (fathom) long. After the Chinese troops had retreated, Cao Khan Moeng then returned to Chiang Lan [to rule] as before.

9.5 CAO KHAN MOENG MARRIES THE LAWA GIRL HÒI SAM CIK

Later, there was a Lawa (Lua) lass, who procured a precious thing, namely a three-pronged conch shell (*hòi sam cik*) as an ornament. She went to the market of Chiang Lan. Cao Khan Moeng saw her and lost his heart to her instantly. Thus [Cao Khan Moeng] took her as his principal consort (*nang tewi*); she was very much loved [by her husband].

9.6 BIRTH OF TAO SIDA KHAM

The Lawa queen had no son; she told her husband:

> My respected husband, we Lawa living on the hills, if we do not have a son, we have to make a cradle adorned with gold [foil] and ask the foster-father to call the soul of a son.

Cao Khan Moeng [followed the words of his wife] and had a cradle adorned with golden [foil] made and sent it to his parents-in-law at Ban Dòi[58] to ask for the soul of a son. [Not long thereafter,] indeed a son was born and he was called Tao Sida Kham.

9.7 THE LAWA QUEEN LOSES HER THREE-PRONGED CONCH SHELL

One day, Nang Lawa went to a balcony to warm herself in the sun. She took the three-pronged conch shell to have a look. Carelessly she let it fall off her hand and it landed [on the ground] below the balcony. A spotted-neck pig bit and broke it [into pieces]. After that Cao Khan Moeng began to find Nang Lawa disgusting. She was sent to his father-in-law's village at Ban Dòi. The villagers were told to cultivate the hill lands and

56. Gao Lishi 1984, 107.

57. According to the Ming sources the above eight rulers reigned before the Ming period (1368–1644). The reign of Cao Khan, who submitted to the Ming court on 20 April 1382, is clearly documented in contemporary Ming sources (see *Taizu shilu*, ch. 143, 2246–47). Obviously the given dates for each reign in Tai Lü sources, which were recorded long after the events and based mainly on oral history, cannot be correct. In the case of Cao Khan Moeng's reign, the error is at least fifty years.

58. Lit., "hill village".

to look after his son well. The village's labour service and land taxes were exempted.[59] When Tao Sida Kham was seven years old, his father brought him back to live with him.

9.8 THE THREE SONS OF CAO KHAN MOENG

Cao Khan Moeng had three sons: The eldest son was Tao Sida Kham, who was born to Nang Lawa, the principal queen, and was invested as crown prince to succeed his father to the throne. The second son was Tao Kumman, who was sent to Na Mün Long as rule. The third son was Peo (Piao) Fai Fa, who was sent to rule Na Saen [at] Chiang Lan.

9.9 ANTI-CHINESE WARS

The reign of Cao Khan Moeng was replete with continuous wars against the Chinese. [The people] in the country could not enjoy happiness.

10. TAO SIDA KHAM, R. 1350–1430

10.1 THE TENTH RULER

Tao Sida Kham succeeded his father to the throne in the year CS 712 (AD 1350).[60] On his succession to the throne he was 40 years old. He reigned 80 years and lived to the age of 120 before passing away in the year CS 792 (AD 1433).[61]

10.2 TAO SIDA KHAM MARRIES A PRINCESS FROM MOENG KHÜN

Cao (Tao) Sida Kham married the younger sister of Phaya Moeng Khün ([i.e., Cao] Chiang Tung) and made her his queen. Phaya Moeng Khün was called Òn Ai.[62] [He] married his younger sister Nang Samoe to the *saenwi fa* Cao (Tao) Sida Kham.

---

59. This is a hint that the "Lua/Lawa", i.e., the pre-Tai autochthonous population, maintained quite strong political and economic positions in dealing with the dominant Tai society of the lowlands. For details see the introduction, part 1, section 3 of this volume.

60. Tao Sida Kham, identified as Dao Xianda in contemporary Ming sources, is first mentioned in Hongwu 24, tenth month, *jiwei* day (2 November 1391). It is also confirmed that he was Dao Kan's son (i.e., Cao Khan Moeng). See *Taizong shilu*, ch. 213, 3148 and Liew-Herres 2003b.

61. The date should be AD 1430. According to MLC-LV1, s. 9.11, he lived to the age of sixty-two and passed away in the year CS 775 (AD 1413), corresponding to the eleventh year of Yongle reign. Dao Xianda is mentioned eighteen times in the MSL. He is last mentioned in Yongle 11, eleventh month, on the *wuwu* day (15 December 1413). He had already passed away when the imperial eunuch emissary Hong Zisheng visited Chiang Rung. See Liew-Herres 2003b.

62. In MLC-LV1, s. 9.1, he is called Ai Òn. There is no corroborative evidence in the Chiang Tung Chronicle (CTC).

10.3 TAO SIDA KHAM'S CHILDREN

Cao (Tao) Sida Kham had one daughter, called Nang Lun Koei, and two sons: the eldest son was called Tao Kü Moeng and the second son was called Cao (Tao) Kham Tet (Tiat).[63]

10.4 PEO FAI FA, HIS MOENG LAEM CONSORT AND THEIR CHILDREN

Cao (Tao) Sida Kham's younger brother Peo Fai Fa married the daughter of Cao Moeng Laem, Phaya Sòng Fa.[64] Peo Fai Fa had three sons: the eldest son was called Daet Ham Ya Pò Tai;[65] the second son was called Thaloem Ka;[66] the third son was called Soe Long Fa (Süa Luang Fa). The eldest son Daet Ham Ya Pò Tai succeeded his father to be the ruler of Na Saen [at] Chiang Lan.

11. TAO KUMMAN, R. 1430–1432

11.1 THE ELEVENTH RULER

Tao Kumman, the younger brother of Tao Sida Kham, succeeded his elder brother to the throne in the year CS 792 (AD 1433 sic/1430). [He] was on the throne one year (sic)[67] and passed away in the year CS 794 (AD 1435 sic/1432).

11.2 THE TWO SONS OF TAO KUMMAN

Tao Kumman had two sons who were not famous: the eldest son was Cao Ai and the second son was Cao Yi; they both ruled Moeng Hing together.[68]

11.3 SOE LONG FA, THE RULER OF MOENG PHONG

Soe Long Fa, the third son of Peo Fai Fa, who was the younger brother of Cao (Tao) Sida Kham, was intelligent, quick-witted, had courage and resourcefulness. Cao (Tao) Sida Kham had already adopted him as his son when he was still a child. [Later], he was sent to rule Moeng Phong and appointed military commander (*cao pon soek*). Moreover, Phaya (Tao) Sida Kham entrusted him as his regent to manage various local matters. Later because [Soe Long Fa] had a licentious affair with the beloved concubine of Tao

63. According to MLC-LV1, s. 9.2, Tao Kham Tiat was invested as the lord of Na Mün Paen.

64. According to MLC-LV1, s. 9.4, Peo Fai Fa married Nang Paeng Kham Daeng, the daughter of the chieftain of Moeng Laem (i.e., Cao Moeng Laem).

65. In MLC-LV1, s. 9.4, his name is Lie Lang Ya (Daet Ham Ya).

66. In MLC-LV1, s. 9.4, his name is E Jia (Ngai Ka).

67. Perhaps he died in the beginning of the year, so that the time that he held the throne was considerably less than two full years.

68. According to MLC-LV1, s. 9.6, Cao Ai and Cao Yi were the sons of [Tao] Saen Nang, the third son of Tao Sida Kham. Tao Kumman had one son, who inherited the fief in Na Mün Luang after his father had passed away.

Sida Kham and was discovered by the *phaya* (lord, ruler), [Soe Long Fa] was driven away. [He] earned his living as a hawker for three years.

11.4 SOE LONG FA MARRIES NANG LUN KOEI

Later, because there was nobody to take over the management [of local affairs], Soe Long Fa was called back. Phaya (Tao) Sida Kham presented his daughter Nang Lun Koei, born to the princess of Chiang Tung, to Soe Long Fa to be his wife and conferred on him three *panna* [of land in] Moeng Hun and Moeng Hai, and let him be the military commander, as before.

11.5 SOE LONG FA'S JUST RULE

{Soe Long Fa treated those who committed crimes [fairly]};[69] those who ought to be executed would be executed; those who ought to be fined would be fined. [Soe Long Fa] had absolute power over the arable land and the properties. There was no war or calamity. Peace prevailed in the land and the people lived and worked in happiness. Wherever he went, good administration and happiness were brought there. The *tao phaya* (here: the provincial rulers) of various places came to offer their submission. At that time the domain [of Moeng Lü] extended to Moeng Maen Nao (Chinese words say *maen ling song saen*).[70]

12. TAO KÜ MOENG, R. 1433–1436

12.1 THE TWELFTH RULER

Tao Kü Moeng, namely the eldest son of Cao (Tao) Sida Kham, succeeded in his uncle's stead in the year CS 755 (or 795) (AD 1435 sic/1433), at the age of thirty-six. [He] was on the throne three years, lived to the age of thirty-nine, and passed away in the year CS 798 (AD 1438 sic/1436).[71]

12.2 TAO KÜ MOENG'S THREE SONS

Tao Kü Moeng had three sons: the eldest son was Tao Bakòng, the second son was Tao Sòng Moeng, and the third son was Tao Sam Pò Lütai. Tao Kü Moeng married the daughter of Tao Hin Pan [called Nang Aen Kòm][72] and made her his queen consort.

69. Gao Lishi 1984, 108.

70. Moeng Maen is the Tai name of the Chinese town of Puer 普洱. See also MLC-LV1, s. 9.10, n. 112 and s. 12.12.

71. Tao Kü Moeng is first mentioned in the contemporary Chinese sources on 15 December 1413. In the *Ming shilu* it states that on arrival of the imperial palace eunuch emissary, Tao Sida Khan had passed away and his eldest son Tao Kü Moeng proclaimed himself the ruler. He, who was arrogant and cruel, could not gain the hearts of his people. He died not long after. See MSG, ch. 189, 31a; *Taizong shilu*, ch. 145, 1717 (Yongle 11, eleventh month, *wu-xu* day). See Liew-Herres 2003b.

72. Her name, given in MLC-LV1, s. 10.1, is also mentioned in the reign of Soe Long Fa, the

12.3 TAO KÜ MOENG, A CRUEL RULER

When Tao Kü Moeng was in power, he neither ruled according to law nor followed the ancestors' injunctions. [He] was cruel and unscrupulous and killed people recklessly. [He] invented [three] means of torture: the pressing tool (mangle) and saw,[73] which [crushed and] sawed people to death an iron hook to hook into the culprit's spinal cord and bone to hang him up; and slicing a piece of flesh each day until [the convicted] died. When a person committed a crime, his siblings and relatives would be killed (i.e., would be incriminated).

12.4 SOE LONG FA FLEES TO MOENG CAE AND MOENG HUN

[Tao Kü Moeng] refused to listen to the advice of Soe Long Fa and others. Soe Long Fa, afraid that he would kill him, sought refuge in Moeng Cae and Moeng Hun.[74]

12.5 DEPORTING TAO KÜ MOENG TO CHIANG FÒNG

In the third year of Tao Kü Moeng's reign, as his younger brother Tao Kham Tet was afraid that he would be murdered [by his elder brother], he ousted Tao Kü Moeng in the year CS 798 (AD 1438 sic/1436)[75] and sent him to live at Fak Thoe before sending him to Chiang Fòng, which is [today's] Ban Chiang Pòm.

12.6 TAO KÜ MOENG'S VIOLENT DEATH AT MOENG KHÒN

Later, the people had a secret discussion. If [Tao Kü Moeng] were to regain his power, he would kill them. So they lied to him saying that they were sending him to Moeng Nun. They lured Tao Kü Moeng, then put him on the back of an elephant and transported him to Moeng Khòn, where he was strangled to death with a rope around his neck. He became a *phi moeng* after his death and oblations are offered to him to the present day.

13. TAO SÒNG MOENG, REIGNING THREE AND A HALF MONTHS BETWEEN 1436–1439

13.1 THE THIRTEENTH RULER

Tao Sòng Moeng succeeded his father to the throne at the age of thirteen.[76] He was still young.

---

sixteenth ruler. See section 16.3 below.

73. See MLC-LV1, s. 10.3. This could have been a sugar cane pressing tool. See Dao Shuren 1989.

74. According to MLC-LV1, s. 10.3, Soe Long Fa sought refuge at Ban Cae of Moeng Hun.

75. According to MLC-LV1, s. 10.4, Tao Kü Moeng was banished in CS 777 (AD 1415).

76. Tao Sòng Moeng is first mentioned in contemporary Chinese sources on 22 December 1416 (Yongle 14, twelfth month, *xinyou* day). He, mistaken for the son of Tao Sida Kham, sent an emissary to offer tribute at the Ming court. See *Taizong shilu*, ch. 183, 1969. Tao Sòng Moeng is mentioned again on 18 February 1417 (Yongle 15, second month, *jiwei* day). He was appointed by the Ming court

13.2 TAO BAKÒNG RETURNES TO CHIANG RUNG

His elder brother Tao Bakòng was the lord (*kin na*) of Moeng Phong. When the mother and son learned of the news that the younger brother [Tao] Sòng Moeng had succeeded to the throne, they discussed [and decided that] according to the right [of primogeniture] the elder son ought to succeed father. {They returned to Chiang Rung forthwith.}[77] Tao Sòng Moeng waited for his elder brother three months and fifteen days before Tao Bakòng returned [to Chiang Rung].[78]

14. TAO BAKÒNG, R. 1439–1441

14.1 THE FOURTEENTH RULER AND HIS DETHRONEMENT

Tao Bakòng succeeded his younger brother at the age of fifteen in the year CS 801 (AD 1440 sic/1439). [His throne] was usurped by his younger paternal uncle Tao Kham Tet (Tiat) in the year CS 803 (AD 1441).[79]

15. TAO KHAM TET (TIAT), R. 1442–1445

15.1 THE FIFTEENTH RULER

Tao Kham Tet ascended the throne in the year CS 804 (AD 1442).[80] Tao Kham Tet was enthroned at the age of thirty-five, reigned three years (lived to the age of thirty-eight), and passed away by the banks of the Nam Thai Fan River in the year CS 807 (AD 1445).[81]

15.2 FRATRICIDAL WARS BETWEEN TWO COUSINS

{The fratricidal struggle for power between Soe Long Fa and Tao Kham Tet will be related in the following.}[82]

Tao Kham Tet asked Cao Soe Long Fa to surrender to him {and sought his help}. Soe Long Fa said:

---

as the vice-pacification commissioner (i.e., *upalaca*) and Tao Long (most probably Soe Long Fa), the grandson of Tao Sida Kham was to be the pacification commissioner (i.e., *saenwi fa*). See *Taizong shilu*, ch. 185, 1981 (Liew-Herres 2003b).

77. Gao Lishi 1984, 109.

78. See MLC-LV1, s. 11.1, n. 126.

79. Tao Bakòng's name is mentioned in contemporary Ming sources in 1 August 1431 (Xuande 6, sixth month, *bingchen* in the memorial of Mu Sheng (1368–1439).

80. He was the younger uncle of Tao Bakòng and Tao Sòng Moeng.

81. In the original Tai Lü text this statement is placed four lines below, inserted after the quotation from Soe Long Fa's talk to Tao Kham Tet. In his Chinese translation, Gao Lishi 1984, 109 (the fifteenth ruler), puts this sentence in its proper place.

82. The above sentence is taken from Gao Lishi 1984, 109, s. 15.2.

> As for [the matter of] deposing the ruler (*cao moeng*, i.e., Tao Bakòng) I do not know; we both have the same position and rank. When my elder uncle (i.e., "Tao Kham Tet's father") [Tao] Sida Kham was on the throne, the administration of all local matters was entrusted to me personally. Now [my] father, the king is dead.[83] The land has been thrown into confusion by you. [You] intend to proclaim yourself king and succeed to the throne; and you want me to go and pay you homage. Even after my death, my spirit (*preta*) would not go to pay you homage.

15.3 SOE LONG FA SEEKS HELP FROM MOENG LAEM

Tao Kham Tet was dissatisfied. He rallied the lords (*cao mòm*) of the various *müang* [along the banks of the] Mekong {and told them to send troops} to attack Ban Ca at Moeng Hun, [where Soe Long Fa's troops were garrisoned]. Naturally Soe Long Fa would not just sit and wait for his sword (i.e., his death). He immediately sought help from his father-in-law at Moeng Laem. Cao Moeng Laem, by the name of Phaya Phai Hom Fa, dispatched his younger brother Kham Ham Fa, leading troops from Moeng Laem to reinforce Soe Long Fa. It was in the year CS 807 (AD 1445).[84]

15.4 THE BATTLE OF HAE NA KHA AND TAO KHAM TET'S RETREAT TO CHIANG LAN

Tao Kham Tet marched to attack [Soe Long Fa], and Soe Long Fa confronted the enemy. In fierce fighting at Hae Na Kha,[85] although Kham Ham Fa from Moeng Laem was wounded in seven places, the elephant ridden by Tao Kham Tet was captured by Soe Long Fa. Defeated, Tao Kham Tet escaped back [to Chiang Lan] and Soe Long Fa took advantage of victory to pursue [his cousin] to Chiang Lan. The people of Chiang Lan were on the side of Soe Long Fa. Tao Kham Tet, having no standing (i.e., no support), fled to {a hillock at} Chiang Ha. Again Soe Long Fa pursued him to {a hillock at} Chiang Ha, where he killed a close and trusted headman of Tao Kham Tet. This place was therefore renamed Còm Süa. Every year oblations are offered [there], to the present day.

15.5 TAO KHAM TET FLEES WITH SEAL AND DIES

Tao Kham Tet took the golden plate with a seal (i.e., a credential or tally) [adorned with] a tiger's head along with him to seek refuge from Cao Lum Fa (i.e., the Heavenly Court). En route he died at [the bank of] the Nam Thai Fan (Th. น้ำถายฟัน).

83. Soe Long Fa, the nephew of Tao Sida Kham, was also his adopted son.

84. According to MLC-LV1, s. 11.4–11.5, he was Phaya Hom Fa and it was in the year CS 790 (AD 1428).

85. According to MLC-LV1, s. 11.5, the battle was fought in Moeng Hun. Soe Long Fa had at that time stationed his troops at Ban Ca in Moeng Hun. Therefore, Hae Na Kha (Th. แรนาคา) is probably a paddy field in Moeng Hun, the location of which could not be identified.

16. SOE LONG FA (SÜA LUANG FA), R. 1446–1466

16.1 THE SIXTEENTH RULER

Soe Long Fa ascended the throne in the year CS 808 (AD 1446). At the time of enthronement he was sixty years old. He reigned twenty years, lived to the age of eighty and passed away in the year CS 828 (AD 1466).

16.2 KHAM HAM FA IS REWARDED AND MARRIES NANG O MING KHAI FOEI

After Kham Ham Fa from Moeng Laem had helped Soe Long Fa in the battle, [he] was going to bring his troops back to Moeng Laem. Soe Long Fa said:

> In this military campaign my younger brother[-in-law] has shown outstanding merit. It is you who has fought and captured the land for me to rule. Moeng Laem is a small land. Moeng Lü-Saenwi Fa in comparison with Moeng Laem is countless times larger.

Consequently [he] conferred a great section of rice fields of ten thousand [units in size] (*na mün long/luang*) on Kham Ham Fa and presented his daughter Nang O (Ua) Ming Khai Foei (the eldest daughter) to Kham Ham Fa to be his wife. Kham Ham Fa then stayed [in Moeng Lü].

16.3 SOE LONG FA MARRIES NANG AEN KÒM

Soe Long Fa married Nang Aen Kòm, the mother of Tao Bakòng and Tao Sòng Moeng, made her his consort, and later promoted her to queen (*nang moeng*).[86]

16.4 SOE LONG FA BANISHES HIS TWO NEPHEWS FROM MOENG LÜ

Tao Bakòng and Tao Sòng Moeng were not able to succeed to the throne (sic); they should have been content and kept quiet. {But they stole and}[87] killed the buffaloes of the *tao phaya* (the nobles and officials) to eat. They formed a gang and went to tend buffaloes. At night they pretended to be nobles (*pen cao pen khun*), dragged away buffaloes belonging to others, killed and ate them. They reared fighting cocks to fight with those of others. Regardless of whether their own cock won or lost, they would take the cock of the other side, kill and eat it. Soe Long Fa believed that if the power and influence of such people were to grow, they certainly would revolt and usurp the throne. Consequently, [Soe Long Fa] had them put on [several] rafts set adrift on the Mekong, and had them live in another place. The two brothers were not allowed to remain in their home land (*müang*). Sent together [with them] on the rafts were fifteen young male attendants (*bao tai*) and twelve young male serfs (*bao kha*).[88] At the time

86. Soe Long Fa married the widow of his cousin Tao Kü Moeng, the daughter of Tao Hin Pan.

87. Gao Lishi 1984, 110.

88. For a similar account, see "The Chronicle of the Forty Rulers of Panna Moeng Hai", Cao Solawong Maha Bunthan version, f° 13/4–9. This narrative resembles the Cao Fa Dek (Lek) Nòi myth

the two brothers were chased away Tao Bakòng was nineteen years old and Tao Sòng Moeng was sixteen years old.[89]

16.5 THE FOUNDING OF CHIANG KHAENG

Sitting on the rafts, they drifted down the river [Mekong] to a shoal where they ran aground. They then left the rafts and went ashore to eat and stay overnight. Hence this place is called "*hat-kang*" {which means blocked by a beach}[90] to the present day. The reason [for calling the place *hat-kang*] was that their rafts went ashore. The fifteen attendants continued the journey with the *cao*; they were all children of *tao phaya*. In the night between midnight and dawn the *cao* (lord)[91] had a dream. He dreamt that Lord Indra told him:

> You have passed the place where you ought to be. You should return to a place where you see an albino pig (*mu phoek*) and an albino hog deer (*fan pòn*) and you should settle there.

On the following day the *cao* told [his] men what he had dreamt. After making a wish and praying to heaven, the river indeed flowed in another direction and the rafts drifted upstream. The *cao* led his men sitting on the rafts. They really saw an albino pig and an albino hog deer. The *cao* said:

> We have reached the place where we should stay. Let us pluck up all our courage and endure staying in this place.

Consequently they settled in that place, which is called "Chiang Khaeng", *chiang* means "city" and *khaeng* means "strong and hardworking"; it is so called to the present day.

---

about the founding of Chiang Khaeng which is recorded in several extant versions of the Chiang Khaeng Chronicle. According to that story, it is Cao Fa Dek Nòi, the son of the ruler of Chiang Rung, who is exiled by his father after an intrigue by the *cao fa*'s Burmese wife. See Grabowsky 2003b; Grabowsky and Renoo 2008.

89. The above account on why and how the two elder brothers of Tao Sam Pò Lütai were sent into exile on rafts and set adrift on the Mekong by their uncle-cum-stepfather is not recorded in MLC-LV1. In MLC-LV1, s. 12.2, the two brothers, afraid that they would be harmed by the supporters of Soe Long Fa, escaped on a raft down the Mekong.

90. Gao Lishi 1984, 110.

91. Here it means Tao Bakòng, same as in the following.

16.6 TAO BAKÒNG MARRIES THE DAUGHTER OF PHAYA MIMO; THE FOUNDING OF WIANG CÒM TÒNG

Later, the ruler took the daughter of Phaya Mimo, who spoke the Lawa language, as his wife.[92] [They] had two sons. When they had grown up, the eldest son went to establish Wiang Còm Tòng [at] Moeng Yu. The second son went to become the ruler of Moeng Khün (Chiang Tung), [where his descendants rule] to the present day.

16.7 THE FOUNDING OF MOENG SING AND CAO FA DEK NÒI

[Later], the ruler of Moeng Yu, named Cao Sali, had a son. When he had grown up he went to establish Wiang Fa Ya Moeng Sing, [which is] the fortified town (*wiang*) of Moeng Sing.[93] The ruler's younger brother Tao Sòng Moeng, of whom nothing is recorded, died in Chiang Khaeng. The ruler (*cao*) of Chiang Khaeng, as he was a son of *cao saenwi*, was called Cao Fa Dek Nòi.[94] He went to found Moeng Sing and took his cousin (the daughter of his father's younger brother) from Moeng Khün (i.e., Chiang Tung) as his wife. The rulers of Moeng Sing were all offspring and descendants of the *saenwi fa*.[95]

16.8 FOUNDING OF MOENG FAN AND OTHER VILLAGES

As for the fifteen male attendants, they founded five villages (*ban*) and all were the headmen of the villages. Cao (Tao) Bakòng told them:

> [As for] the place where I had a dream some villages shall also be established.

The attendants accepted the order and villages were established. One village was called Moeng Fan; *fan* means "dream". Later a portion [of the population of] Moeng Fan was taken to establish a village, which was called Ban Dòn Cai; another portion was taken to establish the villages Ban Ho (Hua) Tui, Ban Sai, Ban Kha—a total of six villages.

---

92. In the Chiang Khaeng Chronicle it is Cao Fa Dek Nòi's wife, the daughter of the Kha chief Phaya Mimo, who is called "the princess with the three-pronged conch shell (*nang hòi sam cik*)". She reminds us of Cao Khan Moeng's principle wife, Nang Lawa. See MLC-LV2, s. 9.7 and 9.8.

93. In Gao Lishi 1984, 110, it is stated: "He was the son-in-law of the ruler of Moeng Phayak [at] Moeng Sing, the fortified town (*wiang*) of Moeng Sing."

94. This mythical figure is called either Cao Fa Lek Nói (*lek* เล็ก, small) or Cao Fa Dek Nòi (*dek* เด็ก, child) in various extant chronicles recording the story of the founding of Chiang Khaeng.

95. It is interesting to note that the Moeng Lü Chronicle confuses Cao Fa Dek Nòi, the legendary founding prince of Chiang Khaeng, with a well-known historical figure Cao Fa Sali Nò Kham (r. 1881–1901), the last ruler of Chiang Khaeng before the principality was divided between French and British colonialists. By placing both *cao fa*—the first and the last ruler—in the same historical context, the Moeng Lü Chronicle obscures the successive transfers of capitals from (Old) Chiang Khaeng, which was situated on the left bank of the Mekong River (nowadays a small village belonging to the Lao district of Moeng Sing), to Moeng Yu (c. 1855) on the now Burmese side of the river and from there finally to the fertile plain of Moeng Sing (1884/86). See Grabowsky 1999b.

16.9 FOUNDING OF BAN PAEK AND OTHER VILLAGES

The twelve male serfs established three villages, namely Ban Paek, Ban Mòk, and Ban Long (Luang). [The villagers] belonged to the Lawa ethnic group.[96]

16.10 HÒ KHAM MOENG SING

Later Moeng Sing developed into a *müang* (polity) and had a *cao fa* (lord). It was then separated from Sipsòng Panna and became Hò Kham Moeng Sing (golden palace of Moeng Sing) which [no longer] belonged to Sipsòng Panna.[97]

16.11 SOE LONG FA SPARES SAM PÒ LÜTAI'S LIFE

[As] Sam Pò Lütai, the younger brother of Tao Bakòng, was still young, he was still with his mother (Nang Aen Kòm). {Soe Long Fa also did not want to spare him.}[98] His mother said to Soe Long Fa:

> My two elder sons have been sent away by you on a raft. It is like having killed [them]. I am already extremely sad. If you still want to kill [their] youngest brother, then I am no longer willing to be the queen mother. I will kill myself by stabbing a small dagger into my throat; death would be more dignified than staying alive.

Soe Long Fa ordered to bring Sam Pò Lütai to show him. Indeed [the baby nephew] had just learned to walk (i.e., just a toddler). Soe [Long Fa] pondered:

> This small boy will not be able to subdue me (i.e., to plot to usurp my throne).

And thus [he] did not [give the order to] kill Tao Sam Pò Lütai.[99]

16.12 SOE LONG FA RANSOMS SEAL AND CREDENTIAL FROM THE CHINESE AUTHORITIES

Tao Kham Tet was defeated by Soe Long Fa. Taking the golden seal [adorned] with a tiger head and the golden warrant along with him he fled and died at [the bank of] the Nam Thai Sai Kham (น้ำถายซายคำ).[100] Cao Lum Fa summoned Soe Long Fa to go and ransom them. Soe Long Fa paid a ransom of one *mün* of [pure] silver and one *saen* of [pure]

96. Lit., "spoke the Lawa language" (*pen phasa lua*, Tr. เปนภาสาล้วะ).

97. The story of the founding of Chiang Khaeng and Moeng Sing is not recorded in MLC-LV1. The same story, differing in detail, is told in Dao Shuren (1989). Most probably the story was a later addition by scribes.

98. This sentence is taken from Gao Lishi 1984, 110.

99. A similar account is given in MLC-LV1, s. 12.2.

100. See also section 15.5 Nam Thai Fan above. See MLC-LV1, s. 11.6, n. 141.

gold[101] to get back the golden seal [adorned] with a tiger head. [He was] still [permitted] to stay [and rule] the land.

16.13 KHAM HAM FA ABANDONS NA MÜN LONG AND MOVES TO MOENG CAE

Kham Ham Fa of Moeng Laem did not govern Na Mün Long for long. On the pretext that Moeng Cae was close to Moeng Laem, he abandoned Na Mün Long and went to govern Moeng Cae. Moreover, he built a Buddhist pagoda (*cetiya*) on a summit at Moeng Cae, and called it Mòn Wiang (i.e., hill of the stockade town).

16.14 THE NINE SONS OF SOE LONG FA

Soe Long Fa had nine sons. The eldest son was called Tao Phasaeng, the second son was called Tao Còm Pha, the third son was called Tao Saeo, the fourth son was called Tao Yòt, the fifth son was called Tao Kham, the sixth son was called Tao Ut, the seventh son was called Tao Som, the eighth son was called Tao Fa Nòi, [and] the ninth son was called Tao Sòt Sòi.

The eldest son Tao Phasaeng, {nominated as crown prince}[102] succeeded his father. The second son Tao Còm Pha was sent to govern Moeng Long.[103] The third son Tao Saeo was sent to govern Na Mün Long. The fourth son Tao Yòt was sent to govern Müang Luang Nam Tha. The fifth son Tao Kham was sent to govern Moeng U-Nüa. The sixth son Tao Ut was sent to govern Moeng Hun. The seventh son Tao Som was sent to govern Moeng Ngat and Moeng Khang. The eighth son Tao Fa Nòi was appointed to govern Na [Mün Long] together with his third brother [Tao Saeo]. The ninth son Tao Sòt Sòi was sent to govern Chiang Lu. At that time Moeng Laem came to attack Sipsòng Panna. Tao Fa Nòi led the troops to counter-attack. [He] pursued [his enemy] straight to Moeng Nim and died of illness at Moeng Nim; he did not die in battle.

16.15 SOE LONG FA'S SIX DAUGHTERS AND THE LANDS CEDED AS DOWRIES

The eldest daughter of Soe Long Fa [Nang O (Ua) Ming Khai Foei] was married to Saen Moeng Cae {i.e., Kham Ham Fa}.[104] She bore [him] a son called [Tao] Laca (Rāja).[105] The second daughter, called Nang Ok Kham Foei, was married to Phaya Lan Cang (Sang), called Phaya Cai Sòngkham who was the ruler (*phaya*) of Moeng Luang Prabang of Moeng Lao (Laos).

---

101. *Ngün mün kham saen* (Th. งินหมื่นคำแสน). *Ngün* (silver) and *kham* (gold) have similar meanings as well as do *mün* (10,000) and *saen* (100,000). This parallel structure simply emphasises the enormous amount of money paid as ransom.

102. Taken from Gao Lishi 1984, 111.

103. The second son Tao Còm Pha was sent to rule his fief Moeng Long.

104. Taken from Gao Lishi 1984, 111.

105. According to MLC-LV1, s. 12.7, they had four sons; the eldest was called Saen Kham Daeng [...] and three daughters. Tao Laca was the son of Soe Long Fa's fifth daughter Nang Kòng Kham who married Saen Kham Daeng. See MLC-LV1, s. 13.11.

At that time the land [of Lan Sang] and the people were all bestowed as the dowry of the *nang* (lady). The two places, Moeng Bun Nüa and Pòng Si Mün, were also given as her dowry. Later, Cao Moeng Lao {i.e., Phaya Lan Sang}[106] asked for Moeng Yò to be also included as dowry. As he demanded several times and Soe Long Fa was sick of listening to him, [the polity] was called Moeng Yò. At that time Pòng Si Mün was a semi-*panna*; therefore it was called Panna Si Fa Khao.[107] Moeng Yò, Moeng Bun, and Hat Sa together formed the [extended] Panna Si Fa Khao.[108] Since then, Phong Sali, [Moeng] Bun, and Moeng Yò were ceded to Moeng Lao. This was in the year CS 873 (AD 1511) (sic).[109] The above were the domains lost in the reign of Soe Long Fa. After that, Hat Sa and Hat Nga were on the border of Moeng Lao.[110]

Soe Long Fa's first and second daughters were born to the eldest daughter of Cao (Tao) Sida Kham, Nang Lun Koei (the principal queen).

The third daughter Nang Ai Mun was married to the prince of Moeng Cung (i.e., Yuanjiang). [They] belonged to a branch of the Tai peoples called Tai Ya and Tai Khae.[111] The fourth daughter Nang Üai Lao was married to Saen Dao Yat of Chiang Ha. The fifth daughter Nang Kòng Kham and the sixth daughter Nang Aen Wang were both married to Saen Wang of Chiang Kham.

Thus the six daughters of Soe Long Fa were all married to various foreign *müang*. All nine sons were sent to become governors (*cao*) of outer *müang* (i.e., within the territory of Moeng Lü). Only the eldest son (Tao Phasaeng) stayed behind to succeed his father.[112]

16.16 TAO SAM PÒ LÜTAI MARRIES THE THIRD DAUGHTER OF SAEN LÒ

[Tao] Sam Pò Lütai grew up gradually. He was then nineteen years old and was very intelligent and capable. Soe Long Fa adopted him, sent him to rule Moeng Phong, and appointed him military commander. [He] took the third daughter of Saen Lò from Moeng Cae as his consort.[113]

---

106. Taken from Gao Lishi 1984, 111.

107. *Panna si fa khao* (Tr. พันนา ๔ ฝา (ผ่า = แบ่งครึ่ง) เข้า), lit., "the *panna* [Pòng] Si [Mün] divided [into two halves]".

108. According to Gao Lishi 1984, 111, s. 16.15, Moeng Yò, Moeng Bun, and Hat Sa formed a semi-*panna*.

109. According to Gao Lishi 1984, 111, s. 16.15, it was in the year CS 823, a *hong sai* year (Tianshun 5, AD 1461). This information is not given in MLC-LV1.

110. The above information is the same as in Gao Lishi 1984, 111 (the sixteenth ruler), but is not given in MLC-LV1, s. 12.6.

111. See MLC-LV1, s. 12.6, n. 161.

112. The above information is identical to that found in Gao Lishi 1984, 111, but is not given in MLC-LV1, s. 12.6.

113. According to MLC-LV1, s. 12.8, Sam Pò Lütai took the three daughters of Saen Lò as his consorts and concubines. See also Gao Lishi 1984, 111, s. 16.16.

16.17 REVOLT OF SOE NGAM FA OF MOENG MAO LONG

Later, there was a Phaya Moeng Fòng[114] called Soe (Süa) Ngam Fa in Moeng Mao Long, called Ce Ciang (Chiang) Saen; he revolted against the Chinese [authorities]. Cao Lum Fa sent one high-ranking official (*khun yai*) called Cang Khui[115] to command troops and march to extirpate [him]. It was in the year CS 814 (AD 1452). Defeated, Soe Ngam Fa fled to Ava (Th. Angwa).[116]

16.18 SOE LONG FA DELIVERS THE HEAD OF A DESERTED COURTIER OF SOE NGAM FA TO CAO LUM FA

One of his courtiers (*amat*) who fled to Moeng Lü was killed by Soe Long Fa. His head was delivered to Cao Lum Fa.[117] [As a result] Cao Lum Fa showered praise and rewards on Cao Moeng Lü, promoted him, and conferred on him the title Kwan Li Waen Thang Ki Ya Min, which means in Tai [Lü] "great hero guarding the national main gate (*patu moeng*) of Cao Lum Fa".[118] The official title [conferred] was higher than those of Moeng Yuan (Yon)[119] (i.e., Lan Na), Moeng Khün (i.e., Chiang Tung), and Moeng Laem. If [the *cao fa* of] these places wanted to pay tribute to Cao Lum Fa, they had to take the route through Moeng Lü and needed an official document with the seal of Cao Moeng Lü before they would be allowed to pass through. If they had no [travel documents] stamped with the seal of Cao Moeng Lü they were not permitted to proceed.

---

114. Here it means the ruler of Moeng Fòng (Hsaenwi).

115. Cang Khui (Tr. ชางคุย) is the Tai Lü rendering of Jiang Gui 蔣貴 (1380–1449) or the marquis of pacifying the west. He was one of the Ming commanders-in-chief in the successive military campaigns against Luchuan-Pingmian in the 1440s. See Liew 1996. The text of MLC-LV2 had obviously been revised in 1963. In MLC-LV1, 11, s. 12.9, based on an earlier generation of Tai Lü manuscripts, he was called Shang Qiu 商球.

116. A similar account is given in Gao Lishi 1984, 111 (the sixteenth ruler). AD 1452 corresponds to the third year of the Jingtai reign of the Ming period. However, the four successive punitive campaigns against Moeng Mao launched by the Ming court ended before 1449. According to contemporary Chinese sources, Soe (Süa) Ngam Fa (Si Ren Fa) fled to Ava in Zhengtong 7 (1442) and died in 1446/47. See Liew 1996: 181ff. The dates given in Tai Lü manuscripts are quite inaccurate.

117. This event is not mentioned in the contemporary Chinese sources. However, Soe Ngam Fa's (i.e., Si Ren Fa's) head was delivered to the Ming court in January 1446. See *Yingzong shilu*, ch. 136, 2704–5 (Zhengtong 10, twelfth month, on *bingchen* day: 14.01.1446). See Liew 1996, 185–86.

118. Gao Lishi 1984, 111, s. 16.18, interprets as "*Guanli yuanzhang ju yamen*". See MLC-LV1, s. 12.18, n. 171; see also MLC-SV1, s. 13, n. 46 and MLC-SV2, s.14, n. 29.

119. The polity (*müang*) of the Tai Yuan means the kingdom of Lan Na. The ethnonym "Yuan" (ยวน) is not a genuine native ethnic name referring to the Tai-speaking population of Lan Na, but was originally a Siamese term for its northern neighbour. The term *yuan*, just like *yun*, is the Burmese name for the Northern Thai still in use; the Pali form yonaka (re-converted into Thai as *yonok* โยนก) can be traced back to the Sanskrit word *yavana* (foreigner). This word was first used by the Indians to refer to the Greek (Ionians), and was later also used for other foreign peoples such as the Persians and the Romans. See Grabowsky 2005.

16.19 RISE OF MOENG MAEN (PUER)

Moeng Ca and Moeng Yuan had one elephant, 7 *sòk* in height, [designed] for paying tribute. Furthermore, Moeng Maen, Moeng [Bò] Tae, Bò Hoek (now Bò Khoe), Moeng Saeng, Khwaen Siao, Si Thong (Thung), Òi (Oi) Loeng, and other places regarded Moeng Maen as the "leading *müang*".[120]

16.20 THE FEES FOR THE SEAL CHOP OF MOENG LÜ

The Heavenly Court notified Moeng Yuan, Moeng Laem, and Moeng Khün of the stamp duty for the seal-chop that they had to pay to Moeng Lü if they wanted to offer tribute to Cao Lum Fa. Moeng Yuan offered in tribute one high-legged golden plate (tray) weighing 700 [units], namely 24 *hòng* and 5 *the*;[121] Moeng Khün offered in tribute 1,000 [units] of silver, namely 35 *hòng*, and Moeng Laem offered in tribute 20 *hòng* of silver. This tradition of paying tribute is observed to the present day.[122]

16.21 INCORPORATION OF MOENG MAEN INTO MOENG LÜ; THE DOMAIN OF HÒ KHAM MOENG CUNG (YUANJIANG)

In the year CS 815 (AD 1453), Cao Lum Fa took back the official seal that had been issued to Moeng Maen and conferred it on Cao Moeng Lü. The [*müang*] originally subordinate to Moeng Maen, including Moeng Maen, were then placed under the jurisdiction of the *saenwi fa* of Sipsòng Panna. Cao Moeng Lü incorporated them into one *panna* and counted it as ten [units] of *na ma* (horse fields) and *na kong* (bow fields), which means that they had to deliver ten horses and ten horsemen armed with bows and arrows to protect Cao Moeng Lü. They were sent to look for Chinese carpenters to build a wall. They were to be held responsible for the cost of labour and materials. They were sent to serve in the palace of the *saenwi fa*, [performing duties] such as blowing the long horns, beating the drums, and watching the city walls.[123] [In return] they were exempted from performing the local labour service. Moeng Saeng, Bò Hoek, Khwaen Siao, Si Thung (Thong), and Òi (Oi) Loeng were held responsible for cultivating the wet rice fields (*na nai hoen*) of the *saenwi fa* Soe Long Fa. They were considered "Lek Nòi". The above was the domain expanded and gained during the reign of Soe Long Fa. Certainly there were also [some other lands] that were lost. At that time the iron bridge and copper bridge (i.e., the iron chain bridge spanning across the Babian River) was taken as the boundary between Sipsòng Panna and Moeng Cung (Yuanjiang). Moeng

120. *Mae moeng* (แม่เมิง), lit., "mother *müang*".

121. According to Gao Lishi 1984, 111, s. 16.20, it is 7 *huo*, i.e. 24.5 *taels*. Gao Lishi obviously translates *hòng* as tael.

122. A rather similar account is recorded in MLC-LV1, s. 12.11.

123. In Gao Lishi 1984, 111 (the sixteenth ruler) instead of "watching the city walls" it is "clear the wild grass in the palace premises".

Cung was a *hò kham* (golden palace); Moeng Lae (Jiangcheng), [Moeng] La Hu, Moeng Thalang, Moeng Lam, and Moeng Sai (Xinping) were all subordinate to Moeng Cung.[124]

16.22 THE TYRANT RULER OF MOENG YÒNG

Later, there was a man called Mün Mu, who was the ruler of Moeng Yòng. His disposition was fierce and cruel. He oppressed the population [until] the people of the entire *müang* were driven beyond their endurance. [They] allied with Moeng Fòng to go against Mün Mu, the ruler of Moeng Yòng. Eventually Mün Mu was arrested and killed. Moeng Yòng became deserted in that year. The Luai River was taken as the boundary between Sipsòng Panna and Moeng Yòng.[125]

16.23 THE COUNTRY PALACES OF SOE LONG FA

During the reign of Soe Long Fa, peace prevailed in the land and the people lived and worked in peace and were content. The *cao mòm*, *cao khun* (lord), and the people lived in peace and happiness. Soe Long Fa inspected various places and wherever he went country palaces were built [for him]. {To the west of the river were}[126] one at Ban Tung, one at Còm Wang, one at Chiang Kang of Moeng Hun, one at Son Khwan, one in the city (*wiang*) of Moeng Cae, one at Nòng Ban, one at Kho Khae, and one at Dòn Coeng of Moeng Hai. To the east of the river were one at Chiang Fòng, one at Moeng Yang, one at Moeng Hing (i.e., Puwen), and one at Moeng Maen.[127] In each country palace, several palace women and concubines were installed. One year [the *cao fa*] toured the east bank of the [Mekong] river, and another year [he] toured the west bank of the river.

16.24 SOE LONG FA PLOTS TO KILL HIS COUSIN THE LORD OF MOENG HING

Subsequently, [Soe Long Fa] incorporated Moeng Kla (Ka), Moeng Bò, and Moeng Pan[128] into the domain of Sipsòng Panna. It was in the *ka rao* year, CS 819 (AD 1447, sic).[129] Soe Long Fa ordered Cao Ai of Moeng Hing (i.e., Puwen) to be the governor of Moeng Bò, Moeng Kla, and Moeng Pan, and the younger brother of Cao Ai, Cao Yi, to be the governor of Moeng Hing.[130] Later, as Cao Ai could not adapt himself to [his new

124. Moeng Cung, from the Chinese perspective was the Yuanjiang aboriginal commission. The above account is not recorded in MLC-LV1.

125. The account recorded in MLC-LV1, s. 12.13 is similar but differs in some details.

126. Gao Lishi 1984, 112 (the sixteenth ruler).

127. These were the key *müang*, located in the north of Chiang Rung.

128. According to Gao Lishi 1984, 112, the three *müang* are in present-day Jinggu County (Tai: Moeng Bò).

129. CS 819 corresponds to AD 1457.

130. According to MLC-LV1, 7, s. 9.6, Cao Ai and Cao Yi were Saen Nang's sons. Saen Nang was the third son of Tao Sida Kham. However, Cao Ai and Cao Yi, lords of Moeng Hing, were Tao Kumman's sons. See section 11.2 above, and Gao Lishi 1984, 108 (the eleventh ruler).

müang], he returned to Chiang Rung. The Council of Nobles (*noe sanam*) sent him to govern Na Saen of Chiang Lan.[131] He attempted to go against Soe Long Fa; Soe Long Fa [plotted to] kill him.

{[Hence he] incited Man Còm Hai to invite Cao Saen of Chiang Lan (i.e., Cao Ai) to go to eat fish. After Cao Saen had come, Man Còm Hai went to cast the net. Pretending that he had seen a big fish, he said that the common people had small luck and could not fish it, whereas Cao Saen's luck was as mighty as the sky. He invited Cao [Saen] to go into the water. As soon as Cao Saen dived into the water, all the people cast their nets. [Cao] Ai, entangled in the nets, was drowned in the deep pond. Cao Saen was the son (sic) of Tao Kü Moeng.[132] He was even more cruel and oppressive towards the people than his father. He plotted to usurp the throne but was killed by the *saenwi fa* in a net with a ruse. [The story] is told to the present day. Since then Moeng Hing (Puwen) was without a ruler and had to look for [a *cao*] in outer *müang*.}[133]

Soe Long Fa was ruler for twenty years and died at the age of eighty.

17. TAO PHASAENG, R. 1466

17.1 THE SEVENTEENTH RULER COMMITS SUICIDE

The eldest son of Soe Long Fa, Tao Phasaeng, succeeded his father in the year CS 828 (AD 1466) [and reigned] five months. He was ousted because the people refused to obey him. He said that he wanted to go [and seek] protection from the Chinese authorities (*cao hò*), but only reached Moeng Hing (Puwen) where he committed suicide.[134]

17.2 THE NOBILITY CONVENES TO ELECT THE NEW RULER

As at that time, the people could not find a successor, the [nobility of] various *müang* convened [in Chiang Rung] to discuss [the matter]:

> What measures shall we take and who ought to be nominated as the [new] ruler? Those who have no support of the people and are disliked by them, will have the [same] ending (fate) as Tao Phasaeng. Whosoever has the support of the people, we will then lead him to ascend the throne.

131. Hence Cao Ai became Cao Saen of Chiang Lan.

132. Tao Kü Moeng had three sons: Tao Bakòng, Tao Sòng Moeng, and Tao Sam Pò Lütai (see above 12.2). Cao Saen (i.e., Cao Ai) was Tao Kü Moeng's nephew.

133. This paragraph is taken from Gao Lishi 1984, 112 (the sixteenth ruler). The above story is not recorded in MLC-LV1. However, according to the Tai Lü text in Dao Shuren (1989), Soe Long Fa was killed by Cao Ai. The opposite is the case according to Dao Shuren's Chinese translation (1989, 235), in which it was Soe Long Fa who had Cao Ai executed. Here, the "outer *müang*" refers to the *müang* beyond the domain of Sipsòng Panna, such as the *müang* in Lan Sang or Lan Na.

134. *Pat khò man* (Tr. ปาดคอมัน), lit., "sliced his own throat".

Moreover, they declared:

> When the name of a candidate is proposed, those who agree shall acclaim; those who disagree shall remain silent.

17.3 SAM PÒ LÜTAI'S NOMINATION

{After the declaration the speaker announced [candidates'] names one after another in a chanting manner}.[135] The first name proclaimed was the second son of Soe Long Fa, Tao Còm Pha. They declared:

> If you all want him, [then] let us acclaim [him as ruler]. If you do not like him [then] keep quiet.

{Thereafter, the names of the various sons of Soe Long Fa were proclaimed in order of seniority.}[136] In the evening they beat the drums and announced [the names] from the palace square to the outside but nobody was acclaimed. They announced [names] for three days but nobody cheered. As the name of Sam Pò Lütai, third son of Tao Kü Moeng, was proclaimed by the announcer, all the people seconded unanimously and cheered for three days. All the *phaya* (princes)[137] said:

> All of you have approved our elder brother,[138] so let our elder brother succeed to the throne. I hope that the *panna* of the hill regions could be reserved for us to cultivate and support ourselves.

17.4 THE CORONATION CEREMONY

The recommendation and election was completed and those who were at the meeting adjourned to the Buddhist temple. Facing the three gems (i.e., the Buddha, the Dhamma, and the Sangha), they took the oath. The silver and golden chisels were used in the oath taking ritual as well.[139] After the ceremony all of them returned to their respective *müang*.

135. The above statement is from Gao Lishi 1984, 112.

136. Ibid.

137. The *phaya* here refer to the younger brothers of Tao Phasaeng.

138. Tao Sam Pò Lütai, the adopted son of Soe Long Fa, was in fact the *phaya*'s cousin.

139. Tr. มีสิ่วงืนสิ่วคำตั้งแล้ว. Here the wording of MLC-LV2, is similar to that of Dao Shuren (1989). However, in MLC-LV1, 13, s. 13.4, it is translated as: "The oath was then engraved in the temple [in two places], one pasted with gold and the other with silver." In Gao Lishi 1984, 112 (the seventeenth ruler), it is: "The oath was engraved on a silver and on a golden plate." It seems that Li Fuyi and Gao Lishi have misinterpreted their respective Tai Lü texts.

18. TAO SAM PÒ LÜTAI, R. 1467–1490

18.1 THE EIGHTEENTH RULER

[Tao] Sam Pò Lütai ascended [the throne] at the age of twenty-six, namely in the year CS 829 (AD 1467). [He] was on the throne twenty-three years and lived to the age of forty-nine and passed away in the year CS 852 (AD 1490).

18.2 OUTBREAK OF FRATRICIDAL WARS

[Five years] after Sam Pò Lütai had ascended the throne, in the year CS 834 (AD 1472), Cao Moeng Long (Tao Còm Pha) and Cao Moeng Hun (Tao Ut) rebelled and colluded with Phaya Tilaka[140] (Tilok) from Chiang Mai of Lan Na (i.e., Kalòm or Kròm)[141] to attack Sam Pò Lütai. Sam Pò Lütai was forced to abandon Chiang Lan and went to build "Wiang Chiang Mu".

18.3 PHAYA TILAKA IS READY TO ATTACK MOENG CAE

Phaya Tilaka (King Tilok) of Lan Na commanded a large force of 200,000 soldiers. Taking Cao Moeng Long, Tao Còm Pha (second son of Soe Long Fa), as [his] guide, [Tilaka] marched [with his troops] to attack Moeng Cae. As Cao Moeng Long and Cao Moeng Cae, called Saen Lò, had a personal feud, Cao Moeng Long pointed out that Cao Moeng Cae and Sam Pò Lütai were of one mind. Saen Lò was his younger brother-in-law and Tao Còm Pha was his wife's elder brother. Saen Lò's wife and Cao Moeng Long Tao Còm Pha both were Soe Long Fa's children.[142] Cao Moeng Long thought:

> He is [my] younger brother-in-law, yet he is against me.

18.4 SAEN LÒ'S RUSE TO REPEL PHAYA TILAKA

At that time, [Phaya Tilaka of] Lan Na-Chiang Mai first launched an attack on Moeng Cae. Saen Lò of Moeng Cae bluffed Phaya Lan Na by saying:

> The old Saen Lò has fled to Chiang Rung. If Lan Na could conquer Chiang Rung all of us are prepared to be the serfs of your Lord (*cao noe ho*, Th. เจ้าเหนือหัว).

---

140. In Tai Lü it is written Tiraka (ติรกา). The ruler of Lan Na is generally known as Tilok (r. 1441–1487/88) in Northern Thai. Tiloka in Pali means "three worlds". He was esteemed by his people as the ruler of the three worlds in the Buddhist cosmology.

141. The ethnic term "Kalòm" (Tr. กลอม), in Lan Na usually written "Kròm" (Tr. กรอม) and pronounced "Khòm", originally refers to the ancient Khmer or to Mon-Khmer speaking peoples in general. However, in Tai Lü usage the term refers to the Tai-speaking population of Lan Na where it is often used instead of the term "Yon" (Yuan). For example, King Tilok of Lan Na is occasionally called Phaya Kalòm. As to the ethnonym "Yuan", see s. 16.18, n.119 above.

142. Saen Lò's wife was the eldest daughter of Soe Long Fa, called Nang Ua Ming Khai Foei, and Cao Moeng Long was Soe Long Fa's second son, Tao Còm Pha. See s. 16.14, and s. 16.15 above.

18.5 PHAYA TILAKA FAILS TO CAPTURE CHIANG RUNG AND MOENG CAE

[The king of] Lan Na believed him truly. Hence [Tilaka] commanded his troops and marched to attack Chiang Rung. The siege [of Chiang Rung] lasted one month and twenty days, [yet] Chiang Rung was not captured. [He] turned back to attack Moeng Cae. Although he had captured three places, he was not able to defeat Moeng Cae.[143] [Thus he] retreated.[144]

18.6 CESSION OF TERRITORIES TO CHIANG TUNG

Phaya Moeng Khün, called Cao Sili Suthammalaca, at that time [had his men] garrisoned in Chiang Tung, sent reinforcements to help Sam Pò Lütai to attack Lan Na. Eventually Lan Na was defeated. After the war, Sam Pò Lütai ceded Moeng Ma and Moeng La Tip to Phaya Moeng Khün to thank and reward him. It was in the year CS 846 (AD 1484). Since then Moeng Ma and Moeng La [Tip][145] were subordinate to Chiang Tung and were no longer under Sipsòng Panna.[146]

18.7 DEFEATED PHAYA TILAKA RETURNS TO LAN NA

Phaya Tilaka retreated to Moeng Yòng. Because of being defeated he was ashamed and did not return to Chiang Mai of Lan Na directly. [He] led his troops via Pak Yòng[147] to Moeng Phong. En route [they] were struck by thunder; [only] then [they] returned [to Chiang Mai]. Sam Pò Lütai ordered the Mün Phong,[148] whose name was Mün Nòn Long and who was a [*pò*] *lam* of the Kha Kao,[149] to lead 4,000 Kha Kao to launch an ambush on [Cao] Lan Na's forces. Countless elephants, horses, and soldiers of Lan Na were lost or killed. [Phaya Tilaka] then returned to his old country (i.e., Lan Na).

---

143. According to Gao Lishi 1984, 113, it is: "After three onslaughts [yet] without defeating Moeng Cae, [he] retreated." The meaning of the passage is a matter of interpretation. It could be that the scribe meant "Cao Lan Na" (i.e., King Tilok) had attacked three places in Moeng Cae, yet he could not conquer it.

144. As for the different perception of the war between Chiang Mai and Chiang Rung as recorded in the chronicles of Lan Na and Sipsòng Panna, see the introduction, part 1, section 9.2 of this volume.

145. In Gao Lishi 1984, 113 (the eighteenth ruler) it is Moeng Ma and Moeng La Tip.

146. No mention of that territorial transfer can be found in the Chiang Tung Chronicle.

147. Lit., "mouth of the Yòng [River]".

148. Kha Kao (Tr. ข้าเก่า) seems to be a particular ethnic group among the hill people. According to Gao Lishi 1984, 113 (the eighteenth ruler), Sam Pò Lü Tai ordered the *pò lam* (i.e., chief official) of the Kha Kao, called Mün Nòn Long, to lead 4,000 Kha Kao to attack Lan Na troops. As to the *pò lam* officials in the traditional administrative system of Sipsòng Panna, see the introduction, part 1, section 4.1 of this volume.

149. The same is given in Gao Lishi 1984, 113 (the eighteenth ruler). Kha Kao refers to the people in the south of Lan Na. See above s. 18.2, n. 141, on Kalòm (Kròm). MLC-LV1, 14, s. 13.9, renders it as *lam kha* [*kao*] (*lanjia*), which he explains in the parenthesis as "representatives stationed at the capital".

18.8 TAO CET DEFECTS TO LAN NA

Later, Cao Moeng Hun (Tao Ut) and Cao Moeng Long (Luang) (Tao Còm Pha) continued to go against Sam Pò Lütai. In the year CS 847 (CS 1475 sic/1485), Soe Long Fa's nephew (sic) Tao Cet, who ruled (*kin na*) Moeng Ngat and Moeng Khang,[150] again sent men to [Chiang Mai-Lan Na] to collude with Phaya Tilaka. Under the escort of 40,000 soldiers from Chiang Rai, he left Moeng Ngat and Moeng Khang in Moeng Lü and proceeded to Lan Na.

18.9 TAO CET RESETTLES HIS FOLLOWERS IN MOENG YÒNG

At that time, Moeng Yòng was depopulated.[151] Tao Cet requested to restore Moeng Yòng, which was approved. Hence he stationed his troops and [resettled his] people there to cultivate [the land]. The population and production of Moeng Yòng increased. Since then Moeng Yòng has been subordinate to Chiang Saen Luang [of Lan Na]. After the year CS 839 (AD 1467 sic/1477) Moeng Yòng was no longer subordinate to Sipsòng Panna.[152]

18.10 REBUILDING OF MOENG NGAT AND MOENG KHANG

Moeng Ngat and Moeng Khang were devastated and depopulated. Thus Phaya Sam Pò Lütai ordered Tao Laca, the son of Saen Kham Daeng of Moeng Cae and a grandson (*lan*) of Soe Long Fa,[153] to rebuild Moeng Ngat and Moeng Khang, which from that time on were [again] populated.[154]

18.11 THE FIVE SONS AND SIX DAUGHTERS OF TAO SAM PÒ LÜTAI

[Tao] Sam Pò Lütai had five sons and six daughters:[155]

---

150. Tao Cet, also called Tao Som, the lord of Moeng Ngat and Moeng Khang, was the seventh son of Soe Long Fa.

151. In Gao Lishi 1984, 113 (the eighteenth ruler) it is stated: "En route they reached Moeng Yòng, which at that time was depopulated."

152. In the chronicles of other Tai polities, including the Moeng Yòng Chronicle, there is no mention that Moeng Yòng had ever been subordinate to Chiang Rung. However, the Chiang Mai Chronicle reports a successful invasion by Chiang Mai troops in the Moeng Yòng area in 1450/51. Since then, Moeng Yòng seems to have been a vassal *müang* of Lan Na. See CMC-HP, Wyatt and Aroonrut 1995, 81; CMC-N, Notton 1932, 112; CMC-TPCM, Udom et al. 1995, 65.

153. Tao Laca was Nang Ua Ming Khai Foei's son. See section 16.15 above. Nang Ua Ming Khai Foei's mother Nang Lun Koei was Tao Sida Kham's daughter. Therefore, Tao Laca's mother and Sam Pò Lütai were cousins. However, according to MLC-LV1, 14, s. 13.11, Tao Laca was Soe Long Fa's fifth daughter Nang Kòng Kham's son and her husband was Saen Kham Daeng.

154. Moeng Ngat (Tr. เมิงงาด) is a small town *müang* situated southeast of Moeng Cae on the route to Moeng Hun, with Moeng Khang (Tr. เมิงขาง) to the north of Moeng Cae. The depopulation of entire *müang* was the result of foreign invasions, internal unrest and natural disasters, and their subsequent resettlement was a widespread phenomenon in traditional Tai polities.

155. According to MLC-LV1, 15, s. 13.5–6, he had six sons and four daughters, but according to MLC-SV1, 51 (16. Sam Khai Noeng), he had only four sons.

The eldest son Tao Yi (the crown prince) was to succeed to his father's throne; the second son was called Cao Moeng Khak (i.e., Cao Am),[156] the third son was called Sam Khai Noeng, the fourth son was called Cao Ai, and the fifth son who was still young was not yet granted any *müang*. The third son, Sam Khai Noeng, was invested as ruler of Moeng U-Nüa, and was concurrently [appointed] military commander (*cao pon soek*); the fourth son Cao Ai was invested as ruler of Moeng Nun.

The eldest daughter [Cao Nang] was married to Tao Saeo's son called Mün Long;[157] [...][158] the fourth daughter was called Nang Chiang Khang; the fifth daughter was Nang Khò Moeng; and the sixth daughter called Nang La died young.

18.12 TAO SAM PÒ LÜTAI ATTACKS HIS COUSIN TAO UT AT MOENG HUN

In the year CS 837 (AD 1475), Tao Sam Pò Lütai fought against [the ruler of] Moeng Hun called Tao Ut, [the sixth] son of Soe Long Fa.[159] Tao Ut fled to Moeng Long to ask for the support of his elder brother [Tao Còm Pha]. Sam Pò Lütai [dispatched his men] to collect the people [that had fled to other places so as] to resettle [them in Moeng Hun]. As the *cao müang* of that land did not care for the people, Moeng Hun became a *na nai hoen*.[160] As a result the people of Moeng Hun killed their own ruler (*cao khao*), namely Tao Ut, and delivered his head to the *saenwi fa* Sam Pò Lütai.

18.13 DEPORTATION OF THE PEOPLE OF MOENG HUN

Sam Pò Lütai said to the people of Moeng Hun:

---

156. According to MLC-LV1, 15 (s. 13.15), his second son was called Cao Moeng, but according to MLC-SV1, 51 (16. Sam Khai Noeng), his second son was called Sam Khai Noeng. Gao Lishi 1984, 113 (the eighteenth ruler), however, states that his name was Cao Am, the ruler of Moeng Khak. Therefore, he was called Cao Moeng Khak. However, he is not to be confused with Phaya Moeng Khün, also called Cao Moeng Khak, who married Tao Sam Pò Lütai's fifth daughter, Nang Khò Moeng. See section 18.14 below.

157. Tao Saeo was the lord of Na Mün Long and Soe Long Fa's third son. See section 16.14 above. So Cao Nang married her father's uncle-cum-stepfather's grandson. However, according to MLC-LV1, 15 (s. 13.16), Cao Nang married Panna Kham Daeng.

158. The second daughter, called Nang Yong Kham, was married to Panna Kham Daeng of Moeng Cae; the third daughter Nang Aen Fòng was married to [...]. See Gao Lishi 1984, 113. However, according to MLC-LV1, 15, s. 13.16, his second daughter Nang Aen Fòng was married to Mün Long's son Tao Saeo. They had two sons: Han Kòng and Chiang Klat.

159. In CS 837, Tao Sam Pò Lütai attacked Cao Moeng Hun called Tao Ut, because he had colluded with Lan Na to create unrest. As Tao Ut could not repulse [the forces of his cousin], he fled to his elder brother in Moeng Long (i.e, to Tao Còm Pha). See Gao Lishi 1984, 113 (the eighteenth ruler).

160. *Na nai hoen* (Tr. นาในเริน), meaning "to be rice fields in [the area of authority] of the household [of a lord]". That would mean that the subjects of Moeng Hun lost their status as *phai moeng* and were directly subordinate to the local governor as *lek nòi* or "petty bondsmen". As to the social categories in old Sipsòng Panna society, see the introduction, part 1, section 4.2 of this volume.

> You all rebel [quite] often.

[Hence] Sam Pò Lütai deported one part of them to Chiang Rung and the other part to Moeng Cae. Moeng Hun was desolate after that.

18.14 TAI KHÜN PRINCE CAO MOENG KHAK MARRIES NANG KHÒ MOENG

Later, the son of Phaya Moeng Khün, called Cao Moeng Khak, married Sam Pò Lütai's [fifth] daughter Nang Khò Moeng. {Hence he stayed to serve Sam Pò Lütai.}[161] Cao Moeng Khak became Phaya Sam Pò Lütai's son-in-law. This son-in-law was a man who loved power and prestige. Whenever he went to have an audience with King Sam Pò Lütai, the king sent men to fetch cushions for him.

18.15 THE CONFLICT BETWEEN THE CROWN PRINCE TAO YI AND CAO MOENG KHAK

[Tao Yi,] the *cao moeng* who was the son, thought:

> I am the crown prince yet dare not behave like this in front of my father, the king. According to the customs and laws, one who has an audience with the great king *saenwi fa* ought not to sit on a cushion. If my father, the king, were to pass away, certainly [he] would fight for the throne with me.

Since then they quarrelled with each other. Sam Pò Lütai intervened by telling his son [Tao Yi]:

> He loves us; therefore he comes to take care of us. My son should not be unfriendly to others.

18.16 TAO YI INVITES CAO MOENG KHAK TO A FEAST

The crown prince, after listening to what his father the king had said, wanted to reconcile with [his brother-in-law]. [He] prepared wine and grilled beef and invited his brother-in-law to a feast in his house. [However], his brother-in-law [was suspicious and] thought that it was an intrigue.

> He might just call me in order to kill me [on the way to the feast].

So he did not go. Tao Yi was even more exasperated. He rallied a gang of young men. After having consumed the alcohol (*kin lao* กินเหล้า) they went to attack Cao Moeng Khak, [Tao Yi's] brother-in-law.

---

161. This statement is taken from Gao Lishi 1984, 113 (the eighteenth ruler).

18.17 THE QUEEN PLOTS AGAINST TAO YI

[His] brother-in-law Cao Moeng Khak quickly ran to hide under the building of his father-in-law. At that time, the queen (*nang tewi*), namely the natural mother of Cao Ai and another wife of his father, wanted to depose Tao Yi [and] to nominate her son-in-law [to be crown prince] and daughter the queen (sic). She went to pay obeisance to the ruler (i.e., Sam Pò Lütai) and said that the crown prince [Tao Yi] was plotting regicide to usurp the throne. [Tao] Sam Pò Lütai, without carefully considering [the slander] and having heard only the queen's words, sent his eldest son-in-law called Mün Long (Tao Saeo's son) to fight his own son (i.e., Tao Yi).

[Mün Long,] believing that Tao Yi was innocent, did not take any action. The queen then hired Panna Kham Daeng from Moeng Cae, giving him 2,200 *cang* (taels) of pure silver. [The queen said to Panna Kham Daeng:]

> You can do what you want; [you can] install your nephew to be the ruler. This should not be beyond your capacity.

Panna Kham Daeng and the queen were siblings; both were the children of Saen Lò. Panna Kham Daeng and Tao Yi had an old grudge. The cause was that Panna Kham Daeng had a beautiful golden embroidered coat. The crown prince once asked for it, [but Panna Kham Daeng] refused to give [it to him]. The crown prince Tao Yi scolded [him and said that] Panna Kham Daeng (lit., "red gold") was not gold but was [just] copper (*tòng daeng*). After that they were at odds. Panna Kham Daeng thus said:

> Now you have insulted me and I will fight you.

Having said that, they fought each other at Kòng Hua Khum [near] Chiang Rung.

18.18 TAO SAM PÒ LÜTAI ATTACKS HIS SON TAO YI

[Panna Kham Daeng] from Moeng Cae was no match for Tao Yi at fighting. However, [Sam Pò Lütai] helped Panna Kham Daeng[162] to fight against his own son. Tao Yi saw that his father was coming to attack him. Feeling that a son ought not to fight with his father, he fled to Moeng Phong.

18.19 UPRISING AGAINST CAO MOENG KHAK

This incident aroused the dissatisfaction of the officials and the people of the whole country (*müang*) with the son-in-law Cao Moeng Khak. They regarded that the root of the chaos and darkness of this land was the son-in-law. The people rose against him. *Cao Saenwi* [Sam Pò Lütai] had his son-in-law hidden in the house of the spirits of the royal family. The people using bows and arrows shot [at his hideout] day and night. The [Tai] Khün son-in-law (i.e., Cao Moeng Khak), having no way to hide, fled to Moeng

162. Panna Kham Daeng was simultaneously Tao Sam Pò Lütai's son-in-law and at the same time his brother-in-law. See MLC-LV1, s. 13.16 and s.13.22; MLC-LV2, s.18.11, n. 158, and s.18.17.

Pai on the upper course of the Mekong, whence [he went] to Moeng Wang, [then] he changed the route [and went] to Moeng Khang, Moeng Ngat, and Moeng Cae. From Moeng Cae [the people escorted him] to Moeng Khün (Chiang Tung).

18.20 TAO YI'S DEATH

Crown prince [Tao Yi] stayed in Moeng Phong. One day, being drunk, he rushed recklessly on an elephant. He knocked at a house and was killed by a spear.

18.21 A REIGN REPLETE WITH WARS AND CALAMITIES

During the reign of [Tao] Sam Pò Lütai the land was replete with wars and calamities. At that time the country (*banmüang*) confronted several attacks from the Kalòm (Kròm).[163] There were already many civil wars [fought] in Sipsòng Panna; waters and lands, the whole country was lost.[164] Moeng Ma and Moeng La Tip were only subordinate to Chiang Tung because they were ceded by Sam Pò Lütai to reward Moeng Khün for their military support after repelling the attack of the Kalòm.

18.22 TAO SAM PÒ LÜTAI'S GRANDSON CAO KHAN MOENG

[Tao Sam Pò Lütai's] sons, Cao Am (the second son) and Tao Yi (eldest son) were not able to succeed to the throne. Cao Am had a son called Cao Khan Moeng.

19. TAO SAM KHAI NOENG, R. 1491–1495

19.1 THE NINETEENTH RULER

[Tao] Sam Pò Lütai's third son Sam Khai Noeng succeeded in his father's stead in the year CS 853 (AD 1490 sic/1491) at the age of twenty-three. He was on the throne five years, lived to the age of twenty-eight, and passed away in the year CS 857 (AD 1495). He had no son. He was the nineteenth ruler of the dynasty.

20. CAO KHAN MOENG, R. 1496–1518

20.1 THE TWENTIETH RULER

Cao Khan Moeng, {namely the son of Cao Am}, succeeded {in his uncle's stead}[165] in the year CS 858 (AD 1495 sic/1496) at the age of twenty-four. He was on the throne twenty-two years, lived to the age of forty-six, and passed away in the year CS 880 (AD

163. Regarding Kalòm (Kròm), see section 18.2 above.

164. A similar account is given in Gao Lishi 1984, 114 (the eighteenth ruler). There we read: "During the reign of Sam Pò Lütai the land was replete with disastrous wars. The Kalòm (Kròm) alone came to attack several times. There were also many civil wars [fought] in Sipsòng Panna and lands and villages were lost."

165. This is taken from Gao Lishi 1984, 114 (the twentieth ruler).

1518). He was the twentieth ruler of the dynasty. Cao Khan Moeng had a son called Cao Sili (Sali) Sompan.

20.2 MOENG SING

{Here [this scribe] wants to relate the history of Moeng Sing. Moeng Sing was founded by the grandson of Cao Sili (Sali) Nòi.[166] He established the fortified city of Wiang Fa Ya in the *lai cai* year, CS 878 (AD 1516).[167] Later, Cao Moeng Sing married the daughter of Cao Fa Chiang Tung. Moeng Sing was a small *Hò Kham* (golden palace) because it was founded by the grandson of the *saenwi fa* [of Chiang Rung]. At that time the frontiers of Cao Fa Moeng Sing were demarcated. Bordering on Burma, Ban Nan Kham (Man Nan Kenmu), from Chiang Kok (Jingge) to Moeng Phayak, was taken as the border; bordering on Laos, Pha Sam Sao (i.e., three-summit hills) and Nam Khao Hu (lit., "water flowing into a cave") were taken as the border; bordering on Chiang Tung, Moeng Pa was taken as the border; Moeng Yu, Moeng Luai, Moeng Si, and Moeng Khang were incorporated into Moeng Sing and became its vassals. Moeng Moeng [was located on] the three borders and belonged to Chiang Tung. Later, Cao Fa Chiang Tung negotiated with the *cao fa* of Moeng Sing. As Moeng Moeng and Chiang Tung were separated by the Mekong, it was inconvenient [for the people] to travel to and fro [across the river]. Hence, Moeng Moeng was incorporated into Moeng Sing and Moeng Si, Moeng Khang, Moeng Yu, and Moeng Luai were incorporated into Chiang Tung. Both sides had reached an agreement [and the lands] were swapped. It was in the year CS 889, *moeng kai* (AD 1527).}[168]

21. CAO SILI (SALI) SOMPAN, R. 1518–1539

21.1. THE TWENTY-FIRST RULER

Cao Sili (Sali) Sompan succeeded his father to the throne in the year CS 880 (AD 1517 sic/1518) at the age of twenty-three. He was on the throne twenty-one years, lived to the age of forty-four and passed away in the year CS 901 (AD 1539). [He was the twenty-first ruler.] Cao Sili (Sali) Sompan had a son called Cao Un (Ong) Moeng.[169]

166. In the sixteenth century there was no *cao phaendin* of Moeng Sing called Cao Sili (Sali) Nòi. A *cao fa* of that name ruled Moeng Sing only in the late nineteenth century (1880/81–1901). If we follow the genealogy of the Chiang Khaeng Chronicle, in CS 878 (AD 1516/17) the fourth ruler of Chiang Khaeng, Cao Moeng Yòt (r. 1502/3–1542/43) was on the throne. However, he did not reside in Moeng Sing but in old Chiang Khaeng. See Grabowsky and Renoo 2008, xiv–xv.

167. CS 878 was indeed a *lai cai* year.

168. The above account on the history of Moeng Sing is taken from Gao Lishi 1984, 114 (the twentieth ruler, Chao Khan Moeng). This interesting account is neither recorded in MLC-LV1, in MLC-LV2, nor in Dao Shuren (1989). The Tai Lü manuscript, on which Gao Lishi's (1984) translation is based, is probably Gao Lishi's own collation of several manuscripts. For details, see the introduction, part 2, section 2 of this volume.

169. He was called Cao Ong Moeng (r. 1560–1588), according to MLC-SV1.

22. CAO UN (ONG) MOENG, R. 1539–1567

22.1 THE TWENTY-SECOND RULER

Cao Un (Ong) Moeng succeeded his father to the throne in the year CS 901 (AD 1539). He was twenty-four years old upon succeeding to the throne. He reigned twenty-eight years, lived to the age of fifty-two, and passed away in the year CS 929 (AD 1567) at Moeng Phayak. He was the twenty-second ruler of the dynasty.

22.2 BURMESE KING FA SUTTHO THAMMALACA CONQUERS SIPSÒNG PANNA

During the reign of Cao Un (Ong) Moeng, there was a Burmese king of Ava (i.e., Fa Suttho Thammalaca)[170] who had accumulated a lot of merit (*puñña*) and become very powerful (*deja-ṛddhi*). Going north and [after] subduing fifty-one *müang* [he] marched to attack the *saenwi fa* [of] Sipsòng Panna in the year CS 925 (AD 1564 sic/1563). The *saenwi fa* Cao Un (Ong) Moeng surrendered.

22.3 MOENG SAI AS A VASSAL OF BOTH SIPSÒNG PANNA AND LAOS

At that time Fa Suttho commanded Cao Un Moeng, the *saenwi fa*, to Moeng Sai (i.e., Xinping) to delimit the boundaries. The boundary between Sipsòng Panna and Moeng Sai was fixed at Ban Kò Nòi [in the plain of] Moeng Sai. The boundary of the domain of Moeng Sai was fifty *lak khwa li* long.[171] Moeng Sai was then a *müang* subordinate to two overlords; tributes were paid to Sipsòng Panna and to Laos. The Lao called them the "[Tai] Lü of Moeng Sai", and the [Tai] Lü [of Sispòng Panna] called them "Lao of Moeng Sai". From Moeng Sai [the frontier] went to Müang Luang Nam Tha.

22.4 DELIMITATION OF THE FRONTIERS OF MOENG SAI

At that time Cao Moeng Lao {and the king of Burma, Fa Suttho}[172] were fixing the frontiers of Moeng Sai (i.e., Xinping). The domain of Sipsòng Panna reached to Pha Sam Sao (lit., "three-summit hills") and Khao Hu River.[173] From here to Müang Luang Nam Tha was a two-day journey. This was the point of convergence of the frontiers of the

---

170. Fa Suttho Thammalaca is mentioned in MLC-LV1, 19 (s. 22.2). According to Gao Lishi 1984, 115 (the twenty-second ruler), the king of Ava was called *Paya maha kaxieben* (Phaya Mahakasat Pun?). Pha Mahakasat Fa Suttho Thammalaca is the Tai name given to the Burmese king Bayinnaung. Also called Braginoco, the king is known in Chinese sources as Mang Yinglong 莽應龍 (r. 1551–1581). He was Tabinshwehti's (Mang Ruiti 莽瑞體) brother-in-law, king of Toungoo dynasty in Myanmar (Burma). He unified his country and conquered the Shan states and Siam, making Myanmar the most powerful kingdom in mainland Southeast Asia.

171. *Lak* (Th. หลัก) is a Tai word for milestone. *Khwa li* is most probably the Tai rendering of the Chinese term *hua li*, which means Chinese *li*. One Chinese *li* equals 0.5 to 0.6 km.

172. The phrase in parenthesis is taken from Gao Lishi 1984, 115 (the twenty-second ruler).

173. Tr. น้ำเข้ารู, lit., "water flowing into a hole".

three [polities], of the Lao, the Yuan, and of Sipsòng Panna. In the south the Huai Sai River was the frontier [of Sipsòng Panna].

22.5 A BODHI TREE AS THE CONVERGENT POINT OF THE FRONTIERS OF THE THREE LANDS

At that time Cao Moeng Lao (i.e., the king of Lan Sang) wanted to have more land allocated to him. [The three polities] resolved that in delimiting the frontiers no territory was to be conceded [to the advantage of] any side. It was to be decided on who had more luck. The three sides were to begin constructing a Buddhist pagoda (*that*, Pali: dhātu) on the same day and at the same time. The size and height of the pagodas were to be the same. The one who completed building the pagoda first would be held to have more luck and more territory would be allocated to him. After the resolution had been passed, [they] started building the pagodas. The result was that all completed the work at the same time.

{King of Burma Fa Suttho}[174] then planted a Bodhi tree in the centre of the fortified city of Müang Luang Nam Tha and this tree was taken as the convergent point of the three frontiers.

22.6 THE POLITIES SUBORDINATE TO MOENG SING

The [polities] subordinate to the *hò kham* of Moeng Sing were Müang Luang Nam Tha, Moeng Long Pukha, Chiang Khaeng, Moeng Müng, Moeng Khang, Moeng Long, and Chiang Kok.[175] These were the Tai villages [in the plains]. As for the hill regions there were even more; there was Hò Kham Nòi, which was subordinate to Sipsòng Panna.

22.7 FA SUTTHO DEMARCATES THE LAND OF CHIANG RAI

Fa Suttho left Müang Luang Nam Tha and went to Chiang Rai. He negotiated with Cao Chiang Rai about demarcating the frontiers. They went to Chiang Saen and decided to take Mae Sai as the frontier. After this, Ta Khi Lek, Moeng Phayak, Moeng Palaeo, and Moeng Yòng were conceded to Burma and no longer subordinate to Chiang Saen. In the past they had been subordinate to Sipsòng Panna.

22.8 CAO UN (ONG) DIES AT MOENG PHAYAK

Fa Suttho {Thamma Laca}[176] returned to Burma from Chiang Saen and Cao Un (Ong) Moeng followed him the whole way. On arriving at Moeng Phayak, [Cao Un (Ong) Moeng] died of illness. This was the year CS 929 (AD 1556 sic/1567). He was the twenty-second ruler of the dynasty.

---

174. The phrase in parenthesis is taken from Gao Lishi 1984, 115 (the twenty-second ruler).

175. This record is anachronistic for the fifteenth century as it describes the territory of the Lao province of Huakhòng formed in 1916 out of the left-bank territories of Chiang Khaeng, which had become a French protectorate in 1896, and territories formerly under the influence of Luang Phabang (such as Luang Nam Tha) and Nan (such as Wiang Pukha). See Lacroze 1994.

176. Here Gao Lishi 1984, 115 (the twenty-second ruler) gives his full name. He is Bayinnaung, see section 22.2, n. 170, above.

22.9 DEMARCATION OF THE BORDERLANDS OF MOENG KHÜN

Fa Suttho returned to Chiang Rung (sic) (i.e., Chiang Tung)[177] and demarcated the borderlands of Moeng Khün and the hill region of Sam Tao (lit., "three lords").[178] He divided [the hill land] into three regions, each region with its own *tao*, because it was at the confluence of the three frontiers. {At that time Moeng Va (Mengwa) and Moeng Khang (Mengkang) were not yet subordinate to Sipsòng Panna.}[179] One *tao* was subordinate to Sipsòng Panna, one *tao* to Chiang Tung, and one *tao* to Chiang Saen. Ever since then, it has been called Sam Tao, to the present day.[180]

22.10 LOST TERRITORIES

During the reign of Cao Un Moeng, Fa Suttho of Burma came to annex a vast territory [of Moeng Lü]. One part [of that territory] was given to the Lao king and another part was handed over to the Moeng Khün.

22.11 THE TWO SONS OF CAO UN (ONG) MOENG

Cao Un Moeng had two sons: the eldest son was called Cao Sali Sunanta and the second son was called Cao In Moeng.

23. CAO SALI SUNANTA, R. 1568–1569

23.1 THE TWENTY-THIRD RULER

Cao Sali Sunanta succeeded his father to the throne in the year CS 930 (AD 1566 sic/1568) at the age of twenty-eight. He was on the throne six months and passed away in the year CS 931 (AD 1567 sic/1569), without a son.

24. CAO IN MOENG, R. 1569–1578

24.1 THE TWENTY-FOURTH RULER

Cao In Moeng succeeded his elder brother to the throne in the year CS 931 (AD 1568 sic/1569) at the age of twenty-four. He was on the throne nine years, lived to the age of thirty-three, and died in the year CS 940 (AD 1578). He had one son called Cao Nò Moeng (i.e., Cao Nò Kham, see below 24.10).

---

177. According to Gao Lishi 1984, 115, Fa Suttho returned to Chiang Tung.

178. They were the Tai Khün, Tai Lü, the Lao, and the hill tribes living in the Golden Triangle on the Mekong. The three *tao* were the three lords of this region. We are not told the identity of the three "tribal lords" nor of the names of the "hill tribes". The most numerous of these hill people in the Chiang Rung–Chiang Tung region were the Akha and Wa (or Bulang).

179. The sentence is taken from Gao Lishi 1984, 115.

180. This is the frontier region known today as the Golden Triangle.

24.2 BURMESE HONOURS TO CAO IN MOENG AND MARRIAGE WITH BURMESE PRINCESS

At that time, Fa Suttho Thammalaca wanted to return [to Burma]. Cao In Moeng dispatched officials (emissaries) to follow Fa Suttho to Ava. The great king of Ava (i.e., Burmese king) conferred on Cao In Moeng *phòi tò*[181] and invested him with the dignified title, Coti Nakkala (Nagara) Maha Caiya Pawala Suthammalaca. An ivory seal was bestowed on him. The seal was three fingers wide. In the middle [of the seal], the Khao Sanero (i.e., the sacred Mount Meru) was engraved, which was surrounded by Khao Sattaphan (sattabhaṇḍa), the "seven mountains", below which was the ocean. There were three supporting pillars and a pair of *anon* fish holding it, on which were a palace, the sun, and the moon. Moreover, Princess Nang Bo Kham (lit., "golden lotus princess") was given to *saenwi fa*, Cao In Moeng, to be his queen (*nang tewi*).

24.3 THE DOWRY OF THE BURMESE PRINCESS

The following gifts were conferred as dowry:

1) two female and two male elephants, height six *sòk.*[182]
2) two high-legged golden trays, each weighing seven *khan* and seven *cap*,[183] with twelve corners, inlaid with gems.
3) two golden bowls, each weighing one *khan* and one and a half *cap.*
4) two silver containers for lime [for chewing betel nuts], each weighing seven and a half *cap.*
5) a pair of small golden lions (*tep sing*), each weighing five *cap.*
6) one golden box [containing] fermented tea, engraved with a one-headed swan (*hangsa* or *haṃsa*) and inlaid with red gems, weighing two *khan* and two and a half *cap.*
7) one golden box [containing] a razor, engraved with a double-headed swan and inlaid with red gems, weighing six *cap.*
8) one golden spoon, weighing one and a half *cap.*
9) one golden crown, inlaid with gems, weighing four *khan*. Moreover, twenty-four golden flowers are placed on the top of the crown {and decorated with five rows of golden borders};[184]

---

181. *Phòi tò* (Tr. ภอยต่อ) is possibly a Burmese loanword. According to MLC-LV1, 19 (s. 19.3), the king of Burma issued a decree and invested the *saenwi fa* with the title Cao Coti Nakhòn Maha Caiya Pawala Suthammalaca (raja). Yet according to Gao Lishi 1984, 116 (the twenty-fourth ruler), Cao Angwa Phaya Mahakasat (i.e., the Burmese king) conferred on Cao In Moeng *phòi tò* (which he translates as "sugar") and the abovementioned title.

182. The elephant is roughly 2 m tall. The same information is given in MLC-LV1, 20, s. 19.4 and Gao Lishi 1984, 116.

183. According to Burmese weight: four *bat* is one *cap* (i.e., the Burmese *kyat*), ten *cap* is one *khan*, ten *khan* is one *còi* or *ku*, one *còi* is one Burmese *jin* (catty) which is about forty-four Chinese *liang* (taels). According to Gao Lishi 1984, 131, one Tai *zha* (*cap*) is 0.44 tael, one *khan* is 4.4 taels, and one *còi* is 44 taels. See MLC-LV1, 22, s. 19.10, n. 308; see also Gao Lishi 1984, 131.

184. This is added in Gao Lishi 1984, 116 (the twenty-fourth ruler).

10) twenty-five small golden *calòy*;[185]
11) one canopied palanquin;
12) one golden water jar inlaid with gems, weighing five *khan*.
13) one golden water jar lid inlaid with gems, weighing two *khan*
14) one golden spittoon weighing five *khan*;
15) ten swords wrapped in golden foil;
16) two golden swords, inlaid with three rows of gems;
17) a pair of pikes (or a long sword) with ivory hilts;
18) a pair of *nārakā* spears,[186] and sixteen spears decorated with golden tassels and silver tassels;
19) a pair of three-layered white parasols, each parasol with a total of thirty-six golden Bodhi leaves;
20) a pair of single-layered white parasols;
21) twelve golden umbrellas;
22) one long-handled umbrella covered with gold;
23) a pair of fans (woven from coconut leaves);
24) a pair of *buzhang* fans;
25) a pair of *pan wan* sunshades (i.e., one of the regalia serving as a sunshade);
26) a pair of cowries (*camòn*);[187]
27) a big gong (*yam long*) covered with gold, with a diameter of five fists;
28) one *cai* drum;[188]
29) a set of nine *cum* drums;[189]
30) a *thing* drum;[190]
31) a *thing ping* drum;[191]
32) one big silver trumpet;
33) a pair of *kha khao kot*;[192]
34) two sets of howdahs covered with gold;
35) two golden hats;

185. *Calòy* is a Burmese loanword from စလွယ်/salwe/, meaning a sash worn as insignia of honour, rank, or office.

186. *Hòk nalaka* (Tr. หอกนารกา). The meaning of this special kind of spear is unclear.

187. According to Cao Maha Khanthawong (personal communication, March 2005), it is one suit of the royal regalia.

188. *Kòng cai* (Tr. กองไช), or "victory drum" (Skt./Pali: jaya = victory).

189. *Kòng cum* (Tr. กองชุม) is a small drum. Both kòng cum and kòng cai are listed as musical instruments used in late nineteenth-century Moeng Sing for royal processions. See Grabowsky and Renoo 2008, 227.

190. *Kòng thing* (Tr. กองตริง), unidentifiable musical instrument.

191. *Kòng thing ping* (Tr. กองตริงปิง), unidentifiable musical instrument.

192. According to Cao Maha Khanthawong (personal communication, March 2005), it is a French horn.

36) a pair of sticks painted red;
37) a pair of sticks painted gold;
38) a pair of insignias in the shape of the hand of God Nārayāṇa;[193]
39) twelve pairs of *phang lang* (i.e., flat, quadrangular iron bells for hanging around the necks of domestic animals);
40) twelve garments with golden embroidery;
41) a palace with a total of twelve rooms on one floor, with two towers and three roofs covered with tiles; four of the pillars are pasted with golden [foil]. The golden throne, four *sòk* high, is adorned with flowers made of oil-ash (ash mixed in oil) and inlaid with coloured glass. In front of the throne a pair of protecting deities, *tewabut* (devaputra), are erected, [each] holding a long knife guarding the front and back of the throne.
42) a piece of shawl woven with golden threads;
43) one red velvet broad-sleeve ceremonial garment, [i.e.,] a short-sleeved robe, [adorned with] a golden border three inches in width;
44) a pair of golden thread shoes; and
45) a pair of *palm-leaf* fans painted with gold.

[The above list] formed the dowry given to Nang Suwanna Patumma Bo Kham and the *saenwi fa*, Cao In Moeng [on their nuptials].

24.4 CHIANG RUNG IS RENAMED CHIANG YUNG

The king of Ava dispatched emissaries, *ahmu-gyi*[194] and *ahmu-mat*[195] of Chiang Rung, to escort [the princess] and [the emissaries of] the *saenwi fa* Cao In Moeng to Chiang Rung. It was in the year CS 932 (AD 1568 sic/1570). Since then Chiang Rung (lit., "city of dawn") was renamed Chiang Yung (lit., "city of peacocks"). Lan Na came to offer submission as well. An edict was issued bestowing [the title] Nakkala (Nagara) Hò Kham on the *saenwi fa*.[196]

24.5 ARRIVAL OF THE BURMESE PRINCESS AND THE MARRIAGE CEREMONY

When the *saenwi fa* learned of this courtesy, he sent the officials of Sipsòng Panna to welcome [the Princess and her entourage] at the half way point [of the journey] and led them in a procession to [the Buddhist monastery of] Wat Yang Pan of Moeng La Tip. From there they proceeded with their gifts to [Ban] Tap Cang Cai (lit., "village of the victorious elephant") at Chiang Rung, where they celebrated for one month. The news

193. Nārayāṇa (Th. Narai) is an important Sanskrit appelation for the Indian god Viṣṇu. Nārayāṇa is also identified as the original man, Puruṣa.

194. *Ahmu-gyi* (အမှူးကြီး) signifies a high-ranking envoy in Burmese.

195. *Ahmu-mat* (အမှူးမတ်) means a high official in the Burmese royal court.

196. See MLC-LV1, 19.5, n. 291; Gao Lishi 1984, 116.

[of the marriage celebrations of the Burmese princess] spread to the high authorities of the Chinese court (sic) at Moeng Sae [Long] (Kunming).[197]

24.6 CAO IN MOENG BECOMES THE *SAENWI FA* OF TWO OVERLORDS

[Consequently], the Chinese authorities at Moeng Sae (Kunming) ordered senior officials (*khun long*) of Moeng La (Simao) and Moeng Maen (Puer) to go to Chiang Yung (Chiang Rung). At that time [the representatives of] the two courts of China and of Burma held friendly negotiations and an agreement was reached. They jointly proclaimed and invested Cao In Moeng as *saenwi fa*. Cao In Moeng paid respect to the Heavenly Court as father and the Burmese court as mother.[198]

At that time the emissary of the Heavenly Court held the right hand of the *saenwi fa* and the emissary of the Burmese side held his left hand and led him to ascend the throne. A grand coronation ceremony was performed and an extraordinary festival was given. An additional title, Coti Nakkala (Nagara) Maha Caiya Pawala Suthammalaca, was conferred on the *saenwi fa*. An additional title, Queen Nang Maha Suwanna Patumma Akka Mahesi Tewi, was conferred on the princess Nang Suwanna Patumma Tewi.

24.7 CEREMONY OF RECEIVING AN IMPERIAL EDICT

As for the ceremony of receiving the imperial edicts, a hall was built, in which the imperial edict was placed. They prepared a mat [made of] the stems of one kind of leaf (*kan tòng*). On it a piece of red cloth and a piece of white cloth were spread. [There were] eight pairs of yellow candles, one water pot made of silver of the ninth grade of purity[199] weighing two *hòi*.[200] The Burmese call [the royal decree] *mintò*. Our Tai word is *atya*.[201]

Panna Bao Cai[202] was entrusted to guard it. On the day of receiving the imperial edict,

---

197. Moeng Sae Long, i.e., Kunming, is the provincial capital of Yunnan. During the Ming period (1368–1644) the provincial governor, or the grand defender, was the Mu clan, the descendants of Mu Ying, who was the adopted son of the founder of the Ming dynasty. The Chinese court at that time was in Beijing (Peking).

198. *Hò pen pò man pen mae* (Tr. ห้อเปนพ่อม่านเปนแม่). This phrase expresses the dual overlordship of China and Burma over smaller polities in the Upper Mekong valley. For details, see the introduction, part 1, section 8 of this volume.

199. It contains the highest degree of silver, i.e., is almost made of pure silver.

200. See MLC-LV1, s. 19.8, n. 298.

201. *Mintò* (Tr. มินตอ)—sometimes written *amingtò* (Tr. อมิงตอ) is the Tai Lü phonetic rendering of the Burmese word /əmeiŋdo/ (အမိန့်တော်) referring to a "royal decree". *Atya* (Th. อาชญา) comes from Skt. ājñā, "order, command".

202. According to MLC-LV1, 54, s. 3.11, the three *panna* located to the west of the Mekong, consisting of ten *müang*, such as Moeng Phong, Moeng Yuan, etc., were the lesser *panna* (*xiao banna*), called Panna Bao Cai (Tr. พันนาบ่าวชาย), whereas the twelve *müang*, such as Moeng La, Simao, Liushun, etc., located to the east of the Mekong, all together nine *panna*, were the greater *panna* (*da banna*). This differs from MLC-LV1, 21, s. 19.8, n. 300, in which it was the *zong shuwu guan* (official in charge of general affairs) who was entrusted to guard the royal edict.

the *saenwi fa* picked up a golden bowl [and the imperial edict] was put on a silver plate. The bowl was covered with a piece of red cloth. The *khun khaek* (secretarial official),[203] who was responsible for receiving [the imperial edict,] carried the imperial edict to the palace of the *saenwi fa* and read it aloud. After reading [the imperial edict], the golden bowl, the silver tray, and the red [square] cloth were kept by the *saenwi fa*. After having opened [and read] the imperial edict, the *saenwi fa* convened the civil and military officials of Sipsòng Panna[204] for a meeting and took the oath of drinking the water of loyalty to the Chinese and Burmese courts facing the three Buddhist jewels (*sòng phanet kaeo cao sam pakan*).

24.8 GIFTS PRESENTED BY CAO IN MOENG TO THE BURMESE EMISSARIES

The gifts presented by the *saenwi fa* to the Burmese emissaries were: one *pan* (33 taels) of silver of the ninth grade of purity for the chief emissary *amuki*,[205] eight *hòi* (1 *hòi* = 3.3 taels) of silver of the ninth grade of purity for the assistant emissary, six *hòi* of silver of the ninth grade of purity for the third-rank emissary, four *hòi* of silver of the ninth grade of purity for the fourth-rank emissary. As for the fourteen members of the retinue, each [was given] one *hòi* of silver of the ninth grade of purity. The chief headman (*nai kao*) of Moeng Khün (i.e., Chiang Tung) was given eight *bat* (1 *bat* = 0.33 tael) of silver of the ninth grade of purity, and the vice-headman six *bat* of silver of the ninth grade of purity. After the end of the coronation ceremony, when the Chinese senior officials had returned but before the Burmese senior officials (*ahmu-gyi-mang sam*) had departed, the *cao saenwi* gave tribute gifts to all the highest-ranking officals (*mang sam*).

24.9 BURMESE EMISSARIES PARTICIPATE IN THE BUDDHIST LENT FESTIVALS

{In the intercalary year, i.e., the year with double ninth months, on the full moon day of the second ninth month, the king of Burma dispatched two emissaries, accompanied by four suites, [to Chiang Yung] to congratulate on the festivals celebrated on the occasion of the beginning and the end of the Buddhist lent.[206] As usual the *saenwi fa* used a *kan tòng* (*dongjing*) mat, two *hòi* of pure silver, a piece of red cloth and a piece of white cloth, and flowery candles for receiving the imperial edict of congratulation. The imperial edict was brought to the palace of the *saenwi fa* to be read. The *saenwi fa* conferred on the chief emissary of Burma six *hòi* of silver of the ninth grade of purity and on the vice emissary four *hòi* of silver [of the ninth grade of purity]; as for the four suites, each one *hòi* of silver [of the ninth grade of purity]. The chief headman of Moeng

203. According to MLC-LV1, 21, s. 19.8, n. 301, it was the secretary or scribe (*shuji guan*). In Gao Lishi 1984, 116, it states that the secretarial official is called *kunqian* (i.e., *khun khaek*). *Khun khaek* (ขุนแขก) were court officials whose duty was to receive visitors and to arrange the proper protocol.

204. *Amat muca* (Tr. อามาดมูชา).

205. *Amuki* (Tr. อมุคี) might be a variant of the Burmese term *ahmu-gyi*. See explanation above.

206. See Doré and Premchit 1992, 258–66; cf. MLC-LV1, s. 19.12, n. 311.

Khün received six *bat* of silver [of the ninth grade of purity] and the suites four *bat* of silver [of the ninth grade of purity].}[207]

24.10 QUEEN SUWANNA PATUMMA BO KHAM GIVES BIRTH TO A SON

In the year CS 934 (AD 1551 sic/1572), Queen Nang Suwanna Patumma Laca Tewi bore a son who was named Cao Nò Kham.[208] In order for her son's name to perpetuate together with the domain of the *saenwi fa*, the queen [commanded] the construction of a vihāra (Buddhist temple building) located in the west of the fortified town (*wiang*). A big statue of the Buddha (*phacao long*) seven *sòk* high was cast and put on an altar. [The Buddha's] face was facing the city of Ava of the king of Burma. The monastery under royal patronage (*wat long*) was named Suwanna Patumma Ārāma, namely the Golden Lotus Temple or Wat Bo Kham in Tai language.

24.11 THE QUEEN'S HOMESICKNESS

Three or four years later the princess missed her parents, the great king [and queen] of Ava. She wanted to pay her respect to her parents and so told the *cao saenwi fa*, her husband, about her desire, and the *cao saenwi fa* was ready to fulfil his wife's wish.

24.12 TRIBUTE GIFTS COLLECTED FROM THE TWELVE *PANNA*

In the year CS 936 Cao (AD 1563 sic/1574), the gifts that the *cao saenwi fa* offered in tribute to the king of Burma were raised from the various *müang* as follows:

I. Chiang Rung (1), Moeng Ham (2),[209] Moeng Nun (3), and Moeng Song (4), [forming] the *panna* under the direct administration of the *saenwi fa*, [offered] one golden ring weighing six *bat*; one silver ring weighing six *bat*;[210] six golden flowers, each weighing one *bat*; six silver flowers, each weighing one *bat*; a pair of candles, [the wax] wrapped in gold weighing one *pan*; two bolts of broad satin (*hae long*); four bolts of narrow satin; four bolts of *nan* (probably dark blue cotton); four bags of salt; four [bamboo] tubes of tea, each tube containing five balls [of tea]; and one horse (of unspecified colour). The golden things were not necessarily of the purest gold.

II. Moeng Cae (5), Chiang Lu (6),[211] Moeng Òng (7), and Moeng Ngat (8), as one *panna*,

207. The above account is taken from Gao Lishi 1984, 117. A similar account is given in MLC-LV1, 22, s. 19.12.

208. I.e., Cao Nò Moeng, see sections 24.1 above and 24.18 below.

209. Moeng Ham is also known as Ganlanba 橄欖壩. See MLC-LV1, index, 12. The Pali name of Moeng Ham was Pathaṭṭharaṭṭha (ปถฏฐรฏฐ).

210. According to MLC-LV1, 23, s. 19.15, they were golden and silver jars instead of rings; likewise below.

211. According to MLC-LV1, index, 12, Chiang Lu (Jinglu 景魯) is located about 10 *li* (c. 5 km) in the south of the then Nanqiao County.

offered in tribute one golden ring weighing eight *the*;[212] one silver ring weighing eight *the*; and two bolts of narrow satin.

III. Moeng Long (9), as one *panna*; Moeng Hun (10) and Moeng Pan (11), as one *panna*; Moeng Hai (12), Chiang Coeng (13), Moeng Yang Nòi (14), Moeng Khòn (15), Moeng Waen (16), and Moeng Hem (17), as one *panna*; Chiang Lò (18), Moeng Mang (19)[213], and [Moeng] Lang Nüa (20),[214] as one *panna*; and Moeng La (21)[215] and Moeng Ban (22), as one *panna*, offered in tribute: one golden ring weighing four *bat*, one silver ring weighing four *bat*, two bolts of narrow satin, and two bolts of *nan* (dark blue cotton).

IV. Moeng Hing (23), and Moeng Bang (24), as one *panna*, offered one golden ring weighing eight *the*, one silver ring weighing eight *the*, two bolts of narrow satin, and two bolts of dark blue cotton.

V. Moeng La (25),[216] and Moeng Wang (26), as one *panna*; Moeng Phong (27), Moeng Mang (28),[217] and Moeng Yuan (29), as one *panna*, offered the same [amount of tribute] as Moeng Hing (30) and Moeng U-Nüa (31) as one *panna*, Chiang Tòng (32),[218] I-pang (33),[219] Bò La (34), and I-ngu (35).[220]

24.13 THE TRADITION OF PAYING OBEISANCE TO *CAO SAENWI FA* IS ESTABLISHED

Before the reign of Cao In Moeng, [Sipsòng Panna] was independent from Burma. However, beginning in his reign this was no longer the case, and submission was offered [to Burma]. The rulers of all provincial *müang* (*ho-moeng*) of Sipsòng Panna came to receive the credentials (*hap moeng*) from the *cao saenwi fa* who conferred on them the insignia of power.[221] [The *cao saenwi fa*] appointed them as the Phaya Nòi and the Phaya

212. According to Gao Lishi 1984, 131, n. 4, *the* is a Tai weight, like the Chinese weight *qian* (1 *qian* = 0.1 tael); 10 *the* = 1 *hom*, i.e., one tael.

213. According to MLC-LV1, index, 12, this is Moeng Man (Meng Man 猛 满) located in the northwest of what was Nanqiao County.

214. According to MLC-LV1, index, 12, it is located in what was Lancang County.

215. According to MLC-LV1, index, 12, this is the Moeng La (Mengla 猛 臘) in the south of what was Zhengyue County (in today's Moeng La). See also Gao Lishi (1984, 117).

216. According to MLC-LV1, 24, s. 19.15, n. 329, this Moeng La (Mengla 猛 拉) is Simao 思 茅.

217. According to MLC-LV1, index, 13, this is Moeng Mang (Mengmang 猛 漭), located in the south of what was Zhenyue County.

218. According to MLC-LV1, index, 13, Chiang Tòng (Zhengdong 整 董) is subordinate to Jiangcheng 江 城 (Moeng Lae).

219. According to MLC-LV1, index, 13, I-pang (Yibang 倚 邦) is located in what was Xiangming County 象 明 縣, then subordinate to Simao (Moeng La). See also Gao Lishi 1984, 118.

220. I-ngu (Yiwu 易 武) is located in what was Zhengyue County. See MLC-LV1, index, 13. According to MLC-LV1, s. 19.15, Moeng Lü was divided into twelve *panna* with thirty *müang* at around AD 1570, six to the east of the Mekong and six to the west of the Mekong.

221. *Khoeng asòng ayot* (Tr. เคิ่งอส่องอโยด) is a hybrid compound. *Khoeng* (Th. *khrüang* เครื่อง) is a Tai word which means "utensils"; *asòng ayot* is probably the phonetic rendering of the Burmese term *ashaung ayaung* (အဆောင်အယောင်) meaning "insignia of office".

Yai, and during the reign of Cao In Moeng [the tradition] of paying obeisance [to the *cao saenwi fa*] at the beginning and end of each Buddhist lent was established.

24.14 LETTER AND TRIBUTE GIFTS PRESENTED TO THE BURMESE KING

The *cao saenwi fa* collected all the gifts to be offered in tribute to the great king of Ava; the tributary gifts of each *panna* were put in one box and all together there were twelve boxes of tributary gifts. After the tributary gifts [from] Sipsòng Panna were handed over, they fell to their knees, clasping their hands together palm to palm, and read [the following] letter:

> I,[222] the ruler of Chiang Yung, whose name is Coti Nakkala (Nagara) Maha Caiya Pawala Suthammalaca, pay my respects and make obeisance to you and prostrate myself at your glorious feet, Sali Suwanna Wala Bat Cak Kham Ekalaca Phawala Ong Long[223] [the great], a man who has accumulated great merit, the conqueror of all kingdoms of the earth, the lord of albino elephants, the lord of red elephants, brave elephants, brave horses, the lord of gold and silver mountains, the lord of the Red Jewel Mountain, the lord of harbours, the lord of the three gems, the Great Lord, the great protector of the whole Jambu continent, the lord of Vejeyyantaprāsāda, God Indra's palace which is shining brilliantly and beautifully like sunrays, a lord as brilliant and luminous as the suvaṇṇa padumma pupphā a[su]vaṇṇa rasmī (lit., "rays of golden lotus flowers"), of endless glory, the lord of five sorts of divine weapons, the lord of the great religion, divine power which had achieved the highest practice, endowed with the qualities of religious precepts (silādhiguṇa) and qualities of wisdom (paññādiguṇa), observer of the ten royal virtues (dasa rājadhamma) and owner of the sevenfold noble treasure (satta ariya dhanaṃ), Lord of the World who has subdued the kings of all countries. I ask you humbly for proper consideration. Now during your reign I present you tribute goods such as the golden and silver flowers (suvaṇṇa rajata pupphā), golden and silver glasses, and silks, according to the ancient customs of the kings of Chiang Yung. I am determined [to do] all this according to the tradition. I order high-ranking officials of Sipsòng Panna to present these gifts at your feet, great king who has accumulated an enormous amount of merit. [I] ask for your royal favour, and that you extend your right hand to receive [my] excellent offerings and best salutations of every kind. I, the leader of the high-ranking officials of Sipsòng Panna, ask for this highest form of happiness only because of Your Majesty's transcendent virtues (pāramī). I would like to become

222. *Kha pha bat* (ข้าพระบาท), lit., "servant of the king's feet".

223. In MLC-LV1, 24, s. 19.16, n. 339, Sali Suwanna Wala Bat Cak Kham Ekalaca Phawala Ong Long is rendered as "the most blessed great emperor" (*zhi fu da huangdi*). Pali/Tai: śrī/siri suvaṇṇa vara pāda cakka *kham* eka rājā braḥ vara *ong long*, lit., "the most blessed supreme king of the golden feet and golden wheel".

your Majesty's serf (i.e., vassal). I prostrate myself to your feet [and] would like to let you know.[224]

24.15 LETTERS FOR THE BURMESE NOBLES

Moreover, several letters were written to be presented to [nobles and officials such as] the *maengsa*,[225] the *lam moeng* (chief translator),[226] the *yung tung* of Moeng Nai (i.e., the ruler of Moeng Nai),[227] and the ruler of Chiang Tung, one letter each.

24.16 LETTERS AND GIFTS FOR THE BURMESE HIGH OFFICIALS

The gifts given to Po Mu Maha Khasat (commander-in-chief)[228] are: five *pan* of golden silk thread, in total one hundred of them; ten sheets of red carpet; one robe of a high-ranking official (*khun*); ten bags of needles; ten pairs of sandals; two [bamboo] tubes of tea; one gold bowl weighing five *cap*; an engraved silver bowl weighing eight *cap*; one sword wrapped in silver foil; and one bolt of broad satin. Apart from [these gifts], small presents were given to the two *maengsa* and to numerous high-ranking Burmese officials. After paying obeisance [and saying farewell], [the delegation] departed.[229]

24.17 THE GIFTS FROM THE KING OF BURMA TO CAO IN MOENG

In return, the king of Burma gave the *cao saenwi fa* gifts including: two pieces of curtains, one piece of silk, four *uk* (one *uk* is twenty pieces) of headgear made of *kasa* cloth (from the city of Kasa in India), four *ho* (bolts) of cloth from foreign countries,[230] four *ho* of yellow cotton thread (*fai*), four *ho* of *nam ban* (variegated cloth), two *pan* of red sandalwood (*can daeng*), two *pan* of white sandalwood (*can khao*), two *pan* of "black medicine" (*ya dam*) (probably opium or black curcuma), two *pan* of asafoetida (*ferula*

224. A similar letter is translated in MLC-LV1, 24–25, s. 19.16. The letter is also translated in Dao Shuren 1989, 238–49 (the twenty-fourth ruler). All three letters are similar in content but vary in wording. Gao Lishi 1984, 118 did not take the trouble to translate the letter.

225. The meaning is unclear. It could be the Tai Lü phonetic rendering of the Burmese word /`miŋ `ða / (မင်းသား), meaning "king's son" or "prince". MLC-LV1, 25, s. 19.17, n. 346, renders it as "crown prince" (*shizi*). According to Dao Shuren 1989, 249, *maengsa* means "prime minister" (*zaixiang*). Gao Lishi 1984, 118, renders *maengsa* (*miaosha*) as "marquis" (*hou*) and states that after *maengsa* is *maengki* (*miaoji*), called "Akkha Maha Sina Luo Huo Kham" (*Ajia maha xina leluo huo han*), which he renders as the "king's prime minister".

226. According to Gao Lishi 1984, 118, *lam moeng* (Tr. ล่ามเมิง) means "minister of inner affairs" (*neiwu da chen*).

227. According to MLC-LV1, 24, s. 19.17, n. 349, it is the Council of Nobles of Moeng Nai. According to Gao Lishi 1984, 118, *yung tung Moeng Nai* means "chieftain of Moeng Nai".

228. According to MLC-LV1, 25, s. 19.17, n. 348, he was field marshal (*da yuanshuai*). Gao Lishi 1984, 118, renders *po mu maha khasat* as "military commander-in-chief".

229. Compare this section with MLC-LV1, 25, s. 19.17.

230. Ai Kham (personal communication) says that this is the cloth for making *sarong*.

scorodosma), two *pan* of pepper (*phik nòi*), one *pan* of *mak pai nam* (หมากปลายหนาม),[231] and two *pan* of sugar (*küa wan*). This was presented to the *cao saenwi fa*. Moreover, the senior officials (*khun long*) of the Council of Nobles (*noe sanam*) who went to pay obeisance (*kantò*)[232] received presents for all the people and all the *müang*. These were the arrangements made [according to the customs of Burma and Sipsòng Panna, which were reintroduced] during the reign of the *cao saenwi fa* [In Moeng, and have been observed] since then.

24.18 CAO IN MOENG'S SON

Cao In Moeng had one son called Cao Nò Moeng (Cao Nò Kham). At the time of his father's death, he was still young, only twelve years old. Therefore his mother ruled as the regent for six years until he was eighteen and succeeded to the throne.

25. CAO NÒ MOENG, R. 1584–1602

25.1 THE TWENTY-FIFTH RULER

Cao Nò Moeng succeeded his father to the throne in the year CS 946 (AD 1584). He was eighteen years old on succeeding to the throne, ruled eighteen years, lived to the age of thirty-six, and passed away in the year 964 (AD 1601 sic/1602). He was the twenty-fifth ruler of the dynasty.

25.2 CAO NÒ MOENG BECOMES A BURMESE VASSAL

After Cao Nò Moeng had ascended the throne, he sent emissaries (*amat*) with a written document to report [the event] to the king of Burma, who invested him as the *saenwi fa* of Sipsòng Panna. Cao Nò Moeng had a son called Cao Sili (Sali) Suthamma.

231. This is probably the fruit of the *bòraphet* tree (*phak ho nam*) or *Tinospora cordifolia tree* (Menispermaceae), one of a genus of about twenty-five woody climbers found in the tropics of Southeast Asia. The stems are used for curing fevers, skin diseases, jaundice, and syphilis.

232. The term *kantò* (กั่นทอ) derives from the Burmese word /*gədo'*/ (ကန်တော့), which, like the Thai *wai* (ไหว้), means "to pay obeisance with one's palms clasped together and raised to touch one's forehead". It can also mean "to present a gift in respect and gratitude". However, the Shan and the Tai Lü use this word in a broader political and cultural context to refer to a ceremony in which people pay respect to their superiors. It also includes the delivery of tribute gifts by the ruler of a vassal state to his suzerain as a token of loyalty. According to Bancop Phanthumetha (1979, 124–27), an inferior person (inferior in social status or age) had to beg his superior for pardon. The superior person could be one's own parents, grandparents, teachers, or other persons of older age and higher rank. In the Burmese Shan states *kantò* ceremonies were usually conducted at the end of the Buddhist lent. During such ceremonies the three gems (Buddha, *dhamma*, and *saṅgha*) were invoked, as well. Puffed rice and flowers were used for decoration. When people paid their obeisance to the *cao fa* in a *kantò* ceremony, they also confessed offences which they had committed intentionally or unintentionally against the *cao fa* and invoked the three gems to help the *cao fa* protect his officials and all his subjects, thereby ensuring good harvests and a flourishing trade.

26. CAO SILI (SALI) SUTHAMMA, R. 1603–1620

26.1 THE TWENTY-SIXTH RULER

Cao Sili (Sali) Suthamma succeeded his father to the throne in the year CS 965 (AD 1602 sic/1603) at the age of sixteen and ruled together with his mother. He was on the throne sixteen years, lived to the age of thirty-two and passed away in the year CS 982 (AD 1618 sic/1620). He was the twenty-sixth ruler of the dynasty.

26.2 A VASSAL OF TWO OVERLORDS

After the Heavenly Court had appointed him *saenwi fa*, he sent the tributary gifts (*kantò*) and [a delegation of] emissaries to report to the king of Burma, who also appointed him *saenwi fa*.

26.3 THE TWO SONS OF CAO SILI SUTHAMMA

Cao Sili Suthamma had two sons: the eldest son was called Cao Mòm Kham Lü and the second son was called Cao Mòm Tao.

26.4 THE TERM *MÒM*

"Mòm" is derived from the Burmese term *maung* and, later, when the Tai Lü used it they pronounced it *mòm*.[233]

27. CAO MÒM KHAM LÜ, R. 1621–1634

27.1 THE TWENTY-SEVENTH RULER

Cao Mòm Kham Lü succeeded his father to the throne in the year CS 983 (AD 1619 sic/1621) at the age of only fourteen; he was still young. Hence he ruled together with his queen mother. Cao Mòm Kham Lü was on the throne fourteen years (sic), lived to the age of twenty-nine, and died in the year CS 996 (AD 1633 sic/1634).

27.2 VASSAL OF TWO OVERLORDS

After Cao Mòm Kham Lü had succeeded to the throne and the Heavenly Court (*cao hò*) had conferred on him [the title *saenwi fa*], he again sent [a delegation of] officials (*khun*) with tributary gifts to report to the king [of Burma], who also bestowed on him [the title] *saenwi fa*.

---

233. Whether both terms have the same meaning is doubtful. The Burmese term *maung* (မောင်) means the younger brother of a woman. It is also a polite term of address when addressing a male younger than oneself. The Tai word *mòm* (Th. หม่อม), on the other hand, is a title for members of a ruling family.

27.3 THE TWO SONS OF CAO MÒM KHAM LÜ

Cao Mòm Kham Lü had two sons: the eldest son was called Cao Saeng Moeng and the second son was called Cao Nò Moeng. They were still young at the time of their father's death. Later, the eldest son Cao Saeng Moeng also died and thus could not succeed his father.

28. CAO MÒM TAO, R. 1634–1641

28.1 THE TWENTY-EIGHTH RULER

Cao Mòm Tao succeeded his elder brother in the year CS 996 (AD 1633 sic/1634). He was at the time of succession twenty-six years old, ruled seven years, lived to the age of thirty-three, and died in the year CS 1003 (AD 1640 sic/1641). He was the twenty-eighth ruler of the dynasty.

28.2 VASSAL OF TWO OVERLORDS

Cao Mòm Tao succeeded to the throne and the Heavenly Court invested him as *saenwi fa*. [He] again sent [a delegation of] emissaries with tributary gifts to report to the king of Burma, who also conferred on him [the title] *saenwi fa*.

28.3 THE SON AND ADOPTED SON OF CAO MÒM TAO

Cao Mòm Tao had a son called Cao Moeng Tao. When Cao Mòm Tao was on the throne, he adopted his elder brother Cao Mòm Kham Lü's second son Cao Nò Moeng {and designated him crown prince}.[234]

29. CAO NÒ MOENG, R. 1642–1655

29.1 THE TWENTY-NINTH RULER

Cao Nò Moeng[235] succeeded his adoptive father (i.e., uncle) to the throne in the year CS 1004 (AD 1647 sic/1642) at the age of eighteen. He was on the throne thirteen years, lived to the age of thirty-one, and died in the year CS 1017 (AD 1644 sic/1655). He was the twenty-ninth ruler of the dynasty.

29.2 VASSAL OF TWO OVERLORDS

Cao Nò Moeng had no son. Both the Heavenly Court and the Burmese king conferred [the title of *saenwi fa*] on Cao Nò Moeng.

234. This is taken from Gao Lishi 1984, 120 (the twenty-eighth ruler).

235. His name is the same as the twenty-fifth ruler, who reigned from 1584 to 1602.

30. CAO MOENG TAO, R. 1655–1668/69

30.1 THE THIRTIETH RULER

Cao Moeng Tao succeeded his elder cousin to the throne in the year of CS 1017 (AD 1644 sic/1655) at the age of twenty.[236] He was on the throne fourteen years, lived to the age of thirty-four, and died in the year CS 1030 (AD 1668). He was the thirtieth ruler of the dynasty.

30.2 VASSAL OF TWO OVERLORDS

Both the emperor of China and the Burmese king conferred [the title of *saenwi fa*] on Cao Moeng Tao. Cao Moeng Tao had a son called Cao Paeng Moeng.

31. CAO PAENG MOENG, R. 1670–1697/98

31.1 THE THIRTY-FIRST RULER AND HIS MOTHER

Cao Paeng Moeng succeeded his father to the throne in the year CS 1032 (AD 1669 sic/1670) at the age of twelve. He reigned together with his mother. He was on the throne twenty-seven years, lived to the age of thirty-nine, and died in the year CS 1060 (AD 1696 sic/1698).[237] His mother lived to the age of seventy-three. He was the thirty-first ruler of the dynasty.

31.2 CAO PAENG MOENG'S TWO SONS

Cao Paeng Moeng (Ch. Zhao Bianmeng) had two sons. His eldest son was called Tao Cin Pao (Ch. Dao Jinbao) and his second son was Tao Sao Wün (Ch. Dao Shaowen). After Cao Paeng Moeng had succeeded to the throne, both the Chinese and Burmese [courts] conferred on him the title *cao saenwi fa*.

31.3 THE UNREST CREATED BY THE WHITE-HEADED BANDIT

During the reign of Cao Paeng Moeng, the white-headed bandit (*kha ho khao*) created unrest. Claiming that he was a man of merit (*cao bun*), he rebelled against the Chinese. The *cao phaendin* and the rulers of the provincial *müang* (*cao ho-moeng*) believed the man of merit (*kha cao bun*) and joined him to oppose the Chinese. At that time the Chinese governor of Moeng Sae (Kunming) sent Chinese [troops] to punish the "white-headed bandit", who lost [the struggle]. The Chinese deported [*cao bun*] to the north

236. According to the *Qing shilu* (Veritable Records of the Qing Dynasty), Tao Moeng Tao (Ch. Dao Mudao) submitted to the Qing court in AD 1660 and he was granted a mink coat, bolts of satin, a saddle, and other things. See Shizu *shilu*, ch. 139, 12 (Shunzhi 17, eighth month, *bingshen* day: 17 September 1660); ch. 143, 9 (Shunzhi 17, twelfth month, *jiawu* day: 13 January 1661).

237. According to the *Qing shilu*, Cao Paeng Moeng (Dao Zhao Bian Meng) passed away in 1726 and the supreme commander of Yunnan-Guizhou, O-er-tai (1680–1745), petitioned to allow Cao

and beheaded the "white-headed bandit".[238] Several bandits were shot. The population (*phai tai*) fled their homes in large numbers. The hill peoples (*kha*) of six of the twelve regions (*khwaen*) fled under the protection of Moeng Laem [which the Cao Hò had raised to the status of *saenfu* (Ch. *xuanfu si*)].[239]

31.4 DIVIDING DRY AND WET FIELDS BETWEEN MOENG LA AND MOENG CAE

Those parts of Sipsòng Panna that did not side with the "white-headed bandit" were Moeng Cae, Moeng Ngat, Moeng La, and Moeng Hing. When the Chinese [emperor] learned this, he was very satisfied with Moeng Cae and raised it to the status of *saenfu*.[240] The hill regions were transferred to [the jurisdiction of] Moeng La (i.e., Simao and Liushun). Since then, there has been the saying: "30,000 dry fields (*hai*) belong to Moeng La and 40,000 rice fields (*na*) belong to Moeng Cae".[241]

31.5 CAO PAENG MOENG'S DAUGHTERS AND THEIR DOWRIES

Cao Paeng Moeng had two daughters: the eldest daughter was married to Cao Moeng Bò (i.e., ruler of Jinggu) and the second daughter was married to Cao Moeng Pan. Moeng Bò and Moeng Pan [were granted] as dowries and became the hereditary principalities

---

Paeng Moeng's son Cao Cin Pao (Dao Zhao Jin Bao) to succeed his father to the post. See *Shizong shilu*, ch. 48, 5 (Yongzheng 4, ninth month, *bingshen* day: 2 October 1726).

238. The white-headed rebellion broke out at the beginning of the eighteenth century. See Kumiko Kato 1997. According to Ai Kham, the *kha ho khao* were the hill tribes in Moeng Laem. In his translation, Gao Lishi 1984, 121, points out that the unrest of the "white-headed bandit" broke out in AD 1688. There is a difference of forty years. The details of the tribal unrest are recorded in Li Fuyi's *Shier banna jinian* (Chronicles of Sipsòng Panna) 1949, 77–78; reprint 1984. It broke out in Kangxi 27 (AD 1688). The 600 to 700 Lua troops attacked and plundered Chashan (tea hills) regions under Sipsòng Panna.

239. A rather similar account is given in Gao Lishi 1984, 121 but is not recorded in MLC-LV1.

240. *Saenfu* is the Tai rendering of the Chinese *xuanfu si*, a pacification commission, a rank lower than *xuanwei si* (*saenwi*). On aboriginal offices (*tusi*) established in Yunnan and mainland Southeast Asia, see Liew-Herres 2003a, 144–86.

241. Indeed, Moeng Cae, situated on west bank of the Mekong, was well-known as the country's rice bowl and its "40,000 rice fields" (*si mün na moeng cae*, Tr. สี่หมื่นนาเมิงแช่). See Yanyong and Ratanaporn 2001; see also the introduction, part 1, section 4.1 of this volume. In Gao Lishi's Chinese translation (1984, 121), it states: "30,000 hill lands (*shan di*) belong to Moeng La and 40,000 wet fields (*shui tian*) belong to Moeng Cae." However, according to Dao Shuren's Chinese translation (1989, 254): "Moeng Cae was divided into *sam mün na* (Th. สามหมื่นนา, i.e., 30,000 rice fields) and *sam mün hai* (Th. สามหมื่นไร่, i.e., 30,000 hill lands)." That Moeng Cae is known as *sam mün na* and *sam mün hai* is derived from this. Yet, according to Dao Shuren's Tai Lü text, it is rendered as: "[...] the hill regions were transferred [under the jurisdiction of Moeng La] (i.e., Simao and Liushun). Since then there is the saying '40,000 dry fields (*hai*) belong to Moeng La and 40,000 rice fields (*na*) belong to Moeng Cae'". This information is not given in MLC-LV1, 30, s. 25.1–3.

of the daughters and sons-in-law;{[and since then these two *müang*] were no longer under the jurisdiction of Sipsòng Panna.}[242]

32. TAO CIN PAO, R. 1698–1707

32.1 THE THIRTY-SECOND RULER

Tao Cin Pao succeeded his father to the throne in the year CS 1060 (AD 1696 sic/ 1698) at the age of twenty-two. He was on the throne nine years, lived to the age of thirty-one, and died in the year CS 1069 (AD 1705 sic/ 1707).[243]

32.2 TAO CIN PAO'S DEAF SON

He had one son called Tao Cao Thao (i.e., Cao Moeng Thao Hu Nok), who was deaf and had a stammer; he could not speak clearly.[244]

33. TAO SAO WÜN, R. 1707–1730

33.1 THE THIRTY-THIRD RULER AS VASSAL OF TWO OVERLORDS

Tao Sao Wün succeeded his elder brother to the throne in the year CS 1069 (AD 1705 sic/1707) at the age of twenty-five. He was on the throne twenty-three years, lived to the age of forty-eight, and died in the year CS 1092 (AD 1728 sic/1730). He was the thirty-third ruler of the dynasty. Tao Cin Pao (sic) was appointed ruler by both the Chinese and the Burmese [courts].

33.2 DISMISSAL OF TAO SAO WÜN

Tao Sao Wün was an incompetent administrator. He plotted against the Chinese; he was feeble and incapable. The Burmese invaded the frontiers frequently, yet no resistance was made. As a result, the inhabitants of Sipsòng Panna fled in great numbers. As a result, he was deposed by the emperor of China (*cao hò*).[245]

---

242. This is taken from Gao Lishi 1984, 121. A similar account is given in Dao Shuren 1989, 254, but in MLC-LV1, 30, s. 25.3, Cao Paeng Moeng had only two sons, with no mention of the daughters.

243. According to the *Qing shilu*, Cao Cin Pao (Dao Jinbao) passed away in AD 1729 (Yongzheng 7). As his son, Tao Cao Thao or Cao Moeng Thao Hu Nok, was his younger brother, Cao Si Mün Na (i.e., Cao Sao Wün) was to be the regent and to care for his nephew. See *Shizong shilu*, ch. 101, 3 (Yongzheng 8, twelfth month, *renyin* day: 15 January 1731); 146, 13 (Yongzheng 12, eighth month, *jisi* day: 23 September 1734).

244. *Hu nok* (Th. หูหนวก) means "to be deaf". See also section 33.4 below; MLC-LV1, s. 26.2; and MLC-SV1, s. 28 (Tao Cin Pao).

245. According to the *Qing shilu*, the stupid and incompetent Tao Sao Wün (Dao Shaowen) was deposed in AD 1766/67. See Gaozong *shilu*, ch. 774, 10–11.

33.3 TAO SAO WÜN'S SIX SONS

Tao Sao Wün had six sons. The eldest son was called Tao Wui Phin, the second son was called Tao Cao Then (Thian), the third son was called Tao Cao Paeng, the fourth son was called Tao Cao Suwan, the fifth son was called Tao Cao Saeng, and the sixth son was called Tao Cao Cai.

33.4 THE FIVE SONS OF CAO MOENG THAO HU NOK (NUAK)

Cao Moeng Thao Hu Nok (i.e., Tao Cao Thao), [son of the ruler's elder brother], had five sons. The people called him "Cao Moe" because he was deaf and had a stammer.[246] The eldest son was called Cao Kang, the second son was called Cao Sü, and the third son was called Cao Saeng who died when he was still young. The fourth son [was called] Cao Mahacai, and the fifth son was called Cao Kham La. The Chinese did not recognise this lineage (*coe khoe*, Th. *chüa khrüa*) and they were excluded from the line of succession. Thus they did not become rulers (*cao*) and were just common descendants [of the royal family].

34. TAO WUI PHIN, R. 1730–1745

34.1 THE THIRTY-FOURTH RULER

Tao Wui Phin succeeded his father to the throne in the year CS 1092 (AD 1729 sic/1730) at the age of twenty-eight.[247] He was on the throne fifteen years, lived to the age of forty-three, and died in the year CS 1107 (AD 1745) in Moeng Sae (Kunming). He was the thirty-fourth ruler of the dynasty.

34.2 THE *UPALACA* TAO CAO THEN'S DEFECTION TO BURMA

Tao Wui Phin succeeded to the throne and his younger brother Tao Cao Then was appointed *upalaca*. Tao Wui Phin had one son called Cao Can, whose sinicised name was Tao Yung Khò. In the reign of Tao Wui Phin, the younger brother Tao Cao Then listened to the slander of his elder brother-in-law Cao Moeng Nai and his son-in-law Cao Kòng of Moeng Yòng. As a result, Tao Cao Then left Sipsòng Panna and abandoned his royal [elder brother] (Cao Wui Phin) and the *sang cao*.[248] He went to Burma, taking along his family. Later, he returned.

---

246. According to MLC-LV1, 30 (s. 26.2), Cao Moe was Cao Thao Hu Nok's son and Cao Moe had five sons.

247. According to the *Qing shilu*, Tao Wui Phin (Dao Weiping), the son of the deposed aboriginal commissioner Tao Sao Wün (Dao Shaowen), succeeded to the post. See *Gaozong shilu*, ch. 910, 8 (Qianlong 37, sixth month, *xinwei* day: CS 1134 or AD 1772).

248. *Sang cao* (Tr. ส่างเจ้า) might be a hybrid compound consisting of the Chinese word *shang* 上 (above, senior) and the Tai word *cao* for "lord". Hence, *sang cao* could refer to the superior lord in Simao (Moeng La Hò).

34.3 REPLACEMENT OF TAO WUI PHIN BY HIS YOUNGER BROTHER TAO CAO SUWAN

The Heavenly Court (*cao hò*) believed Tao Wui Phin was wrong and sent high officials down to [Chiang Rung] to investigate [the situation]. First his younger brother Tao Cao Suwan was summoned to Moeng Sae (Kunming). Later, Tao Wui Phin, together with the official seal, was brought to Moeng Sae (Kunming). He went to meet Tao Cao Suwan at Moeng Maen (Puer) and together with his younger brother they went to Moeng Sae (Kunming). Tao Wui Phin was deposed and the official seal (*cum yin*)[249] and the letter of conferment (*pu ca kao ci*)[250] were surrendered [to the Manchu authorities]. Only the official seal of the *saenwi fa* of Sipsòng Panna (*Coeli swaenwi sisü*)[251] was put under the care of his younger brother Tao Cao Suwan. Tao Wui Phin lived in Moeng Sae (Kunming) three years before dying of illness.[252] Tao Cao Suwan was then sent back to Sipsòng Panna to succeed to the throne.[253]

35. TAO CAO SUWAN (TAO SUWAN), R. 1746–1763

35.1 THE THIRTY-FIFTH RULER AS VASSAL OF TWO OVERLORDS

Tao Cao Suwan succeeded his elder brother to the throne in the year CS 1108 (AD 1746) at the age of thirty-six.[254] He was also appointed by the emperor of China as well as by the king of Burma. He was on the throne seventeen years, lived to the age of fifty-three and died in the year CS 1125 (AD 1764 sic/1763).

35.2 THE THREE SONS OF TAO CAO SUWAN

Tao Cao Suwan had three sons and four daughters. {These four daughters were born to the princess of Puwen (Moeng Hing).}[255] The eldest son, called Tao Thai Phin, whose Tai name was Cao Mòm Mahasang or Cao Kumman, died young. The second son was Cao Mòm Maha Wong, whose sinicised name was Tao Thai Khò. The third son was Cao Mòm Maha Wang, whose sinicised name was Tao Thai Khang.

---

249. In the original Tai Lü manuscript it is *cum yin*, translated as "official seal".

250. In the original Tai Lü manuscript it is *pu ca kao ci*, translated as *guafeng zhaozhi* 掛封照紙 (see MLC-SV1, 60–61, s. 34, n. 88) meaning the "letter of appointment" or "letter of conferment".

251. This is the Tai Lü transliteration of the Chinese official title *Cheli xuanwei shisi* 車里宣慰使司 (pacification commissioner of Cheli) conferred on the Tai Lü king.

252. According to Dao Shuren (1989) he was arrested by *cao hò* (the Chinese authorities) and was killed in Moeng Sae (Kunming).

253. Tao Wui Phin (Dao Weiping) and Tao Cao Then are well documented in the *Qing shilu*, from Qianlong 37 to 43 (AD. 1772 to 1777). *Gaozong shilu*, ch. 910–1043.

254. According to the *Qing shilu*, Tao Suwan (Dao Shiwan) became the tribal ruler in Qianlong 42 (AD 1777). See *Gaozong shilu*, ch. 1034, 15–16.

255. The above statement, not in MLC-LV2, is in Gao Lishi 1984, 122 (the thirty-fifth ruler). As to Cao Mòm Suwan's children (i.e., Tao Cao Suwan), see MLC-LV1, 32, s. 29.4.

35.3 THE FOUR DAUGHTERS OF TAO CAO SUWAN AND THEIR CONSORTS

His eldest daughter Nang Paeng Moeng Long (Luang) was married to the ruler of Moeng Laem, and Moeng Ping and Moeng Lam were granted as [her] dowry. Since then the two *müang*, Moeng Ping and Moeng Lam, have been under the jurisdiction of Cao Moeng Laem.[256] The second daughter Nang Kang was married to Cao Moeng U-Nüa. The third daughter Nang Saeng Pin was married to Cao Sü-ao and they had no child. The fourth daughter Nang Kòi Fòng was married to the ruler of Moeng Phong. She bore two sons: the eldest son was called Cao Mahacai and the second son was called Cao Paka Kumman.

35.4 THE TWO SONS OF *UPALACA* TAO CAO THEN

Tao Cao Then, the *upalaca*, had two sons: the eldest son was called Cao Maha Phom, and the second son was called Cao Maha Khanan. The Chinese and Burmese courts did not want to appoint him (or them?) as ruler.[257]

The younger (sic) youngest brother of [Tao] Cao Suwan (i.e., Tao Cao Cai) had three sons and four daughters.[258]

36. TAO THAI KHÒ (CAO MÒM MAHA WONG), R. 1764–1770

36.1 THE THIRTY-SIXTH RULER

Tao Thai Khò, whose Tai name was Cao Mòm Maha Wong, succeeded his father to the throne in the year CS 1126 (AD 1764) at the age of twenty-eight. He was on the throne six years, lived to the age of thirty-four, and died in the year CS 1132 (AD 1770).

256. See also Gao Lishi 1984, 122. According to MLC-LV1, 56, s. 3.12, *panna* Ping and *panna* Lam were granted to Cao Moeng Laem as dowry in CS 1156 (AD 1794).

257. In Gao Lishi 1984, 122, s. 35.4, it is stated: "Tao Cao Then, the *upalaca*, had two sons; the eldest son was called [Cao] Maha Phom. He had two sons and four daughters. The two sons died young and without heirs. As for the four daughters: the eldest daughter was married to Cao Moeng Khaeng (i.e., the *cao fa* of Chiang Khaeng); the second daughter was married to Cao Moeng Nun; the third daughter was married to Cao Mahacai of Moeng Phong. It is not clear [to whom] the fourth daughter was married. The second son of Tao Cao Then, called Cao Mòm Maha Khanan, married two wives. The principle wife, who was the elder sister of Phaya Sing Kham (叭 興 罕), bore a daughter called Nang Can Kham (婻 占 罕). She was married to Cao Maha Nòi (召 麻 哈 囡) and bore a son. The concubine bore a daughter named Nang Po Kham (婻 波 罕). She was married to Cao Moeng U-Nüa." See MLC-LV1, s. 30.4, n. 448.

258. The same is recorded in Dao Shuren 1989, 257. Gao Lishi 1984, 122, s. 35.6, records: "The youngest brother of Tao Cao Suwan, [Tao] Cao Cai, had three sons and four daughters. The eldest son was called Cao [Maha] Phom; the second son was called Cao Cai (the same name as his father); and the third son was called Cao Nò Kham. The eldest daughter was called Nang Cin Kham (婻 金 罕); and the second daughter, called Nang Kang Noeng (婻 岡 能), was married to Cao Moeng La; the third daughter, called Nang Saeng Bin (婻 香 炳), was married to Cao Moeng Man. She bore a son. The fourth daughter was named Nang Po Kham (婻 波 罕)." Yet, according to MLC-LV1, s. 27.2, he had only two sons and a daughter. The two sons were Cao Maha Pung (Phom) and Cao Kha Thian.

36.2 TAO THAI KHÒ'S SON TAO SUNWU (CAO MAHA NÒI)

He had one son, who, at the age of two months, was given the sinicised name Tao Sunwu (Dao Shengwu) and whose Tai name was Cao Maha Nòi.[259]

36.3 CREATION OF DUAL *SAENWI FA*

Cao Mòm Maha Wong (Tao Thai Khò) had succeeded to the throne, [the *cao phaendin*] dispatched officials to Moeng Nai and Ava to beg the king of Burma for another conferment. [However], the king of Burma dispatched an emissary[260] to go summon the *upalaca* Tao Cao Then to Burma. As [the *upalaca*] was the subject of both sides, he could not obey the command of one side to proceed [there] personally. Forthwith [Tao Cao Then] sent Phaya Long Khoen[261] from Moeng Cae and Phaya U-ten from Chiang Rung to Burma to pay respect [and explain the situation]. {The king of Burma approved and granted the *upalaca* Tao Cao Then the title *saenwi fa* of the Burmese side.}[262] [Thus, it happened that] the uncle (i.e., Tao Cao Then) and the nephew (i.e., Tao Thai Khò) both became *saenwi fa*; one was established by the Heavenly Court and one by the Burmese side.

36.4 BURMESE KING DESTROYS THE REBELLIOUS TAO CAO THEN

More than a year later, the *upalaca* [Tao Cao Then] listened to the malicious talk of Cao Kòng from Moeng Yòng. [As a result he] defied the order of the king [of Burma] (i.e., Bodaw-hpaya) and was removed from his post. It was in the year CS 1128 (AD 1766). The Burmese king sent a general (*khun*) to capture Cao Kòng of Moeng Yòng, and [Cao Kòng] was beheaded.[263] [The Burmese] continued their march to Chiang Yung (Chiang Rung) but they could not find the *cao upalaca* who was hiding in the forests. So the Burmese burnt the palace of the *cao upalaca* at Chiang Dòn Long and then withdrew to Ava. The *cao upalaca* [Tao Cao Then] died in the year CS 1130 (AD 1768).

---

259. Tao Sunwu was two months old when his father Tao Thai Khò passed away. See MLC-SV1, s. 33, Tao Thai Khang. Gao Lishi 1984, 123, places the following at the end of this reign: "Tao Thai Khò had one son called Cao Maha Nòi, whose sinicised name was Tao Sunwu (i.e. Dao Shengwu)." Cao Maha Nòi is also known as Cao Mòm Maha Nòi. See section 38.1 below.

260. In MLC-LV1, 33, s. 30.1, it is stated that the king of Burma rejected this request because Tao Thai Khò was [still] young. Forthwith the Burmese dispatched Yela with a missive to summon Tao Cao Thian to Burma to declare that he agreed to be the subject and servant (i.e. vassal) of the Heavenly and Burmese courts.

261. Phaya Long Khoen (Tr. พระยาหลวงเขิน) was the ruler of Moeng Cae. See section 39.25 below.

262. This sentence is from Gao Lishi 1984, 122 (the thirty-sixth ruler).

263. The Burmese troops marched into [Tao] Cao Then's camp, arrested Cao Kòng, and killed him. His head, together with his daughter Nang Tip, was delivered under escort to the king of Burma. See MLC-LV1, 33, s. 30.3. A very similar account is given in Gao Lishi 1984, 122. The Burmese general was called Da-ma-sui 達 瑪 隋 in Gao Lishi's translation.

36.5 TAO THAI KHÒ'S PREMATURE DEATH

The *cao saenwi fa* Maha Wong (Tao Thai Khò) sent officals (*khun*) to Burma [with tribute?] to pay obeisance[264] to the king of Burma.[265] The king of Burma agreed and appointed Tao Thai Khò as *cao saenwi fa*. The Burmese emissary was ordered to bring the letter of appointment [to Chiang Rung]. On arriving at Chiang Tung he heard that Tao Thai Khò had died. The Burmese[266] letter of appointment could not be delivered.

36.6 TAO THAI KHÒ'S SON TAO SUNWU (CAO MAHA NÒI)

Tao Thai Khò had one son called Cao Maha Nòi, whose sinicised name was Tao Sunwu (Dao Shengwu). He was still young, just two months old (see section 36.2 above).

37. CAO FA CAN (TAO YUNG KHÒ), R. 1770–1779

37.1 THE THIRTY-SEVENTH RULER DIES IN NAN

Cao Fa Can, whose sinicised name was Tao Yung Khò, succeeded his cousin [Tao Thai Khò or Cao Maha Wong][267] to the throne in the year CS 1132 (AD 1770) at the age of thirty-one. He was on the throne nine years and lived to the age of forty. {In the year CS 1141, *jihai* (*kat kai* year), Qianlong 44, AD 1779},[268] he passed away in Nan.[269]

37.2 DIVIDED ALLEGIANCE IN SIPSÒNG PANNA

After Cao Fa Can had succeeded to the throne, he dispatched nobles (*khun*) to pay respect to the king [of Burma]. The king [of Burma] approved and appointed Cao Fa Can as *saenwi fa*.

Later, Cao Fa Can and Cao Maha Phom (the two cousins) were not on friendly terms. Cao Fa Can sent soldiers (*kaeo-han*) and had Cao Maha Phom killed.[270] The six *panna* to the east of the river Mekong sided with Cao Maha Phom. Under the leadership of the Cao Fa of Moeng Phong they commanded troops and marched to attack Cao Fa Can. The

264. *Kantò* (Th. กั๋นทอ). See explanation in n. 232 above.

265. According to Gao Lishi 1984, 123, s. 36.4, Tao Thai Khò sent Phaya Long Kheo Kham Paen from Chiang Rung and Cao Laca Cai of Moeng Cae to Burma, with a letter for the king of Burma. A very similar account is given in MLC-LV1, s. 30.5; Dao Shuren 1989.

266. In the original text it is "Chinese" (*hò*), which is probably a scribal error. The above translation is rectified by the translators.

267. Tao Yung Khò was Tao Wui Phin's son, and Tao Thai Khò was Cao Mòm Suwan's son. Cao Mòm Suwan was the fourth younger brother of Tao Wui Phin (the eldest son of Tao Sao Wün).

268. This is taken from Gao Lishi 1984, 123. According to MLC-LV1, 34, s. 31.3, it is in CS 1168 (AD 1806).

269. According to MLC-LV1, 34, s. 31.3, Tao Yung Khò followed Kawila and defected to Chiang Mai, where he passed away without an heir.

270. According to MLC-LV1, 33,s. 30.7, Cao Maha Phom was killed at Chiang Lò.

six *panna* to the west of the river [Mekong] favoured Cao Fa Can, but could not triumph over the six *panna* to the east of the river.

37.3 CAO FA CAN PLOTS TO REGAIN POWER BUT FAILS

Cao Fa Can was forced to take his wives and seek protection from the Cao Fa of Chiang Tung (Moeng Khün). They lodged at Ban Mai Tòi. Later he proceeded personally to Ava. He was willing to offer the six *panna* to the west of the river to Burma, while the six *panna* to the east of the river were still to be under the Heavenly Court (*cao wòng*). The king of Burma believed there was no precedent for this. [He] had Cao Fa Can thrown into the royal prison for the crime of harbouring the intention of instigating conflicts between China and Burma. [Cao Fa Can] was handed over to "Maengki Satò"[271] who banished him to Moeng Nai for more than one year.

37.4 CAO FA CAN DEFECTS TO "KAWILA" AND DIES AT MOENG NAN

At that time Kawila of Chiang Mai, Phrae, and Nan marched [north] to conquer Sipsòng Panna.[272] The king of [Burma] ordered the Burmese chief official (*khun long*) to take Cao [Fa] Can to Moeng Laem, [whence they finally] arrived at Moeng Cae. Cao Fa Can offered tribute to Kawila, who was encamping at Moeng Ta Lò. In the letter Kawila was told that he should come to escort [Cao Fa] Can. When Kawila learned of this [request] he sent [soldiers] to camp at the Nòng Wat Lake [near] Ban Phasat [in] Chiang Coeng. Cao Fa Can persuaded his family to visit Kawila's camp and, then [Cao Fa Can] went to Moeng Nan with Kawila's troops. He died in Moeng Nan childless.

37.5 MASS DEPORTATIONS FROM SIPSÒNG PANNA TO LAN NA

At that time Kawila deported large numbers of the population of Sipsòng Panna to Phrae, Nan, and Chiang Mai.

38. CAO MÒM MAHA WANG (TAO THAI KHANG), R. 1780–1785 (AS REGENT), R. 1786–1809, AND CAO MAHA NÒI (TAO SUNWU)

38.1 ENLISTING REFUGEES TO REBUILD SIPSÒNG PANNA

The Heavenly Court (*cao hò*) appointed Cao Mòm Maha Wang, whose sinicised name was Tao Thai Khang, to be the acting *saenwi fa*. He and his nephew Cao Mòm Maha Nòi {whose sinicised name was Tao Sunwu}[273] were held responsible for gathering the officials and the people who had fled {to other places, and for persuading them} back

271. *Maengki satò* (Th. แมงคีซาต่อ) is derived from the Burmese term *min-gyi sa-taw* (မင်းကြီးစားတော်) signifying the supreme commander of the royal capital. MLC-LV1, 34, s. 30.8, n. 459, renders *maengki satò* as supreme commander (*zongdu*).

272. See MLC-LV1, s. 31.2, n. 461.

273. Taken from Gao Lishi 1984, 123.

to Chiang Yung to reconstruct their homeland. {Cao Mòm Maha Wang served as acting *saenwi fa* six years, from CS 1142 (AD 1780) to CS 1147 (AD 1785)}.[274]

38.2 THE THIRTY-EIGHTH RULER CAO MÒM MAHA WANG, R. 1786–1809

Cao Mòm Maha Wang succeeded to the throne in the year CS 1148 (AD 1787 sic/1786) at the age of thirty-eight. He was on the throne twenty-three years, lived to the age of sixty-one, and died in the *kat mao* year CS 1171 (AD 1810 sic/1809). {At that time, in Chiang Khaeng, Moeng Yòng, Chiang Tung, Moeng Laem, and other places, all those who had fled in confusion from [their homelands] because of Kawila returned to rebuild their homes.}[275] The Heavenly Court then issued the seal and the credential to Cao Mòm Maha Nòi, whose sinicised name was Tao Sunwu, [authorising him] to rule.

38.3 APPOINTING CAO MAHA WANG AS THE BURMESE *SAENWI FA*

At that time, the Burmese king summoned Cao [Mòm] Maha Nòi (nephew) and [Cao Mòm] Maha Wang (elder paternal uncle) [to Ava], but they were unable to go and so ordered an official (*tao khun*) to pay their respects to the king. The king was angry that Cao Maha Nòi and Cao Maha Wang did not come. He entrusted Cao Mahacai of Ta Lò with a royal decree (*amintò*) summoning them [to come] forthwith. As [Cao] Maha Nòi, who was the seal-holder, could not go [to Ava in person], Cao Maha Wang, who was the younger paternal uncle (sic), had to go with all the provincial rulers to Ava. [When he did so,] the king was delighted and conferred [on Cao Maha Wang] the title Cao Saenwi Fa Coti Nakkala Maha Wongsa Laca.[276]

38.4 POWER STRUGGLE BETWEEN UNCLE AND NEPHEW

The uncle and nephew ruled together one year. Later, because of a power struggle, they were not on friendly terms. Cao Maha Nòi {being aware that he was isolated and weak}[277] went to Moeng La on the pretext of gaining knowledge. The rulers (*cao*) of five *müang* to the east of Mekong went with him.

Later, Cao Maha Nòi grew dissatisfied with the senior Chinese official [of Simao or Moeng La] and ordered Cao Khanan, the ruler of Moeng Bang (sic),[278] to take tribute (*bannakan*) to persuade Kawila of Phrae and Nan[279] to come and attack Cao Maha Wang. They [did so, but] were defeated and fled. Cao Maha Wang pursued them to Moeng Yò and Moeng Bun (now in Laos).

274. The bracketed statement is given in Gao Lishi 1984, 123, in parenthesis.

275. The bracketed statement is from Gao Lishi 1984, 123.

276. Th. เจ้าแสวนหวีฟ้าโชตินัคครมหาวงสาราชา. This title consists of the Tai word *cao* (lord), the Chinese-derived title *saenwi fa* (*xuanwei shi*, pacification commissioner), followed by the Pali phrase joti nagara mahā vaṃsa rājā (lit., "light, splendour, city, great, dynasty, king").

277. Taken from Gao Lishi 1984, 124.

278. According to MLC-LV1, s. 31.9 and Gao Lishi 1984, 124, s. 38.4, that polity was Moeng Òng.

279. For Kawila as a generic term, see MLC-LV1, s. 31.2, n. 461.

38.5 IMPRISONING CAO MAHA NÒI IN AVA AND HIS LATER DETENTION IN SIMAO (MOENG LA)

At that time the Burmese king sent a commander-in-chief (*khun long*) with over 150 brave soldiers to march directly to Chiang Yung. At that time, as Cao Maha Nòi was afraid that the high Chinese authorities (*phu yai hò*) would punish him, he abandoned his wives and children in Moeng La (Simao) and went to Bò La (forest in I-pang/Yibang). The Burmese commander arrested him and took him to Ava. The king of Burma ordered Cao Maha Wang to move against Cao Maha Nòi. Cao Maha Nòi could not gain a victory over [Cao] Maha Wang. Cao Maha Nòi committed a crime and was thrown into the royal prison in Ava. Later, the Heavenly Court (*cao hò*) sent Wui Yaen[280] to Ava to bring Cao Maha Nòi back. They returned to Moeng Sae (Kunming) and Cao Maha Nòi was then sent to Moeng La (Simao) where [he] stayed six years. Cao Maha Nòi paid gold to hire Lua [and] Musoe at Moeng La, Moeng Bang, Chiang Tòng, and Moeng U to [help him] fight Cao Maha Wang at the foothills of Dòi Nam Yang Mountain, but they were defeated.

38.6 CAO MAHA NÒI FLEES WITH SEAL AND CREDENTIAL

Then Cao Maha Nòi feared that the Chinese court would punish him, so he abandoned his wife and children at Moeng La and fled to Moeng Sò in the territory of the Kaeo (Vietnamese).[281] He had taken the seal and the inscribed plate (credential) with him; later, he disappeared.[282]

38.7 CAO MAHA WANG'S PEACEFUL REIGN

During the reign of Cao Maha Wang as *saenwi fa* there was neither war nor calamity. The land was powerful and the people could live in peace and were happy.

38.8 THE RULER'S TWO SONS

Cao Maha Wang had two sons: the eldest son was Tao Coen Cong (in Pinyin, Dao Zhengzong), whose Tai name was Cao Mòm Suca Wanna; the second son was Cao Lamma (i.e., Cao Lamma Awuttha Kumman), whose sinicised name was Tao Soen Cong (in Pinyin, Dao Chengzong).

---

280. *Wui yaen* (Th. วุยแย้น) is the Tai Lü transcriptions of the Chinese term *weiyuan* 委 員, which means commissioner. It is not a personal name. In Gao Lishi 1984, 124, the Chinese envoy was the "Old Commissioner Cai" (Lao Cai weiyuan 老 蔡 委 員).

281. According to Dao Shuren 1989, 260, Moeng Sò is in Dien Bien Phu.

282. According to a report in the *Qing shilu*, Dao Shengwu (Tao Sunwu) had already fled to Moeng Nai in Burma with the seal in Daoguang 3, eleventh month, *bingyin* day (3 December 1823). See *Xuanzong shilu*, ch. 61, 2.

39. CAO MÒM SUCA WANNA (TAO COEN CONG), R. 1788–1818

39.1 THE THIRTY-NINTH RULER AND HIS YOUNGER BROTHER AS *UPALACA*

Cao Mòm Suca Wanna succeeded his father to the throne in the year CS 1150 (AD 1789 sic/1788) at the age of thirty-two.[283] He was on the throne eighteen years, lived to the age of fifty, and died in the year CS 1180 (AD 1819 sic/1818). Cao Lamma Awuttha Kumman (hereafter abbreviated to Cao Lamma) was conferred the title of *upalaca* (viceroy).

39.2 THE TWO BROTHERS RECEIVE CONFERMENTS FROM THE BURMESE KING

{Cao Mòm Suca Wanna dispatched Phaya Long Sai, Cao Moeng Hing (Puwen), Phaya Moeng Cae, Phaya Phom of Chiang Tòng, and Phaya Pala as emissaries to Burma to bring a missive to inform the king of Burma.}[284] The *upalaca* sent [a delegation of Tai Lü] nobles (*khun*) [as emissaries to Burma] to offer tributes to the king [of Ava].[285] [The king] appointed [Cao Mòm Suca Wanna] as *saenwi fa* [conferring on him the honorary title] [*Cao*] Coti Nakkala (Nagara) Maha Wongsa Laca (Joti Nagara Mahā Vaṃsa Rājā), and conferring on his younger brother [Cao Lamma Awuttha Kumman] the honorary title Sili Wanna Upalaca (Siri Vaṇṇa Uparājā). Forthwith, [the Tai Lü] emissaries (*amuki*, i.e., *ahmu-gyi*), who had been dispatched [to Burma], were entrusted to bring the letters of appointment back [to Chiang Yung (Rung)].

39.3 CAO MAHA KHANAN FIGHTS FOR THE THRONE

In the year CS 1163 (AD 1802 sic/1801), Cao Maha Khanan,[286] Cao Cai,[287] Cao Nò Kham,[288] and Cao Phom,[289] who were the leaders, [as well as] Phaya Long Cang, Phaya

---

283. The *Qing shilu* states that Tao Thai Khang's eldest son, Tao Coen Cong (Dao Zhengzong), was allowed to succeed to the post of Cheli in 1834. See *Xuanzong shilu*, ch. 252, 15–17 (Daoguang 14, fifth month, *guiwei* day: 25 June 1834).

284. The above information is taken from Gao Lishi 1984, 124.

285. A similar account is given in MLC-LV1, 37, s. 32.3. According to MLC-LV1, in CS 1199 (AD 1837), Dao Zhengzong (Tao Coen Cong or Cao Mòm Suca Wanna) and his younger brother sent Phaya Long Sai, Cao Moeng Cae, Cao Moeng Hing, Phaya Phom of Chiang Tóng, and Phaya Pala of Moeng Phong (namely the Tai Lü nobles) to deliver a memorial to the king of Burma. A similar account is recorded in Gao Lishi 1984, 124, with only a difference in the recorded year.

286. He was the second son of Tao Cao Then and grandson of Tao Sao Wün. See section 35.4 above.

287. According to Gao Lishi 1984, he was the second son of Tao Cao Cai (the sixth son of Tao Sao Wün). MLC-LV1, s. 27.2 states that Tao Cao Cai's sons were Cao Maha Pung and Cao Kha Thian. The Cao Cai here is probably Tao Cao Cai.

288. According to MLC-LV1, s. 27.2, Cao Nò Kham was the eldest son of Cao Maha Khanan and a great-grandson of Tao Sao Wün, but according to Gao Lishi (1984), he was the third son of Tao Cao Cai who was the sixth son of Tao Sao Wün.

289. Cao Phom was probably the eldest son of Tao Cao Cai and a grandson of Tao Sao Wün,

Long Cana Lücai, and Phaya Còm Kham mobilised together three hundred soldiers and plotted to take over the country from the two brothers (i.e., the ruler and the viceroy). They mobilised their troops to besiege the city (*wiang*) [of Chiang Yung] and argued that after the murder of the two rulers (*cao*) they themselves would become rulers. At that time Cao Chiang Ha (i.e., president of the *noe sanam*)[290] and the various provincial nobles (*khun ho-moeng*) of Sipsòng Panna disagreed. [So] they pretended that they wanted to cooperate [with them]. Cao Chiang Ha immediately ordered Cao Moeng Phong to bring the two *cao* (i.e., the *saenwi fa* and the *upalaca*), who were brothers, secretly across the river (Mekong) in the middle of the night and had them hidden in Ban Na Kha, [where they later] fled to Moeng La (Simao).

39.4 CAO CHIANG HA'S RUSE

The ruler (sic) of (the ruler's) Cao Chiang Ha, who was the leader, thus invited Cao Nò Kham to ascend the throne. He told Cao Nò Kham respectfully:

> If you please, do promote Phaya Long Cang, Phaya Long Cana Lücai, and Phaya Còm Kham to be the high-ranking officials (*amat ton phu yai*) [of the *noe sanam*].

[Afterwards,] Cao Nò Kham called the three of them to assume their [respective] offices. When they came to the meeting hall at his request, they were captured in an ambush and were killed forthwith at the Council of Nobles (*noe sanam*). Cao Nò Kham perceived the situation; frightened, he fled to a hideout in the forests.

39.5 CHINESE INVESTIGATION OF THE MATTER

The Chinese officials in Moeng La (Simao) on seeing the arrival of the two brothers (Cao Mòm Suca Wanna and Cao Lamma Awuttha) immediately sent envoys to Chiang Yung to investigate [the situation]. They made a report to the *cung tu* at Moeng Sae.[291] He gave an order to the ruler of Sipsòng Panna led by Cao Chiang Ha (president of the Council of Nobles), which stated:

> Cao Maha Khanan and his sons conspire to usurp the throne and create disturbances in the land, [but they] are unsuccessful. [Moreover,] there is a letter calling for *cao saenwi fa* to return as ruler (*cao*). Phaya Long Cang and the other two men (i.e., Phaya

---

but according to MLC-LV1, s. 27.2, Cao Phom was Cao Nò Kham's younger brother, thus a great grandson of Tao Sao Wün.

290. As to the institution of *noe sanam*, the Council of Nobles, see the introduction, part 1, section 4.1 of this volume.

291. *Cung tu* is the Tai Lü transliteration of the Chinese *zongdu*, i.e., supreme commander. The full title in Chinese is *zongdu Yunnan junwu* 總督雲南軍務 (supreme commander of the military affairs of Yunnan), with the seat in Moeng Sae (Kunming). It is rendered as the Yunnan *zongdu* by Gao Lishi 1984, 125.

Long Cana Lücai, and Phaya Còm Kham) have all been killed. Cao Maha Khanan and his sons have created tremendous troubles, so we have to eradicate all of them, roots and branches.

39.6 CAO NÒ KHAM LAUNCHES ANOTHER ATTACK WITH THE HELP OF THE HILL TRIBES

Under the leadership of Cao Chiang Ha, all the provincial leaders of Sipsòng Panna cooperated to get rid of them (i.e., Cao Maha Khanan, his family, and relatives). Cao Nò Kham fled to hide in the forests, and learned that [the nobility of] Sipsòng Panna had exterminated his father and the entire family. Thus he fled to Moeng Pan (in Jinggu) and [from there to] Moeng Küng Ma (i.e., Gengma). He came back to mobilise all the Lua [and] the Kha Kui Pha Phüng[292] to fight [against the troops of] Sipsòng Panna. [However], he was defeated by the troops of Sipsòng Panna, who crushed the Kha Kui Pha Phüng forces.

39.7 CHIANG TUNG GIVES PROTECTION TO CAO NÒ KHAM

The ruler of Chiang Tung appointed Tao Bun Hoeng (Roeng) as leader to command fifty valourous soldiers to a village of the Kha Wa peoples to take Cao Nò Kham. This village was called Ban Chiang Can. They took Cao Nò Kham from amidst the troops of the Kha Kui, the Lua, and the Musoe. While the forces of Sipsòng Panna were fighting against the Kha Kui, Cao Nò Kham was brought to Chiang Tung; he was placed under the protection of the *cao fa* of Chiang Tung.[293]

39.8 CAO NÒ KHAM AND CAO MAHA PHOM ATTACK SIPSÒNG PANNA TROOPS

The *cao fa* of Chiang Tung then summoned Cao Maha Phom and Cao Nò Kham and ordered them to lead military forces to attack in a guerrilla manner the Sipsòng Panna troops at Moeng Laem; at the time Sipsòng Panna was fighting the Kha Kui. When the Sipsòng Panna [side] learned that Cao Nò Kham had already arrived in [the territory of] Sipsòng Panna and Moeng Laem, they came to fight against the Tai Khün at Ban Na Ngòi [in] Moeng Pan. The Tai Khün troops were defeated by the forces of Sipsòng Panna.[294]

---

292. Syntactically, it is not clear whether Pha Phüng (Th. ผาผึ้ง), lit., "bees rock", is an extension of Kha Kui (a Tibeto-Burman ethnic group of the mountains) or the name of a third ethnic group.

293. A similar account is given in MLC-LV1, s. 32.8.

294. See MLC-LV1, s. 32.9. The *Moeng Laem Chronicle* gives a different account of the battles. It emphasises that Moeng Laem tried to stay neutral in the conflict with the ruling house of Chiang Rung. Moeng Laem was nevertheless dragged into the quagmire and had to ward off a massive attack from Chiang Tung. The victory over the Tai Khün forces, however, is not ascribed to a military alliance with the Chiang Rung loyalists but to military support of the Wa who helped the Moeng Laem army repulse the invaders and even to seize border areas, such as Moeng Yang, from Chiang Tung. See *Moeng Laem Chronicle*, Long Co Pan-Bang Yang version, ff° 45/3–47/7.

39.9 CHINESE AND BURMESE ENVOYS ARE SENT TO END THE CIVIL WAR

The combined forces of Sipsòng Panna and Moeng Laem seized the advantage of victory to pursue [the enemies] to Moeng Ma. The news reached the Chinese and the Burmese sides. On the side of the Heavenly Court, the Chinese officials of Moeng La (Simao) sent the district magistrate Wei and the district magistrate Chen (Shen) [to Chiang Yung] to end the hostilities. [On the Burmese side,] the commander-in-chief of Moeng Nai sent *pyanki*[295] Nòratha (a senior official), the *sitkè*[296] of Chiang Tung to stop[297] them.

39.10 PEACE NEGOTIATIONS

The Chiang Rung forces were led by Cao Puttha Phommawongsa Mangkala Singhalaca of Moeng Chiang Ha, the military commander of Sipsòng Panna. The troops of Moeng Laem were led by Cao Puttha Phommawongsa Cotikalatha (Cotikaraṭha) Wòlalaca.[298] The forces of Chiang Tung were under the command of Phaya Long Khaek Compu. They all were servants of the lord-kings of the two halves of heaven (i.e., of China and Burma) and could not violate the orders (*ahmu-gyi*) of [their] two lords. Thus they discussed how to act according to the oath of allegiance that the three *müang* had sworn to the two parties. Chiang Tung had violated the oath, as it only listened to the words of Cao Nò Kham and sent troops to fight against Sipsòng Panna, [but this time] they would not be able to defy the orders of the royal representatives (*ahmu-gyi*) of both sides.[299]

39.11 PEACE TREATY WITH CHIANG RUNG, MOENG LAEM, AND CHIANG TUNG

The three parties reached an agreement. Five copies of the agreement were [made and] given [to the following parties]: one to the *ahmu-gyi* of the Chinese side and one to the *ahmu-gyi* of the Burmese side, who were the two witnesses; one copy for each of the Maha Nakòn (Sipsòng Panna and Chiang Tung) and [one copy] for [Moeng Laem]. The [two] *cao ahmu-gyi* of both sides (China and Burma) acted as witnesses [as well]. They all drank the water of the oath of allegiance at Wat Yang Pan [in] Moeng Ta Lò. They swore to the Three Gems and the witnesses were the deities, Lord Indra, Lord Brahma, the Garuda, the dragons (*nak*), the lords of all the four worlds (*tao tang si*), the princess of the earth (*nang thòlani*), and the guardian spirits of the three great cities (*maha nakòn*).

295. *Pyanki* (Tr. ปฺย่านคี) means "the great [personality who] translates" and derives from Burmese *pyan-gyi* (ပြန်ကြီး), *pyan* (ပြန်) meaning "to translate", and *gyi* (ကြီး) meaning "great".

296. The *cekkai* (Tr. เช็กคาย), called *sitkè* (စစ်ကဲ) in Burmese, was a police and military commander who assisted the provincial civilian governor. A *cekkai* or *sitkè* was based in the strategically most important Burmese vassal states such as Müang Nai, Chiang Mai, and Chiang Saen.

297. *Ham ta sita* (ห้ามทะซีตา). *Ham* (ห้าม) and *ta* (ทะ) are Tai words, and /`hsi/ (ဆီး) and /`ta/ (တား) are Burmese words. All these words mean "to block", "to prevent", "to obstruct".

298. Tr. เจ้าพุทธพรมฺมวงสาโชติกรฐวรราชา, cao buddha braḥma vaṃsā joti raṭha vara rājā.

299. Compare with MLC-LV1, s. 32.10.

39.12 CAO NÒ KHAM IS PLACED IN CUSTODY OF CAO CHIANG TUNG

The *ahmu-gyi* of the Chinese side asked for handing over Cao Nò Kham who was in Chiang Tung. [The authorities of] Chiang Tung replied:

> We all will take Cao Nò Kham in custody.

Then the Chinese side said:

> You say that you have taken Cao Nò Kham in custody. You shall not release him. Protect him well! Don't let him go out to destroy the country of Sipsòng Panna!

39.13 SUPPLEMENTARY TREATY SECURING CAO NÒ KHAM'S RIGHT

Chiang Tung gave his guarantee and promised to be loyal to all the three great cities:

> If, in the future, there is no heir in the [direct] lineage of the *saenwi fa*, then the five copies of treaty will be brought together. Cao Nò Kham will then be permitted to return to succeed to the throne.

As there was fear that an oral promise would lack solid proof, five copies of a [supplementary] treaty were made and one copy was delivered to the Chinese and one to the Burmese; the three parties each kept a copy as proof.

39.14 CAO NÒ KHAM IS SENT TO AVA

The *cao fa* of Chiang Tung ordered Cao Nò Kham to go to Ava to serve the Burmese king. At that time the king [of Burma] was absent. Thus the [highest-ranking] official (*khun*) of Ava issued a decree (*amintò*) on the eighth waning day of the first month[300] with the following content:

> Cao Nò Kham, who was the commander of the troops, should not depart for [Ava]. And the *upalaca* [together with his] mother and children should not go down [to Chiang Tung?]. Both parties should for the moment be kept in custody at Moeng Nai and wait until the king has returned to Ava. I will issue another decree when the king has returned to Ava.

39.15 CHINESE OFFICIALS ARE PREVENTED FROM GOING TO AVA

The chief Burmese *sitkè* thus ordered General Ye Suai Tòng Nòratha and Cao Phommawong [of] Moeng Cae to summon the *cao saenwi fa*. The *cao saenwi fa* did not

300. According to Li Fuyi, MLC-LV1, s. 32.11, the event occurred in CS 1201, making the day above correspond to Friday, 29 November 1893 (1201 Karttika 23).

come. The Chinese authorities (*cao hò*) of Moeng La (Simao) and Moeng Maen (Puer) recruited troops, placed them under the command of a *fu yae*[301] and sent them to Chiang Yung. They came with the Burmese *ahmu-gyi* and the ruler of Moeng U who had led [the delegation of] Sipsòng Panna and travelled to Chiang Tung. They said that they planned to go to Ava. Thus they wrote a letter to Moeng Nai to give their respects to the king of Ava. The reply from Ava said:

> According to the tradition, the Chinese guests never go to discuss matters with Ava. Tell them that they shall not come. Let them return. Let Cao Nò Kham depart for [the north]. Let the *upalaca*, his mother and [her] children (i.e., the *upalaca*'s younger siblings) come to Ava.

39.16 *UPALACA* TAO SOEN CONG ARRIVES AT AVA

On the fourteenth waxing of the seventh month,[302] the *upalaca* (i.e., Tao Soen Cong; in Pinyin, Dao Chengzong), his mother, and siblings reached Ava.

39.17 BURMESE TROOPS MARCH TO CHIANG YUNG

After the chief Burmese *sitkè* Kani Nguan had brought Cao Nò Kham to Chiang Tung, he appointed Nakham Mòng (Maung) So [and] Nakham Ne Myo[303] to lead a force of three thousand men to Chiang Yung.

39.18 CAO NÒ KHAM RETURNS TO CHIANG YUNG; ABORTIVE CHINESE-BURMESE PEACE NEGOTIATIONS

The *cao saenwi fa*, Suca Wanna, and his retainers (*kha phai tai*) crossed the Mekong and went to the eastern bank of the river. Only the rulers of Moeng Cae and Cao Moeng Hun went to welcome him (Cao Nò Kham). Cao Nò Kham [and his men] encamped at Chiang Lan and at the Buddhist monastery of Ban Puak Nòi at Chiang Tü on the western bank of the Mekong.

The Chinese officials of Moeng La (Simao) sent the rulers of Moeng Phong, Moeng La, Moeng Hing, Moeng Long (Luang), and Moeng Ham, as well as Phaya Long (Luang) Mangkala Paya, Phaya Long Sai to follow the vice-magistrate Laeo (Liao) who had commanded the troops to [Chiang Yung]; they encamped at the ferry crossing of Ta Kò at Ban Chiang Laeng. The Burmese [troops] crossed the Mekong and negotiated with

301. *Fu yae* is the Tai rendering of the Chinese *fuye* 副 爺, i.e., the respectful way of addressing the vice-magistrate or an imperial official.

302. According to Li Fuyi MCL-LV1, s. 32.11, the event occurred in CS 1201, making the day above would be equivalent to Saturday, 27 April 1839 (1201 Vaiśaka 14).

303. *Nakham* (นะข่าม) is probably the phonetic rendering of the Burmese word *nakhan*[*-daw*] (နားခံတော်), a title designating an officer who presented applications and petitions to the king for decision and relayed the king's orders to persons concerned.

the Chinese side for two months, but no agreement was reached. [Finally] the Chinese authorities (*cao hò*) and the Sipsòng Panna forces withdrew.

39.19 BURMESE-SUPPORTED CAO NÒ KHAM BECOMES THE *SAENWI FA*; EXECUTION OF OPPONENTS

At that time, Cao Nò Kham and the Burmese [mistakenly] thought that the Heavenly Court and Sipsòng Panna were cowards, and had been routed. Carried away by their success, they encouraged Cao Nò Kham to ascend the throne in the palace and had Phaya Long Sing, the headman of Chiang Yung, as well as Phaya Long Sulaye Paeng of Moeng Laem, and an official (*amat*) of Moeng Phong executed.

39.20 RANSOM DEMANDED

The officials (*tao khun*) of Sipsòng Panna whom the *upalaca* had entrusted to get the money to ransom them [were also detained by the Burmese troops stationing in Chiang Yung]. For one headman they demanded two *khan* (8.8 taels) and for one suite six *khan* (26.4 taels).[304] Thus the goods and horses of the Chinese traders who went to Chiang Yung to do business were confiscated by the Tai (i.e., the officials of the *upalaca*); some of the Chinese traders were also killed.[305]

39.21 EXPULSION OF CAO NÒ KHAM AND HIS BURMESE ALLIES

As a result, the Chinese officials in Moeng La (Simao) and Moeng Maen (Puer) immediately ordered the rulers of Moeng Phong and Moeng La [Tai] (เมิงล้า) to lead the Sipsòng Panna troops to drive—in violation of all custom and tradition—Cao Nò Kham as well as the Burmese, the Tai Khün, and the [Tai of Moeng] Yang out of Chiang Yung. [The Chinese and Tai] pursued [Cao Nò Kham] and encamped at Chiang Tung. Moreover, a document was prepared and it was forwarded to the king of Burma via Cao Moeng Nai.[306] The king of Burma learned about [this]; thus [His Majesty] had the *upalaca*, his mother, and his siblings detained in the royal guardhouse (*lacawat*, Skt. rājavati).

304. The same amount is recorded in Gao Lishi 1984, 127. But according to MLC-LV1, 42, s. 32.26, the amount of ransom demanded for a headman was one *còi* and two *khan* (ca. 52.8 taels) of silver and for a soldier six *khan* (26.4 taels). The amount given in Li Fuyi is more plausible.

305. Here it remains unclear as to who robbed the Chinese traders. In the revised version of the Moeng Lü Chronicle, transcribed and translated by Renoo Wichasin (2001, 308–9), it is said that the officials sent by the *upalaca* had taken money to redeem him. However, Cao Nò Kham imprisoned them and ordered people to rob the Chinese traders. This narrative seems to be clearer and is better suited to the context. Later, Cao Nò Kham was accused of having put the country into political disorder. According to Gao Lishi 1984, 127, it was the Burmese who robbed the Chinese traders doing business in Chiang Rung. The same is recorded in MLC-LV1, 42, s. 32.26.

306. Moeng Nai (Burmese: Monè), situated on the right bank of the Salween, was one of the largest *müang* in the southern Shan region. In the second half of the nineteenth century it had a substantial minority of ethnic Burmese. It was from here that the Burmese controlled the southern Shan states.

39.22 ACQUITTAL OF THE *UPALACA* AND HIS MEN

Later, the Burmese military commander Mu Pakhan Maeng,[307] who was faithful, learned the truth:

> The *saenwi fa* is not guilty; [Cao Nò Kham and the Burmese troops], beyond being unable to care for the country, also robbed and killed the people. Thus the people hate them. If someone has mismanaged the affairs, it is the Burmese troops and Cao Nò Kham.

[The king of Burma] sent the chief *sitkè* Mòng (Maung) Kintuk[308] as commander-in-chief to lead a force of two thousand Komui (Khamu?) and march to Chiang Tung.[309] After an investigation was conducted the *saenwi fa* was acquitted. The chief culprits were the Burmese emissaries. An order was given to arrest *sitkè* Kani Nguan, Nakham Mòng (Maung) So, Nakham Ne Myo, Nakham Canthabuli,[310] and Mòng [Ta] Li. [They] were escorted to the royal guardhouse. The *upalaca*, his mother and siblings, as well as all officials (*amat*) were acquitted and released from the royal guardhouse. They remained in Ava.

39.23 TAO COEN CONG SENDS CAO MOENG U-NÜA TO OFFER TRIBUTE TO BURMA

The *cao saenwi fa*, who was the ruler of Sipsòng Panna, appointed the ruler of Moeng U-Nüa to lead a delegation taking tribute gifts (*khüang kantò*) as well as one dark-skinned horse with [...] eyes and one white horse with black eyes, and two elephants, via Moeng Laem through Mang Loen, and Saenwi (Moeng Fòng/Pòng), down to Sipò (Hsipaw). The Burmese king sent an *ahmu-gyi* (emissary) to go and fetch the *kantò* (tribute) at Sipò. He divided the tribute gifts into two parts [and] took one part [together with] an elephant to Moeng Nai. Afterwards they were brought to Chiang Tung and entrusted to Cao Nò Kham to deliver them [to the Burmese king].[311]

39.24 TAO SOEN CONG AND HIS MOTHER OFFER TRIBUTE TO THE BURMESE KING

Then the ruler of Moeng U, who was the leader, went down to Ava, taking with him [the other part of the] tribute gifts to present to the *upalaca*, his mother, and children. The *upalaca*, his mother, and his siblings offered the gifts to the Burmese king, but the king said neither good nor bad.

See Scott and Hardiman 1901, 431–37 (part 1, vol. 2); cf. Grabowsky and Turton 2003, 218–19. The Cao Moeng Nai was probably the brother-in-law of Tao Cao Then. See section 34.2 above.

307. Personal Burmese name unidentifiable.

308. Personal Burmese name unidentifiable.

309. In MLC-LV1, 43, s. 32.28, it is stated: "[...] reinforcing his troops with two thousand men. In the sixth month of the *ka mao* year, CS 1205 (Daoguang 23, AD 1843), they reached Chiang Tung. Gao Lishi 1984, 127, s. 39.33, records two thousand soldiers.

310. As to the meaning of the Burmese terms *sitkè* and *nakham/nakhan-daw*, see nn. 296 and 303 above.

311. See MLC-LV1, s. 32.29; Gao Lishi 1984, 127, s. 39.34.

39.25 THE BURMESE KING REJECTS THE TRIBUTE GIFTS; CAO NÒ KHAM IS ASKED TO PAY TRIBUTE IN PERSON

Then the *cao saenwi fa* sent a delegation led by the ruler of Chiang Tòng and Phaya Long Khoen [of] Moeng Cae to bring a horse with a yellow head and four white legs, as well as a cow with three eyes to Chiang Tung, whence through Moeng Nai to Ava. The king of Burma did not grant permission to [accept the tribute] offered. He ordered the delegation to return. Cao Nò Kham was ordered to pay his respect and to offer tribute gifts personally.

39.26 EXECUTION OF THE FOUR CULPRITS

Cao Nò Kham, who was the leader, and the ruler of Moeng Cae[312] brought the tribute gifts to Ava and presented them to the king of Burma. [The king of Burma] gave two elephants to the *upalaca*, his mother, and younger siblings. The *sitkè* Kani Nguan died one month [after he had been put into prison]. Nakham Mòng (Maung) So, Nakham Canthabuli, Nakham Ne Myo, and Mòng (Maung) Ta Li were brought to Moeng Nai under escort. At the order of the king of Burma, the four men were executed at the border of Moeng Nai for the crime of creating unrest in Sipsòng Panna.

39.27 CAO SILI WANNA (TAO SOEN CONG) MARRIES IN MOENG LONG AND THE BIRTH OF CAO MÒM SÒ

Not long after, Cao Sili Wanna, the *upalaca* (i.e., Tao Soen Cong), who was the leader of all the officials (*amat*) of Sipsòng Panna, [in the company of] his mother and children, returned with his followers to Sipsòng Panna. Upon arrival at Moeng Long (Luang), he took a wife who bore him a son. [The prince] was called Cao Mòm Khung Kham for his purple skin (*phio sò*). After [the prince] had grown up he was called Cao Mòm Sò.[313]

39.28 CAO MÒM SUCA WANNA (TAO COEN CONG) ADOPTS CAO MÒM SÒ

As Cao Mòm Suca Wanna had no son,[314] he adopted his younger brother's son. [When the prince] was young he became a monk. At the age of eighteen, he went to Ava. A year later he left Ava and returned to [Sipsòng Panna] after becoming a layman again.

39.29 MUSLIM UNREST AND ASSASSINATION OF CAO MÒM SUCA WANNA

In the reign of Cao Mòm Suca Wanna (i.e., Tao Coen Cong) a war between the Chinese Muslims (*hò phasi*) and the [forces] loyal to the emperor of China (*hò long*) broke out. The [forces of the] emperor of China won. Cao Mòm Suca Wanna was ordered to appear

312. It is unclear why the ruler of Moeng Cae, who had quarelled with Cao Nò Kham, should have brought the tribute gifts together with Cao Nò Kham.

313. His Chinese name is Tao Cin An (in Pinyin, Dao Jun'an 刀鈞安). See section 40.1 below; and MLC-SV1, 63, s. 36. See also Gao Lishi 1984, 127, s. 39.38.

314. However, according to Gao Lishi 1984, 128, s. 39.42, Cao Mòm Suca Wanna had a young son called Cao Mòm Saeng.

personally [before the Chinese authorities]. On the way to Moeng Hing (Puwen) he was assassinated by Muslims at Kat Han (market). His body was carried back to Moeng Yang Nòi and buried on the foothills of Dòi Ai Haeng Long. He was the thirty-ninth ruler of the dynasty.

39.30 UNREST IN SIPSÒNG PANNA; DEATH OF CAO LAMMA AWUTTHA (TAO SOEN CONG)

In the reign of Cao Mòm Suca Wanna when he was still the ruler, Cao Mahacai of Moeng Phong launched an attack [on Chiang Yung], causing much unrest in Sipsòng Panna, and the country (*banmüang*) was depopulated. The *cao upalaca* was killed by the military commander (*khun han*) of Moeng Phong.

40. CAO MÒM SÒ (CAO MÒM KHUNG KHAM), R. 1863–1879

40.1 THE FORTIETH RULER

Cao Mòm Sò (Cao Mòm Khung Kham), Chinese name Tao Cin An,[315] succeeded his adoptive father (i.e., uncle) to the throne in the year CS 1225 (AD 1864 sic/1863) at the age of twenty. He was on the throne sixteen years, lived to the age of thirty-six, and died in the year CS 1241 (AD 1879).

40.2 CAO MÒM SAENG USURPS THE THRONE AND KILLS CAO MÒM SÒ

Later his younger brother Cao Mòm Saeng[316] usurped the throne. He led warriors to chase Cao Mòm Sò out of the palace. Cao Mòm Sò fled to the monastery of Wat Ho (Hua) Nòng[317] in Moeng Ham, Cao Mòm Saeng sent warriors to pursue him and had his elder brother (in fact, cousin) killed at Wat Ho (Hua) Nòng.

{Later his younger brother Cao Mòm Saeng usurped the throne. Together with Khun Han and Phaya Long he led warriors to chase [Cao Mòm Sò] out of the palace. Cao Mòm Sò fled to take refuge with the ruler of Moeng Cae. He stayed at Wat Ban Sa. When Khun Han and Cao Mòm Saeng learned of this, they came to fight him at Wat Ban Sa. [Cao Mòm Sò] fled with his family on a boat to Wat Ban Ho Nòng in Moeng Ham. Cao Mòm Saeng ordered Khun Han to kill [Cao Mòm Sò] at Wat Ban Ho Nòng.}[318]

{Later his younger brother Cao Mòm Saeng usurped the throne. He led warriors to chase Cao Mòm Sò out of the palace. Cao Mòm Sò fled to the Wat Ho Nòng Buddhist temple in Moeng Ham. Cao Mòm Saeng sent warriors to pursue him and had his elder

315. In Pinyin, Dao Jun'an 刀鈞安. See MLC-SV1, 63, s. 36.

316. According to MLC-LV2, Cao Mòm Suca Wanna had no son. Cao Mòm Saeng's Chinese name is Tao Sin Fu. See section 41.1 below.

317. In Dao Shuren 1989, this is Wat Ban Hua Nòng.

318. Taken from Dao Shuren 1989.

brother (in fact cousin) killed in the Buddhist temple of Ho Nòng. This was a fratricidal war and power struggle.}[319]

40.3 BÒ TIAN AND BÒ PET ARE SOLD TO THE FRENCH

In the reign of Cao Mòm Sò there was a Chinese official called magistrate Taeo (Tiao), who was from Laengkwang.[320] He sold Bò Tian and Bò Pet, in the domain of Sipsòng Panna, to the French. The territory (*nam din*) belonged to Moeng La. The people were *lek nòi* of Moeng La.

40.4 SOCIAL UNREST AND REVOLTS AGAINST THE CHINESE

During the reign of Cao Mòm Sò chaos prevailed in Sipsòng Panna. There were three armed rebellions against the Heavenly Court, supported by the double U (i.e., Moeng U-Nüa and Moeng U-Tai) to the east of the river. However, none of the three were victorious. The three wars against the double Guang (i.e., Guangdong and Guangxi) caused the people in the east of the river to flee. Some of them fled to Moeng Kaeo Nòi (Vietnam), Moeng Lao (Laos), and Moeng Thai (Thailand). As a result, the villages were depopulated and the arable lands deserted. There was also the uprising of Cao Mòm Nòi of Moeng La, which also led to war and unrest. The people of Moeng Hing (Puwen) fled in chaos to Moeng La and Moeng Hing became depopulated. The [rest of the] people (lit., "families") left the *müang*. [Cao Mòm Sò] was the fortieth ruler of the dynasty.

41. CAO MÒM SAENG (TAO SIN FU), R. 1880–1883

41.1 THE FORTY-FIRST RULER

Cao Mòm Saeng, Chinese name Tao Sin Fu, succeeded his elder brother (cousin) to the throne in the year CS 1242 (AD 1881 sic/1880) at the age of eighteen. He was on the throne three years, lived to the age of twenty-one, and died in the year CS 1245 (AD 1883).

41.2 MOENG LA RAISES TROOPS AND KILLS CAO MÒM SAENG

During his reign, Cao Mòm Saeng killed Cao Ya Long of Moeng La. As a result, they assembled the troops of the various *müang* in the east of the Mekong under the leadership of Moeng La to attack Cao Mòm Saeng. They had him killed in the north of the village of Ban Sa.[321] Cao Mòm Saeng had no son.

319. Taken from Gao Lishi 1984, 128, s. 40.2.

320. The magistrate Daeo refers to Dao daren 刀大人 (i.e., magistrate Dao). Langkwan is obviously the Tai Lü rendering of the Chinese Liangguang (lit., "two *guang*"), the generic abbreviation of Guangdong and Guangxi Provinces. See Gao Lishi 1984, 128, s. 40.3.

321. According to Gao Lishi 1984, 128, s. 41.2, Ban Sa is a village in the district of Chiang Rung.

41.3 MOENG U-NÜA AND MOENG U-TAI ARE SOLD TO THE FRENCH

During the reign of Cao Mòm Saeng, the Magistrate (*tayin*, i.e., Ch. *taren* 大 人) Taeo (Tiao 刁) sold the double Moeng U (เมิง ๒ อู, i.e., Moeng U-Nüa and U-Tai) to the French for 12,000 "thorn-headed" piastres.[322]

41.4 CAO MÒM SÒ'S DAUGHTER

Cao Mòm Sò had a daughter called Sa Keng (Kiang) Kham who was married to Cao Moeng Ham.

41.5 THE THREE SONS OF CAO MÒM SÒ IN CHIANG TUNG

Cao Mòm Sò had three sons: the eldest son was called Cao Mòm Kham Lü (Tao Soen Oen), the second son was called Cao Mòm Phomma, and the third son was called Cao Mòm Còm Moeng.[323] When Cao Mòm Saeng (Tao Sin Fu) committed a crime against their father [Cao Mòm Sò], one official (*khun*) sent [the three boys] to Chiang Tung [to put them] under the protection of the *cao fa*. When they had grown up, Cao Mòm Saeng died. As there was no heir from the direct lineage to succeed to the throne of Sipsòng Panna, [the nobles] looked for a direct descendant of the *saenwi fa* and learned that Cao Mòm Sò still had three sons living in Chiang Tung. [They] then brought his eldest son Cao Mòm Kham Lü back to be ruler and succeed [to the throne].[324]

{Cao Mòm Saeng succeeded to the throne in the *kot si* year, CS 1242 (AD 1880), at the age of eighteen. He was on the throne three years, and was age twenty-one when he died. As for the ruler's death, Cao Mòm Soek of Moeng La (เมิงลา) came to kill Cao Han Long of Moeng La (เมิงล้า). The nobles (*khun*) and commoners (*phai tai*) of Moeng La (เมิงล้า) on the east bank of the Mekong were united. The military leader (*cao soek*) of Moeng La (เมิงลา) came to kill Cao Ya Long of Moeng La (เมิงล้า). Cao Mòm Saeng was the mastermind of that plan. Thus they fought against Cao Mòm Saeng. Cao Mòm Saeng sought protection in Chiang Tung. Cao Khun Han captured him at Ho (Hua) Ban Sa and killed him there.

During the reign of [Cao] Mòm Saeng a Chinese called Taeo Tayin Laengkwang (i.e.,

---

322. *Man ho nam* (Tr. หมันหัวหนาม), rupees with the effigy of the French "Marianne" on the front side of the coin, wearing a crown. The *man* (หมัน), originally a unit of measurement of weights, became the name of the Indochinese piastre in northern Laos. The French in Indochina introduced a silver piastre in 1885. It weighed 27.2156 grammes (pure silver of 0.9000 fine). See www.viettouch.com/numis. The piastre at the turn of the century was therefore the close equivalent (in silver weight) to the Mexican-Spanish dollar and the US silver dollar, and equal to approximately 1.81 Thai baht (15 g silver). The amount of money paid by the French to the Chinese government for the cession of the two Moeng U is confirmed in the The Chronicle of the Forty Rulers of *Panna* Moeng Hai Cao Solawong Maha Buntan version (f° 52/4).

323. According to MLC-SV1, 63, s. 36, Cao Mòm Sò (i.e., Dao Jun'an or Cao Mòm Khung Kham) had four sons: Tao Soen Oen (Dao Cheng'en) or Cao Mòm Kham Lü, Cao Phom[ma], Cao Còm Moeng, and Cao Khòng (Khung) Kham.

324. As for a very similar account compare with The Chronicle of the Forty Rulers of *Panna* Moeng Hai, Cao Solawong Maha Buntan version, f° 41/5–10.

Governor Dao of Guangdong and Guangxi) illegally sold the territory of Sipsòng Panna. He sold [Moeng] U-Tai and [Moeng] U-Nüa to the French at the price of 12,000 "thorn-headed" piastres. Cao Mòm Saeng had no children. At that time [Sipsòng Panna] had no ruler. Thus the nobles (*khun*) of Sipsòng Panna convened to discuss [the political situation] and made a list of the members of the royal dynasty. They learned that Cao Mòm Sò's daughter, whose name was Nang Keng Kham, had become the daughter-in-law of [the ruler of] Moeng Ham. [Cao] Mòm Sò had three sons. The eldest son was called Cao Mòm Kham Lü; the second son was called Cao Mòm Phomma; the third son was called Cao Mòm Còm Moeng. When [Cao] Mòm Saeng committed a crime against their father [Cao Mòm Sò], the three sons were brought by an official of a *panna* to Tu Long Fa Hao; they were placed in the custody of the *cao fa* of Chiang Tung, where they grew up. When the officials of Sipsòng Panna learned that [these princes] were in Chiang Tung, they delivered tribute gifts (*bannakan*) to the *cao fa* of Chiang Tung and asked the eldest [of the three princes], [Cao Mòm] Kham Lü, to return [to Chiang Rung] to become ruler. The thirty-sixth (thirty-seventh) generation ruler [of the dynasty] had come to an end.}[325]

42. CAO MÒM KHAM LÜ OR TAO SOEN OEN (DAO CHENG' EN), R. 1884–1924

42.1 THE FORTY-SECOND RULER

Cao Mòm Kham Lü, Chinese name Tao Soen Oen (Dao Cheng'en), succeeded to the throne in the year CS 1246 (AD 1885 sic/1884) at the age of twenty. He was on the throne forty years, lived to the age of sixty, and died in the year 1286 (AD 1924). He was the forty-second ruler of the dynasty.

42.2 THE FIRST WIFE NANG MÒM WAEN TIP FROM CHIANG TUNG

After Cao Mòm Kham Lü had succeeded to the throne, he married the elder sister of the *cao fa* of Chiang Tung, called Nang Mòm Waen Tip. He had eight wives.

42.3 THE SECOND WIFE NANG CAN HÒM AND HER CHILDREN

The second wife was Nang Can Hòm, who bore [him] three sons and two daughters: The eldest son was called Cao Mòm Suwanna Phakhang (Tao Tung Laeng, i.e., Dao Dongliang) (eldest son); the second son was called Cao Mòm Saeng Moeng (Tao Tung Thin, i.e., Dao Dongting) (the sixth son); the third son was called Cao Mòm Mani Kham (Tao Tung Sin, i.e., Dao Dongxin) (the ninth son). The eldest daughter was called Nang Mòm Pu and was married to Cao Moeng Long (Luang); the second daughter was called Nang Mòm Yong (Yuang) (the fourth daughter) and was married to Cao Moeng Yu.

325. This is taken from Dao Shuren 1989. According to Gao Lishi 1984, 128, s. 41.4, they were the three sons of Cao Mòm Sò's daughter.

42.4 THE THIRD WIFE NANG LÒT AND HER CHILDREN

The third wife was Nang Lòt, who bore [him] three sons and three daughters: The eldest son was Cao Mòm Kang (Tao Tung Kwang, i.e., Dao Donggang) (the second son); the second son was Cao Mòm Kham Cün (also called Cao Mòm Mahacai) (Tao Tung Khwa, i.e., Dao Donghua) (the third son); the third son was Cao Mòm Còm Moeng (also called Cao Mòm Tui) (the fourth son). The eldest daughter was Mòm Còm Fòng (the third daughter); the second daughter was Mòm Sili Wanna (the fifth daughter); the third daughter was Mòm Nuan (Non) Ta (the seventh daughter).

42.5 THE FOURTH WIFE NANG KÒNG AND HER CHILDREN

The fourth wife was Nang Kòng,[326] who bore [him] two sons and three daughters: The eldest son was Cao Mòm Khòng Kham (also called Cao Mòm La) (Tao Tung Cai, i.e., Dao Dongcai) (the fifth son); the second son was Cao Mòm Khung Kham (Tao Tung Yi, i.e., Dao Dongyu) (the seventh son). The eldest daughter was Mòm Bo Kham (the second daughter); the second daughter was [Nang] Mòm Khan Kham (the sixth daughter), and the third daughter was [Nang] Mòm Pem (the eighth daughter).

42.6 THE FIFTH WIFE NANG BO KHAM AND THE SIXTH WIFE NANG IN KHAM AND THEIR CHILDREN

The fifth wife was Nang Bo Kham, who bore [him] one son called Cao Mòm Phomma (Tao Tung Sün, i.e., Dao Dongchen) (the eighth son). He was also called Cao Mòm Maha Khu (Khru).

The sixth wife was Nang In Kham, who bore [him] a daughter, called Nang Mòm Bo Kham (the ninth daughter) and also called Mòm Mo. She was blind and did not marry.

42.7 THE SEVENTH WIFE NANG LAO AND THE EIGHTH WIFE NANG TAN

The seventh wife was Nang Lao[327] [who was barren]. The eighth wife was Nang Tan, who was barren.

42.8 THE NINE SONS AND NINE DAUGHTERS OF CAO MÒM KHAM LÜ

Later Cao Mòm Kham Lü divorced [Nang] Mòm Waen Tip, who returned to Chiang Tung. His nine sons are listed [below] according to their seniority in age, without regard [for the status] of the wife they were born to; likewise for his daughters.

The eldest son Cao Mòm Suwanna Phakhang, Chinese name Tao Tung Laeng (Dao Dongliang), succeeded his father to the throne.

The second son Cao Mòm Kang, Chinese name Tao Tung Kwang (Dao Donggang), [was the vice-*saenwi fa* (*upalaca*)].

The third son Cao Mòm Kham Cün, also called Cao Mòm Mahacai, Chinese name Tao

326. According to Dao Shuren 1989, she was called Nang Koang Saeng.

327. According to Dao Shuren 1989, she was called Nang Tan Kham.

Tung Khwa (Dao Donghua), lived on his principality in Moeng Phong and died in Moeng Phong without a son.

The fourth son Cao Mòm Còm Moeng (also called [Cao] Mòm Tui) lived on his principality in Moeng Hun.

The fifth son Cao Mòm Khòng Kham (also called [Cao] Mòm La), Chinese name Tao Tung Sai (sic, Cai) (Dao Dongcai), shared a principality with his elder brother in Moeng Hun.

The sixth son Cao Mòm Saeng Moeng, Chinese name Tao Tung Thin (Dao Dongting), lived on his principality in Moeng Ham until Liberation (AD 1950).

The seventh son was Cao Mòm Khung Kham and his Chinese name was Tao Tung Yi (Dao Dongyu).

The eighth son was Cao Mòm Phomma[328] and his Chinese name was Tao Tung Sün (sic) (Dao Dongchen).

The ninth son, Cao Mòm Mani Kham, whose Chinese name was Tao Tung Sin (Dao Dongxin), lived on his principality in Moeng Ham seven years. The people of Moeng Ham revolted against him. He was forced to return to Chiang Rung. His sixth elder brother Cao Mòm Saeng [Moeng] was sent to take his place.

The eldest daughter [Nang] Mòm Pu was married to Cao Moeng Long.

The second daughter [Nang] Mòm Bo Kham died of illness [when she was young].

The third daughter [Nang] Mòm Còm Fòng was married to Cao Moeng (the aboriginal official of Chiang Lò).

The fourth daughter [Nang] Mòm Yong (Yuang) was married to Cao Moeng Yu (in Chiang Tung). She was divorced later, and came to stay with her elder sister (no. 1) at Moeng Long. She then married Phaya Long Saeng Moeng of Moeng Long.

The fifth daughter [Nang] Mòm Sili Wanna was married to Cao Moeng Cae.

The sixth daughter [Nang] Mòm Khan Kham was married to Cao Moeng Nun.

The seventh daughter [Nang] Mòm Nuan (Non) Ta was married to Cao Moeng Hai.

The eighth daughter [Nang] Mòm Pem was married to the younger brother of Cao Moeng Hai, Cao Kang.

The ninth daughter Mòm Bo Kham[329] was blind and did not marry.

Cao Mòm Kham Lü had a total of nine daughters and nine sons.

42.9 THE DIVORCED WIFE MOBILISES TROOPS TO ATTACK HER FORMER HUSBAND

The princess of Chiang Tung, the divorced wife of Cao Mòm Kham Lü, twice mobilised troops to attack Sipsòng Panna. During the later attack, Cao Mòm Kham Lü avoided [the

328. In Gao Lishi 1984, 129, s. 42.9, he was also called Cao Mòm Phomma. But he was also called Cao Mòm Maha Khu (Khru). See section 42.6 above. In MLC-SV1, 63, s. 37, he was also known as Cao Mòm Maha Khu (Khru).

329. She was also called Mòm Mo. See section 42.6 above.

onslaught] by going to hide in Xiting (Gao Lishi: Xiding 西定) and Cangdang (Gao Lishi: Zhanglan 章瀾) of Moeng Cae.

42.10 CAO MÒM KHAM LÜ BREAKS HIS PROMISE

Previously the *cao phaendin* (sovereign) made a promise: If [Cao Moeng Cae] cared for and protected the *cao phaendin* well, Xiting and Cangdang would be granted to Cao Moeng Cae. Later, when the unrest had been pacified and [Cao Mòm Kham Lü] had again ascended the throne of *cao phaendin*, he had no intention of keeping his promise.

42.11 CHINA AND CHIANG RUNG SEND TROOPS AGAINST MOENG CAE

Eventually a war broke out in which Chiang Rung lost against Moeng Cae.[330] The *cao phaendin* submitted a letter reporting this to the Chinese governor in Moeng Sae (Kunming). [The Chinese governor] sent soldiers to reinforce the *cao phaendin* in the fight against Moeng Cae. The ruler of Moeng Cae then established his camps at the fortified town (*wiang*) of Chiang Coeng. The troops of Sipsòng Panna [and the Chinese troops] attacked Moeng Cae. They fought for three years, but neither [side] could gain a victory. At that time the ruler of Moeng Sae (Kunming), called Thang Yaen Suai (Marshal Tang),[331] ordered three high officials, namely Li Ta Yin, Ma Ta Yin, and Khwang Ta Yin,[332] to lead an army down to help the *cao phaendin* fighting Moeng Cae and Chiang Coeng. However, they could not win.

42.12 KHÒ SU SIN (KE SHUXUN) AND THE POLL TAX

Later another high official called Khò Su Sin (Ke Shuxun)[333] was sent [to Sipsòng Panna]. He defeated Moeng Cae and Chiang Coeng and was appointed general administrator and stationed in Chiang Rung to administer the whole [domain of] Sipsòng Panna. After this, a household tax (*ngün ho hoen*, a kind of poll tax) was imposed. Each household was to pay two piastres (*man*) and four *hao*. Later [the household tax] increased yearly.

42.13 *UPALACA* CAO MÒM PHOMMA AND HIS FAMILY

After Cao Mòm Kham Lü's younger brother Cao Mòm Phomma (i.e., the second son of Cao Mòm Sò, see 41.5 above) had been promoted to *upalaca* (viceroy), he departed

330. As to the revolt of Moeng Cae, see Dao Shuren's record of the "Cow's Cushion War" of 1913 (following the translation of MLC-LV2), cf. the introduction, part 1, section 11 of this volume.

331. *Yaen suai* is the Tai Lü rendering of the Chinese *yuanshuai* 元帥 (marshal). According to Gao Lishi 1984, 130, s. 42.12, he was Tang yuanshuai 唐元帥.

332. *Ta yin* is the Chinese rendering of the Chinese *daren* 大人, a formal way of addressing the district magistrate. According to Gao Lishi 1984, 130, s. 42.12, they were Magistrate Li 李, Magistrate Ma 馬, and Magistrate Huang 黃.

333. Ke Shuxun 柯樹勳 (1862–1926), the general departmental chief (*zong juzhang* 總局長) of the Frontier Headquarters of Pusi. He was the author of the *Treatise of Pusi Frontier* (*Pusi yanbian zhi lüe*). He was the father-in-law of Li Fuyi (born in 1901).

for Chiang Tung to assume [the position of] Cao Moeng Khak (i.e., governor of Moeng Khak) and married a wife who bore [him] a daughter called Nang Nói. After Nang Nòi was married, she also gave birth to a daughter called Nang Keng (Kiang). The *cao upalaca* (i.e., Cao Mòm Phomma) died in Moeng Khak.

42.14 CAO MÒM CÒM MOENG AND HIS FAMILY

Cao Mòm Còm Moeng (the fourth son, also called Cao Mòm Tui) defected to Chiang Tung. Later he was appointed the ruler (*cao moeng*) of Lang Sa Long and married a Burmese girl and also took a Moeng Khün girl. The Burmese wife bore him two sons: the eldest son was called Cao Mòm Thun Òng and the second son was called Cao Mòm Thun Cing. The [Moeng] Khün wife bore him five sons: the eldest son called Cao Long, the second son called Cao Kò, the third son Cao Tòng, the fourth son called Cao Num, and the fifth son called Cao Sing Cai. All five sons stayed in Chiang Tung. Cao Mòm Còm Moeng married the younger sister of the *cao fa* of Moeng Sing.[334] [They] had two sons in Moeng Sing whose names are not known. Cao Mòm Còm Moeng [finally] went to Chiang Tung where he died.

42.15 BÒ TEN (TIAN) SALT MINE IS SOLD TO THE FRENCH

During the reign of Cao Mòm Kham Lü the Chinese [official] Foei Ta Yin[335] came to sell a salt mine called Bò Ten (Tian) for three thousand "thorn-headed" piastres to the French.

43. CAO MÒM SUWANNA PHAKHANG OR TAO TUNG LAENG (DAO DONGLIANG), R. 1927–1943

43.1 THE FORTY-THIRD RULER

Cao Mòm Suwanna Phakhang, whose Chinese name is Tao Tung Laeng (Dao Dongliang), succeeded his father to the throne in the year CS 1289 (AD 1929 sic/ 1927), on the ninth waxing day of the twelfth month,[336] at the age of forty-one. He was on the throne sixteen years, lived to the age of fifty-seven, and died in the year CS 1305 (AD 1944 sic/1943), on the second waning day of the eighth month.[337]

334. The marriage took place in May 1897. The Chiang Khaeng Chronicle records: "On an auspicious day during the seventh month (covering the period from 2 May to 31 May 1897), the royal father, the royal mother, the nobles, the councillors, and the dignitaries came together to celebrate the marriage of the young couple. As to the son of Cao Sani Fa (i.e., *xuanwei shi*), ruler of Chiang Rung, his name was Cao Maha Sali Còm Müang." See CKC-WTP, f° 64/7–10, Grabowsky and Renoo 2008, 163.

335. According to Gao Lishi 1984, 130, the Chinese official was District Magistrate Fei (Fei daren 費大人).

336. 1289 Asvina 9 = Wednesday, 5 October 1927.

337. 1305 Jyestha 17 = Saturday, 19 June 1943.

43.2 CAO MÒM SUWANNA PHAKHANG'S CHILDREN

Cao Mòm [Suwanna] Phakhang had two sons. The eldest son was called Cao Mòm In Moeng (Tao Si Tae; in Pinyin, Dao Shide), and the second son was called Cao Mòm Mahacai (Dao Shigui). He adopted the son of his younger brother Cao Mòm Saeng Moeng (no. 6 son) named Cao Mòm Kham Lü, whose sinicised name was Tao Sü Sin (Dao Shixun). Cao Mòm [Suwanna] Phakhang had three daughters: The eldest daughter, called Mòm Patumma, was married to the ruler of Chiang Lò; the second daughter, called Mòm Waen, was married to the ruler of Chiang Tòng. The third daughter, called Mòm Kham Mun, was married to the ruler of Moeng La.

43.3 CAO MÒM SUWANNA PHAKHANG AND HIS THREE WIVES

Cao Mòm Suwanna Phakhang, the *saenwi fa*, took a princess of Moeng La (เมิงลา) called Sa Thao Kham as his principal wife. They had two daughters. The eldest daughter was called Mòm Patumma and the second daughter was called Mòm Kham Mun.

The second wife was Nang Keng (Kiang) who had one daughter called Mòm Waen.

The third wife, called Nang Tan, was his stepmother.[338] After his father's death, he married his stepmother and she bore [him] two sons: The eldest son was Cao Mòm In Moeng, whose Chinese name was Tao Si Tae (Dao Shide). The second son was [Cao] Mòm Mahacai, whose Chinese name was Tao Si Kui (Dao Shigui).

44. CAO MÒM KHAM LÜ OR TAO SÜ SIN (DAO SHIXUN), R. 1947–1950

44.1 THE FORTY-FOURTH RULER

Cao Mòm Kham Lü, whose Chinese name is Dao Shixun (Tao Sü Sin), succeeded to the throne in the year CS 1309 (AD 1947). On the eighth waxing day of the fourth Tai month,[339] the water spreading ceremony of the coronation was performed and he was promoted to *saenwi fa*. At succession, he was twenty-two years old (sic), and ruled more than a year before he went to study Chinese in Moeng Sae (Kunming). The head of the Council of Nobles (*tao phaya noe sanam*) acted as the regent. He did not return after graduation. At that time the country (*banmüang*) (i.e., China) was liberated.[340] He married a Chinese woman and lived [with her] in China (Moeng Hò). At present he is still living in China. From the times of Phaya Coeng [to the end of the dynasty], there were altogether forty-four rulers in the dynasty and more than eight hundred years have passed.

338. She was the eighth wife of Tao Soen Oen (Cao Mòm Kham Lü). See section 42.7 above.

339. 1307 Magha 8 = Saturday, 9 February 1946.

340. Sipsòng Panna fell under communist rule in late 1949 and early 1950.

{Cao Mòm Kham Lü, Chinese name Dao Shixun, succeeded to the throne in the *moeng kai* year, CS 1309 (AD 1947). On the eighth day of the fourth month the water spreading ceremony of the coronation was performed and he was promoted to *saenwi fa*. At succession, he was twenty-two years old (sic);[341] he ruled over a year, then the land was liberated. Before liberation he was studying in Kunming. After liberation, he graduated from university and married a Chinese wife. He then worked in Beijing (Currently he is the researcher of the Institute of Nationalities of Yunnan, an assistant research worker. He is [also] the dean of the Institute of the Languages of Nationalities and a standing member of the Provincial Council).}[342]

{Cao Mòm Kham Lü, Chinese name Dao Shixun (Tao Sü Sin), succeeded to the throne in the *dap mao* year, CS 1307 (AD 1947). On the eighth waxing day of the fourth Tai month[343] the water sprinkling ceremony of coronation was performed and he was promoted to *saenwi fa*. He was twenty-two years old (sic) on succession, and ruled over a year before he went to study Chinese [in Kunming]. The head of the Council of Nobles (*khun* [*noe*] *sanam*) acted as the regent. He did not return after graduation. At that time the country (*banmüang*) was liberated (1949). He married a Chinese woman and lived [with her] in Moeng Sae (Kunming).}[344]

THE "COW'S CUSHION WAR" OF 1913[345]

In Moeng Hai the "Cow's Cushion War" broke out because the [Cao] La, the nephew of Cao Ya Mai, borrowed a cow's cushion at Ban Hin. Ca Kap Kham [also called Ca Pò Bo] came to trade for them. When they returned, the cow's cushions were missing. These cow's cushions belonged to a general (*saen pon*) at Ban Laeng. Cao La sent them back to Ban Laeng. The *saen pon* at Ban Laeng blamed Cao La: "The new cow's cushions have become old ones". Cao La replied: "They were old when I got them from Ca Kap Kham".

Thereafter they accused each other.

341. Cao Mòm Kham Lü was born in AD 1928. He was nineteen years old when he became *cao phaendin*. He lives with his wife in Kunming.

342. Taken from Gao Lishi 1984, 131. s. 44.1. In the colophon Gao Lishi writes: "As for the genealogy of the *cao phaendin* it begins with the *saenwi fa* Phaya Coeng (it should have been *cao phaendin*, as the official title of *saenwi fa* began during the Yuan dynasty) and ends in Dao Shixun, a total of forty-four reigns. From CS 532, a *gengyin* year (Qiandao 6 of the Song dynasty, AD 1170) down to CS 1318 (i.e., AD 1956, the peaceful negotiation of land reform and the abolition of the feudal land ownership), giving a total of 786 years [of history of the Tai Lü kingdom]."

343. 1307 Magha 8 = Saturday, 9 February 1946.

344. Taken from Dao Shuren 1989.

345. This section is taken from Dao Shuren 1989, 472–78

[The *saen pon*) asked for compensation. The people of Ban Laeng were not content and they discussed the matters with Ca Kap Kham at Ban Hin. The people of Ban Hin were not content as well and refused. [After their refusal] was turned down, they approached Cao Ya Mai. [Finally] a war broke out with Ca Kap Kham and the *saen pon* of Ban Laeng fought against each other. Cao La sided with Ban Hin and Cao Ya Mai sided with Ban Laeng. The struggle ended without a victory on either side. Thereafter the people were on Cao Ya Mai's side. Then Ban Hin was defeated. General (*saen han*) Pothiyak of Ban Hin, who was a native of Moeng Cae, went to recruit troops from Moeng Cae to fight with Cao Ya Mai.

At that time Cao Ya Mai approached the *cao phaendin*. Moeng Hai and Chiang Rung cooperated to fight against Moeng Cae. They marched to Moeng Cae taking the route via Ban Kao. Saen Pothiyak was separated from his troops and came to Ban Kun. Cao Ya Mai's soldiers were able to catch him and then executed him in the vicinity of the monastery of Wat Ban Kun. The troops of Moeng Cae were unwilling [to surrender]. They asked [Moeng] Laem for support.[346] Xiting, Bata, Cangdang, and Ho (Hua) Thoen came to give support to Moeng Cae and Cao La and his two—altogether three—brothers. They blamed Cao Chiang Rung for being partial (lit., "not in the middle"). They came to attack Chiang Rung. Moeng Hai supported Chiang Rung. [Chiang Rung and Moeng Hai] decided to write a letter together to Cao Moeng Sae. Then Cao Moeng Sae sent troops to help the *cao phaendin* against Moeng Cae. After the ruler of Moeng Cae had withdrawn his troops to Chiang Coeng, they deployed their troops and fought against each other. The fighting lasted two to three months. As the forces of Moeng Cae outnumbered those of Chiang Rung and Moeng Hai, Moeng Cae succeeded in entering the stockaded town (*wiang*) of Moeng Hai. The Wat Long (main monastery) was crowded with people. They (i.e., the forces of Moeng Cae) who had invaded the town, killed Nang Pan, the younger sister of Cao Ya Sipò. Thus Moeng Hai ordered Han Cai Nam Lek and Ca Kham Phai, who was the leader of the seven men. Together with Han Nòi of Ban Sao (village), they besieged the troops of Moeng Cae at Wat Long (Luang) and [finally] gained a victory. Later the Hò (Chinese) advised the *cao phaendin*:

> You should write a letter and send it to the authorities of Moeng Sae (Kunming) to ask for additional support. The fighting is not yet over, as the three *cao*, who are brothers, are still unwilling [to submit]. They have the desire to defeat the younger uncle (Cao Ya Mai).

After the governor of Moeng Sae (Kunming) [called] Thang Yaen Suai had received the letter, he [appointed] the three *nai luang hua sük* (i.e., military commanders) whose

346. The Moeng Laem Chronicle (ff° 48/11–49/3) mentions a military involvement of Moeng Laem only on the side of Chiang Rung and the imperial Chinese forces. After his defeat the "ruler of the forty thousand rice fields of Moeng Cae" fled to Moeng La.

names were Li Ta Yin Cang, Ma Ta Yin Cang, and Kwang Ying Cang, as the supreme military commanders and sent them down [to Chiang Rung].

When the Moeng Cae side learned that, a letter was written to inform the *cao mòn* of Moeng La (Simao) and Moeng Maen (Puer); they were sent to Lan Sang and fighting broke out between the Guangxi-Guangdong forces and the imperial Chinese forces (*hò luang*). In both forces Chinese as well as Tai soldiers [were recruited]. An easy victory over Moeng Cae was not possible.

Then the governor of Moeng Sae (Kunming) ordered [two] other officials (*khun nai*), whose names were Khò Su Sin (i.e., Ke Shuxun) [and] Khun Khò Ta Yin to lead a force of three thousand Guangxi-Guangdong soldiers to Sipsòng Panna. They discussed how to fight with wisdom and divided the troops into several smaller units to cross the San Thaen (mountain) to Moeng Ngat. One unit entered Moeng Hai and [finally] [reached] via Ban Kao to Sala Kap Pò. Then they [marched] along the Moeng Cae side [along the river bank?] till Ban Kho Lom. They marched during daytime and took a rest at nighttime. They marched on this route three days and three nights in rotation. All the people [in Moeng Cae] were aware that

> The Guangxi-Guangdong troops, amounting to millions of soliders, have come to fight against Moeng Cae. They have been marching three days and three nights without taking a rest. This news has reached us.

The people in Moeng Cae, however, were not discouraged and sent a letter to the ruler of Moeng Khak to ask him to send reinforcements.

At that time as the news was spread to the *cao fa* of Chiang Tung, he mobilised troops with the strength of 3,000 soldiers for the Chinese. After the "black people" (?) had entered Moeng Cae, fighting broke out at Chiang Coeng. Ho Khò's forces were defeated and the "White Chinese" troops were surrounded. [The Tai] set fire to their country besides the fire set from outside (i.e., by the Chinese). Four persons were arrested and brought to Chiang Rung. The Moeng Hai side had already caught the two English military commanders, father and son. Not much later, the "White Chinese" troops of Moeng Cae were defeated and Khò Ta Yin (i.e., Ke Shuxun) led 700 Chinese soldiers to Chiang Tung. After the *cao fa* of Chiang Tung had submitted, Kho Ta Yin encamped at La Tip. Khò Ta Yin returned to make his obeisance to the authority in Moeng Sae (Kunming). He left three generals (*khun*) and 700 Chinese soldiers [stationing in Moeng Cae]. They collected money from the households of Moeng Cae and the amount raised was much more than that raised from other *müang*. The inhabitants of [Moeng] Cae became angry and wrote a letter to the ruler of Moeng Khak. The ruler of Moeng Khak wrote a letter to the *cao fa* of Chiang Tung who mobilised 500 Burmese troops to fight the Chinese at La Tip. The Chinese were defeated by the Burmese. Out of more than 700 Chinese soldiers only 200 survived. The three generals (*khun*) returned to Moeng Sae (Kunming) to inform the authority. The governor of Moeng Sae (Kunming) was furious at the three officers and had all of them executed.

Later on, Khò Ta Yin received an order from the governor of Moeng Sae (Kunming), and he returned to Chiang Rung as [Chinese] governor (*cung pan*) [whose task was] to supervise the whole administration in Sipsòng Panna. He organised [the tax system] on the basis of household clusters (*hua hoen tham*). Each household had to pay two *man* (i.e., piastres) and four *kwa* (*kao*?). [However,] later the taxes increased.

III. Genealogy of the *Cao Phaendin* of Moeng Lü or Sipsòng Panna (MLC-SV1)

Translators' note: The Tai Lü text is contained in *Recension of the Genealogy of the* Saenwi Fa *of Sipsòng Panna* (Ch. *Cheli xuanwei shixi kaoding*), by Li Fuyi, Kunming: 1947 edition, pp. 44–63. This Tai Lü manuscript by Tao Coen Cong (Cao Mòm Suca Wanna Laca) was kept in Chiang Rung, and was copied around AD 1944 by Luo Zeguang for Li Fuyi. It is most probably the oldest extant Tai Lü manuscript of the short version of the Moeng Lü Chronicle. It records the genealogies of thirty-eight rulers in twenty-eight generations.

The following records the genealogy of the pacification commissioners (*cao phaendin cao saenwi fa*). [The reigns of the successive rulers] are as follows:

1. CAO PHAYA COENG (ZHAO BA ZHEN), D. 1180

The *cao saenwi fa* Cao Phaya Coeng, and his queen (*maha tewi*) Rammanni[1] had four sons: the eldest son, named Lao Yoe Hoeng (Roeng),[2] was invested as the ruler of Lan Cang (Lan Sang, i.e., Laos) and Lan Na (Chiang Mai);[3] the second son, named Ai Hung,[4] was invested as the ruler of Moeng Kaeo (i.e., Vietnam); the third son, named Yi Kham Loeng,[5] was invested the ruler of Wiang Can (Vientiane); [and] the fourth son, named

1. In MLC-LV1, 1, s. 1.4, she is called Nang Akkha Mahesī (Niang A-ga Ma-xie-xi), lit., "principal queen"; in MLC-SV2, 83, s. 1, her personal name was Nang Lam Ma.

2. In MLC-LV1, 2, s. 1.5, he is called Tao Peng Leng (Tao Pung Loeng).

3. In MLC-SV2, 83, s. 1, his principality/kingdom was only Lan Na.

4. In MLC-LV1, 2, s. 1.5, he was Tao Ai Beng (Tao Ai Pung).

5. In MLC-LV1, 2, s. 1.5, he was Tao Yi Kang Leng (Tao Yi Kham Hoeng/Roeng); in MLC-SV2, 83, s. 1, he was Yi Kham Loeng.

Sam Khai Noeng,[6] succeeded his father to the throne (*taen sak pò*)[7] as ruler of Moeng Saenwi Fa-Sipsòng Panna[8] in Moeng Chiang Rung (i.e., Cheli). Cao Phaya Coeng passed away (*cuti*)[9] in the year [cunla]sakkalaca (hereafter CS) 542, [a *kot cai* year], (AD 1180). He was the founder of the dynasty.

2. SAM KHAI NOENG (SAN KAILENG), R. 1180–1201

Sam Khai Noeng succeeded his father to the throne [in the first year] *kin thawai waennaen*.[10] In the year CS 542 (*kot cai*) (AD 1180), the Cao Lum Fa,[11] by the name of Pothiyan,[12] conferred on [him an official] seal adorned with a golden sword and a tiger-

6. In MLC-LV1, 2, s. 1.5, he was Tao Kang Leng (Tao Khai Noeng). In MLC-SV2, 83, s. 1, he was Sam Khai Noeng, whose fief was in Moeng Chiang Rung.

7. Li Fuyi (MLC-SV1, 45) translates it *ji fu wei* 繼父位 (succeed in his father's stead), which could be translated "succeed his father to the throne". From the Chinese point of view it is "succeed his father to the post of pacification commissioner", but from the Tai Lü perspective it is "succeed to his father's throne as supreme ruler of Sipsòng Panna", i.e., *cao phaendin*.

8. Li Fuyi (MLC-LV1, 45) translates Sipsòng Panna rather literally into the "Kingdom of Twelve Thousand Rice Fields".

9. The Tai Lü word *cutti* derives from the Pali *cuti*, (Skt. *cyuti*), which means "he vanishes, passes away". The use of this word indicates the high status of the deceased person. Note the subtle differences in the choice of words in Chinese for death. In Li Fuyi (MLC-LV1 and MLC-SV1) the word *hong* 薨 (death of a prince or a feudal lord) is used throughout the translation, whereas in Li Fuyi 1983a and 1983b, the revised editions of MLC-LV1 and MLC-SV1 respectively, Li Fuyi changes all to *zu* 卒 (death of a person). This has a political implication. In Chinese *beng* 崩 (lit., "collapse like a mountain") is used for the death of an emperor; *hong* 薨, is used for the death of a feudal lord or a prince; and *zu* 卒 is for the death of an official or an ordinary person. The reason for using the term hong 薨 is that in the Republican Period (1912–1949) the ruler of Chiang Rung was still recognised as the "feudal lord" or vassal of China, and Li Fuyi was a Chinese official. For details on using the various euphemisms for "death" or "to die" in Tai Lü texts, see the introduction, part 2, section 7 of this volume.

10. The Tai Lü term *kin thawai waennaen* is interpreted by Li Fuyi (MLC-SV1, 45) as *Jingtai yuannian* 景泰元年, which means "the first year of Jingtai reign". However, "the first year of Jingtai reign" of the Ming period corresponds to AD 1450. The rendering of *kin thawai waennaen* into Chinese as *Jingtai yuan nian* by Li Fuyi (MLC-SV1) is hard to accept. It probably means "the first year of Jiatai reign" (i.e., AD 1201). See Li Fuyi 1947c; Dao Yongming 1989, 7; Dao Shuren 1989, 221; Chen Xujing 1994, 42. If Sam Khai Noeng was enthroned in AD 1180, there is a difference of twenty-one years.

11. Here *cao lum fa* (Tai Lü) is rendered as "son of heaven of China" (*Zhongguo tianzi* 中國天子) by Li Fuyi (MLC-SV1, 45). However, on p. 49 (in the section "thirteenth ruler"), *cao lum fa* is translated into *tianchao huangdi* 天朝皇帝 (emperor of the Heavenly Court).

12. Here the emperor by the name of Pothiyan probably referred to Duan Zhixing (r. 1173–1200), king of the Later Dali (1096–1253).

head (*cum yin dap kham ho soe*) and appointed [him] the pacification commissioner (*cao saenwi fa*).[13] The domain under the jurisdiction of the pacification commission was to be his principality. [Moreover], taxes (*suai li*) were raised. [It was fixed that] for every five years a lesser tribute (*saeo kung*) was to be paid, and for every nine years a major tribute (*ta kung*) was to be paid.[14]

Sam Khai Noeng was fifty-nine years old on his succession [to the throne]. He was on the throne twenty-one years before he became ill and passed away (*cuti*) at the age of eighty in the *ruang rao* (or *hung lao*) year, [CS 563 (AD 1201)]. This is the second generation (second ruler) of the dynasty.[15]

3. AI KUNG (AI GONG), R. 1201–1224

Sam Khai Noeng had two sons: the eldest was called Ai Kung[16] and the second was Yi Poeng.[17] Ai Kung succeeded his father to the throne as pacification commissioner (*cao saenwi fa*) at the age of forty-seven. He was on the throne twenty-three years and passed away (*cuti tai*)[18] at the age of seventy in the *kap san* year, CS 586 (AD 1224). This is the third generation (third ruler) of the dynasty.[19]

---

13. In AD 1180 (corresponds to Chunxi 7 of the Southern Song dynasty) the *cao phaendin* of Moeng Lü was not yet conferred the title *xuanwei shi* 宣慰使 (pacification commissioner), rendered into Tai as *saenwi fa*, by China. The supreme ruler of Moeng Lü was conferred *xuanwei shi* in the reign of Dao Kan (Cao Khan Moeng), the eighth ruler, by the Ming court. However, the title also appears in the translation of Gao Lishi (MLC-SV2). This shows that both manuscripts on which the translations are based, have been revised by the later scribes and the title *saenwi fa* was simply added to the rulers before Cao Khan Moeng.

14. The Tai Lü terms *saeo kung* (Tr. แซวกูง) and *ta kung* (Tr. ต่ากูง) are obviously loanwords of the Chinese *xiao gong* 小 貢 and *da gong* 大 貢 respectively. This was an ancient tradition of offering tribute, which could be traced back to the Eastern Zhou era (770–256 BC) or the Spring and Autumn Period (722–481 BC).

15. According Gao Lishi's translation (MLC-SV2) he reigned twenty years, from 1180 to 1200, and passed away at the age of eighty.

16. In MLC-LV1, 2, s. 2.2, he was called Tao Beng (Tao Pung or Ai Pung).

17. In MLC-LV1, 2, s. 2.2, he was Ai Yi Beng (Ai Yi Peng).

18. *Cuti tai* (Tr. จุตติตาย) is a combination of Pali and Tai Lü respectively. In Sanskrit it is *cyuti*, which literally means "he passed away" (third person plural), and *tai* means "to die". The term *cuti tai* refers to the decease of a prince or a very high-ranking personality. Li Fuyi (MLC-SV1, 45) renders it as *hong* 薨, which means the death of a prince or a feudal lord.

19. In MLC-SV2, 83, s. 3, Ai Kòng succeeded his father to the throne in the same year (AD 1200), reigned twenty-three years, and passed away at the age of seventy in CS 583 (AD 1221).

4. TAO RUNG (HUNG) KAEN CAI (DAO LONG PIAN ZAI), R. 1224–1247

Ai Kung had one son called Tao Rung Kaen Cai, who succeeded his father in the *kap san* year, CS 586 (AD 1224). He had one son, named Tao Haeng Long (Luang) and a daughter named Nang O Ming Khai Fa.[20] When the daughter was a bit older (*yai*),[21] she was renamed to Nang Ok Aen;[22] when she married the ruler (*cao*) of Chiang Rai,[23] she was given another name, Nang Kham Kai.[24] At the time when Tao Rung Kaen Cai succeeded his father to the throne as ruler of the land he was thirty-nine years old. He was [on the throne of] *cao saenwi fa* twenty-three years and passed away (*cuti*) at the age of sixty-two in the *moeng met* year, CS 609 (AD 1247). This is the fourth generation (fourth ruler) of the dynasty.[25]

5. TAO HAENG LONG (DAO LIANG LONG), R. 1247–1263

Tao Haeng Long succeeded his father to the throne as ruler (*cao*). He had two sons: the elder was named Tao Putok,[26] and the second son was named Yi Peng (Piang) Lak Sai. Tao Haeng Long was thirty-eight years old when he succeeded to [the throne]. He was on the throne sixteen years and passed away (*cuti tai*) at the age of fifty-four in the *ka kai* year CS 625 (AD 1263). This is the fifth generation (fifth ruler) of the dynasty.[27]

6. TAO PUTOK (DAO BUDA), R. 1263–1277

Tao Putok succeeded his father to the throne in the *ka kai* year, CS 625 (AD 1263).

20. In MLC-LV1, 3, s. 4.1, she was called [Niang] Wo Min Zhuang Meng (Nang O/Ua Ming Còm Moeng); in MLC-SV2, 83, s. 4, her name is Nang O Moeng; in Gao Lishi 1984, 106, s. 4.2, her name was Nan Wo Min Kai Fa (Nang O/Ua Ming Khai Fa).

21. In MLC-SV1, 45, Li Fuyi adds a parenthesis and explains that she was a toddler.

22. In MLC-LV1, 3, she was then called Niang Wo Bian (Nang O/Ua Paeng), similar to MLC-SV2, 83, s. 4.

23. Here Li Fuyi (MLC-SV1, 45) renders "Cao Chiang Rai" as the "chieftain (*qiu* 酋) of Chiang Rai".

24. In MLC-LV1, 3, she was then called Niang Kang Kai (Nang Kham Khai); in MLC-SV2 her name is Nan Han Kai (Nang Kham Kai).

25. According to the translation of Gao Lishi (MLC-SV2, 83, s. 4), Tao Hung Kaen Cai succeeded his father in CS 583 (AD 1221), on the throne twenty-four years, and passed away at the age of sixty-two in the year CS 605 (AD 1243).

26. In other sources the eldest son's name is Ai Buwa or Tao Puwak. See MLC-LV1, 4–5, s. 5.2 and s. 6.1; MLC-SV2, 83, s. 6; MLC-LV1, s. 5.3; MLC-LV2, s. 6.1.

27. In MLC-SV2, s. 5, Tao Haeng Luang was on the throne sixteen years, and passed away at the age of fifty-four in the year CS 621 (AD 1259).

Previously, Yi Peng Lak Sai[28] had been invited to be the successor of Moeng Fòng because Cao Moeng Fòng,[29] whose name was Fa Kham Kòng, had no son. When he was about to leave for [Moeng Fòng, his wife] gave birth to a son called Cao Ai. After he had arrived in Moeng Fòng, he married [another wife], who [also] bore him a son. Later when Cao Fa Moeng Fòng[30] passed away (*cuti pai sia*),[31] Yi Peng Lak Sai succeeded his adoptive father as the ruler of Moeng Fòng. From then onwards, the Cao Fa Moeng Fòng is addressed as pacification commissioner (*cao saenwi fa*), [down] to the present day.[32] Yi Piang Lak Sai had two sons.

His elder brother Tao Putok became a ruler at the age of thirty-eight. He was on the throne fourteen years and passed away (*cuti*) at the age of fifty-two in the *moeng pao* year, CS 639 (AD 1277), without an heir. This prompted the people (nobles) of Sipsòng Panna to hold a conference, at which they decided to go to Moeng Fòng and welcome [Yi Peng Lak Sai] back to succeed his elder brother. Moreover, his son Tao Ai (i.e., Cao Ai), who was born in Moeng Lü (i.e., before he went to Moeng Fòng), was to be brought back to Moeng Lü. [However, his second son],[33] who was born in Moeng Fòng, was to remain there and be the ruler of Moeng Fòng.

7. YI PENG LAK SAI (YI BING LA SAI), R. 1277

Yi Peng Lak Sai returned to succeed his elder brother to the throne, but died less than a year later, in the *moeng pao* year, CS 639 (AD 1277). This is the sixth generation (seventh ruler) of the dynasty.[34]

8. TAO AI (DAO AI) OR CAO AI (ZHAO AI), R. 1277–1318

Tao Ai succeeded his father to the throne in CS 639, the *moeng pao* year, at the age of thirty-nine. He was on the throne forty-one years and passed away (*cuti tai*) at the age

28. In MLC-LV1, s. 6.2, he was Yi Lak Sai.

29. Here Li Fuyi (MLC-SV1, 47) renders Cao Moeng Fòng as "chieftain of Moeng Fòng", which is rectified here.

30. Here Li Fuyi (MLC-SV1, 47), adds a parenthesis: namely the ruler of Moeng Fòng, Fa Kham Kòng, the abbreviation of Cao Fa Moeng Fòng.

31. Here Li Fuyi (MLC-SV1, 47), uses the word *si* 死 (died), instead of *hong* 薨 (death of a feual or vassal lord).

32. Most probably Moeng Pòng (Fòng) refers to Moeng Hsaenwi (Ch. Mubang). The Anglicised name of Moeng Pòng, Hsaenwi, is obviously derived from *saenwi fa*, which is derived from the Chinese *xuanwi shi*, translated into "pacification commissioner".

33. Here Li Fuyi (MLC-SV1, 47) renders it as *shuzi* 庶 子, which means sons not born by the principal wife, i.e., sons of concubines.

34. This account is not recorded in MLC-SV2.

of eighty in the *poek sanga* year, CS 680 (AD 1318). This is the seventh generation (eight ruler) of the dynasty.

9. CAO KHAN MOENG (DAO KAN), R. 1318–1362

Tao Ai had a son called Cao Khan Moeng.[35] He succeeded his father to the throne in the *poek sanga* year, CS 680, at the age of thirty-nine. He was on the throne forty-four years and passed away (*cuti tai*) at the age of eighty-three in the *tao yi* year, CS 724 (AD 1362). This is the eighth generation (ninth ruler) of the dynasty.

Cao Khan Moeng had three sons: The eldest son was called Tao Sida Kham, who was born to his principal wife, namely the queen who got a three-pronged conch shell.[36] The second was Tao Kumman and the youngest son was Peo (Piao) Fai Fa.

10. CAO SIDA KHAM (DAO XIANDA), R. 1362–1442

Cao (Tao) Sida Kham succeeded his father to the throne in the *tao yi* year, CS 724 (AD 1362), at the age of forty. He was on the throne eighty years and passed away (*cuti tai*) at the age of 120 in the *tao set* year, CS 804 (AD 1442). Cao Sida Kham had two sons: the elder son was Tao Kü Moeng, and the second son was called Tao Kham Tet (Tiat).[37]

11. TAO KUMMAN (DAO GONGMAN), R. 1442–1443

Tao Kumman, the younger brother of Cao (Tao) Sida Kham, succeeded his elder brother to the throne in the *tao set* year, CS 804 (AD 1442). He had no son (i.e., was without an heir). In the *ka kai* year, CS 805 (AD 1443), he was deposed by Tao Kham Tet.[38] Tao Kü Na (Tao Kü Moeng) was to become ruler subsequently.[39]

35. According to Dao and Kang 1989a, 285, his name is Cao Khan Moeng.

36. "Three-pronged conch shell" refers to [Nang] Hòi Sam Cik (Tr. [นาง]หอย ๓ จิก).

37. Most probably he was Tao Kham Daeng. See MLC-LV1, 7, s. 9.2. In MLC-SV2, s. 9, it is recorded that Tao Sida Kham, the eldest son of Phaya Khan Moeng, succeeded his father to the throne. According to Dao and Kang (1989a, 285), the ruler's name was Tao Kham Tet.

38. According to MLC-LV2, s. 11.2, Tao Kumman had two sons, Cao Ai and Cao Yi; but according to MLC-LV1, s. 9.3, he had one son. In Gao Lishi's translation of MLC-SV2, 84, s. 9, we learn that Tao Kumman died of illness, but in MLC-SV1, 49, he was ousted by Tao Kham Tet.

39. The last sentence in the Tai Lü text is not translated into Chinese by Li Fuyi in MLC-SV1, 49. According to this source, Tao Kü Na (Kü Moeng) was the fourteenth ruler of Moeng Lü. But "Tao Kü Na" (r. 1355–1385) was the king of Lan Na, not the king of Moeng Lü. The mistake is obviously

12. TAO KHAM TET (DAO DIAN), R. 1443–1444

Tao Kham Tet (or Tao Kham Daeng) was on the throne one year. However, as Soe Long Fa and Peo Fai Fa were dissatisfied [with him], they sent troops to attack him. Tao Kham Tet could not repulse [their forces], so he took the [official] seal adorned with a golden sword and fled to Nam Ngai Sai Kham,[40] where he died in the *kap cai* year, CS 806 (AD 1444).

13. SOE LONG FA (SÜA LUANG FA; SHE LONG FA), R. 1444–1464

Soe Long Fa succeeded [Tao Kham Tet] to the throne. Cao Lum Fa[41] summoned him to go to get the [official] seal adorned with a golden sword. Thus, Soe Long Fa presented one *saen* of pure gold and one *saen* of white silver[42] to Cao Lum Fa to obtain [the official seal]. Cao Lum Fa then gave him a golden seal [of office], like previous [rulers]. Peace prevailed in the land during the reign of Soe Long Fa.

In the *lai yi* (*rai yi*) year, CS 808 (AD 1446), a prince ([*cao*] *fa*) of Moeng Fòng, by the name of Soe (Süa) Tham Fa,[43] who was the lord of Moeng Mao Long (Luang), revolted against the Cao Lum Fa.[44] Consequently, Cao Lum Fa appointed the senior official Cang Sui (Zhang Shui)[45] as military commander [to take his troops and] go attack him. Soe

---

ascribed to the scribe. It should have been Tao Kü Moeng. Tao Kü Moeng and Tao Kü Na were not contemporary.

40. According to Li Fuyi (1947b), 49 and Dao Shuren (1989), 231, Nam Ngai Sai Kham is the Golden Sand River (probably the Upper Yangzi River). MLC-LV1, 9, s. 11.6 states, "En route he stopped at Moeng Nam Thai Fan (Pan), where he died." Nam Thai Fan is interpreted by Li Fuyi as Nanjing, the then capital of China. In Gao Lishi (1984), 109, s. 15.5, it states, "On the way he died by the bank of Nam Thai River." The location of Nam Thai is unknown. On Nam Ngai/Thai Sai Kham and Nam Thai Fan, see also MLC-LV1, s. 12.3; MLC-LV2, s. 15.5 and s. 16.12.

41. *Cao lum fa* (in Tai Lü) literally means "lord under heaven", i.e., "universal monarch". Li Fuyi (MLC-S V1, 49) renders it as *tianchao huangdi* 天朝皇帝, which means "emperor of the Heavenly Court".

42. One *saen* (Th. แสน) of Tai Lü weight is slightly more than 200 *jin* 斤 (catty) according to the treasure-scale, *kuping* 庫平, for silver. See MLC-SV1, 49.

43. Soe Tham Fa is also known as Soe Ngam Fa. See MLC-SV1, 49. Soe Ngam Fa or Cao Ngam Pha or Tao Ngam Pha all refer to the same lord of Moeng Mao, known in contemporary Chinese sources as Si Ren Fa. See Liew 1996.

44. Here *cao lum fa* is rendered as *tianchao* 天朝 (Heavenly Court) by Li Fuyi (MLC-SV1, 49).

45. Here Li Fuyi (MLC-SV1, 49) adds a parenthesis: In [his] addition A (i.e., his 1933 translation), he was Zhang Hong 張洪. Zhang Shui 張水 is unknown to Liew-Herres. However, Zhang Hong was an imperal envoy, the author of *Shi Mian Lu* 使緬錄 (Record of an envoy to Burma), sent to Luchuan and Burma during the early Ming period. The commanders-in-chief of the third military campaign

Tham Fa, unable to defend against [the attack], fled to Burma (Moeng Man). One of his senior officials (*khun phòng*) fled to Moeng Lü. Soe Long Fa caught and killed him. His head was delivered to Cao Lum Fa. Thus, [Soe Long Fa] gained the firm trust [of Cao Lum Fa]. He was promoted to the [military] rank of *khwan waen cang ki kòn sae khin ya min*.[46] He was also placed in charge of Lan Na (Chiang Mai), Lan Cang (Sang), Moeng Khün, [and] Moeng Laem. The whole territory was divided into the *müang* of Moeng Maen (Ninger), Bò Hoek (Mohei), Moeng Saeng (Mengxiang), Moeng Tae (Mengdie), Khwaen Siao (Quanxiu), Na Kot Si Thung (Na ge xi tong), Òi Loeng (Huaileng), etc. All these lands were to be his vassal states. Soe Long Fa ascended the throne at the age of sixty. He was on the throne twenty years, and passed away (*cuti tai*) at the age of eighty in the *kap san* year, CS 826 (AD 1464). This is the ninth (sic) tenth generation (thirteenth ruler) of the dynasty.

14. TAO KÜ MOENG (DAO GENG MENG), R. 1464–1467

Soe Long Fa had a total of nine sons: the eldest son was Tao Phasaeng, the second son Tao Còm Pha, the third son Tao Saeo, the fourth son Tao Yòt, the fifth son Tao Kham, the sixth son Tao Ut, the seventh son Tao Som, the eighth son Tao Fa Nòi, and the ninth son Tao Sòt Sòi. None of his nine sons were allowed to become [his] heir. They were sent to various *panna* as governors (*cao panna*).[47] However, Tao Kü Moeng, the son of Tao Sida Kham [and] the adopted son (*samuti*)[48] (sic) of Soe Long Fa, succeeded [Soe Long Fa to the throne] at the age of eighteen. He was on the throne three years and passed away (*cuti*) at the age of twenty-one in the *moeng kai* year, CS 829 (1467 AD). This is the tenth generation (fourteenth ruler) of the dynasty.

---

against Luchuan were neither Zhang Shui nor Zhang Hong. The imperial troops were led by Wang Ji 王驥 (1378–1460) and Jiang Gui 蔣貴 (1380–1449). See Liew 1996.

46. Li Fuyi (MLC-SV1, 51) explains in the parenthesis that probably the post referred to the "Bureau of Yuanjiang Route Command (Yuanjiang zongguanfu 元江總管府)", but there was no such post at that time. Yuanjiang 元江 is the Chinese rendering of the Tai Lü Moeng Cung. The above transcriptions are close to (in Pinyin): *Guan Yuanjiang zongguan xingsheng yamen* 管元江總管行省衙門, i.e., commander of the Yuanjiang (Moeng Cung) Route Command. See also MLC-SV2, s. 14, n. 29.

47. Here *panna*, a tax-paying administrative unit, can best be translated as "district".

48. *Samuti* (Tr. สมุติ). The Siamese word *sommut* (สมมุติ) means to assume, or to suppose; in Pali *sammuti* means consent, permission, or choice. In colloquial Tai a different term would be used. According to the Tai Lü text on which Li Fuyi's (MLC-SV1) translation is based, Tao Kü Moeng was Soe Long Fa's adopted son. However, according to the translation of Li Fuyi (MLC-SV1, 51), Tao Sida Kham's son Tao Kü Moeng, succeeded Soe Long Fa [to the throne] at the age of eighteen. In fact Tao Kü Moeng and Soe Long Fa were cousins. Soe Long Fa adopted Tao Kü Moeng's son Tao Sam Pò Lütai. See MLC-LV1, 11, s. 12.8.

15. TAO SAM PÒ LÜTAI (SAN BAO LIDAI), R. 1467–1497

Tao Kü Moeng had three sons: the eldest [son] was Tao Bakòng, the second son Tao Sòng Moeng, and the third son was called Tao [Sam] Pò Lütai. Tao Bakòng and Tao Sòng Moeng both died before they could succeed to the throne.[49] Thus, at that time Tao [Sam] Pò Lütai was to succeed to the throne as ruler at the age of twenty. He was on the throne thirty years and passed away at the age of fifty in the *moeng sai* year, CS 859 (AD 1497). This is the eleventh generation (fifteenth ruler) of the dynasty.

16. SAM KHAI NOENG (SAN KAI LENG), R. 1497–1502

[Tao Sam] Pò Lütai had four sons: the eldest son was called Tao Yi, the second son was Sam Khai Noeng, the third son was Cao Am, and the youngest son was Tao Ai.[50] Tao Yi died before he could succeed to the throne and had no son. [Hence], Sam Khai Noeng succeeded his father to throne in the *moeng sai* year, CS 859 (AD 1497), at the age of fifteen. He was on the throne five years and passed away (*cuti tai*) at the age of twenty in the *tao set* year, CS 864 year (AD 1502), without an heir. This is the twelfth generation (sixteenth ruler) of the dynasty.

17. CAO KHAN [MOENG] (ZHAO KAN), R. 1502–1523

The third son of [Tao] Sam Pò Lütai, Cao Am, died (*siang mòranna sia*)[51] before he could succeed to the throne and had no heir. The fourth son Cao Ai also could not succeed

49. This statement is unfounded. According to MLC-LV1, 9, 2. 11.1–2; MLC-LV2, s. 13 and s. 14; and MLC-SV2, s. 12–11, Tao Bakòng and Tao Sòng Moeng both ruled for a short period. According to other sources, such as Gao Lishi 1984, they and their attendants were put on several rafts and sent down the Mekong by Soe Long Fa. Tao Bakòng was allegedly the founder of Chiang Khaeng. Moreover, Tao Bakòng (Dao Bagong) and Tao Sòng Moeng (Dao Shuang Meng) are mentioned many times in contemporary Chinese sources. See the Liew-Herres (2003b) translation of Chinese sources on Cheli.

50. According to MLC-LV1, 15, s. 13.15, he had six sons (Tao Yi, Cao Moeng, Sam Khai Noeng, Cao Am, Cao Ai, and Cao Khan Moeng); according to MLC-LV2, s. 18.11 and Gao Lishi 1984, 113, s. 18.11, he had five sons (Tao Yi, Cao Am, Sam Khai Noeng, Cao Ai, and the fifth son, still young). The names of the ruler's sons are quite confusing. In Tai Lü the first son is usually called "Ai", the second son "Yi", and the third one "Sam". It is not likely that the fourth/fifth son was called "Tao Ai" and the eldest son called "Tao Yi". A possible explanation is that Tao Sam Pò Lütai had two wives. The first wife had borne him four sons but the eldest had already died when his second wife gave birth to a son, who was the fourth surviving son of the ruler but *her* first son, thus he was called Tao Ai.

51. In Tai Lü *siang* means "to come to an end", *sia* means "to lose", and *mòrana*, which is derived from Pali *maraṇa*, means "death".

[to the throne]. [He] had a son by the name of Cao Khan [Moeng], who succeeded to the throne as ruler in the *tao set* year, CS 864 (AD 1502), at the age of sixty-four. He was on the throne twenty-one years and passed away (*cuti tai*) at the age of eighty-five in the *ka met* year, CS 885 (AD 1523). This is the thirteenth generation (seventeenth ruler) of the dynasty.

18. CAO SALI SOMPAN (ZHAO SHILI SONGBAN), R. 1523–1560

Cao Khan [Moeng] had one son called Cao Sali Sompan who succeeded his father to the throne in the *ka met* year, CS 885 (AD 1523), {at the age of thirty}. He was on the throne thirty-seven years and passed away (*cuti tai*) in the *khot san* year, CS 922 (AD 1560), {at the age of sixty-seven}.[52] This is the fourteenth generation (eighteenth ruler) of the dynasty.

19. CAO ONG MOENG (DAO YUN MENG), R. 1560–1588

Cao Sali Sompan had one son called Cao Ong Moeng who succeeded his father to the throne in the *khot san* year, CS 922 (AD 1560), at the age of sixteen. As counted he was on the throne twenty-eight years, [and died] at the age of forty-four. In the *poek cai* year, CS 950 (AD 1588), he was taken hostage by the king of Moeng Kham[53] Ava-Hongsa[wati] and died (*cuti tai*) in Moeng Phaya Yòt.[54] This is the fifteenth generation (nineteenth ruler) of the dynasty.[55]

20. CAO SALI SUNANTA (ZHAO SHILI SUNANDA), R. 1588–1595

Cao Ong Moeng[56] had two sons: the eldest son was called Cao Sali Sunanta; the second son was called Cao Un (On) Moeng.[57] Cao Sali Sunanta succeeded his father to the throne

52. The information in { } is given in Dao & Kang 1989a, 288.

53. Moeng Kham (เมิงคำ) means "golden kingdom" (or polity).

54. Phaya Yòt is probably a corrupt form of Phayak, a town situated in the southeast of Chiang Tung (Keng Tung).

55. According to Dao and Kang 1989a, 288, he is Cao Ong (Un) Moeng.

56. His name is transcribed into Cao Ong (Un) Moeng. See Dao and Kang 1989a, 288.

57. In Li Fuyi's Chinese translation of MLC-SV1, 53, it says that Cao Ong Moeng had two sons. The eldest son was Cao Sali Sunanta and the second son was Cao In Moeng. According to MLC-LV1, 19, s. 18.1, the second son of Cao Nò (Ong) Moeng was Cao In Moeng (r. 1569–1598), who was the younger brother of Cao Sali Sunanta. According to MLC-LV2, s. 22.11, the second son of Cao Un (Ong) Moeng was Cao In Moeng (r. 1569–1578), the younger brother of Cao Sali Sunanta.

in the *poek cai* year, CS 950 (AD 1588), at the age of sixteen. He was on the throne seven years and passed away (*cuti*) at the age of twenty-three in the *dap met* year, CS 957 (1595 AD). This is the sixteenth generation (twentieth ruler) of the dynasty.

21. CAO NÒ MOENG (DAO NUO MENG), R. 1595–1609

Cao Un (On) Moeng had one son by the name of Cao Nò Moeng who succeeded [his paternal elder uncle] to the throne in the *dap met* year, CS 957 (AD 1595), at the age of twenty-eight. He was on the throne fourteen years and passed away (*cuti tai*) at the age of forty-two in the *kat lao* year, CS 971 (AD 1609). This is the seventeenth generation (twenty-first ruler) of the dynasty.[58]

22. CAO SALI SUTHAMMA (ZHAO SHILI SUTANMA), R. 1609–1620

Cao Nò Moeng had one son named Cao Sali Suthamma, who succeeded his father to the throne in the *kat lao* year, CS 971 (AD 1609), at the age of sixteen. He was on the throne eleven years and passed away (*cuti tai*) at the age of twenty-seven in the *kot san* year, CS 982 (AD 1620). This is the eighteenth generation (twenty-second ruler) of the dynasty.

23. CAO [MÒM] KHAM LÜ (ZHAO KAN LE), R. 1620–1623

Cao Sali Suthamma had two sons: the eldest son was called Cao [Mòm] Kham Lü, and the second son was called Cao Mòm Tao. Cao [Mòm] Kham Lü succeeded his father to the throne in the *kot san* year, CS 982 (AD 1620), at the age of twenty-two. He was on the throne three years and passed away (*cuti tai*) at the age of twenty-five in the year CS 985 (AD 1623). [This is the nineteenth generation (twenty-third ruler) of the dynasty.]

24. CAO MÒM TAO (DAO MU DAO), R. 1623–1628

Cao [Mòm] Kham Lü had two sons: The eldest son Cao Mòm Saeng Moeng died before he could succeed his father to the throne. The second son by the name of Cao Nò Moeng[59] was still young when his father passed away. His younger paternal uncle (*ao* อาว), Cao

58. Cao In Moeng's name and reign is not recorded in MLC-SV1. According to MLC-LV1, 19, s. 18.1, Cao Sali Suthamma who reigned only six months was succeeded by his younger brother Cao In Moeng (r. 1568–1598). See also MLC-LV2, s. 24.1 and Gao Lishi 1984, 115, s. 24.1.

59. Note that his name is the same as his great-grandfather, the twenty-first ruler.

Mòm Tao, brought him up as his son (adopted him). After the decease of Cao [Mòm] Kham Lü, Cao Mòm Tao succeeded his elder brother to the throne in the *ka kai* year, CS 985 (AD 1623), at the age of seventeen. He was on the throne five years and passed away (*cuti*) at the age of twenty-two in the *poek si* year, CS 990 (AD 1628). This is the nineteenth generation (twenty-fourth ruler) of the dynasty.[60]

25. CAO NÒ MOENG (DAO NUO MENG), R. 1628–1640

Cao Mòm Tao had one son whose name was Cao Moeng Tao.[61] After the death of Cao Mòm Tao, Cao Nò Moeng succeeded in his younger paternal uncle's stead in the *poek si* year, CS 990 (AD 1628), at the age of thirteen. He was on the throne twelve years and passed away (*cuti tai*) without an heir {in the *khot si* year, CS 1002 (AD 1640)}.[62] This is the twentieth generation (twenty-fifth ruler) of the dynasty.

26. CAO MOENG TAO (DAO MENG TAO), R. 1640–1644

Cao Moeng Tao had one son called Cao Paeng Moeng. Cao Moeng Tao succeeded his elder brother[63] (sic) to the throne in the *khot si* year, CS 1002 (AD 1640), at the age of seventeen. He was on the throne four years and passed away (*cuti tai*) at the age of twenty-one in the *kap san* year, CS 1006 (AD 1644). This is the twenty-first generation (sic) (twentieth generation) (twenty-sixth ruler) of the dynasty.[64]

27. CAO PAENG MOENG (ZHAO BIAN MENG), R. 1666–1708

When Cao Paeng Moeng succeeded his father to the throne, he was still young. The queen mother (*nang tewi*) held the regency. [She ruled as regent] from the year *kap san* (AD 1644) on down to the *lai* (*rai*) *sanga* year, CS 1028 (AD 1666), until Cao Paeng Moeng was twenty-two years old and came of age. The queen then handed the rule to him {but still helped him to rule the land}.[65]

60. Cao Mòm Kham Lü and Cao Mòm Tao belonged to the same generation.

61. His name is very close to that of his father Cao Mòm Tao (Dao Mu Dao).

62. For the information in braces, see Dao and Kang 1989a, 289.

63. In fact Cao Nò Moeng and Tao Moeng Tao were cousins.

64. In 1644 the Ming dynasty (1368–1644) was overthrown by the Manchu, who founded the Qing dynasty (1644–1911).

65. See Dao and Kang 1989a, 290.

In the *ka pao* year, CS 1035 (AD 1673), the queen mother died at the age of seventy-three. Cao Paeng Moeng [formally] became ruler at the age of twenty-two. He was on the throne sixty-four years and passed away (*cuti tai*) at the age of eighty-six in the year *poek cai*, CS 1070 (AD 1708), the year Yongzheng 2 (*Yung cün nai* 2), on the thirteenth day of the waxing moon in the second month (AD 1724).[66] This is the twenty-second generation (sic) (in fact twenty-first) [ruler of the dynasty].

28. TAO CIN PAO (DAO JINBAO), R. 1708–1713

Cao Paeng Moeng had two sons: the eldest son was called Tao Cin Pao, and the second son was called Tao Sao Wün. Tao Cin Pao succeeded his father to the throne in the *poek cai* year, CS 1070 (AD 1708), at the age of sixteen and was on the throne five years (i.e., until AD 1713). [He] had a son called Cao Thao Hu Nok, who suffered from a speech impediment (a stammer) and was unable to pronounce words clearly. {This is the twenty-second generation (twenty-eighth ruler) of the dynasty}.[67]

29. TAO SAO WÜN (DAO SHAOWEN), R. 1713–1766

As a result, Tao Cin Pao's younger brother Tao Sao Wün [was nominated] to succeed him as ruler at the age of twelve. [He ruled until] he was fifty-three years old (AD 1754), never thoughtful[68] in running the country's administration[69] or dealing with the Heavenly Court and the Burmese court.[70] As a result, he was deposed.[71] He passed away at the age of sixty-three in the *lai* (*rai*) *set* year, CS 1128 (AD 1766).

Tao Sao Wün had six sons: the eldest son was Tao Wui Phin, the second son Tao Cao [Then] (Thian), the third son Tao Cao Paeng, the fourth son Tao [Khamòm] Suwan, the fifth son Tao Saeng Moeng, and the sixth son Tao Cao Cai. [This is also the twenty-second generation (twenty-ninth ruler) of the dynasty].

66. This date is equivalent to CS 1070 Margasirsha 13 or Sunday, 25 November 1708.

67. This information is not given in MLC-SV1, 57, but added in Li Fuyi 1983b, 99, i.e., the revised edition of his 1947 edition of MLC-SV1.

68. *Bò toei* (Tr. บ่เตย).

69. *Kan ban moeng* (Tr. การบ้านเมิง).

70. *Kan hò man* (Tr. การห้อม่าน). Here Li Fuyi (MLC-SV1, 57) renders it as *tianchao* 天 朝 (Heavenly Court), i.e., the incumbent Manchu court, and the *mianchao* 緬 朝 (Burmese court). In the original Tai Lü text it says *kan hò man*, lit., "activities [pertaining to] the Chinese [and] the Burmese". Li Fuyi's translation is rather free but appropriate.

71. This sentence differs totally from that of Dao and Kang 1989a. He was deposed because he was incompetent, which is confirmed by MLC-LV1, 31, s. 27; MLC-LV2, s. 33.2; Gao Lishi 1984, 121, s. 33.2. According to MLC-LV1, 31, he was deposed in the year CS 1129 (AD 1767).

30. TAO WUI PHIN (DAO WEIPING), R. 1766–1781

After Tao Sao Wün had been deposed, [his eldest son] Tao Wui Phin was [nominated] forthwith to succeed his father. It was in the *lai* (*rai*) *set* year, CS 1128 (AD 1766), when he was forty-one years old. Later, because of listening to the slanderous talk of Cao Moeng Nai, his younger brother Tao Cao Then's son-in-law, he led his father and members of the royal family to desert Sipsòng Panna. They broke with the realm and with the superior officials (*sang sü*),[72] and proceeded to Burma. Later, he returned to the country (to Chiang Rung), but because Tao Wui Phin's behaviour was disloyal and insincere, the high-ranking Chinese officials lost confidence in him. A superior official arrived to take his fourth younger brother Tao Khamòm Suwan (i.e., Tao Suwan) to the Chinese domain (in Simao or Kunming). Afterwards, Tao Wui Phin was [arrested and] interrogated. The superior official, taking along the official seal with him, was escorted to Moeng Maen (Ninger), [whence] he and his younger brother [Tao Suwan] were transferred to Moeng Sae Long (Kunming) under escort. The official seal of "Cheli Military-cum-Civilian Pacification Commission"[73] was confiscated from [Tao] Wui Phin and given to Tao Suwan. He was ordered to return to [Chiang Rung] and succeed his eldest brother to the throne to rule Sipsòng Panna. [As for Tao] Wui Phin he was detained in Moeng Sae Long (Kunming). [Tao] Wui Phin was on the throne a total of fifteen years. He died in Moeng Sae Long at the age of twenty-five (sic) in the *hong pao* year, CS 1143 (AD 1781), namely in Qianlong (*khaen nung*) 44 (sic) (AD 1779).[74] {This is the twenty-third generation (thirtieth ruler) of the dynasty}.[75]

31. CAO MÒM SUWAN (DAO SHIWAN), R. 1781–1797

In that year the superior official issued a new seal of the Cheli Pacification Commission (*choeli saenwi*)[76] to Cao Mòm Suwan (Tai: Khamòm Suwan), and the old seal was

72. The Tai Lü term *sang sü* is obviously a loanword of the Chinese *shangsi* 上司 (superior authority). Here it probably means the senior officials in Kunming (Moeng Sae Long) or Simao (Moeng La).

73. According to the original Tai Lü text it is: "The official seal of *choeli kwin min saenwi*", rendered into Chinese by Li Fuyi (MLC-SV1, 59) as 車里軍民宣慰[使司] (in Pinyin, *cheli junmin xuanwei* [*shisi*]), translated into English as "Cheli Military-cum-Civilian Pacification Commission". This is the official post of the Ming court for Moeng Lü.

74. The year CS 1143 (AD 1781) corresponds to Qianlong 46 (AD 1781). If Cao Mòm Suwan ascended the throne at the age of forty-one and ruled fifteen years, he was fifty-six years old when he died in Kunming.

75. This is taken from MLC-SV1, 59, translated by Li Fuyi.

76. The words engraved on the seal, according to the seal used by Dao Cheng'en (Tao Soen

surrendered to [the Qing court]. Cao Mòm Suwan succeeded his elder brother to the throne in the *hong pao* year, CS 1143 (AD 1781), Qianlong 44 (sic) (AD 1779).[77] Both the emperor of China (*cao hò*) and the Burmese king (*man*)[78] had appointed [him as their vassal ruler]. He was at that time age thirty-six. He was on the throne seventeen years and passed away (*cuti tai*) at the age of fifty-three in the *moeng sai* year, CS 1159 (AD 1797), Jiaqing 1 (*ca khing waen*), on the fourth day of the waxing moon in the fifth month.[79] This is the twenty-third generation (thirty-first ruler) of the dynasty.

32. TAO THAI KHÒ (DAO TAIHE) OR CAO MÒM MAHA WONG, R. 1798–1801

The superior officials [of China] were annoyed that Tao Cao Then had listened to the words of his son-in-law Cao Moeng Nai and brought his officials and royal relatives to Burma. Therefore, he was not allowed to succeed to [the throne], to hold the powers and seal [of office]. Tao Cao Paeng died before he could succeed to [the throne] and left no heir. Tao Cao Saeng Moeng (Tao Saeng Moeng) also died before he could inherit [the throne]. When Tao [Khamòm] Suwan was the ruler, he had three sons: The eldest son, namely [my] elder paternal uncle Tao Thai Phin (in Pinyin, Dao Taiping),[80] died early without an heir. The second son was [the scribe Tao Coen Cong's] elder uncle Tao Thai Khò (or Cao Mòm Maha Wong), and the third son, namely [the scribe Tao Coen Cong's] father Tao Thai Khang (Cao Mòm Maha Wang). After the death of [my (the scribe Tao Coen Cong's)] grandfather Tao [Khamòm] Suwan, Tao Thai Khò succeeded his father to the throne to rule the land. This was in the *poek sanga* year, CS 1160 year (AD 1798), in the year Jiaqing 2 (1797 AD) (sic), and he was twenty-eight years old. He was on the throne three years and passed away (*cuti tai*) at the age of thirty in the *hong lao (ruang rao)* year, CS 1163 (AD 1801), in the year Jiaqing 5, on the eighth day of the waxing moon in the eighth month (sic).[81] This is the twenty-fourth generation (thirty-second ruler) of the dynasty.

Oen) since the end of the Qing period, should read: "The seal of Yunnan Simao Ting Pacification Commission", twelve characters, in two lines, each character in seal script.

77. The year CS 1143 corresponds to 1781 AD and Qianlong 46.

78. *Cao hò an man tan hü* (เจ้าห้ออ่านม่านทานหื้อ) can also be translated as "the Heavenly Court and the court of Ava had appointed [him as vassal ruler]".

79. Sunday, 18 February 1798. The year CS 1159 corresponds to AD 1797 and Jiaqing 2.

80. Here Li Fuyi (MLC-SV1, 59) adds a parenthesis: this is from Tao Coen Cong's (i.e., Cao Mòm Suca Wanna Laca's) perspective. Thus the chronicle was probably recorded by Tao Coen Cong. Li Fuyi (MLC-SV1) uses the term *bofu* 伯 父, which in Chinese means the paternal elder uncle, i.e., the elder brother of one's father.

81. 1163 Jyeṣṭha 8 or Wednesday, 20 May 1801.

33. TAO THAI KHANG (DAO TAIKANG) OR CAO MÒM MAHA WANG, R. 1802–1817

[My] elder paternal uncle Tao Thai Khò (or Cao Mòm Maha Wong) and [his consort] Nang Paen Moeng La[82] had a son, who was namely my elder brother (sic)[83] Tao Sunwu (Cao Maha Nòi). [My elder uncle] died [when his son] was just two months [old].[84] At that time the Son of Heaven (Cao Fa Wong)[85] conferred the official seal (*cum yin*)[86] and letter of appointment (*khao si*)[87] on my father Tao Thai Khang (Cao Mòm Maha Wang). He was to administer the affairs of the land[88] on behalf of [his infant nephew], and to succeed his elder brother (refers to Tao Thai Khò) to rule Sipsòng Panna. It was in the *tao set* year, CS 1164 (AD 1802), in Jiaqing 7 (1802) (*ca khing* 7), [and he was] eighteen years old. {This is also the twenty-fourth generation (thirty-third ruler) of the dynasty.}[89]

34. TAO SUNWU (DAO SHENGWU) OR CAO MAHA NÒI, R. 1817–1833

[My (Tao Coen Cong's)] father (Tao Thai Khang) acted as the regent sixteen years, until his nephew Tao Sunwu (Cao Maha Nòi) came of age and could take over administrating the land. Then Tao Thai Khang (Cao Mòm Maha Wang) reported the matter to the superior officials (*sangi sü*, i.e., Ch. *shangsi*) [in Simao or Kunming], requesting that they issue the official seal (*com yin*),[90] and formally appoint Tao Sunwu to succeed

82. Here Li Fuyi (MLC-SV1, 61 explains in parenthesis that she was namely the daughter of the Liushun aboriginal commission, i.e., the daughter of the Cao Moeng La (i.e., Liushun).

83. Here it means the scribe's elder brother (*phi kha*). But in fact Tao Sunwu (Ch. Dao Shengwu) and Tao Coen Cong (Ch. Dao Zhengzong) were cousins.

84. Here Li Fuyi (MLC-SV1, 61) explains in parenthesis: It means the death of the elder uncle Tao Thai Khò instead of Tao Sunwu.

85. *Cao fa wong* is a combination of *cao fa* (Tai Lü: lord of heaven) and *wong* (Ch. *wang* 王, king). Here Li Fuyi (MLC-SV1, 61) renders it as *tianzi* 天子 (son of heaven), i.e., the emperor of China.

86. The Tai Lü term *cum yin* is most probably a Chinese loanword *zhong yin* 中印 (Chinese seal), translated by Li Fuyi (MLC-SV1, 61) into *yinxin* 印信 (seal and credential).

87. The Tai Lü term *khao si* is most probably a loanword of the Chinese *zhaozhi* 照紙, which is a letter of appointment. Li Fuyi (MLC-SV1, 61) renders it as *yinxin zhaozhi* 印信照紙, which means seals and letter of appointment, a sort of credential.

88. Here Li Fuyi (MLC-SV1, 61) renders it as "affairs of the commission" (*siwu* 司務); here *si* 司 is the abbreviation of *xuanwei si* 宣慰司 (pacification commission).

89. The statement is not taken from Li Fuyi 1983b, 103.

90. Here Li Fuyi (MLC-SV1, 61) renders it as *gua feng zhao zhi* 掛封照紙, which means "letters of appointment".

my father to the throne. It was in the *moeng pao* year, CS 1179 (AD 1817). In the year Daoguang (*tao khang*) 13 (AD 1833), when my elder brother (cousin) Tao Sunwu was deposed, he took the seal and fled. At this time the superior officials forbade his son to succeed him.

Tao Thai Khang (Cao Mòm Maha Wang) had two sons: The elder was Tao Coen Cong (in Pinyin, Dao Zhengzong, i.e., the scribe), whose Tai name was Cao Mòm Suca Wanna Laca; the second son was Tao Soen Cong (in Pinyin, Dao Chengzong), whose Tai name was Lamma Awuttha Kumman. [My] father Tao Thai Khang (Cao Mòm Maha Wang) looked for his nephew Tao Sunwu (Cao Maha Nòi) without success. So he made me (i.e., Tao Coen Cong or Cao Mòm Suca Wanna Laca) his (i.e., Tao Thai Khò) adopted son (*luk kep*) and heir to the throne (lit., "holder of the [official] seal"). This is the twenty-fifth generation (thirty-fourth ruler) of the dynasty.[91]

35. TAO COEN CONG (DAO ZHENGZONG) OR CAO MÒM SUCA WANNA LACA, R. 1837–1865

Tao Thai Khang (Cao Móm Maha Wang) was born (*koet*) in the year CS 1198 (AD 1836) and died[92] in the *lai* (*rai*) *san* year.[93] In the *hong pao* year, CS 1203 (AD 1841), Cao Nò Kham[94] leading Burmese troops, encamped at Ta Kò[95] and killed Phaya Long Sing.[96]

Tao Coen Cong (Cao Móm Suca Wanna Laca), born in the *ka met* year [CS 1185] (AD 1823), succeeded his father as the ruler at the age of fourteen (in AD 1837). He was on the throne twenty-eight years and died (*sang bun sia*) in the foothills of Dòi Ai Laeng Hap Long (i.e., in AD 1865). This is the twenty-fifth generation (thirty-fifth ruler) of the dynasty.

91. From the context, the authorship of this part of the genealogy is ascribed to Tao Coen Cong (i.e., Cao Mòm Suca Wanna Laca).

92. *Sang bun* (Siam.: สร้างบุญ) means "to acquire merit". Here Li Fuyi (MLC-SV1, 61) uses the word *zu* 卒, which means "die" or "pass away", instead of *hong* 薨 (death of a feudal lord or prince).

93. Here the scribe might have made a mistake. It could have been that Tao Thai Khang (Cao Móm Maha Wang) died in the *lai* (*rai*) *san* year CS 1198 (AD 1836). According to Li Fuyi (MLC-SV2, 61), Tao Thai Khang died in CS 1186 (1836), the *bingshen* (*lai san*) year.

94. Cao Nò Kham was the grandson of Tao Cao Then (the second son of Tao Sao Wün). Tao Cao Then was the younger brother of Tao Wui Phin. See MLC-LV1, 31, s. 27.2.

95. Located on the east of the Mekong in Chiang Rung.

96. Phaya Long Sing was a high civil official of Chiang Rung under the *saenwi fa*. See Li Fuyi 1933, 107 (Cheli); MLC-LV2, s. 39.19; Gao Lishi 1984, 127, s. 39.30.

36. TAO CIN AN (DAO JUN'AN), CAO MÒM KHUNG KHAM, OR CAO MÒM SÒ, R. 1866–1878

Cao Mòm Khung Kham (Tao Cin An or Cao Mòm Sò)[97] was born in the *moeng met* year, CS 1209 (AD 1847), on the third day of the waxing moon in the tenth month.[98] In the *kap cai* year, CS 1226 (AD 1864), at the age of eighteen, he went to Ava. [He returned] at the age of twenty to succeed his elder uncle [Cao Mòm] Suca Wanna [Laca] to the throne (i.e., in AD 1866). [Cao Mòm Khung Kham] had four sons. The eldest son was called Cao Mòm Kham Lü (Tao Soen Oen), the second son was Cao Phomma, the third son was Cao Còm Moeng, and the fourth son was Cao Khòng (Khung) Kham. Tao Cin An (Cao Mòm Sò) reigned twelve years and passed away at the age of thirty-one in the *poek yi* year, CS 1240 (AD 1878). This is the twenty-sixth generation (thirty-sixth ruler) of the dynasty.

37. CAO MÒM KHAM LÜ OR TAO SOEN OEN (DAO CHENG'EN), R. 1878–1922

At that time, Cao Mòm Kham Lü, whose [sinicised] name was Tao Soen Oen (Dao Cheng'en),[99] was [nominated] to succeed his father to the throne at the age of twenty. He was on the throne forty-four years and passed away (*sang bun pai*) at the age of sixty-four in the *tao set* year, CS 1284 (AD 1922). This is the twenty-seventh generation (thirty-seventh ruler) of the dynasty.

Cao [Mòm] Kham Lü (i.e., Tao Soen Oen) had nine sons: the eldest son was Cao Mòm Long Khòng Kham,[100] the second son was Cao Mòm Kang, the third son was Cao Mòm Mahacai,[101] the fourth son Cao Mòm Tui, the fifth son Cao Mòm La, the sixth son Cao Mòm Saeng Moeng, the seventh son Cao Mòm Khung Kham, the eighth son Cao Mòm Maha Khu Phomma or Cao Mòm Phomma, and the ninth son was Cao Mòm Mani Kham.[102]

97. Tao Cin An (Dao Jun'an), whose Tai Lü name is Cao Khamòm Khung Kham, was also called Tao Mòm Sò for his skin was rather dark purple. Tao Cin An, the son of Tao Soen Cong (Cao Lamma Awuttha Kumman) and his wife of Moeng Long, was adopted by his uncle Dao Zhengzong (Tao Coen Cung or Cao Mòm Suca Wanna Laca). See MLC-LV2, s. 39.27; Gao Lishi 1984, 127.

98. 1209 Śrāvaṇa 3 or Saturday, 14 August 1847.

99. According to Gao Lishi 1984, 128, Cao Mòm Kham Lü was the grandson of Tao Cin An (or Cao Mòm Sò, i. e., Cao Khamòm Khung Kham), namely the eldest son of his daughter. He grew up in Chiang Tung (Keng Tung). See also MLC-LV2, s. 41.5

100. He was also known as Cao Mòm Suwanna Phakhang (alias Tung Laeng).

101. His sinicised name was Dao Weiying. See Li Fuyi 1983b, 54, revised edition of MLC-SV1.

102. His sinicised names were Dao Zixin or Dao Dongxin. See Li Fuyi 1983b, revised edition of MLC-SV1. For the nine sons of Cao Mòm Kham Lü, see also MLC-LV2, 42.8.

38. CAO MÒM LONG KHONG KHAM (DAO DONGLIANG), R. 1926–1943

Cao Mòm Long [Khong Kham] (Tao Tung Laeng) succeeded his father to the throne at the age of forty, in the *lai* (*rai*) *yi* year, CS 1288, (AD 1926). He was on the throne seventeen years and passed away at the age fifty-seven in the *ka met* year, CS 1305, on the second day of the waning moon in the eighth month.[103] {This is the twenty-eighth generation (thirty-eighth ruler) of the dynasty.}[104] Cao Mòm Long Khong Kham had two sons: the eldest [son] was called Cao Mòm In Moeng,[105] and the second son was Cao Mahacai. The two brothers were still young.[106]

103. 1305 Jyeṣṭha 17 or Saturday, 19 June 1943.

104. This sentence is neither in MLC-SV1, 63, nor in the Tai Lü text, but added in Li Fuyi 1983b, 109, the revised edition of MLC-SV1.

105. The eldest son's sinicised name was Dao Shide. See Li Fuyi 1983b, revised edition of MLC-SV1.

106. The genealogy ends in 1943 when Li Fuyi translated the MLC-SV1 into Chinese and published it in Kunming in April 1947. According to Li Fuyi 1983b/2008b, 109, revised edition of MLC-SV1, the seal of the *saenwi fa* of Sipsòng Panna was lost in Daoguang 13 (1833) when Tao Sunwu (Dao Shengwu) fled with it.

Two Tai Ya women near Moeng Yang, Sipsòng Panna (Volker Grabowsky, 2005)

Tai and Kha vendors sell vegetables at a market in Chiang Tung (Apiradee Techasiriwan, 2004)

Tai Lü villagers near Chiang Rung, in 1944 (Reprinted from Smith and Clark 1954)

Traditional Tai Lü house at Ban Mòng near Chiang Rung (Volker Grabowsky, 2005)

Tai Lü village near Chiang Rung (Volker Grabowsky, 2005)

Wat Pa Cae Mahā Rājasathān Sipsòng Panna, Chiang Rung (Volker Grabowsky, 2005)

The guilded stupa of Wat Phrathat Kham Moeng Laem (Volker Grabowsky, 2005)

Main stupa and *vihan* of Wat Phasat Ceng (Chiang) Coeng, Moeng Cae (Renoo Wichasin, 2005)

Stupa near the remains of Wiang Phakhang (Kannikar Wimonkasem, 2005)

Ubosot of Wat Phasat Ceng (Chiang) Coeng, Moeng Cae (Volker Grabowsky, 2005)

Present-day trading centre of Moeng Hai
(Renoo Wichasin, 2006)

Building belonging to the complex of the *hò kham* (ruler's palace) of Moeng Laem (Volker Grabowsky, 2005)

Tea trading centre in Simao city
(Renoo Wichasin, 2005)

Shop owned by Chinese Muslims (*hò phasi*) in Simao
(Renoo Wichasin, 2005)

Terraced rice fields along the route from Moeng Laem to Moeng Cae
(Volker Grabowsky, 2005)

Tai Lü house near Chiang Rung (Kannikar Wimonkasem, 2005)

The Chinese characters say: *Cheli xuanwei shisi yishiting,* "The Council of Nobles (*noe sanam*) of the Cheli Pacification Commission." Cultural Bureau of Sipsòng Panna Prefecture. (Volker Grabowsky, 2002)

Monastic library (*hò tham*) of Wat Luang Ceyyavaṃsa Mahā Rājasathān Śrī Còm Moeng, Moeng Cae (Renoo Wichasin, 2005)

Stupa (*phathat*) at Wat Ban Foei Lung, Moeng Long (Volker Grabowsky, 2002)

Entrance to monastery in Chiang Tung, c. 1890
(British Library, OIOC [Sir J. George Scott collection], 92/5 (55))

Vihan of Wat Luang Rājasathān Wiang Kang (Klang), Moeng Laem (Volker Grabowsky 2005)

Mural painting at Wat Ban Ca, Moeng Ham (Volker Grabowsky, 2002)

ภยาเวสนฺตรทานช้างเผิกแก้วงางอน ไภ่อสดอนสมเสด ไภ่เมิงเคด ขับหนี ไพเข้าบวดเปน ชีปล่าไม้
Prince Vessantra (Phaya Wetsandòn) offers his precious albino elephant. The people mock him and, full of anger, they chase him away to live henceforth as an ascetic in the forest.

Mural painting of the Buddha's life at Wat Ban Cong, Moeng Laem
(Renoo Wichasin, 2005)

Li Fuyi and Foon Ming Liew-Herres in Li Fuyi's apartment in Taibei (Foon Ming Liew-Herres, 1 November 2008)

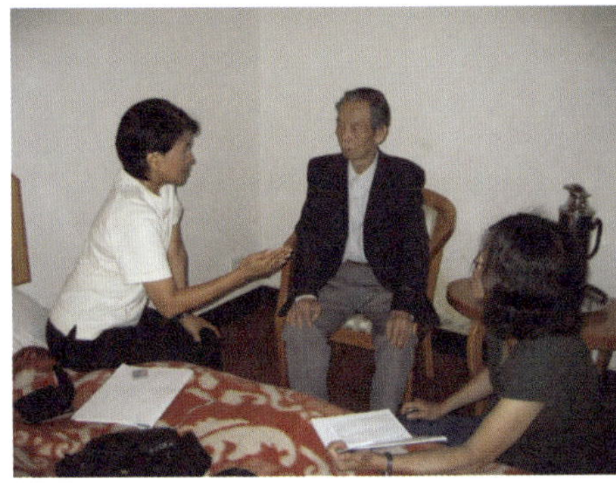

Interview of the co-authors Renoo Wichasin (left) and Foon Ming Liew-Herres (right) with Cao Maha Khanthawong in Chiang Rung (Volker Grabowsky, 9 April 2005)

Cao Mòm Kham Lü, December 1999 in Chiang Rung (Reprinted from Yanyong and Ratanaporn 2001)

From left to right: the owner of the manuscript of the *Moeng Laem Chronicle*, the abbot of Wat Phathat Kham Moeng Laem, and a monk of Wat Phathat Kham Moeng Laem (Volker Grabowsky, 2005)

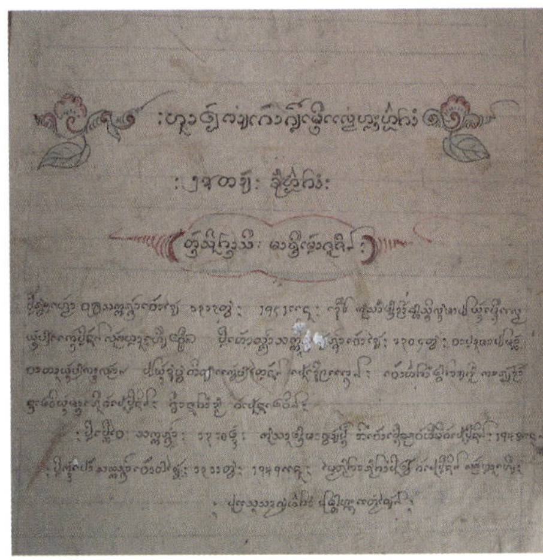

Cover folio of a mulberry paper manuscript of the *Moeng Laem Chronicle*, dated 1984 (Volker Grabowsky, 2005)

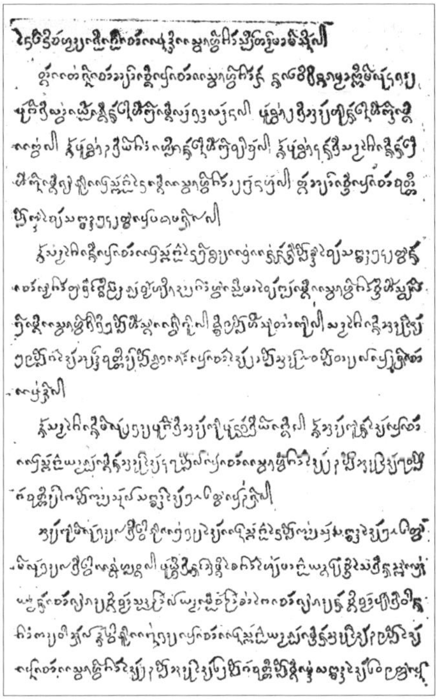

First page of MLC-SV1 chronicling the first four *cao fa* (rulers) of Moeng Lü (Li Fuyi 1947b, 44)

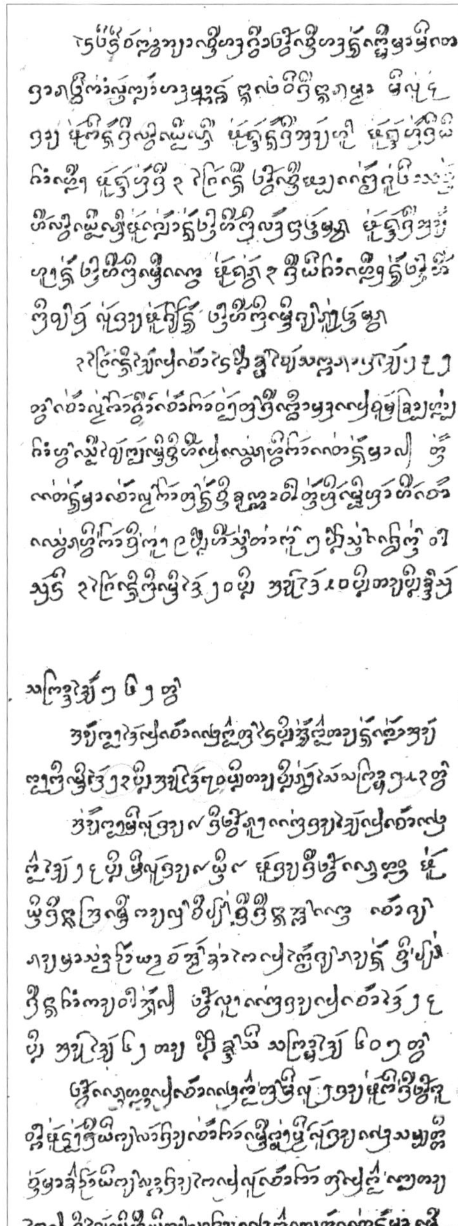

First page of MLC-SV2 chronicling the first five *cao fa* (rulers) of Moeng Lü (Gao Lishi 1982, 83)

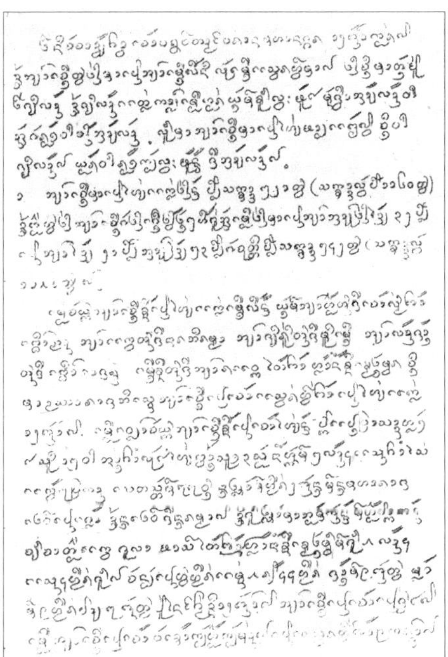

First page of the MLC-LV2 chronicling the first ruler (*cao phaendin*) of Moeng Lü, Phaya Coeng (Cüang) (Unpublished 1963, 1)

Remains of the ancient city wall of Moeng Phong (Volker Grabowsky, 2002)

The wall from above (Volker Grobowsky, 2002)

City gate of Moeng Mao (Aranya Siriphon, 2006)

Pa Daeng Gate in the town of Chiang Tung (Apiradee Techasiriwan, 2004)

City gate of Chiang Rung (Reprinted from Smith and Clark, 1954)

IV. Genealogy of the *Cao Phaendin* of Sipsòng Panna (MLC-SV2)

1. PHAYA COENG HAN (BA ZHEN HAN)

Here the events of Phaya Coeng Han (Phaya Coeng) will be related. He was [highly revered and][1] very powerful. His queen, named Nang Lamma (Nan langma), bore four sons: The eldest was named Lao Yoe Hoeng (Roeng), the second son was named Ai Hung, the third son was named Yi Kham Loeng, and the fourth son was named Sam Khai Noeng. Tao Coeng defeated various lands and enfeoffed his eldest son with Lan Na as his domain; the second son was given Moeng Kaeo[2] to rule; the third son was given Wiang Can (Vientiane)[3] to rule, and the youngest son was given Moeng Ceng Hung (i.e., Moeng Chiang Rung)[4] to rule.

2. SAM KHAI NOENG (SANG KAI NENG), R. 1180–1200

Sam Khai Noeng succeeded to the throne[5] in the *khot cai* year,[6] *sakkalaca* (cūḷasakarāja, hereafter abbreviated to CS) 542 (AD 1180). The *cao lum fa* (lord under heaven), namely

1. This phrase is added by Gao Lishi (MLC-SV2, 83); it is not in the original Tai Lü text printed alongside.

2. Vietnam is known by the Tai as Moeng Kaeo (Mengjiao), i.e., Jiaozhi (Annam). See MLC-SV2, 90, n. 4.

3. *Wiang* (เวียง), pronounced *weng* in Tai Lü, means "walled city", *can* (Th. จันทร or จันทน์) means "moon" or "sandalwood" (from Skt. candra or candana respectively).

4. Here "Moeng Ciang" or "Ceng Hung" does not only refer to the township of Chiang Rung; it also alludes to the whole polity of Moeng Lü (or Sipsòng Panna). See MLC-SV2, 90, n 6.

5. *Pen cao* (Tr. เปนเจ้า), lit., "to be ruler or lord". Ch. *wei* 位, meaning "position", here is interpreted as "throne" (*wang wei* 王 位).

6. The Tai, like the Chinese, use ten *tiangan* 天 干 (*mae pi* แม่ปี) and twelve *dizhi* 地 支 (*luk pi* ลูกปี) to number the years. See MLC-SV2, 90, n. 7.

the *cao fa wòng* (a Tai Lü expression for the emperor of China) by the name of Pothiman (Bodhimāna),[7] bestowed on him a seal in the form of a golden plate adorned with a tiger's head. From that point on, he held [the title] *saenwi fa*.[8] At that time Cao Lum Fa said with pity: From now on, the *saenwi fa*[9] is to present a major tribute once every nine years and a lesser tribute once every five years. {This will be sufficient.}[10]
Sam Khai Noeng was on the throne twenty years, lived to the age of eighty, and died in the *khot san* year, CS 562 (AD 1200).

3. AI KÒNG (AI GUANG), R. 1200–1221

Ai Kòng[11] succeeded his father to the throne in the year his father passed away (*tai*). Ai Kòng was on the throne twenty-three years[12] and died (*tai*) in the *hong sai* year, CS 583 (AD 1221), at the age of seventy.

4. TAO HUNG (RUNG) KAEN CAI (DAO LONG JIAN ZAI), R. 1221–1243

Ai Kòng had a son by the name of Tao Hung Kaen Cai, who succeeded his father. [The ruler] had one son and one daughter. The son was called Tao Haeng Long, and the daughter was named Nang O Moeng, later renamed Nang Ok Paeng. When Cao Chiang Rai[13] wanted to marry her, she was renamed Nang Kham Kai. Tao Hung Kaen Cai was on the throne twenty-four years, lived sixty-two years, and passed away (*tai*) in the *khot si* year,[14] CS 605 (AD 1243).

---

7. In other versions of the Moeng Lü Chronicle, such as MLC-LV2, and Dao Shuren 1989, his name is Pothiyan, (Bodhiyāna), lit., "the Buddha's vehicle", which is correct. The mistake here is a scibe's error. See MLC-SV2, 90, n. 10.

8. The term *saenwi fa* is a combination of the Chinese term *xuanwei* (proclaim and pacify) and the Tai term *fa* (sky/heaven). For details, see the introduction, part I, 6.1 and 6.3 in this volume.

9. Hereafter Gao Lishi (MLC-SV2, 83) translates *saenwi fa* as *xuanwei shi* (pacification commissioner). See MLC-SV2, 90, n. 11.

10. The sentence in parenthesis is taken from MLC-SV2, 83.

11. In MLC-LV1, s. 3.1, he was called Tao Beng (Tao Pung or Ai Pung); in MLC-LV2, s. 3.1, he was Ai Kung.

12. According to calculation he was on the throne twenty-one years.

13. Cao Chiang Rai means the "lord of Chiang Rai". Chiang Rai was founded in 1262 by King Mangrai who took up his residence in this city. For three decades Chiang Rai remained the capital of Lan Na. However, after the conquest of Hariphunchai (in 1292) Mangrai moved first to Wiang Kum Kam (near present-day Chiang Mai airport) and finally founded Chiang Mai (lit., "new city") as the new capital of his enlarged kingdom.

14. According to MLC-SV2, 90, n. 14, the year CS 605 was not a *gengchen* (*kot si*) year, but a *guimao* (*ka mao*) year.

5. TAO HAENG LONG (DAO LIANG LONG), R. 1243–1259

Tao Haeng Long succeeded his father to the throne (*pen cao taen pò*). He had two sons: the eldest son was Tao Puwak and the second son was Yi Peng Lak Sai. At that time Cao Fa Moeng Pòng had no son to succeed him. He took Yi Peng Lak Sai as adopted son. Later, after the death of his adoptive father (*pò kep*, Th. พ่อเก็บ), Yi Peng Lak Sai stayed to succeed his adoptive father to rule the country. Since then Cao Moeng Pòng was called *cao saenwi*, and [this title] is used until now (i.e., when the chronicle was written). Cao Haeng Long was on the throne (lit., "was ruler", *pen cao*) sixteen years, and passed away in the *kat met* year, CS 621 (AD 1259) at the age of fifty-four.

6. TAO PUWAK (DAO BUWA), R. 1259–1272

The eldest son of Tao Haeng Long, Tao Puwak, succeeded his father to the throne. He was on the throne fourteen years. He had one son named Tao Ai (Dao Ai). Tao Puwak passed away at the age of forty-five in the *tao san* year, CS 634 (AD 1272).

7. TAO AI (DAO AI), R. 1272–1308

Tao Ai succeeded his father to the throne and reigned forty-one years (sic). He passed away in the *poek san* year,[15] CS 670 (AD 1308).

8. CAO KHAN MOENG (ZHAO KAN MENG), R. 1308–1341/1351

Tao Ai had one son named Cao Khan Moeng. He succeeded his father to the throne. Cao Khan Moeng had three sons: the eldest son was Cao Sida Kham, born to the girl of the Lawa tribe (*nang lua/lawa*), who had procured the three-pronged conch shell (*hòi sam cik*). The second son was Tao Kumman,[16] and the third son was Peo Fai Fa. Phaya Khan Moeng was on the throne forty-four years (sic) and passed away at the age of eighty-three in the *hong mao* year, CS 703 (sic) (AD 1341).[17]

---

15. According to MLC-SV2, 90, n. 16, the *wushen* (*poek san*) year corresponds to the year CS 670 (AD 1308). In this case he reigned thirty-six years.

16. *Kumman*, which is derived from Skt./P. kumāra, means a young boy or son. See MLC-SV2, 90, n. 18.

17. According to MLC-SV2, 90, n. 19, the Chinese *xinmao* (i.e., *hong mao*) year corresponds to the year CS 713 (AD 1351), instead of CS 703; hence he was on the throne forty-three years.

9. TAO SIDA KHAM (DAO XILA HAN), R. 1341–1381 (SIC); R. 1451–1531

Tao Sida Kham, eldest son of Phaya Khan Moeng, succeeded his father to the throne. His younger brother Tao Kumman died [of illness]. Peo Fai Fa had one son called Soe Long Fa (Süa Luang Fa). Before Peo Fai Fa passed away he entrusted the upbringing of his son Soe Long Fa to his elder uncle (*lung*).[18] Tao Sida Kham had one son named Tao Kü Moeng. Tao Sida Kham was on the throne eighty (sic) years and passed away in the *hong kai* year, CS 743 (sic)[19] (AD 1381).

10. TAO KÜ MOENG (DAO KE MENG), R. 1381–1383 (SIC); R. 1431–1433

Tao Kü Moeng, the son of Tao Sida Kham, succeeded his father to the throne. He had three sons: the eldest son was named Tao Bakòng, the second son was named Tao Saeng (sic)[20] (Sòng) Moeng, and the third son was named Tao Sam Pò Lütai. Tao Kü Moeng was on the throne three years. He passed away in the *ka pao* year, CS 745 (sic) (AD 1383).[21]

11. TAO BAKÒNG (DAO BAGONG), R. BETWEEN 1383 AND 1436

Tao Bakòng—then six years old—was the eldest son of Tao Kü Moeng, and was nominated by all [the people] to succeed his father to the throne. He was on the throne three years and was ousted by Tao Kham Tet (Tiat) in the *dap mao* year, CS 798 (AD 1436).[22]

12. TAO SÒNG MOENG (DAO SHUANG MENG), R. 1436

Thus the three-year-old younger brother Tao Sòng Moeng was nominated to succeed his father (sic) (his elder brother) to the throne. He was on the throne only two months and fifteen days before he died (*tai sia*).[23]

18. The elder uncle of Soe Long Fa was namely Tao Sida Kham.

19. According to MLC-SV2, 90, n. 20, the Chinese *xinhai* (i.e., *hong kai*) year corresponds to CS 793 (AD 1431); thus he was on the throne eighty years.

20. According to the Tai Lü manuscript, it is "Saeng", which is a scribal error. But later he was called Tao Sòng Moeng.

21. According to MLC-SV2, 90, n. 21, the Chinese *guichou* (i.e., *ka pao*) year corresponds to CS 795 (AD 1433). If it were CS 745 (AD 1383), it is fifty years less; hence a mistake.

22. According to MLC-SV2, 90, n. 22, the Chinese *yimao* (i.e., *dap mao*) year corresponds to CS 797 (AD 1435), thus he was on the throne only two years.

23. According to other sources Tao Bakòng and Tao Sòng Moeng were sent into exile on a raft

13. TAO KHAM TET (DAO HAN DI), R. 1436–1437

Tao Kham Tet, the son of Tao Sida Kham, succeeded to the throne. Just a year later, Soe Long Fa (Süa Luang Fa) was dissatisfied [with him], and so raised troops to attack him. The fighting could not be stopped. Tao Kham Tiat was defeated and fled with the golden seal to Na Thawai where he died in the *lai* (*rai*) *si* year, CS 799 (AD 1437).[24]

14. SOE LONG FA (SHE LONG FA), R. BETWEEN 1437 AND 1525

Soe Long Fa (Süa Luang Fa), son of Peo (Piao) Fai Fa, succeeded to the throne. He had nine sons: the eldest son was Cao Basaeng (i.e., Tao Phasaeng), the second son was Cao Còm Pha, the third son was Tao Saeo, the fourth son was Tao Yòt, the fifth son was Tao Kham, the sixth son was Tao Ut, the seventh son was Tao Som, the eighth son was Tao Fa Nòi, and the ninth son was Tao Sòt (i.e., Tao Sòt Sòi).

During the time when Soe Long Fa was on the throne, peace prevailed in the region and the people lived in peace and attended to their occupations.[25] At that time there was a Cao Fa Moeng Pòng, whose domain was in Moeng Mao Long, by the name of Soe Ngam Fa.[26] He revolted against Cao Lum Fa. In the *poek sanga* year, CS 800 (AD 1438), Cao Lum Fa sent a senior minister by the name of Sang Sui (Cang Kui, i.e., Jiang Gui)[27] to command troops to fight against [Soe Ngam Fa]. Soe Ngam Fa fled to Moeng Man.[28] One important Shan official (*khun phòng yai*) escaped to Moeng Lü (Sipsòng Panna). After he had been killed by the *cao saenwi fa* Soe Long Fa, his head was chopped off and presented to Cao Lum Fa (i.e., Emperor Zhengtong). [Consequently, Soe Long Fa] gained the appreciation of Cao Lum Fa and was granted the [additional] title *khai waen cang ki kwin swaen kin ya*

---

down the Mekong River. Tao Bakòng is given credit as founder of Chiang Khaeng, now in Laos. See Gao Lishi 1984, 110, s. 16.4. As to the mythical founding of Chiang Khaeng, see Grabowsky 2003b; Grabowsky and Renoo 2008.

24. According to MLC-SV2, 90, n. 23, the Chinese *bingchen* (i.e., *lai/rai si*) year corresponds to CS 798 (AD 1436).

25. According to MLC-SV2, 90, n. 24, the original text reads: *sug[g]ati gamana*, in P. *sugati* means "happiness; bliss", and *gamana* means "pursuit; striving for". Thus the phrase means, "in pursuit of happiness".

26. Moeng Mao Long (Luang) is in present-day Ruili, Dehong Prefecture, southwestern Yunnan. This refers to the four Luchuan-Pingmian campaigns launched by the Ming court in the Zhengtong reign (1436–1449). See Liew 1996.

27. Gao Lishi (MLC-SV2, 85) transcribes Cang Kui (in Tai Lü) into Zhang Zhui 張 綴 (in Pinyin). Gao points out that the transcriptions of the Chinese name into Tai is not accurate. He was probably Jiang Gui 蔣 貴 (1380–1449). See MLC-SV2, 90, n. 26. Jiang Gui (1380–1449) was the Earl of Pacifying the West, one of the commanders-in-chief sent to quell the unrest in Moeng Mao (i.e., Luchuan-Pingmian). Liew 1996. CS 800 corresponds to the year Zhengtong 3 (AD 1438).

28. The Tai Lü usually called Burma "Moeng Man" (เมิงม่าน).

mün.[29] The official post conferred on [him] was higher than that on Lan Cang (Sang),[30] Lan Na, Moeng Khün,[31] [and] Moeng Laem. Moreover, additional territories, [including] Moeng Cung (Mengzhong, i.e., Yuanjiang), Moeng Maen (Mengmian, i.e., Puer), Bò Hoek (Mohei), Moeng Saeng (i.e., Puer and Mengxian region), Moeng Tae (Mengdi), Khwaen Siao (Quanxiu), [and] Nam Kot (Naguo), were granted to the *cao saenwi fa* as his vassals. Soe Long Fa was on the throne twenty years and passed away at the age of eighty in the *dap kai* year, CS 887 (AD 1525).[32] He was the seventeenth (sic)[33] ruler of the dynasty.

15. TAO BAKÒNG'S (DAO BAGONG'S) SON (SIC), R. 1525

The son of Tao Bakòng succeeded to the throne and died [of illness] four months later.[34]

16. TAO SAM PÒ LÜTAI (DAO SAN BO LEDAI), R. 1525–1528

Tao Sam Pò Lütai succeeded to the throne. He had four children: the eldest child was Tao Yi, the second child was Sam Khai Noeng, the third child was Cao Am, and the fourth child was Cao Ai. [Tao] Sam Pò Lütai was on the throne three years (sic) and passed away at the age of fifty in the *dap sai* year, CS 890 (AD 1528).[35]

29. This is a Chinese official title given to Soe Long Fa, which has been transcribed by the scribe into Tai Lü, who probably had heard it from some Chinese officials who could not speak proper Beijing dialect, on which Mandarin is based. It is so poorly transcribed that it is not possible to reconstruct the Chinese title completely. *Khai* could mean "to open" or "to establish"; *waen cang* probably means "Yuanjiang 元 江", i.e., Moeng Cung; *ki kwin swaen kin* is unintelligible; *ya mün* means "government office". Gao Lishi also could not figure out what the title really means. See MLC-SV2, 90, n. 28; MLC-VS1, s. 13, n. 46.

30. Lan Sang means "land of a million elephants"; Lan Sang, pronounced Lan Cang in Tai Lü, is the old kingdom of Laos.

31. The Chinese transcription of Moeng Khün is Menggen 孟 艮, i.e., Chiang Tung (Keng Tung), in present-day Burma.

32. According to MLC-SV2, 90, n. 31, the Chinese *yihai* (i.e., *dap kai*) year corresponds to CS 817 (AD 1455). Thus he was on the throne twenty years. If it were the year CS 887 (AD 1525), then he was not 80, but rather 150 years old, which is an error.

33. According to our calculation there were only fourteen rulers so far.

34. Here most probably a scribal error has occured. He was most probably Tao Pasaeng, the eldest son of Soe Long Fa.

35. According to MLC-SV2, 90, n. 32, the Chinese *yisi* (i.e., *dap sai*) year corresponds to the year CS 847 (AD 1485). He was thus on the throne thirty years.

17. CAO AI (ZHAO AI), R. 1528

The father's throne was reserved for his fourth son Cao Ai to succeed. But after one month [of his rule], all [the people] of the *müang* were dissatisfied. They refused to support the younger brother to inherit the throne while the elder brother was still alive. So they all dismissed him.

18. CAO KHAN MOENG (ZHAO KAN MENG) (SIC), SAM KHAI NOENG (SANG KAI NENG), R. 1528–1548

The people nominated his elder brother Cao Khan Moeng[36] to succeed his younger brother. [He was on the throne] twenty-one years and passed away at the age of sixty-seven in the *poek set* year, CS 910 (AD 1548).[37]

19. PHAYA AEN (BA YAN) FROM MOENG U (MENGWU), R. 1548–1555

[The people] then nominated Phaya Aen, the son of [Cao Khan Moeng], who had been sent to govern Moeng U, to succeed to the throne (*pen cao*). He was on the throne seven years and passed away in the *dap kai* year, CS 917 (AD 1555).[38]

20. SALI SUNANTA LACA (XILI SHUNIANDA LAZHA), R. 1555–1592

[Then] all [the people] nominated the son of his elder brother by the name of Sali Sunanta Laca to succeed to the throne (*pen cao*). He was on the throne thirty-seven years and passed away at the age of sixty-three in the *tao si* year, CS 954 (AD 1592).

---

36. Tao Ai had no elder brother called Cao Khan Moeng. He was probably Sam Khai Noeng. See MLC-SV2, 91, n. 33. Cao Khan Moeng was the son of Tao Ai, ruler no. 8. However, according to MLC-SV1, 53, s. 17, Cao Khan Moeng (Zhao Kan) was the son of Cao Ai who was Tao Sam Pò Lütai's fourth son. This is the same as given in Dao and Kang 1989a, 287.

37. According to MLC-SV2, 91, n. 34, the Chinese *wuxu* year (i.e., *poek set*) corresponds to the year CS 900 (AD 1538). In this case he was on the throne fifty-two years.

38. According to MLC-SV2, 91, n. 36, CS 917 corresponds to the Chinese *yimao* (i.e., *dap mao*) year, namely AD 1555. In this case he was on the throne seventeen years.

21. UPALACA (WUBALAZHA), R. 1592–1606

[Then] all [the people] nominated Kaeo[39] Moeng, the *upalaca*[40] who lived in Chiang Khòng, to succeed to the throne. They held a very grand coronation ceremony, and celebrated with festival activities (*ut sa phi sek*).[41] An honorary title, Maha Thammalaca[42] was conferred on him. He was on the throne fifteen years and passed away in the *lai sanga* year, CS 968 (AD 1606).

22. CAO UN MOENG (ZHAO WEN MENG), R. 1606–1625

The people[43] nominated Cao Un Moeng to be the pacification commissioner (*cao saenwi fa*). He was in office twenty-eight years. The Burmese king by the name of Suttho Thammalaca[44] commanded troops to invade the domain (*müang*) of the [*cao*] *saenwi fa*. It is noted that the territory under Fa Suttho Thammalaca was very extensive. The [incumbent] *cao saenwi fa* Cao Un Moeng was captured and died at Moeng Phayak in the year CS 987 (AD 1625).[45]

23. SUTHAMMA (SUTANMA), R. 1625–1632

Later the people invited the *upalaca* (viceroy) from Chiang Aen to [come and be] the [new] ruler. His name was Suthamma. He was in office seven years and passed away in the *tao san* year, CS 994 (AD 1632).

---

39. Kaeo Moeng (Tr. แก้วเมิง) appears to be a personal name. However, as the semi-vowel *wò waen* (ว), written in subscript, is very similar to the subscript form of the final consonant *mò ma* (ม), *kaeo* could easily be mistaken for *kaem*. *Kaem Moeng* (Tr. แกมเมิง) is an archaic appellation of the viceroy or *upalaca* among the Tai Lü and Tai Khün. Thus Kaem Moeng-Upalaca seems to be a tautological term.

40. *Upalaca* (Tr. อุปราชะ) means viceroy (P. uparāja).

41. According to MLC-SV2, 91, n. 38, *utsa* means "celebrate happily", and *phisek* means "extraordinary". Gao's interpretation is wrong. In fact, *ussalacaphiset* (Tr. อุสสาราชภิเสด), a Pali compound consisting of ussā[ha], "strength, power" + raja, "king" + abhiseka, "consecration, inauguration" (Skt. abhiṣeka).

42. According to MLC-SV2, 91, n. 39, the title is derived from a Pali term (mahādhamma rāja), which means the "great Buddhist, righteous king".

43. *Tanglai* (Tr. ทังหลาย), lit., "all [the people]".

44. He was the Burmese king Bayinnaung (Fa Suttho Thammalaca), r. 1551–1581.

45. According to MLC-SV2, 91, n. 41, the year CS 987 corresponds to the Chinese *yichou* (i.e., *dap pao*) year (AD 1625), the reign of Tianqi 5. If Cao Un Moeng had reigned from AD 1606 to 1625, he was on the throne nineteen years.

24. CAO NÒ MOENG (ZHAO NUO MENG), R. 1632–1645

Cao Nò Moeng, who was namely *upalaca* of Chiang Khòng, the grandson of Sali Suthamma, was enthroned. Cao Nò Moeng had two sons: the eldest son was Cao Kham Lü, and the second son was Cao Mòm Tao. Cao Nò Moeng was in office fourteen years. He passed away at the age of forty-two in the *dap lao* year, CS 1007 (AD 1645).

25. CAO KHAM LÜ (ZHAO HAN LE), R. 1645–1659

Cao Kham Lü succeeded his father to the throne. He had two sons: the eldest son was Cao Saeng Moeng, and the second son was Cao Nò Moeng. Cao Kham Lü was in office seven years and he passed away in the *kat pao* year, CS 1021 (AD 1659).

26. CAO MÒM TAO (ZHAO MENG DAO), R. 1659–1662

Cao Mòm Tao, the younger brother of Cao Kham Lü, succeeded his elder brother to the throne. He had one son and ruled three years. Cao Mòm Tao passed away at the age of twenty in the *tao yi* year, CS 1024 (AD 1662).

27. CAO SAENG MOENG (ZHAO XIANG MENG), R. 1662–1670

Cao Saeng Moeng, the eldest son of Cao Kham Lü, succeeded his paternal younger uncle (*ao*) to the throne. He was in office nine years and passed away at the age of fifteen in the *moeng met* year, CS 1032 (AD 1670).[46]

28. CAO NÒ MOENG (ZHAO NUO MENG), R. 1670–1677

Cao Nò Moeng succeeded his elder brother to the throne. He passed away at the age of fifteen in the *moeng met* year, CS 1039 (AD 1677).[47]

46. According to MLC-SV2, 86, it should have been the Chinese *gengxu* (i.e., *kot set*) year.

47. According to MLC-SV2, 86, it should have been the Chinese *dingsi* (i.e., *moeng sai*) year.

29. CAO MOENG TAO (ZHAO MENG DAO), R. 1677–1682

The son of Cao Mòm Tao was enthroned.[48] He was on the throne eight years. He had one son called Cao Paeng Moeng. The *cao* was in office three years[49] and passed away at the age of twenty in the year *tao set*, CS 1044 (AD 1682).

30. CAO PAENG MOENG (ZHAO BIAN MENG), R. 1682–1726

Cao Paeng Moeng succeeded his father to the throne. As he was still young, his Nang Tewi (i.e., the mother dowager) acted as regent. The mother and son held the seal and credential (i.e., rule) for altogether twenty-nine years. The mother dowager passed away in the *hong mao* year, CS [1073] (AD 1711)[50] at the age of fifty-three. After the death of the mother dowager (*cao nang ton mae*), Tao Paeng Moeng ruled formally. Tao Paeng Moeng had two sons: the eldest son was Tao Cin Pao and the second son was Tao Sao Wün. [...].[51]

31. TAO CIN PAO (DAO JINBAO), R. 1726–1729

Tao Cin Pao succeeded his father and had been in office three years when he died. [...].[52]

32. TAO SAO WÜN (DAO SHAOWEN), R. 1729–1782

Cao Tao Sao Wün succeeded his elder brother to the throne. He had six sons: the eldest son was Tao Wui Phin, the second son was the *upalaca*, the third son was Mòm Cai Long, the fourth son was Tao Khamòm Suwan, the fifth son was Cao Mòm Saeng Moeng, and the sixth son was Cao Mòm Cai Nòi, who was the youngest son.

48. In the original Tai Lü manuscript the name of Tao Mòm Tao's son is not stated. Gao Lishi points out that according to other manuscripts his name is Cao Moeng Tao (Zhao Meng Dao). See MLC-SV2, 91, n. 43.

49. It should have been five years.

50. According to MLC-SV2, 91, n. 44, the original manuscript is torn. It was in the year CS 1073 (AD 1711).

51. According to MLC, 91, n. 45, the original manuscript is torn. However, according to calculation Cao Paeng Moeng was on the throne fifteen years and passed away in the Chinese *bingwu* (*lai/rai sanga*) year, the year CS 1088 (AD 1726).

52. According to MLC-SV2, 91, n. 46, the original manuscript is torn. According to calculation he should have died in the Chinese *jiyou* (i.e., *dap lao*) year, CS 1091 (AD 1729).

{Before Tao Cin Pao's son was born, Tao Sao Wün was already an old Khamòm Thao.}[53] Both princes (*latcabut sòng pha-ong*)[54] ruled until then. Henceforth, [the chronicles] should continue to be recorded carefully.

Cao Khamòm Thao, namely Tao Sao Wün, was enthroned at the age of twelve. He was in office fifty-three years and passed away at the age of sixty-five in the *tao yi* year, CS 1144 (AD 1782).

SUPPLEMENTS TO THE ORIGINAL MANUSCRIPT

1. SUPPLEMENTARY RECORD

Here the events from the first generation founder are to be expounded. After Somdet Cao Phaya Coeng had ascended the throne,[55] [the territories] under his jurisdiction extended to Lan Na, Moeng Kaeo, and Moeng Lao. The king (*somdet pha pen cao*)[56] Phaya Coeng had four sons:

The eldest son Tao Bun Loeng was enfoeffed in Lan Na; the second son Tao Ai Hung (Rung) was enfoeffed in Moeng Kaeo; the third son Tao Yi Kham Hoeng (Roeng) was enfoeffed in Moeng Lao; and the fourth son was Tao Kham Hoeng, who succeeded his father to the throne.

[From the reign of Phaya Coeng] down to the year Jingtai 1 (1450)[57] when Somdet Tao Kham Hoeng submitted to the Chinese, called *Min Sao Khin Thai Waen Naen*,[58] no dates were recorded. After this *cao fa*[59] had ascended the throne, the regulations set for offering tribute were: A major tribute was to be paid once every nine years (*cin kun*

53. This statement is taken from Gao Lishi's Chinese translation. See MLC-SV2, 87.

54. *Latcabut* (Tr. ราชบุตฺต), lit., "royal son" (P. rājaputra). Here it refers to Tao Cin Pao. *Pha-ong* is a Sanskrit/Pali-derived honorific prefix for members of royalty. Here it refers to Tao Sao Wün.

55. The original Tai Lü text in hybrid Pali-Khmer is *sawoei latca-sombat*. *Sawoei* means "to eat" or "to consume"; *latca* means "king" (Skt./P. rāja); *sombat* (P. saṃpatti) means "fortune, property, attainment, bliss". Thus the phrase means "possess the fortune of a king"; it can be rendered as "ascend to the throne" or "rule the kingdom". This phrase resembles semantically the Tai Lü *kin moeng*. See also MLC-SV2, 91, n. 48.

56. *Somdet pha pen cao*, which means sovereign, is a royal title prefixed to the name of all the rulers of Moeng Lü. "*Somdet*" is a respectable title for kings and monks. See MLC-SV2, 91, n. 49.

57. According to Gao Lishi, the second ruler Sam Khai Noeng succeeded his father to the throne in the year Chunxi 7 of the Song dynasty (i.e., AD 1180). See MCL-SV2, 91, n. 50. The reign Jingtai 1 (1450 AD) appearing in several manuscripts, including MLC-LV1, is obviously a scribal error. The mistake has been perpetuated by the subsequent scribes.

58. These Tai Lü transliterations correspond to Chinese (in Pinyin) *Mingchao Jingtai yuannian* 明朝景泰元年, which means the reign of Jingtai 1 of the Ming dynasty (i.e., AD 1450). Probably here the Tai scribe means Emperor Jingtai of the Ming Dynasty.

59. It means "son of heaven", i.e., emperor.

yai) and a lesser tribute (*cin kun nòi*)[60] was to be paid once every five years. Moreover, Somdet Tao Kham Hoeng was conferred the title Kio Cang Wang (i.e., the king of Chiang Rung).[61] After the fourth generation[62] ruler Tao Haeng Long had ascended the throne, the Chinese emperor conferred the surname Dao (lit., "knife")[63] on him. Since then, it has been used [as a surname] to the present day.

Until the eighteenth generation,[64] [in the reign of] the ruler (*pha pen cao*) by the name of Tao Kham Lü (Tao Mòm Kham Lü), that *sun ci cao ta sin* (i.e., the ruler Shunzhi of the Great Qing) defeated the original (sic) [Ming] emperor ([*cao*] *wòng*). Emperor Shunzhi ascended the throne.[65] Somdet Pha Pen Cao Tao Kham Lü submitted. In the year Shunzhi 18 (i.e., CS 1023; AD 1661), the seal and letter of appointment were conferred on him and [Emperor] Shunzhi granted [him the title] *cao saenwi fa*. The *khao lang* (land tax paid in kind)[66] offered in tribute amounted to 1,084 *tan* (piculs)[67] and the domain of Moeng Cung (i.e., Yuanjiang) was incorporated into [Sipsòng Panna].

Not long after (i.e., CS 1035; AD 1673), this Wu Sangui (1612–1678) defeated Emperor Shunzhi (r. 1644–1661).[68] Wu Sangui proclaimed himself emperor; [he then] had the seal and credential conferred by Shunzhi confiscated and issued a new seal to Tao Nò Moeng (i.e., Cao Nò Moeng, LV2: r. 1642–1655). Until the nineteenth (sic) generation,[69] the one who ascended the throne was his younger brother (*ton nòng*), called [Cao] Moeng Tao.

In the year Kangxi 20 (i.e., CS 1043; AD 1681), [after the Qing court] had defeated

---

60. The Tai Lü *cin kun* is derived from the Chinese *jin gong* 進 貢, which means "offer in tribute".

61. The section of Mekong River in Sipsòng Panna is also called Jiulong Jiang (lit., "nine dragons river") by the Chinese, namely Chiang Rung River, and the king or *saenwi fa* of Sipsòng Panna was also called the king of Jiujiang (king of Chiang Rung) of Cheli.

62. It should have been the fifth generation ruler.

63. *Dao* 刀 is the Chinese rendering of *tao/cao* (lord or ruler); now it has become the surname of many former nobles, i.e., the descendants of the aristocratic clans, of the Tai peoples in Yunnan.

64. It should have been the twenty-fifth generation.

65. *Sun ci cao ta sin* (Tr. สุ่นจีเจ้าต่าซิ้น) is the Tai Lü transcription of the Chinese *Shunzhi chao da Qing* 順 治 朝 大 清, i.e., the Shunzhi reign of the Great Qing (r. 1644–1661). It could be interpreted as Shunzhi Cao, i.e., Emperor Shunzhi of the Great Qing. Here it refers to the year Shunzhi 2 (AD 1645), CS 1007. The last emperor of the Ming dynasty, Chongzhen (Zhu Youjian, 1611–1644), committed suicide on the Coal Hill in Beijing on 25 April 1644.

66. According to Gao Lishi, *kao lang* is a combined term of Tai and Chinese. *Kao* in Tai means grain; *lang*, i.e., derived from the Chinese *liang* 糧, also means grain. Thus *kao lang* means grain offered in tribute to the emperor of China. See MLC-SV2, 91, n. 52.

67. According to Gao Lishi, one *dan* 石 (*picul*) of paddy grain is 300 *jin* 斤 (catties). MLC-SV2, 88.

68. Wu Sangui 吳 三 桂, a native of Liaodong, was a Ming northeast frontier general. He first submitted to the Manchu but later founded the short-lived kingdom of Zhou (1678–1681) in southern China. He did not defeat Emperor Shunzhi as the Moeng Lü Chronicle claims. See ECCP II, 877–880.

69. It should have been the twenty-sixth generation.

Wu Sangui (sic),[70] Kangxi (r. 1662–1722) ascended the throne and sent troops down [to Yunnan] to attack and kill [him]. Somdet [Cao] Mòm Tao came to offer his allegiance. Emperor Kangxi conferred the seal and credential on the twentieth generation of *cao saenwi fa*,[71] Paeng Moeng, and made him the ruler of Sipsòng Panna and of Kha Sipsòng Ho Khwaen.[72]

2. THE DOMAIN

The domain previously conferred on the sovereign [of Moeng Lü], the *somdet pha pen cao phaendin* (or *cao saenwi fa*), by the emperor of the Heavenly Court covered:

The lower flowage of the Mekong River, [beginning] at Pha Sam Sao Nam Khao Hu (lit., "water flowing into the cave of the three-summit hills"), where there is a cave from which the water flows into the Ton Mi Long (lit., "great bear hill") and runs along the ridge to Moeng Long Pukha;[73] then, from the That Pu Kok (lit., "Pu Kok Pagoda"), straight across the *müang* to Kòng Hae (Rae) Daeng (lit., "pale red stony hills"),[74] bordering on Lan Sang (Laos), is the domain under the [*cao*] *saenwi fa*.

In the north, from Nòng Tao Sai (lit., "sandy turtle pond")[75] to the beach, Hat Tao Pu Taen (lit., "beach of the royal throne"), through Nam Kang (Kang River), joining Nam Cian (Jian River) and Nam Tae (Tae River) to Moeng Cung (Yuanjiang), to Ai Sa Kham Khoe, to Ngòn Long, to Nam Ang, to Nam Lam, and following the Nam Lam to Sam Tao (lit.,"three lords")—one *tao* (lit., "lord") belongs to the domain (*müang*) of *saenwi fa*, one *tao* belongs to Chiang Tung, and one *tao* belongs to Chiang Saen. [It runs] from the *tao* belonging to the [*cao*] *saenwi fa* to the old border at Long Noe (Luang Nüa) and to Moeng Phayak, and going back to Pha Sam Sao Nam Khao Hu, which is the starting point. The domain previously under the jurisdiction (*khet anaratha*) of the [*cao saenwi fa*] covered these [regions].

70. Wu Sangui died of illness on 2 October 1678. He was succeeded by his eldest grandson Wu Shifan, who was confined in Yunnan and committed suicide on 7 December 1681. See ECCP II, 877–80.

71. It should have been the thirtieth generation.

72. *Kha* means slave/serf and the *kha* here refers to the hill tribes, apart from the Tai Lü in Sipsòng Panna. *Ho* means headman or chief and *khwaen* is an administrative unit similar to *panna*. The *cao phaendin* of Sipsòng Panna divided the regions inhabited by the hill tribes into twelve administrative districts for levying taxes, called *ho khwaen*. See Gao Lishi 1982, 91, n. 55.

73. In the east of Mengla County, in present-day Laos.

74. *Kòng hae daeng* (Tr. กองแรแดง) means "red silk/taffeta way".

75. *Nòng tao sai* (Tr. หนองเต่าซาย) means "sandy turtle pond".

3. THE KHA SIPSÒNG HO KHWAEN[76]

1) Khwaen Khòng (Quan Kuan)
2) Khwaen Kham Te (Quan Handi)
3) Khwaen Lòt (Quan Luo)
4) Khwaen Mang Pha (Quan Mangpa)
5) Khwaen Sam Sa (Quan Xisa)
6) Khwaen Khoe Kham (Quan Gehan)
7) Khwaen Hu Lang (Quan Hulang)
8) Khwaen Mò (Quan Mo)
9) Khwaen Lai (Quan Lai)
10) Khwaen Dai (Quan Lai)
11) Khwaen Kai (Quan Jie)
12) Khwaen ... (Quan ...)[77]

These are the "Kha Sipsòng Panna".

---

76. As for the meaning of *ho khwaen*, see above n. 72.

77. The paper of the original manuscript is torn. See MLC-SV2, 89. According to MLC-LV1, s. 3.15 above, it is Khwaen Nòng.

Appendix 1

Genealogical Table of the Rulers of Moeng Lü or Sipsòng Panna

NOTES

i. The original Tai names as well as the sinicised names of Tai Lü rulers have been transcribed by various translators into different Chinese characters. Below, they are transcribed into standard Pinyin Romanisation, followed by the complex Chinese characters.

ii. The modern Thai transcription of the names of Tai Lü rulers follows the transcription of Renoo (2001) with some modifications.

Abbreviation	Title/Translator/Year of Publication
MLC-LV1	History of Moeng Lü (*Leshi*), translated into Chinese by Li Fuyi, February 1947
MLC-LV2	The Chronicle of the Forty-Four Reigns of the *Cao Phaendin* of Sipsòng Panna, the 1963 version of the Moeng Lü Chronicle
MLC-SV1	The Genealogy of the *Cao Phaendin* of Moeng Lü, the Lineage of the Saenwi Fa of Cheli, translated into Chinese by Li Fuyi, April 1947, with the Tai Lü text printed alongside
MLC-SV2	The Genealogy of the *Cao Phaendin* of Sipsòng Panna, translated into Chinese by Gao Lishi, 1982, with the Tai Lü text printed alongside

The forty-four Tai Lü rulers, the *cao phaendin*	MCL-LV1 Li Fuyi (1947a)	MLC-LV2 1963-MLC	MLC-SV1 Li Fuyi (1947b)	MLC-SV2 Gao Lishi (1982)
Name in Thai	Reign (AD)	Reign (AD)	Reign (AD)	Reign (AD)
1) Cao Phaya Coeng (เจ้าภยาเจิง)	1) Ba Zhen 叭 真 (Phaya Coeng), r. 1180–1192	1) Phaya Coeng, r. 1159–1180	1) Cao Phaya Coeng (Zhao Ba Zhen 詔 叭 真), d. in 1180	1) Phaya Coeng Han, d. 1180
2) Tao Khai Noeng (ท้าวไค้เนิง) Sam Khai Noeng (สามไค้เนิง)[1]	2) Tao Kangleng 匋 鈧 冷, r. 1192–1211 (Tao Khai Noeng), r. 1192–1211	2) Sam Khai Noeng, r. 1180–1201	2) Sam Khai Noeng (Sang Kaineng 三 凱 冷), r. 1180–1201	2) Sam Khai Noeng, r. 1180–1200
3) Tao Pung (ท้าวพูง) Ai Kung (อ้ายกูง)[2]	3) Tao Beng 匋 伻, (Tao Pung or Ai Kung), r. 1211–1234	3) Ai Kung, r. 1201–1206	3) Ai Kung (Ai Gong 愛 恭), r. 1201–1224	3) Ai Kòng, r. 1200–1221
4) Tao Hung Kaen Cai (ท้าวรุ่งแก่นชาย)[3]	4) Tao Long Jian Zai 匋 隴 建 仔, (Tao Hung Kaen Cai) r. 1234–1257	4) Tao Hung Kaen Cai, r. 1206–1227	4) Tao Rung (Hung) Kaen Cai (Dao Long Bian Zai 刀 隴 匾 仔), r. 1224–1247	4) Tao Hung (Rung) Kaen Cai, r. 1221–1243
5) Tao Haeng Long (ท้าวแรงหลวง)[4]	5) Dao Lianglong 刀 兩 龍, (Tao Haeng Long) r. 1257–1273	5) Tao Haeng Long, r. 1228–1254	5) Tao Haeng Long (Dao Lianglong 刀 兩 龍), r. 1247–1263	5) Tao Haeng Long, r. 1243–1259
6) Tao Puwak (ท้าวพูวาก)[5]	6) Dao Buwa 刀 補 瓦 (Tao Puwak), r. 1273–1287	6) Tao Puwak, r. 1255–1269	6) Tao Putok (Dao Buda 刀 補 達), r. 1263–1277	6) Tao Puwak, r. 1259–1272
7) Yi Peng Lak Sai (ยี่เพียงลากซาย)[6]	Yi La Sai 伊 拉 諟, r. 1287 (1983 edition of *Leshi*)	7) Cao Yi Peng (Piang) Lak Sai, r. 1270–1271	7) Cao Yi Peng Lak Sai (Yi Bing La Sai 伊 丙 拉 諟), r. 1277	
8) Tao Ai (ท้าวไอ่), or Cao Ai (เจ้าไอ่)[7]	7) Dao Ai 刀 愛 (Cao Ai), r. 1287–1347	8) Cao Ai, r. 1271–1311	8) Tao Ai or Cao Ai (Dao Ai 刀 愛), r. 1277–1318	7. Tao Ai, r. 1272–1308
9) Cao Khan Moeng (เจ้าคานเมิง)[8]	8) Dao Kan 刀 坎 (Cao Khan Moeng), r. 1347–1391	9) Cao Khan Moeng, r. 1312–1350	9) Cao Khan Moeng (Dao Kan 刀 坎), r. 1318–1362	8) Cao Khan Moeng, 1308–1341/1351

1. He was the fourth son of Cao Phaya Coeng.
2. He was the eldest son of Sam Khai Noeng (the second ruler).
3. He was the son of Ai Kung.
4. He was the son of Tao Hung Kaen Cai.
5. He was the eldest son of Tao Haeng Long.
6. He succeeded his elder brother Tao Puwak, or Tao Putok (MLC-SV1), and died less than a year later.
7. He was the eldest son of Yi Peng Lak Sai.
8. He was the son of Cao Ai.

10) Tao (Cao) Sida Kham (ท้าวสิดาคำ)[9]	9) Dao Xianda 刀暹答, (Tao Sida Kham), r. 1391–1413	10) Tao (Cao) Sida Kham, r. 1350–1430	10) Tao Sida Kham (Dao Xianda 刀暹答), r. 1362–1442	9) Tao Sida Kham, r. 1341–1381 (sic); r. 1451–1531
11) Tao Kumman (ท้าวกุมมาร)[10]	Not listed as a ruler	11) Tao Kumman, r. 1430–1332	11) Tao Kumman (Dao Gongman 刀公滿), r. 1442–1443	
12) Tao Kü Moeng (ท้าวกือเมิง)[11]	10) Dao Gengmeng 刀更猛, (Tao Kü Moeng) r. 1413–1415	12) Tao Kü Moeng, r. 1433–1436	14) Tao Kü Moeng (Dao Gengmeng 刀更孟), r. 1464–1467[12]	10) Tao Kü Moeng, r. 1381–1383 (sic); r. 1431–1433
13) Tao Kham Tet (ท้าวคำเทียด)[13]	11) Dao Dian 刀典, (Tao Kham Tet), r. 1415–1428 (11 years)	15) Tao Kham Tet (Tiat), r. 1442–1445 Dao Handi	12) Tao Kham Tet (Dao Dian 刀典), r. 1443–1444[14]	13) Tao Kham Tet, r. 1436–1437
14) Soe Long Fa (เสือล่วงฟ้า)[15]	12) She Long Fa 奢隴法 (Soe Long Fa), r. 1428–1457	16) Soe Long Fa (Süa Luang Fa), r. 1446–1466	13) Soe Long Fa (Süa Luang Fa; She Long Fa 奢隴法), r. 1444–1464	14) Soe Long Fa, r. between 1437 and 1525
15) Tao Sòng Moeng (ท้าวสองเมิง)[16]	11. Dao Shuangmeng 刀雙孟 (Tao Sòng Moeng), r. for 2½ months in 1415	13) Tao Sòng Moeng, r. for 3½ months between 1436 and 1439	Tao Sòng Moeng (Dao Shuangmeng 刀雙孟), died before he could succeed	12) Tao Sòng Moeng, r. 1436
16) Tao Bakòng (ท้าวบากอง)[17] or Tao Phakang (ท้าวปราคาง)	Dao Bagong 刀霸供 (Tao Bakòng), not listed as a ruler	14) Tao Bakòng, r. 1439–1441	Tao Bakòng (Dao Bagong 刀霸供), died before he could succeed	11) Tao Bakòng, r. between 1383 and 1436

9. He was the eldest son of Cao Khan Moeng.

10. He was the second son of Cao Khan Moeng, succeeded his elder brother Tao Sida Kham, but was disposed of by Dao Dian (Tao Kham Tet).

11. He was the eldest son of Tao Sida Kham.

12. According to MLC-SV1, Tao Kü Moeng, the eldest son of Tao Sida Kham, succeeded Soe Long Fa (Süa Luang Fa).

13. He was the second son of Tao Sida Kham, probably also called Tao Kham Daeng (see MLC-LV1, s. 9.2) or Dao Handi (Tao Kham Tet).

14. Dao Dian (Tao Kham Tet), ruled only one year, fled to Nam Ngai Sai Kham (Irrawaddy), and died in 1444.

15. Soe Long Fa was the third son of Poe Fai Fa, who was the third younger brother of Tao Sida Kham. Hence, Soe Long Fa was the nephew of Tao Sida Kham and grandson of Cao Khan Moeng. Soe Long Fa was referred to as Dao Silong (Tao Soe Long) or Dao Long (Tao Long) in the Ming sources. See *Yingzong shilu*, ch. 292, 6242 (Tianshun 2, sixth month, *renshen* day: 26 July 1458).

16. He was the second son of Tao Kü Moeng.

17. He was the eldest son of Tao Kü Moeng. According to MLC-LV1 and other Tai Lü sources the two elder sons of Tao Kü Moeng, namely the elder brothers of Tao Sam Pò Lütai, fled to the Mekong for their lives or were sent into exile by his uncle-cum-stepfather Soe Long Fa. Dao Bagong (Tao Bakòng) was allegedly the founder of Chiang Khaeng, in Laos.

17) Tao Phasaeng (ท้าวปราแสง)[18]	12b) Dao Baxian 刀霸羨 (Tao Pha-saeng), r. 1457 r. 2 months	17) Tao Phasaeng,[19] r. 1466	Tao Phasaeng (Dao Baxian 刀霸羨), not allowed to succeed	15) Tao Bakòng's son (sic),[20] r. 1525
18) Tao Sam Pò Lütai (ท้าวสามพ่อลือไท)[21]	13) San Bao Lidai 三寶歷代 (Tao Sam Pò Lütai), r. 1457–1497	18) Tao Sam Pò Lütai, r. 1467–1490	15) Tao Sam Pò Lütai (San Bao Lidai 三寶歷代), r. 1467–1497	16) Tao Sam Pò Lütai, r. 1525–1528
				17) Cao Ai,[22] r. 1528
19) Tao Sam Khai Noeng (สามไค้เนิง)[23]	14) San Kaileng 三凱冷 (Tao Sam Khai Noeng), r. 1497–1502	19) Tao Sam Khai Noeng, r. 1491–1495	16) Sam Khai Noeng (San Kaileng 三凱冷), r. 1497–1502	
20) Cao Khan Moeng (เจ้าคานเมิง)[24]	15) Zhao Kan 詔侃 (Cao Khan Moeng), r. 1502–1523	20) Cao Khan Moeng, r. 1496–1518	17) Cao Khan [Moeng] (Zhao Kan 詔侃), r. 1502–1523	18) Cao Khan Moeng (sic), Sam Khai Noeng,[25] r. 1528–1548
				19) Phaya Aen,[26] r. 1548–1555
21) Cao Sili Sompan (เจ้าสรีสมภาร)[27]	16) Zhao Shili Songban 詔室利崧版 (Cao Sili Sompan), r. 1523–1530	21) Cao Sili (Sali) Sompan, r. 1518–1539	18) Cao Sali Sompan (Zhao Xili Songban 詔室利崧版), r. 1523–1560	
22) Cao Ong Moeng (เจ้าองเมิง)[28] or Cao Un Moeng (เจ้าอุ่นเมิง)	17) Dao Nuomeng 刀糯猛 (Cao Nò Moeng),[29] r. 1530–1568	22) Cao Un (Ong) Moeng], r. 1539–1567	19) Cao Ong Moeng (Dao Yunmeng 刀韞猛), r. 1560–1588	

18. He was the eldest son of Soe Long Fa.

19. He ruled five months and was ousted; he committed suicide at Moeng Hing on the way to China (see MLC-LV2, s. 17.2).

20. He was most probably Tao Phasaeng, Soe Long Fa's eldest son.

21. He was the youngest son of Tao Kü Moeng, adopted by his uncle, Soe Long Fa, who married his mother after the death of his father.

22. He was the fourth son of Tao Sam Pò Lütai.

23. He was the third son of Tao Sam Pò Lütai.

24. According to MLC-LV1, 25, he was the sixth son of Tao Sam Pò Lütai.

25. He was the second son of Tao Sam Pò Lütai.

26. He was the lord of Moeng U, the son of Cao Khan Moeng.

27. He was the son of Cao Khan Moeng.

28. He was the son of Cao Sili Sompan.

29. Here he was Dao Nuomeng (Cao Nò Moeng), probably a muddle of names.

23) Cao Sili Sunanta (เจ้าสรีสุนันทา)[30]	18) Zhao Shili Sunanda 詔室利穌赧打 (Cao Sili Sunanta), r. in 1568	23) Cao Sali Sunanta), r. 1568–1569	20) Cao Sali Sunnata (Zhao Shili Sunanda 詔室利穌赧打), r. 1588–1595	20) Sali Sunanta Laca, r. 1555–1592
				21) Upalaca Kaeo Moeng,[31] r. 1592–1606
24) Cao In Moeng (เจ้าอิ่นเมิง)[32]	19) Dao Yingmeng 刀應猛 (Cao In Moeng), r. 1569–1598	24) Cao In Moeng, r. 1569–1578	Not listed as a ruler	22) Cao Un Moeng,[33] r. 1606–1625
25) Cao Nò Moeng (เจ้าหน่อเมิง)[34]	20) Dao Yunmeng 刀韞猛 (Cao Ong Moeng),[35] r. 1598–1628	25) Cao Nò Moeng, r. 1584–1602	21) Cao Nò Moeng (Dao Nuomeng 刀糯猛), r. 1595–1609	23) Suthamma[36] r. 1625–1632
26) Cao Sili Suthamma (เจ้าสรีสุธัมมา)[37]	21) Zhao Shili Sutanma 詔室利穌坦瑪 (Cao Sili Suthamma), r. 1628–1639	26) Cao Sili (Sali) Suthamma, r. 1603–1620	22) Cao Sali Suthamma (Zhao Shili Sutanma 詔室利穌坦瑪), r. 1609–1620	24) Cao Nò Moeng,[38] r. 1632–1645
27) Cao Kham Lü (เจ้าคำลือ) or Cao Mòm Kham Lü (เจ้าหม่อมคำลือ)[39]	22) Zhao Kangle 詔銃勒 (Cao Mòm Kham Lü), r. 1639–1669	27) Cao Mòm Kham Lü, r. 1621–1634	23) Cao [Mòm] Kham Lü (Zhao Kangle 詔銃勒), r. 1620–1623	25) Cao Kham Lü,[40] r. 1645–1659
28) Cao Mòm Tao (เจ้าหม่อมท้าว)[41]	Not listed as a ruler	28) Cao Mòm Tao, r. 1634–1641	24) Cao Mòm Tao (Dao Mudao 刀穆禱), r. 1623–1628	26) Cao Mòm Tao,[42] r. 1659–1662

30. Reigning only six months, he was the eldest son of Tao Ong (Un) Moeng and elder brother of Cao In Moeng..

31. He was the *upalaca* from Chiang Khòng.

32. He was the second son of Cao Ong (Un) Moeng and younger brother of Cao Sili Sunnanta.

33. He died at Moeng Phayak in AD 1625.

34. He was the son of Cao In Moeng.

35. Here Li Fuyi (MLC-LV1) had probably mixed up his name with that of Cao Ong (Un) Moeng. He was born in 1570, was the son of Cao In Moeng and his queen, a Burmese princess, Nang Bo Kham, or Nang Suwanna Patumma Tewi.

36. He was the *upalaca* from Chiang Aen.

37. According to MLC-LV1, he was the son of Dao Yunmeng [Tao Ong (Un) Moeng]; but according to MLC-SV1 he was the son of Cao Nò Moeng.

38. He was the *upalaca* of Chiang Khòng, the grandson of Sali Suthamma.

39. He was the eldest son of Cao Sili (Sali) Suthamma.

40. He was the eldest son of Cao Nò Moeng.

41. He was the second son of Cao Sili (Sali) Suthamma.

42. He was the younger brother of Cao Kham Lü.

				27) Cao Saeng Moeng,[43] r. 1662–1670
29) Cao Nò Moeng (เจ้าหน่อเมิง)[44]	23) Dao Nuomeng 刀懦猛 (Cao Nò Moeng), r. 1669–1681	29) Cao Nò Moeng, r. 1642–1655	25) Cao Nò Moeng (Dao Nuomeng 刀懦猛), r. 1628–1640	28) Cao Nò Moeng,[45] r. 1670–1677
30) Cao Moeng Tao (เจ้าเมิงท้าว)[46]	24) Dao Mudao 刀穆禱 (Cao Moeng Tao), r. 1681–1684	30) Cao Moeng Tao, r. 1655–1668/69	26) Cao Moeng Tao (Dao Mengtao 刀猛桃), r. 1640–1644	29) Cao Moeng Tao,[47] r. 1677–1862
31) Cao Paeng Moeng (เจ้าแพงเมิง)[48]	25) Zhao Bianmeng 詔匾猛 (Cao Paeng Moeng), r. 1684–1724	31) Cao Paeng Moeng, r. 1670–1697/98	27) Cao Paeng Moeng (Zhao Bianmeng 詔匾猛), r. 1666–1708 [49]	30) Cao Paeng Moeng, r. 1682–1726
32) Tao Cin Pao (เท่าชิ่นเพา)[50]	26) Dao Jinbao 刀金寶 (Tao Cin Pao), r. 1724–1729	32) Tao Cin Pao, r. 1698–1707	28) Tao Cin Pao (Dao Jinbao 刀金寶), r. 1708–1713	31) Tao Cin Pao, r. 1726–1729
33) Tao Sao Wün (เท่าเส่าวิ้น), or Cao Mòm Tao (เจ้าหม่อมท้าว)[51]	27) Dao Shaowen 刀紹文 (Tao Sao Wün), r. 1729–1767	33) Tao Sao Wün, r. 1707–1730	29) Tao Sao Wün (Dao Shaowen 刀紹文), r. 1713–1766	32) Tao Sao Wün, r. 1729–1782
34) Tao Wui Phin (เท่าวุ้ยภิ้น)[52]	28) Dao Weiping 刀維屏 (Tao Wui Phin), r. 1767–1777	34) Tao Wui Phin, r. 1730–1745	30) Tao Wui Phin (Dao Wieping 刀維屏), r. 1766–1781	
35) Tao Suwan (เท่าสุวัณณ์), Cao Mòm Suwan (เจ้าหม่อมสุวัณณ์), or Tao Mòm Suwan (เท่าหม่อมสุวัณณ์)[53]	29) Dao Shiwan 刀士宛 (Tao Suwan), r. 1777–1796	35) Tao Cao Suwan (Cao Suwan), r. 1746–1763	31) Cao Mòm Suwan (Dao Shiwan 刀士宛), r. 1781–1797	

43. He was the eldest son of Cao Kham Lü.

44. He was the second son of Cao Mòm Kham Lü and his uncle Cao Mòm Tao (twenty-eighth ruler) acted as the regent.

45. He was the younger brother of Cao Saeng Moeng. He was not Cao Nò Moeng, the *upalaca* of Chiang Khòng, the twenty-fourth ruler according to MLC-SV2.

46. He was the son of Cao Mòm Tao (twenty-eighth ruler).

47. He was the son of Cao Mòm Tao.

48. He was the son of Dao Mudao or Dao Mengtao (Cao Moeng Tao) and his mother Nang Tewi acted as the regent.

49. Cao Paeng Moeng's mother, who died in 1673, acted as the regent from 1644 to 1666, until her son was twenty-two years old.

50. He was the eldest son of Cao Paeng Moeng.

51. He was the second son of Cao Paeng Moeng.

52. He was the eldest son of Tao Sao Wün.

53. He was the fourth son of Tao Sao Wün.

36) Tao Thai Khò (เท่าถ่ายค้อ),[54] Cao Mòm Maha Wong (เจ้าหม่อมมหาวง)	30) Dao Taihe 刀太和 (Tao Thai Khò), r. 1797–1802	36) Tao Thai Khò (Cao Mòm Maha Wong), r. 1764–1770	32) Tao Thai Khò (Dao Taihe 刀太和) or Cao Mòm Maha Wong, r. 1798–1801	
37) Cao Can (เจ้าจัน) or Tao Yung Khò (ท้าวยูงค้อ)[55]	Dao Yonghe 刀永和 (Tao Yung Khò), or Zhao Zhan 詔占 (Cao Fa Can), r. 1802	37) Cao Fa Can (Tao Yung Khò), r. 1770–1779		
38) Cao Mòm Maha Wang (เจ้าหม่อมมหาวัง)[56]	Dao Taikang 刀太康 (Tao Thai Khang), as regent, r. 1802–1817	38) Cao Mòm Maha Wang (Tao Thai Khang), r. 1780–1785 (as regent), r. 1786–1809	33) Tao Thai Khang (Dao Taikang 刀太康) or Cao Mòm Maha Wang, r. 1802–1817[57]	
38b) Tao Sunwu (เท่าซุ้นวู), or Cao Mòm Maha Nòi (เจ้ามหาน้อย)[58]	31) Dao Shengwu 刀繩武 (Tao Sunwu) or Cao Maha Nòi, r. 1817–1833	38b) Cao Mòm Maha Nòi (Tao Sunwu), 1809–	34) Tao Sunwu (Dao Shengwu 刀繩武) or Cao Maha Nòi, r. 1817–1833	
39) Cao Mòm Suca Wanna or Cao Mòm Suca Wanna Latcabut (เจ้าหม่อมสุชาวัณณ์ราชบุตร)[59]	32) Dao Zhengzong 刀正綜 (Tao Coen Cong), r. 1834–1864	39) Cao Mòm Suca Wanna (Tao Coen Cong), r. 1788–1818	35) Tao Coen Cong (Dao Zhengzong 刀正綜) or Cao Suca Wanna Laca, r. 1837–1865	
40) Tao Cin An (เท่าชิ่นอ่าน); Cao Mòm Khung Kham (เจ้าาหม่อมขุงคำ), or Cao Mòm Sò (เจ้าหม่อมส้อ)[60]	Not listed	40) Cao Mòm Sò (Cao Mòm Khung Kham or Tao Cin An), r. 1863–1879	36) Tao Cin An (Dao Jun'an 刀鈞安), Cao Mòm Khung Kham or Cao Mòm Sò, r. 1866–1878	

54. He was the second son of Dao Shiwan (Tao Suwan or Tao Cao Suwan), appointed by China. Dao Zhao Ding (Tao Cao Then/Thien), the second son of Tao Sao Wün, was appointed by Burma; he died in 1800.

55. He was the only son of Tao Wui Phin.

56. He was the third son of Dao Shiwan (Tao Cao Suwan).

57. He passed away in 1836.

58. He was the son of Tao Thai Khò (Cao Mòm Maha Wong) and his queen from Moeng La, dismissed in Daoguang 13 (1833 AD).

59. He was the eldest son of Dao Taikang (Tao Thai Khang, or Cao Mòm Maha Wang).

60. He was the son of Dao Chengzong (Tao Soen Cong or Cao Lamma Awuttha Kumman) and was adopted by his uncle Dao Zhengzong (Tao Coen Cong or Cao Mòm Suca Wanna).

41) Tao Thai Khang (ท้าวถ่ายคัง), Tao Sin Fu (เท่าซิ่นฟู), or Cao Mòm Saeng (เจ้าหม่อมแสง)[61]	Not listed	41) Cao Mòm Saeng, (Tao Sin Fu), r. 1880–1883		
42) Tao Soen Oen (เท่าเซิ้นอ่าน), or Cao Mòm Kham Lü (เจ้าหม่อมคำลือ)[62]	Not listed	42) Cao Mòm Kham Lü or Tao Soen Oen), r. 1884–1924	37) Cao Mòm Kham Lü or Tao Soen Oen (Dao Cheng'en 刀承恩), r. 1878–1922	
43) Tao Tung Laeng (เท่าตุ๋งแล้ง), Cao Mòm Long Khong Kham (เจ้าหม่อมหลวงขงคำ), or Cao Mòm Suwanna Phakhang (เจ้าหม่อมสุวัณณปราคาง)[63]	Not listed	43) Cao Mòm Suwanna Phakhang or Tao Tung Laeng, r. 1927–1943	38) Cao Mòm Long Khong Kham or Tao Tung Laeng (Dao Dongliang 刀棟樑), r. 1926–1943	
44) Tao Sü Sin (เท่าสื่อซิ่น), or Cao Mòm Kham Lü (เจ้าหม่อมคำลือ)[64]	Not listed	44) Cao Mòm Kham Lü or Tao Sü Sin (Dao Shixun 刀世勳), r. 1947–1950		

61. According to MLC-LV2, s. 41.1, his Chinese name is Tao Sin Fu, not Tao Thai Khang as given in Gao Lishi 1984, 128 (forty-first ruler). He was the son of Dao Zhengzong (Cao Mòm Suca Wanna) and died without a son.

62. According to Gao Lishi 1984, he was the eldest son of Cao Mòm Sò's (Tao Cin An's) daughter who grew up in Keng Tung; but according to Dao Shuren (1989), he was the eldest son of Cao Mòm Sò (Tao Cin An) who sought refuge in Keng Tung.

63. He was the eldest son of Dao Cheng'en (Tao Soen Oen or Cao Mòm Kham Lü).

64. Dao Shixun (Tao Sü Sin or Cao Mòm Kham Lü) was the eldest son of Dao Dongting (Tao Tung Thin or Cao Mòm Saeng Moeng), the sixth son of Dao Cheng'en (Tao Soen Oen or Cao Mòm Kham Lü). He was formally enthroned in 1943 and abdicated in 1950. He is living in Kunming with his wife and two children, a son and a daughter.

Appendix 2
Bilingual Memorials Submitted by Tao Sam Pò Lütai to the Ming Court

A memorial presented by the ruler of Cheli to the Ming court contained in the *Babai guan biaowen* 八百館表文 ([Memorials of] the Bureau of Babai), in *Xiyu tongwen biao* 西域同文表 (Bilingual memorials of the Western Regions), a Ming work, original Qing manuscript copy, in the holdings of Tōyō Bunko; Tokyo.

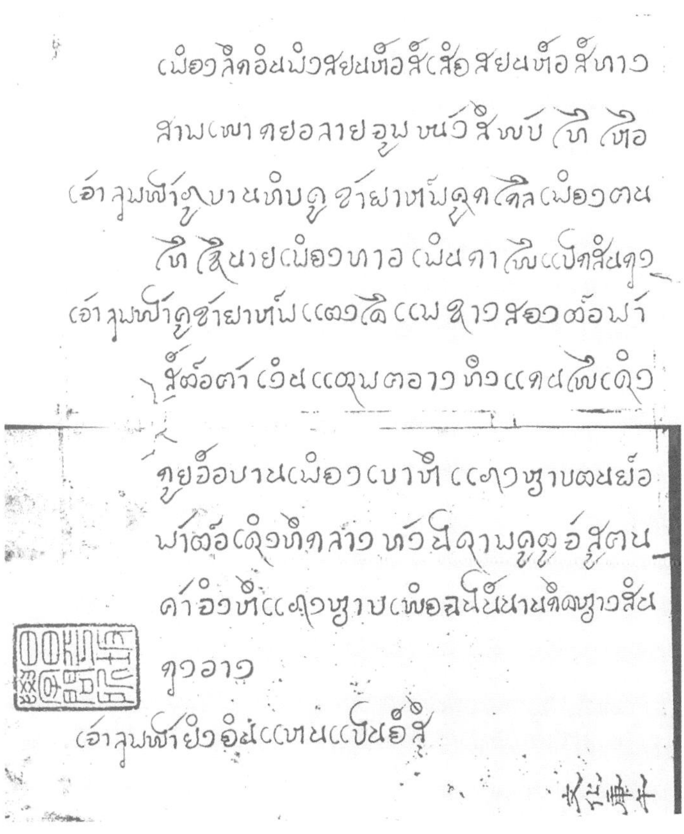

I. INTRODUCTION

Contained in the *Xiyu tongwen biao*, under the various translation bureaux of the *Siyi guan* 四夷館 (Translators' Institute) at the capital, are many rare and valuable bilingual memorials submitted by the local kings in Yunnan, Mainland Southeast Asia, and other vassal states from the Western Regions to the Ming court. The *Babai guan* (Translation Bureau of Lan Na) was one of them. One of these bilingual memorials from *Babai guan* is translated here. The Tai version written in the so-called tamarind pod script (*tua aksòn fak kham*) was submitted by a ruler of Sipsòng Panna (Cheli), Tao Sam Pò, to the Ming court. In 2002, when F. M. Liew-Herres was in Tokyo, Tōyō Bunko kindly allowed her to photocopy some of these bilingual memorials for the DFG project "Traditional Polities of the Tai". The English translation by F. M. Liew-Herres is based on the Chinese translation of the memorial in Tai Yuan, which is not reproduced in facsimile here. It is translated for those who can read the old Tai Yuan so that they can compare it with the original Tai Yuan memorial themselves. The corresponding memorial in Chinese is given below with the Pinyin transcription. The original memorial in tamarind pod script was transcribed into modern Thai script and translated into English by Volker Grabowsky and Renoo Wichasin.

II. THE CORRESPONDING CHINESE MEMORIAL (NOT A FACSIMILE REPRODUCTION)

Line 1:	車里軍民宣慰使司宣慰 *Cheli junmin xuanwei shisi xuanwei*
Line 2:	使刀三保具印信文書奏 *Shi Dao Sanbao ju yinxin wenshu zou*
Line 3:	天皇帝知道我奴婢是遠方夷 *Tian huangdi zhidao wo nubi shi yuanfang yi*
Line 4:	人差頭目刀門戛去進貢 *ren chai toumu Dao Menjia qu jingong*
Line 5:	天皇帝我奴婢辦得象二隻馬 *Tian huangdi wo nubi ban de xiang liang zhi ma*
Line 6:	四匹金銀器皿等件行至 *si pi jin yin qimin deng jian xing zhi*
Line 7:	貴州地方不肯應付人夫 *Gui-zhou di-fang bu-ken ying-fu ren fu*
Line 8:	馬匹到處都問我每要人 *ma pi dao chu dou wen wo mei yao ren*
Line 9:	事纔肯應付因此誤進 *shi cai ken yingfu yinci wu jin*
Line 10:	貢望 *gong wang*

Line 11: 天皇帝可憐見便益
Tian huangdi kelian jian bian yi

III. THE TRANSLATION

"The Pacification Commissioner Tao Sam Pò [Lütai from] the Cheli Military-cum-Civilian Pacification Commission has drawn up a memorial with the seal and credential. The Celestial Emperor knows [that] I, [your] slave, a foreigner from a distant land, have sent headman (*cao mòm*) Tao Moen Ka to offer tribute to the Celestial Emperor. I, the slave, manage to provide two elephants [and] four horses [as well as] gold and silver wares [and] other things. [On] arriving in Guizhou land [the local authority] refuses to supply [us with] servants [and] horses. Everywhere [they] ask us [for presents]. Every time [we] have to give presents so as to get services. Therefore [our] tribute offering is being delayed. [I] hope for the mercy of the Celestial Emperor to grant us the conveniences."

IV. COMMENTARY

The memorial is a solid proof that tribute envoys from Sipsòng Panna had visited the capital of Ming China. This unique document is the evidence of the sustaining tribute relationship between Sipsòng Panna and China during the Ming period. The memorial was sent during the reign of Tao Sam Pò Lütai (1457–1497).

V. TRANSCIPTION OF THE MEMORIAL INTO MODERN THAI

(1) เมืองลื้อ*กวินมิง*[1] เสียนหวีสือเสือ เสียนหวีสือทาง[2]

(2) สามเพา(พ่อ) *เกียว*[3] ลายจุ้ม หนังสือพับไทไหว้

(3) เจ้าลุ่มฟ้ารู้*บานทีป*[4] *คูข้า*[5] *ผาหม*[6] ถูกไกลเมืองฅน

---

1. แปลงจากคำจีนว่า *junmin* ซึ่งหมายถึง ด้านทหาร (*jun*) และ พลเรียน (*min*)

2. น่าจะเป็นคำว่า ท้าว

3. เป็นคำจีน แปลว่า เตรียม

4. อาจสันนิษฐานความหมายได้ ๒ แบบ คือ ๑) ยินดีเป็นอย่างยิ่ง โดยพิจารณาจากคำว่า บาน ๒) อาจเป็นชื่อของ เจ้าลุ่มฟ้า หรือ "อ๋อง" กษัตริย์จีนที่ยูนนาน ซึ่งใน *Zimme Yazawin* ระบุชื่อว่า อุทิปวา (Utibwa) โดยพิจารณา จากคำว่า รูบานทิป (ดูใน *Zimme Yazawin* หน้า 41-42 ประเด็นนี้ รองศาสตราจารย์กรรณิการ์ วิมลเกษม เป็นผู้ตั้งข้อสังเกต)

5. กูข้า คือ สรรพนามบุรุษที่ ๑ ซึ่งแสดงความนอบน้อม

6. ควรเขียนเป็นผาห่ม กูข้าผาห่ม หมายถึง ข้าพเจ้าซึ่งเป็นผู้ปกครอง (ผา อาจเป็นคำเดียวกับ ฝา หมายถึง สิ่งที่ใช้ปกห่ม ปกคลุม ดังนั้น ฝาห่มจึงหมายถึง ผู้ปกครอง ในที่นี้เป็นสรรพนามบุรุษที่ ๑

(4) ไท ใช้นายเมือง ท้าวเมิน(หมื่น)กา *ไพ*[7]แปก สิน*กุง*[8]

(5) เจ้าลุ่มฟ้า คูข้าผาห์มแต่งได้แม่ช้างสองตัว ม้า

(6) สี่ตัว คำเงิน แถม*ควาง*[9]*ทึง*[10]*แกน*[11]ไพเถิง[12]

(7) กูยจีว บ้านเมือง *เบาหื้อ*[13]แรงฮาบ(หาบ)ตนผัว

(8) ม้า ตัวเถิง[14]ทือกลาง *ทัง*[15] นั[น] ถามคู *ตู*[16] จักสู่[17]คน

(9) ค้า จิงหื้อแรงฮาบ เพื่อฉันนี้ นานกืด[18] *ฮาง*[19]สิน

(10) กุง*วาง*[20]

(11) เจ้าลุ่มฟ้า *เยิงอิน*[21]แหน*แปนอิ*[22]สือ

VI. TRANSLATION FROM THE ORIGINAL TAI MEMORIAL INTO ENGLISH

(1) The Moeng Lü Military-cum-Civilian Pacification Commission.

(2) The pacification commissioner Tao Sam Pò has drawn up a memorial with the seal and credential in Tai script to submit [it] respectfully to

---

7. ไป
8. แปลงจากคำจีนว่า *jin gong* แปลว่า ส่งส่วย หรือ มอบบรรณาการ
9. คำนี้ น่าจะเขียนผิด ควรเป็นคำว่า คัว/ครัว แปลว่า สิ่งของ
10. ทั้ง, ทุก
11. คำนี้คงมาจากคำจีนว่า *jian* 件 ซึ่งเป็นคำลักษณนามใช้กับสิ่งของทั่ว ๆไป
12. ถึง
13. ไม่ให้
14. คำนี้ควรเขียนเป็น เถิก หรือ ถึก หมายถึง สัตว์เพศผู้ เป็นวลีว่า ม้าตัวเถิก
15. คำนี้ควรเขียนเป็น ทาง ทือกลางทางนั้น หมายถึง ในระหว่างทางนั้น
16. คำนี้ควรเขียนเป็น ทาง ทือกลางทางนั้น หมายถึง ในระหว่างทางนั้น
17. ไปเยี่ยม, แบ่งให้, แบ่งปัน
18. กึด ภาษาไทพหญ่ แปลว่า หยุด ค้าง
19. ควรเขียนเป็น ห้าง แปลว่า จัดเตรียม(เครื่องบรรณาการ)
20. วาง เป็นคำจีนแปลว่า หวัง หวังว่า
21. คำนี้ควรเป็น ยินอินดู — ตกคำว่า ดู ไปคำหนึ่ง แปลว่า — มีความเมตตากรุณา
22. แปนอิ เป็นคำจีน *bian yi* แปลว่า อย่างสะดวก

(3) the Celestial Emperor (*cao lum fa*[23]). [You] know [that] I [your] slave, a foreigner from a distant land,

(4) have sent governor (*nai müang*) Tao Moen Ka to carry tribute

(5) to the Celestial Emperor. I, the slave, manage to provide two female elephants [and]

(6) four horses [as well as] gold and silver wares [and] other things. [On] arriving in

(7) Guizhou the local authority (*ban-müang*) refuses to supply [us with] servants

(8) [and] male horses. Everywhere [they] ask us [for presents].

(9) [Every time] we have to share [presents with] merchants so as to get services. Therefore

(10) [our] tribute offering is being delayed.

(11) [I] hope for the mercy of the Celestial Emperor to grant us the conveniences.

23. Lit., "lord under heaven".

Appendix 3
Cheli as Described in the *Ming shilu*

DOCUMENT 1

事
上曰兵部臣曰岷莊王葬金山與許悼王及懷獻世子墳
園同處宜於武成中衛撥官三員旗軍三百戶守護將見有校
充軍役者補之○以故太監劉順王瑾等莊田賜太監曹吉祥
○已故昌平侯楊洪妾李氏奏長子俊犯法已正典刑孫冰復
發充軍遺下家產伏望恩旨許妾變賣餘俊支過祿米二百四
十石無人糴納乞以賣房銀折還官從之○雲南總兵官都督
同知沐璘奏車里軍民宣慰司宣慰使刀霸羨自殺其弟板雅
忠等已推充三寶歷代掌管地方今板雅忠等又作亂糾合八
百借倩人馬讎殺欲調官軍撫安而春煖瘴高未宜動眾輕進
上曰三寶歷代係庶孽奪嫡謀害刀霸羨以致板雅忠等借兵
攻殺璘等其差的當官員去撫諭板雅忠等及體勘何人應襲
宣慰職事具奏定奪令各罷兵以息爭端○辛酉禮部引會試

TRANSLATION

In the year Tianshun 1, second month, on *gengshen* day (21 March 1457), the regional commander (*zong bingguan*) of Yunnan cum Cheli vice-commissioner-in-chief (*dudu tongzhi*), Mu Lin 沐璘, memorialised:

> The pacification commissioner (*xuanwei shi*) of the Cheli (Moeng Lü) Military-cum-Civilian Pacification Commission, Dao Baxian 刀霸羡 (Tao Phasaeng), had committed suicide. The younger brothers Banya Zhong 板雅忠 (Phaya Còm) et al. have already elected their elder brother San Bao Lidai 三寶歷代 (Tao Sam Pò Lütai) to rule the land on behalf of them. Now Banya Zhong (Phaya Còm) again creates troubles and bands together with Babai (Lan Na). He borrows the men and horses and kills out of vengeance (blood feuds). We intend to transfer government troops to pacify and quell [the revolt] but the warm spring is approaching and the epidemic attributed to miasma is flourishing. We should not yet mobilise the troops and march on recklessly.

The emperor replied:

San Bao Lidai (Sam Pò Lütai), the son of a concubine (*shunie*), has usurped [the post] of the son of a legal consort (*di*) and murdered (*mouhai*) Dao Baxian (Tao Phasaeng), prompting Baya Zong (Phaya Còm) to borrow troops [from Babai] to attack and kill. [Mu] Lin and others should send suitable officials to pacify and instruct Baya Zhong (Phaya Còm), et al., and make investigation to find out who is the legal heir to the post of the pacification commissioner (*saenwi fa*). The cause of the succession conflict is to be reported and they should be ordered to withdraw their forces and settle their conflicts.

Translated from *Yingzong shilu* 275, 5860 (Tianshun 1, second month, *gengshen* day: 21 March 1457) by Foon Ming Liew-Herres.

DOCUMENT 2

之地命還于雲南城中○勅鎮守雲南西平侯沐晟爾奏以車
里宣慰使刀暹荅侵害威遠欲興兵討之兵重事也危道也不
若且令雲南都司移文諭之如此格心向化即兵可止若諭之
不悛加兵未晚爾其訓練將士以俟○戊戌以刑科給事中蕭
銑為戶科左給事中工科給事中陳敬宗為戶科右給事中兵
科給事中萬奉為本科給事中○前軍都督府臣奏貴州都司
言普定衛達鎮撫甯忠往普安道經善利驛所乘馬蹂踐王館
請罷之　上曰驛館以備過使止宿朝廷未嘗設王館若是諸
王經過不過暫時留止豈是常制忠不足罪其是之○己亥修
魯王府宮殿○遣內官李興等賚勅諭暹羅國王昭祿羣膺哆
囉帝剌並賜王文綺帛四十匹及銅錢麝香諸物其貢使偕行
○禮部尚書李至剛奏日本國遣使使入貢已至寧波府凡番

TRANSLATION

[In Yongle 1, ninth month], on *dingyou* day (8 October 1403), an imperial decree was issued to the Grand Defender of Yunnan and the Marquis of Pacifying the West, Mu Sheng, [which said]:

> You have submitted a memorial and said that on account that the pacification commissioner of Cheli, Dao Xianda (Tao Sida Kham), has invaded and inflicted harm on Weiyuan, you want to raise troops against him. Sending troops concerns important matter and it is a dangerous path. It is better to tell the Regional Military Commission of Yunnan to send an official letter to admonish him. If he changes his heart and reforms, troops will be withdrawn immediately. If he does not repent after admonition, it is not too late to use forces. You should train the commanders and soldiers instead and wait.

Translated from *Taizong shilu* 23, 426 (Yongle 1, ninth month, on *dingyou* day: 8 October 1403) by Foon Ming Liew-Herres.

DOCUMENT 3

及四夷朝使○戊戌車里故宣慰使刀暹答次子刀賽遣兄刀
怕弄等來朝貢象馬金銀器初朝廷遣中官洪仔生齎勑往賜
刀暹答錦綺等物既至而刀暹答已卒長子刀良孟自立驕慢
很愎失其良心無幾病卒衆推刀賽權司事至是遣刀怕弄等
謝頒其父之恩并請襲職從之○庚子改四川酉陽宣撫司之
邑梅洞長官司隸重慶府八百大甸宣慰刀歆遣頭目孟都魯
由等進象馬等物賜之鈔幣○辛丑代王桂第六子生賜名遜
烇○行在户部言臣言河南汝寧等府所屬十六州縣連年水
災田穀不登所徵税粮宜令折輸鈔帛就河南布政司收貯官
用爲便從之　別失八里王馬哈麻火州王子哈三土魯番萬
户賽因帖木兒柳城萬户觀音奴俱遣使從給事中傅安等貢
名馬海青賜賚其使有差復遣使齎勑慰諭馬哈麻等并賜之

TRANSLATION

In Yongle 11, eleventh month, on *wuxu* day (15 December 1413), the second son of the late pacification commissioner Dao Xianda (Tao Sida Kham), Dao Sai (Tao Sai), sent his elder brother Dao Palong (Tao Phaeng Long) and others to pay tribute to the Ming court, presenting elephants, horses, gold and silver utensils. Earlier, the Ming court sent palace eunuch Hong Zaisheng, carrying with him an imperial decree, brocades (*jin*), fine silks (*qi*), and other things, [to Cheli]. On arrival he found out that Dao Xianda was already dead and his eldest son Dao Genmeng (Tao Kü Moeng) who was arrogant and cruel, had succeeded to the post himself. He could not gain the hearts of his people. Not long after he died of illness. The people recommended Dao Sai (Tai Sai) to be administrator of the [tusi] post for the time being. Dao Palong thanked the Ming court for the kindness shown to his [deceased] father and begged for the permission to succeed to the post which was approved.

Translated from *Taizong shilu* 145, 1717 (Yongle 11, eleventh month, *wuxu* day: 15 December 1413) by Foon Ming Liew-Herres.

Appendix 4
Seals of Cheli

SEAL OF THE CHELI PACIFICATION COMMISSION (車里宣慰司印)

This seal, made of wood, is engraved with Chinese and Manchu characters and looks quite worn. As a rule the seals issued by the court of imperial China were not made of wood, so perhaps the original seal was lost and the incumbent *saenwi fa* of Moeng Lü made a wooden one for himself pending the issuing of a new one.

图 28 车里宣慰司印

Tao Sunwu (Cao Mòm Maha Nòi), the *saenwi fa* of China, and his uncle Tao Thai Khang (Cao Mòm Maha Wang), the *saenwi fa* of the Burmese court, were not on good terms. Around Daoguang 13 (AD 1833), Tao Sunwu took the official seal and absconded secretly to Moeng Sò. When Tao Coen Cong (Cao Mòm Suca Wanna) succeeded his father, Cao Mòm Maha Wang, as *saenwi fa* the following year, he had no seal (see MLC-LV1, s. 32.1). This wooden seal was probably cast during that time.

SEAL OF SIMAO BUREAU OF THE CHELI PACIFICATION COMMISSION (雲南思茅廳車里宣慰司之印)

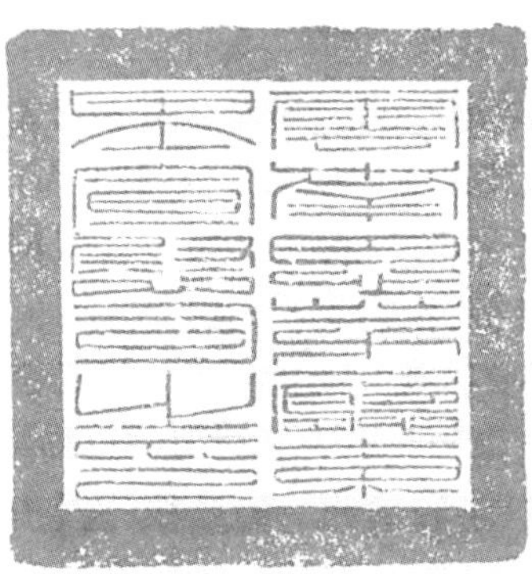

图 29 云南思茅厅车里宣慰司之印

This wooden seal was probably issued by the warlord and commissioner-in-chief (*dudu* 都督) of Yunnan, Tang Jiyao 唐繼堯 (fl. 1911–1927).

Both photographs are reproduced from Xiao Minghua 蕭明華 and Zou Yongqiong 鄒永瓊, 1989, 36–37.

Appendix 5

Inscription at a Monastery in Moeng Cae

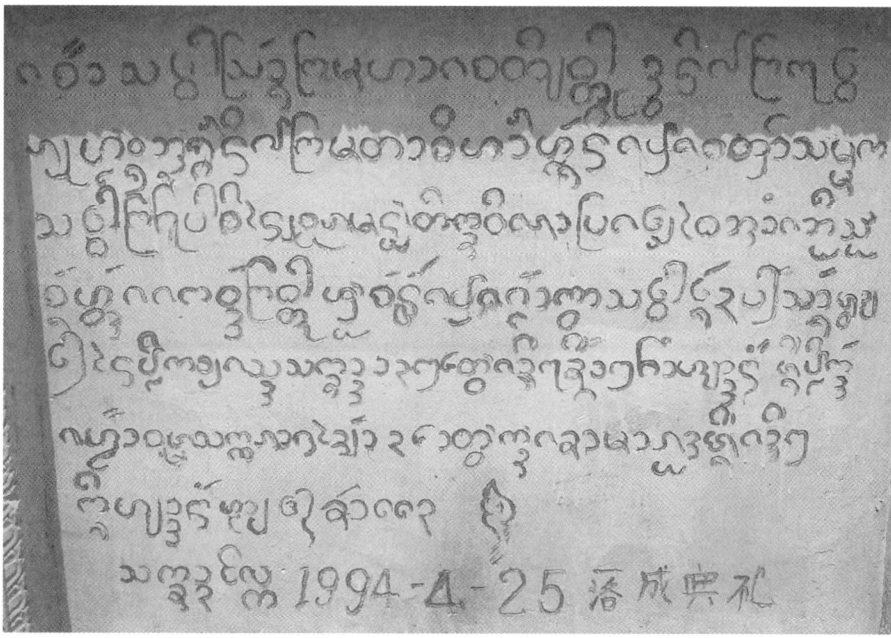

TRANSCRIPTION INTO MODERN THAI

(1) เจ้าสัทธาสร้างพระมหาเจติยธาตุ ดวงนิแล พระพุทธ

(2) รูปหลวงองค์นิแล พระมหาวิหารหลังนิเปนเจตนาสมฺมณ

(3) สัทธาพระฅูบาวิไนยวรมนอ(มโน)ติกขวิโร ประเทศไธ(ไทย)อำเภอสอง

(4) จังหวัดแพ่(แพร่) วัดพระธาตุหนองจันท์เปนเคล้ากว่าสัทธาทัง ๓ บ้าน สร้างถวาย

(5) ทานในปสีกาบเลด ลกฺขาด ๑๓๕๖ ตัว เติน (เดือน) ๗ ขึ้น ๑๕ ค่ำหยาดน้ำ ถึงปลีกัต

(6) เหม้าจุฬสกฺกราชได้ย ๑๓๖๑ ตัว กดเข้ามาถึงเดิน (เดือน) ๕

(7) พิง(เพ็ง)หยาดน้ำหมายทานข้าแด

(8) สกฺขาดโลก ๑๙๙๔-๔-๒๕

TRANSLATION

(1) The Buddhist faithfully built this great stupa and
(2) great Buddha image. This great vihāra is the good intention of Samaṇo
(3) Saddhā Khuba Winai Wòramanatikkhawiro (Vinaya Varamanatikkhaviro) from Thailand, Sòng District,
(4) Phrae Province, monastery of Wat Phrathat Luang Can, who is the head of the faithful of all three villages. It was built [and] donated
(5) in the *kap set* year, [cūla]sakarāja 1356, in the seventh month, on the fifteenth day of the waxing moon.[1] In the *kat*
(6) *mao* year, [cūla]sakarāja 1361, in the fifth month,
(7) the consecration ceremony will be held.
(8) International Era (AD) 25 April 1994.

1. Monday, 25 April 1994.

Bibliography

I. ARCHIVAL SOURCES

BRITISH LIBRARY, INDIA OFFICE AND ORIENTAL COLLECTIONS, LONDON

Archer, W. J. 1891a. "Report on a Journey in the Më-kong Valley, by Mr. W. J. Archer, First Assistant in Her Majesty's Consular Service in Siam." In *Parliamentary Papers*, vol. 79.

McLeod's Journal. 1868/69. "A Journal kept by Captain W. C. McLeod, Assistant to the Commissioner in the Tenasserim Provinces, during his Mission from Moulmein to the Frontiers of China." In *Parliamentary Papers*, vol. 46.

Scott, J. G. 1891. "Memorandum by Mr. J. G. Scott, Officiating Superintendent, Shan States, on a Visit to the Kyaington-Chiengmai Boundary to Meung Hsing and to Chieng Hung." In *Scott Papers* [Mss Eur F 278/73].

Scott, J. G. 1896. "A few notes about the Chinese frontier and provinces of Mong Lem, Keng Hung, and Chien Pien, vide map in pocket." In *Scott Papers* [Mss Eur F 278/90].

Warry, W. 1888–1895. Photocopies of selected official and private papers of William Warry (1854–1936), acting assistant Chinese secretary, Peking 1881–82, special service, Government of India from 1885, political officer, Bhamo, Mandalay and Shwegu 1867–89, adviser to the Chief Commissioner, Burma, on Chinese affairs 1890–1904; including photocopies of maps of the Trans-Salween section of the Burmo-Chinese frontier.

CAO MAHA KHANTHAWONG COLLECTION, CHIANG RUNG

Cao phaendin sipsòng panna เจ้าแผ่นดินสิบสองพันนา (The Rulers of Sipsòng Panna), Tai Lü manuscript. 53 ff.

GRABOWSKY/LIEW-HERRES COLLECTION

Moeng Lü Chronicle (MLC) – *Khao nitan kakun cao phaendin tangmuan mi sisip-si cao lae* ค่าวนิทานกะกุนเจ้าแผ่นดินทังมวนมี ๔๔ เจ้าแล (The Chronicle of the Forty-Four Rulers [of Sipsong Panna], in Tai Lue language and script). Manuscript composed for the Department of Culture and History

(DCH), Government of the Sipsòng Panna Tai Autonomous Prefecture, 1963. Abbreviation: MLC-LV2.

Moeng Laem Chronicle พื้นเมิงแลม (in Tai Laem language und Tai Lue script), manuscript-copy made by Po Saeng Sam, Wat That Long, Moeng Laem. 63 ff°.

Pap pün moeng sisip cin cao panna moeng hai พับพื้นเมิงสี่สิบชิ่นเจ้าพันนาเมิงราย (The Chronicle of the Forty Rulers of *panna* Moeng Hai), Cao Solawong Maha Bunthan version, Tai Lü manuscript. 48 ff°.

Pap pün sipsòng panna saenwi fa pen pün tai lü hao lae พับพื้นสิบสองพันนาแสนหวีฟ้าเปน พื้นไทลื้อเรา แล (The Chronicle of the Pacification Commissioners of Sipsòng Panna: A Tai Lü Chronicle), Tai Lü manuscript from Moeng Long. 57 ff°.

Pün moeng ham พื้นเมิงรำ (Moeng Ham Chronicle), Khanan Nakkasen version, Tai Lü manuscript. 23 ff°.

Pün moeng long พื้นเมิงลวง (Moeng Long Chronicle), Ban Foei Lung version, Tai Lü manuscript. 43 ff°.

PRESERVATION OF LAO MANUSCRIPTS PROGRAMME (PLMP), VIENTIANE

Pawat müang siang khaeng ປະຫວັດເມືອງຊຽງແຂງ (The History of Chiang Khaeng), Tai Lü manuscript. Wat Ta Pao, Müang Sing District, Luang Nam Tha Province, Inventory Code: 03.02.12.14.001.00, 78 ff. (Quoted as "Chiang Khaeng Chronicle, Wat Ta Pao version") [CKC-WTP].

PUBLIC RECORD OFFICE (PRO), LONDON

Archer, W. J. 1891b. "Mr. Archer to the Government of India", enclosure 4 in document no. 34, "Selection of Papers respecting the Affairs of Siam" [FO 422/34].

———. 1891c. "Mr. Archer to the Government of India", enclosure 10 in document no. 57, "Burma. Part 8" [FO 881/6216].

———. 1893. "Memorandum by Mr. Archer on the Sipsong Panna", 18 November 1893 [FO 881/6459].

Bourne. 1885. "Mr. Bourne's report of a journey in S.W. China", 9 December 1885 [FO 97/484].

O'Conor, N. 1895. "Sir N. O'Conor to the Earl of Kimberley", 20 June 1895 [FO 422/4].

"Siam, France, and China." 1895. Confidential document by G. N. C., dated 13 August 1895 [FO 881/6699].

Warry, Mr. 1895. "[Report sent] to the Chief Secretary to the Chief Commissioner, Burmah." (Moulmein, 10 May 1895) In: *Further Correspondence respecting the Affairs of Siam*, part 7: July to December 1895 [PRO, FO 422/43].

SOCIAL RESEARCH INSTITUTE (SRI), CHIANG MAI UNIVERSITY

Pün wongsa mahakhasat tanglai tangtae phaña samantalat pon ma lae pün wongsa caonai ton sawoei latcasombat nai müang pua lae müang nan พื้นวงสามหากระสัตรทังหลายตั้งแต่พระยา สมันตราชโพ้นมา และพื้นวงสาเจ้านายตนเสวยราชสมบัติในเมืองพัวแล เมืองน่าน (The Chronicle of Rulers Since the Reign of Phaya Samantalat and the Chronicle of the Nobles who Ruled in Müang Pua and Müang Nan), Tai Yuan manuscript. Wat Phranet, tambon Wiang Nüa, amphoe Müang, Nan, SRI 82.107.05.043–043, 240 ff.

Tamnan müang chiang rung: phün müang ratchasamnak 12 panna chiang rung, chabap kraisi nimmanhemin ตำนานเมืองเชียงรุ่ง: พื้นเมืองราชสำนัก ๑๒ ปันนา เชียงรุ่ง ฉบับอาจารย์ ไกรศรี นิมมานเหมินท์ (The Chronicle of Chiang Rung: The Chronicle of the Royal Residence of Sipsòng Panna-Chiang Rung, manuscript of Kraisi Nimmanahaeminda). Tai Lü manuscript, 114 ff., inv. no. 90.166.01.01.025–025.

II. PUBLISHED SOURCES AND SECONDARY LITERATURE

A. IN WESTERN LANGUAGES

Afanassieva, Elena. 1998. "Baan and müang as polysemantic expressions for Tai key conceptions." *Tai Culture* 3 (2): 27–30.

Baker, Chris. 2002. "From Yue to Tai." *Journal of the Siam Society* 90: 1–25.

Chiranan Prasertkul. 1989. *Yunnan Trade in the Nineteenth Century. Southwest China's Cross-Bounderies Functional System*. Bangkok: Institute of Asian Studies, Chulalongkorn University.

Chu Hsi-tsu 朱希祖. 1932. "Some Explanations of Wu San-kuei's Chou Regime." *Academia Senica* (Bulletin of the National Research Institute of History and Philosophy) 2 (4): 393–401.

Collis, Maurice S. 1938. *Lord of the Sun Set: A Tour of the Shan States*. London: Faber and Faber.

Daniels, Christian. 2000. "The Formation of Tai Polities Between the 13th to 16th Centuries: The Role of Technological Transfer." *The Memoirs of the Toyo Bunko* 58: 51–98.

Davis, Sara L. M. 2006. *Song and Silence: Ethnic Revival on China's Southwest Borders*. Chiang Mai: Silkworm Books.

Diller, Anthony. 2000. "The Tai Language Family and the Comparative Method". In: *Proceedings of the International Conference on Tai Studies, July 29–31, 1998*. Bangkok: Institute of Language and Culture for Rural Development, Mahidol University, 1–32.

Dodd, William C. 1996. *The Tai Race: Elder Brother of the Chinese*. Repr. Bangkok: White Lotus (Cedar Rapids, Iowa, 1923).

Eade, J. C. 1989. *Southeast Asian Ephemeris: Solar and Planetary Positions, A.D. 638–2000*. Ithaca, N.Y.: Southeast Asia Program, Cornell University.

———. 1995. *The Calendrical Systems of Mainland Southeast Asia*, Handbuch der Orientalistik. Leiden: E. J. Brill.

———. 1996. *The Thai Historical Record: A Computer Analysis*. Tokyo: The Centre for East Asian Cultural Studies for Unesco.

Fairbank, John K. 1941. "On the Ch'ing Tributary System." *Journal of Asian Studies* 6: 135–246.

Fernquest, Jon. 2006. "Crucible of War: Burma and the Ming in the Tai Frontier Zone (1382–1454)." *SOAS Bulletin of Burma Research* 4 (2): 27–81.

Garnier, Francis 1996. *Further Travels in Laos and in Yunnan. The Mekong Exploration Commission Report (1866–1868)—Vol. 2*. Translated by Walter Tips. Bangkok: White Lotus.

Gedney, William. 1999 (1964). *The Lue Language: Glossaries, Texts and Translations*. Ann Arbor: University of Michigan Press.

Goodrich, L. Carrington and Fang Chaoying (eds.). 1976. *Dictionary of Ming Biography*. 2 vols. New York: Columbia University Press.

Grabowsky, Volker. 1999a. "Forced Resettlement Campaigns in Northern Thailand during the Early Bangkok Period." *Journal of the Siam Society* 87: 45–86.

———. 1999b. "Introduction to the History of Müang Sing (Laos): The Fate of a Lü Principality." *Bulletin de l'École française d'Extrême-Orient* 86: 233–91.

———. 2001. "Note on kep phak sai sa kep kha sai müang." *Aséanie* 8: 67–71.

———. 2003a. "Chiang Khaeng 1893–1896: A Lue Principality in the Upper Mekong Valley at the Centre of Franco-British Rivalry." In *Contesting Visions of the Lao Past*, edited by Christopher E. Goscha and Søren Ivarsson, 37–70. Copenhagen: NIAS Press.

———. 2003b. "Cao Fa Dek Nòi and the Founding Myth of Chiang Khaeng", 95–143. In *Cultural Diversity and Conservation in the Making of Mainland Southeast Asia and Southwest China: Regional Dynamics in the Past and Present*, edited by Hayashi Yukio and Thongsa Sayavongkhamdy, 144–86. Vientiane/Kyoto: Department of Museums and Archaeology, Ministry of Information and Culture/Center for Southeast Asian Studies, Kyoto University.

———. 2004. *Bevölkerung und Staat in Lan Na: Ein Beitrag zur Bevölkerungsgeschichte Südostasiens*. Wiesbaden: Harrassowitz Verlag.

———. 2005. "Population and state in Lan Na prior to the mid-sixteenth century", in: *Journal of the Siam Society* 93: 1–68.

———. 2008. "The Tai Polities in the Upper Mekong and Their Tributary Relationships with China and Burma." *Aséanie* 21: 1–53.

Grabowsky, Volker and Andrew Turton. 2003. *The Gold and Silver Road of Trade and Friendship: The Richardson and McLeod Missions to Tai states in 1837*. Chiang Mai: Silkworm Books.

Grabowsky, Volker and Renoo Wichasin. 2008. *Chronicles of Chiang Khaeng: A Tai Lü Principality of the Upper Mekong*. Honolulu: Center for Southeast Asian Studies, University of Hawai'i.

Jagacinski, Ngampit. 1987. "The Lue of Xishuangbanna in China's Yunnan Province: Description and a study of the OV order in the *?AU* construction", Ph.D. diss., The Ohio State University.

Hall, D. G. E. 1981. *A History of Southeast Asia*. London: Macmillan Asian Histories Series.

Hartmann, John F. 1984. *Linguistic and Memory Structures in Tai-Lue Oral Narratives*. Canberra: Research School of Pacific Studies, The Australian National University.

Hasegawa, Kiyoshi. 2002. "Cultural Revival and Ethnicity: The Case of the Tai Lue in the Sipsong Panna, Yunnan Province." In *Dynamics of Ethnic Cultures Across National Boundaries in Southwestern China and Mainland Southeast Asia: Relations, Societies, and Languages*, edited by Hayashi Yukio and Yang Guangyuan, 121–37. Chiang Mai. Ming Muang Printing House.

Hsieh, Shi-Chung. 1989. "Ethnic-political Adaptation and Ethnic Change of the Sipsong Panna Dai: An Ehnohistorical Analysis." Ph.D dissertation, University of Washington.

Hsi, Angela. 1975. "Wu San kuei in 1644: A reappraisal." *Journal of Asian Studies* 34 (2): 443–53.

Hucker, Charles O. 1985. *A Dictionary of Official Titles in Imperial China*. Stanford, Calif.: Stanford University Press.

Hummel, Arthur W., ed. 1943–1944. *Eminent Chinese of the Ching Period, 1644–1912*. 2 vols. Washington: US Government Printing Office.

Kahnt, Helmut and Bernd Knorr. 1987. *Alte Maße, Münzen und Gewichte*. Mannheim/Wien/Zürich: Meyers Lexikonverlag.

Kato, Kumiko. 1994. "Muang Polities in Sipsongpanna: A Comparison of the Categories of Land and People among the Muang." *The Journal of the Faculty of Letters Nagoya University, History* 40: 25–50.

———. 1997. "Changes in Sipsongpanna in the Eighteenth Century: Focusing on 1720s–1730s", in: *The Journal of the Faculty of Letters Nagoya University, History* 43: 1–18.

———. 1998. "Control of Irrigation by müang Political Power: The case of Müang Chiang Hung (Möeng Cheng Hung) of Sipsongpanna." *Tai Culture* 3 (2): 49–71.

———. 1999. "The main trade routes between China and Burma through Sipsongpanna before the 1950s." In *Linguistic and Anthropological Study on the Shan Culture Area*, 201–22. Tokyo: Institute for the Study of Languages and Cultures of Asia and Africa.

Keyes, Charles. 1987. *Thailand: Buddhist Kingdom as Modern Nation-State.* Boulder, Colo.: Westview Press.

Lacroze, Luc. 1994. *Monographie de deux provinces septentrionales du Laos: Phong Saly et Houa Khong.* Les cahiers de Péninsule no. 1. Metz.

Leach, E. R. 1954. *Political Systems of Highland Burma.* Boston: Beacon Press.

Lefèvre-Pontalis, Pierre. 1897. "L'invasion Thaïe en Indo-Chine." *T'oung Pao* 8 (1): 53–78.

Lemoine, Jacques. 1987. "Tai Lue Historical Relations with China and the Shaping of the Sipsong Panna Political System." In *Proceedings of the International Conference on Thai Studies, The Australian National University, Canberra, 3–6 July, 1987*, edited by Anne Buller, 121–32.

———. 1997. "Féodalité Taï chez les Lü des Sipsong Panna et les Taï Blancs, Noirs et Rouges du Nord-ouest du Viêt-nam." *Péninsule* 35 (2): 171–217.

Lieberman, Victor B. 1984. *Burmese Administrative Cycles: Anarchy and Conquest, c. 1580–1760.* Princeton, N.J.: Princeton University Press.

Li, Fang Kuei. 1964. "The Phonemic System of the Tai Lü Language." *Bulletin of the Institute of History and Philology* (Academia Sinica) 35: 7–14.

———. 1977. *A Handbook of Comparative Tai.* Honolulu: University of Hawai'i Press.

Liew (-Herres), Foon Ming. 1984. *Tuntian Farming of the Ming Dynasty.* Hamburg: Gesellschaft für Natur- und Völkerkunde Ostasiens e.V., (MOAG, vol. 97.)

———. 1996. "The Luchuan-Pingmian Campaigns (1438–1449)." *Oriens Extremus* 39 (2): 162–203.

———. 1998. *The Treatises on Military Affairs of the Ming Dynastic History (1368–1644).* 2 vols. Hamburg: Gesellschaft für Natur- und Völkerkunde Ostasiens e.V.; (MOAG, vol. 129.)

———. 2003a. "The Aboriginal Tribes and the Tribal Principalities in Yunnan as Presented in the Ming and Early Qing Historiography: A Preliminary Survey." In *Cultural Diversity and Conservation in the Making of Mainland Southeast Asia and Southwest China: Regional Dynamics in the Past and Present*, edited by Hayashi Yukio and Thongsa Sayavongkhamdy, 144–86. Vientiane/ Kyoto: Department of Museums and Archaeology, Ministry of Information and Culture/ Center for Southeast Asian Studies, Kyoto University.

———. 2003b. *The Traditional Tai Polity of Lan Na and of the Tai Polities Around: A Documentation of Sino-Tai Relations and Inter-Tribal Conflicts. Collection of Records from Chinese Sources covering the Period from 13th to 18th Centuries.* In manuscript.

———. 2007. "Intra-dynastic and Inter-Tai Conflicts in the Old Kingdom of Moeng Lü in Southern Yunnan." *SOAS Buletin of Burma Research* 5: 51–112.

Liew, Foon Ming (in collaboration with Volker Grabowsky). 2004. "An Introduction to the Tai Lü

Sources of the History of Müang Lü (Sipsòng Panna): Various Tai Lü Manuscript-copies on the 'Dynastic History of Müang Lü' that have been translated into Chinese or transcribed into Thai and the salient studies of the History of Müang Lü (*Leshi*), 1947–2001." *Aséanie* 14: 149–94.

Liew-Herres, Foon Ming and Volker Grabowsky (in collaboration with Aroonrut Wichienkeeo). 2008. *Lan Na in Chinese Historiography: Sino-Tai Relations as Reflected in the Yuan and Ming Sources (13th to 17th Centuries)*. Bangkok: Institute of Asian Studies, Chulalongkorn University.

Liu Yan. 1999. *An On-the-spot Investigation into the Southernly Emigration of the Dai Race*. Translated by Wang Yi and Liu Biao. Kunming: Xishuang Autonomous Prefecture Nationality Research Institute, Yunnan Nationality Press.

Luce, Gordon H. 1961. *The Man Shu* (Book of the Southern Barbarians). Data Paper: Number 44, Southeast Asia Program. Department of Far Eastern Studies, Cornell University, Ithaca, New York.

McFarland, George Bradley. 1944. *Thai-English Dictionary*. Stanford, Calif.: Stanford University Press.

Morey, Stephen. 2004. "Tones in the Tai languages of Assam." *Indian Journal of Tai Studies* 4: 53–68 (Moranhat, Assam: Institute of Tai Studies and Research).

Mote, Frederick W. 1999. *Imperial China, 900–1800*. Cambridge, Mass. and London: Harvard University Press.

Mote, Frederick W. and Denis Twitchett (eds.) 1988. *The Cambridge History of China, Volume 7: The Ming Dnyasty, 1368–1644, Part I*. Cambridge: Cambridge University Press.

Mühlmann, Wilhelm. 1964. *Rassen, Ethnien, Kulturen*. Neuwied and Berlin: Luchterhand.

Myanmar-English Dictionary. 1998. Rangoon: Department of the Myanmar Language Commission, Ministry of Education.

Notton, M. Camille, transl. 1932. *Annales du Siam, IIIe volume: Chronique de Xieng Mai*. Paris: Librairie Orientaliste Paul Geuthner.

Placzek, Jim A. 1999. "New Evidence on the Origins of the Thais". Paper presented at the International Conference on the Tai Peoples before the Coming of Civilization, Thai Khadi Research Institute, Thammasat University, 27–28 May 1999.

Ratanapañña. 1968. *The Sheaf of Garlands of the Epochs of the Conqueror*, being a translation of Jinakālamālīpakaraṇam (translated by N. A. Jayawickrama). London: Pali Text Society.

Ratanaporn Sethakul. 2000a. "Tai Lue of Sipsongpanna and Müang Nan in the Nineteenth Century". In *Civility and Savagery: Social Identity in Tai States*, edited by Andrew Turton, 319–29. Richmond, Surrey: Curzon.

———. 2000b. "Community Rights of the Lü in China, Laos and Thailand: A Comparative Study." *Tai Culture* 5 (2): 69–103.

Rhys Davids, T. W. 1989. *Pali-English Dictionary*. New Dehli: Munshiram Manoharlal Publishers (originally published in 1921–23 by Pali Text Society, London).

Rujaya Abhakorn, M. R. 1984. "Ratburi, an Inner Province: Local Government and Central Politics in Siam, 1868–1892." Ph.D. diss., Ithaca N.Y.: Cornell University.

Sai Kam Mong. 2004. *The History and Development of the Shan Scripts*. Chiang Mai: Silkworm Books.

Sāimöng Mangrai, Sao. 1981. *The Pāḍaeng Chronicle and the Jengtung State Chronicle Translated*. (Michigan Papers on South and Southeast Asia, no. 19). Ann Arbor: The University of Michigan, Center for South and Southeast Asian Studies.

Sarassawadee Ongsakul. 2005. *History of Lan Na.* Translated by Chitraporn Tanratanakul. Chiang Mai: Silkworm Books.

Scott, James G. and John P. Hardiman. 1900. *Gazetteer of Upper Burma and the Shan States.* part 1, vol. 1. Rangoon: Superintendent of Government Printing and Stationary.

Smith, Nicol and Blake Clark. 1954. *Into Siam: The Underground Kingdom.* New York and Indianapolis: The Bobbs-Merrill Company.

Stuart-Fox, Martin. 1998. *The Lao Kingdom of Lān Xāng: Rise and Decline.* Bangkok: White Lotus.

Suebsaeng Promboon. 1971. "Sino-Siamese Tributary Relations, 1282–1853." Ph.D. diss., University of Wisconsin-Madison.

Sun Laichen. 2000. "Ming-Southeast Asian overland interactions, c. 1368–1644." Ph.D. diss., University of Michigan.

Souneth Phothisane. 1996. "The Nidān Khun Borom: Annotated Translation and Analysis." Ph.D. diss., University of Queensland.

Tambiah, Stanley, J. 1976. *World Conqueror and World Renouncer: A Study of Buddhism and Polity in Thailand against a Historical Background.* Cambridge: Cambridge University Press.

Tanabe, Shigeharu. 1988. "Spirits and Ideological Discourses: The Tai Lü Guardian Spirits in Yunnan." *Sojourn* 3 (1): 1–25.

Tern Moen, Sao. 1995. *Shan-English Dictionary.* Kensington, Maryland: Dunwoody Press.

Terwiel, B. J. 1978. "The Origins of the T'ai Reconsidered." *Oriens Extremus* 25 (2): 249–58.

The Yunnan Ethnic Groups and their Cultures. 2000. Kunming: Yunnan University International Exchange Series I.

Turton, Andrew. 2000. "Introduction to *Civility and Savagery.*" *Civility and Savagery: Social Identity in Tai States: Social Identity in Tai States*, edited by Andrew Turton, 3–31. Richmond, Surrey: Curzon.

Twitchett, Denis and Fairbank, John K. (eds.) 1980. *The Cambridge History of China, Volume 11, Late Ch'ing 1800–1911. Part 2.* Cambridge: Cambridge University Press.

Wade, Geoffrey Philip. 2000. "The 'Ming Shi-lu as a source for Southeast Asian history—Fourteenth to Seventeenth Centuries." *Journal of Southeast Asian Studies* 21 (2): 249–94.

Wyatt, David K. and Aroonrut Wichienkeeo. 1995. *The Chiang Mai Chronicle.* Chiang Mai: Silkworm Books.

Yule, Henry. 1968. *A Narrative of the Mission to the Court of Ava in 1855, together with the Journal of Arthur Phayre to the Court of Ava.* Kuala Lumpur: Oxford University Press.

Yos Santasombat. 2001. *Lak Chang: A reconstruction of Tai identity in Daikong.* Canberra: Pandanus Books/Research School of Pacific and Asian Studies, Australian National University.

B. IN CHINESE

Banna wenshi ziliao xuanji 版納文史資料選輯 (Collections of historical sources pertaining to [Sipsòng] banna). Special issue in the series *Xishuang banna shiliao jilu* 西雙版納史料輯錄, No. 2) Kunming renmin chubanshe: 1987.

Cheli xuanwei shixi jianshi 車里宣慰世系簡史, edited and collated by Dao Guang Xiang 刀光祥 (Tao Kòng Saeng) and Yan Han 岩罕 (Ai Kham). In the series *Bannan wenshi ziliao xuanji*, No. 1. Kunming): Yunnan renmin chubanshe, 1987.

Chen Xujing 陳序經. 1994. *Leshi manbi: Xishuang banna lishi shibu* 泐史漫筆：西雙版納歷史釋補 (History of Moeng Lü from an Unrestrained Pen: Interpretations and Supplements to the History of Sipsòng Panna). Guangzhou: Zhongshan daxue.

Da Ming Huidian 大明會典 (Collected Statutes of the Great Ming). 1976. 228 chapters, compiled upon imperial order under the direction of Li Dongyang 李東楊 (1447–1516) and Shen Shixing 申時行 (1535–1614). Revised edition, completed in 1587 and printed during the Wanli and Tianqi periods. Photographic reprint of the Wanli edition in 5 vols. by Taibei: Xin wenfeng, 1976.

Da Ming yitong zhi 大明一統志 (Comprehensive Geography of the Great Ming Dynasty). By Li Xian 李賢 (1408–1467), et. al., first printed in 1461; photographic reprint by Taibei: Wenhai chubanshe, 1965.

Dao Shuren 刀述仁, transl. 1989. "Sishisi dai Zhao Pianling shixi" 四十四代召片領世系 (The Genealogy of the Forty-Four *Cao Phaendin* of the Dynasty). In Cheli xuanwei shi shixi jijie 車里宣慰使世系集解, pp. 218–82. (Chinese translation) and 377–480 (Tai Lü original text). Kunming: Yunnan minzu chubanshe. Translated into English by F. M. Liew-Herres, V. Grabowsky, and Renoo Wichasin, unpublished manuscript.

Dao Yongming 刀永明 and Kang Langzhuang 康朗莊, transl. 1989a. "Cheli xuanwei shixi" 車里宣慰世系 (The Genealogy of the Pacification Commissioners of Sipsòng Panna). In Cheli xuanweishi shixi jijie 車里宣慰使世系集解, 283–314. Kunming: Yunnan minzu chubanshe.

——— 1989b. "Xianwang shixi" 先王世系 (The Genealogy of the Late Kings). In *Cheli xuanweishi shixi jijie* 車里宣慰使世系集解, 315–47. Kunming: Yunnan minzu chubanshe.

Dian Kao 滇考. (Study of Yunnan by Feng Su) 馮甦, Daoguang 1 (1821) edition; photographic reprint by Taibei: Chengwen chubanshe, 1967.

Dian Xi 滇繫 (Collected Source Material on Yunnan), by Shi Fan 師範, 1808 edition.

Dushi fangyu jiyao 讀史方輿紀要, by Gu Zuyu 顧祖禹 (1631–1692). Block Print, 1879; reprinted in Shanghai, 1937.

Gao Lishi 高立士, transl. 1982. "*Xishuang Banna Zhao Pianling shixi yizhu*" 西雙版納召片領世系譯註 (Genealogy of the Rulers of Sipsòng Panna: An Annotated Translation). With the Chinese translation based on the Moeng Lü Chronicle in Tai Lü and the Tai Lü texts printed alongside. *Minzu xuebao* 民族學報 (*Journal of Nationalities*) 2: 81–91. Yunnan: Minzu chubanshe 民族出版社 (Nationalities Publishers). Abbreviation: MLC-SV2.

———. transl. 1984. "*Xishuang Banna Zhao Pianling sishisi shi shimu*" 西雙版納召片領四十四世始末 (Chronicle of the Forty-Four Cao Phaendin of Sipsòng Panna). *Mingzu diaocha yanjiu* 民族調查研究 (Study and Investigation of the Nationalities), 102–131. Kunming: Yunnan minzu chubanshe (reprinted in 1992, 121–70). Translated into English by Liew-Herres in 2004, in an unpublished manuscript.

Gaozong shilu 高宗實錄 in *Qing shilu. See Banna wenshi ziliao xuanji* 版納文史資料選輯 (special issue, 1987).

Guoque 國榷 (State Discourse), c. 1653, by Tan Qian 談遷 (1594–1658). Printed by Beijing: Zhonghua shuju 中華書局, 1958 (reprint 1988), 6 volumes.

Huang Kaihua 黃開華. 1968. "Ming dai tusi zhidu sheshi yu xi'nan kaifa" 明代土司制度與西南開發 (The establishment of the system of the aboriginal commissions during the Ming period and the development of the southwest). *Ming dai tusi zhidu* 明代土司制度 (The system of the aboriginal commissions of the Ming dynasty), edited by Bao Zunpeng, 27–217. Taibei.

Jinghong xianzhi 景洪縣志 (Local Gazetteer of Chiang Rung). 2000. Kunming: Yunnan renmin chubanshe.

Li Fuyi 李拂一. 1912. *Dianbian shidi Menggen tusi zhi kaocha* 滇邊失地孟艮土司之考察 (A study of the lost territory of Moeng Khün Aboriginal Commission on Yunnan frontier). In *Yongchang fu wenzheng* 永昌府文徵, edited by Li Genyuan 李根源 (1879–1976), chapter 36, 9–12.

———. 1933. *Cheli* 車里 (Chiang Lü or Sipsòng Panna). In *Shidi xiao congshu* 史地小叢書. Shanghai: Commercial Press.

———. 1942. "*Cheli ming ming kao* 車里命名考" (Study of the toponym Cheli). In *Bianjiang tongxun* 邊疆通訊 3:5; reprinted in Li Fuyi 2003, 31–37.

———. 1947a. *Leshi* 泐史 (History of Moeng Lu). In *Xinan yanjiu congshu* 西南研究叢書 (Collectanea of Southwest Studies), No. 8. Kunming: Chongwen shuju 崇文書局 (revised and printed by Taibei: Furen shuwu 復仁書局, 1983; revised and printed in 2008). Abbreviation: MLC-LV1.

———. 1947b. *Daile wen Cheli xuanwei shixi* 歹仂文車里宣慰世系. *Fu Hanwen duizhao* 附漢文對照 (Genealogy of the *saenwi* [*fa*] of Sipsòng Panna in Tai Lü script supplemented by the Chinese translation). Printed in *Cheli xuanwei shixi kaoding* 車里宣慰世系考訂 (see Li Fuyi 1947c), 43–63. Kunming: Chongwen shuju 崇文書局 (revised and printed by Taibei: Furen shuwu 復仁書屋, 1983; revised and printed by Taibei: Furen shuwu in 2008). Abbreviation: MLC-SV1.

———.1947c. *Cheli xuanwei shixi kaoding* 車里宣慰世系考訂 (Recension of the Genealogy of the *Saenwi Fa* of Sipsòng Panna), printed together with *Daile wen Cheli xuanwei shixi* 歹仂文車里宣慰世系. *Fu Hanwen duizhao* 附漢文對照 (Genealogy of the *saenwi* [*fa*] of Sipsòng Panna in Tai Lü script supplemented by the Chinese translation). (See Li Fuyi 1947b). In *Xinan yanjiu congshu* 西南研究叢書, no. 9, 1–41. Kunming: Chongwen shuju 崇文書局 (revised and printed by Taibei: Furen shuwu 復仁書屋, 1983; revised and printed by Taibei: Furen shuwu in 2008).

———. 1949. *Shier banna jinian* 十二版納紀年 (Chronicle of Sipsòng Panna). Kunming: Dingxin (reprinted in Taibei: 1984).

———. 1955. *Shier banna zhi* 十二版納誌 (Treatise on Sipsòng Panna). In *Xinan bianyao*. Taibei: Zhengzhong shuju.

———. 1983a. See Li Fuyi 1947a.

———. 1983b. See Li Fuyi 1947b.

———. 1984. *Zhenyue xian xin zhi gao* 鎮越縣新志稿 (Draft of the new treatise on Zhenyue County). Taibei: Furen shuwu.

———. 2003a. *Nanhuang neiwai* 南荒內外 (Within and beyond the southern fringes), collected articles by Li Fuyi. Taibei: Furen shuwu 復仁書屋 (reprint of the 1979 edition).

———. 2003b. "*Cheli ming ming xinkao* 車里命名新考" (A new study of the toponym of Cheli). In *Nanhuang neiwai* 南荒內外, 197–200.

———. 2008a. See Li Fuyi 1947a.

———. 2008b. *Cheli xuanwei shixi kaoding gao* 車里宣慰世系考訂稿. *Chongding ben* 重訂本 (Revised edition of the Draft of the genealogy of the *saenwi* [*fa*] of Sipsòng Panna). Taibei: Furen shuju 復仁書局 (See Li Fuyi 1947b).

Liu Boqiu 1946. *Zhong Mian jiwu wenti* 中緬機務問題 (Burmese-Chinese Border Issues). Chongqing: Zhengzhong shuju.

Ling Chunsheng 凌純聲 1968. *Mingdai zai zhongnan bandao suo zhi shi xuanwei si* 明代在中南半島所置十宣慰司 (The ten pacification commissions established in China and Mainland Southeast Asia during the Ming period), originally printed in Dalu zazhi 大陸雜誌; reprinted in Ming shi luncong 明史論叢, vol. 5. Taibei: Xuesheng shuju.

Man Shu 蠻書 (Book of the Southern Barbarians). By Fan Chuo 樊綽 (Tang period). *Man Shu jiaozhu* 蠻書校注 (An Annotated Edition of the Book of the Southern Barbarians), annotated by Xiang Da 向達. Beijing: Zhonghua shuju, 1962. For an English translation of *Man Shu*, see Luce, Gordon H. 1961.

Menghai xianzhi 猛海縣志 (Local Gazetteer of Moeng Hai County). 1997. Kunming: Yunnan renmin chubanshe.

Mengla xianzhi 猛臘縣志 (Local Gazetteer of Moeng La County). 1994. Kunming: Yunnan renmin chubanshe.

Mingshi 明史 (History of the Ming Dynasty) (completed in 1736). Edited by Zhang Tingyu 張廷玉 (1672–1755) et al. Beijing: Zhonghua shuju.

Mingshi gao 明史稿 (Draft of the History of the Ming Dynasty) (completed in 1723). Edited by Wang Hongxu 王鴻緒 (1645–1723), Wan Sitong 萬斯同 (1638–1702) et al. Photographic reprint of the original edition in Japan, 1973; repr. in reduced size by Taibei: Wenhai chubanshe, 1985. Abbreviation: MSG.

Ming shilu 明實錄 (Veritable Records of the Ming Dynasty). Taibei 1961–1966 (repr. 1984). Abbreviation: MSL.

Nanhuang neiwai 南荒內外, see Li Fuyi 2003.

Puer fu zhi 普洱府志 (Gazetteer of Puer Prefecture), edited by Chen Zonghai 陳宗海. Printed in Guangxu 23 (1897).

Pusi yanbian zhilüe 普思沿邊志略, by Ke Shuxun 柯樹勳. In manuscript copy and printed in 1916.

Qingshi Gao 清史稿 (Draft of the History of the Qing Dynasty) (compiled in 1914–1927) under Zhao Erxun 趙爾巽, Ke Shaomin 柯劭忞 et al. Beijing: Zhonghua shuju, 1928 (repr. 1977).

Shenzong shilu 神宗實錄. *See Ming shilu.*

Shi Mian lu 使緬錄 (Record of an envoy to Burma) by Zhang Hong 張洪 (1364–1447).

Shizong shilu 世宗實錄. *See Ming shilu.*

Taizong shilu 太宗實錄. *See Ming shilu.*

Tan Qixiang 譚其驤 (chief editor) et al. 1982. *Zhongguo lishi ditu ji* 中國歷史地圖集 (Historical Altas of China), vol. 7. Shanghai: Cartographic Publishing House.

Xiao Minghua 蕭明華 and Zou Yongqiong 鄒永瓊. 1989. *Yunnan shaoshu minzu guanyin ji* 雲南少數民族官印集 (Seals of the Minority Peoples in Yunnan). Kunming: Yunnan renmin chubanshe.

Xishuang banna shiliao jilu 西雙版納史料輯錄. In *Banna wenshi ziliao xuanji* 版納文史資料選輯 (special issue). Jinghong: 1987.

Xuanzong shilu 宣宗實錄. See *Ming shilu.*

Yuanshi 元史 (History of the Yuan Dynasty). Edited by Song Lian 宋濂 (1310–1381), et al., completed in 1370; reprinted in 1739 (Wuyingdian edition); modern reprint with punctuations, in 15 volumes by Beijing: Zhonghua shuju, 1976.

Yuanshi jishi benmo 元史紀史本末 (Narrative of Yuan History from the beginning to the end). Edited by Chen Bangzhan 陳邦瞻 (obtained *jinshi* degree in 1598), completed in 1606, reprinted in Beijing: Zhonghua shuju, 1979.

Zhaobu zonglu 招捕總錄, by an author of the Yuan period, edited by Qian Xizuo 錢熙祚 in 1844 and reprinted in 1889 in the *Shoushange congshu* 守山閣叢書.

C. IN THAI

Aphiradi Techasiriwan. (อภิรดี เตชะศิริวรรณ). 2003. *Phatthanakan aksòn lae akkharawithi nai ekkasan tai lü* พัฒนาการอักษรและอักขรวิธีในเอกสารไทลื้อ (The Development of Script and Orthography in Tai Lü documents). M.A. thesis, Chiang Mai University.

Aroonrut Wichienkeeo (อรุณรัตน์ วิเชียรเขียว) 1996a. *Photcananukrom sap lan na chaphò kham thi prakot nai bai lan* พจนานุกรมศัพท์ล้านนา เฉพาะคำที่ปรากฏในใบลาน (The Northern Thai Dictionary of Palm-leaf Manuscripts). Chiang Mai: Silkworm Books.

———. 1996b. *Photcananukrom phasa thin phak nüa* พจนานุกรมภาษาถิ่นภาคเหนือ (The Northern Thai Dictionary). Chiang Mai: Chiang Mai Teachers College.

Aroonrut Wichienkeeo and Anan Ganjanapan (Kancanaphan) (eds.). (อรุณรัตน์ วิเชียรเขียว และอานันท์ กาญจนพันธุ์). 1988. "Tamnan müang yòng" ตำนานเมืองยอง (The Müang Yòng Chronicle). In *Nangsü pariwat cak khamphi bai lan chut tamnan müang lae kotmai* หนังสือปริวรรตจากคัมภีร์ใบลาน ชุดตำนานเมืองและกฎหมาย (Transcription of Palm-leaf Manuscripts, Volume on Chronicles and Customary Law Codes). Chiang Mai: Chiang Mai Teachers College und University of Chiang Mai.

Aroonrut Wichienkeeo (อรุณรัตน์ วิเชียรเขียว) and David K. Wyatt. 2004 (1999). *Tamnan phün müang chiang mai* ตำนานพื้นเมืองเชียงใหม่ (The Chiang Mai Chronicle). Chiang Mai: Silkworm Books.

Bancop Phanthumetha (บรรจบ พันธุเมธา). 1979. *Pai sòp kham thai/tai* ไปสอบคำไท (Investigating Tai languages). Bangkok: Khana anu-kammakan phoei-phrae ekkalak khòng thai.

———. 1961. *Ka le man tai* กาเลหม่านไต . Bangkok: Samakhom phasa lae nangsü.

Bunchuai Sisawat (บุญช่วย ศรีสวัสดิ์). 2004 (1954). *Thai sipsòng panna* ไทยสิบสองปันนา (The Thai/Tai of Sipsòng Panna). 2 vols. Bangkok: Samnakphim sayam.

Cia Yaencòng (alias Yanyong Ciranakhòn) (เจีย แยนจอง หรือ ยรรยง จิระนคร). 2005. *Khon tai mai chai khon thai tae pen khrüa yat chat phasa* "คนไท" ไม่ใช่ "คนไทย" แต่เป็นเครือญาติชาติ ภาษา ("Tai" Does not Mean "Thai" but an Ethno-linguistic Family). Bangkok: Sinlapa-watthanatham.

Cit Phumisak (จิตร ภูมิศักดิ์). 1976. *Khwam pen ma khòng kham sayam thai lao lae khòm lae laksana thang sangkhom khòng chü chonchat* ความเป็นมาของคำสยาม ไทย ลาว และขอม และลักษณะทางสังคมของชื่อชนชาติ (The Origins of the Terms Siam, Thai, Lao, Khòm and Their Socio-Ethnic Characteristics). Bangkok: Duang Kamol.

Lamun Canhòm (ลมูล จันทน์หอม). 2004. *Phap nithan kha 4 saen mòn ma* พับนิทานข้า ๔ แสนหมอนม้า (Chronicle of the Servants of the 400,000 Horse Cushions). Chiang Mai: Chiang Mai Rajabhat University.

Natcha Laohasirinadh (ณัชชา เลาหศิรินาถ). 1998. *Sipsòng phanna rat carit* สิบสองพันนา รัฐจารีต (Sipsòng Panna: A Traditional State). Bangkok: The Thailand Research Fund.

Patithin 250 pi, ph.s. 2304 thüng 2555 ปฏิทิน ๒๕๐ ปี พ.ศ. ๒๓๐๔ ถึง ๒๕๕๕ (The 250 Year Calendar, AD 1761–2012). 1954. Bangkok.

"Phongsawadan müang chiang rung" พงศาวดารเมืองเชียงรุ้ง (The Chiang Rung Chronicle). 1964. In *Prachum phongsawadan* ประชุมพงศาวดาร (Collected Chronicles) 9–9: 1–37. Bangkok: Khurusapha.

"Phongsawadan müang chiang rung" พงศาวดารเมืองเชียงรุ้ง (The Chiang Rung Chronicle). 2002. In *Prachum phongsawadan chabap kancanaphisek* ประชุมพงศาวดารฉบับกาญจนาภิเษก (Collected Chronicles, Kāñcanābhiṣeka version). vol. 8, 404–35. Bangkok: Krom Silpakorn.

"Phongsawadan müang chiang tung" พงศาวดารเมืองเชียงตุง (The Chiang Tung Chronicle). 1990. Translit. by Thawi Swangpanyangkoon (ทวี สว่างปัญญางกูร). In *Nangsü caek pen bat phli ngan phraratchathan phloeng sop cao mae thipphawan na chiang tung* หนังสือแจกเป็นบัตรพลีงานพระราชทานเพลิงศพเจ้าแม่ทิพวรรณ ณ เชียงตุง (Cremation volume for Cao Mae Thipphawan of Chiang Tung).

"Phongsawadan müang chiang tung tòn cop" พงศาวดารเมืองเชียงตุง ตอนจบ (The Chiang Tung Chronicle, final part). 1993. Translit. by Thawi Swangpanyangkoon (ทวี สว่างปัญญางกูร). *Ruam botkhwam prawattisat* รวมบทความประวัติศาสตร์ (Collection of historical articles) 15: 12–20.

Prawat khwaen sipsòng panna ประวัติแคว้นสิบสองปันนา (The History of the Sipsòng Panna Region). 1982. *Thalaeng ngan prawattisat ekkasan borannakhadi* แถลงงานประวัติศาสตร์และเอกสารโบราณคดี (Historische Studies and Archaeological Documents) 16 (1) 29–47.

Pricha Phinthong (ปรีชา พิณทอง). 1989. *Saranukrom phasa isan thai angrit* สารานุกรมภาษาอีสานไทยอังกฤษ (Isan-Thai-English Encyclopedia). Ubon Ratchathani: Rongphim Siritham.

Renoo Wichasin (เรณู วิชาศิลป์), transl. 2001. *Chüa khrüa cao saenwi sipsòng panna* เชื้อเครือเจ้าแสนหวีสิบสองพันนา (The Genealogy of Cao Saenwi of Sipsòng Panna), compiled by Thao Khwang Saeng and Ai Kham (เท่าคว่างแซ้ง และ อ้ายคำ เรียบเรียง). Chiang Mai: Silkworm Books.

Sarassawadee Ongsakul (สรัสวดี อ๋องสกุล), translit. and ed. 1993. *Lakthan prawattisat lan na cak ekkasan khamphi bai lan lae phapnangsa* หลักฐานประวัติศาสตร์ล้านนาจาก เอกสารคัมภีร์ใบลานและพับหนังสา (Documents on the history of Lan Na from palm-leaf and leporello manuscripts). Chiang Mai: Chiang Mai University.

———. 1996a. *Prawattisat lan na* ประวัติศาสตร์ล้านนา (History of Lan Na) (2nd edition). Bangkok: Amarin.

———. translit. and ed. 1996b. *Phün müang nan chabap wat phra koet* พื้นเมืองน่านฉบับวัดพระเกิด (The Nan Chronicle, Wat Phra Kaet version). With a preface by Nitthi Iaosiwong (นิธิ เอียวศรีวงศ์). Bangkok: Amarin.

Social Research Insitute (SRI) (สถาบันวิจัยสังคม). 1981. *Tamnan phün müang lan na chiang mai*, ตำนานพื้นเมืองล้านนาเชียงใหม่ (Chronicle of Lan Na-Chiang Mai). Chiang Mai: SRI, Chiang Mai University.

Somphong Witthayasakphan (สมพงศ์ วิทยศักดิ์พันธุ์). 2001. *Prawattisat thai yai* ประวัติศาสตร์ไทใหญ่ (History of the Shan). Bangkok: Samnakngan kòngthun sanapsanun kan wicai.

Srisakara Vallibhotama (ศรีศักร วัลลิโภดม). 1989. "Watthanatham sipsòng panna" วัฒนธรรมสิบสองพันนา (Sipsòng Panna Culture). *Warasan Müang Boran* วารสารเมืองโบราณ (Müang Boran Journal) 15 (3): 27–42.

Sumit Pitiphat (สุมิตร ปิติพัฒน์). 1983. "Khon thai nai sipsòng panna" คนไทยในสิบสองปันนา (The Thai in Sipsòng Panna). *Warasan thammasat* วารสารธรรมศาสตร์ (The Thammasat University Journal). 12 (1): 123–37.

Tamnan phün müang chiang mai ตำนานพื้นเมืองเชียงใหม่ (Chiang Mai Chronicle). 1971. Bangkok: Samnak nayok ratthamontri.

Tao Kòng Saeng and Ai Kham. 1990. *Chüa khrüa cao saenwi fa sipsòng panna* เชื้อเครือเจ้าแสนหวีฟ้าสิบสองพันนา (Dynastic History of the Rulers of Sipsòng Panna). Kunming: Yunnan minzu chubanshe.

Thawi Sawangpanyangkun (ทวี สว่างปัญญางกูร) translit. and ed. 1984. *Tamnan müang yòng* ตำนานเมืองยอง (The Müang Yòng Chronicle). Chiang Mai: Social Research Institute.

———. translit. and ed. 1986. *Tamnan phün müang sipsòng panna* ตำนานพื้นเมืองสิบสองพันนา (Chronicle of Sipsòng Panna). Chiang Mai: Chiang Mai University Library.

———. translit. and ed. 1990. "Phongsawadan müang chiang tung" พงศาวดารเมืองเชียงตุง (The Chiang Tung Chronicle). In *Nangsü caek pen bat phli ngan phraratchathan phloeng sop cao mae thipphawan na chiang tung* หนังสือแจกเป็นบัตรพลีงานพระราชทานเพลิงศพเจ้าแม่ทิพวรรณ ณ เชียงตุง (Book distributed on the occasion of the cremation ceremony of Princess Thipphawan of Chiang Tung).

———. translit. and ed. 1993. *Chüa khrüa phaendin saenwi fa (twelve panna)* เชื้อเครือแผ่นดินแสนหวีฟ้า (สิบสองพันนา) (Genealogy of Rulers of *Saenwi Fa*—Sipsòng Panna). In *Ruam bothkhwam prawattisat* รวมบทความประวัติศาสตร์ (Collected Articles on History), vol. 15, 1–11.

Thongthaem Nartchamnong (ทองแถม นาถจำนง). 1989. "Thinthan khòng chao tai nai sipsòng panna" ถิ่นฐานของชาวไตในสิบสองพันนา (The Areas of Settlement of the Tai in Sipsòng Panna). *Warasan müang boran* วารสารเมืองโบราณ (Müang Boran Journal) 16 (3): 51–65.

Udom Roongruangsri (อุดม รุ่งเรืองศรี). 1991. *Photcananukrom lan na thai chabap mae fa luang* พจนานุกรมล้านนา-ไทย ฉบับแม่ฟ้าหลวง (The Lan Na-Thai Dictionary, Mae Fa Luang version), 2 vols. Bangkok: Munlanithi mae fa luang lae thanakhan thai phanit (Mae Fa Luang Foundation and Thai Commercial Bank).

Udom Rungruangsri et al. (อุดม รุ่งเรืองศรี และคณะ). 1995. *Tamnan phün müang chiang mai chabap chiang mai 700 pi* ตำนานพื้นเมืองเชียงใหม่ ฉบับเชียงใหม่ ๗๐๐ ปี (The Chiang Mai Chronicle, 700th Anniversary Edition). Chiang Mai: Sun watthanatham cangwat chiang mai lae Sathaban ratchaphat chiang mai.

Wimon Khetta (วิมล เขตตะ). 2000. *Phap phün khao (khlao) chüa khrüa cao sawaenwi fa sipsóng phanna: kan süksa nüaha thang prawattisat* พับพื้นเคล้าเชื้อเครือเจ้าแสวนหวีฟ้าสิบสองพันนา: การศึกษาวิเคราะห์เนื้อหาทางประวัติศาสตร์ (Manuscripts on the Genealogy of Cao Saenwi Fa-Sipsòng Panna: An Analytical Study of Historical Subject Matters). M.A. thesis, Bangkok: Silpakorn University.

Winai Pongsripian (วินัย พงศ์ศรีเพียร) (ed.). 1996. *Pa pai si fu – pa pai ta tian: chiang mai nai ekkasan prawattisat cin boran* ปาไป่สีฟู่–ปาไป่ต้าเตี้ยน เชียงใหม่ในเอกสารประวัติศาสตร์จีนโบราณ (Babai-xifu– Babai-dadian: Chiang Mai in Old Chinese Sources). Bangkok: Prime Minister's Office.

Yanyong Ciranakhòn and Ratanaporn Sethakul (ยรรยง จิระนคร และรัตนาพร เศรษฐกุล). 2001. *Prawattisat sipsòng panna* ประวัติศาสตร์สิบสองปันนา (History of Sipsòng Panna). Bangkok: Amarin.

INTERNET WEBSITES

http://epress.nus.edu.sg/msl (Southeast Asia in the Ming Shi-lu: An Open Access Resource).

http://www.viettouch.com/numis ("Indochinese Coins").

http://de.wikipedia/org/wiki.

Index